TRANS-METRO-POLITAN:

ONE MORE TIME

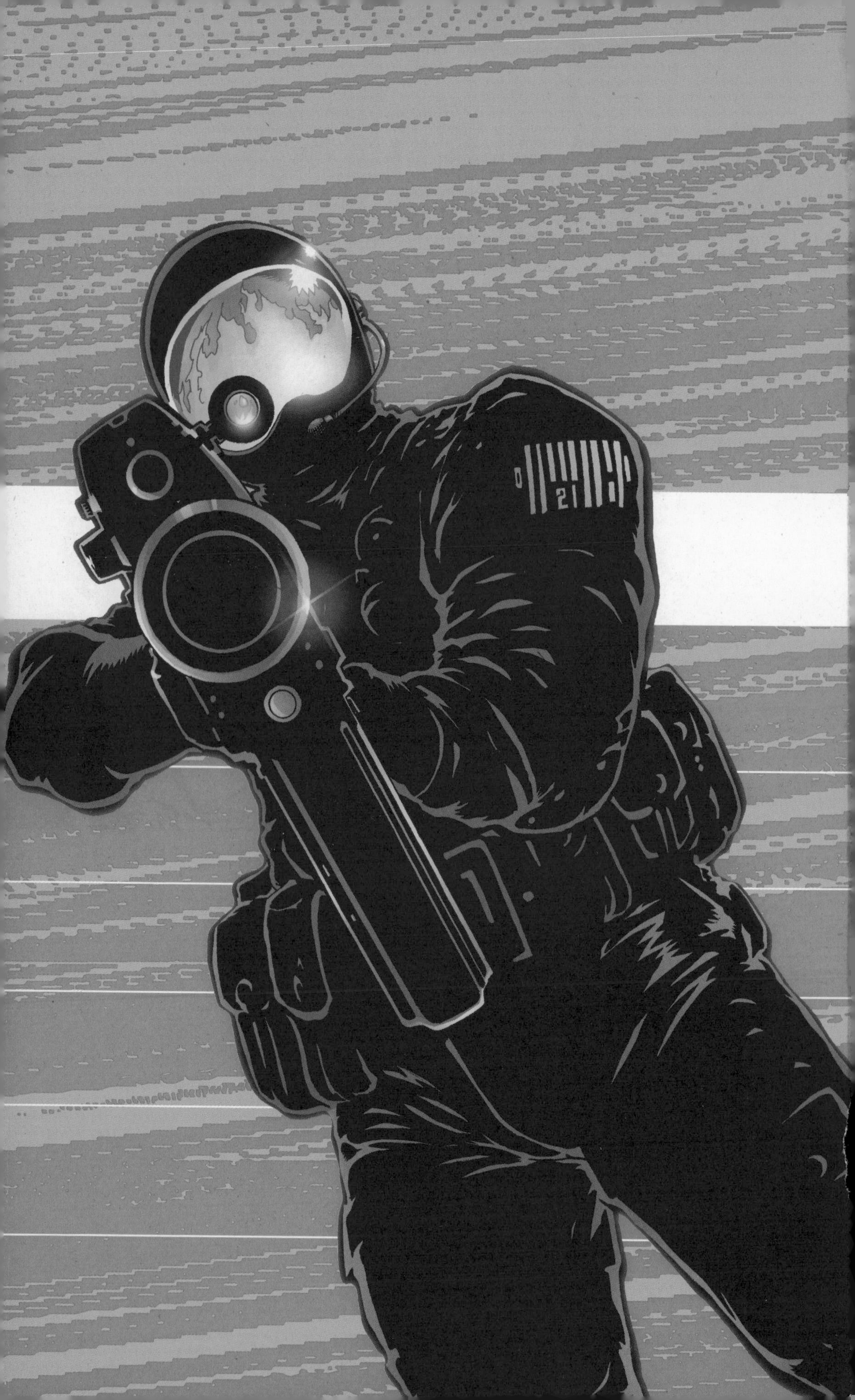

TRANS-
METRO-
POLITAN:
ONE MORE TIME

Warren_Ellis
Writer

Darick_Robertson
Penciller

Rodney_Ramos
Inker

Nathan_Eyring
Colorist

Clem_Robins
Letterer

Gene Ha (#55-57)
Darick Robertson (#58-60)
Original Series Covers

TRANSMETROPOLITAN created by
Warren_Ellis and Darick_Robertson

Heidi MacDonald Zachary Rau Axel Alonso Tony Bedard Editors – Original Series Jennifer Lee Tammy Beatty Assistant Editors – Original Series
Scott Nybakken Editor Robbin Brosterman Design Director – Books Curtis King Publication Design

Shelly Bond Executive Editor – Vertigo Hank Kanalz Senior VP – Vertigo and Integrated Publishing

Diane Nelson President Dan DiDio and Jim Lee Co-Publishers Geoff Johns Chief Creative Officer
John Rood Executive VP – Sales, Marketing and Business Development Amy Genkins Senior VP – Business and Legal Affairs
Nairi Gardiner Senior VP – Finance Jeff Boison VP – Publishing Planning Mark Chiarello VP – Art Direction and Design
John Cunningham VP – Marketing Terri Cunningham VP – Editorial Administration Alison Gill Senior VP – Manufacturing and Operations
Jay Kogan VP – Business and Legal Affairs, Publishing Jack Mahan VP – Business Affairs, Talent Nick Napolitano VP – Manufacturing Administration
Sue Pohja VP – Book Sales Courtney Simmons Senior VP – Publicity Bob Wayne Senior VP – Sales

Cover illustration by Darick Robertson.

TRANSMETROPOLITAN: ONE MORE TIME

DC Comics, 1700 Broadway, New York, NY 10019. A Warner Bros. Entertainment Company. Printed in Canada. Third Printing.
ISBN: 978-1-4012-3124-8

Library of Congress Cataloging-in-Publication Data

Ellis, Warren, author.
Transmetropolitan. Vol. 10, One more time / Warren Ellis, Darick Robertson, Rodney Ramos.
pages cm
"Originally published in single magazine form as Transmetropolitan 55-60, Transmetropolitan: I hate it here and Transmetropolitan: filth of the city."
ISBN 978-1-4012-3124-8
1. Journalists–Comic books, strips, etc. 2. Graphic novels. I. Robertson, Darick, illustrator. II. Ramos, Rodney, illustrator. III. Title. IV. Title: One more time
PN6728.T68 E443 2011
741.5'973–dc23
2012376098

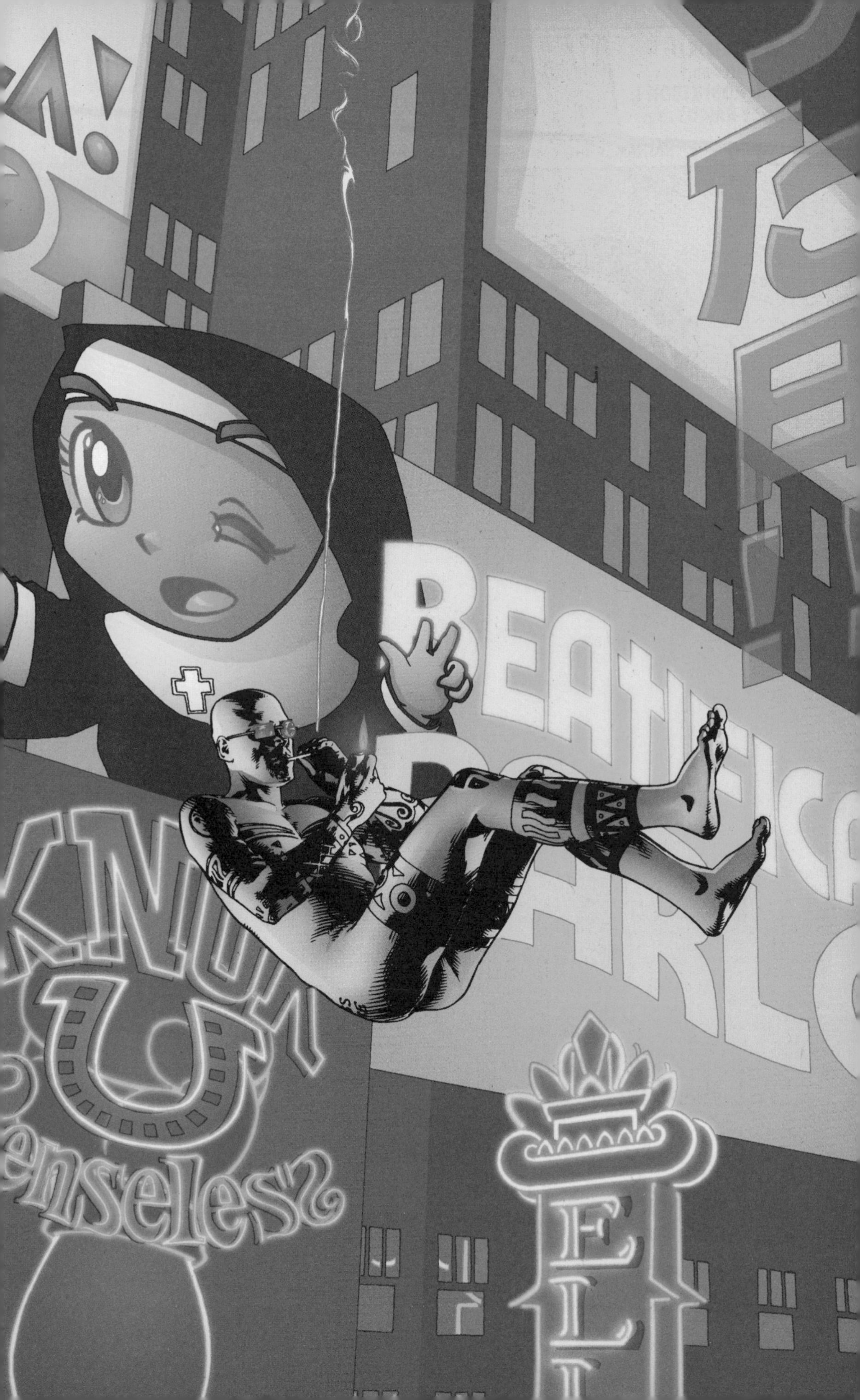

WARREN ELLIS writes and **DARICK ROBERTSON & RODNEY RAMOS** draw

HEADLONG ONE OF THREE

CLEM ROBINS, letterer **NATHAN EYRING**, color & separations **GENE HA**, cover **ZACHARY RAU**, ass't editor **HEIDI MacDONALD**, editor

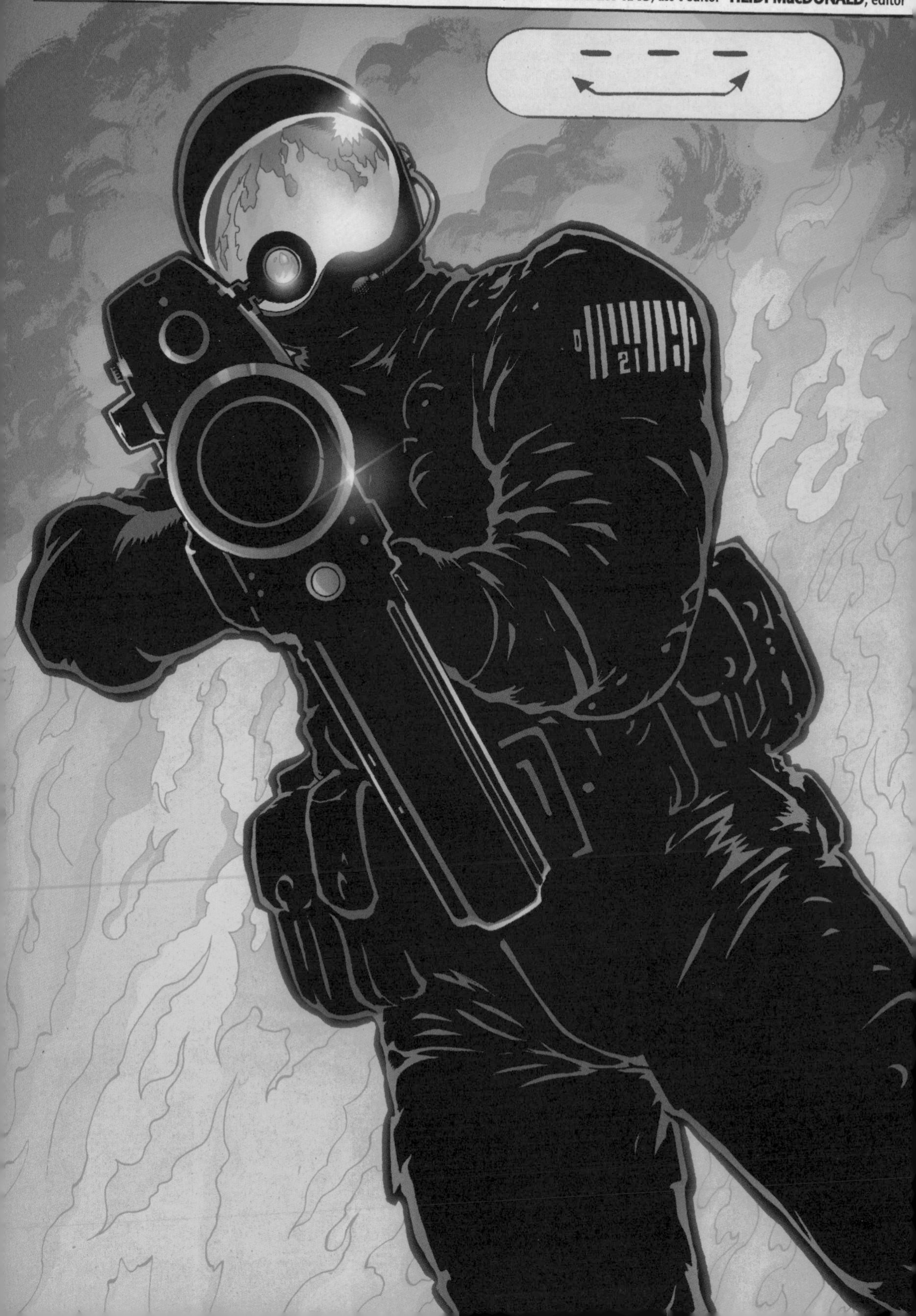

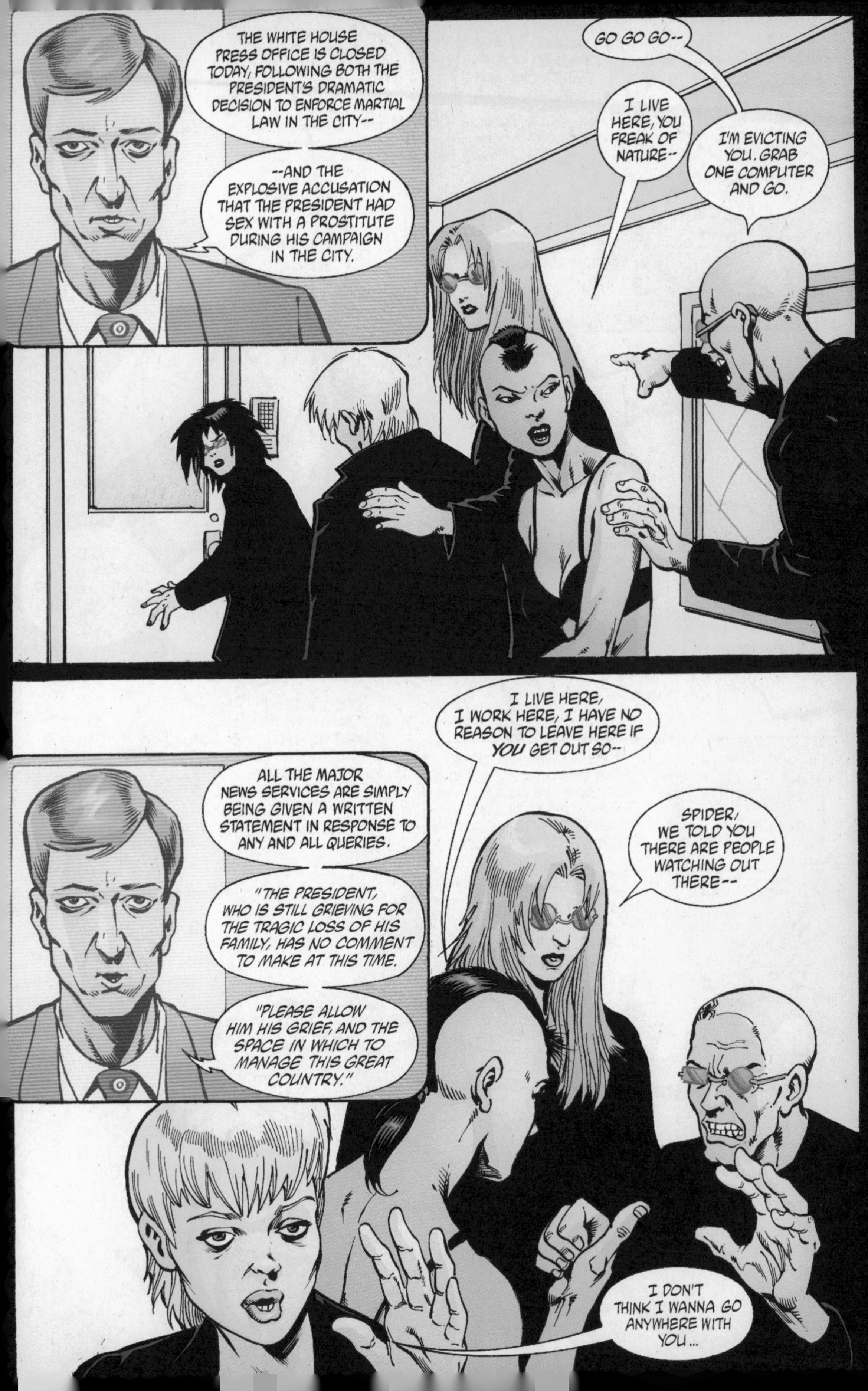
THE WHITE HOUSE PRESS OFFICE IS CLOSED TODAY, FOLLOWING BOTH THE PRESIDENT'S DRAMATIC DECISION TO ENFORCE MARTIAL LAW IN THE CITY--
--AND THE EXPLOSIVE ACCUSATION THAT THE PRESIDENT HAD SEX WITH A PROSTITUTE DURING HIS CAMPAIGN IN THE CITY.
GO GO GO--
I LIVE HERE, YOU FREAK OF NATURE--
I'M EVICTING YOU. GRAB ONE COMPUTER AND GO.
ALL THE MAJOR NEWS SERVICES ARE SIMPLY BEING GIVEN A WRITTEN STATEMENT IN RESPONSE TO ANY AND ALL QUERIES.
"THE PRESIDENT, WHO IS STILL GRIEVING FOR THE TRAGIC LOSS OF HIS FAMILY, HAS NO COMMENT TO MAKE AT THIS TIME.
"PLEASE ALLOW HIM HIS GRIEF, AND THE SPACE IN WHICH TO MANAGE THIS GREAT COUNTRY."
I LIVE HERE, I WORK HERE, I HAVE NO REASON TO LEAVE HERE IF YOU GET OUT SO--
SPIDER, WE TOLD YOU THERE ARE PEOPLE WATCHING OUT THERE--
I DON'T THINK I WANNA GO ANYWHERE WITH YOU...

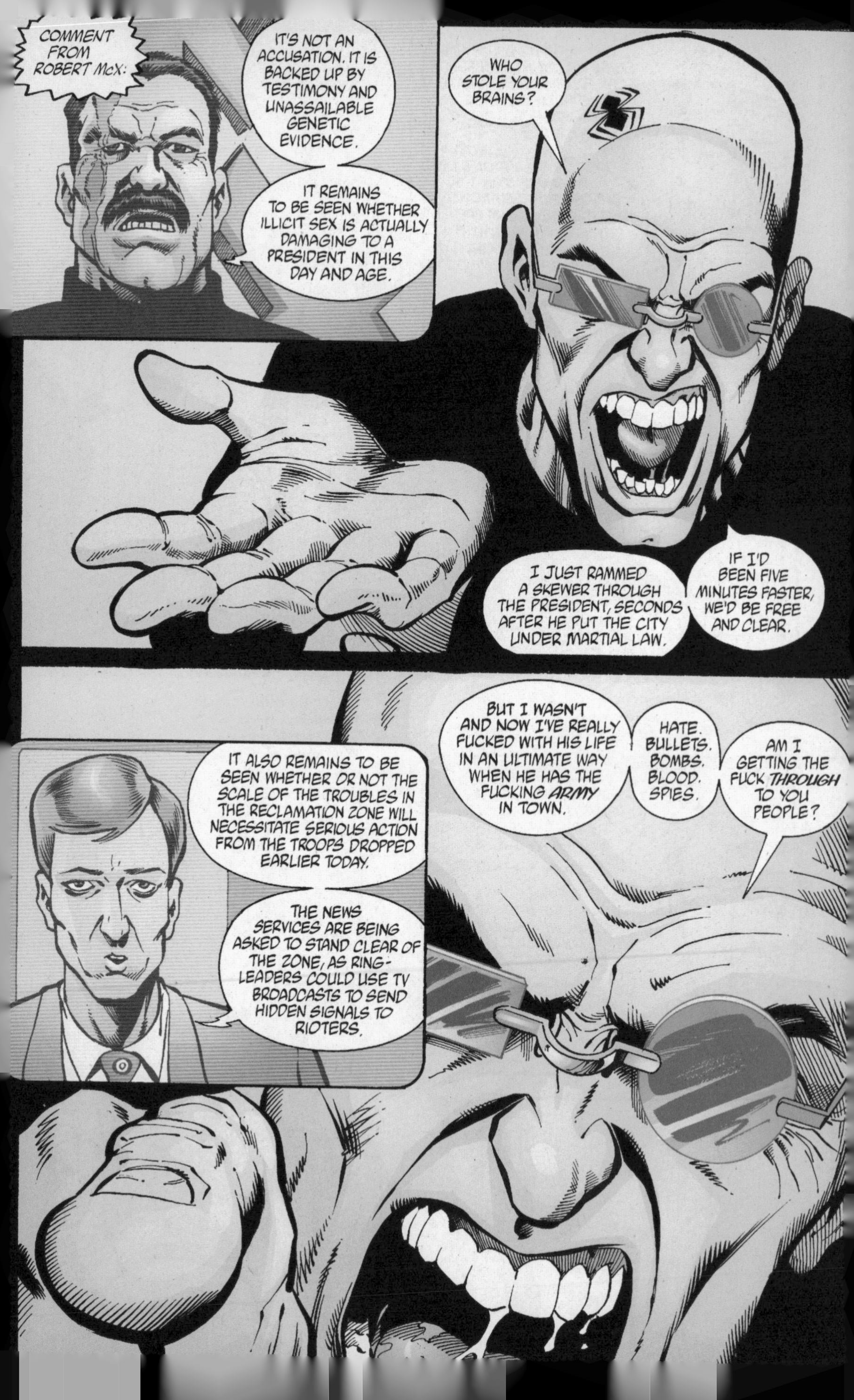
COMMENT FROM ROBERT McX:
IT'S NOT AN ACCUSATION. IT IS BACKED UP BY TESTIMONY AND UNASSAILABLE GENETIC EVIDENCE.
IT REMAINS TO BE SEEN WHETHER ILLICIT SEX IS ACTUALLY DAMAGING TO A PRESIDENT IN THIS DAY AND AGE.
WHO STOLE YOUR BRAINS?
I JUST RAMMED A SKEWER THROUGH THE PRESIDENT, SECONDS AFTER HE PUT THE CITY UNDER MARTIAL LAW.
IF I'D BEEN FIVE MINUTES FASTER, WE'D BE FREE AND CLEAR.
IT ALSO REMAINS TO BE SEEN WHETHER OR NOT THE SCALE OF THE TROUBLES IN THE RECLAMATION ZONE WILL NECESSITATE SERIOUS ACTION FROM THE TROOPS DROPPED EARLIER TODAY.
THE NEWS SERVICES ARE BEING ASKED TO STAND CLEAR OF THE ZONE, AS RING-LEADERS COULD USE TV BROADCASTS TO SEND HIDDEN SIGNALS TO RIOTERS.
BUT I WASN'T AND NOW I'VE REALLY FUCKED WITH HIS LIFE IN AN ULTIMATE WAY WHEN HE HAS THE FUCKING *ARMY* IN TOWN.
HATE. BULLETS. BOMBS. BLOOD. SPIES.
AM I GETTING THE FUCK *THROUGH* TO YOU PEOPLE?

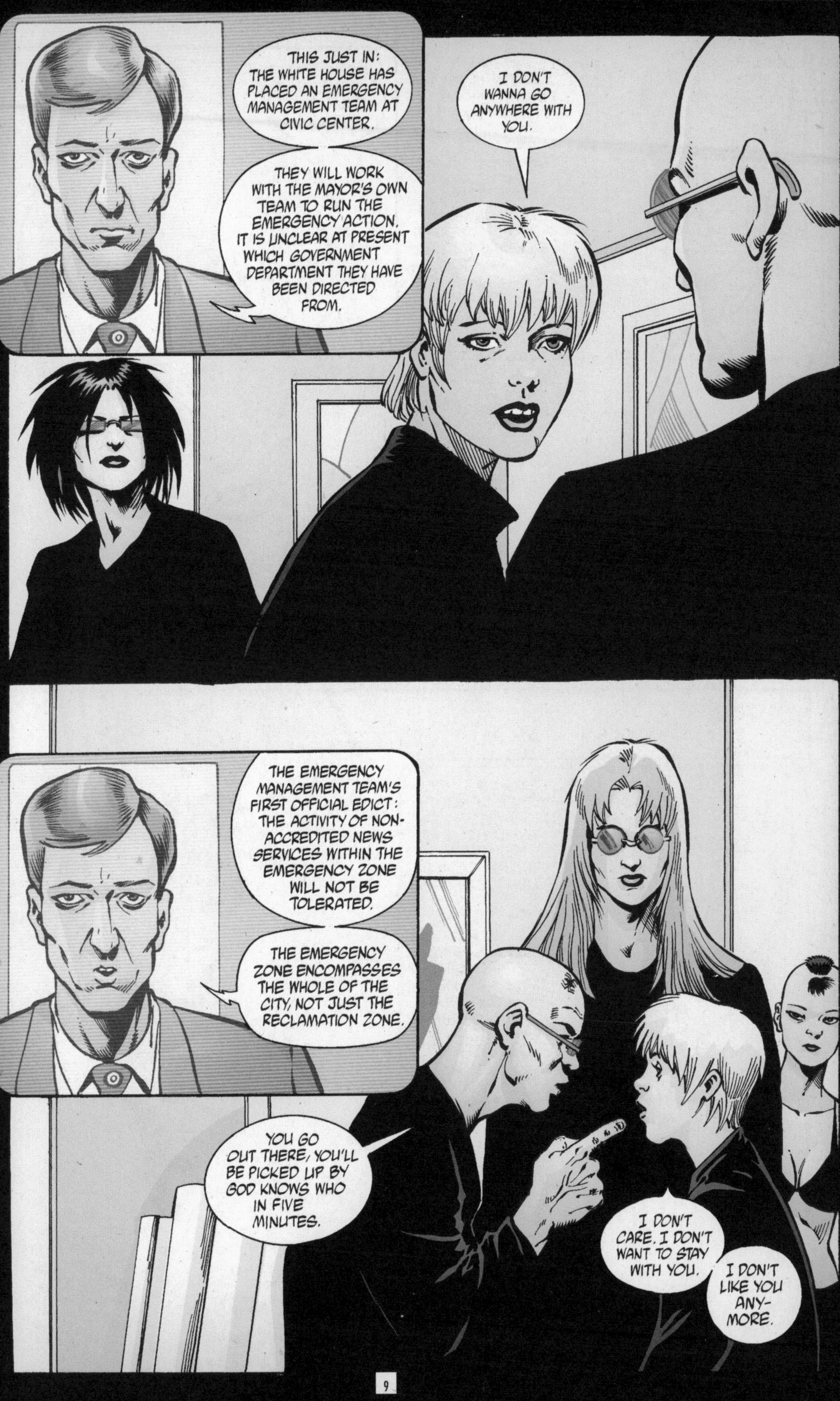
THIS JUST IN: THE WHITE HOUSE HAS PLACED AN EMERGENCY MANAGEMENT TEAM AT CIVIC CENTER.
THEY WILL WORK WITH THE MAYOR'S OWN TEAM TO RUN THE EMERGENCY ACTION. IT IS UNCLEAR AT PRESENT WHICH GOVERNMENT DEPARTMENT THEY HAVE BEEN DIRECTED FROM.
I DON'T WANNA GO ANYWHERE WITH YOU.
THE EMERGENCY MANAGEMENT TEAM'S FIRST OFFICIAL EDICT: THE ACTIVITY OF NON-ACCREDITED NEWS SERVICES WITHIN THE EMERGENCY ZONE WILL NOT BE TOLERATED.
THE EMERGENCY ZONE ENCOMPASSES THE WHOLE OF THE CITY, NOT JUST THE RECLAMATION ZONE.
YOU GO OUT THERE, YOU'LL BE PICKED UP BY GOD KNOWS WHO IN FIVE MINUTES.
I DON'T CARE. I DON'T WANT TO STAY WITH YOU.
I DON'T LIKE YOU ANY-MORE.

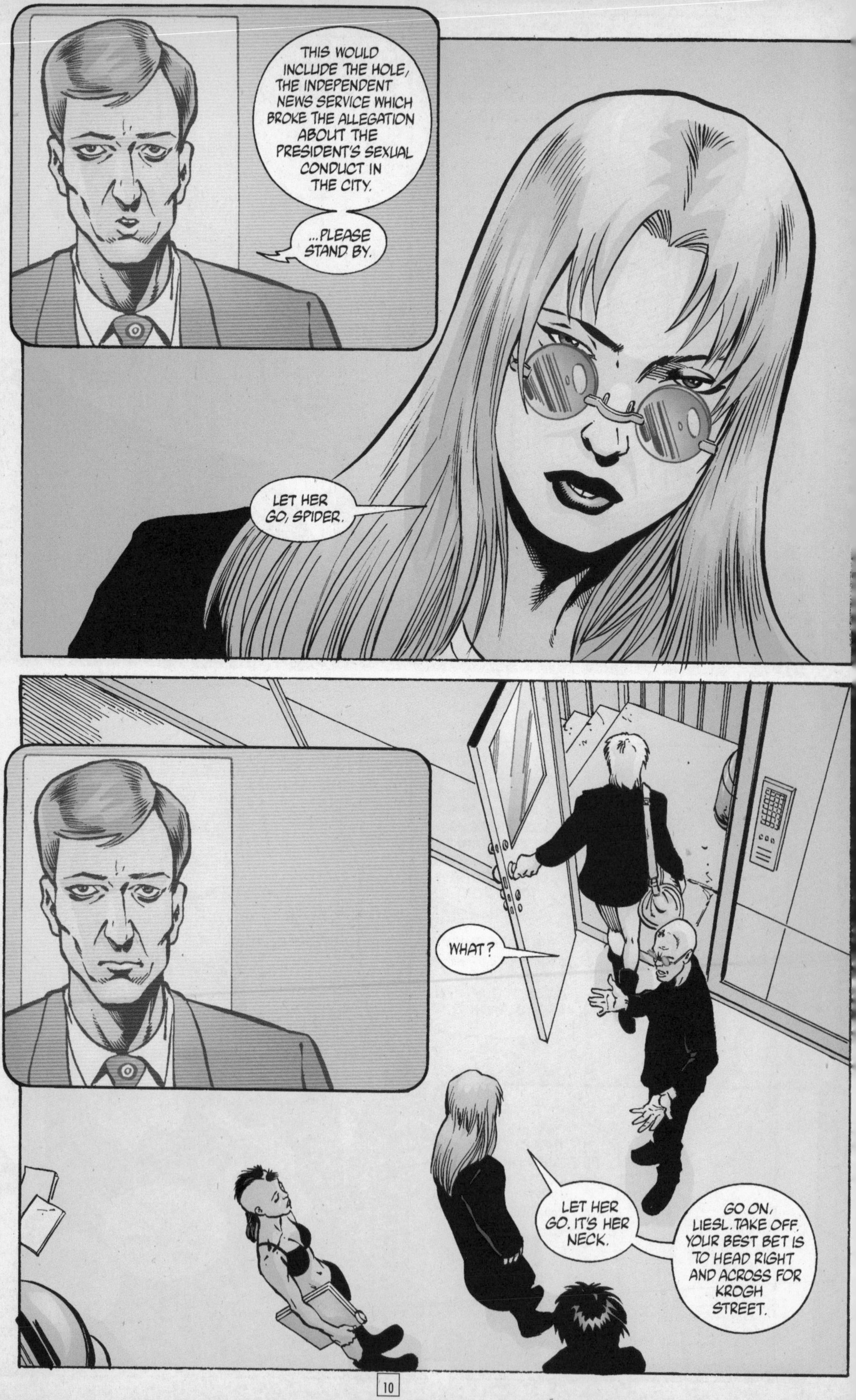
THIS WOULD INCLUDE THE HOLE, THE INDEPENDENT NEWS SERVICE WHICH BROKE THE ALLEGATION ABOUT THE PRESIDENT'S SEXUAL CONDUCT IN THE CITY.
...PLEASE STAND BY.
LET HER GO, SPIDER.
WHAT?
LET HER GO. IT'S HER NECK.
GO ON, LIESL. TAKE OFF. YOUR BEST BET IS TO HEAD RIGHT AND ACROSS FOR KROGH STREET.

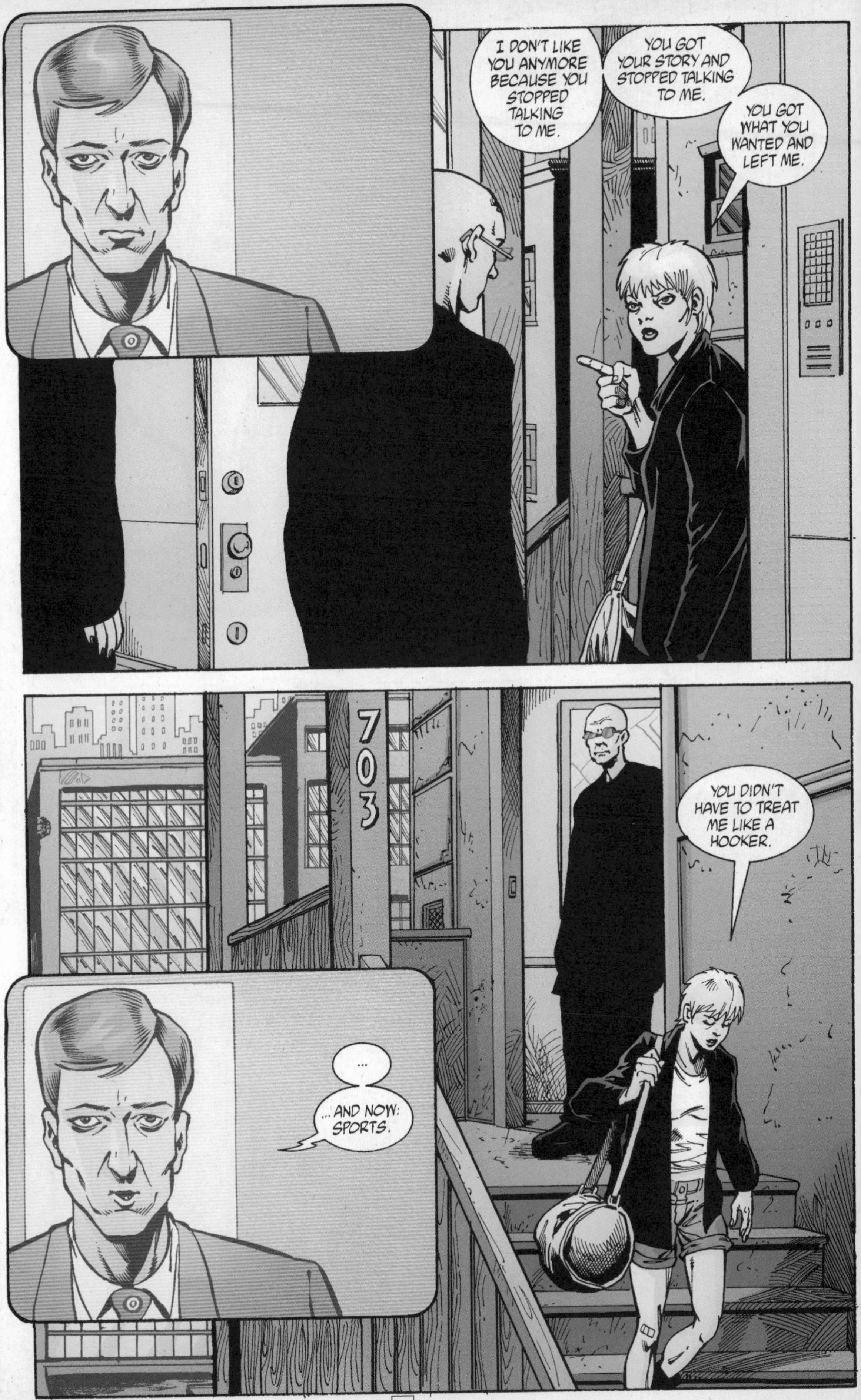
I DON'T LIKE YOU ANYMORE BECAUSE YOU STOPPED TALKING TO ME.
YOU GOT YOUR STORY AND STOPPED TALKING TO ME.
YOU GOT WHAT YOU WANTED AND LEFT ME.
703
YOU DIDN'T HAVE TO TREAT ME LIKE A HOOKER.
...
...AND NOW: SPORTS.

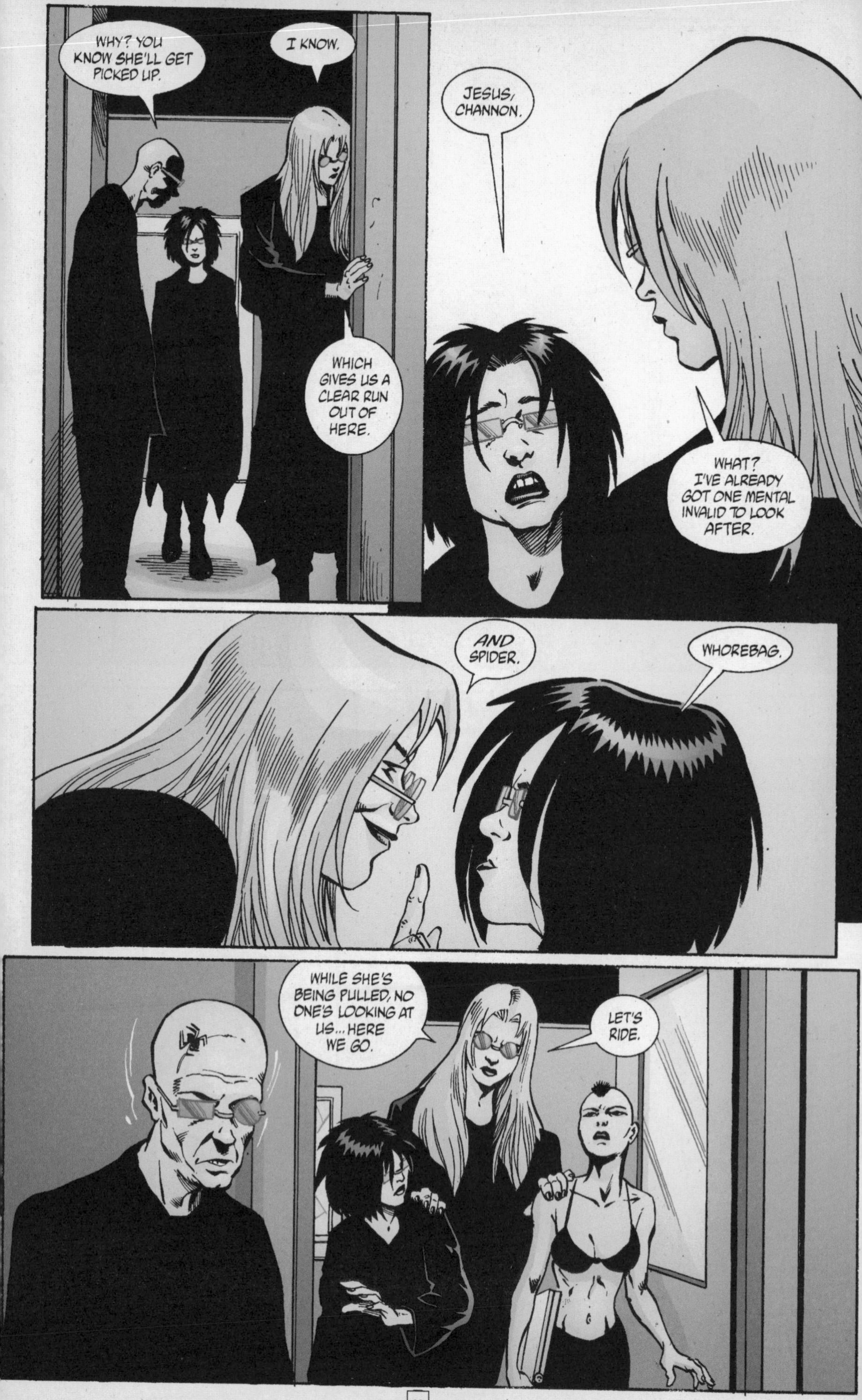
WHY? YOU KNOW SHE'LL GET PICKED UP.
I KNOW.
WHICH GIVES US A CLEAR RUN OUT OF HERE.
JESUS, CHANNON.
WHAT? I'VE ALREADY GOT ONE MENTAL INVALID TO LOOK AFTER.
AND SPIDER.
WHOREBAG.
WHILE SHE'S BEING PULLED, NO ONE'S LOOKING AT US... HERE WE GO.
LET'S RIDE.

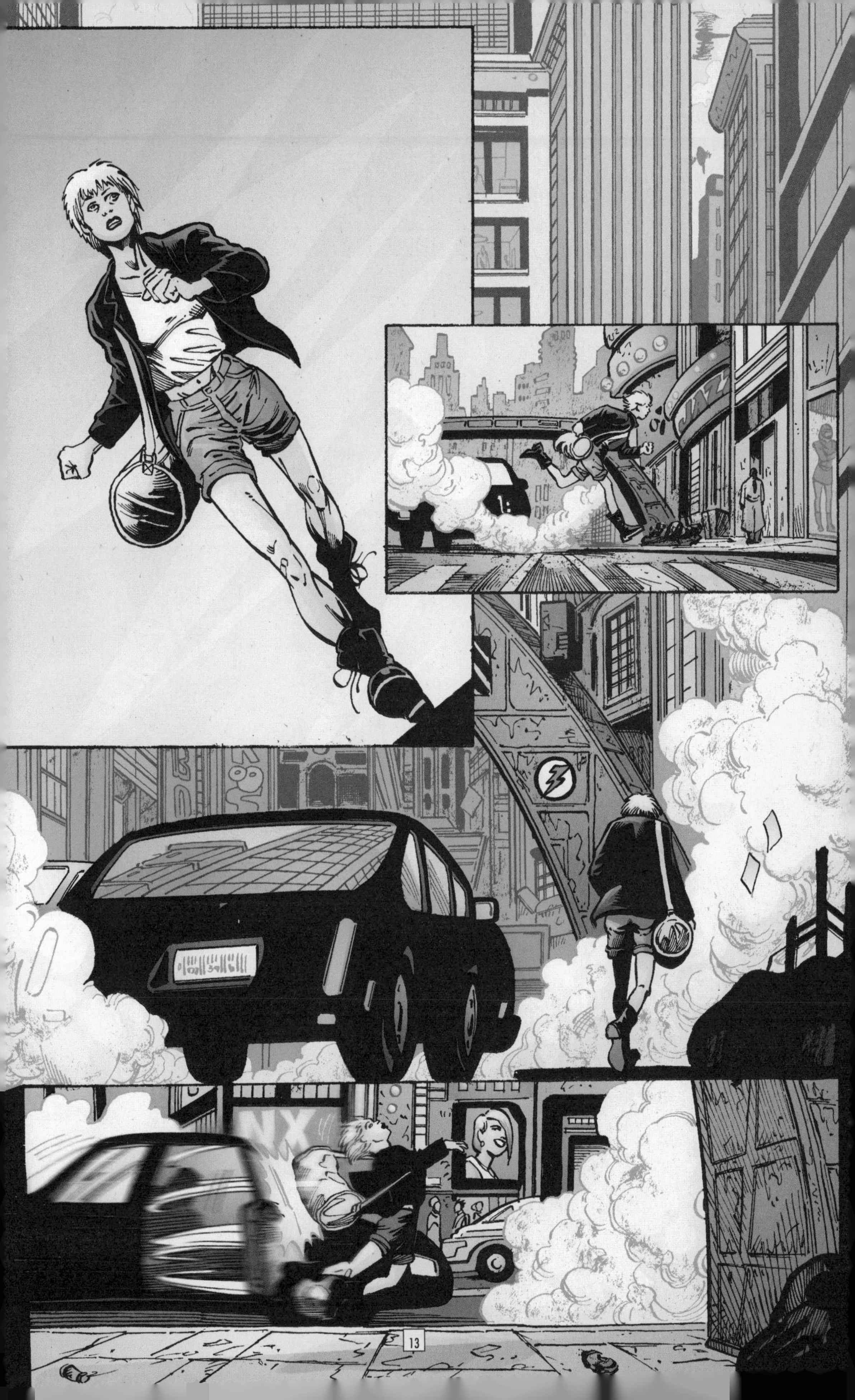

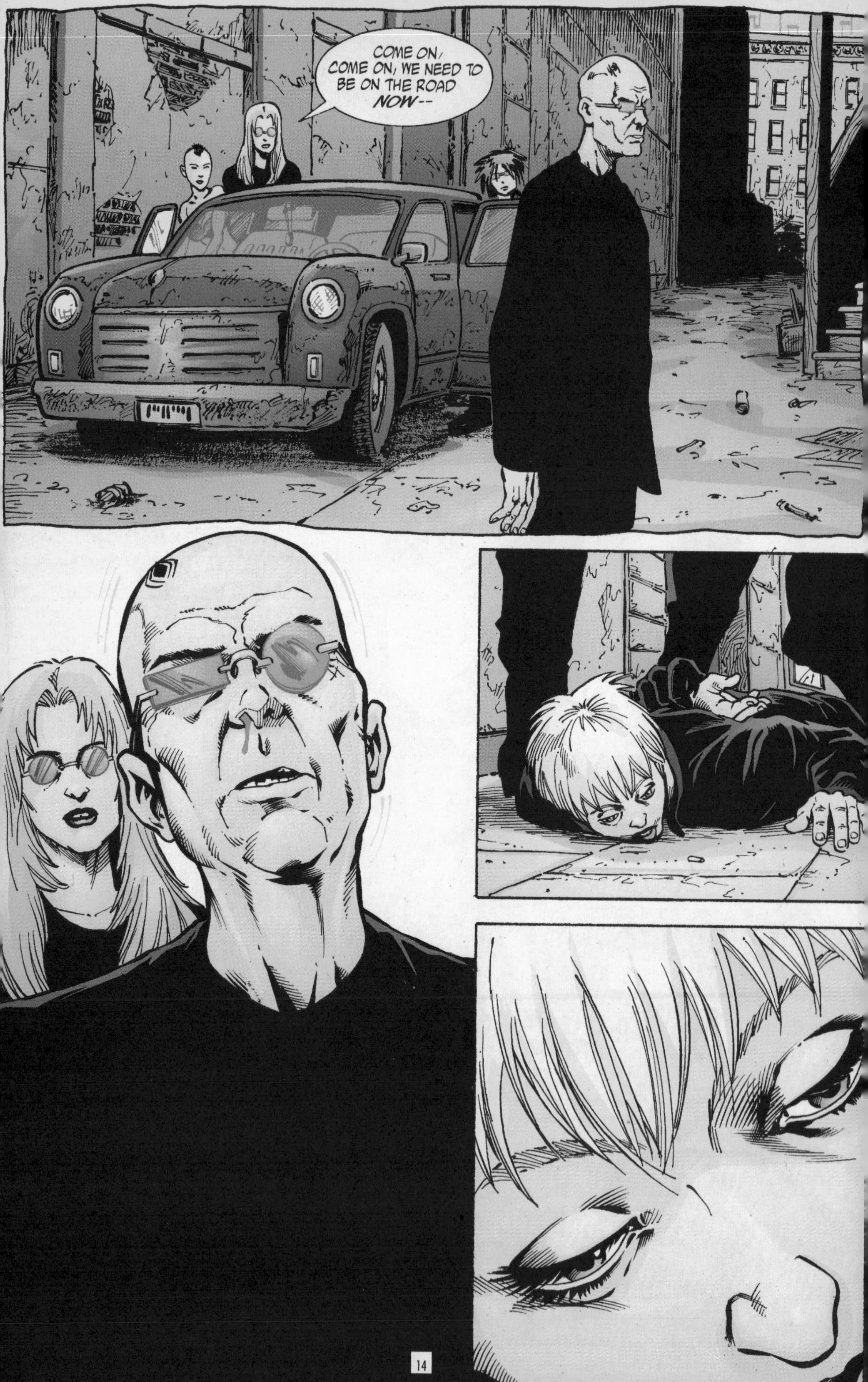
COME ON, COME ON, WE NEED TO BE ON THE ROAD NOW--

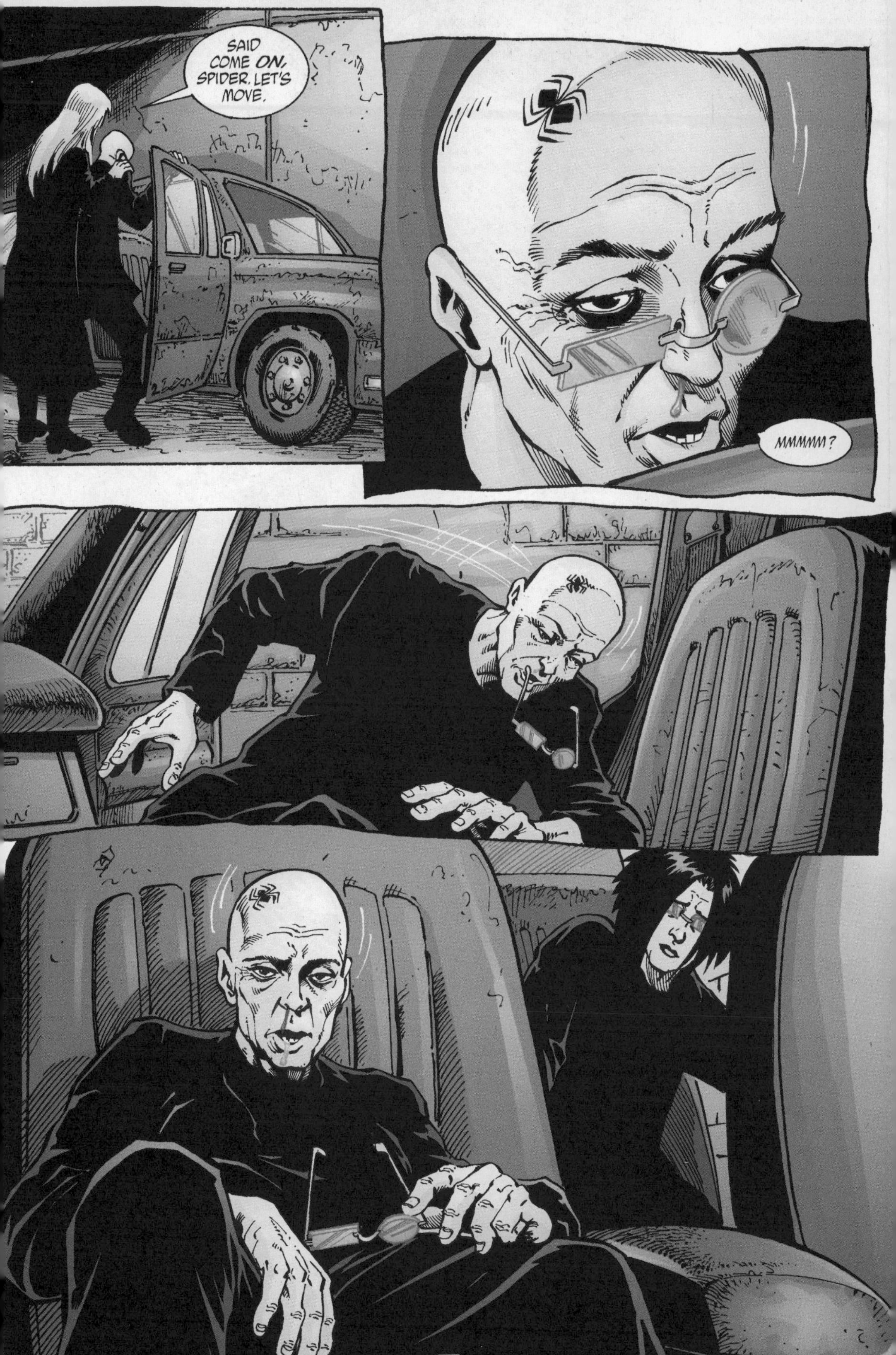
SAID COME ON, SPIDER. LET'S MOVE.
MMMMM?

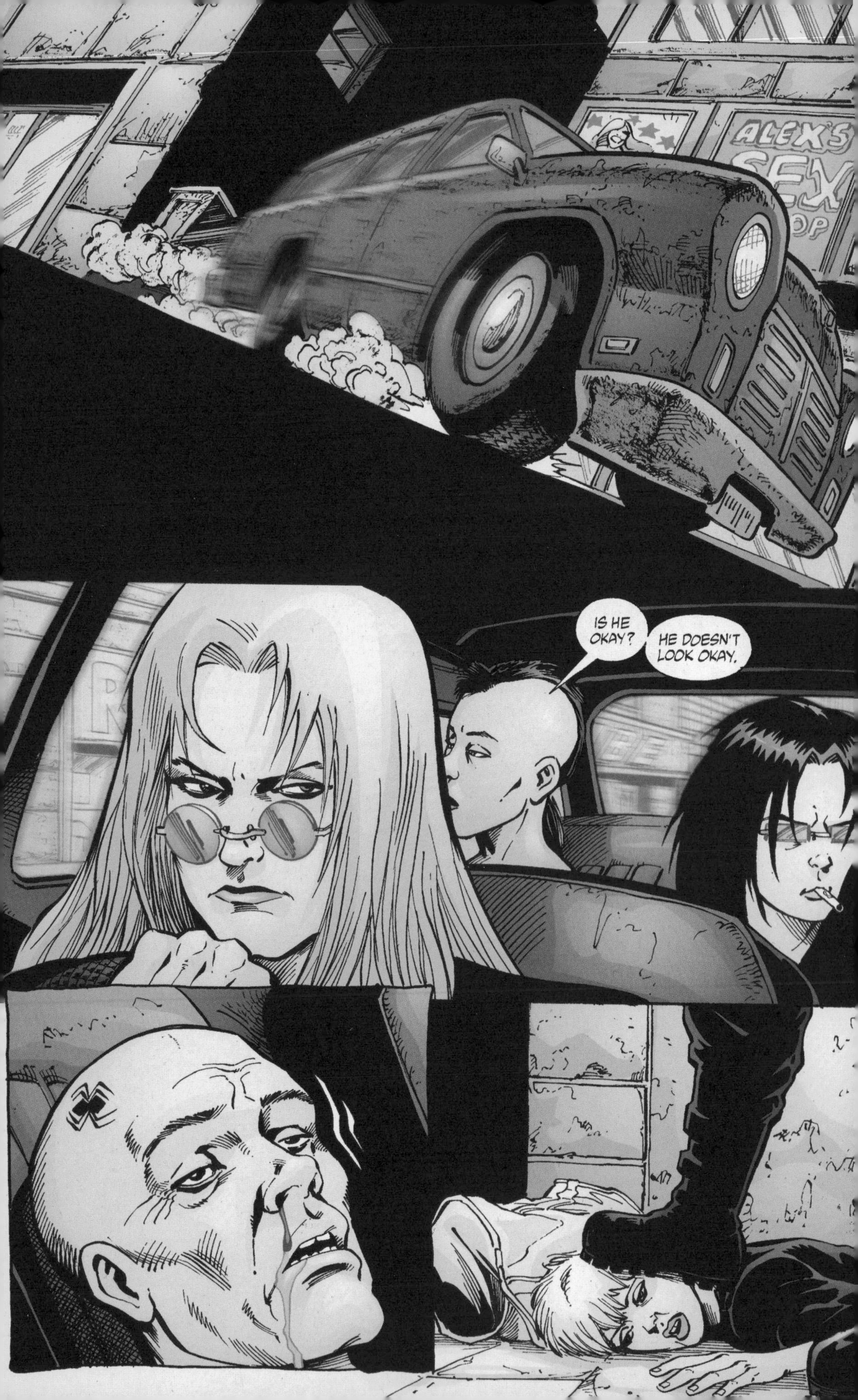
ALEX'S
SEX
IS HE OKAY?
HE DOESN'T LOOK OKAY.

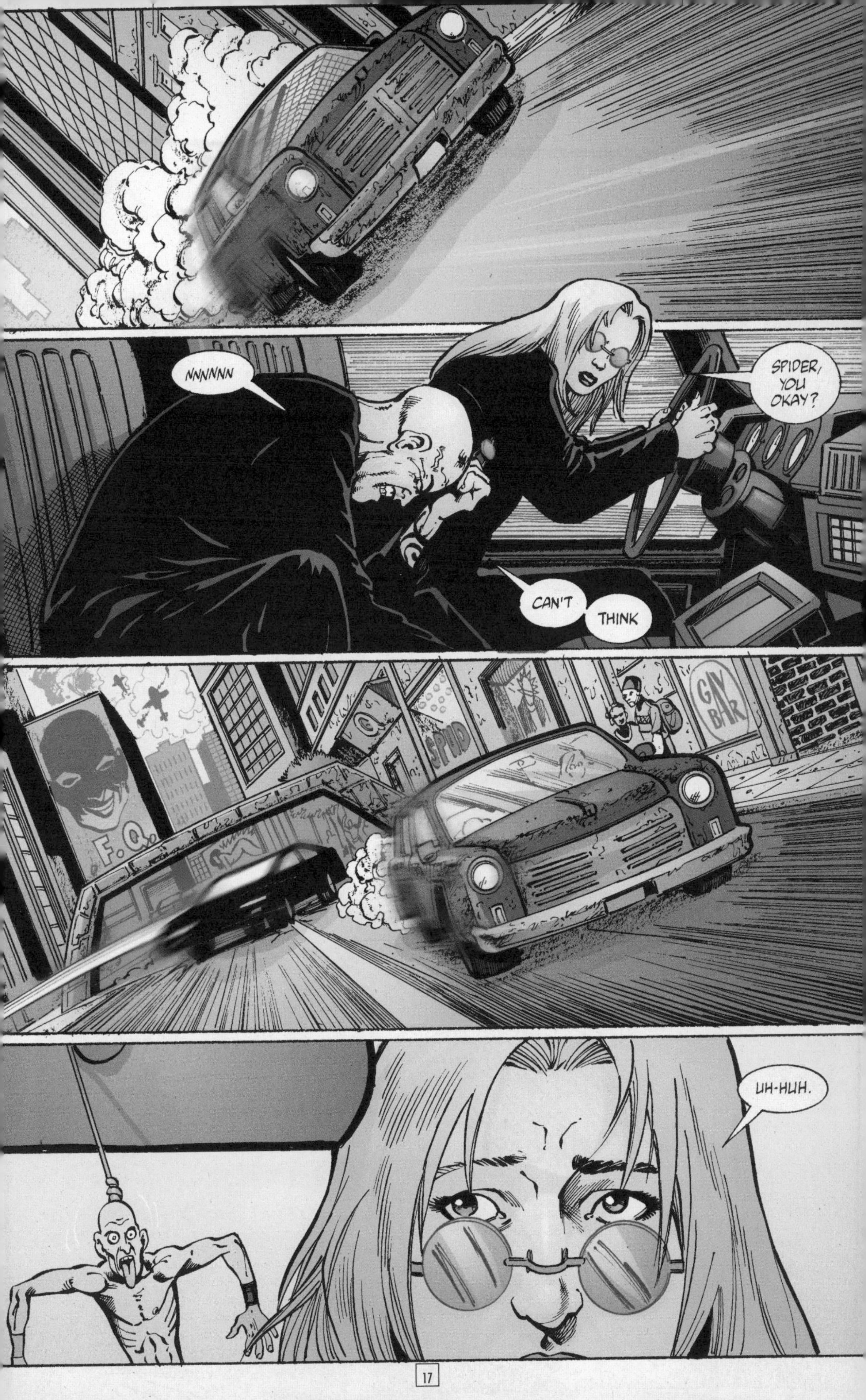
NNNNNN
SPIDER, YOU OKAY?
CAN'T
THINK
SPUD
GAY BAR
F.C.
UH-HUH.

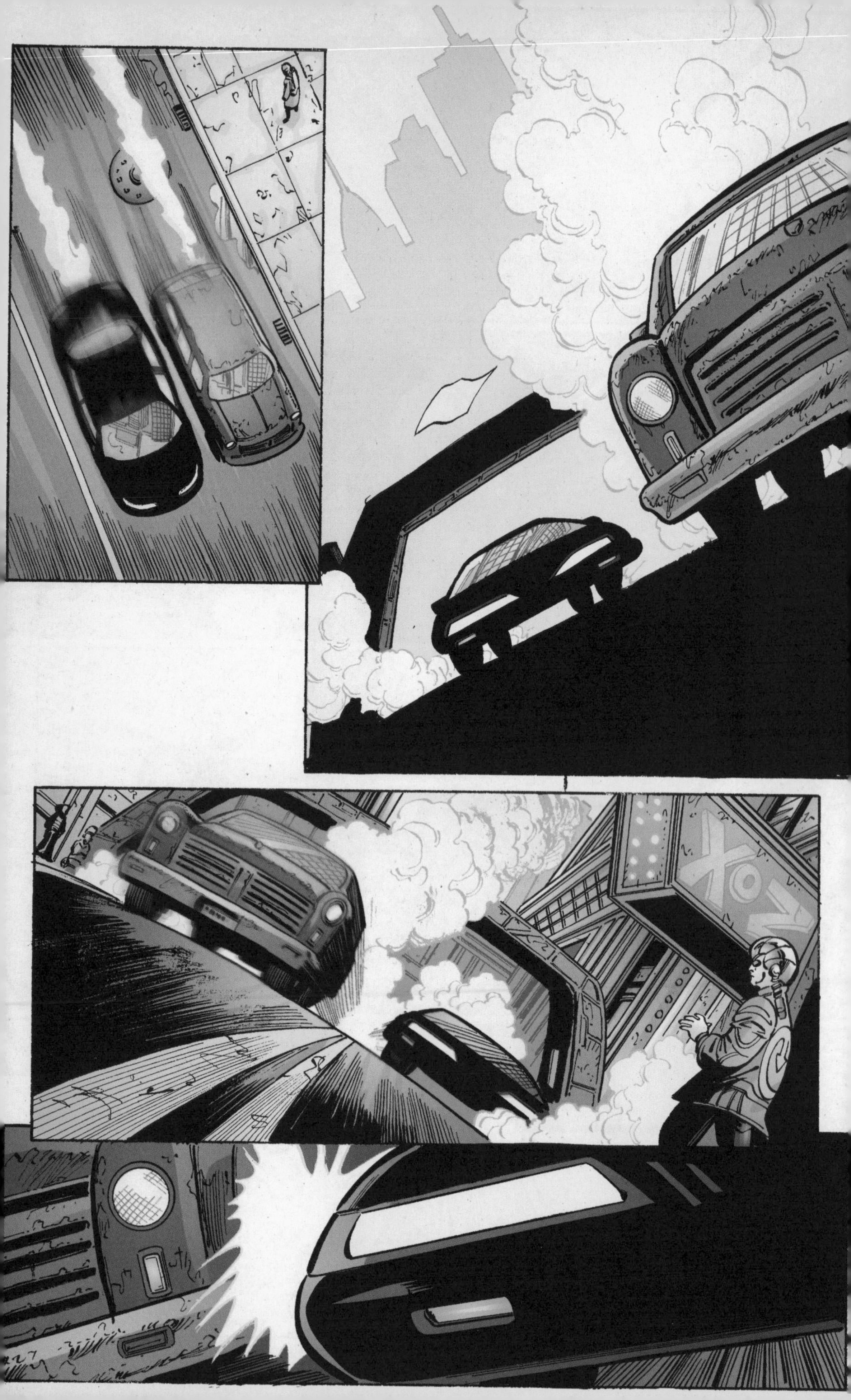

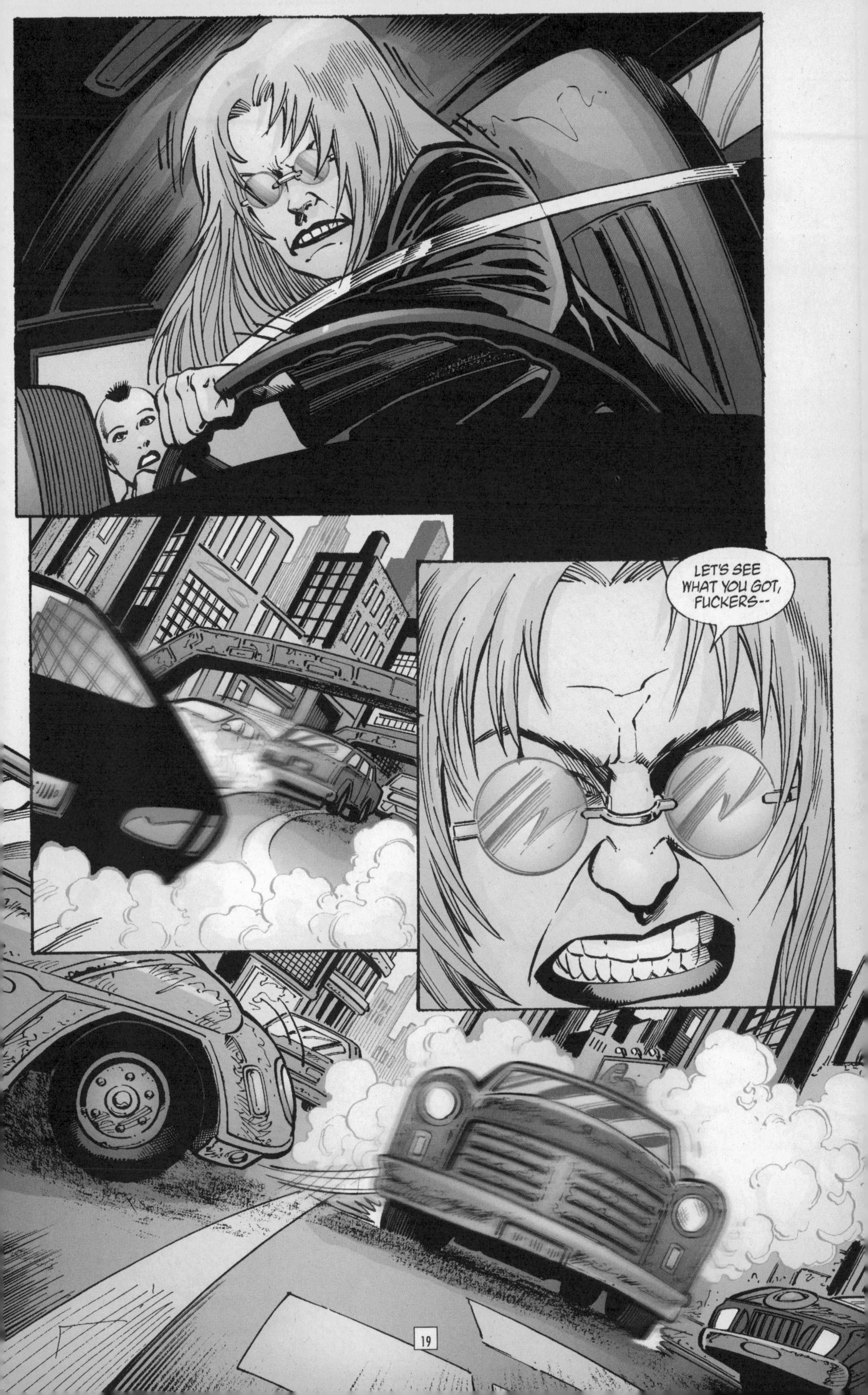
LET'S SEE WHAT YOU GOT, FUCKERS--

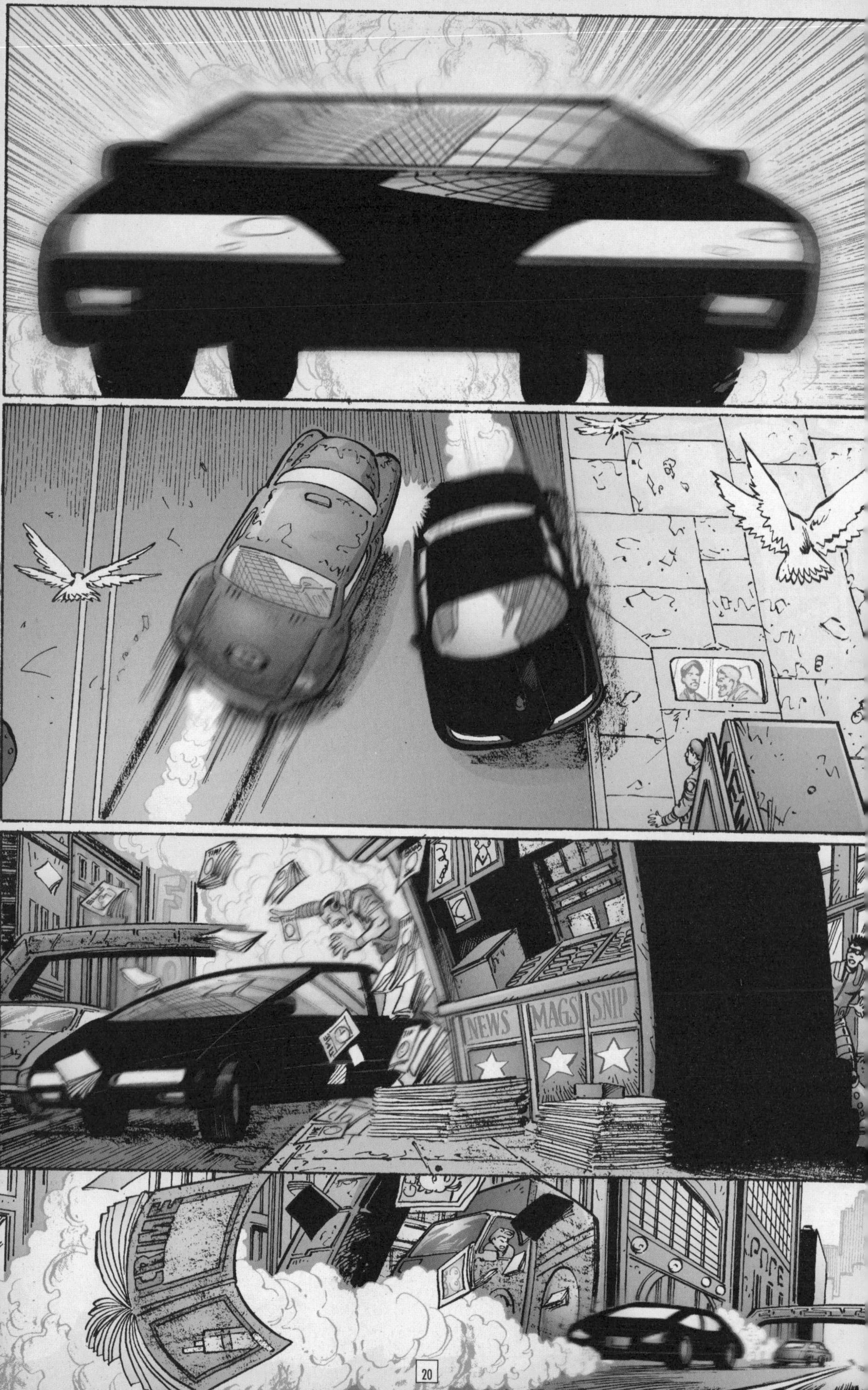
NEWS
MAGS
SNIP
CRIME

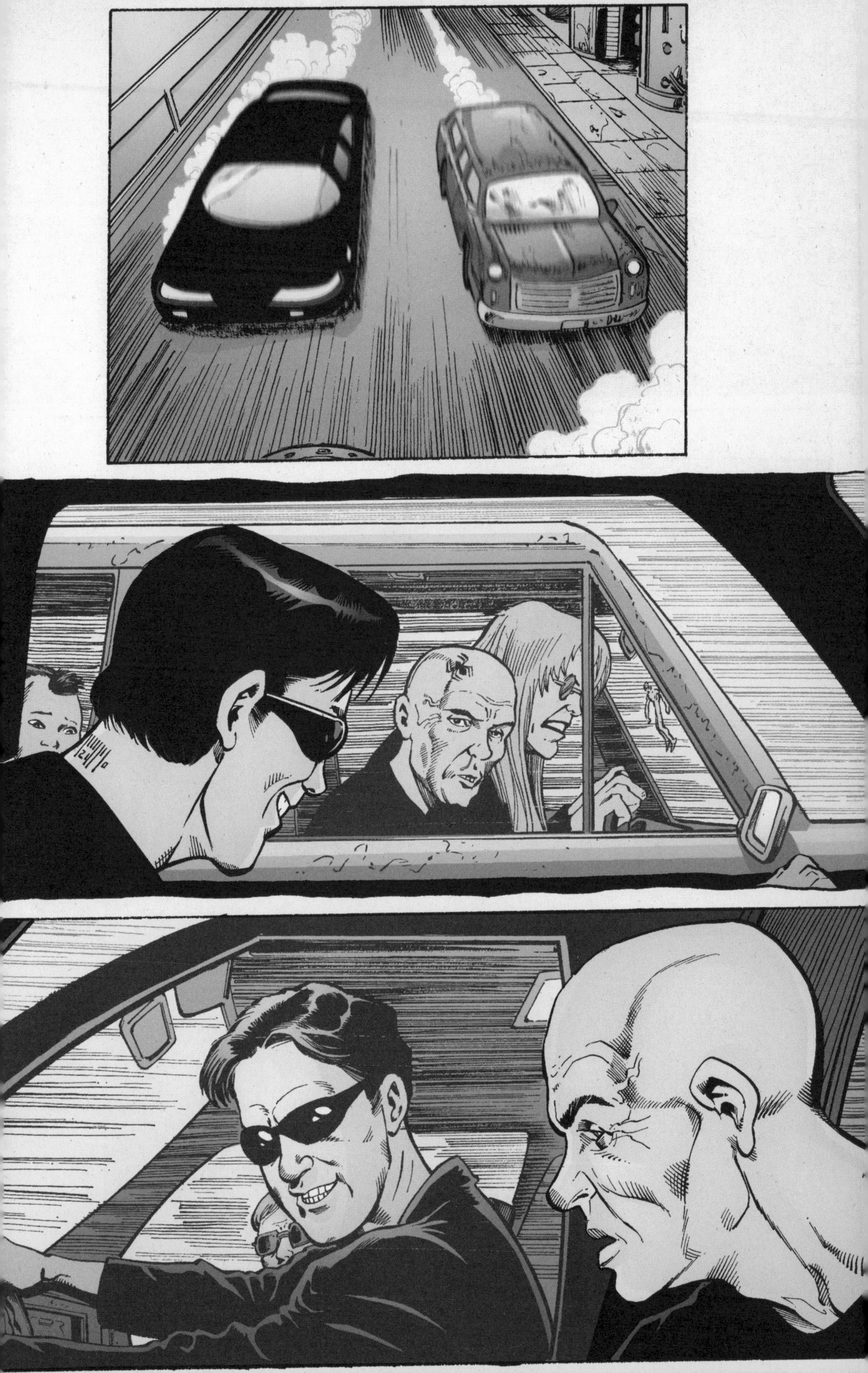

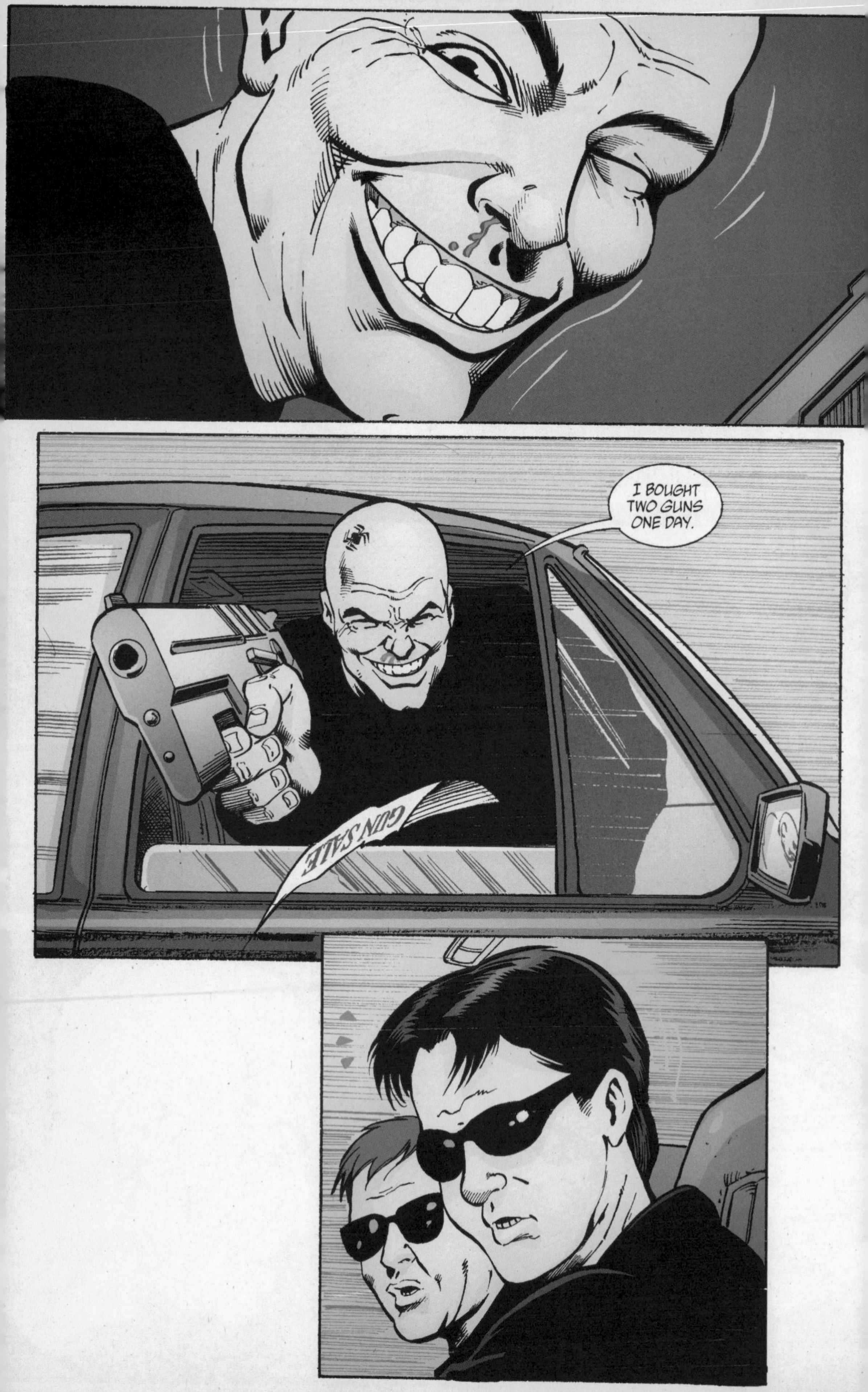
I BOUGHT TWO GUNS ONE DAY.
GUN SALE

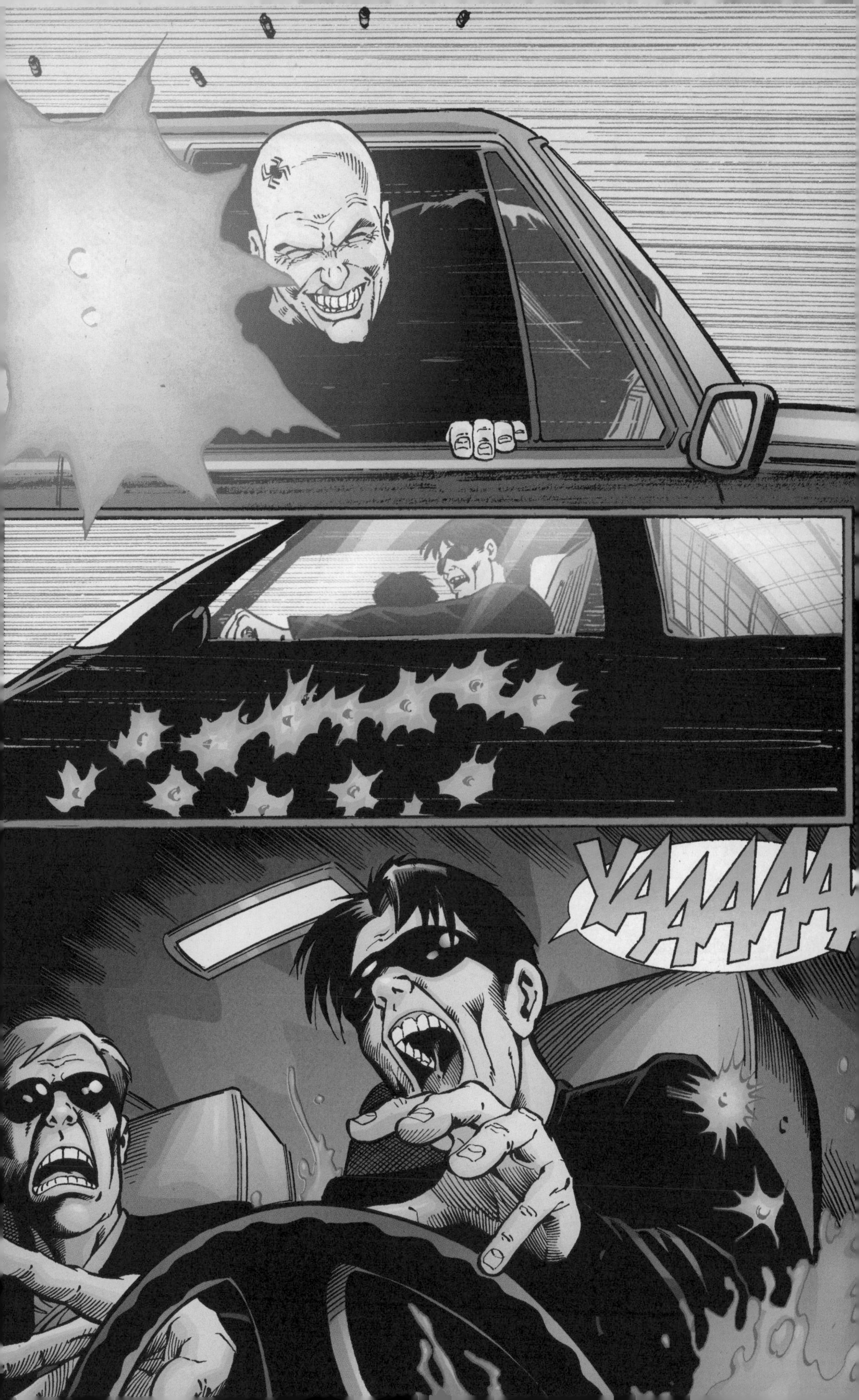
YAAAAA

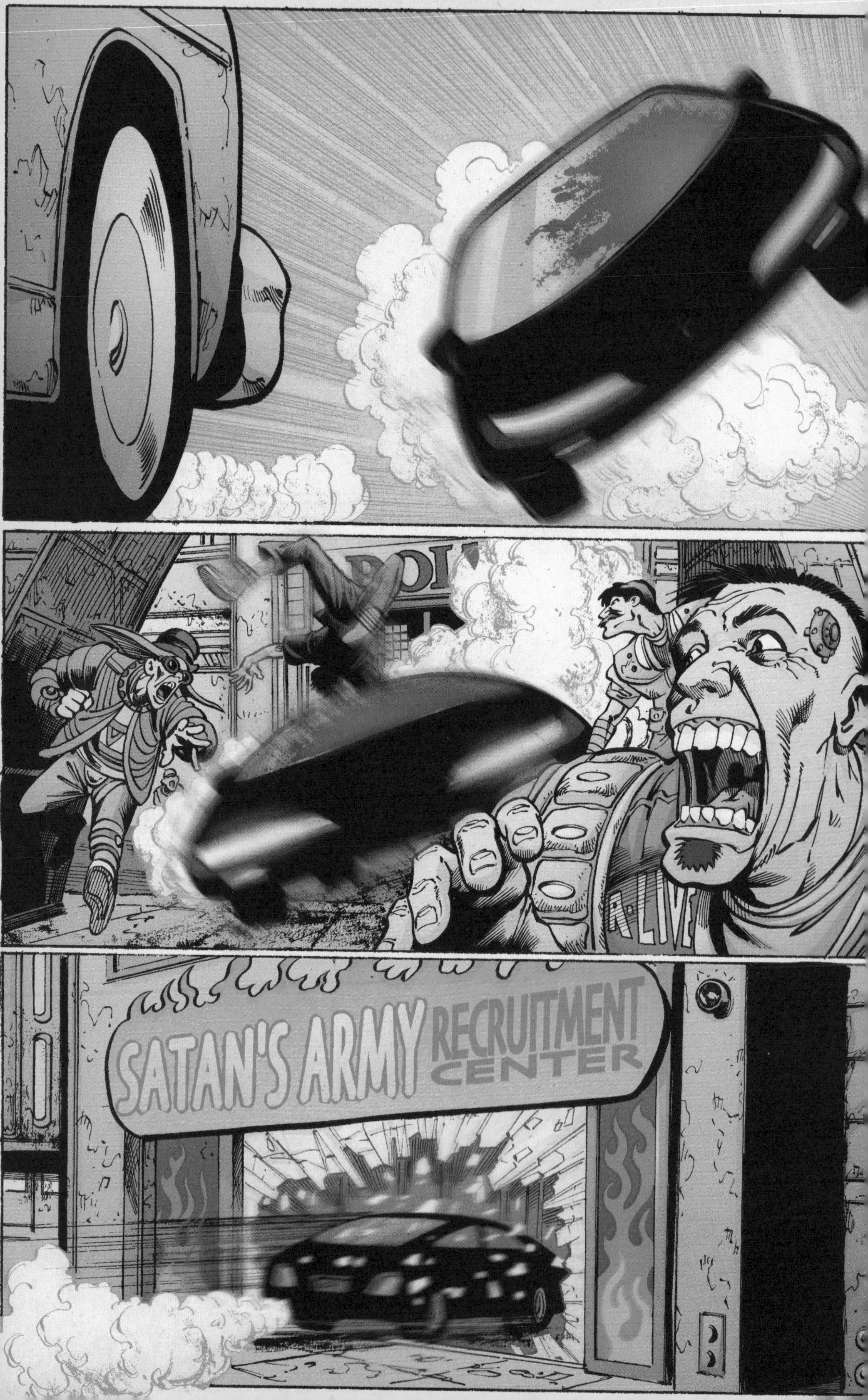
SATAN'S ARMY
RECRUITMENT CENTER

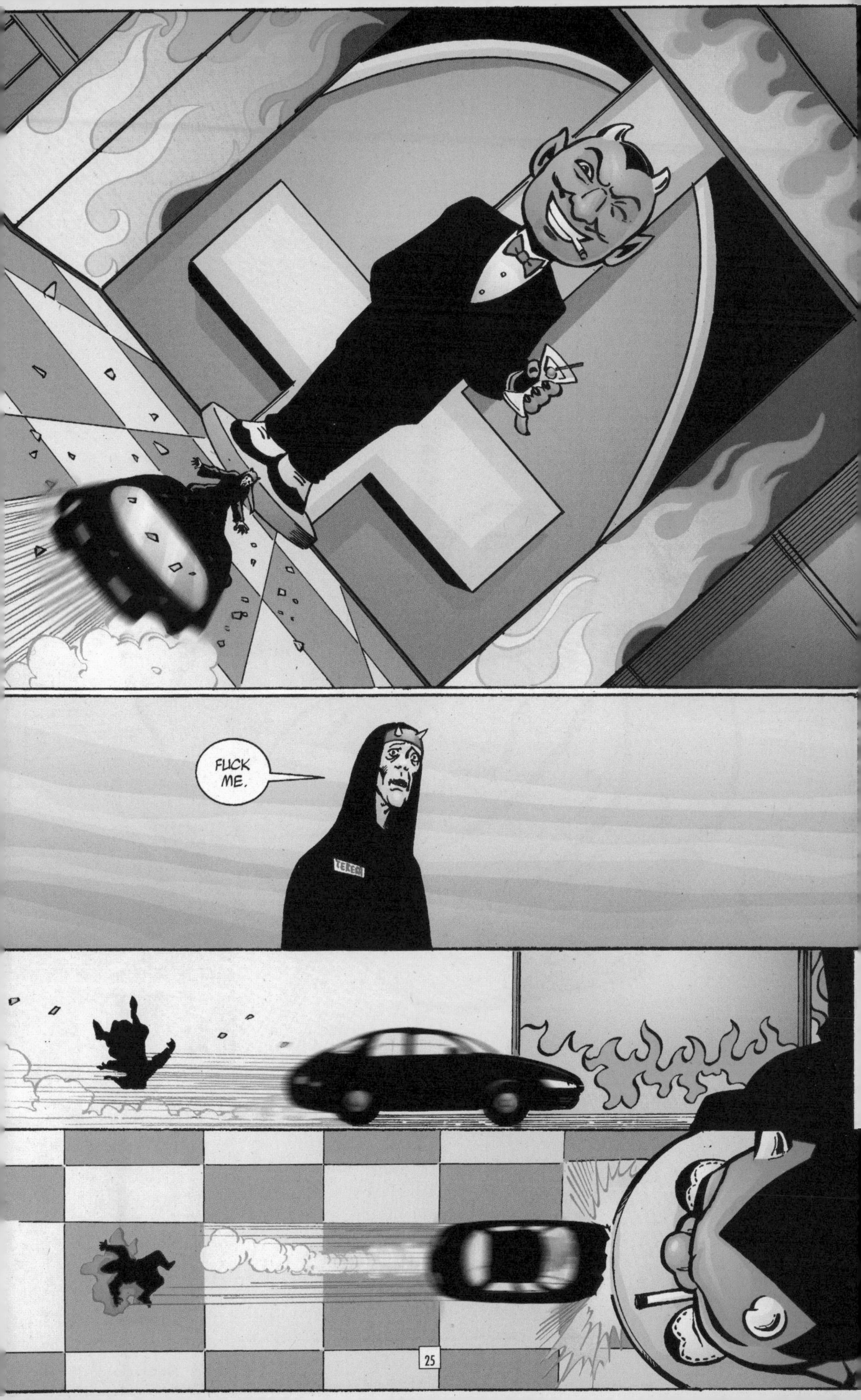
FUCK ME.
TEREM

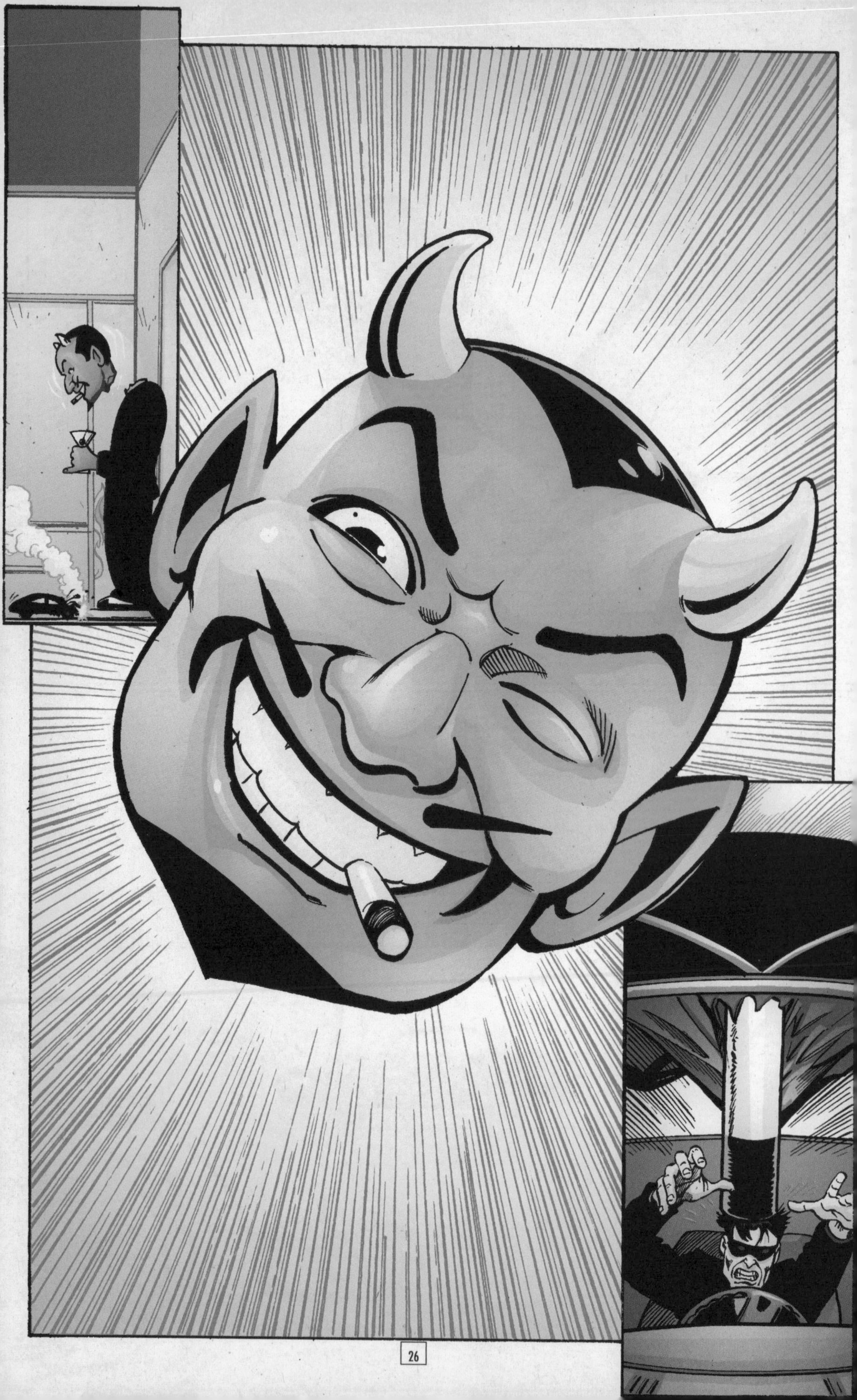

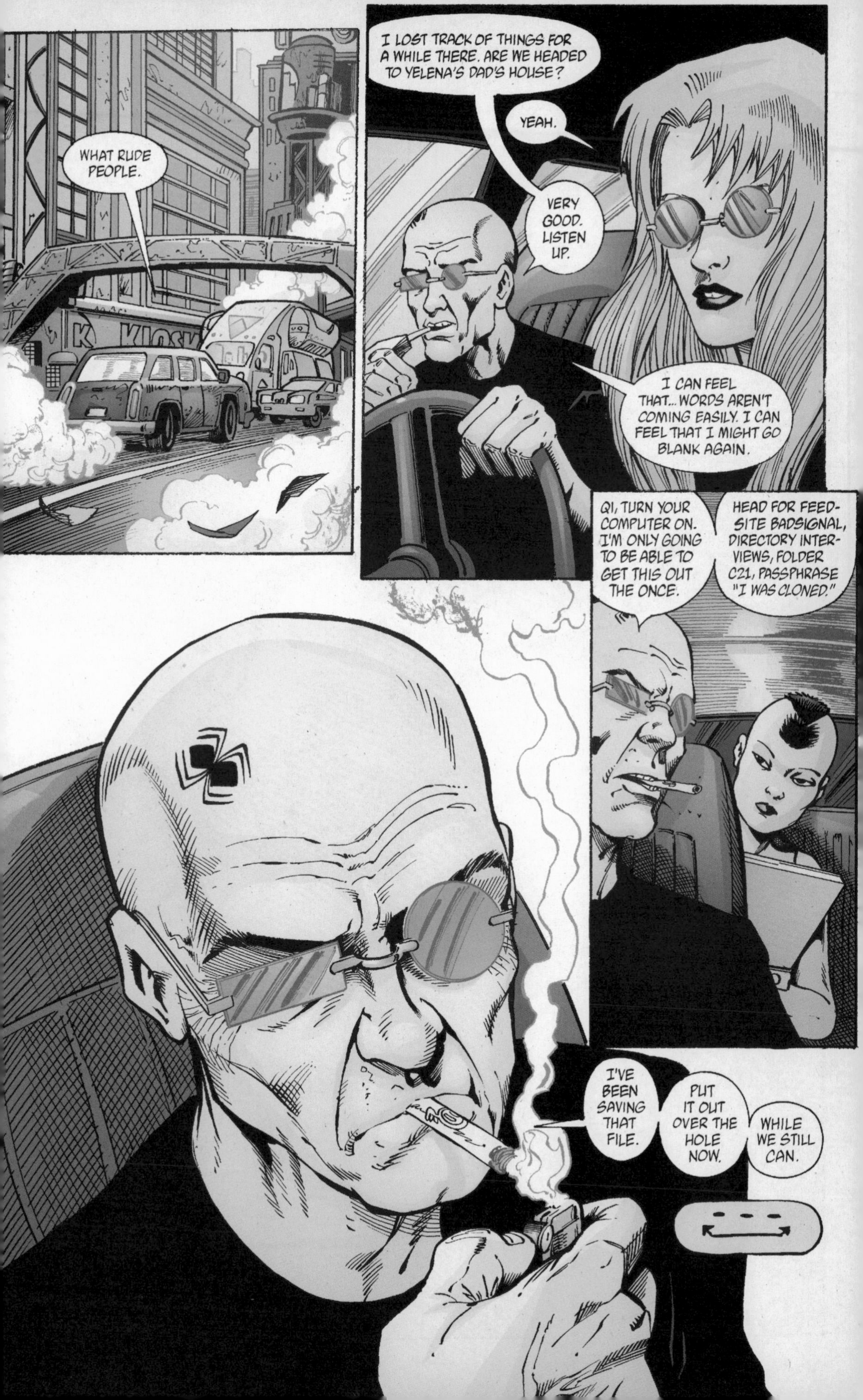
WHAT RUDE PEOPLE.
KIOSK
I LOST TRACK OF THINGS FOR A WHILE THERE. ARE WE HEADED TO YELENA'S DAD'S HOUSE?
YEAH.
VERY GOOD. LISTEN UP.
I CAN FEEL THAT... WORDS AREN'T COMING EASILY. I CAN FEEL THAT I MIGHT GO BLANK AGAIN.
QI, TURN YOUR COMPUTER ON. I'M ONLY GOING TO BE ABLE TO GET THIS OUT THE ONCE.
HEAD FOR FEED-SITE BADSIGNAL, DIRECTORY INTERVIEWS, FOLDER C21, PASSPHRASE "I WAS CLONED."
I'VE BEEN SAVING THAT FILE.
PUT IT OUT OVER THE HOLE NOW.
WHILE WE STILL CAN.

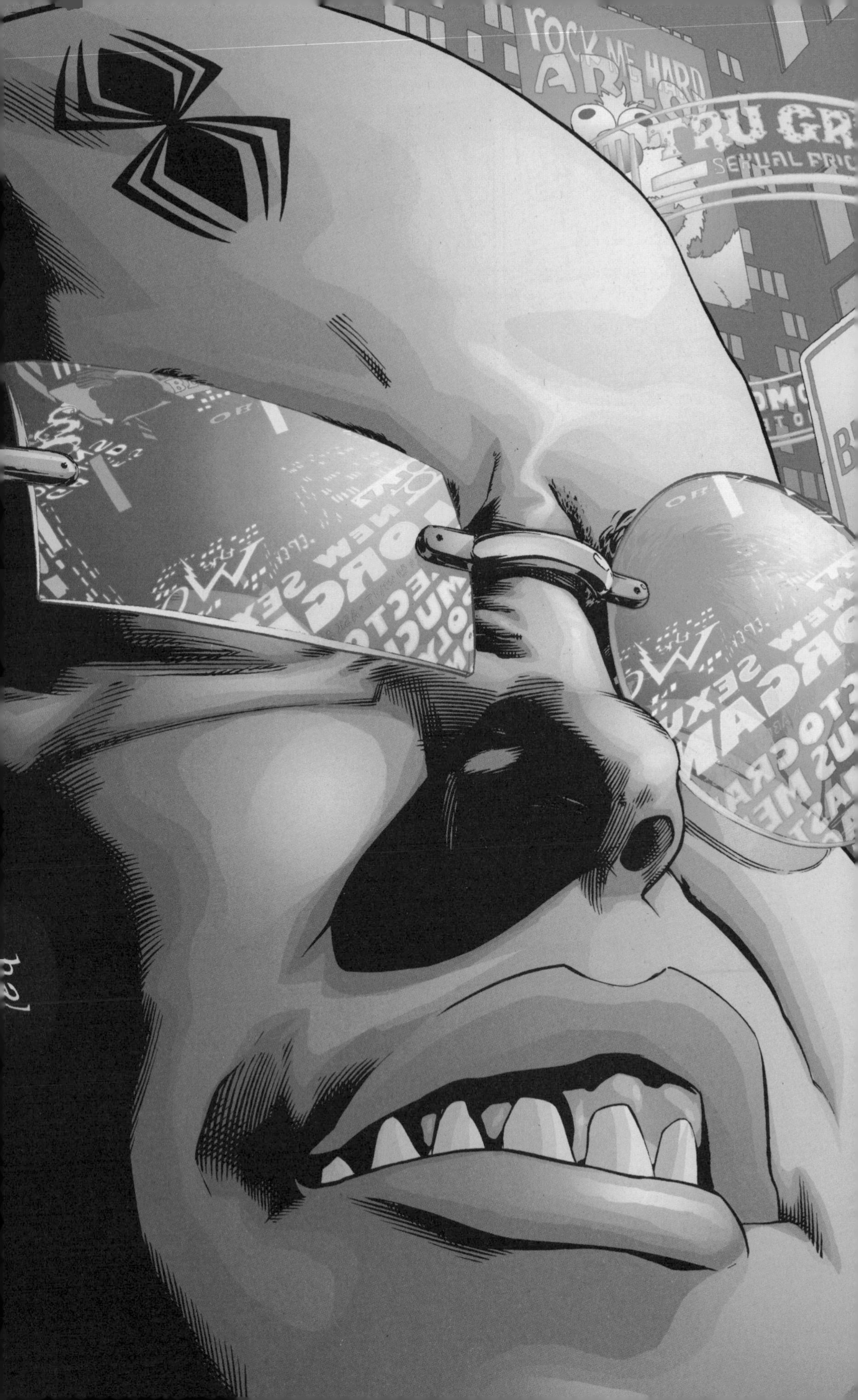
ROCK ME HARD

WARREN ELLIS writes and DARICK ROBERTSON & RODNEY RAMOS draw

HEADLONG

CLEM ROBINS, letterer NATHAN EYRING, color & separations GENE HA, cover ZACHARY RAU, ass't editor HEIDI MacDONALD, editor

2 of 3

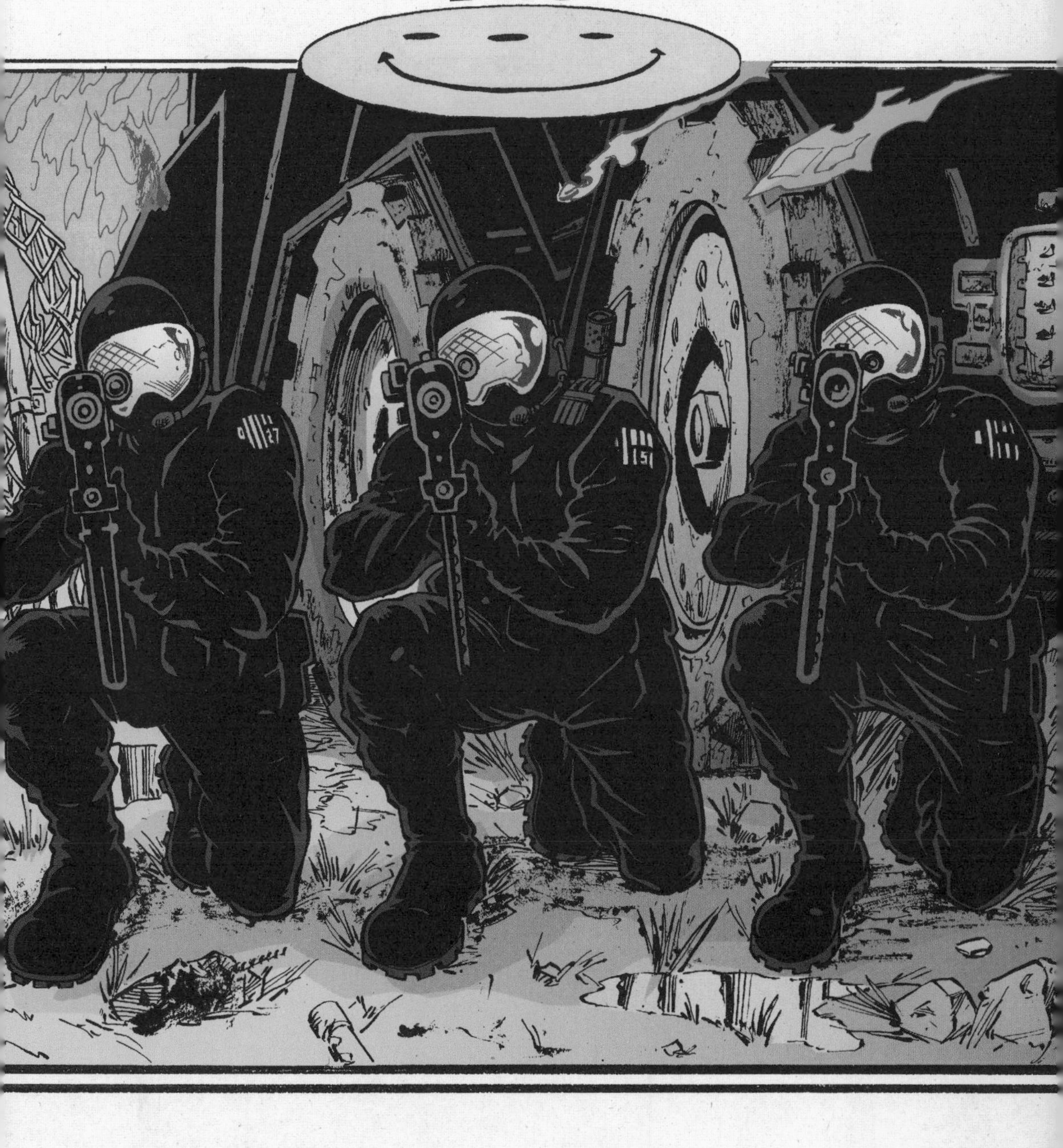

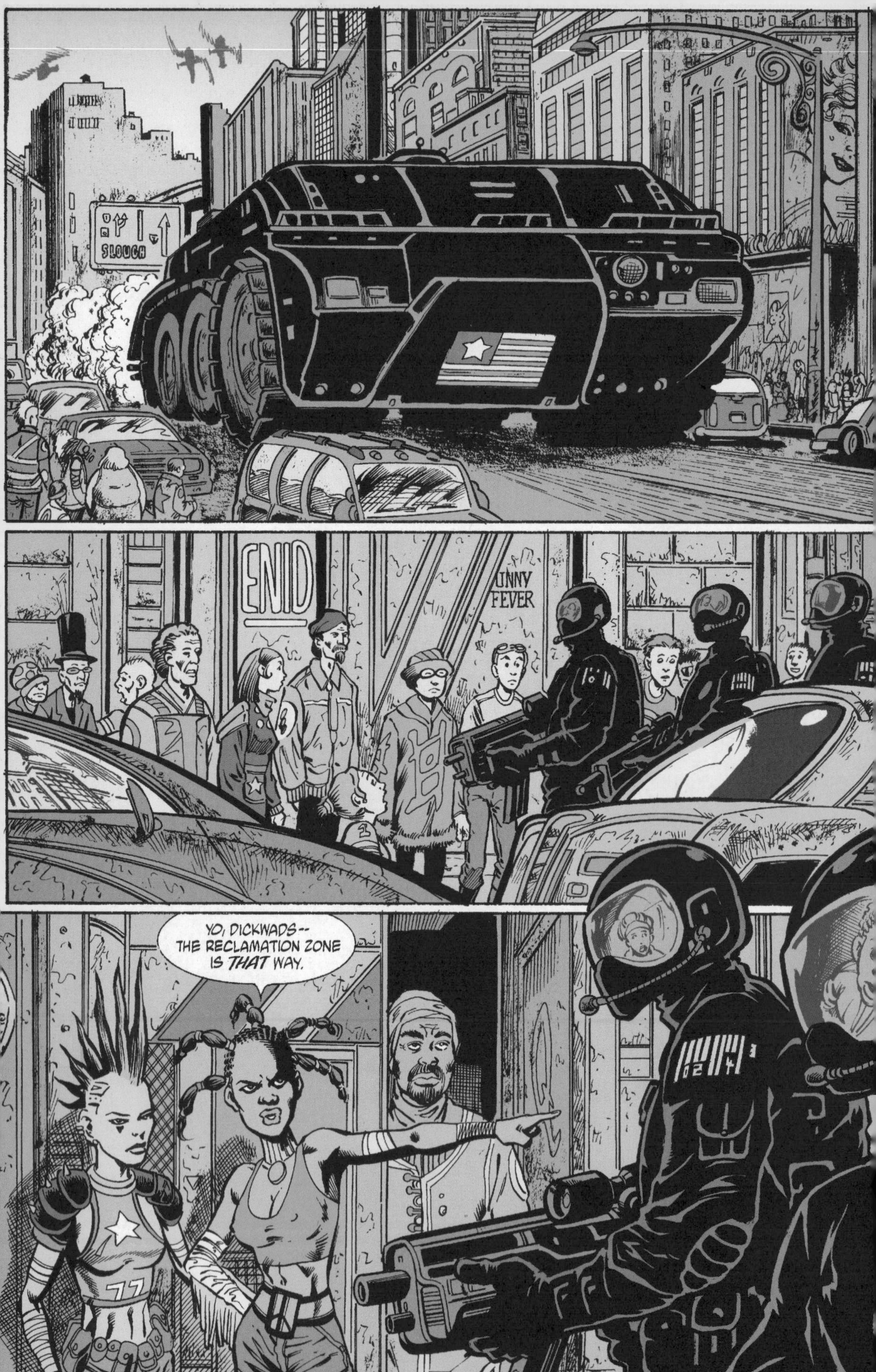
SLOUGH
ENID
UNNY
FEVER
YO, DICKWADS--
THE RECLAMATION ZONE
IS THAT WAY.

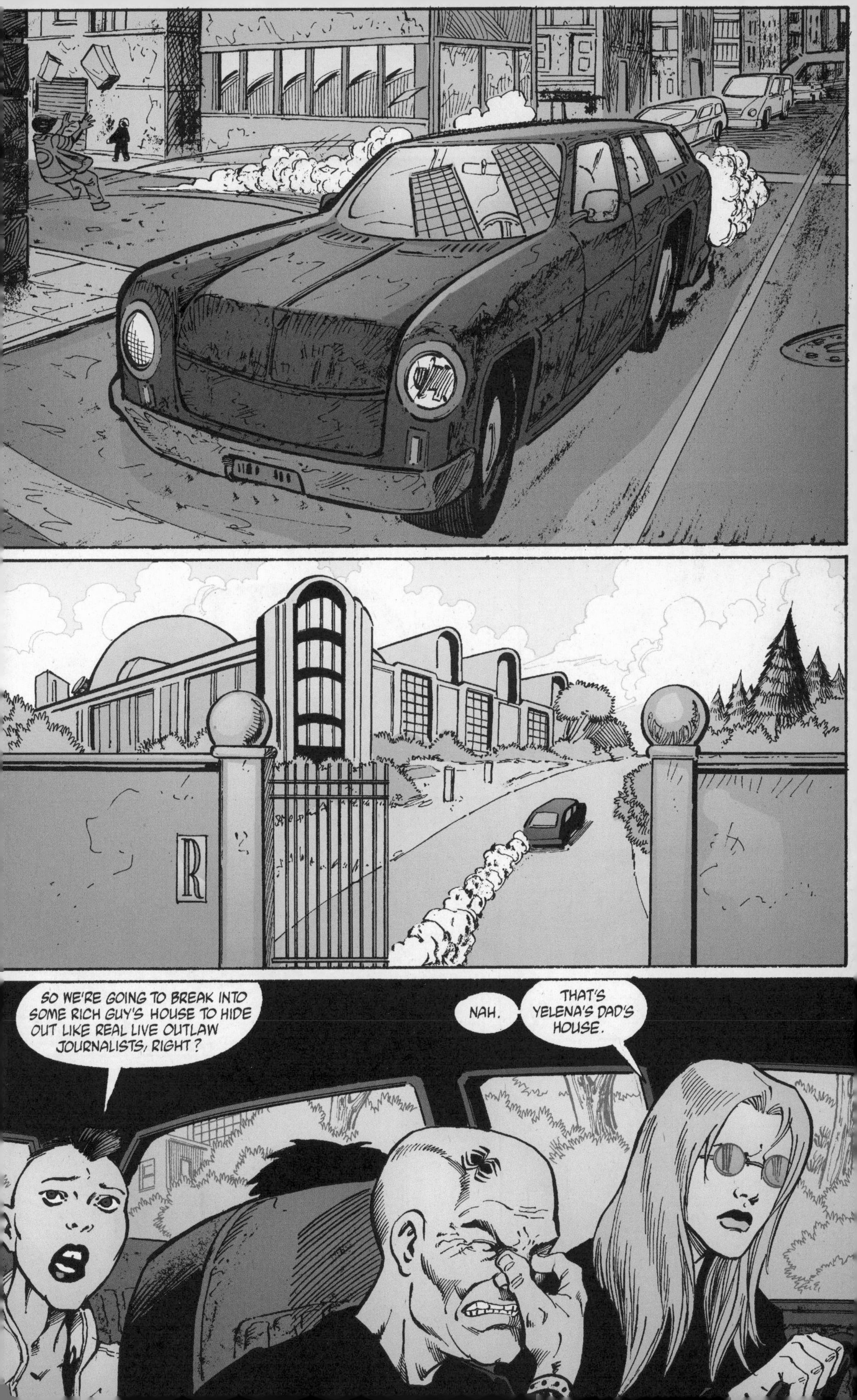
SO WE'RE GOING TO BREAK INTO SOME RICH GUY'S HOUSE TO HIDE OUT LIKE REAL LIVE OUTLAW JOURNALISTS, RIGHT?
NAH.
THAT'S YELENA'S DAD'S HOUSE.

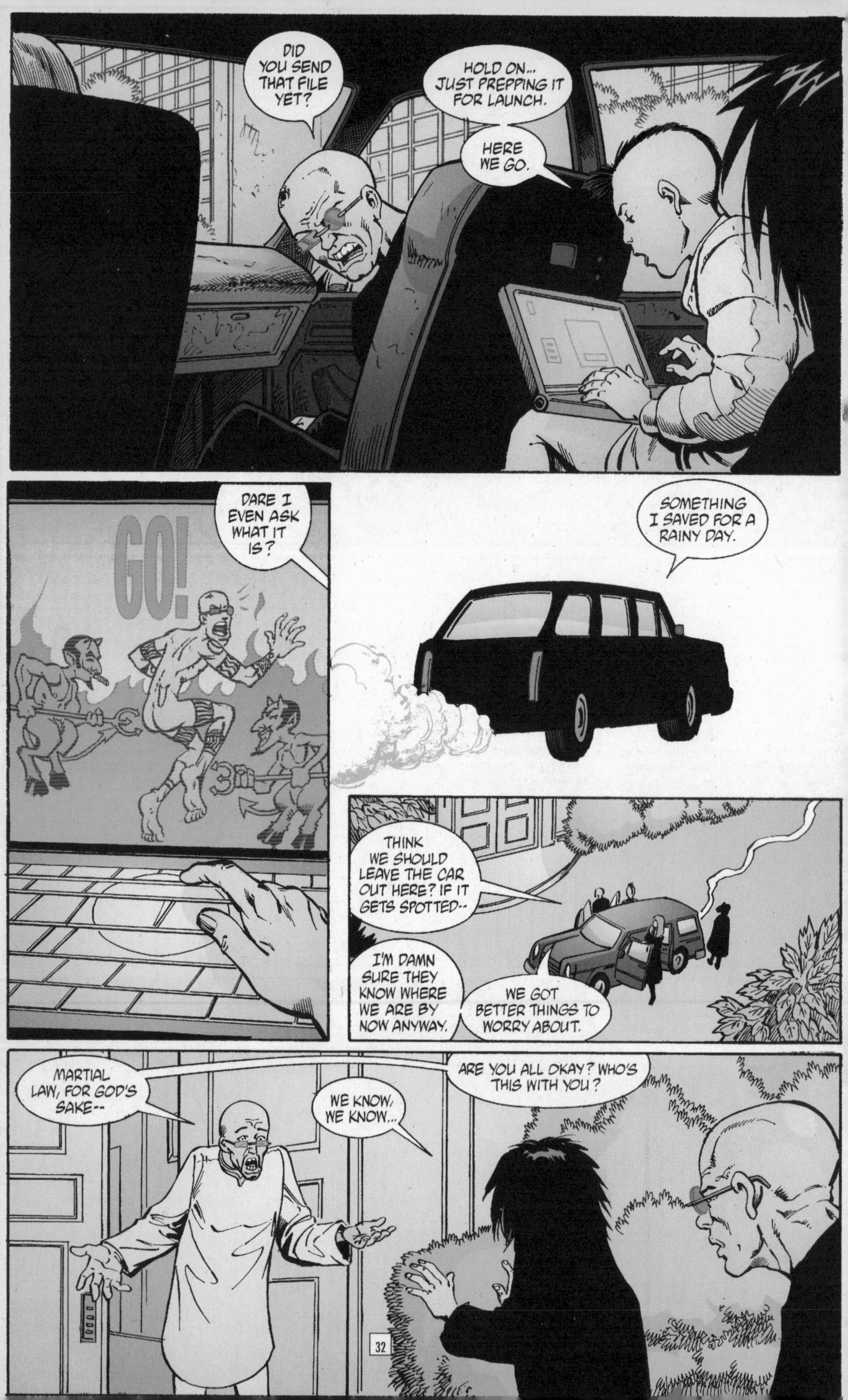
DID YOU SEND THAT FILE YET?
HOLD ON... JUST PREPPING IT FOR LAUNCH.
HERE WE GO.
DARE I EVEN ASK WHAT IT IS?
GO!
SOMETHING I SAVED FOR A RAINY DAY.
THINK WE SHOULD LEAVE THE CAR OUT HERE? IF IT GETS SPOTTED--
I'M DAMN SURE THEY KNOW WHERE WE ARE BY NOW ANYWAY.
WE GOT BETTER THINGS TO WORRY ABOUT.
MARTIAL LAW, FOR GOD'S SAKE--
ARE YOU ALL OKAY? WHO'S THIS WITH YOU?
WE KNOW, WE KNOW...

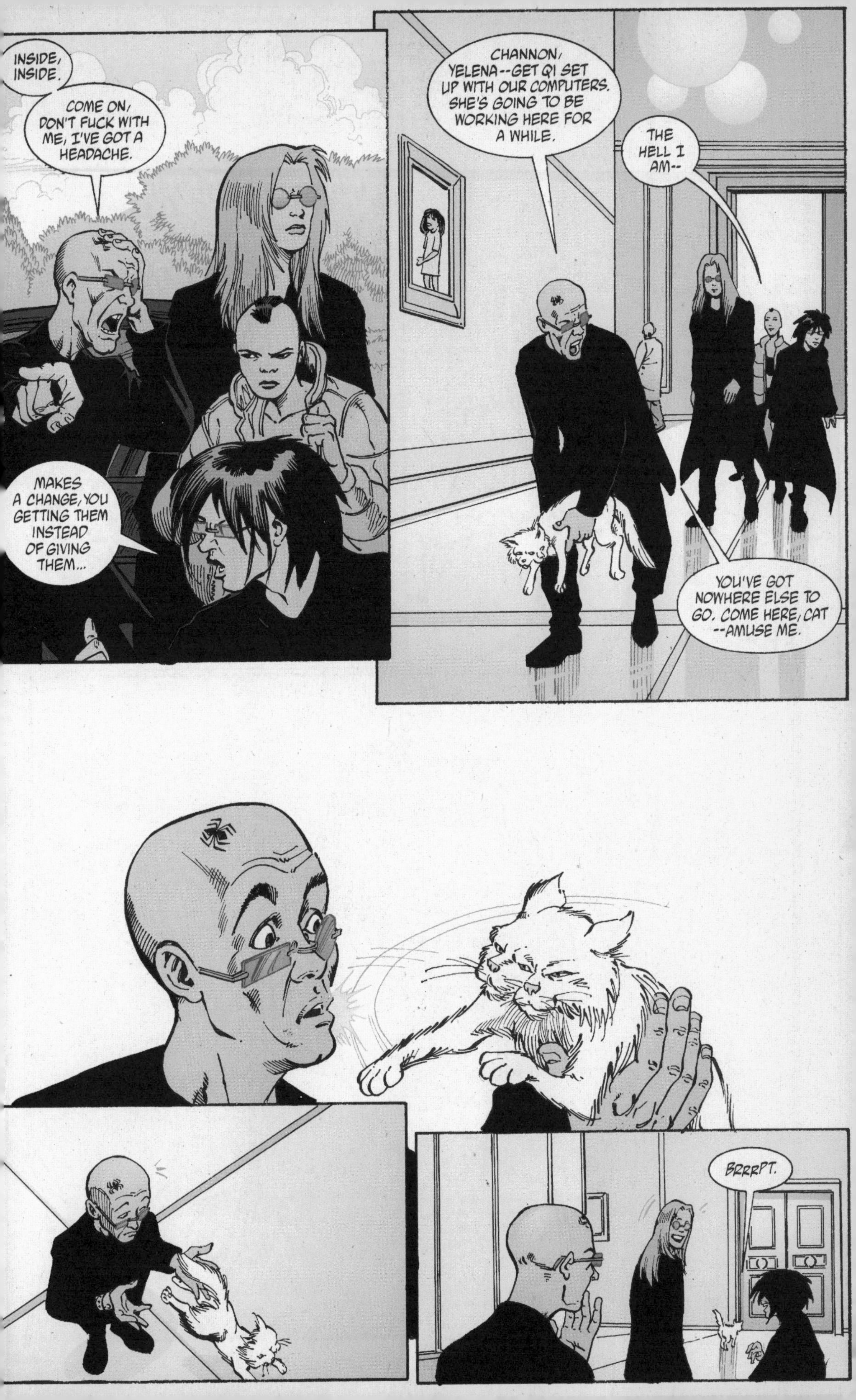
INSIDE, INSIDE.
COME ON, DON'T FUCK WITH ME, I'VE GOT A HEADACHE.
MAKES A CHANGE, YOU GETTING THEM INSTEAD OF GIVING THEM...
CHANNON, YELENA--GET QI SET UP WITH OUR COMPUTERS. SHE'S GOING TO BE WORKING HERE FOR A WHILE.
THE HELL I AM--
YOU'VE GOT NOWHERE ELSE TO GO. COME HERE, CAT --AMUSE ME.
BRRRPT.

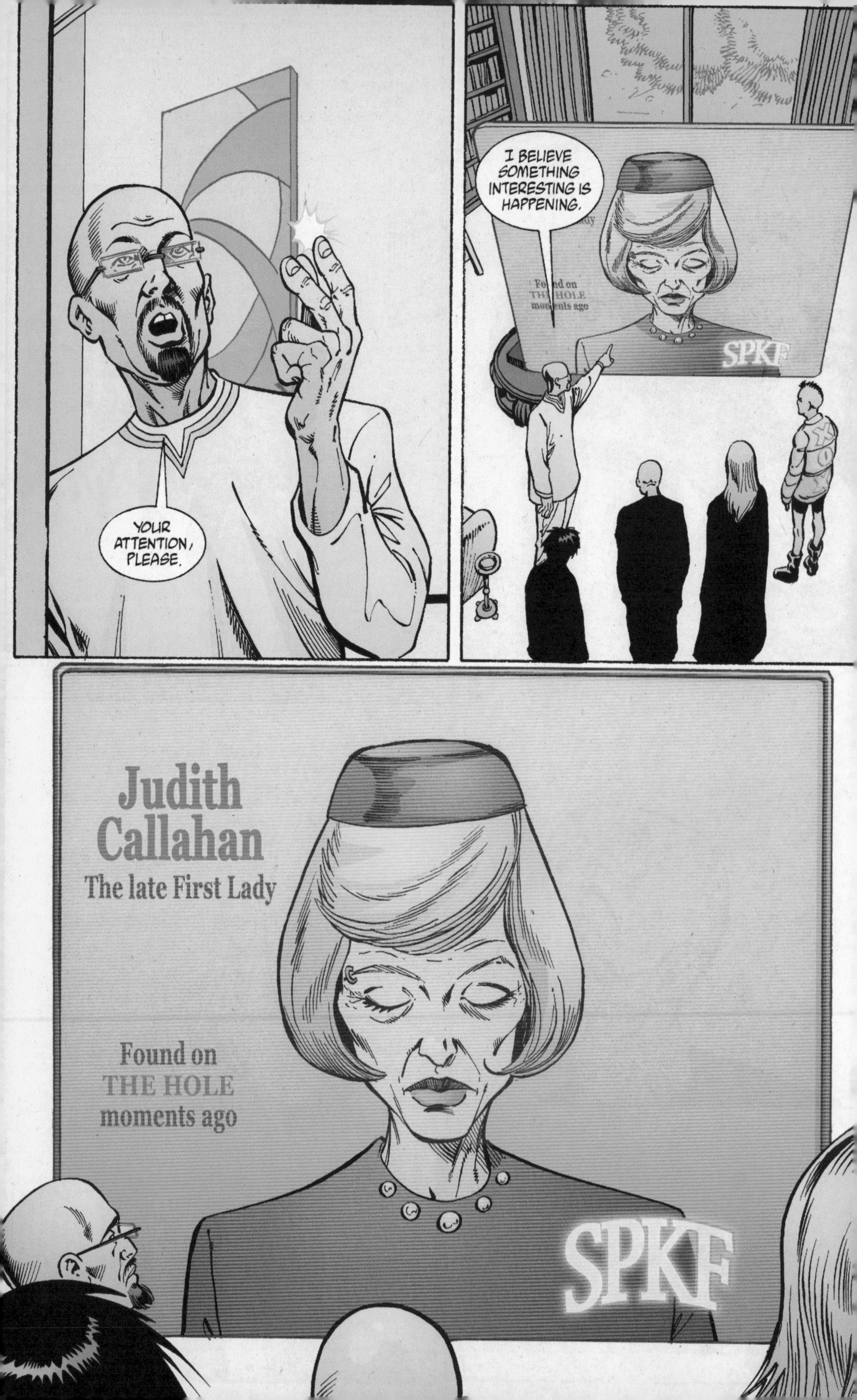
YOUR ATTENTION, PLEASE.
I BELIEVE SOMETHING INTERESTING IS HAPPENING.
Found on THE HOLE moments ago
SPKF
Judith Callahan
The late First Lady
Found on
THE HOLE
moments ago
SPKF

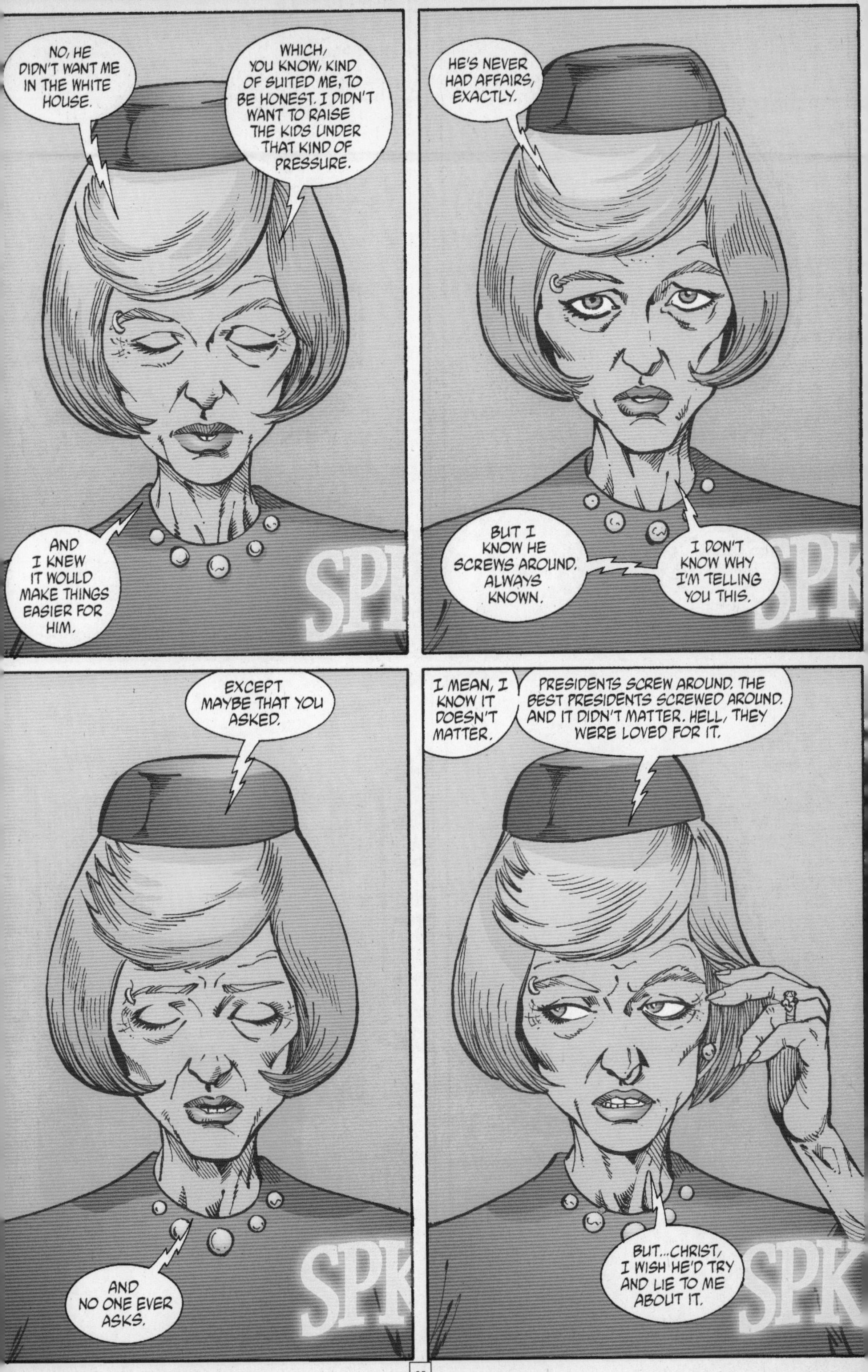
NO, HE DIDN'T WANT ME IN THE WHITE HOUSE.
WHICH, YOU KNOW, KIND OF SUITED ME, TO BE HONEST. I DIDN'T WANT TO RAISE THE KIDS UNDER THAT KIND OF PRESSURE.
AND I KNEW IT WOULD MAKE THINGS EASIER FOR HIM.
SPK
HE'S NEVER HAD AFFAIRS, EXACTLY.
BUT I KNOW HE SCREWS AROUND. ALWAYS KNOWN.
I DON'T KNOW WHY I'M TELLING YOU THIS.
SPK
EXCEPT MAYBE THAT YOU ASKED.
AND NO ONE EVER ASKS.
SPK
I MEAN, I KNOW IT DOESN'T MATTER.
PRESIDENTS SCREW AROUND. THE BEST PRESIDENTS SCREWED AROUND. AND IT DIDN'T MATTER. HELL, THEY WERE LOVED FOR IT.
BUT...CHRIST, I WISH HE'D TRY AND LIE TO ME ABOUT IT.
SPK

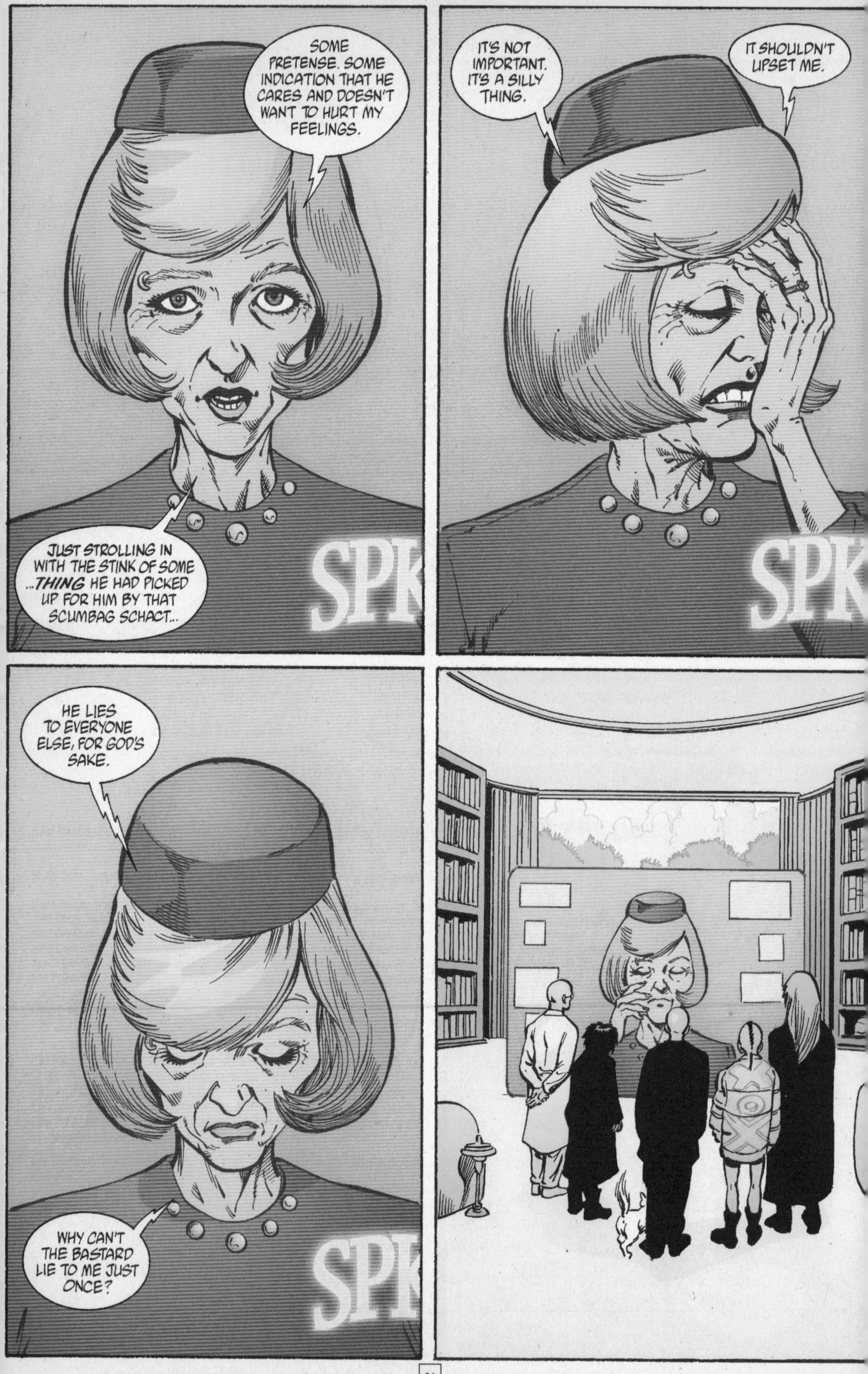
SOME PRETENSE. SOME INDICATION THAT HE CARES AND DOESN'T WANT TO HURT MY FEELINGS.
JUST STROLLING IN WITH THE STINK OF SOME ...THING HE HAD PICKED UP FOR HIM BY THAT SCUMBAG SCHACT...
SPK
IT'S NOT IMPORTANT. IT'S A SILLY THING.
IT SHOULDN'T UPSET ME.
SPK
HE LIES TO EVERYONE ELSE, FOR GOD'S SAKE.
WHY CAN'T THE BASTARD LIE TO ME JUST ONCE?
SPK

IS THAT THE FILE I SENT? WHERE THE HELL DID THAT COME FROM?

GET ME TO A KEYBOARD. I FEEL THE POWER MOVING IN ME ONCE MORE.

SPKF

SPIDER?

THE FARSIGHT COMMUNITY SENT ME TO CALIFORNIA USING AN UNMONITORED TELEPRESENCE PROCESS, BACK DURING THE ELECTION.

I INTERVIEWED MRS. CALLAHAN. I USED A LOT OF THAT INTERVIEW TO CAUSE TROUBLE.

BUT YOU SAVED THIS.

THAT'S RIGHT. I NEVER USED THIS. I HID IT.

WHY?

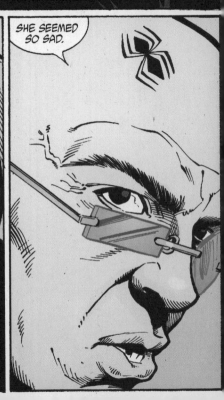

SHE SEEMED SO SAD.

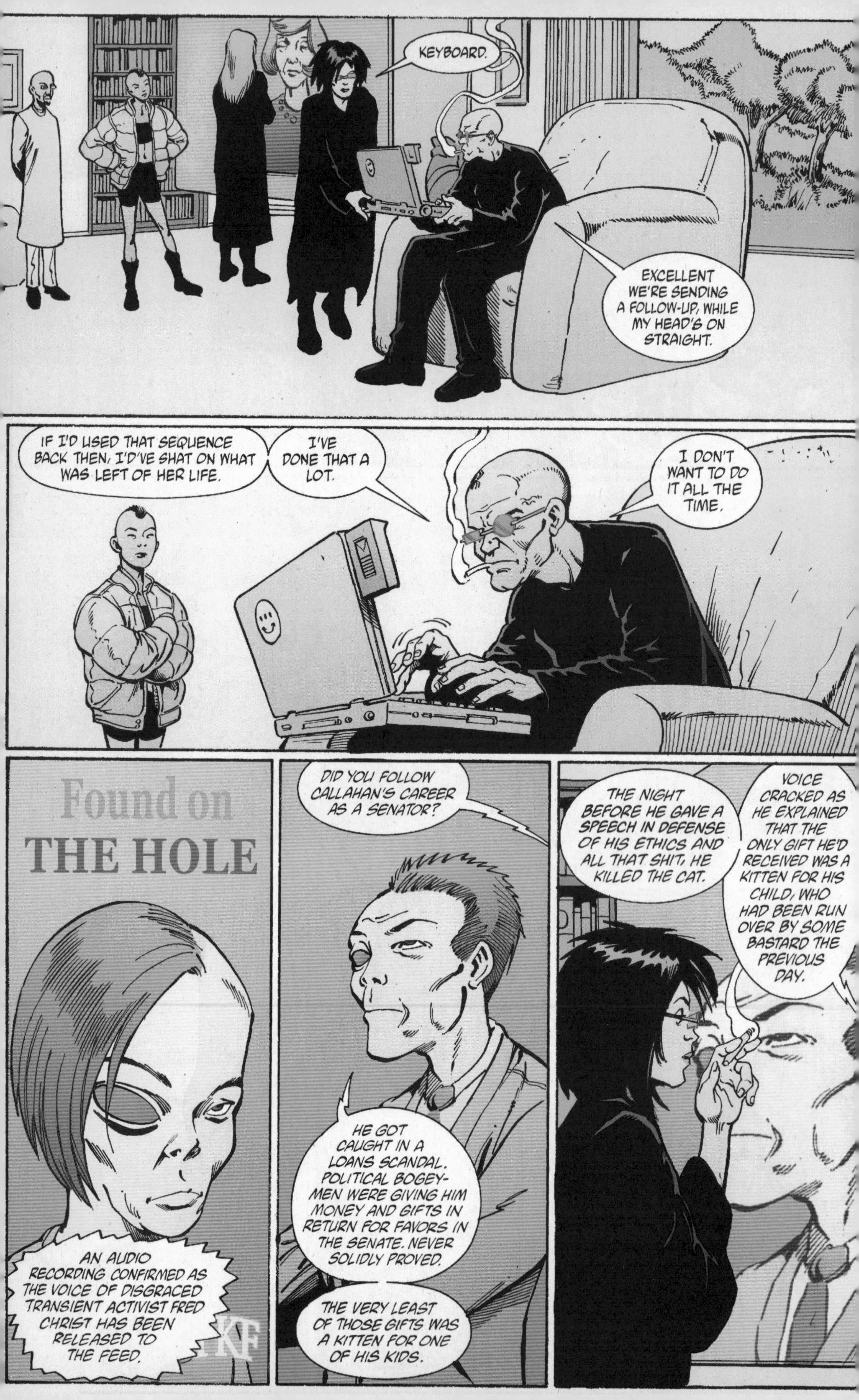
KEYBOARD.
EXCELLENT WE'RE SENDING A FOLLOW-UP, WHILE MY HEAD'S ON STRAIGHT.
IF I'D USED THAT SEQUENCE BACK THEN, I'D'VE SHAT ON WHAT WAS LEFT OF HER LIFE.
I'VE DONE THAT A LOT.
I DON'T WANT TO DO IT ALL THE TIME.
Found on
THE HOLE
AN AUDIO RECORDING CONFIRMED AS THE VOICE OF DISGRACED TRANSIENT ACTIVIST FRED CHRIST HAS BEEN RELEASED TO THE FEED.
DID YOU FOLLOW CALLAHAN'S CAREER AS A SENATOR?
HE GOT CAUGHT IN A LOANS SCANDAL. POLITICAL BOGEY-MEN WERE GIVING HIM MONEY AND GIFTS IN RETURN FOR FAVORS IN THE SENATE. NEVER SOLIDLY PROVED.
THE VERY LEAST OF THOSE GIFTS WAS A KITTEN FOR ONE OF HIS KIDS.
THE NIGHT BEFORE HE GAVE A SPEECH IN DEFENSE OF HIS ETHICS AND ALL THAT SHIT, HE KILLED THE CAT.
VOICE CRACKED AS HE EXPLAINED THAT THE ONLY GIFT HE'D RECEIVED WAS A KITTEN FOR HIS CHILD, WHO HAD BEEN RUN OVER BY SOME BASTARD THE PREVIOUS DAY.

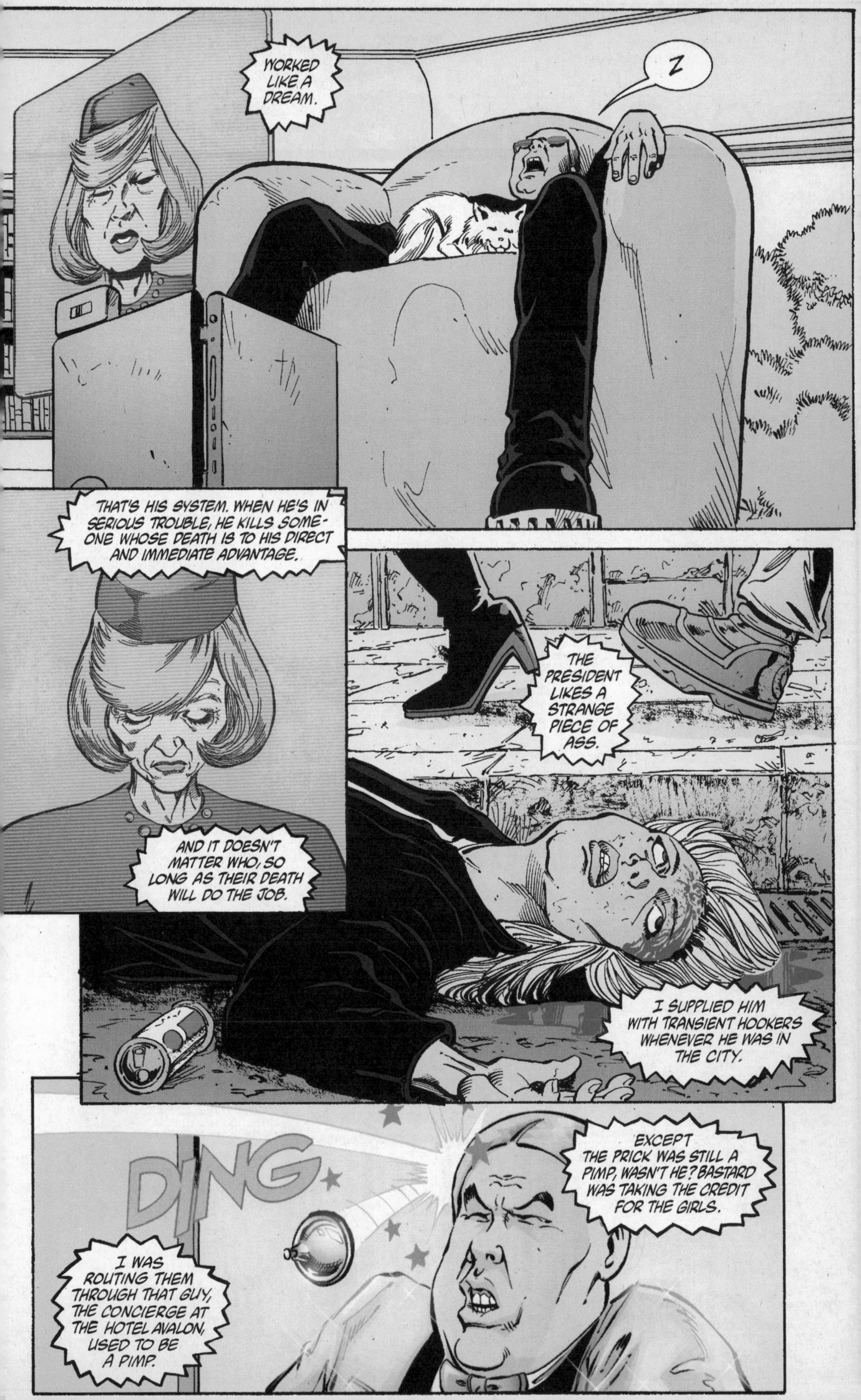
WORKED LIKE A DREAM.
Z
THAT'S HIS SYSTEM. WHEN HE'S IN SERIOUS TROUBLE, HE KILLS SOME-ONE WHOSE DEATH IS TO HIS DIRECT AND IMMEDIATE ADVANTAGE.
AND IT DOESN'T MATTER WHO; SO LONG AS THEIR DEATH WILL DO THE JOB.
THE PRESIDENT LIKES A STRANGE PIECE OF ASS.
I SUPPLIED HIM WITH TRANSIENT HOOKERS WHENEVER HE WAS IN THE CITY.
DING
I WAS ROUTING THEM THROUGH THAT GUY, THE CONCIERGE AT THE HOTEL AVALON, USED TO BE A PIMP.
EXCEPT THE PRICK WAS STILL A PIMP, WASN'T HE? BASTARD WAS TAKING THE CREDIT FOR THE GIRLS.

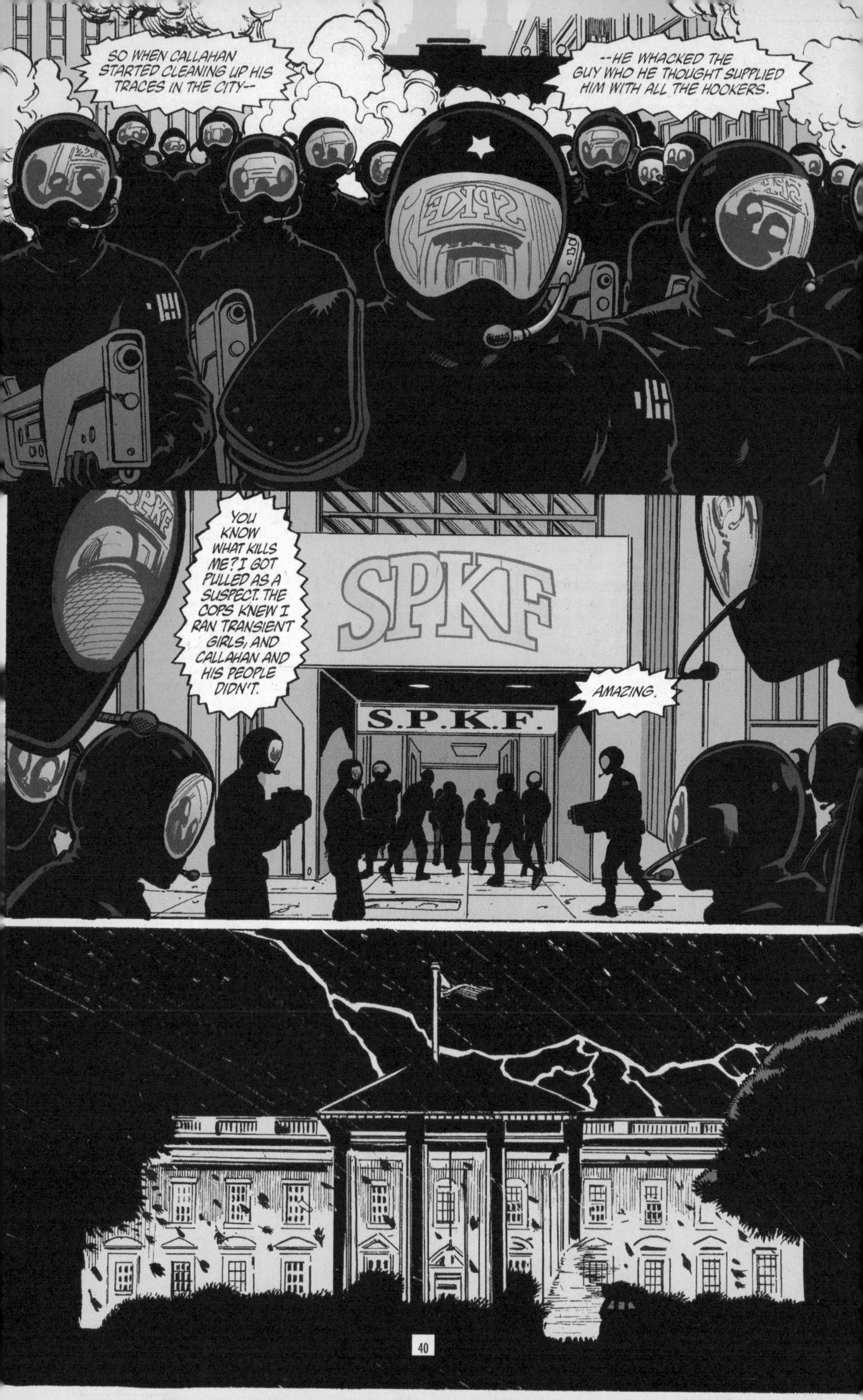
SO WHEN CALLAHAN STARTED CLEANING UP HIS TRACES IN THE CITY--
--HE WHACKED THE GUY WHO HE THOUGHT SUPPLIED HIM WITH ALL THE HOOKERS.
YOU KNOW WHAT KILLS ME? I GOT PULLED AS A SUSPECT. THE COPS KNEW I RAN TRANSIENT GIRLS, AND CALLAHAN AND HIS PEOPLE DIDN'T.
SPKF
S.P.K.F.
AMAZING.

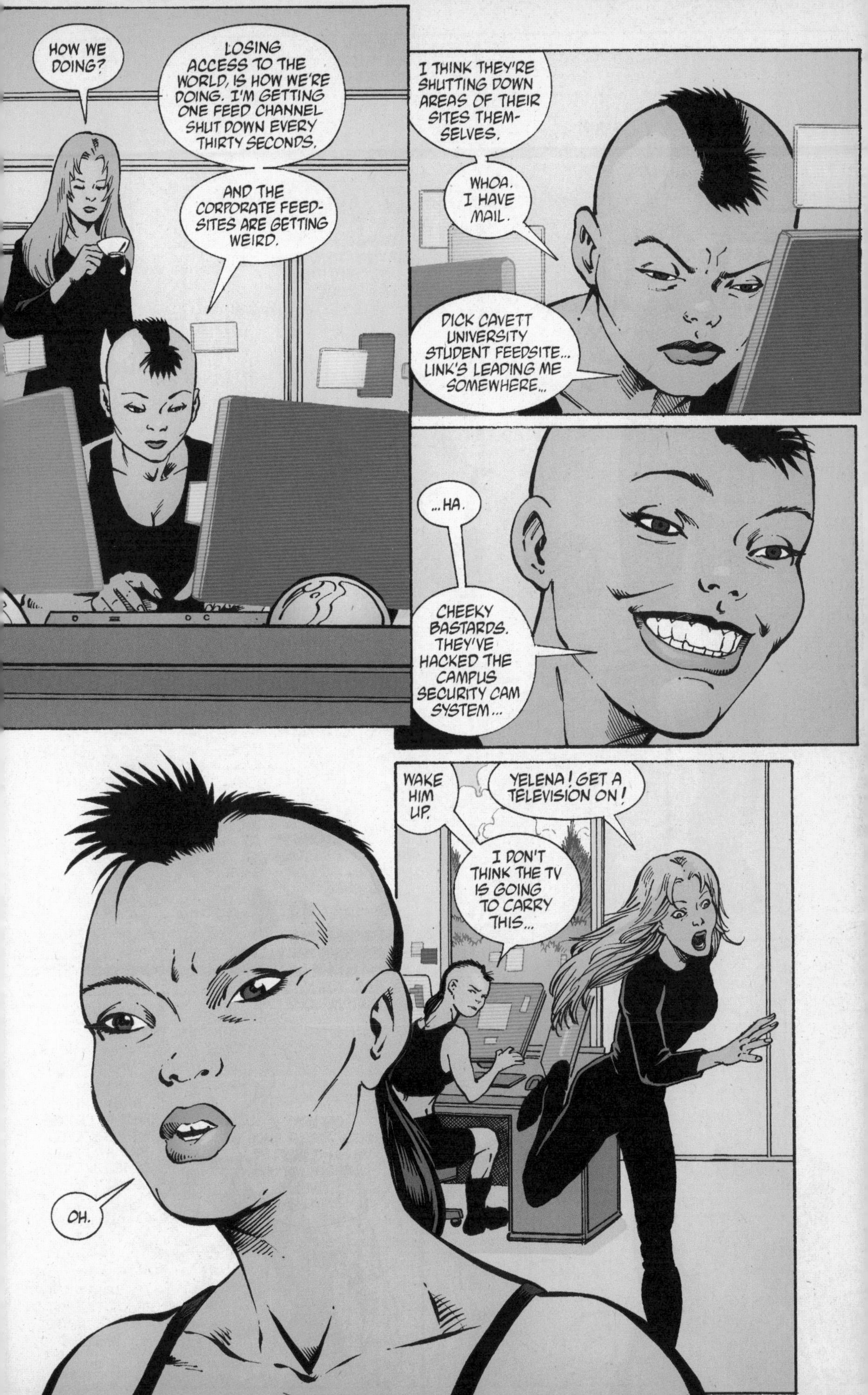

HOW WE DOING?
LOSING ACCESS TO THE WORLD, IS HOW WE'RE DOING. I'M GETTING ONE FEED CHANNEL SHUT DOWN EVERY THIRTY SECONDS.
AND THE CORPORATE FEED-SITES ARE GETTING WEIRD.
I THINK THEY'RE SHUTTING DOWN AREAS OF THEIR SITES THEM-SELVES.
WHOA. I HAVE MAIL.
DICK CAVETT UNIVERSITY STUDENT FEEDSITE... LINK'S LEADING ME SOMEWHERE...
...HA.
CHEEKY BASTARDS. THEY'VE HACKED THE CAMPUS SECURITY CAM SYSTEM...
OH.
WAKE HIM UP.
YELENA! GET A TELEVISION ON!
I DON'T THINK THE TV IS GOING TO CARRY THIS...

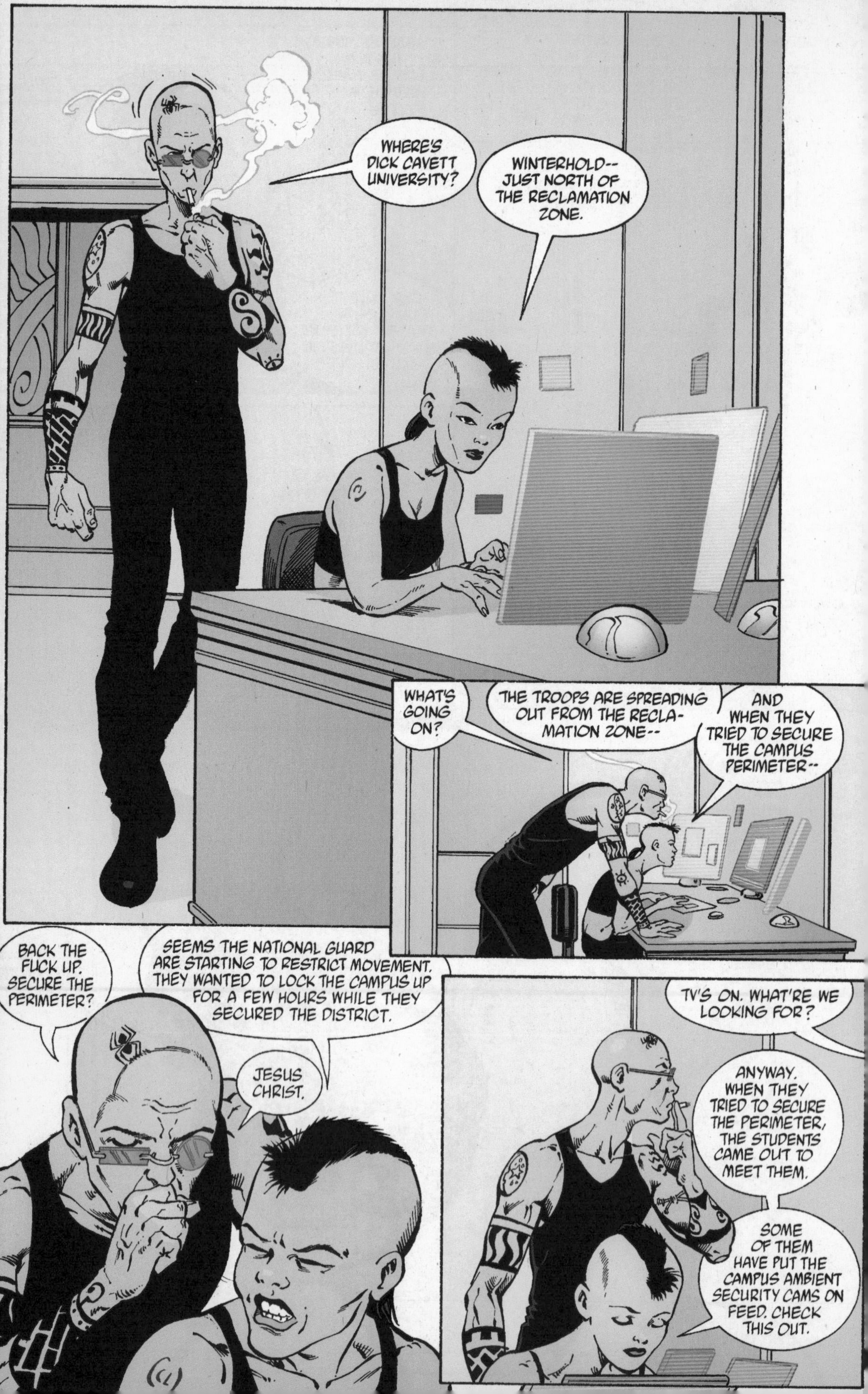
WHERE'S DICK CAVETT UNIVERSITY?
WINTERHOLD-- JUST NORTH OF THE RECLAMATION ZONE.
WHAT'S GOING ON?
THE TROOPS ARE SPREADING OUT FROM THE RECLAMATION ZONE--
AND WHEN THEY TRIED TO SECURE THE CAMPUS PERIMETER--
BACK THE FUCK UP. SECURE THE PERIMETER?
SEEMS THE NATIONAL GUARD ARE STARTING TO RESTRICT MOVEMENT. THEY WANTED TO LOCK THE CAMPUS UP FOR A FEW HOURS WHILE THEY SECURED THE DISTRICT.
JESUS CHRIST.
TV'S ON. WHAT'RE WE LOOKING FOR?
ANYWAY. WHEN THEY TRIED TO SECURE THE PERIMETER, THE STUDENTS CAME OUT TO MEET THEM.
SOME OF THEM HAVE PUT THE CAMPUS AMBIENT SECURITY CAMS ON FEED. CHECK THIS OUT.

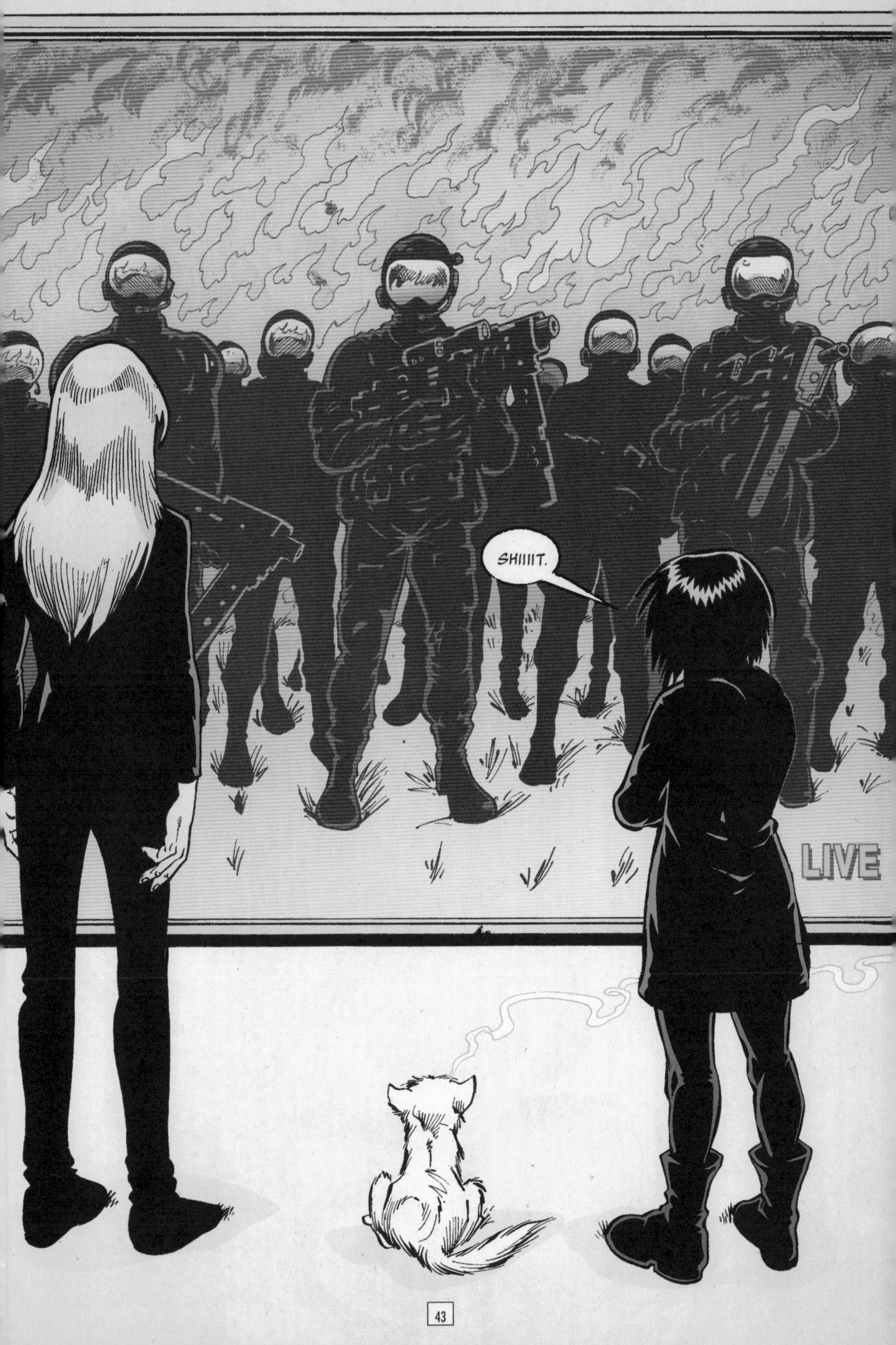
LIVE
SHIIIIT.

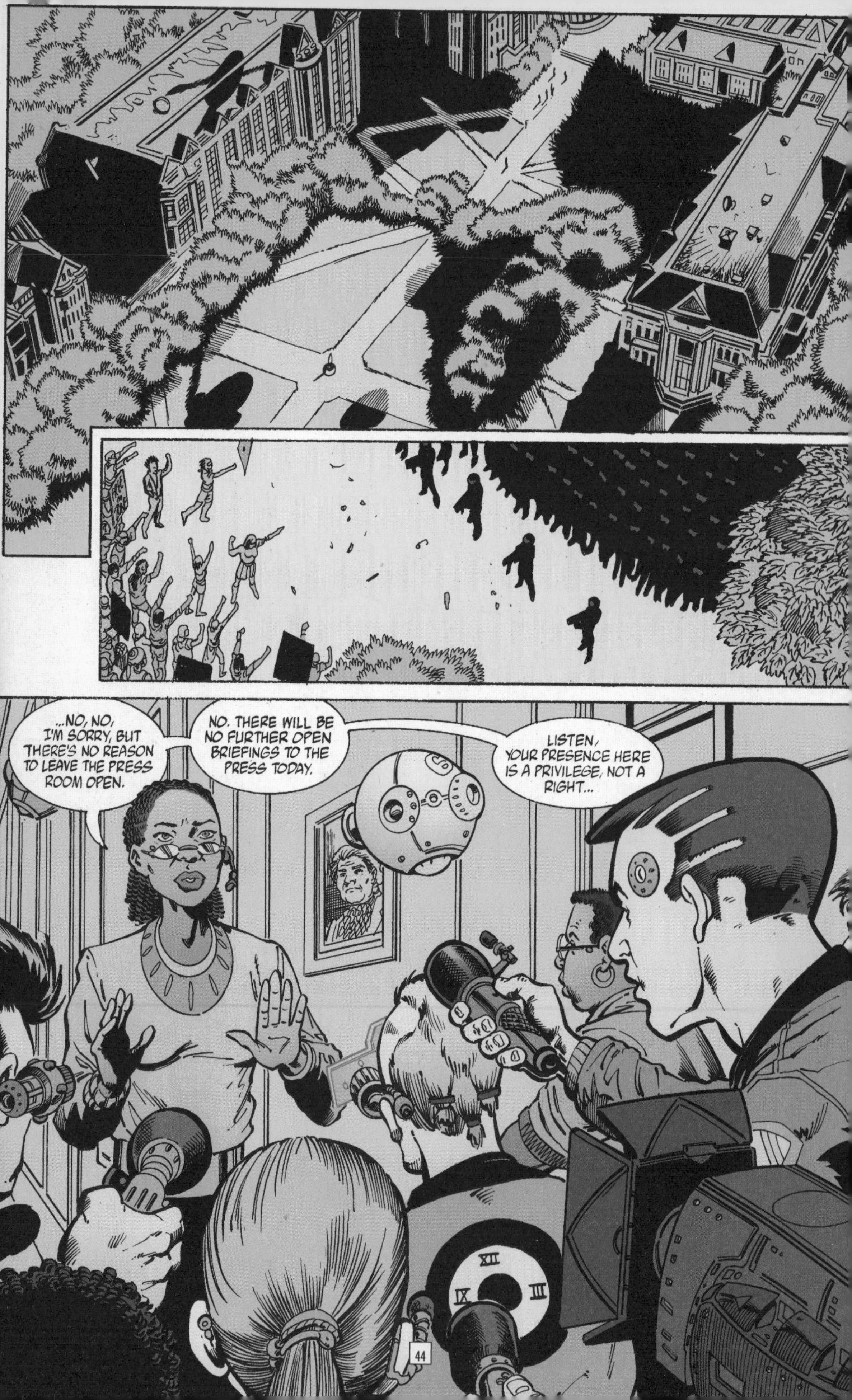
...NO, NO, I'M SORRY, BUT THERE'S NO REASON TO LEAVE THE PRESS ROOM OPEN.
NO. THERE WILL BE NO FURTHER OPEN BRIEFINGS TO THE PRESS TODAY.
LISTEN, YOUR PRESENCE HERE IS A PRIVILEGE, NOT A RIGHT...

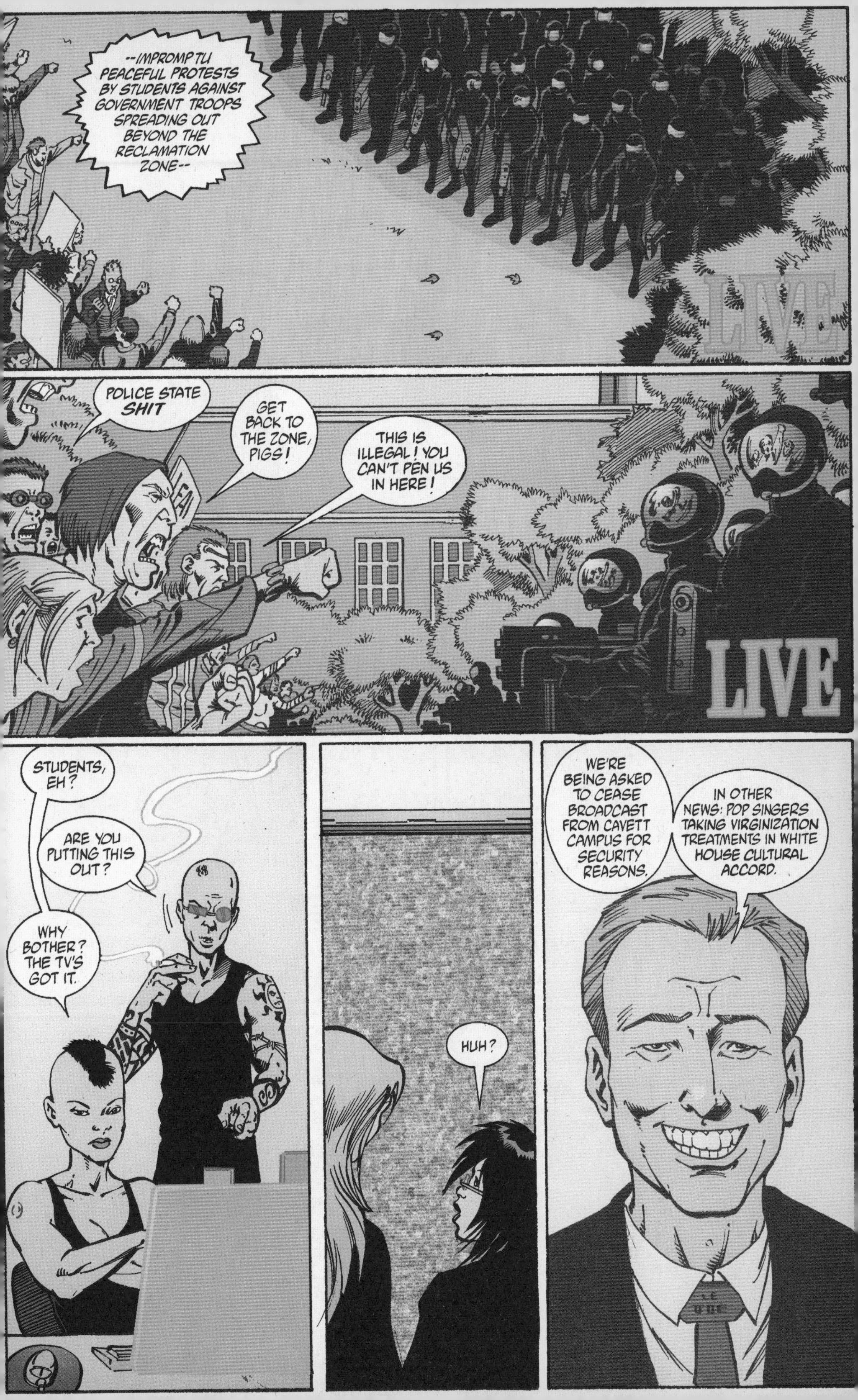
--IMPROMPTU PEACEFUL PROTESTS BY STUDENTS AGAINST GOVERNMENT TROOPS SPREADING OUT BEYOND THE RECLAMATION ZONE--
LIVE
POLICE STATE SHIT
GET BACK TO THE ZONE, PIGS!
THIS IS ILLEGAL! YOU CAN'T PEN US IN HERE!
LIVE
STUDENTS, EH?
ARE YOU PUTTING THIS OUT?
WHY BOTHER? THE TV'S GOT IT.
HUH?
WE'RE BEING ASKED TO CEASE BROADCAST FROM CAVETT CAMPUS FOR SECURITY REASONS.
IN OTHER NEWS: POP SINGERS TAKING VIRGINIZATION TREATMENTS IN WHITE HOUSE CULTURAL ACCORD.

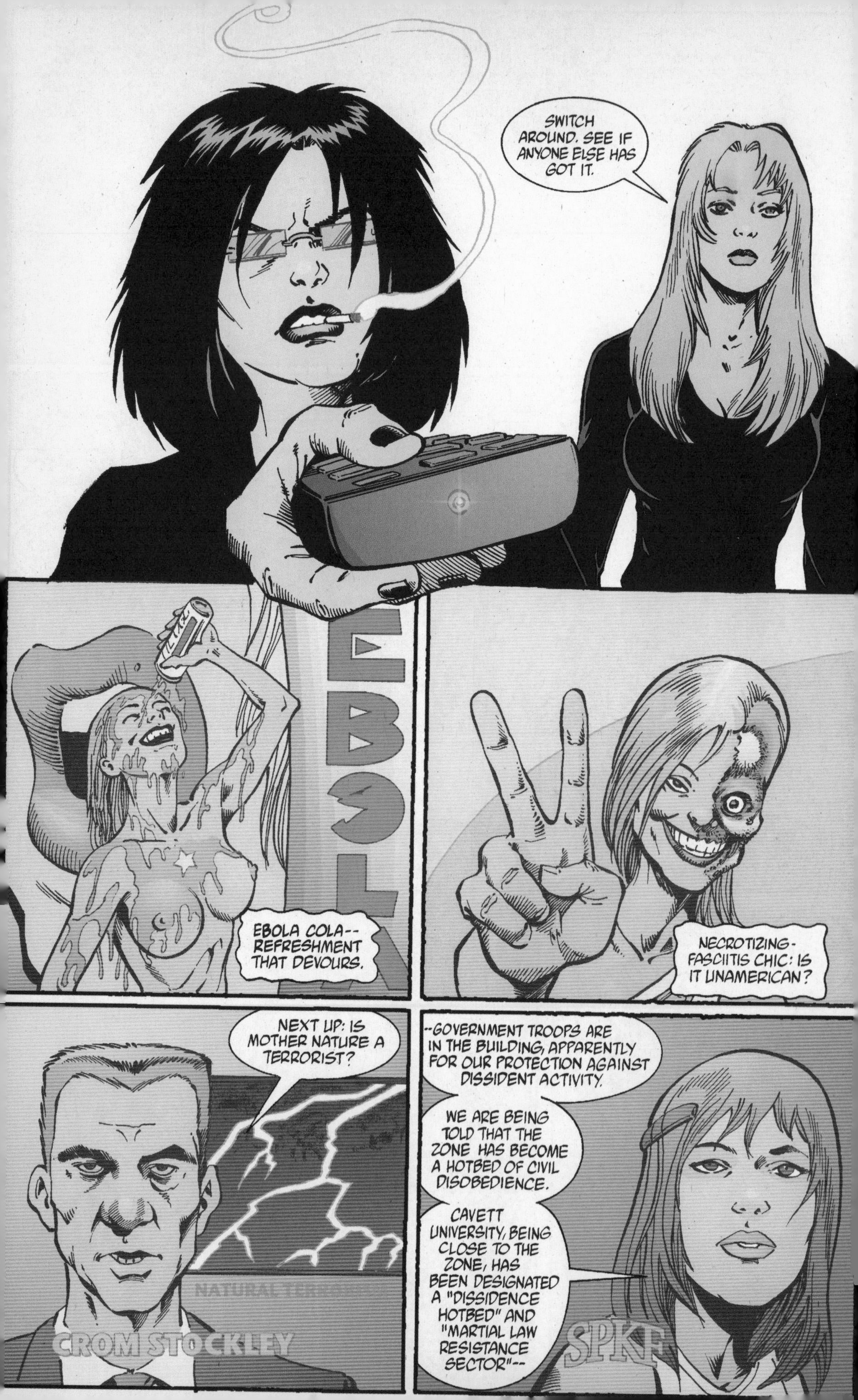
SWITCH AROUND. SEE IF ANYONE ELSE HAS GOT IT.
EBOL
EBOLA COLA-- REFRESHMENT THAT DEVOURS.
NECROTIZING-FASCIITIS CHIC: IS IT UNAMERICAN?
NEXT UP: IS MOTHER NATURE A TERRORIST?
CROM STOCKLEY
--GOVERNMENT TROOPS ARE IN THE BUILDING, APPARENTLY FOR OUR PROTECTION AGAINST DISSIDENT ACTIVITY.
WE ARE BEING TOLD THAT THE ZONE HAS BECOME A HOTBED OF CIVIL DISOBEDIENCE.
CAVETT UNIVERSITY, BEING CLOSE TO THE ZONE, HAS BEEN DESIGNATED A "DISSIDENCE HOTBED" AND "MARTIAL LAW RESISTANCE SECTOR"--
SPKF

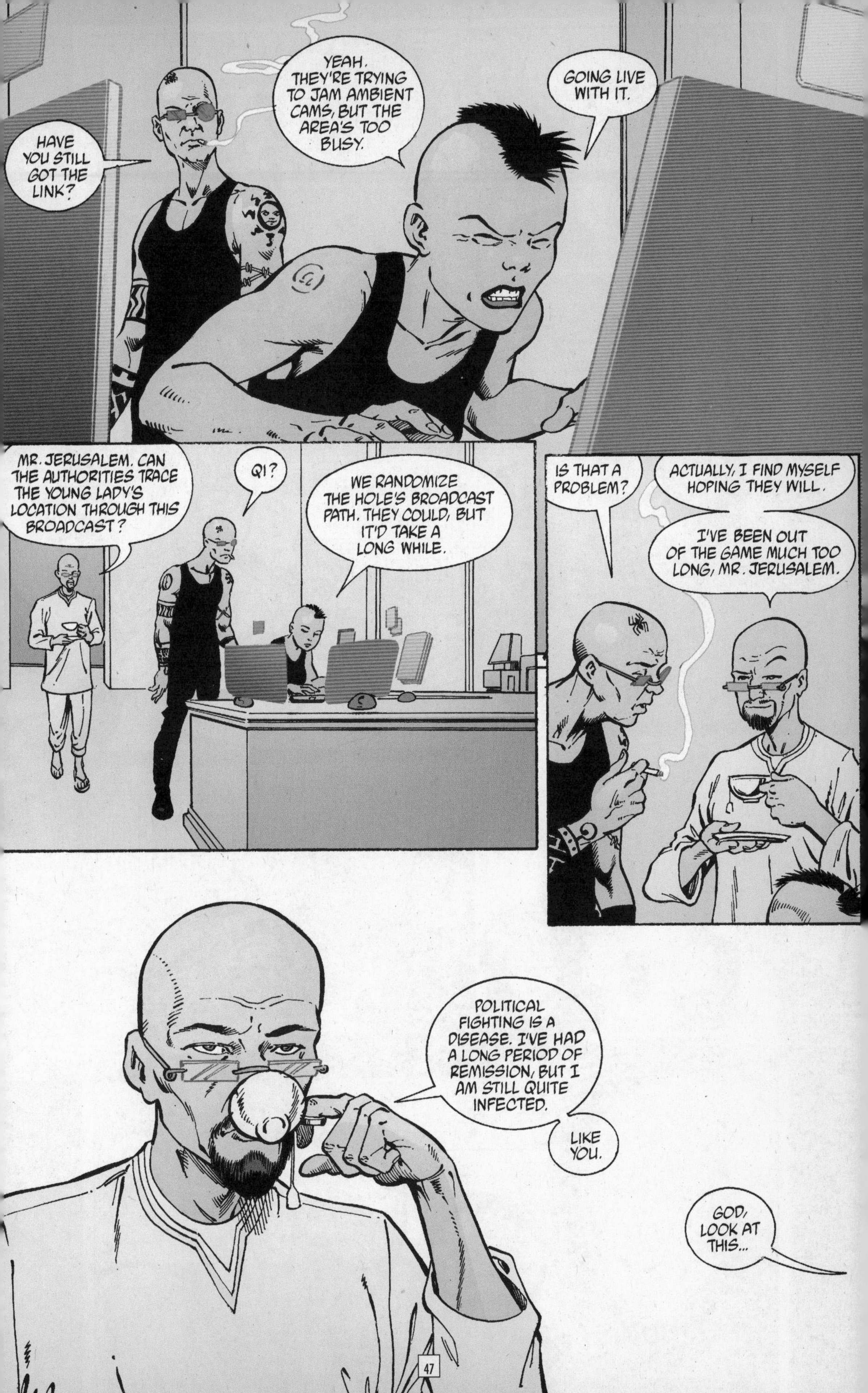
HAVE YOU STILL GOT THE LINK?
YEAH. THEY'RE TRYING TO JAM AMBIENT CAMS, BUT THE AREA'S TOO BUSY.
GOING LIVE WITH IT.
MR. JERUSALEM. CAN THE AUTHORITIES TRACE THE YOUNG LADY'S LOCATION THROUGH THIS BROADCAST?
QI?
WE RANDOMIZE THE HOLE'S BROADCAST PATH. THEY COULD, BUT IT'D TAKE A LONG WHILE.
IS THAT A PROBLEM?
ACTUALLY, I FIND MYSELF HOPING THEY WILL.
I'VE BEEN OUT OF THE GAME MUCH TOO LONG, MR. JERUSALEM.
POLITICAL FIGHTING IS A DISEASE. I'VE HAD A LONG PERIOD OF REMISSION, BUT I AM STILL QUITE INFECTED.
LIKE YOU.
GOD, LOOK AT THIS...

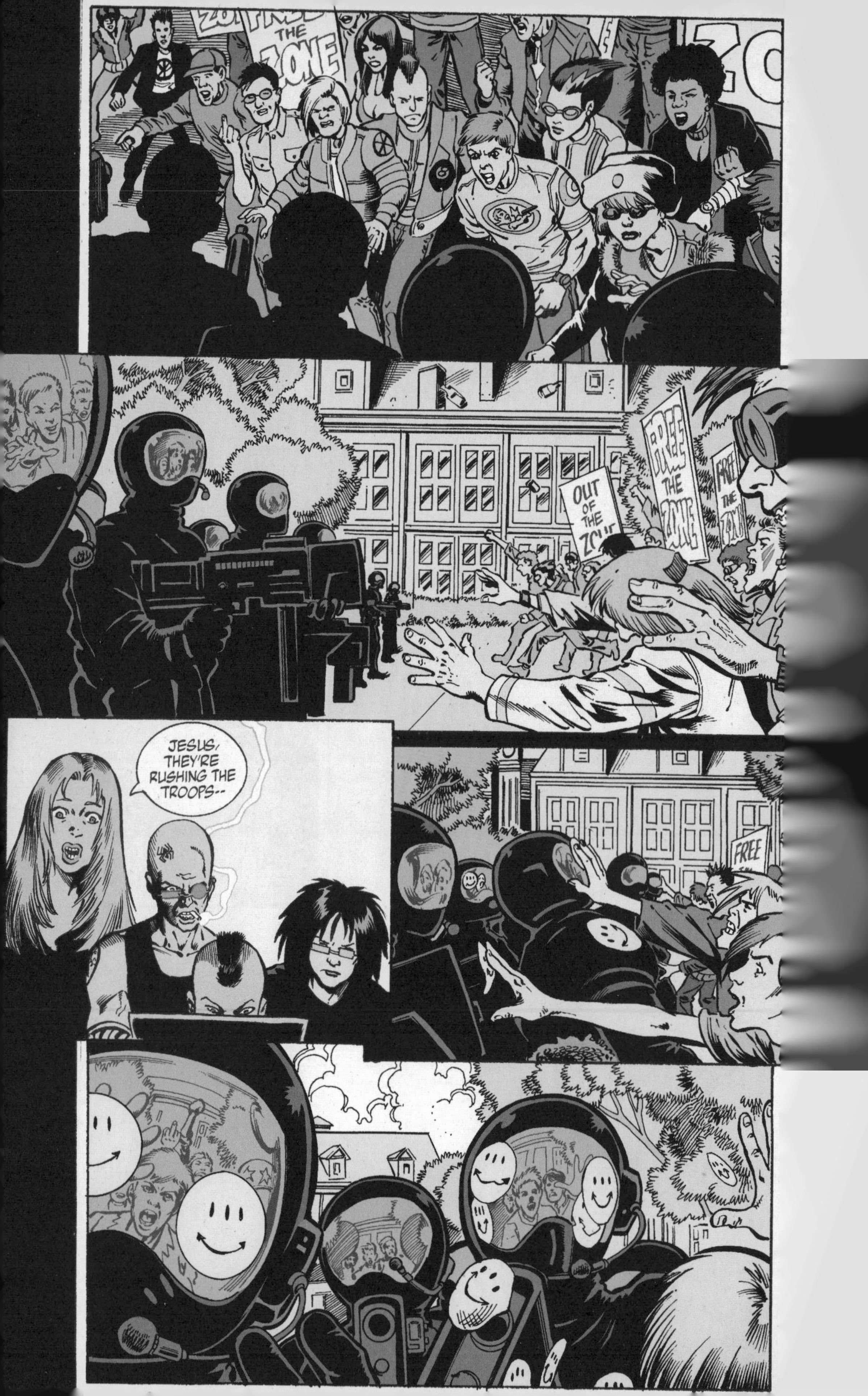
THE ZONE
FREE THE ZONE
OUT OF THE
JESUS, THEY'RE RUSHING THE TROOPS--
FREE

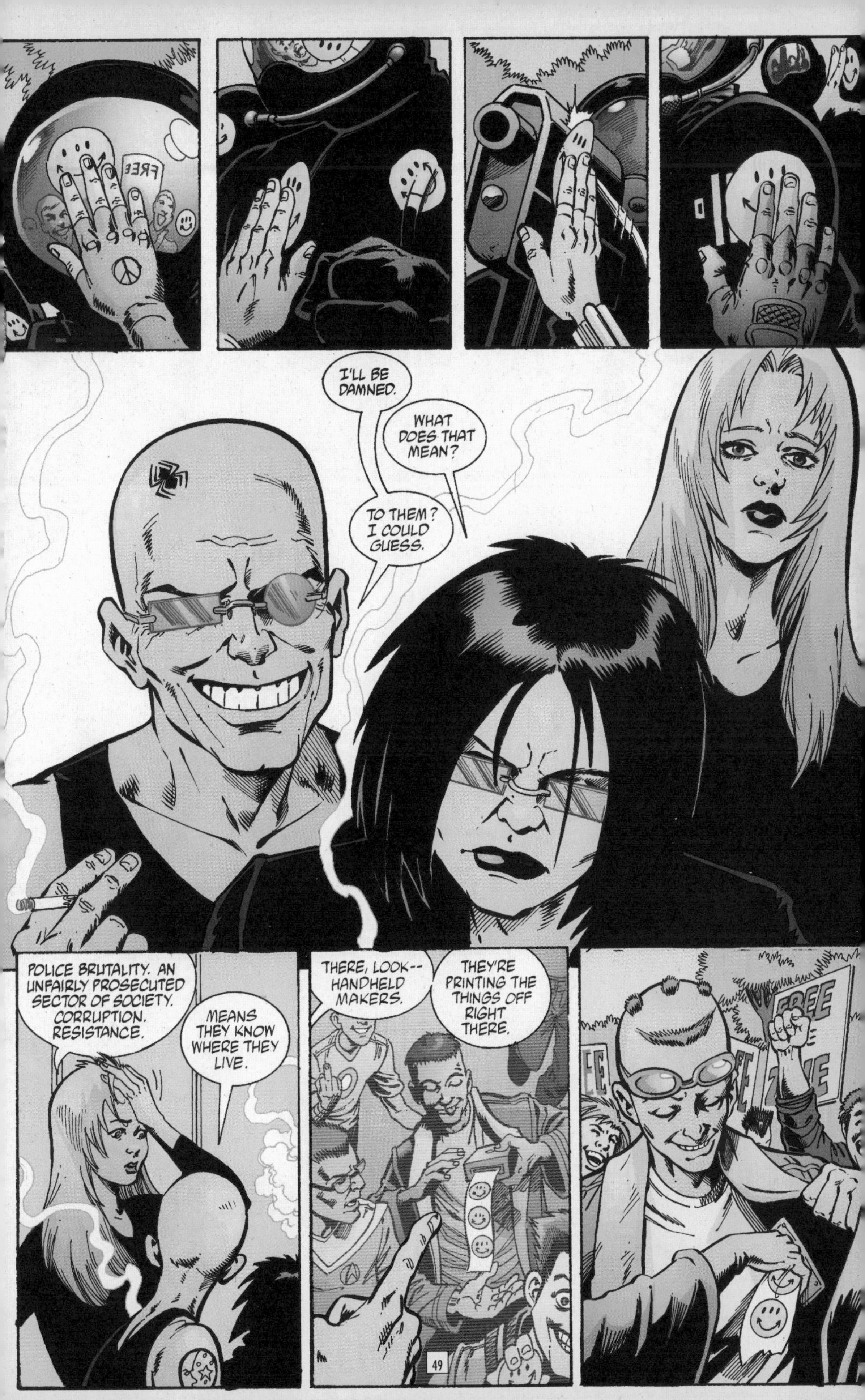
FREE
I'LL BE DAMNED.
WHAT DOES THAT MEAN?
TO THEM? I COULD GUESS.
POLICE BRUTALITY. AN UNFAIRLY PROSECUTED SECTOR OF SOCIETY. CORRUPTION. RESISTANCE.
MEANS THEY KNOW WHERE THEY LIVE.
THERE, LOOK-- HANDHELD MAKERS.
THEY'RE PRINTING THE THINGS OFF RIGHT THERE.
FREE

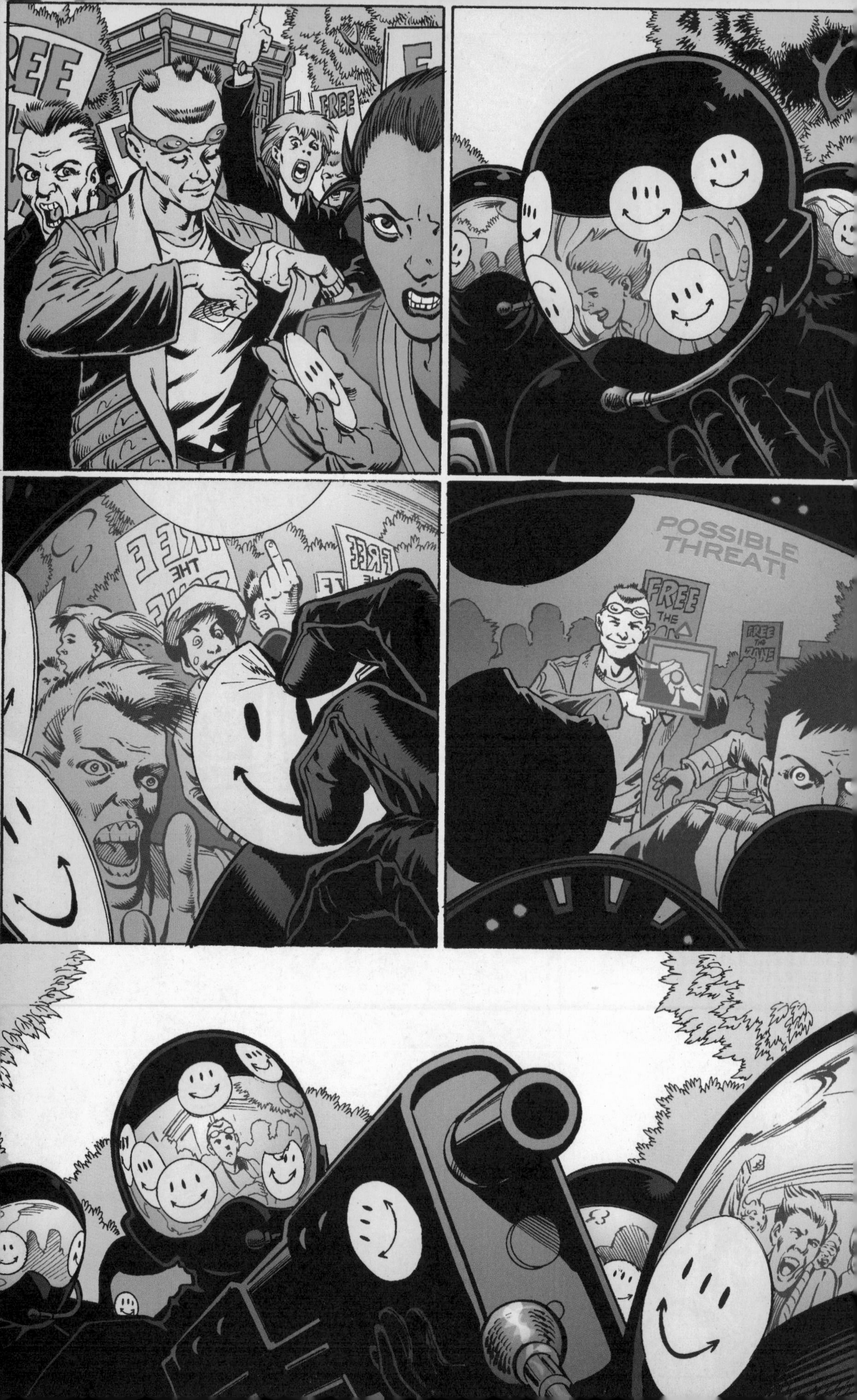
FREE
POSSIBLE THREAT!
FREE THE ZONE

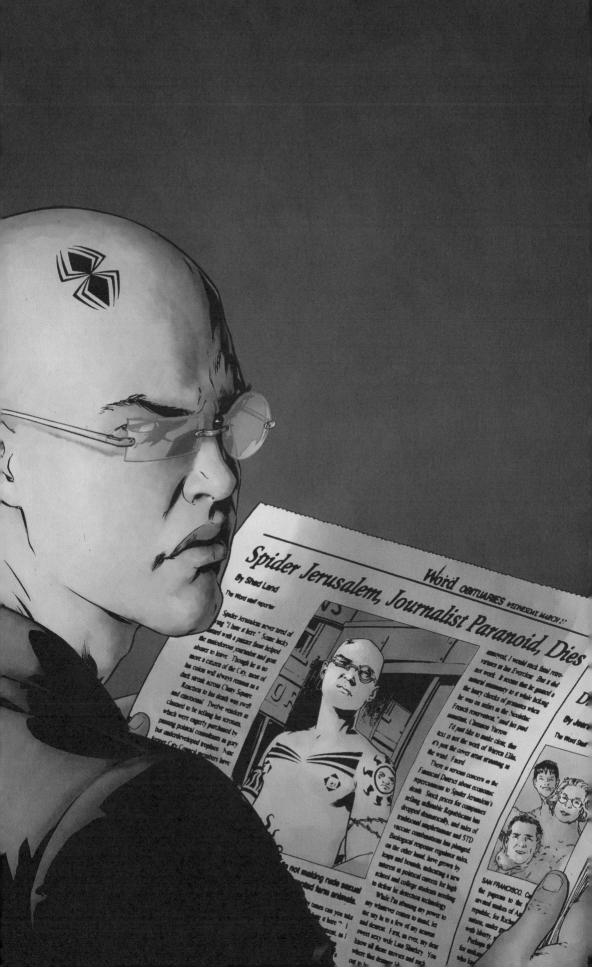

Spider Jerusalem, Journalist Paranoid, Dies

By Shud Land
The Word staff reporter

Spider Jerusalem never tired of saying "I hate it here." Some lately claimed with a pointer finger helped the malodorous journalist and poet abuses to leave. Though he is no more a citizen of the City, most of his codes will always remain as a dark streak across Chimy Square.

Reaction to his death was swift and emotional. Twelve vendors at claimed to be selling his screams, which were eagerly purchased by passing political commuters as gory but underdeveloped trophies. Nine former City Council members have

...not making rude gestures... ...pted farm animals...

Word OBITUARIES WEDNESDAY, MARCH 17

...removed, I would such fatal retro-...
...vences in his Everclear. Dies it did...
...not work. It seems that he gained a...
...natural immunity to it while licking...
...the furry chords of jennettes when...
...he was on safari at the Neolithic...
...French reservation," said his paid...
...assassin. Omarosa Yarrow.

I'd just like to make clear, this...
...text is just the work of Warren Ellis,...
...it's just the cover artist screwing in...
...the word. Fnord.

There is serious concern as the...
Financial District about economic...
repercussions to Spider Jerusalem's...
death. Stock prices for companies...
selling unlistenable Republicrats has...
dropped dramatically, and sales of...
radioactive amphetamines and STD...
vaccine combinations has plunged...
on the other hand, have grown by...
leaps and bounds, indicating a new...
interest in political careers for high...
school and college students needing...
to define his deficient sociology.

While I'm abusing my power to...
any whatever comes to mind, let...
me say hi to a few of my nearest...
and dearest. I yam, as ever, my dear...
sweet sexy wife Lisa Sharkey. You...
know all those movies and such...
...where that dumasse gale...

D

By Jea
The Word Staf

SAN FRANCISCO, Ca.
the pygmies to the
arv and snakes of An
republic, for Ricky
action, under g
with liberty
Package
...for an...
who la...

WARREN ELLIS writes and **DARICK ROBERTSON** & **RODNEY RAMOS** draw

HEADLONG

THREE of Three

CLEM ROBINS, letterer **NATHAN EYRING**, color & separations **GENE HA**, cover **ZACHARY RAU**, ass't editor **HEIDI MacDONALD**, editor

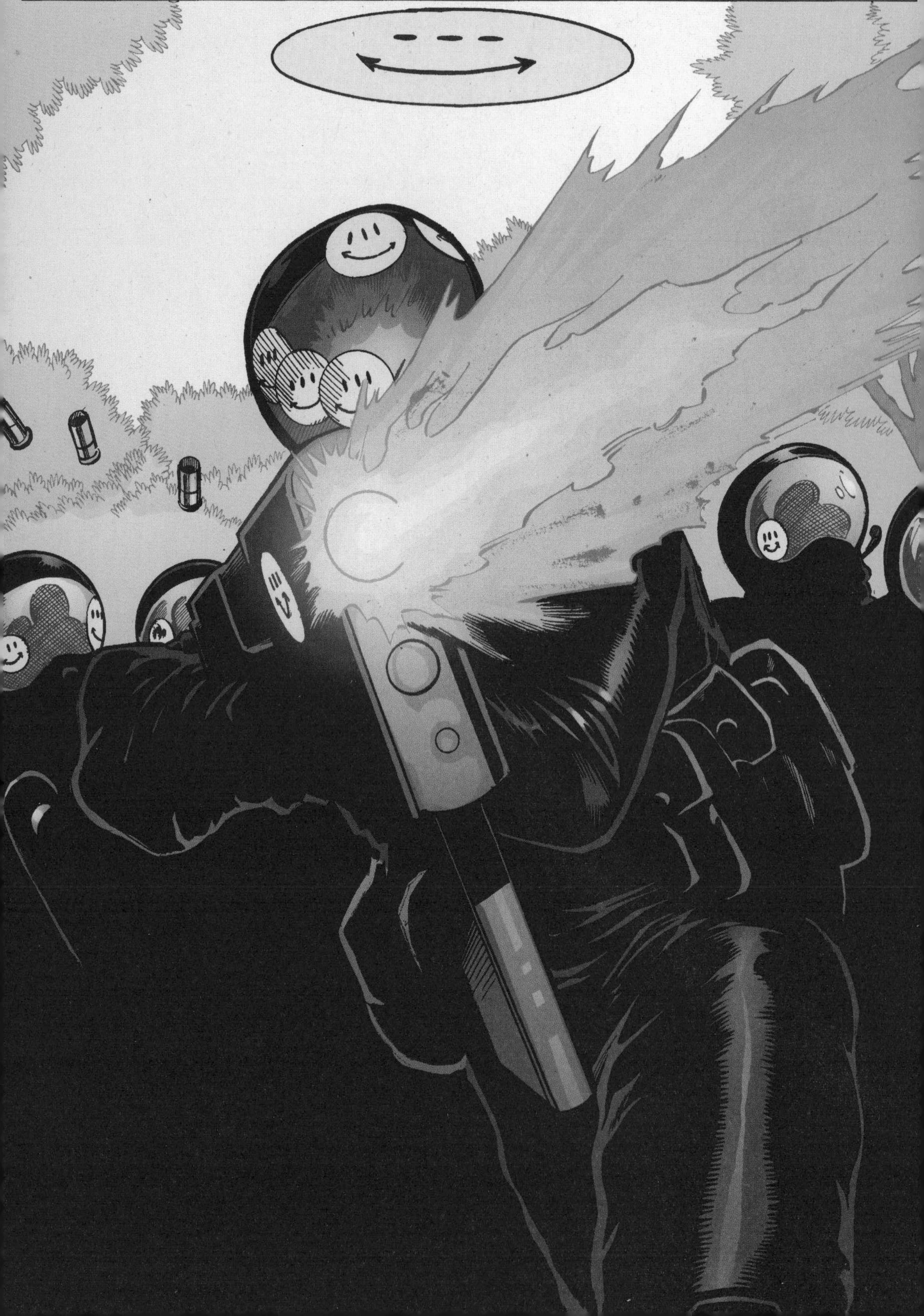

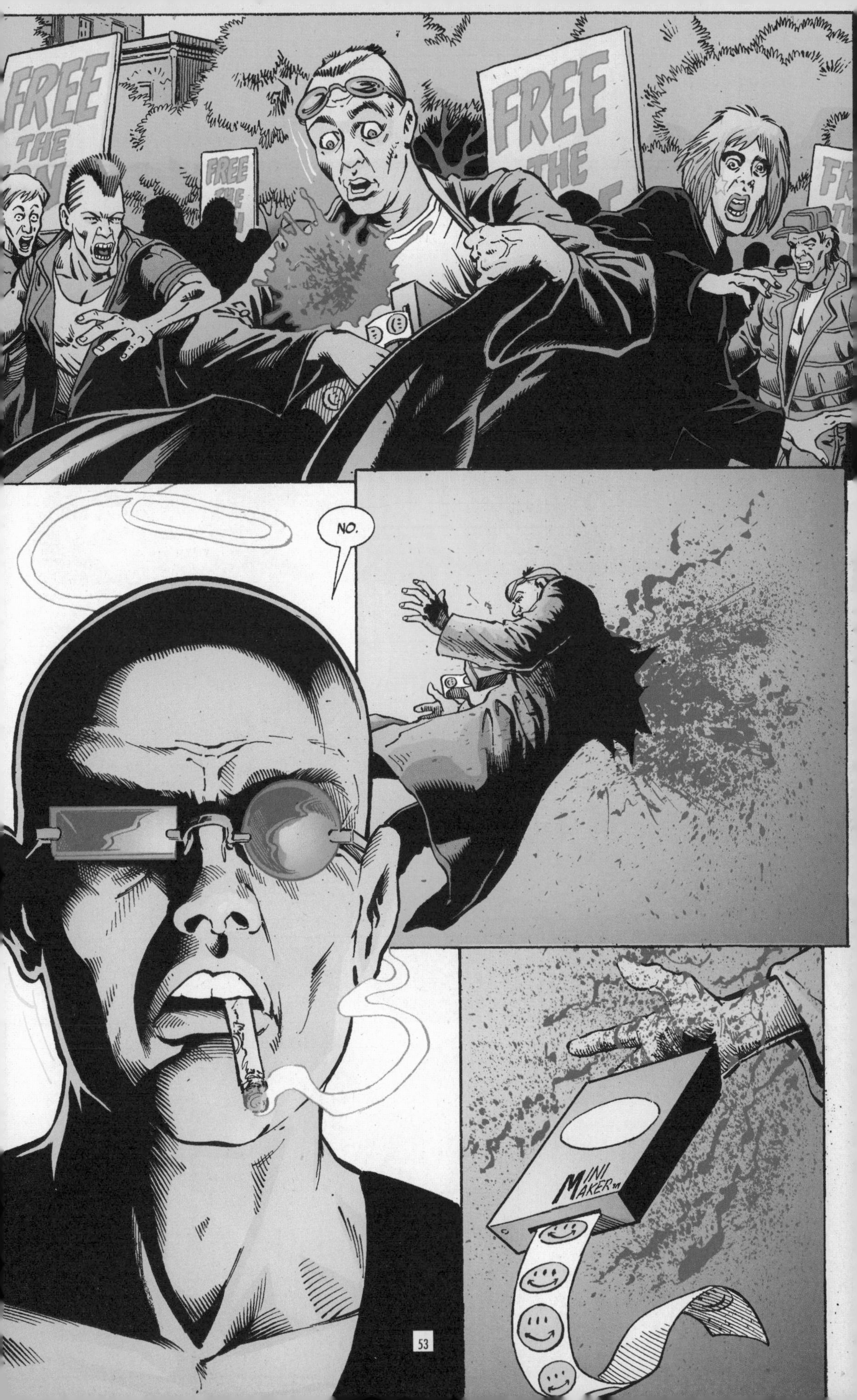
FREE THE
FREE
NO.
MINI MAKER

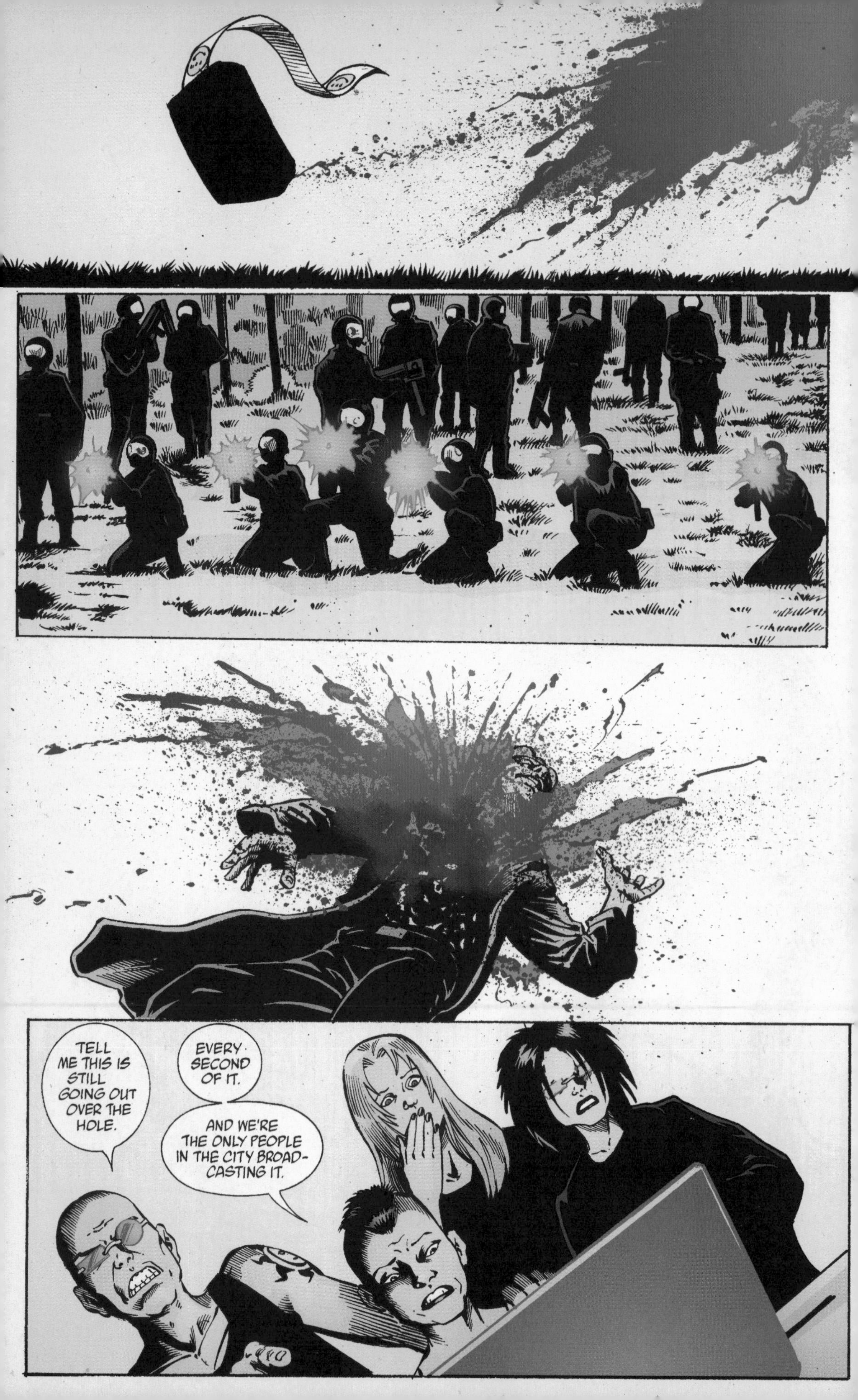
TELL ME THIS IS STILL GOING OUT OVER THE HOLE.
EVERY SECOND OF IT.
AND WE'RE THE ONLY PEOPLE IN THE CITY BROAD-CASTING IT.

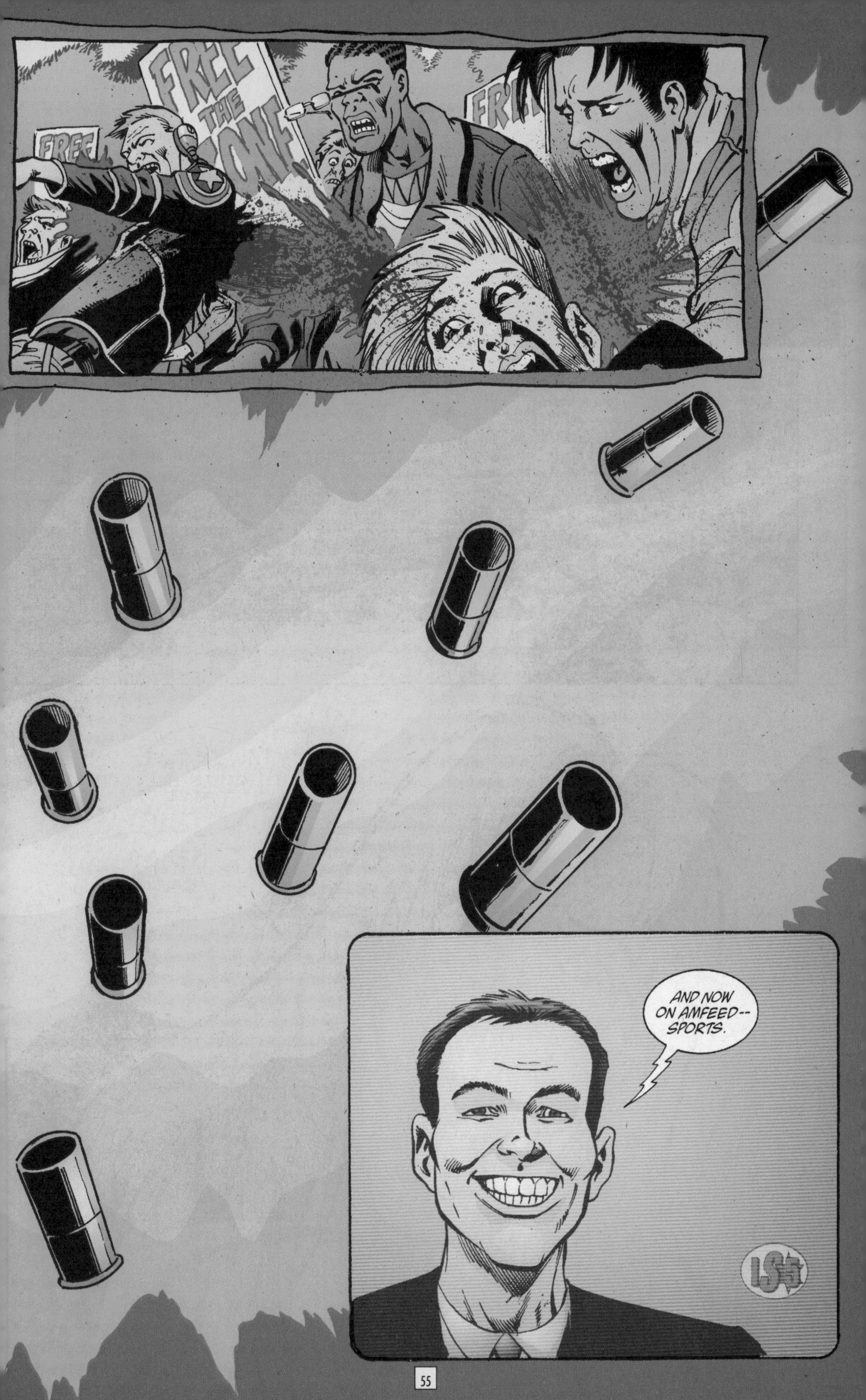
FREE THE ZONE
FREE
AND NOW ON AMFEED-- SPORTS.

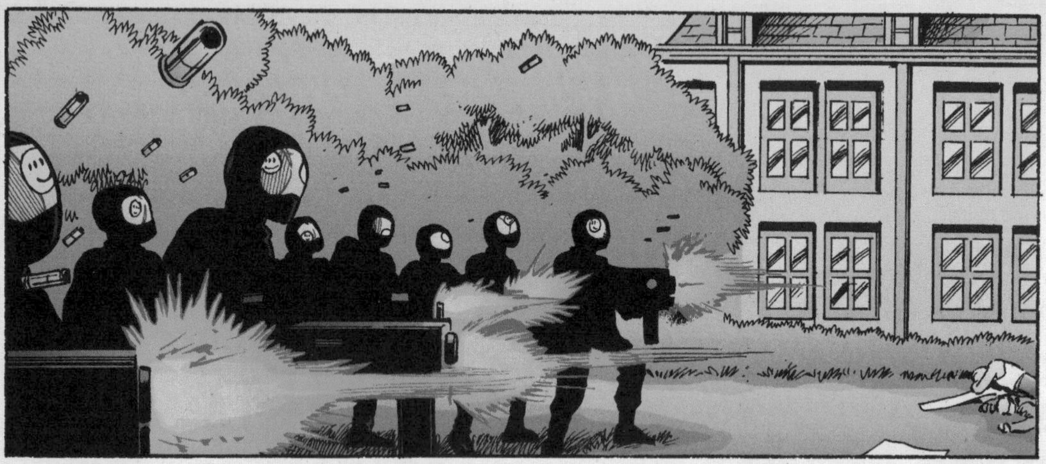

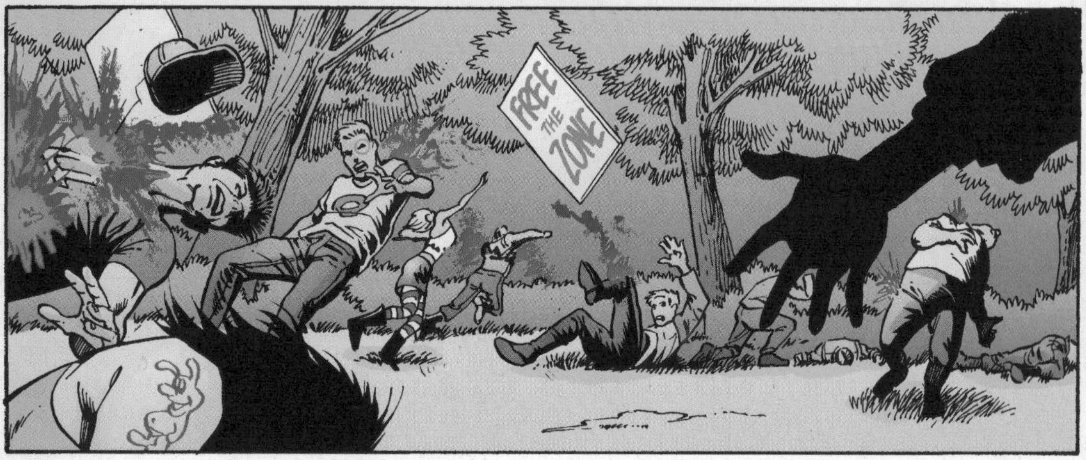
FREE THE ZONE

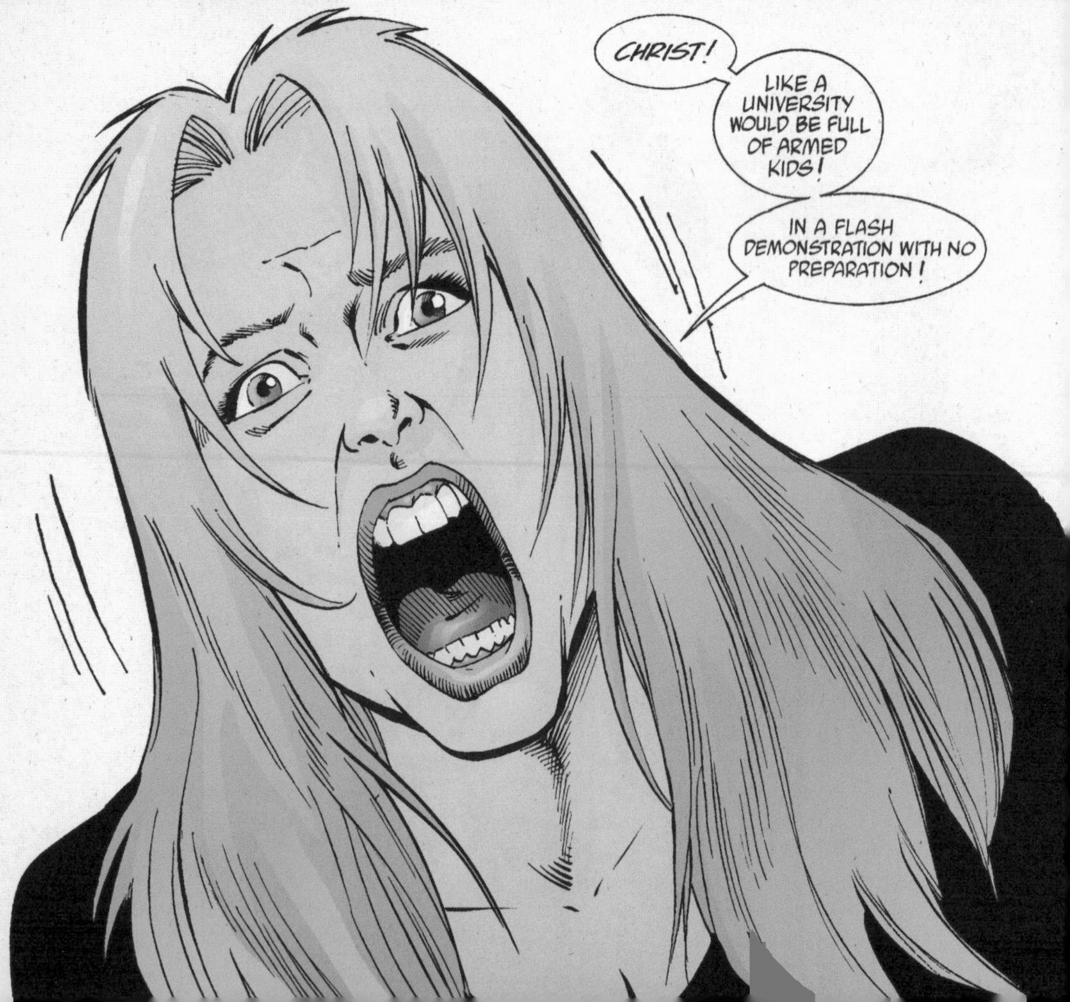
CHRIST!
LIKE A UNIVERSITY WOULD BE FULL OF ARMED KIDS!
IN A FLASH DEMONSTRATION WITH NO PREPARATION!

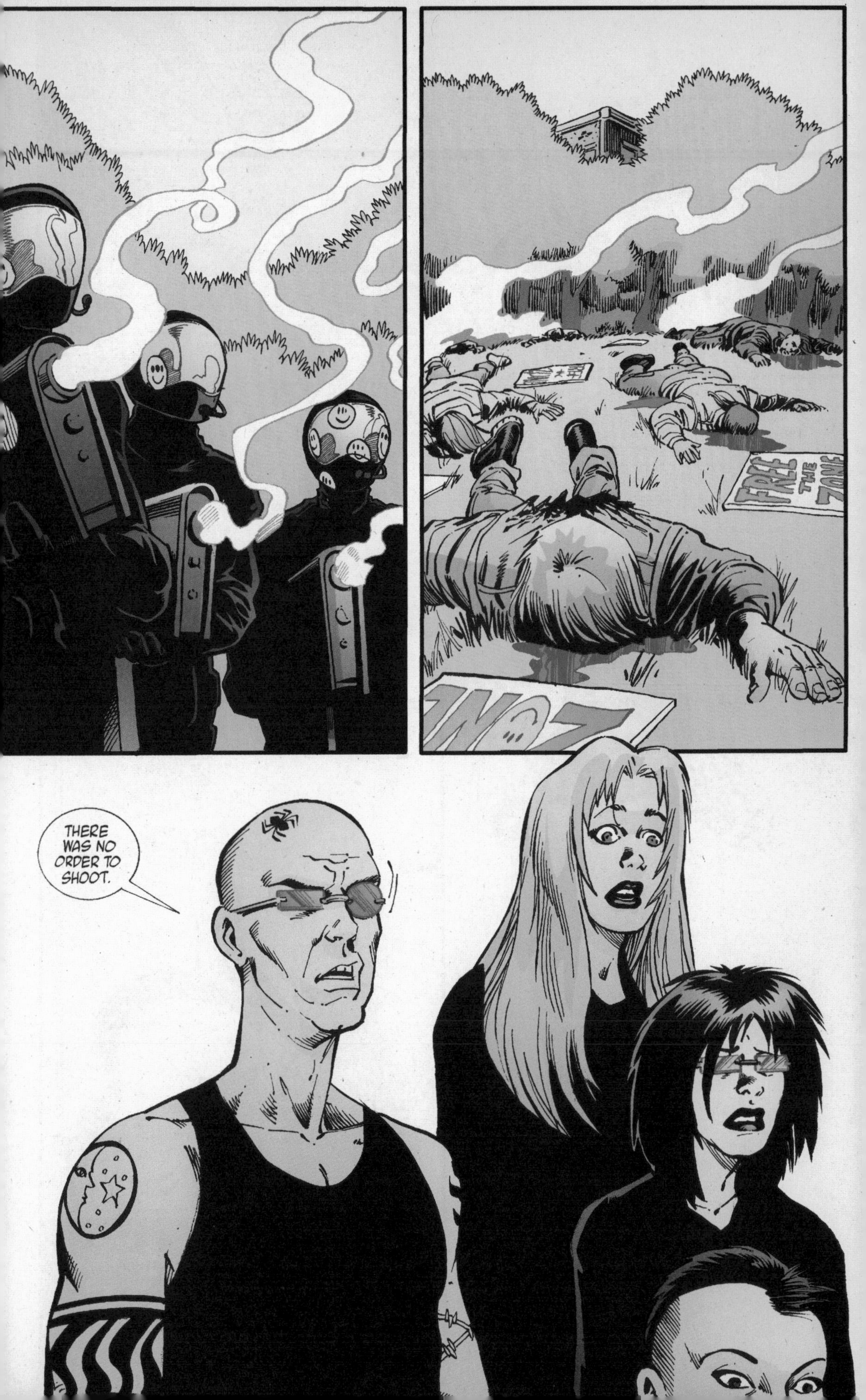
FREE THE ZONE
THERE WAS NO ORDER TO SHOOT.

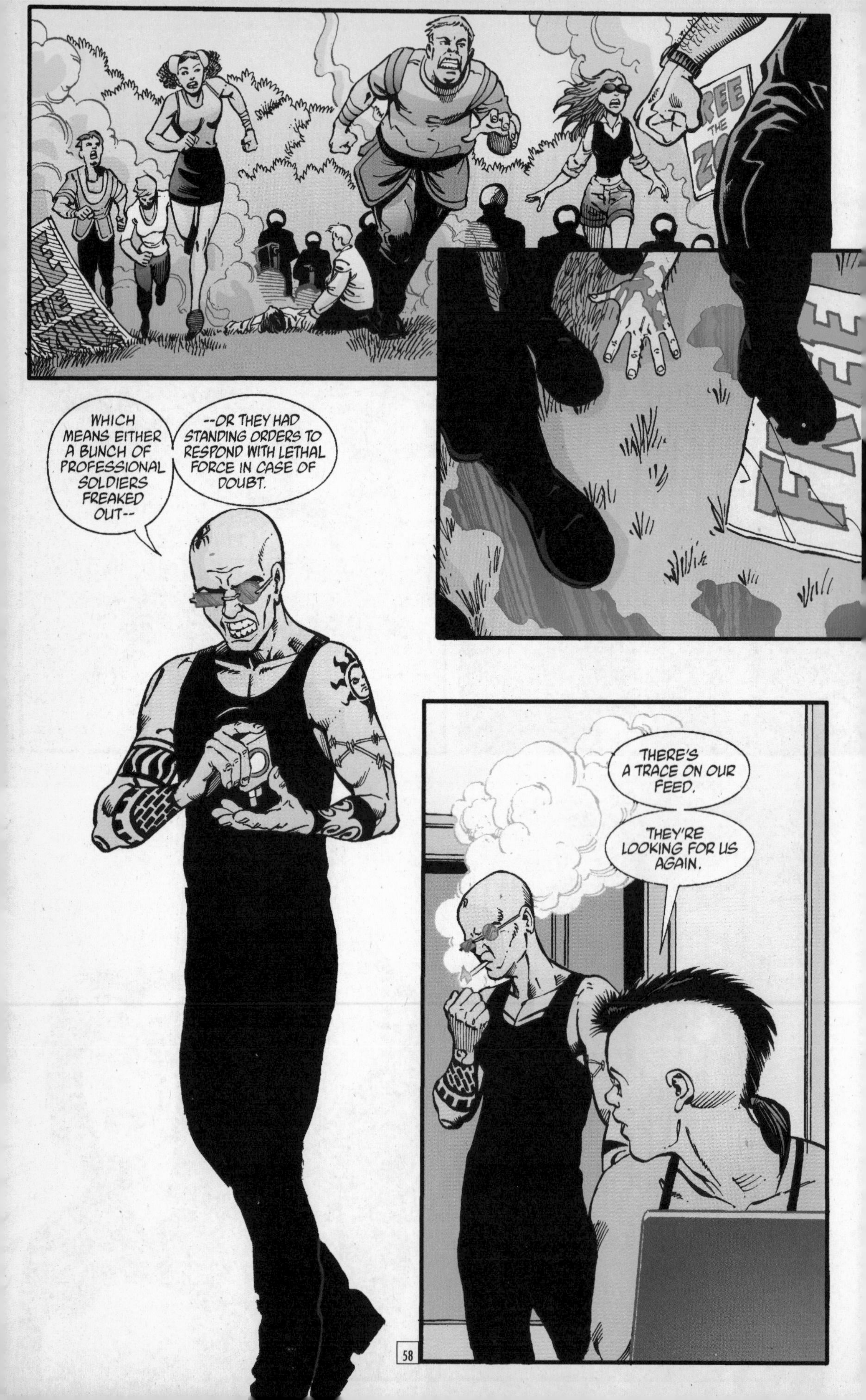
FREE THE ZONE
WHICH MEANS EITHER A BUNCH OF PROFESSIONAL SOLDIERS FREAKED OUT--
--OR THEY HAD STANDING ORDERS TO RESPOND WITH LETHAL FORCE IN CASE OF DOUBT.
THERE'S A TRACE ON OUR FEED.
THEY'RE LOOKING FOR US AGAIN.

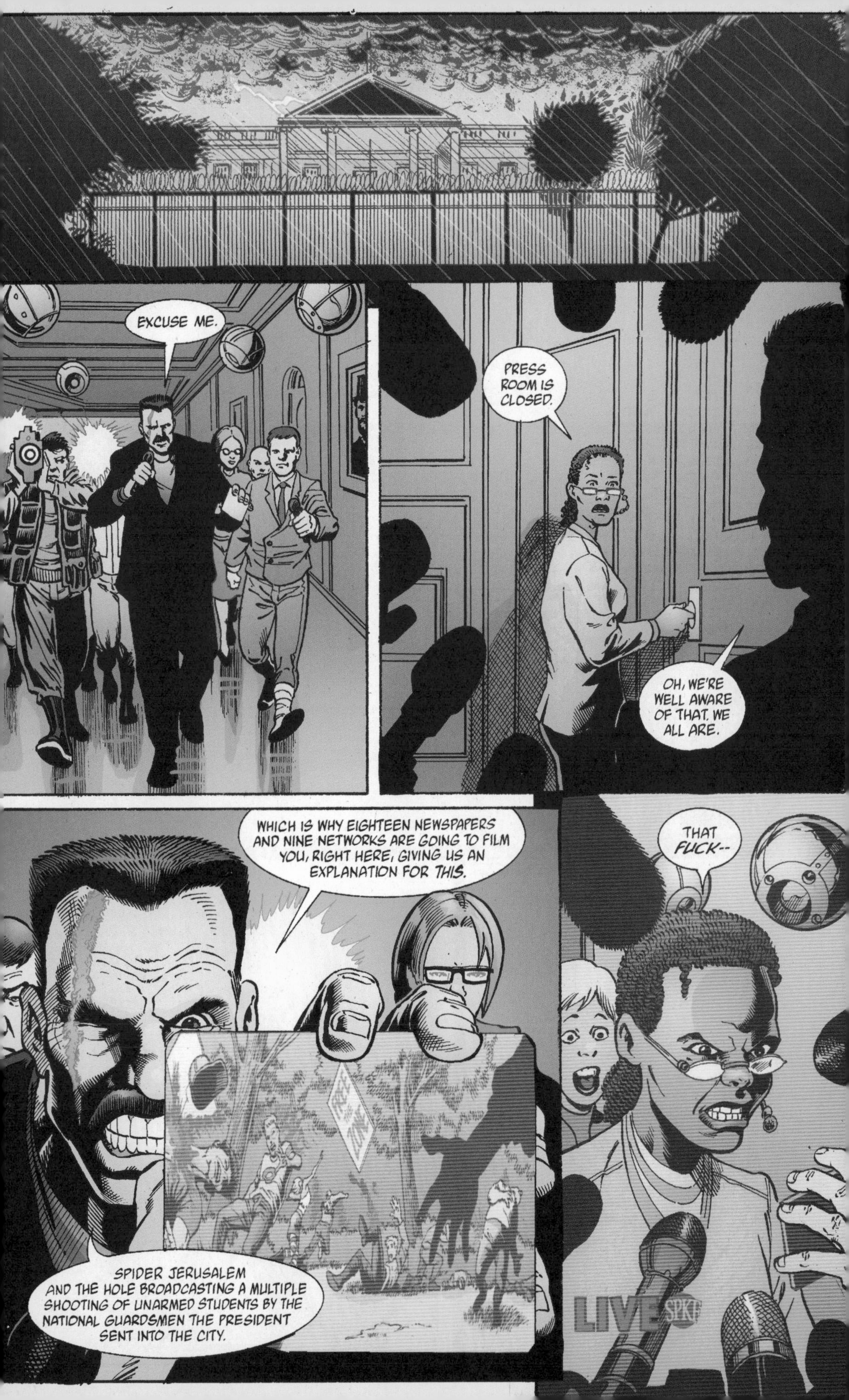
EXCUSE ME.
PRESS ROOM IS CLOSED.
OH, WE'RE WELL AWARE OF THAT. WE ALL ARE.
WHICH IS WHY EIGHTEEN NEWSPAPERS AND NINE NETWORKS ARE GOING TO FILM YOU, RIGHT HERE, GIVING US AN EXPLANATION FOR THIS.
SPIDER JERUSALEM AND THE HOLE BROADCASTING A MULTIPLE SHOOTING OF UNARMED STUDENTS BY THE NATIONAL GUARDSMEN THE PRESIDENT SENT INTO THE CITY.
THAT FUCK--
LIVE

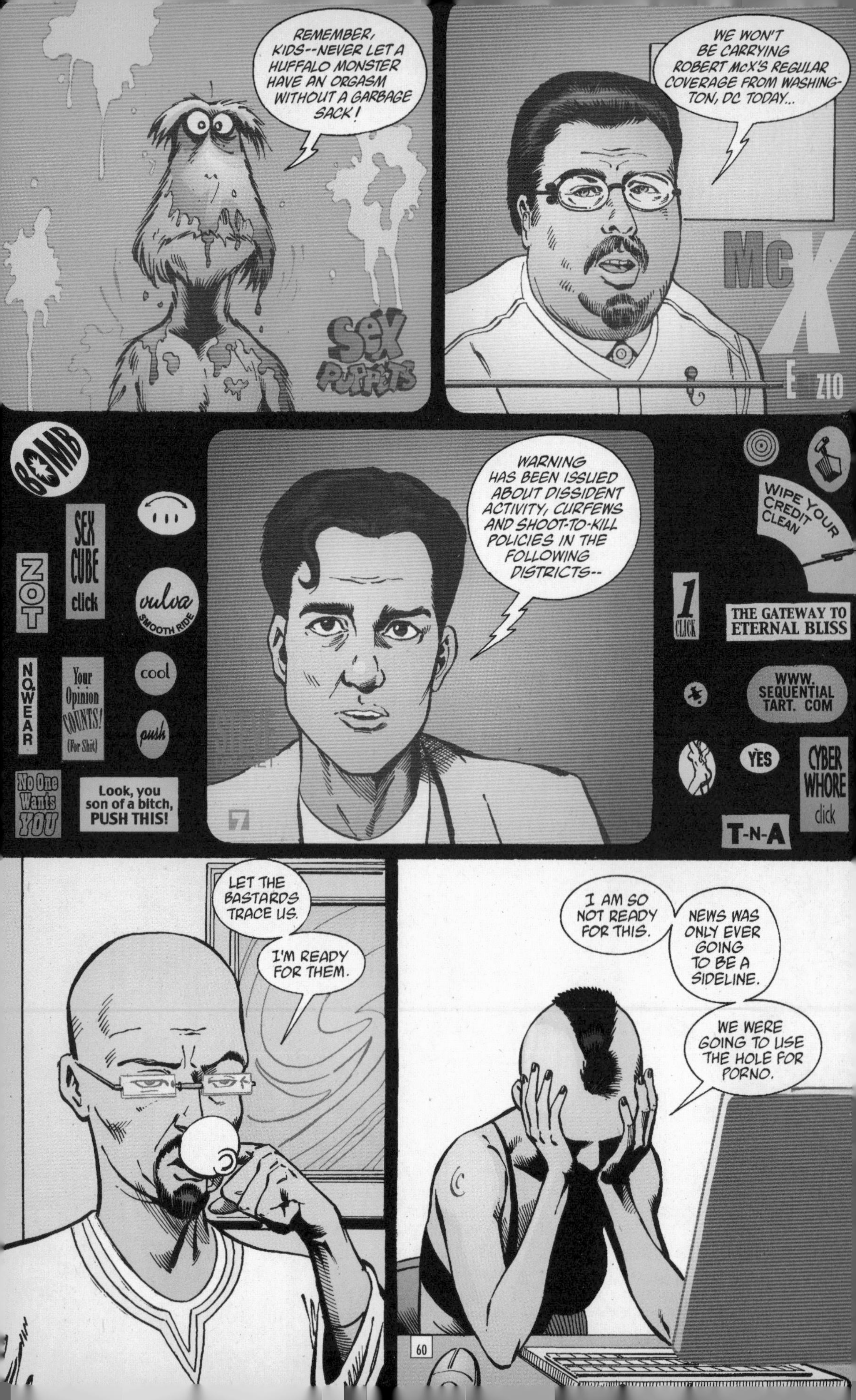
REMEMBER, KIDS--NEVER LET A HUFFALO MONSTER HAVE AN ORGASM WITHOUT A GARBAGE SACK!
SEX PUPPETS
WE WON'T BE CARRYING ROBERT McX'S REGULAR COVERAGE FROM WASHINGTON, DC TODAY...
McX
WARNING HAS BEEN ISSUED ABOUT DISSIDENT ACTIVITY, CURFEWS AND SHOOT-TO-KILL POLICIES IN THE FOLLOWING DISTRICTS--
BOMB
SEX CUBE click
ZOT
vulva SMOOTH RIDE
cool
push
NO.WEAR
Your Opinion COUNTS! (For Shit)
No One Wants YOU
Look, you son of a bitch, PUSH THIS!
WIPE YOUR CREDIT CLEAN
1 CLICK
THE GATEWAY TO ETERNAL BLISS
WWW. SEQUENTIAL TART. COM
YES
CYBER WHORE click
T-N-A
LET THE BASTARDS TRACE US.
I'M READY FOR THEM.
I AM SO NOT READY FOR THIS.
NEWS WAS ONLY EVER GOING TO BE A SIDELINE.
WE WERE GOING TO USE THE HOLE FOR PORNO.

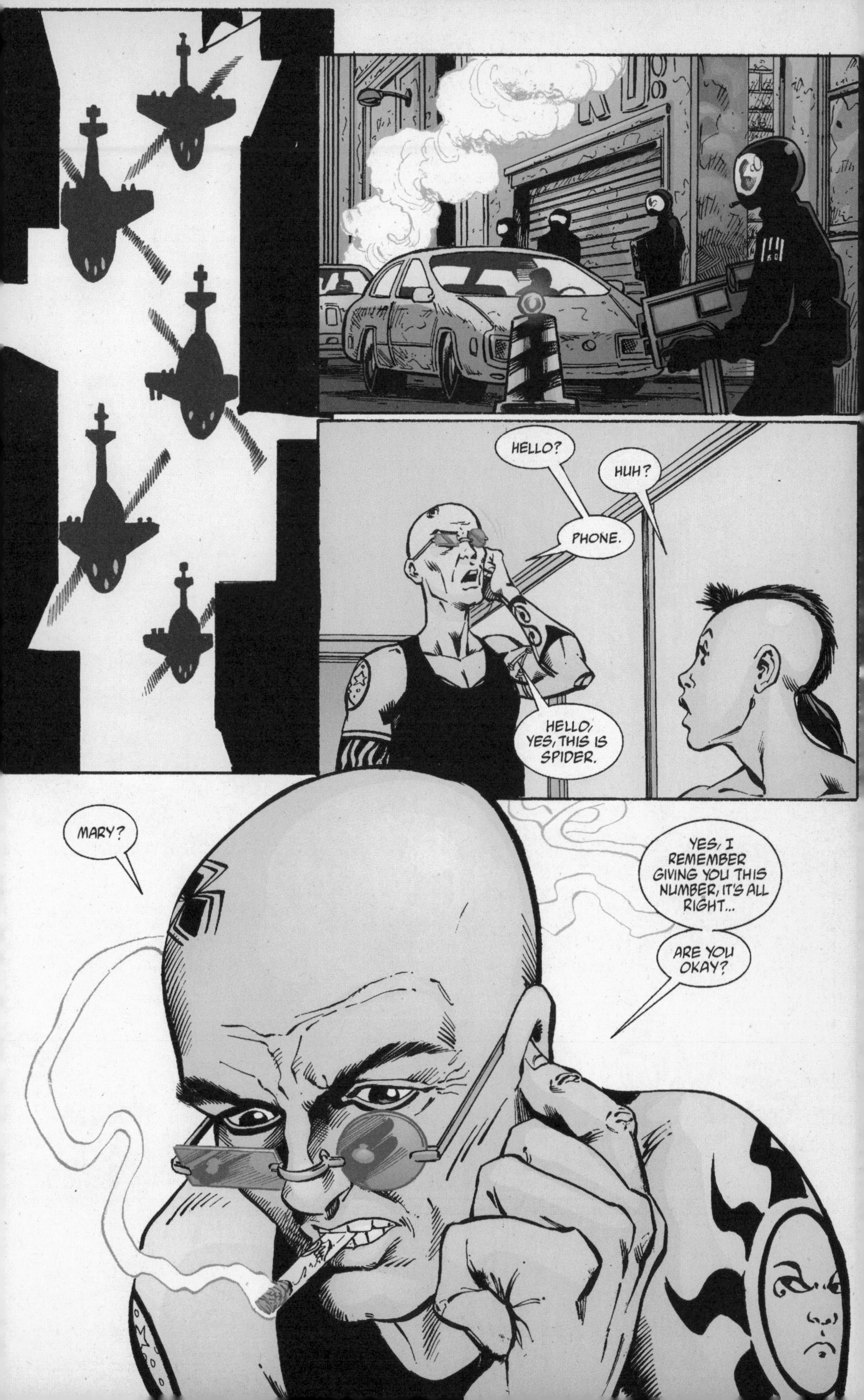
HELLO?
HUH?
PHONE.
HELLO, YES, THIS IS SPIDER.
MARY?
YES, I REMEMBER GIVING YOU THIS NUMBER, IT'S ALL RIGHT...
ARE YOU OKAY?

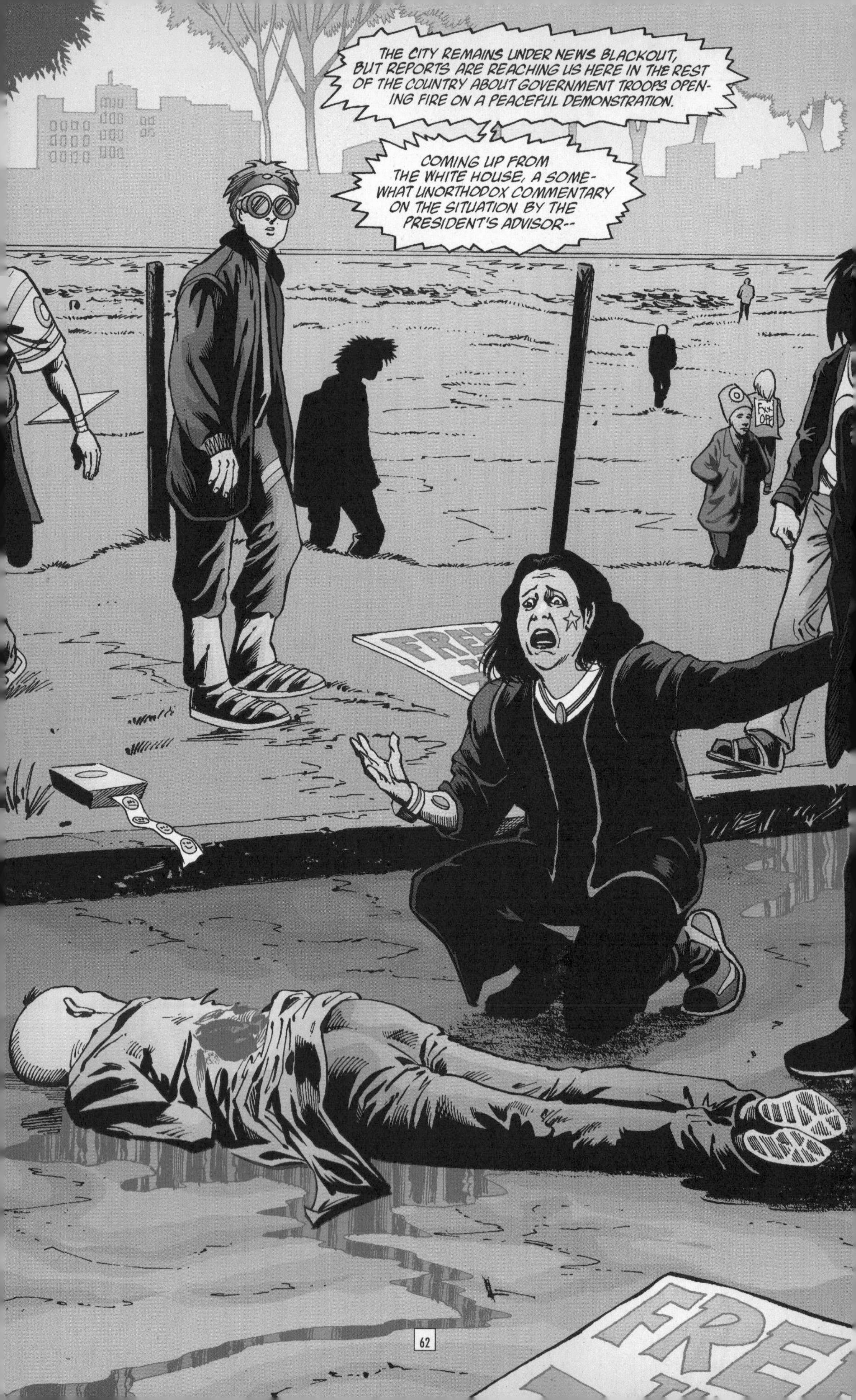

THE CITY REMAINS UNDER NEWS BLACKOUT, BUT REPORTS ARE REACHING US HERE IN THE REST OF THE COUNTRY ABOUT GOVERNMENT TROOPS OPENING FIRE ON A PEACEFUL DEMONSTRATION.
COMING UP FROM THE WHITE HOUSE, A SOMEWHAT UNORTHODOX COMMENTARY ON THE SITUATION BY THE PRESIDENT'S ADVISOR--

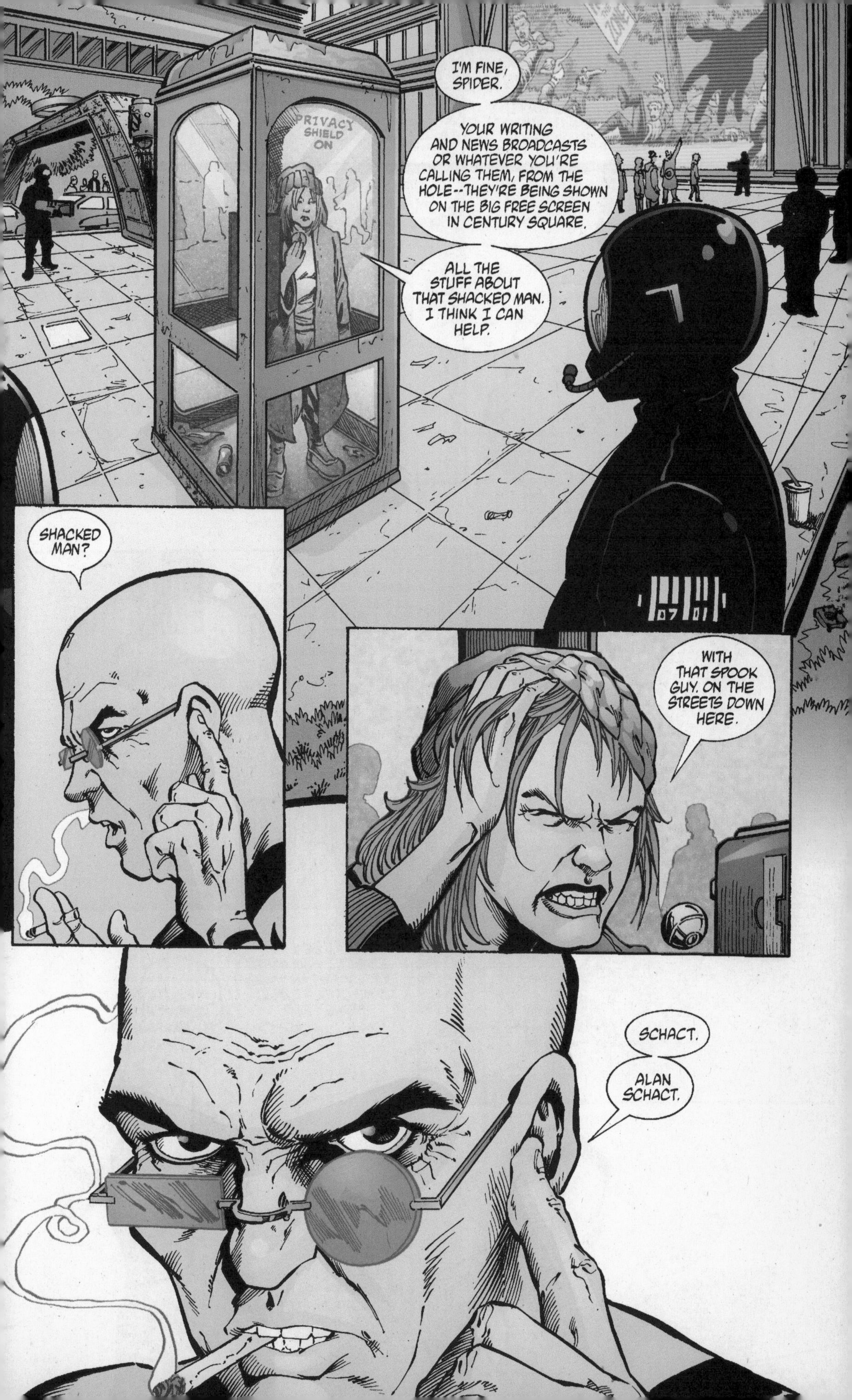

PRIVACY SHIELD ON
I'M FINE, SPIDER.
YOUR WRITING AND NEWS BROADCASTS OR WHATEVER YOU'RE CALLING THEM, FROM THE HOLE--THEY'RE BEING SHOWN ON THE BIG FREE SCREEN IN CENTURY SQUARE.
ALL THE STUFF ABOUT THAT SHACKED MAN. I THINK I CAN HELP.
SHACKED MAN?
WITH THAT SPOOK GUY. ON THE STREETS DOWN HERE.
SCHACT.
ALAN SCHACT.

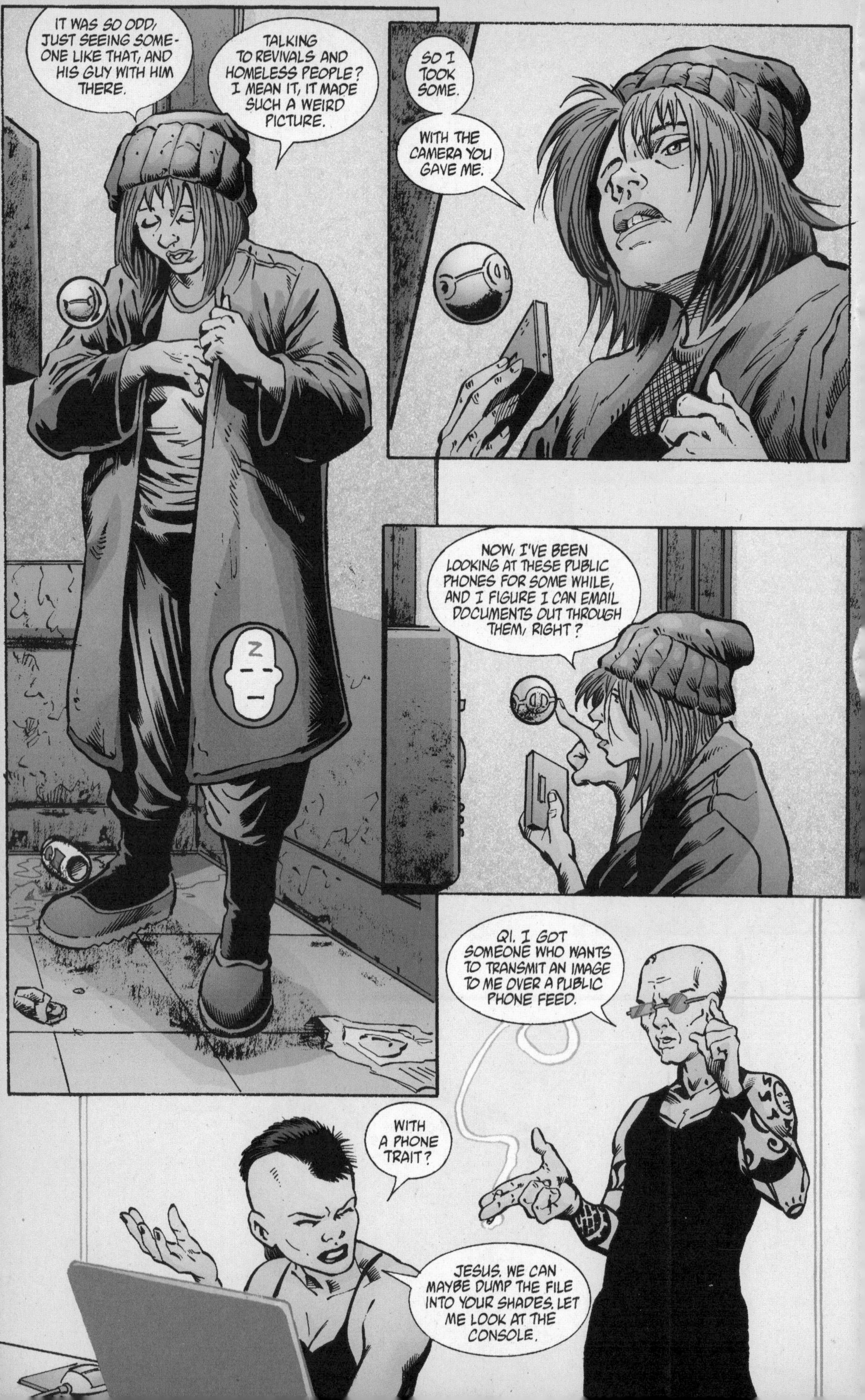
IT WAS SO ODD, JUST SEEING SOME-ONE LIKE THAT, AND HIS GUY WITH HIM THERE.
TALKING TO REVIVALS AND HOMELESS PEOPLE? I MEAN IT, IT MADE SUCH A WEIRD PICTURE.
SO I TOOK SOME.
WITH THE CAMERA YOU GAVE ME.
NOW, I'VE BEEN LOOKING AT THESE PUBLIC PHONES FOR SOME WHILE, AND I FIGURE I CAN EMAIL DOCUMENTS OUT THROUGH THEM, RIGHT?
QI. I GOT SOMEONE WHO WANTS TO TRANSMIT AN IMAGE TO ME OVER A PUBLIC PHONE FEED.
WITH A PHONE TRAIT?
JESUS. WE CAN MAYBE DUMP THE FILE INTO YOUR SHADES. LET ME LOOK AT THE CONSOLE.

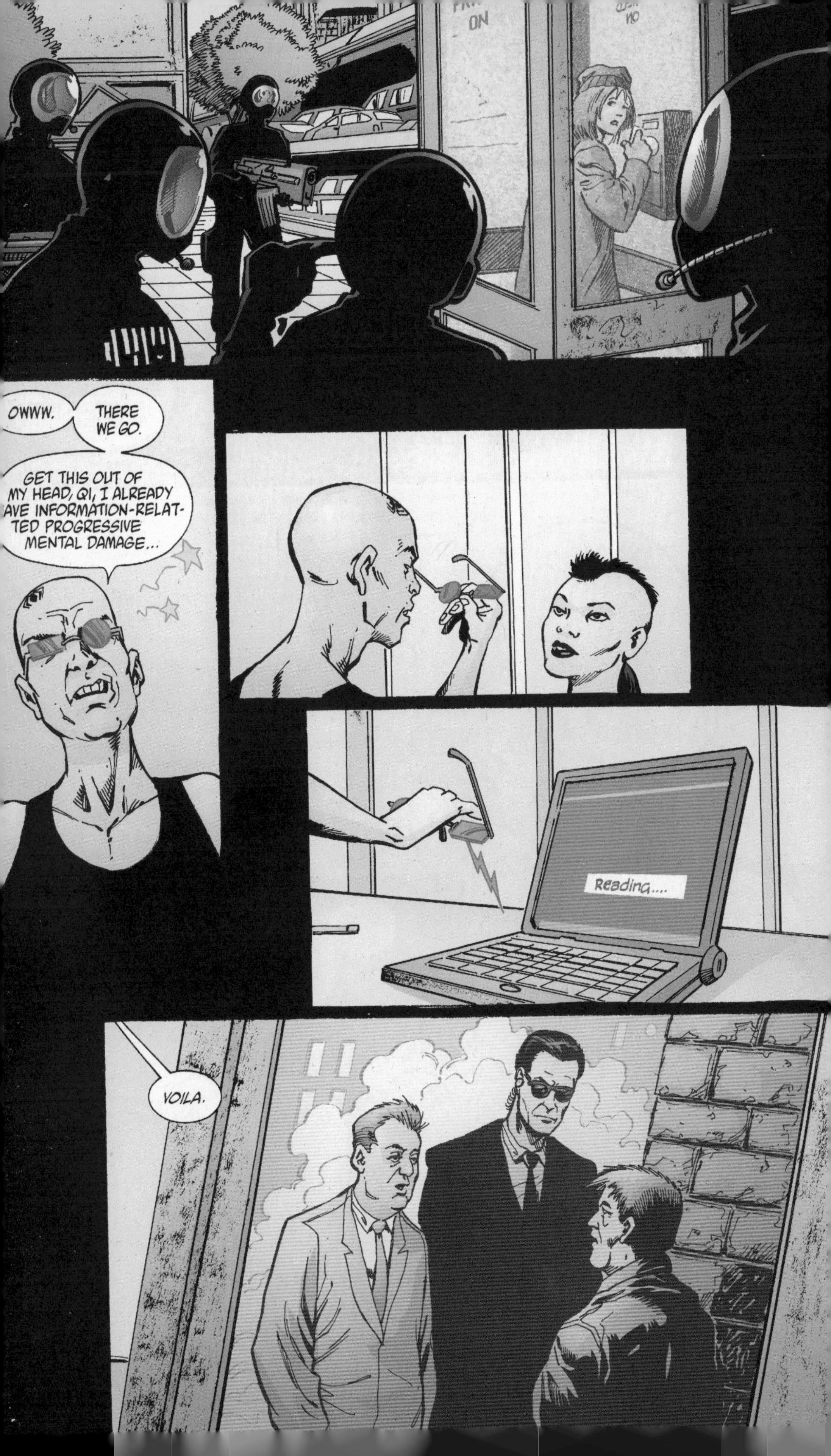
OWWW.
THERE WE GO.
GET THIS OUT OF MY HEAD, QI, I ALREADY AVE INFORMATION-RELAT-TED PROGRESSIVE MENTAL DAMAGE...
Reading....
VOILA.

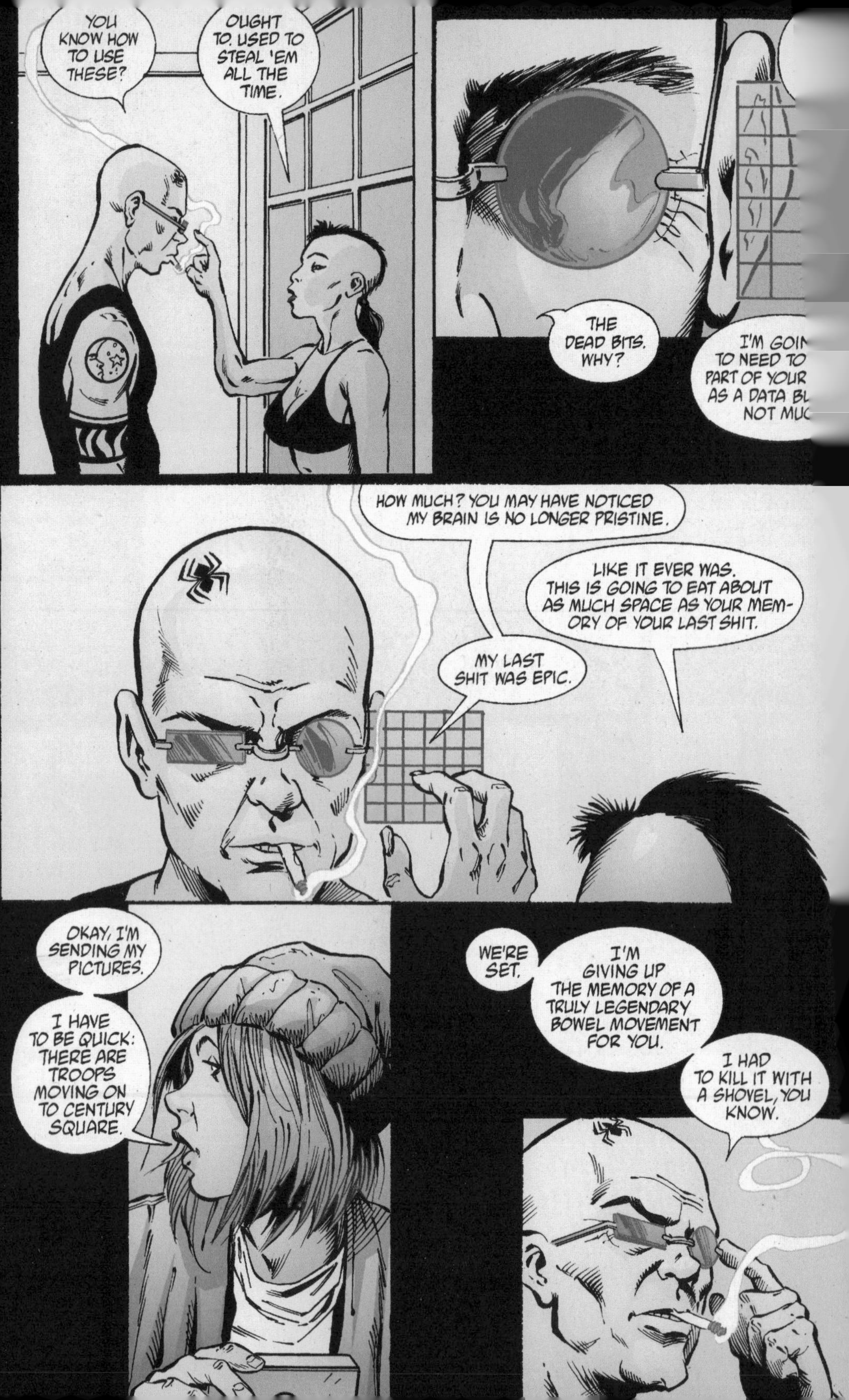
YOU KNOW HOW TO USE THESE?
OUGHT TO. USED TO STEAL 'EM ALL THE TIME.
THE DEAD BITS. WHY?
I'M GOIN TO NEED TO PART OF YOUR AS A DATA BL NOT MUC
HOW MUCH? YOU MAY HAVE NOTICED MY BRAIN IS NO LONGER PRISTINE.
LIKE IT EVER WAS. THIS IS GOING TO EAT ABOUT AS MUCH SPACE AS YOUR MEMORY OF YOUR LAST SHIT.
MY LAST SHIT WAS EPIC.
OKAY, I'M SENDING MY PICTURES.
I HAVE TO BE QUICK: THERE ARE TROOPS MOVING ON TO CENTURY SQUARE.
WE'RE SET.
I'M GIVING UP THE MEMORY OF A TRULY LEGENDARY BOWEL MOVEMENT FOR YOU.
I HAD TO KILL IT WITH A SHOVEL, YOU KNOW.

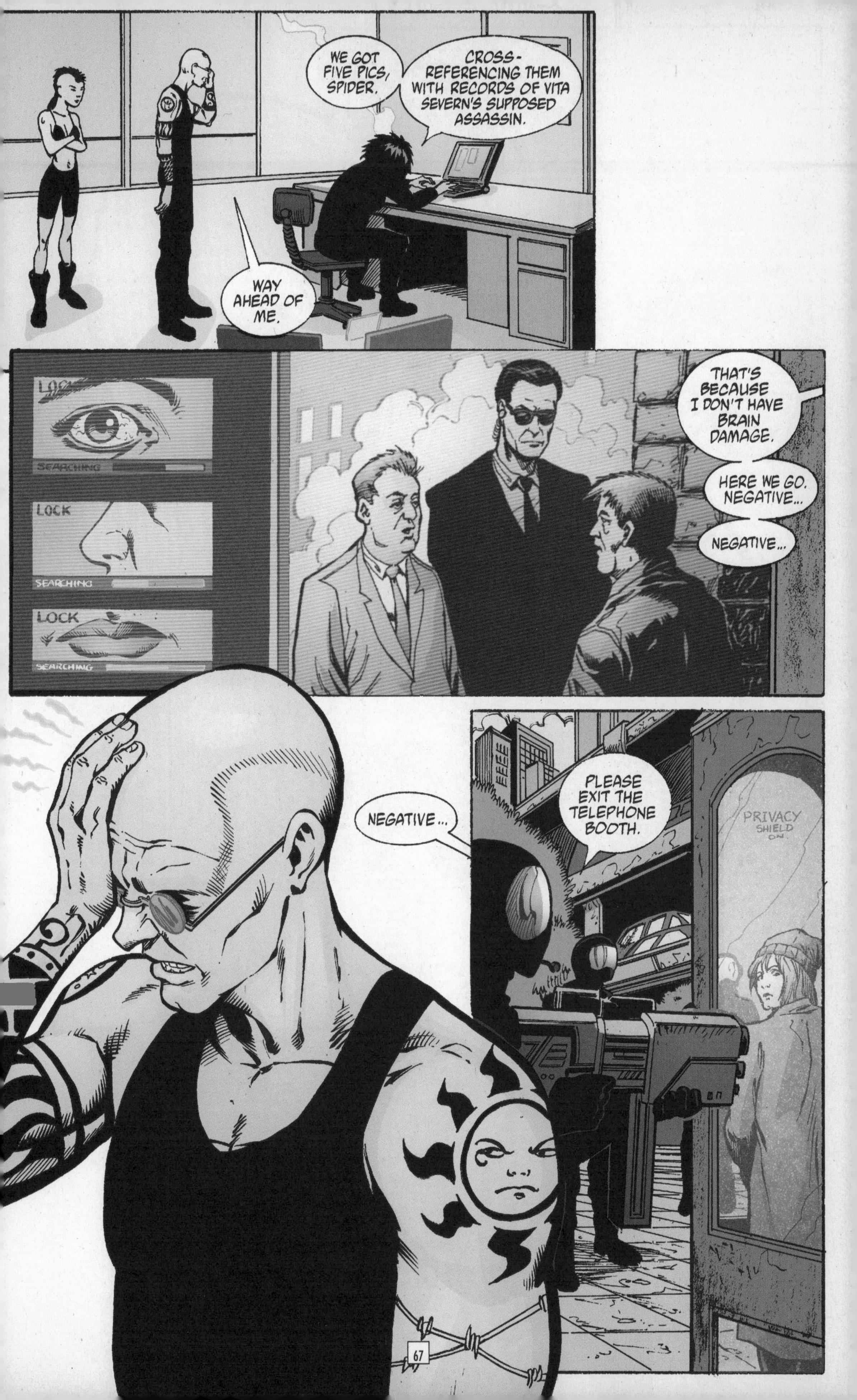
WE GOT FIVE PICS, SPIDER.
CROSS-REFERENCING THEM WITH RECORDS OF VITA SEVERN'S SUPPOSED ASSASSIN.
WAY AHEAD OF ME.
LOCK
SEARCHING
LOCK
SEARCHING
LOCK
SEARCHING
THAT'S BECAUSE I DON'T HAVE BRAIN DAMAGE.
HERE WE GO. NEGATIVE...
NEGATIVE...
NEGATIVE...
PLEASE EXIT THE TELEPHONE BOOTH.
PRIVACY SHIELD ON.

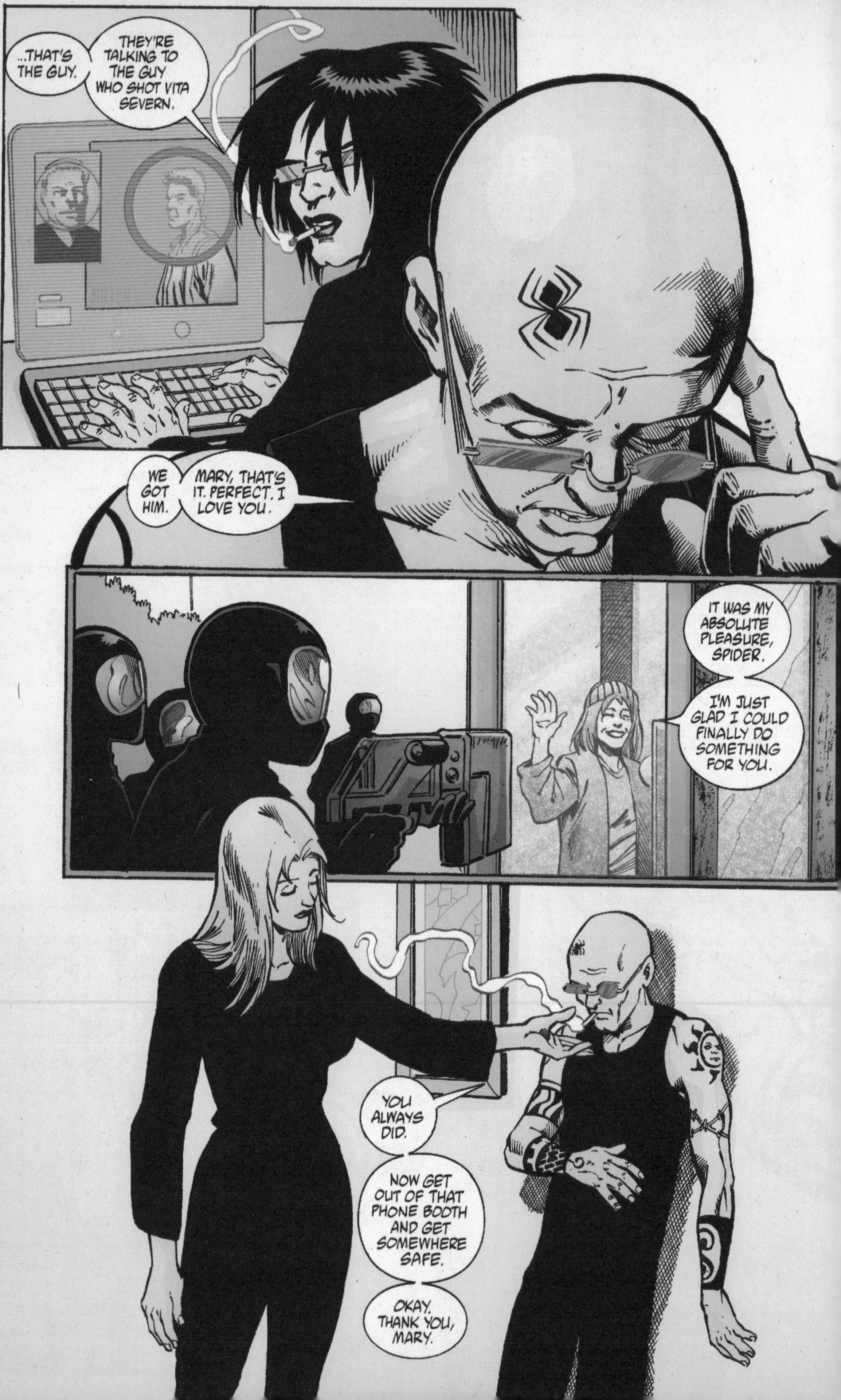
...THAT'S THE GUY.
THEY'RE TALKING TO THE GUY WHO SHOT VITA SEVERN.
WE GOT HIM.
MARY, THAT'S IT. PERFECT. I LOVE YOU.
IT WAS MY ABSOLUTE PLEASURE, SPIDER.
I'M JUST GLAD I COULD FINALLY DO SOMETHING FOR YOU.
YOU ALWAYS DID.
NOW GET OUT OF THAT PHONE BOOTH AND GET SOMEWHERE SAFE.
OKAY. THANK YOU, MARY.

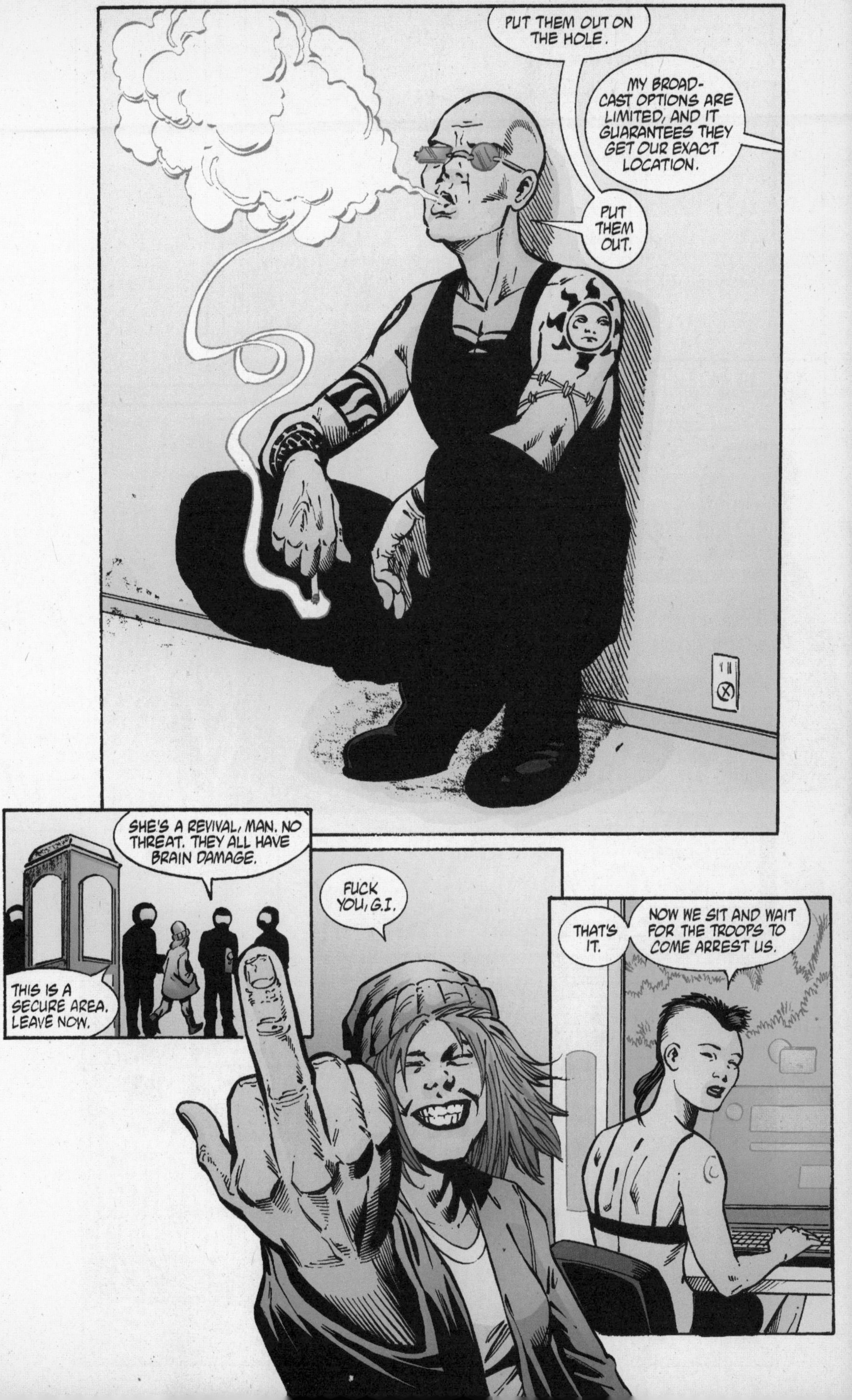
PUT THEM OUT ON THE HOLE.
MY BROAD-CAST OPTIONS ARE LIMITED, AND IT GUARANTEES THEY GET OUR EXACT LOCATION.
PUT THEM OUT.
SHE'S A REVIVAL, MAN. NO THREAT. THEY ALL HAVE BRAIN DAMAGE.
THIS IS A SECURE AREA. LEAVE NOW.
FUCK YOU, G.I.
THAT'S IT.
NOW WE SIT AND WAIT FOR THE TROOPS TO COME ARREST US.

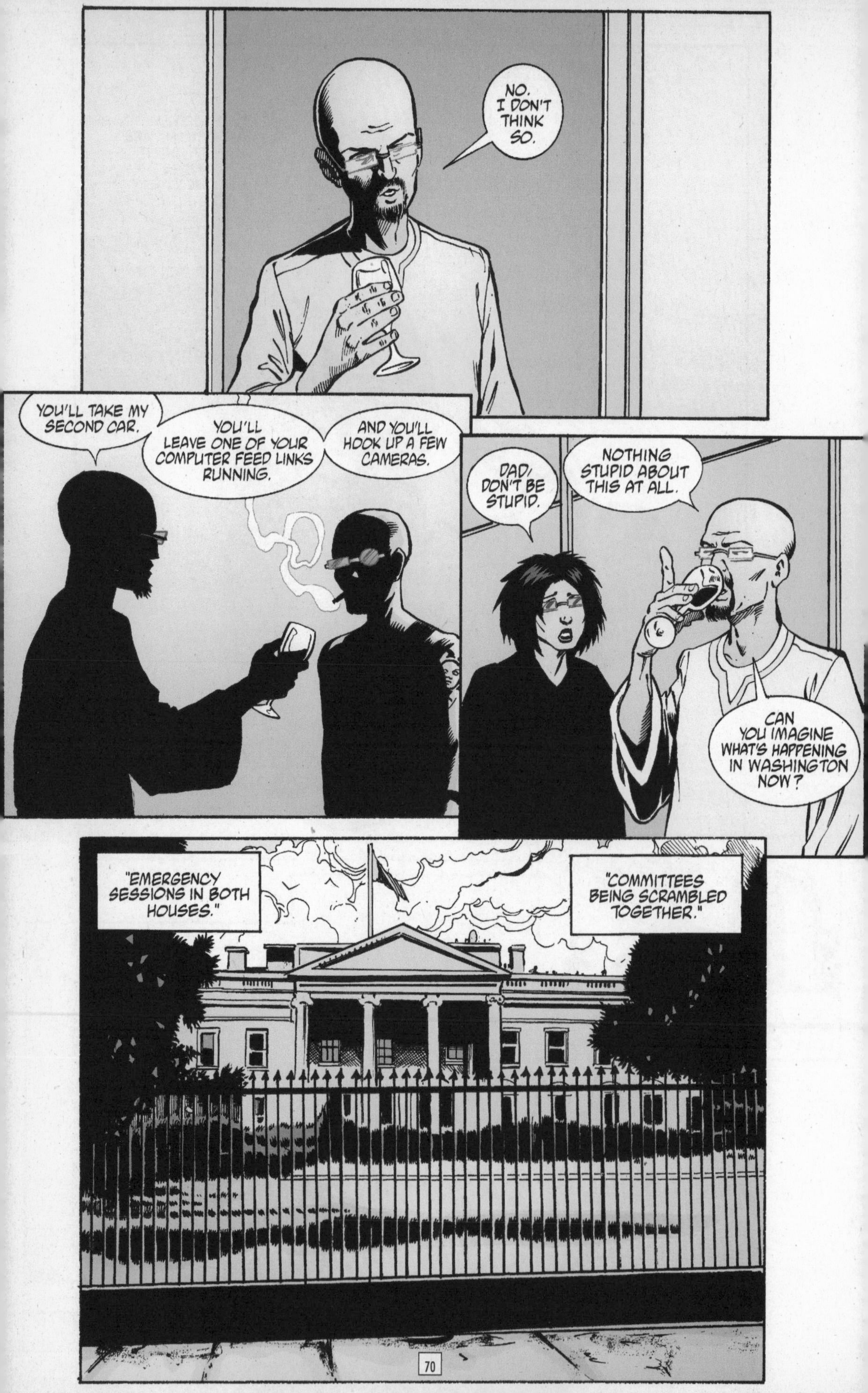
NO. I DON'T THINK SO.
YOU'LL TAKE MY SECOND CAR.
YOU'LL LEAVE ONE OF YOUR COMPUTER FEED LINKS RUNNING.
AND YOU'LL HOOK UP A FEW CAMERAS.
DAD, DON'T BE STUPID.
NOTHING STUPID ABOUT THIS AT ALL.
CAN YOU IMAGINE WHAT'S HAPPENING IN WASHINGTON NOW?
"EMERGENCY SESSIONS IN BOTH HOUSES."
"COMMITTEES BEING SCRAMBLED TOGETHER."

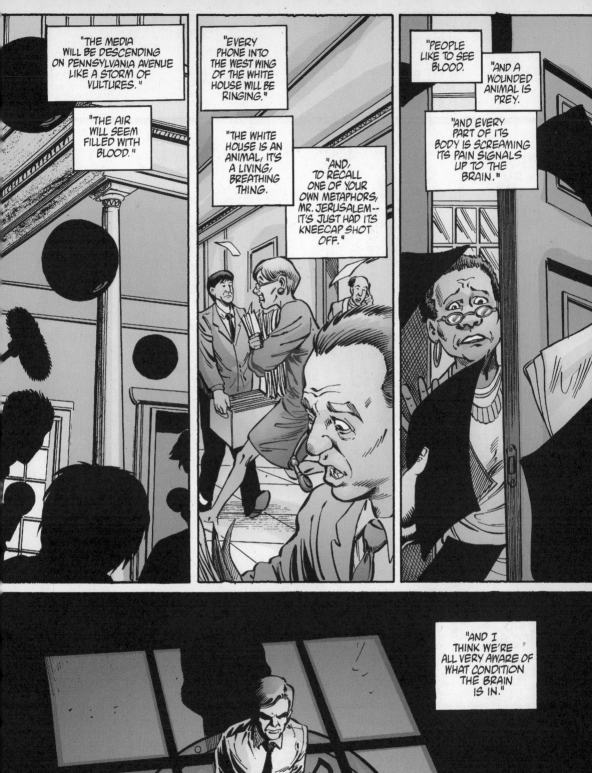

"THE MEDIA WILL BE DESCENDING ON PENNSYLVANIA AVENUE LIKE A STORM OF VULTURES."

"THE AIR WILL SEEM FILLED WITH BLOOD."

"EVERY PHONE INTO THE WEST WING OF THE WHITE HOUSE WILL BE RINGING."

"THE WHITE HOUSE IS AN ANIMAL, IT'S A LIVING, BREATHING THING.

"AND, TO RECALL ONE OF YOUR OWN METAPHORS, MR. JERUSALEM-- IT'S JUST HAD ITS KNEECAP SHOT OFF."

"PEOPLE LIKE TO SEE BLOOD.

"AND A WOUNDED ANIMAL IS PREY.

"AND EVERY PART OF ITS BODY IS SCREAMING ITS PAIN SIGNALS UP TO THE BRAIN."

"AND I THINK WE'RE ALL VERY AWARE OF WHAT CONDITION THE BRAIN IS IN."

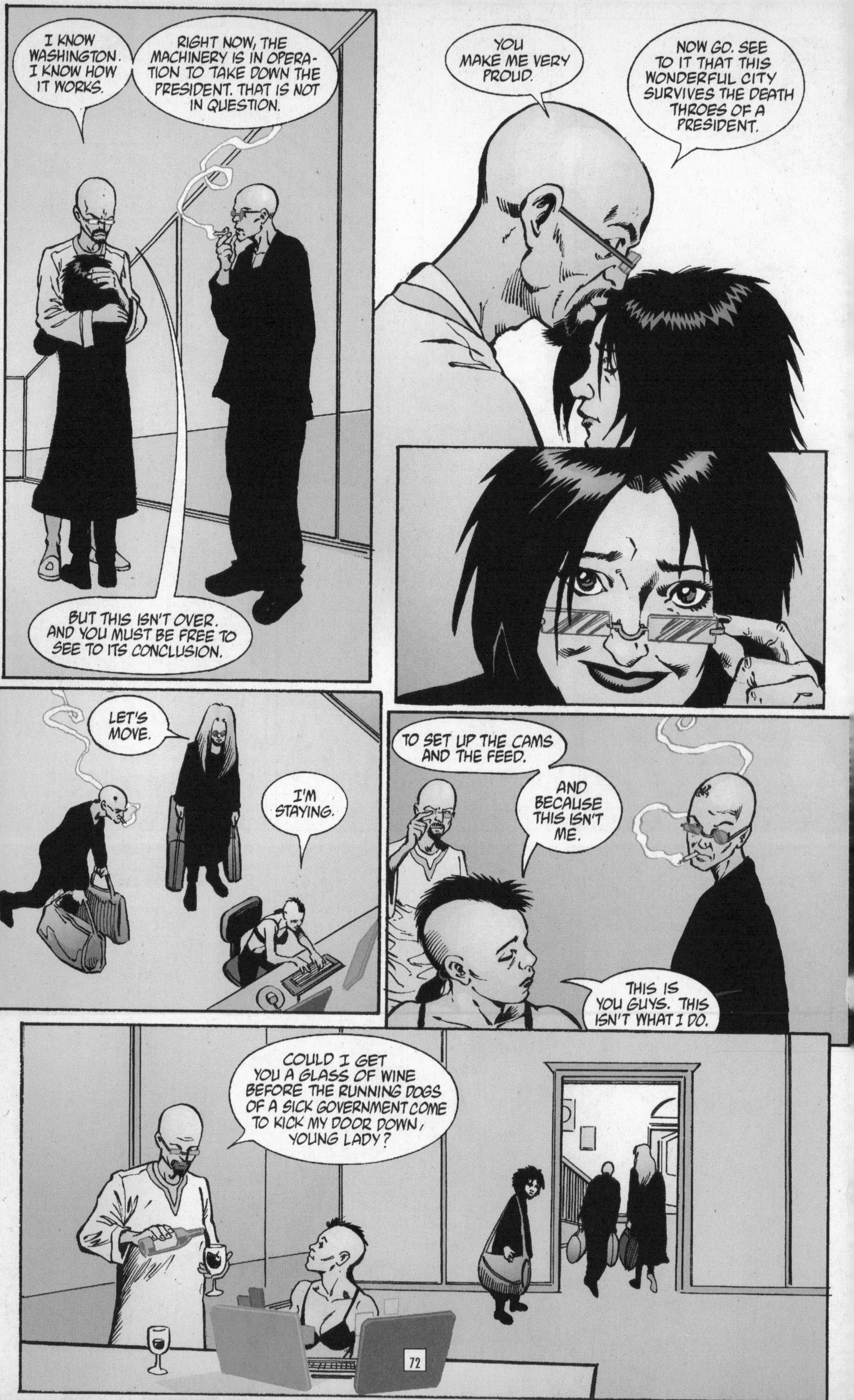
I KNOW WASHINGTON. I KNOW HOW IT WORKS.
RIGHT NOW, THE MACHINERY IS IN OPERATION TO TAKE DOWN THE PRESIDENT. THAT IS NOT IN QUESTION.
BUT THIS ISN'T OVER. AND YOU MUST BE FREE TO SEE TO ITS CONCLUSION.
YOU MAKE ME VERY PROUD.
NOW GO. SEE TO IT THAT THIS WONDERFUL CITY SURVIVES THE DEATH THROES OF A PRESIDENT.
LET'S MOVE.
I'M STAYING.
TO SET UP THE CAMS AND THE FEED.
AND BECAUSE THIS ISN'T ME.
THIS IS YOU GUYS. THIS ISN'T WHAT I DO.
COULD I GET YOU A GLASS OF WINE BEFORE THE RUNNING DOGS OF A SICK GOVERNMENT COME TO KICK MY DOOR DOWN, YOUNG LADY?

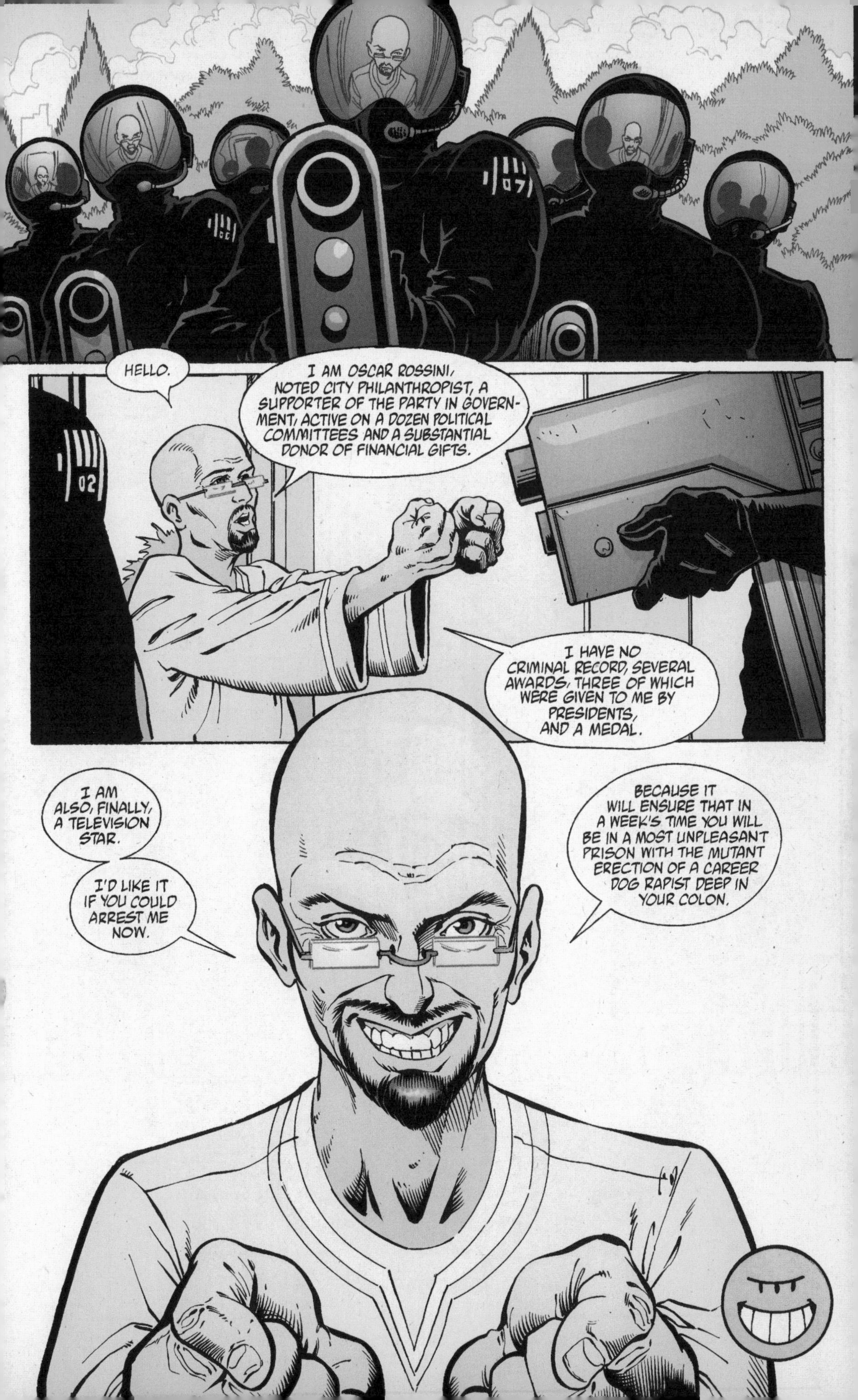

HELLO.
I AM OSCAR ROSSINI, NOTED CITY PHILANTHROPIST, A SUPPORTER OF THE PARTY IN GOVERNMENT, ACTIVE ON A DOZEN POLITICAL COMMITTEES AND A SUBSTANTIAL DONOR OF FINANCIAL GIFTS.
I HAVE NO CRIMINAL RECORD, SEVERAL AWARDS, THREE OF WHICH WERE GIVEN TO ME BY PRESIDENTS, AND A MEDAL.
I AM ALSO, FINALLY, A TELEVISION STAR.
I'D LIKE IT IF YOU COULD ARREST ME NOW.
BECAUSE IT WILL ENSURE THAT IN A WEEK'S TIME YOU WILL BE IN A MOST UNPLEASANT PRISON WITH THE MUTANT ERECTION OF A CAREER DOG RAPIST DEEP IN YOUR COLON.

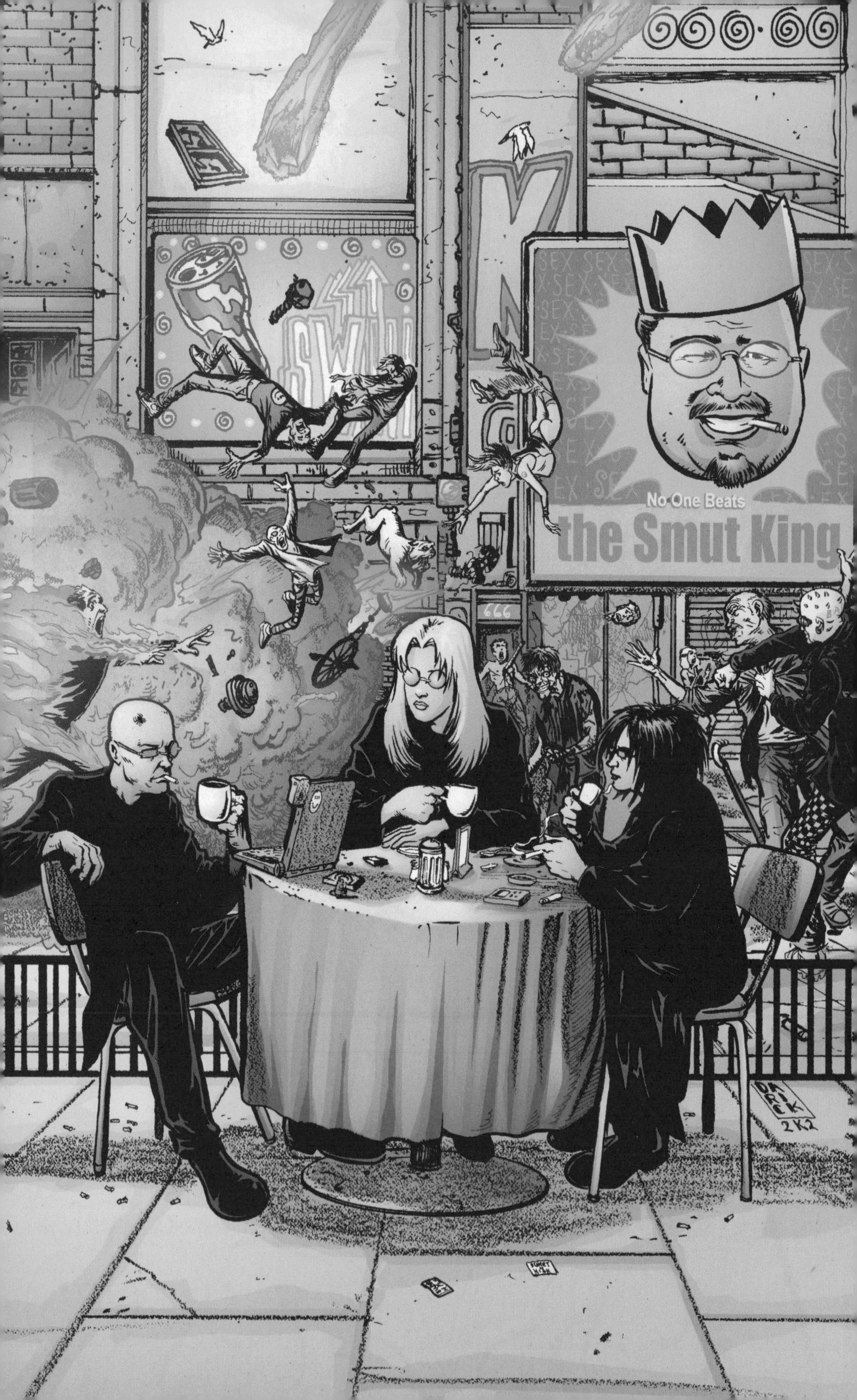

No One Beats
the Smut King
666
DARICK 2K2

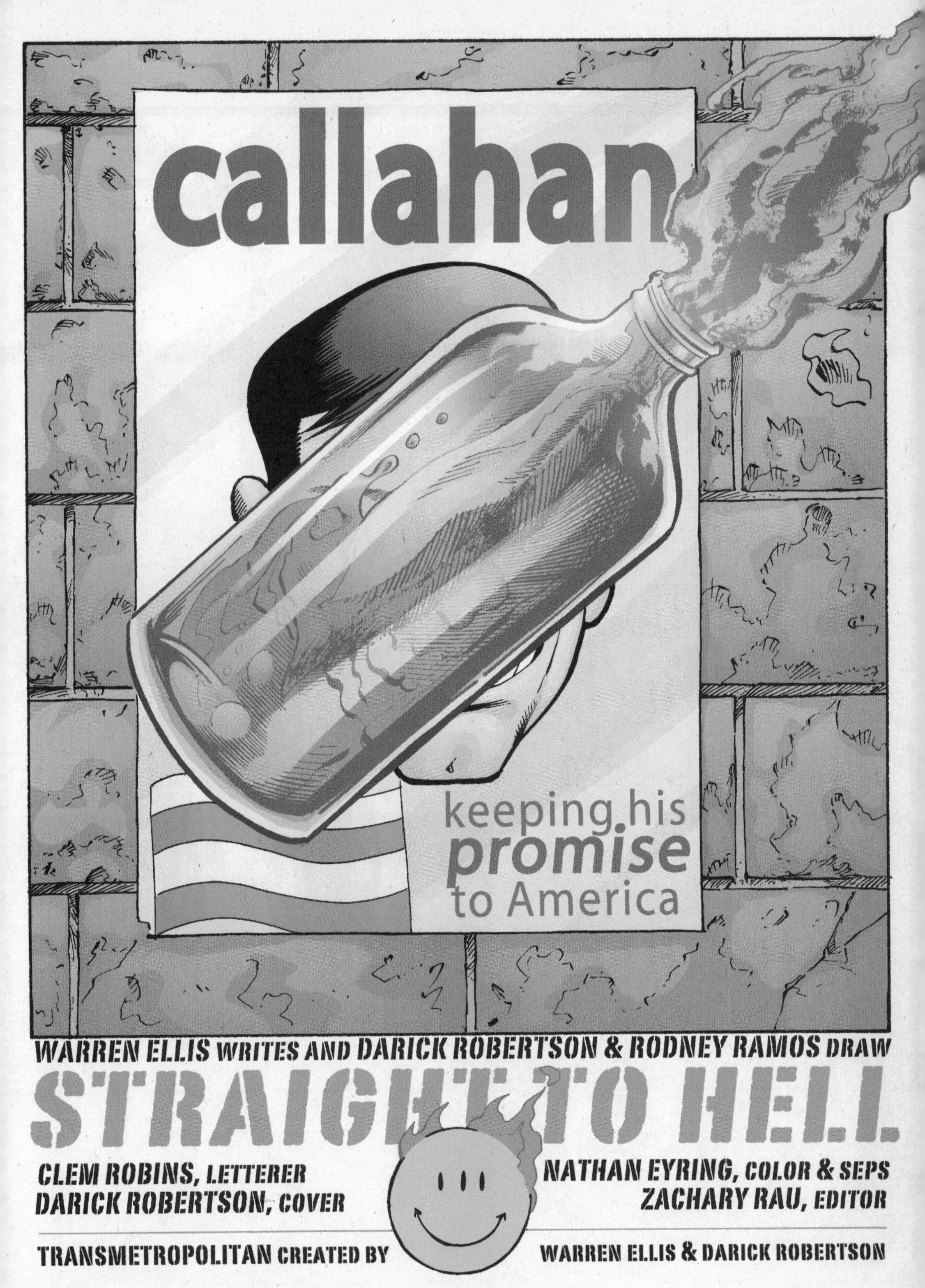
callahan
keeping his
promise
to America

WARREN ELLIS WRITES AND DARICK ROBERTSON & RODNEY RAMOS DRAW

STRAIGHT TO HELL

CLEM ROBINS, LETTERER
DARICK ROBERTSON, COVER

NATHAN EYRING, COLOR & SEPS
ZACHARY RAU, EDITOR

TRANSMETROPOLITAN CREATED BY WARREN ELLIS & DARICK ROBERTSON

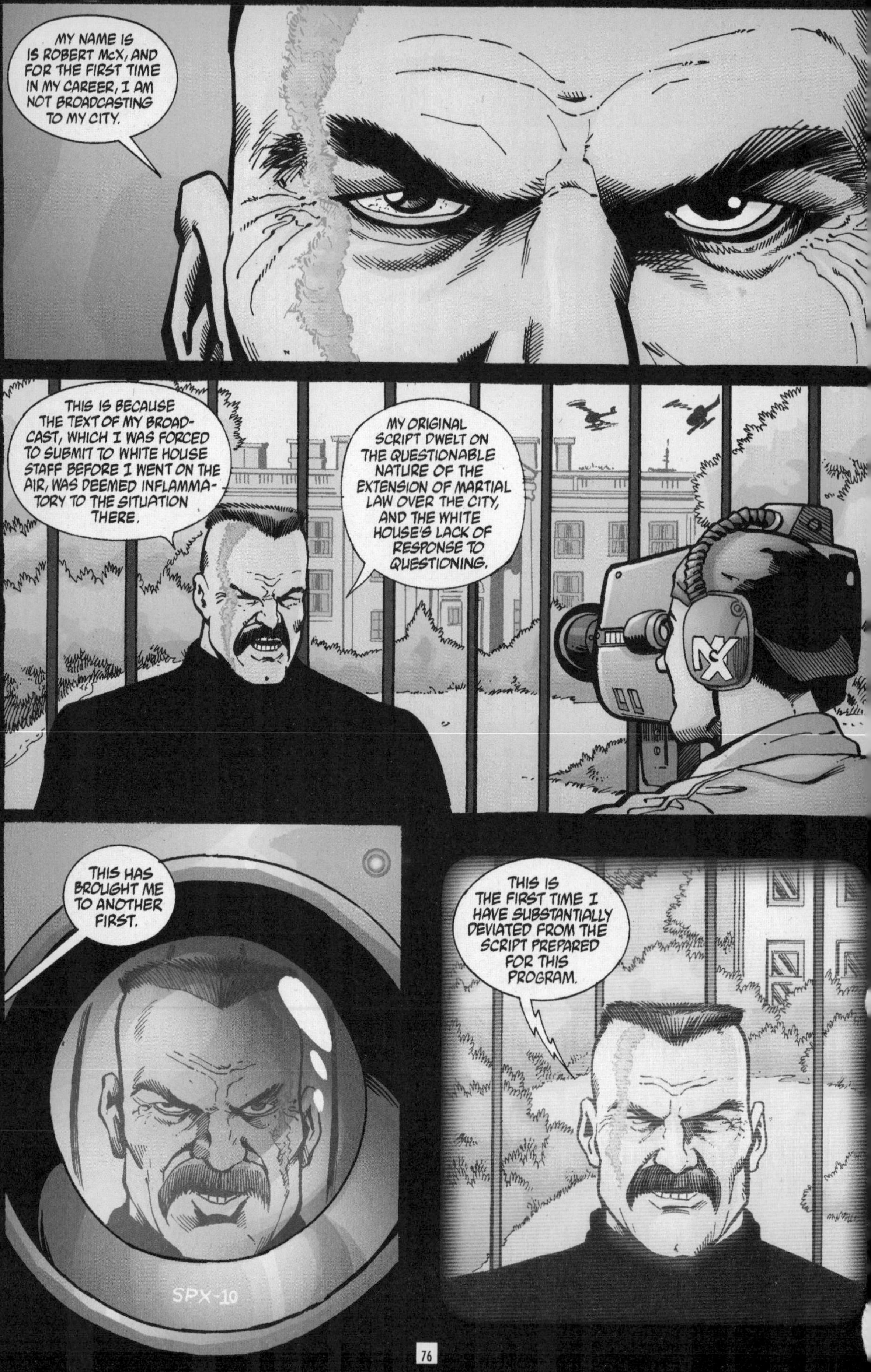
MY NAME IS IS ROBERT McX, AND FOR THE FIRST TIME IN MY CAREER, I AM NOT BROADCASTING TO MY CITY.
THIS IS BECAUSE THE TEXT OF MY BROAD-CAST, WHICH I WAS FORCED TO SUBMIT TO WHITE HOUSE STAFF BEFORE I WENT ON THE AIR, WAS DEEMED INFLAMMA-TORY TO THE SITUATION THERE.
MY ORIGINAL SCRIPT DWELT ON THE QUESTIONABLE NATURE OF THE EXTENSION OF MARTIAL LAW OVER THE CITY, AND THE WHITE HOUSE'S LACK OF RESPONSE TO QUESTIONING.
THIS HAS BROUGHT ME TO ANOTHER FIRST.
SPX-10
THIS IS THE FIRST TIME I HAVE SUBSTANTIALLY DEVIATED FROM THE SCRIPT PREPARED FOR THIS PROGRAM.

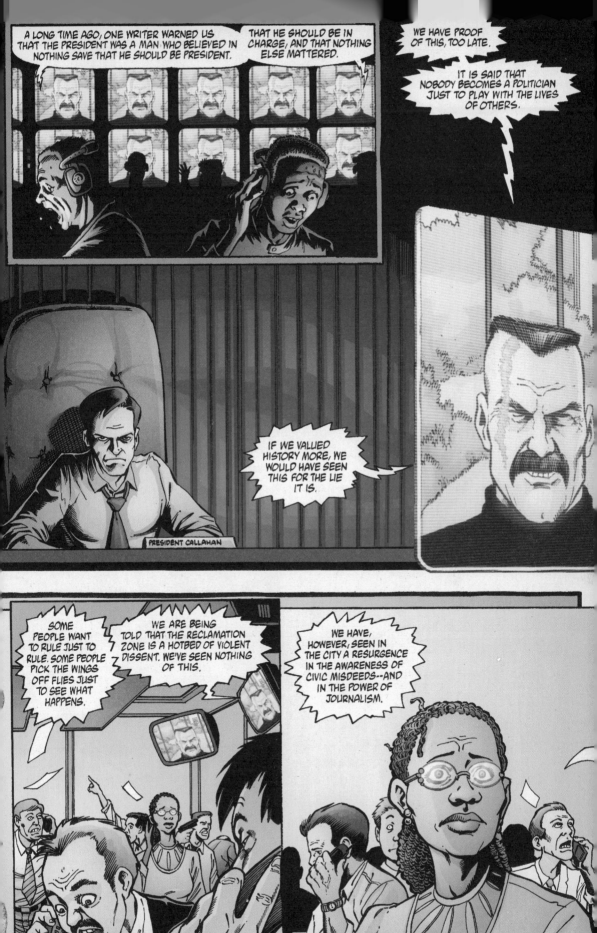

A LONG TIME AGO, ONE WRITER WARNED US THAT THE PRESIDENT WAS A MAN WHO BELIEVED IN NOTHING SAVE THAT HE SHOULD BE PRESIDENT.

THAT HE SHOULD BE IN CHARGE, AND THAT NOTHING ELSE MATTERED.

WE HAVE PROOF OF THIS, TOO LATE.

IT IS SAID THAT NOBODY BECOMES A POLITICIAN JUST TO PLAY WITH THE LIVES OF OTHERS.

IF WE VALUED HISTORY MORE, WE WOULD HAVE SEEN THIS FOR THE LIE IT IS.

PRESIDENT CALLAHAN

SOME PEOPLE WANT TO RULE JUST TO RULE. SOME PEOPLE PICK THE WINGS OFF FLIES JUST TO SEE WHAT HAPPENS.

WE ARE BEING TOLD THAT THE RECLAMATION ZONE IS A HOTBED OF VIOLENT DISSENT. WE'VE SEEN NOTHING OF THIS.

WE HAVE, HOWEVER, SEEN IN THE CITY A RESURGENCE IN THE AWARENESS OF CIVIC MISDEEDS--AND IN THE POWER OF JOURNALISM.

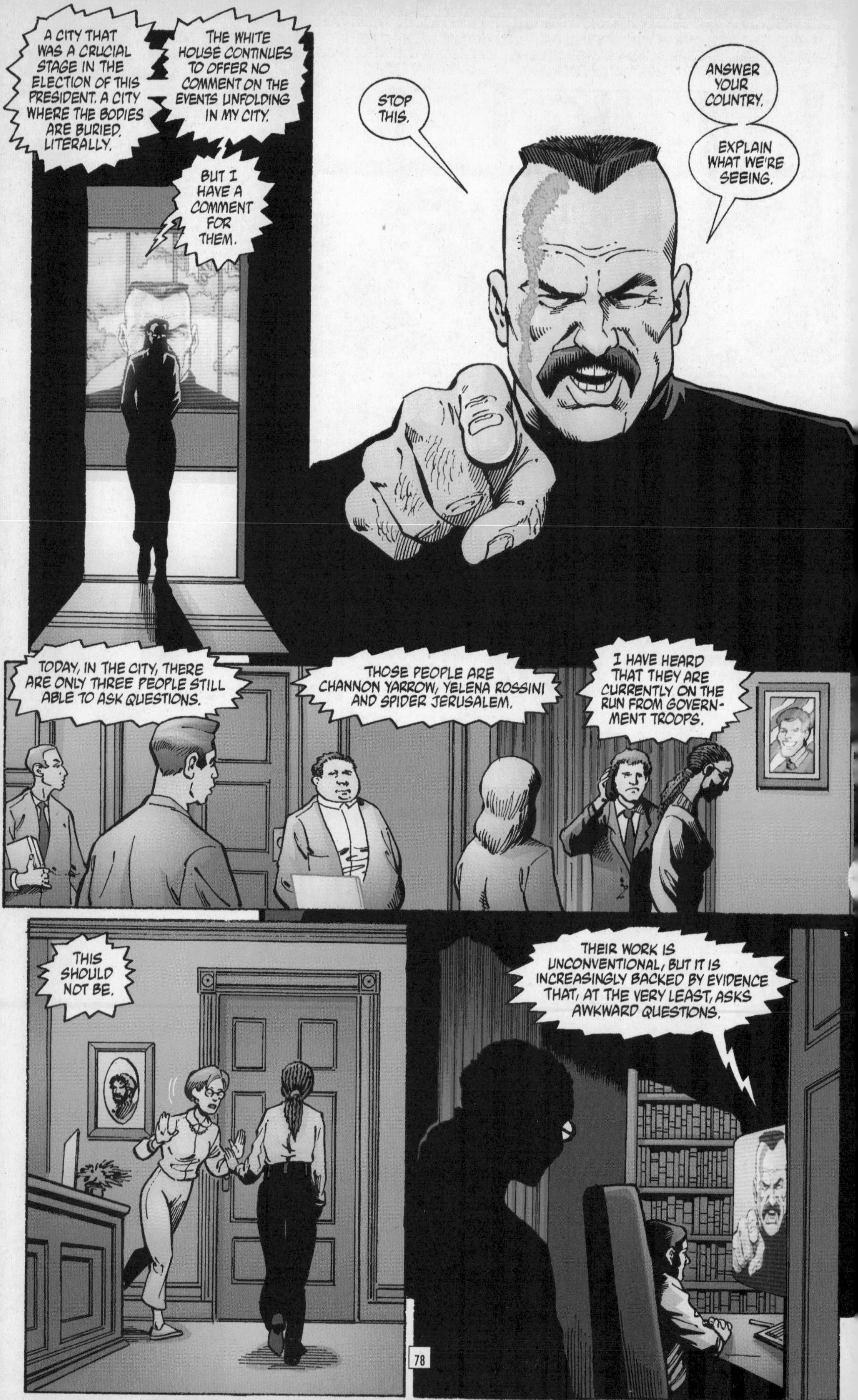
A CITY THAT WAS A CRUCIAL STAGE IN THE ELECTION OF THIS PRESIDENT. A CITY WHERE THE BODIES ARE BURIED. LITERALLY.
THE WHITE HOUSE CONTINUES TO OFFER NO COMMENT ON THE EVENTS UNFOLDING IN MY CITY.
BUT I HAVE A COMMENT FOR THEM.
STOP THIS.
ANSWER YOUR COUNTRY.
EXPLAIN WHAT WE'RE SEEING.
TODAY, IN THE CITY, THERE ARE ONLY THREE PEOPLE STILL ABLE TO ASK QUESTIONS.
THOSE PEOPLE ARE CHANNON YARROW, YELENA ROSSINI AND SPIDER JERUSALEM.
I HAVE HEARD THAT THEY ARE CURRENTLY ON THE RUN FROM GOVERNMENT TROOPS.
THIS SHOULD NOT BE.
THEIR WORK IS UNCONVENTIONAL, BUT IT IS INCREASINGLY BACKED BY EVIDENCE THAT, AT THE VERY LEAST, ASKS AWKWARD QUESTIONS.

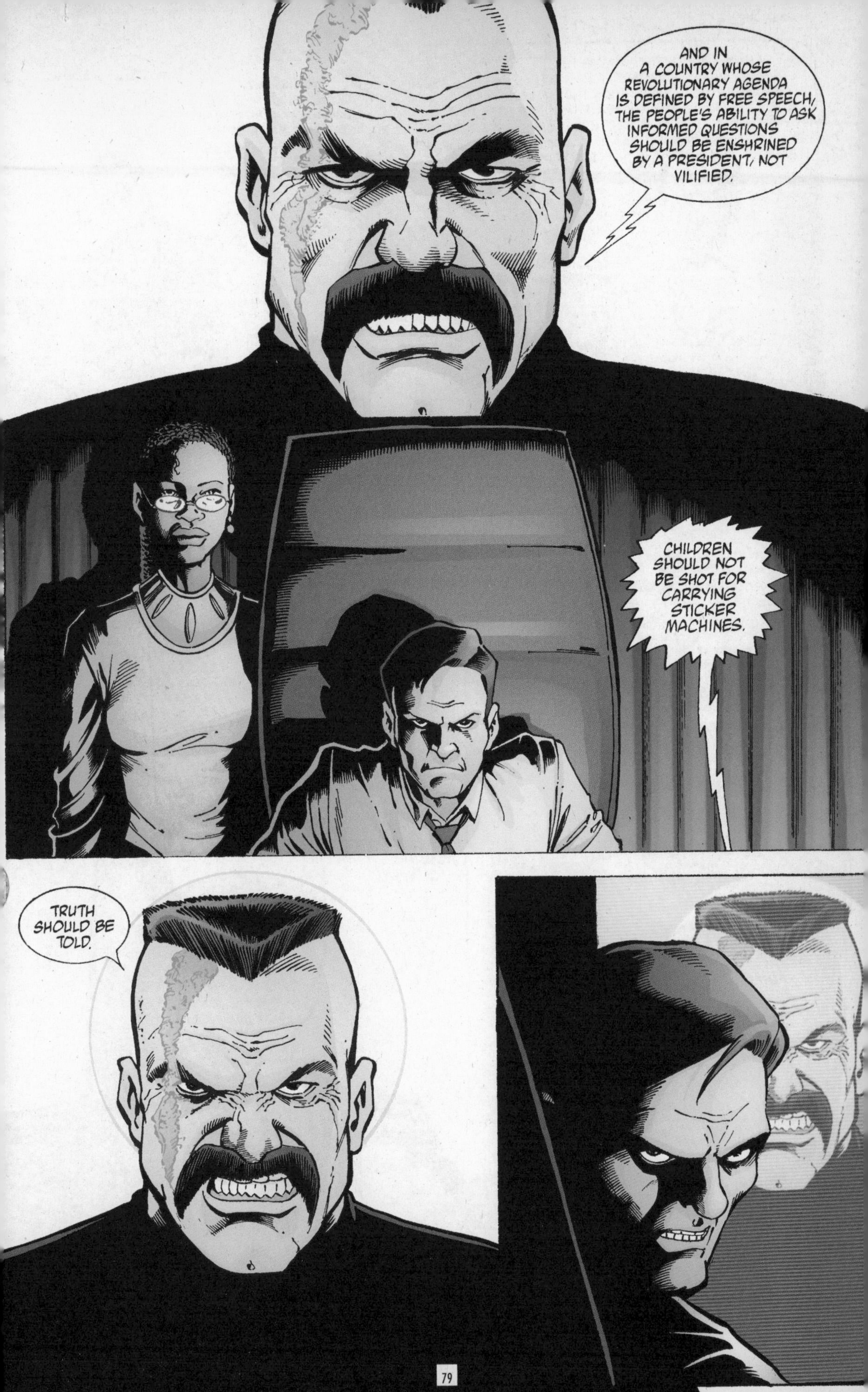
AND IN A COUNTRY WHOSE REVOLUTIONARY AGENDA IS DEFINED BY FREE SPEECH, THE PEOPLE'S ABILITY TO ASK INFORMED QUESTIONS SHOULD BE ENSHRINED BY A PRESIDENT, NOT VILIFIED.
CHILDREN SHOULD NOT BE SHOT FOR CARRYING STICKER MACHINES.
TRUTH SHOULD BE TOLD.

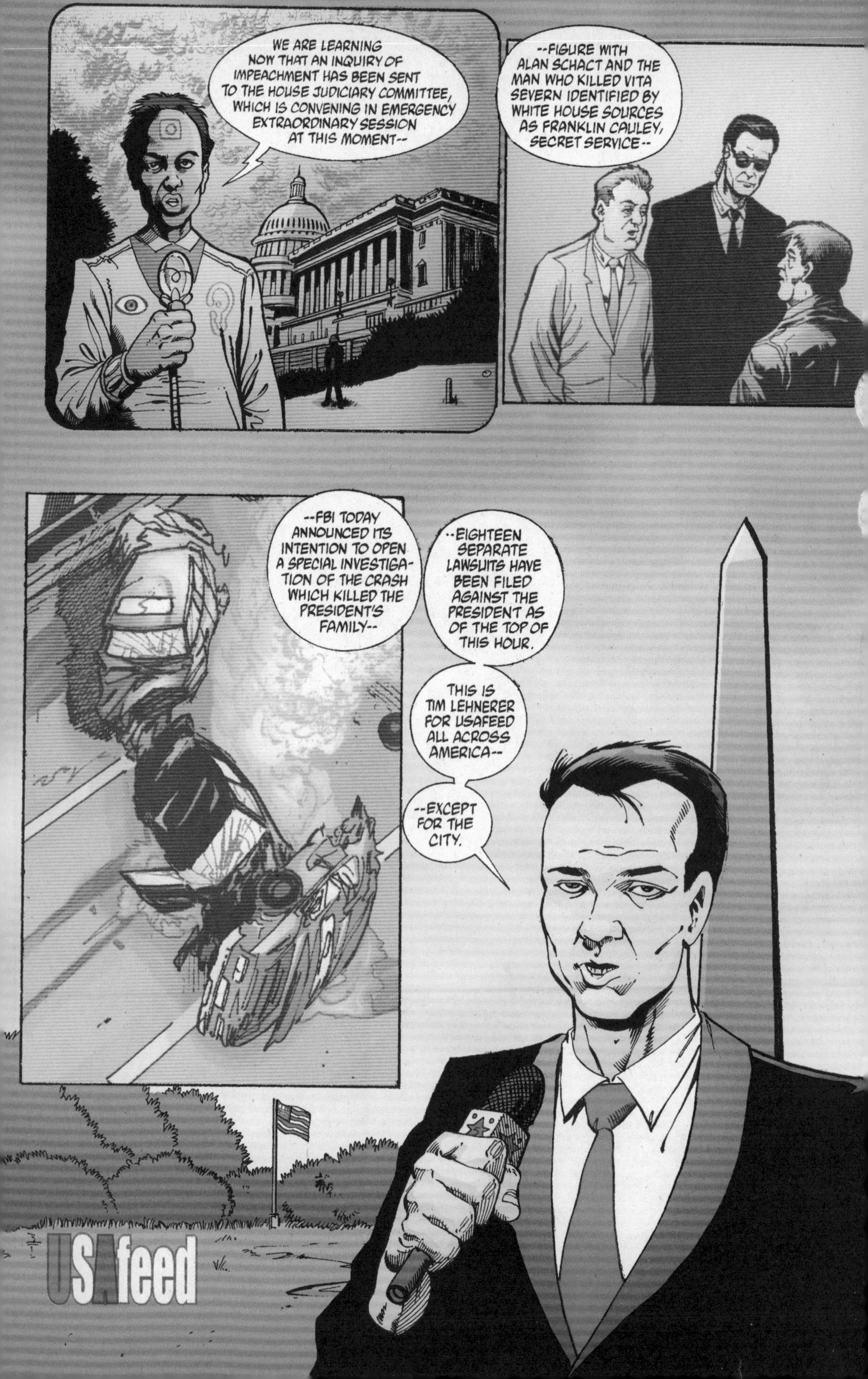
WE ARE LEARNING NOW THAT AN INQUIRY OF IMPEACHMENT HAS BEEN SENT TO THE HOUSE JUDICIARY COMMITTEE, WHICH IS CONVENING IN EMERGENCY EXTRAORDINARY SESSION AT THIS MOMENT--
--FIGURE WITH ALAN SCHACT AND THE MAN WHO KILLED VITA SEVERN IDENTIFIED BY WHITE HOUSE SOURCES AS FRANKLIN CAULEY, SECRET SERVICE--
--FBI TODAY ANNOUNCED ITS INTENTION TO OPEN A SPECIAL INVESTIGATION OF THE CRASH WHICH KILLED THE PRESIDENT'S FAMILY--
--EIGHTEEN SEPARATE LAWSUITS HAVE BEEN FILED AGAINST THE PRESIDENT AS OF THE TOP OF THIS HOUR.
THIS IS TIM LEHNERER FOR USAFEED ALL ACROSS AMERICA--
--EXCEPT FOR THE CITY.
USAfeed

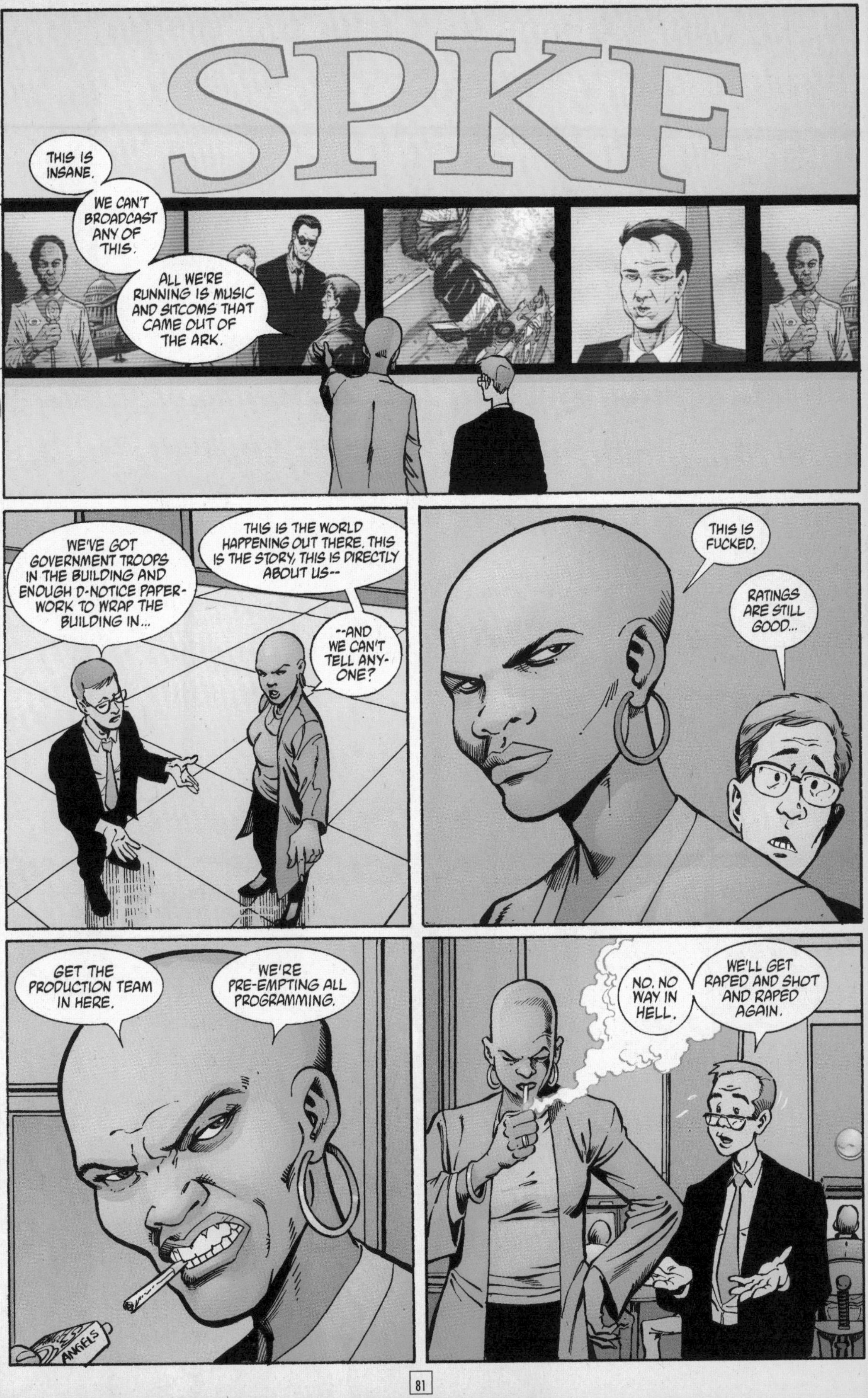
SPKF
THIS IS INSANE.
WE CAN'T BROADCAST ANY OF THIS.
ALL WE'RE RUNNING IS MUSIC AND SITCOMS THAT CAME OUT OF THE ARK.
WE'VE GOT GOVERNMENT TROOPS IN THE BUILDING AND ENOUGH D-NOTICE PAPER-WORK TO WRAP THE BUILDING IN...
THIS IS THE WORLD HAPPENING OUT THERE. THIS IS THE STORY, THIS IS DIRECTLY ABOUT US--
--AND WE CAN'T TELL ANY-ONE?
THIS IS FUCKED.
RATINGS ARE STILL GOOD...
GET THE PRODUCTION TEAM IN HERE.
WE'RE PRE-EMPTING ALL PROGRAMMING.
NO. NO WAY IN HELL.
WE'LL GET RAPED AND SHOT AND RAPED AGAIN.

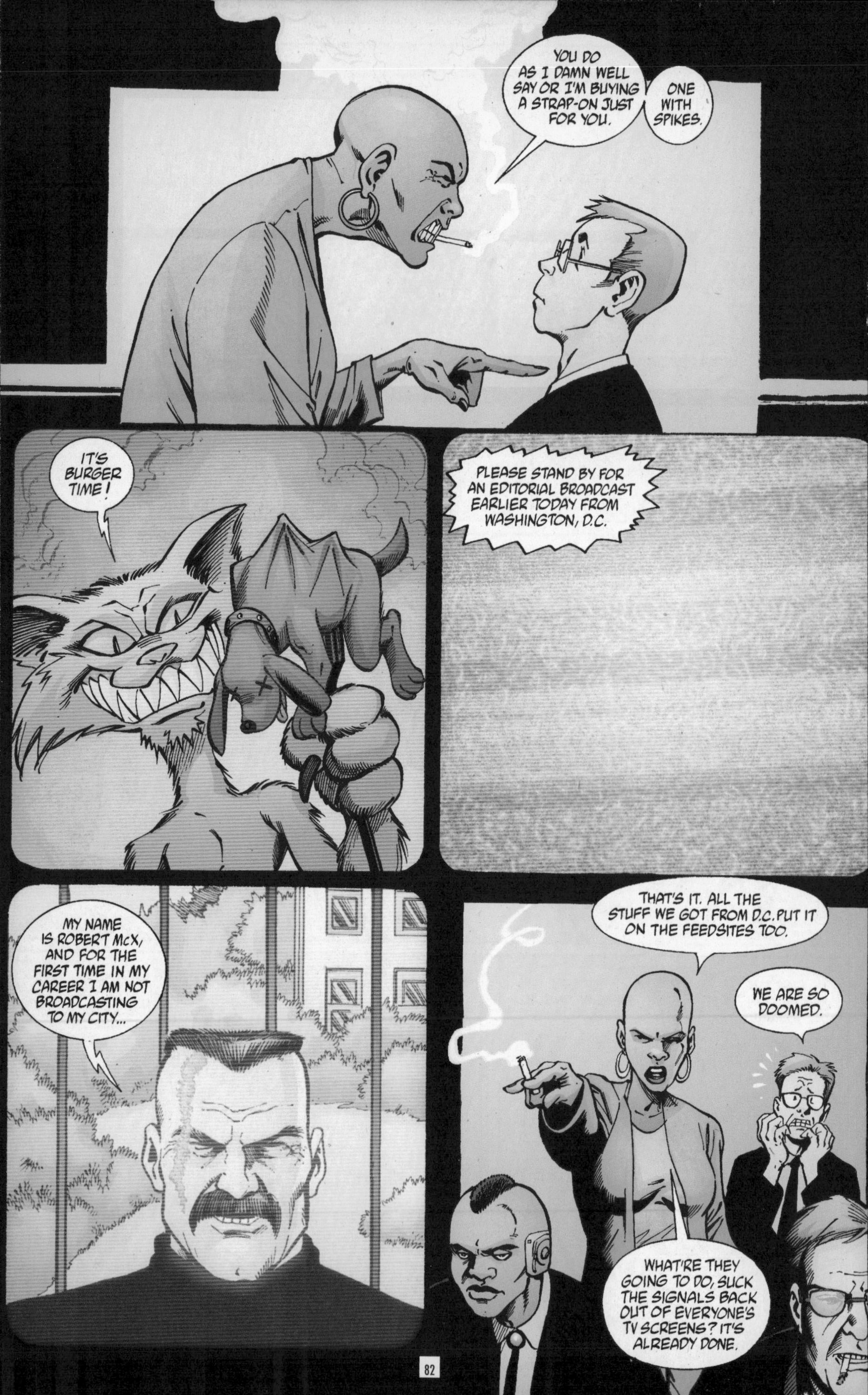
YOU DO AS I DAMN WELL SAY OR I'M BUYING A STRAP-ON JUST FOR YOU.
ONE WITH SPIKES.
IT'S BURGER TIME!
PLEASE STAND BY FOR AN EDITORIAL BROADCAST EARLIER TODAY FROM WASHINGTON, D.C.
MY NAME IS ROBERT McX, AND FOR THE FIRST TIME IN MY CAREER I AM NOT BROADCASTING TO MY CITY...
THAT'S IT. ALL THE STUFF WE GOT FROM D.C. PUT IT ON THE FEEDSITES TOO.
WE ARE SO DOOMED.
WHAT'RE THEY GOING TO DO, SUCK THE SIGNALS BACK OUT OF EVERYONE'S TV SCREENS? IT'S ALREADY DONE.

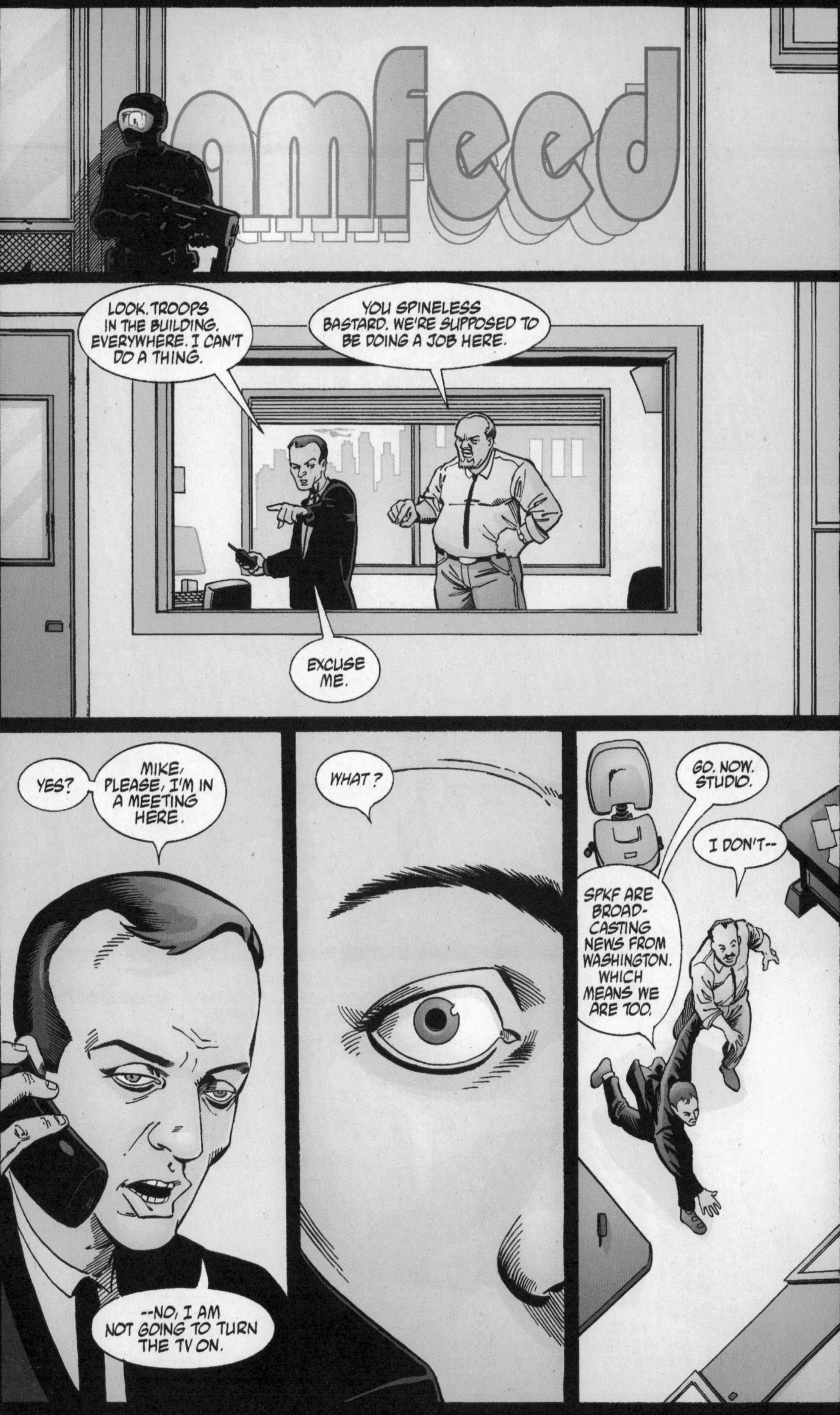
amfeed
LOOK. TROOPS IN THE BUILDING. EVERYWHERE. I CAN'T DO A THING.
YOU SPINELESS BASTARD. WE'RE SUPPOSED TO BE DOING A JOB HERE.
EXCUSE ME.
YES?
MIKE, PLEASE, I'M IN A MEETING HERE.
--NO, I AM NOT GOING TO TURN THE TV ON.
WHAT?
GO. NOW. STUDIO.
I DON'T--
SPKF ARE BROAD-CASTING NEWS FROM WASHINGTON. WHICH MEANS WE ARE TOO.

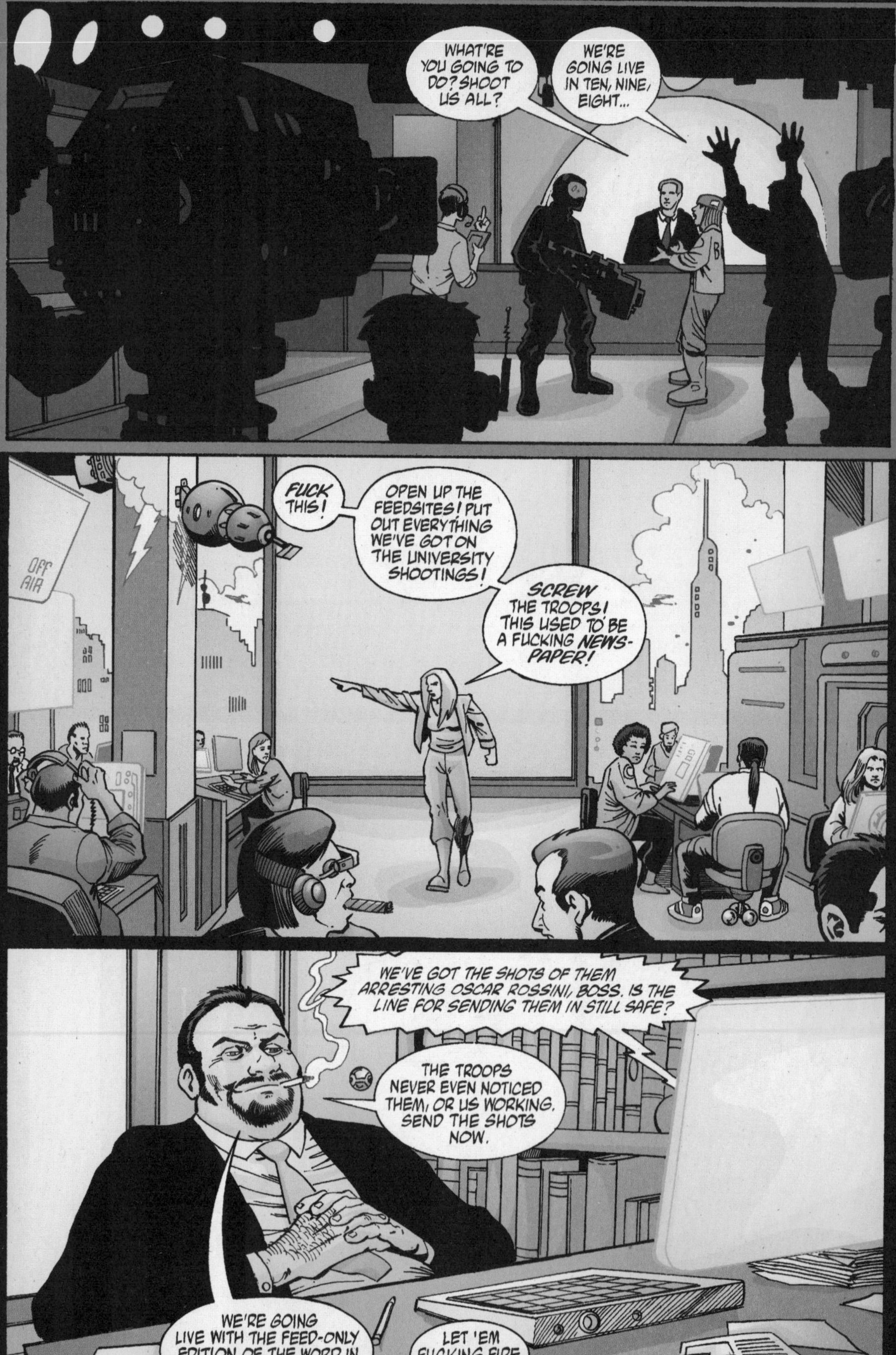
WHAT'RE YOU GOING TO DO? SHOOT US ALL?
WE'RE GOING LIVE IN TEN, NINE, EIGHT...
OFF AIR
FUCK THIS!
OPEN UP THE FEEDSITES! PUT OUT EVERYTHING WE'VE GOT ON THE UNIVERSITY SHOOTINGS!
SCREW THE TROOPS! THIS USED TO BE A FUCKING NEWS-PAPER!
WE'VE GOT THE SHOTS OF THEM ARRESTING OSCAR ROSSINI, BOSS. IS THE LINE FOR SENDING THEM IN STILL SAFE?
THE TROOPS NEVER EVEN NOTICED THEM, OR US WORKING. SEND THE SHOTS NOW.
WE'RE GOING LIVE WITH THE FEED-ONLY EDITION OF THE WORD IN FIVE MINUTES.
LET 'EM FUCKING FIRE ME.

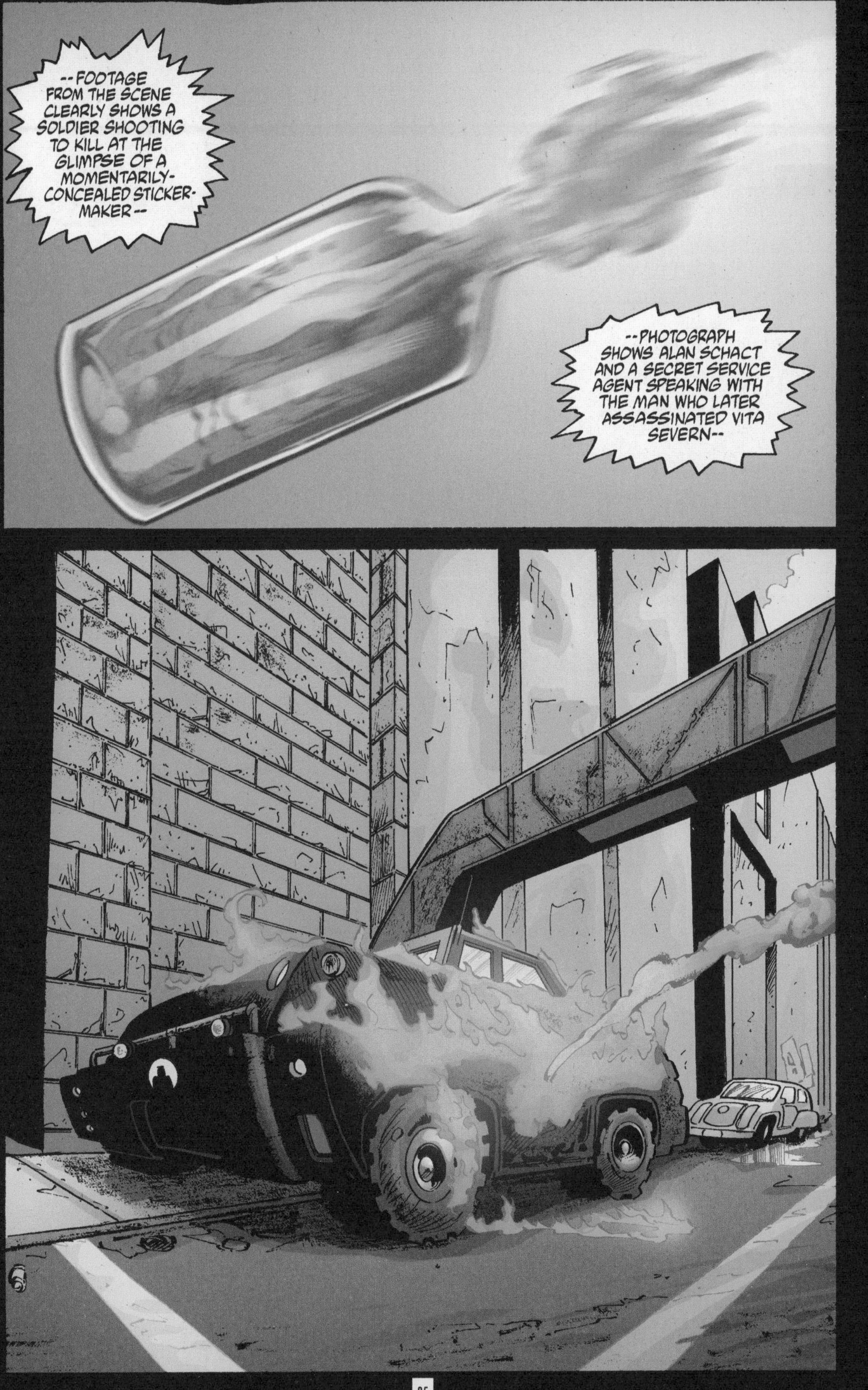
--FOOTAGE FROM THE SCENE CLEARLY SHOWS A SOLDIER SHOOTING TO KILL AT THE GLIMPSE OF A MOMENTARILY-CONCEALED STICKER-MAKER--
--PHOTOGRAPH SHOWS ALAN SCHACT AND A SECRET SERVICE AGENT SPEAKING WITH THE MAN WHO LATER ASSASSINATED VITA SEVERN--

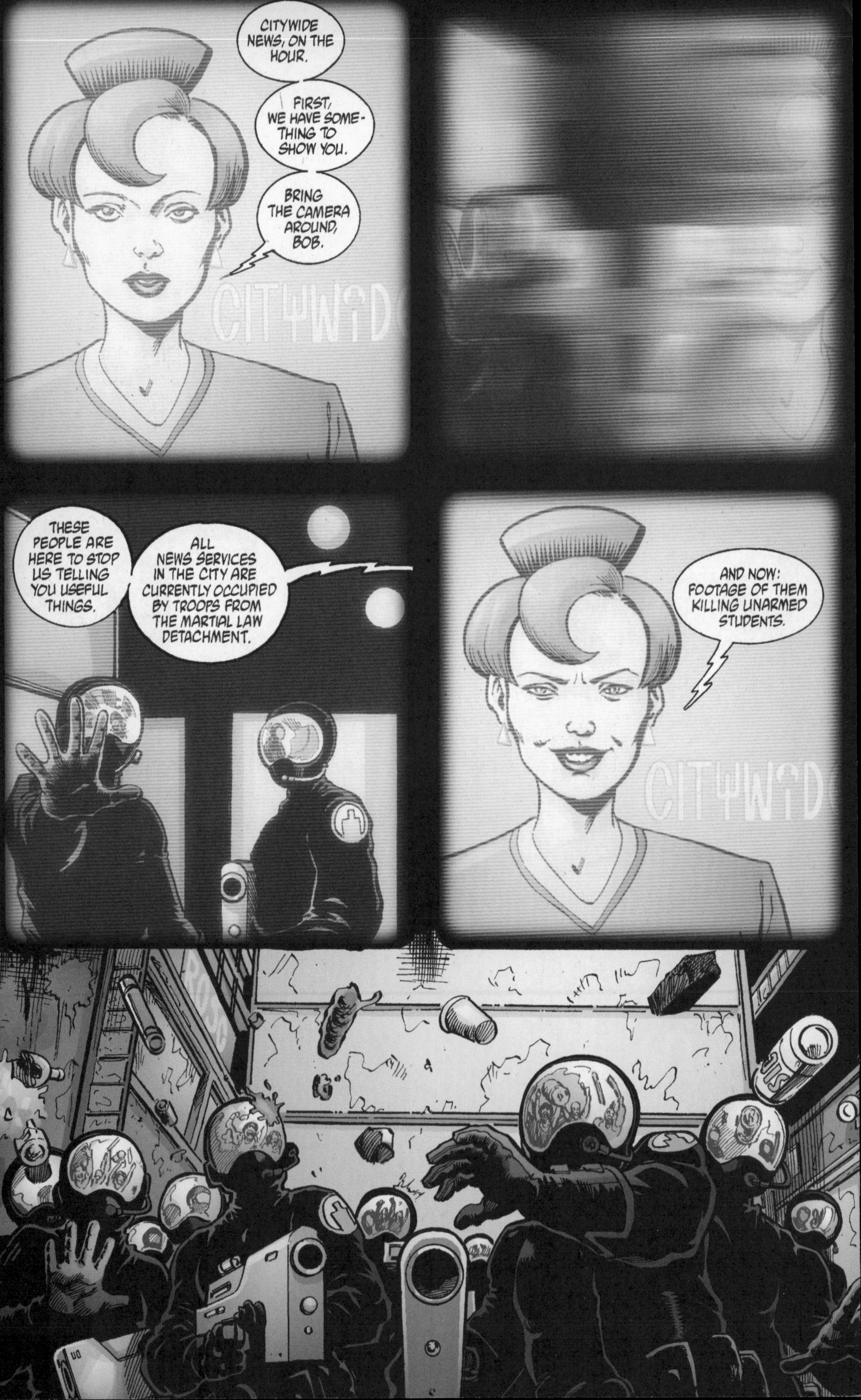
CITYWIDE NEWS, ON THE HOUR.
FIRST, WE HAVE SOME-THING TO SHOW YOU.
BRING THE CAMERA AROUND, BOB.
CITYWID
THESE PEOPLE ARE HERE TO STOP US TELLING YOU USEFUL THINGS.
ALL NEWS SERVICES IN THE CITY ARE CURRENTLY OCCUPIED BY TROOPS FROM THE MARTIAL LAW DETACHMENT.
AND NOW: FOOTAGE OF THEM KILLING UNARMED STUDENTS.
CITYWID

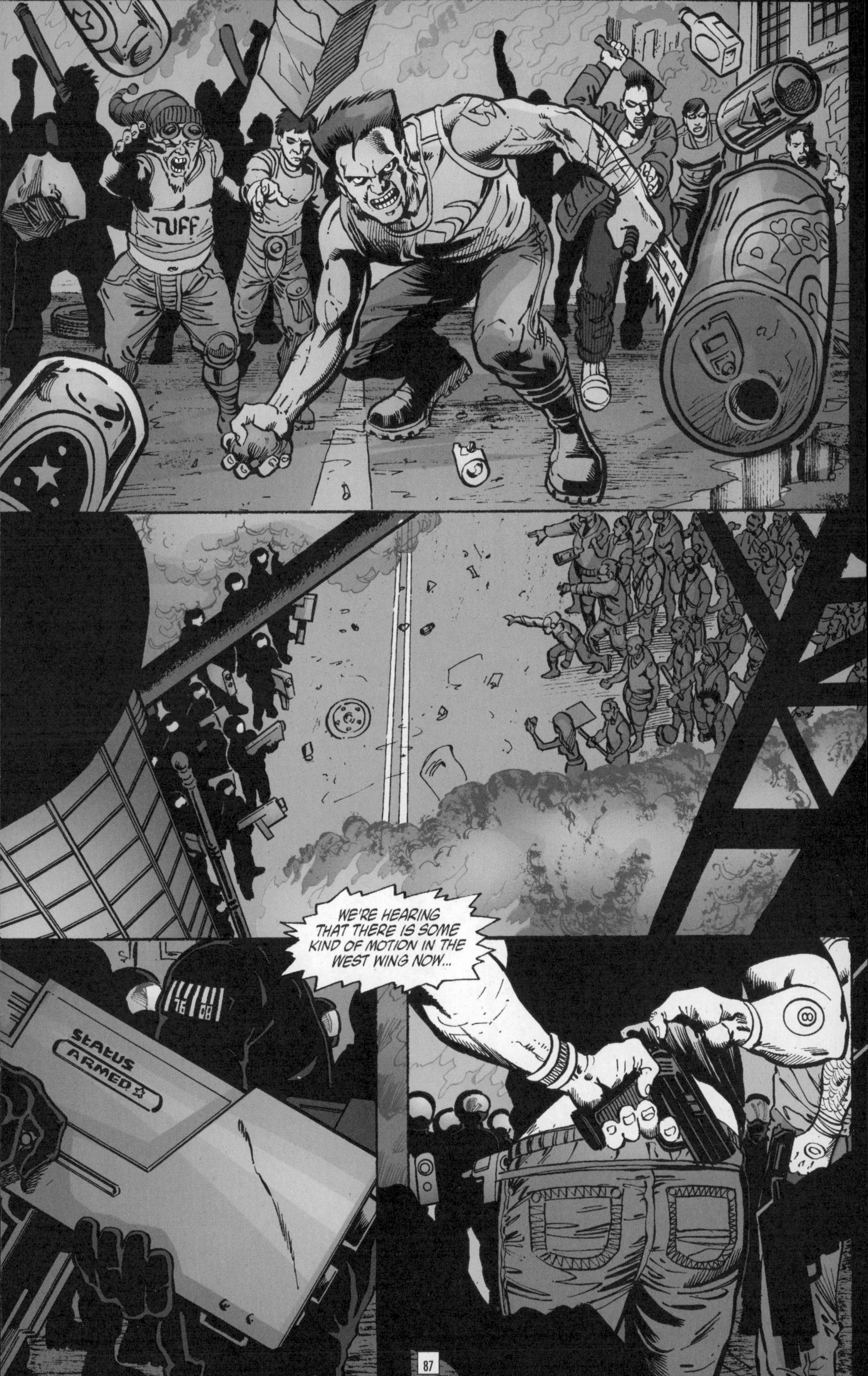
TUFF
PISS
WE'RE HEARING THAT THERE IS SOME KIND OF MOTION IN THE WEST WING NOW...
76 08
STATUS
ARMED

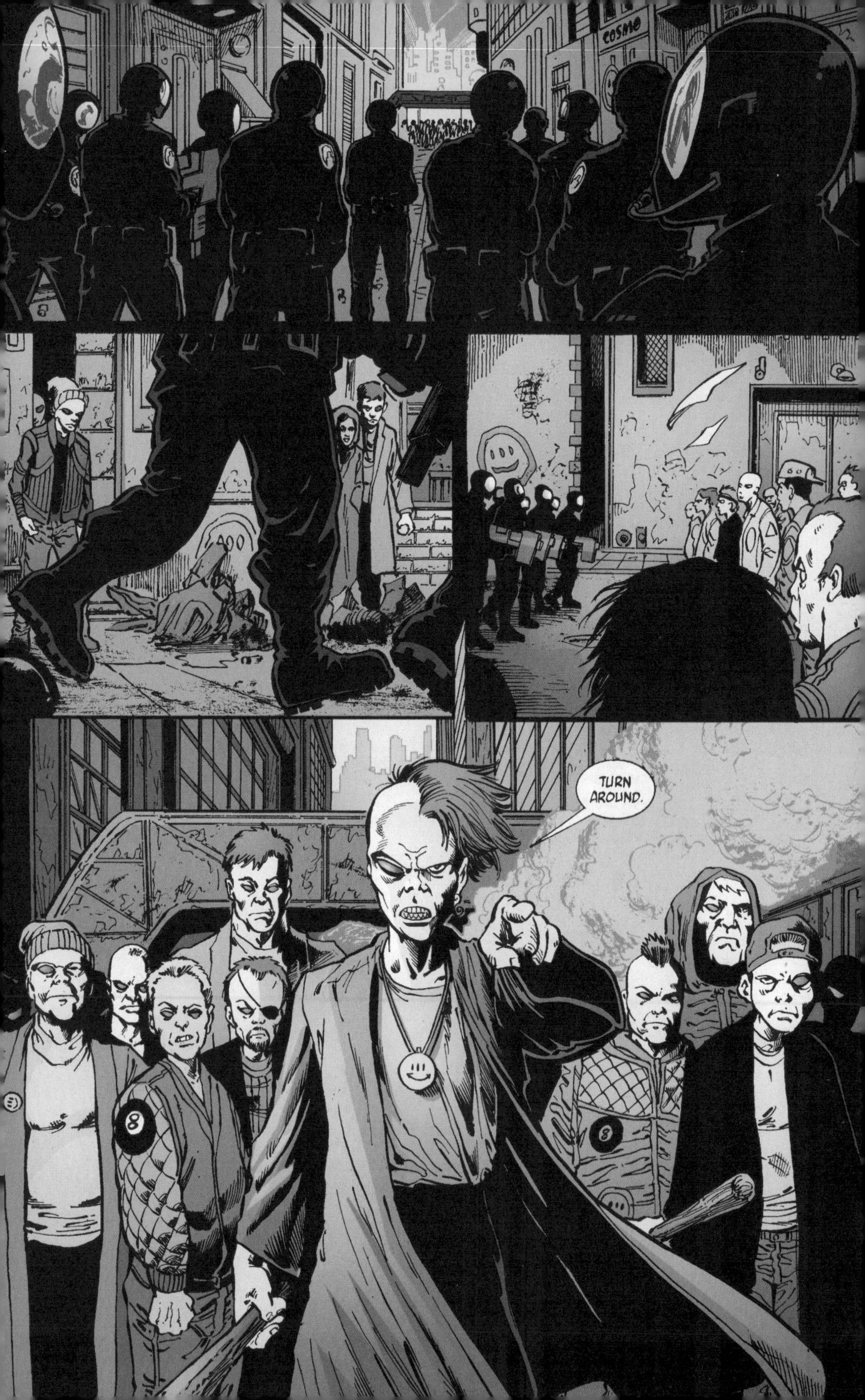
COSMO
TURN AROUND.

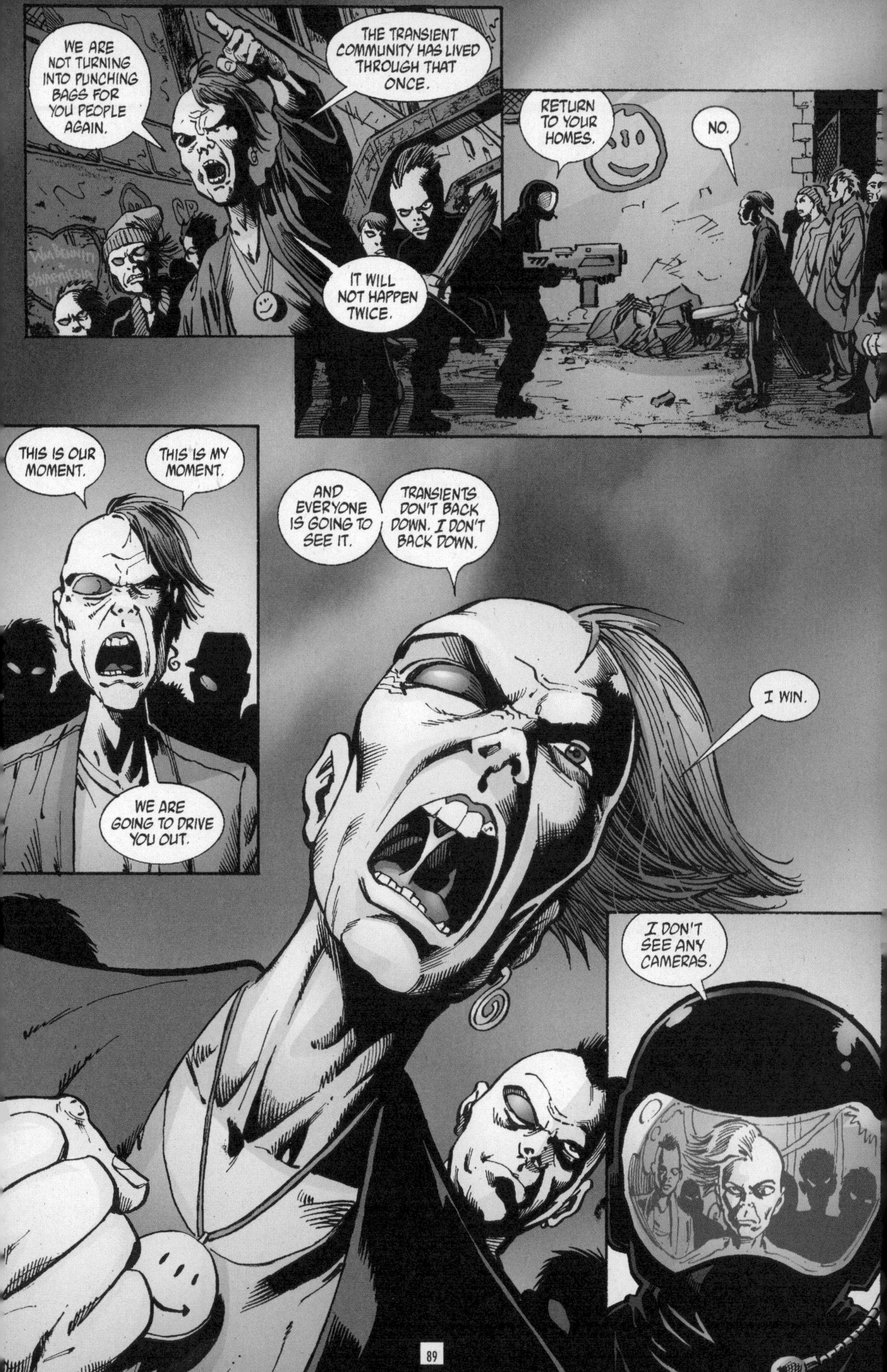

WE ARE NOT TURNING INTO PUNCHING BAGS FOR YOU PEOPLE AGAIN.
THE TRANSIENT COMMUNITY HAS LIVED THROUGH THAT ONCE.
IT WILL NOT HAPPEN TWICE.
RETURN TO YOUR HOMES.
NO.
THIS IS OUR MOMENT.
THIS IS MY MOMENT.
WE ARE GOING TO DRIVE YOU OUT.
AND EVERYONE IS GOING TO SEE IT.
TRANSIENTS DON'T BACK DOWN. I DON'T BACK DOWN.
I WIN.
I DON'T SEE ANY CAMERAS.

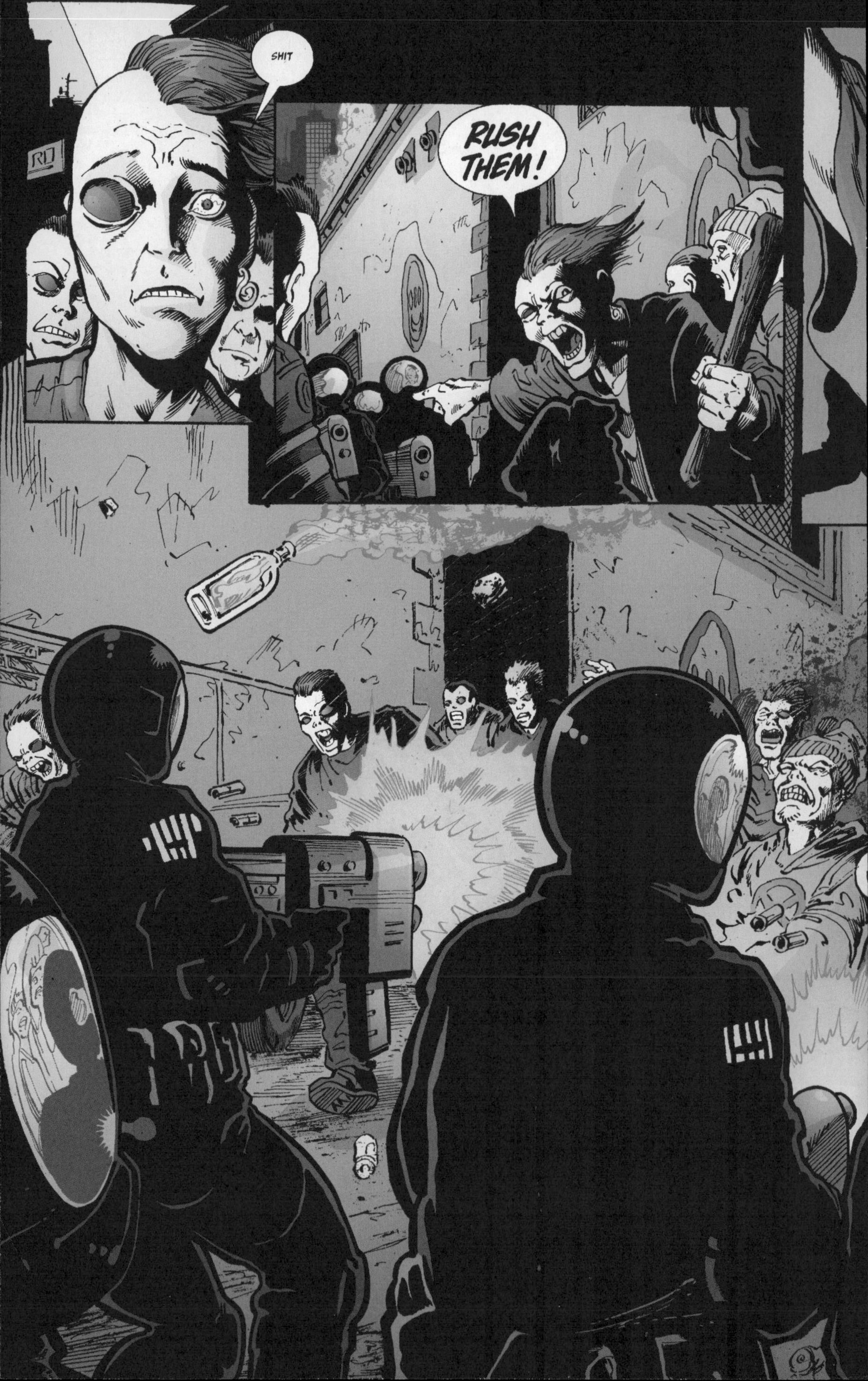
SHIT
RUSH THEM!

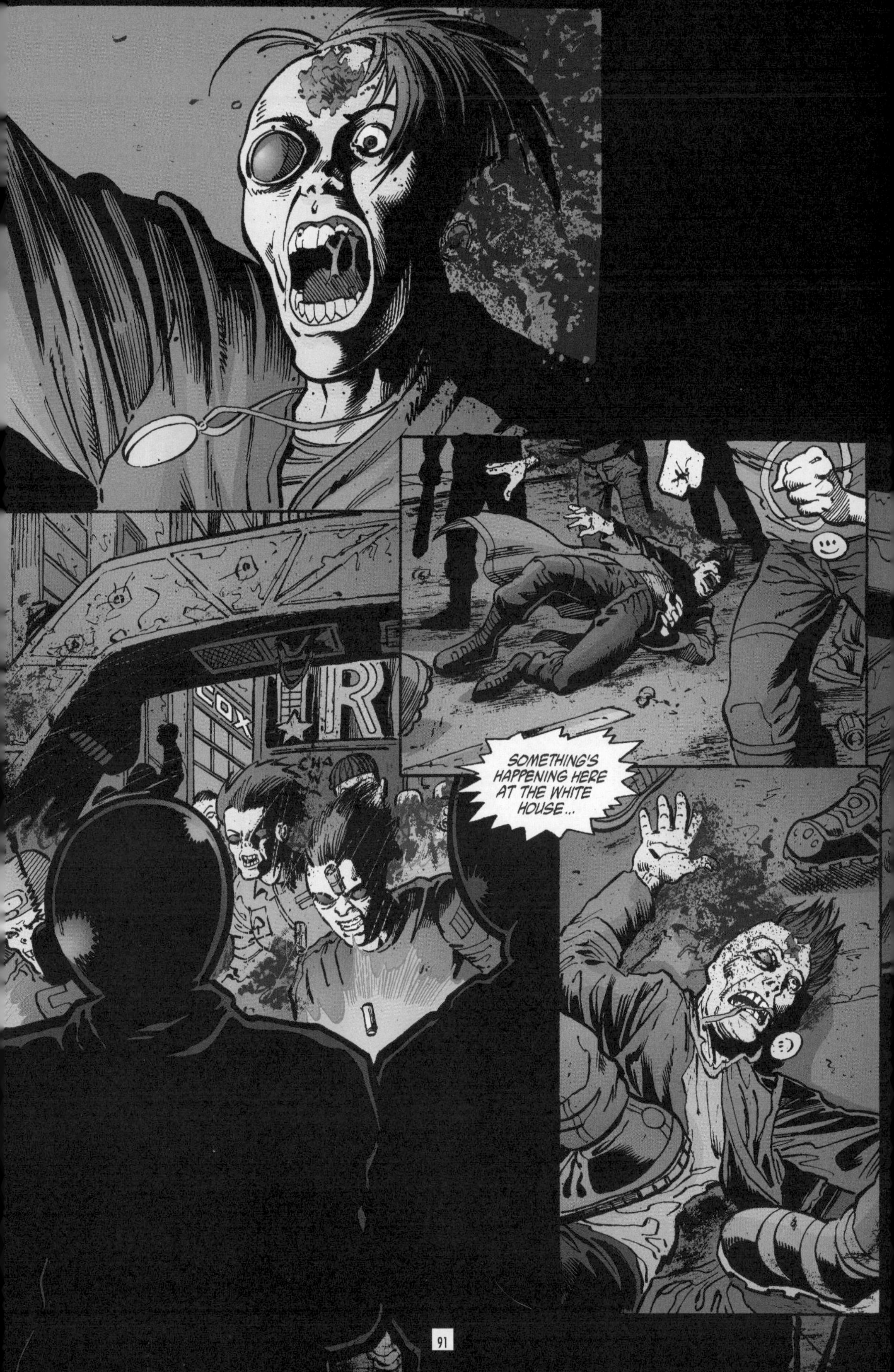
SOMETHING'S HAPPENING HERE AT THE WHITE HOUSE...

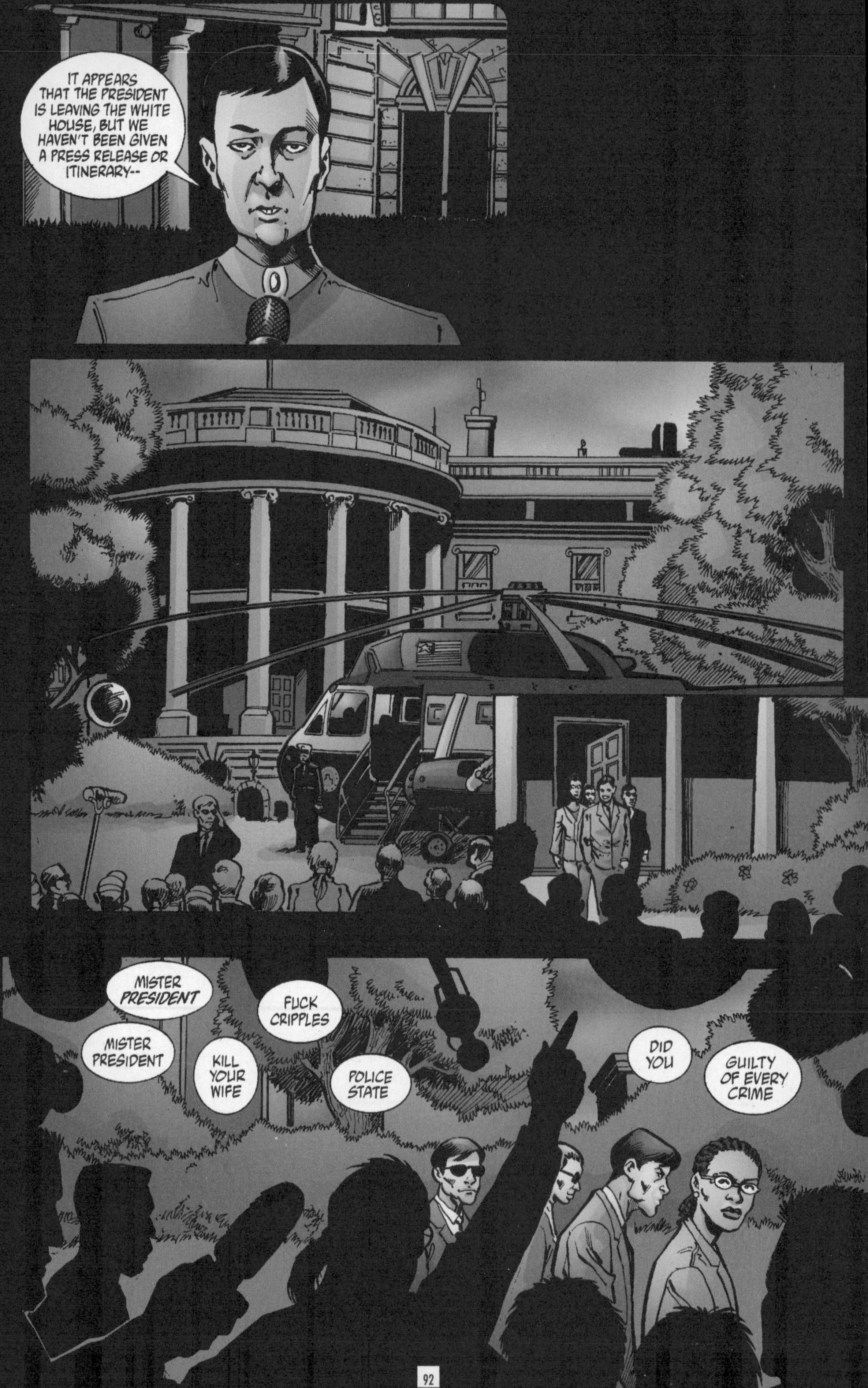
IT APPEARS THAT THE PRESIDENT IS LEAVING THE WHITE HOUSE, BUT WE HAVEN'T BEEN GIVEN A PRESS RELEASE OR ITINERARY--
MISTER *PRESIDENT*
MISTER PRESIDENT
KILL YOUR WIFE
FUCK CRIPPLES
POLICE STATE
DID YOU
GUILTY OF EVERY CRIME

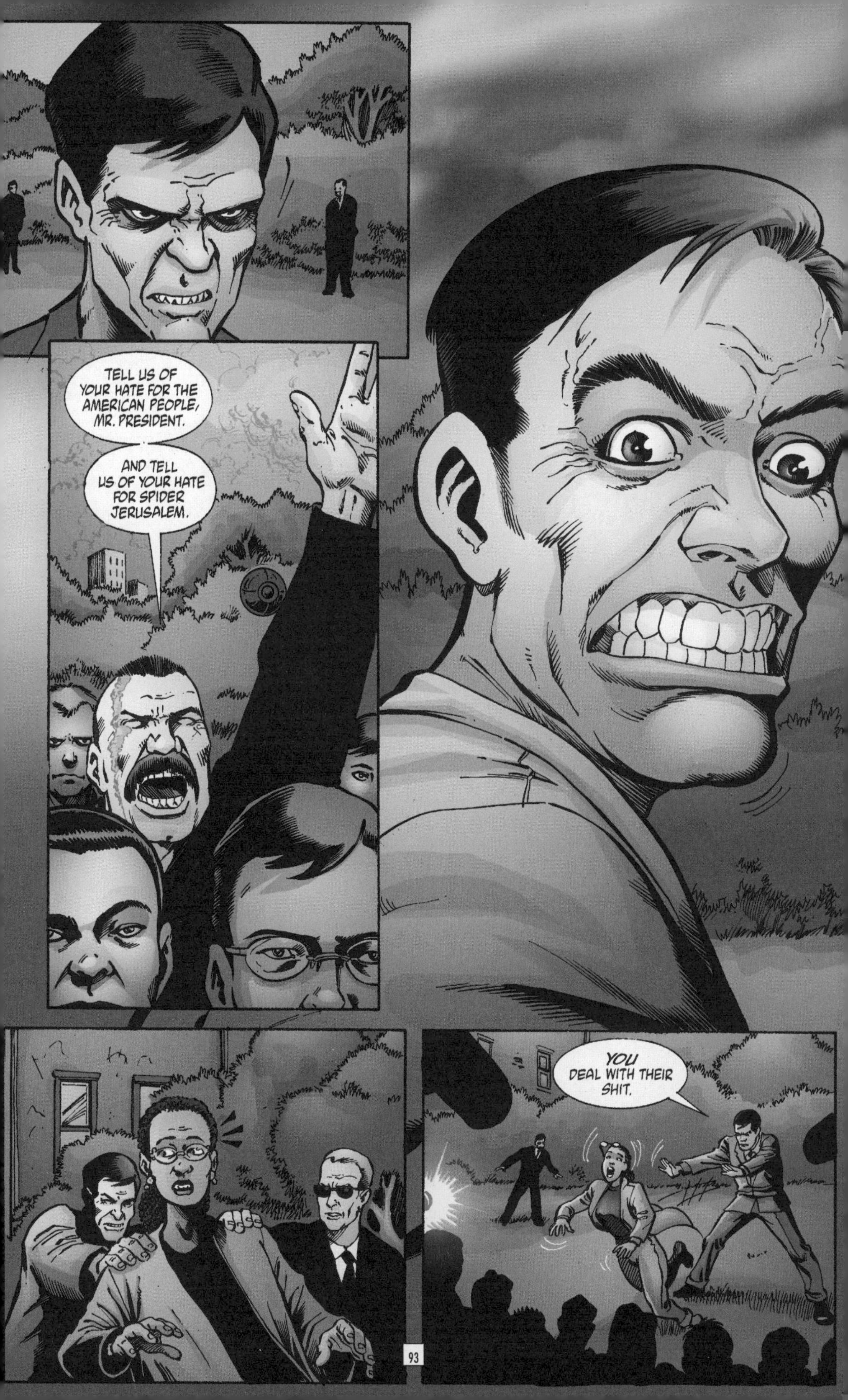
TELL US OF YOUR HATE FOR THE AMERICAN PEOPLE, MR. PRESIDENT.
AND TELL US OF YOUR HATE FOR SPIDER JERUSALEM.
YOU DEAL WITH THEIR SHIT.

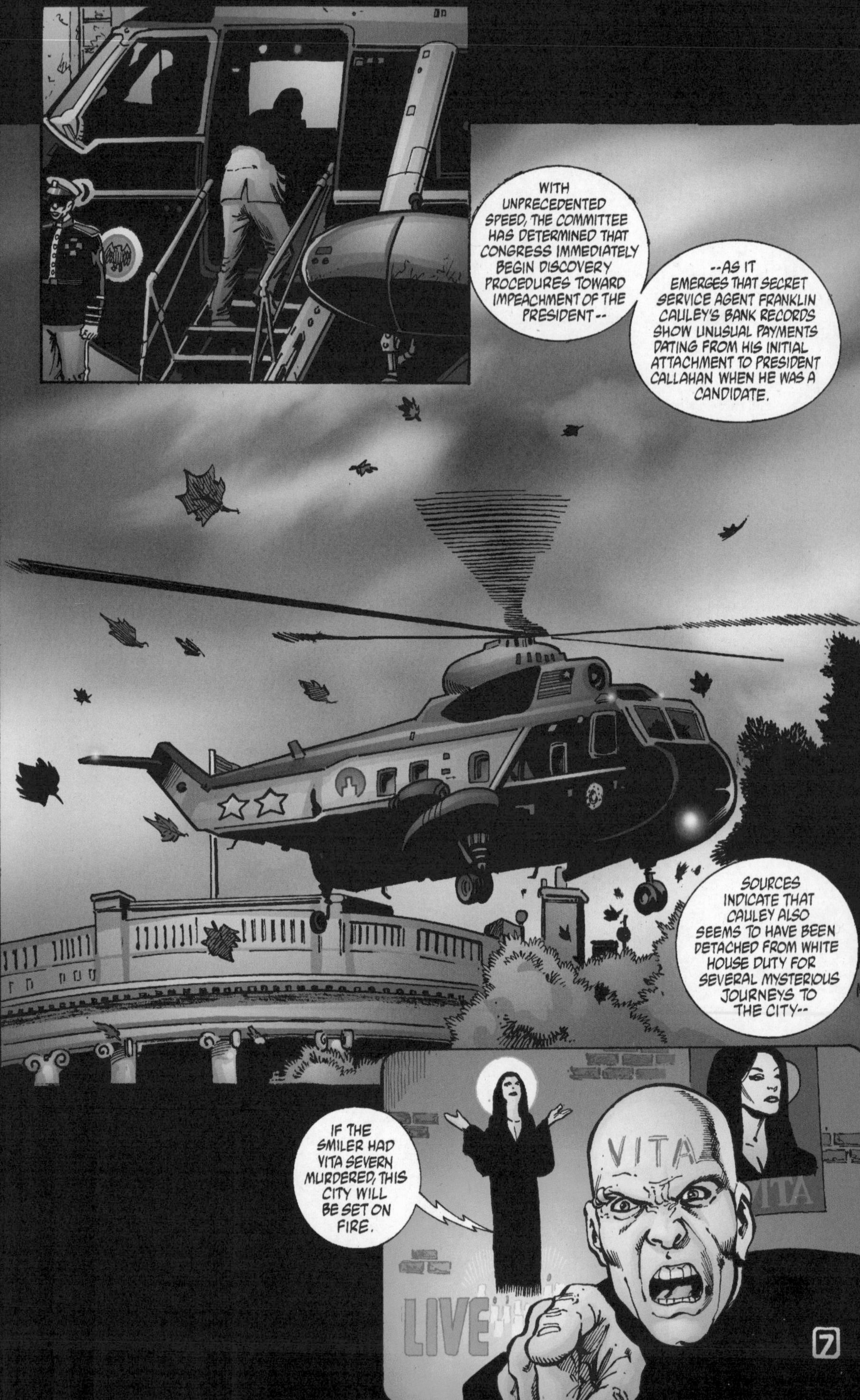
WITH UNPRECEDENTED SPEED, THE COMMITTEE HAS DETERMINED THAT CONGRESS IMMEDIATELY BEGIN DISCOVERY PROCEDURES TOWARD IMPEACHMENT OF THE PRESIDENT --
--AS IT EMERGES THAT SECRET SERVICE AGENT FRANKLIN CAULEY'S BANK RECORDS SHOW UNUSUAL PAYMENTS DATING FROM HIS INITIAL ATTACHMENT TO PRESIDENT CALLAHAN WHEN HE WAS A CANDIDATE.
SOURCES INDICATE THAT CAULEY ALSO SEEMS TO HAVE BEEN DETACHED FROM WHITE HOUSE DUTY FOR SEVERAL MYSTERIOUS JOURNEYS TO THE CITY--
IF THE SMILER HAD VITA SEVERN MURDERED, THIS CITY WILL BE SET ON FIRE.
VITA
LIVE

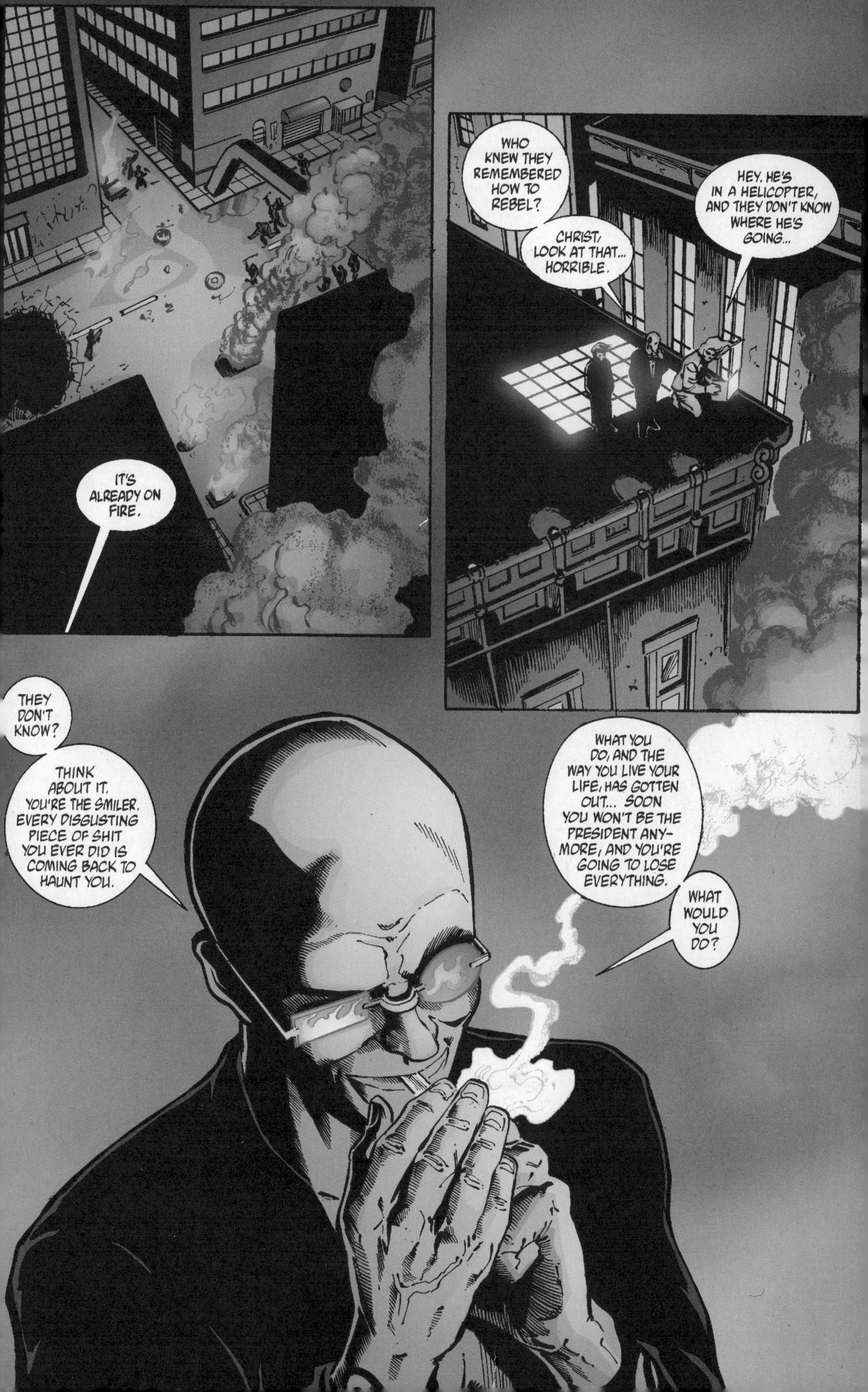
IT'S ALREADY ON FIRE.
WHO KNEW THEY REMEMBERED HOW TO REBEL?
CHRIST, LOOK AT THAT... HORRIBLE.
HEY, HE'S IN A HELICOPTER, AND THEY DON'T KNOW WHERE HE'S GOING...
THEY DON'T KNOW?
THINK ABOUT IT. YOU'RE THE SMILER. EVERY DISGUSTING PIECE OF SHIT YOU EVER DID IS COMING BACK TO HAUNT YOU.
WHAT YOU DO, AND THE WAY YOU LIVE YOUR LIFE, HAS GOTTEN OUT... SOON YOU WON'T BE THE PRESIDENT ANY-MORE, AND YOU'RE GOING TO LOSE EVERYTHING.
WHAT WOULD YOU DO?

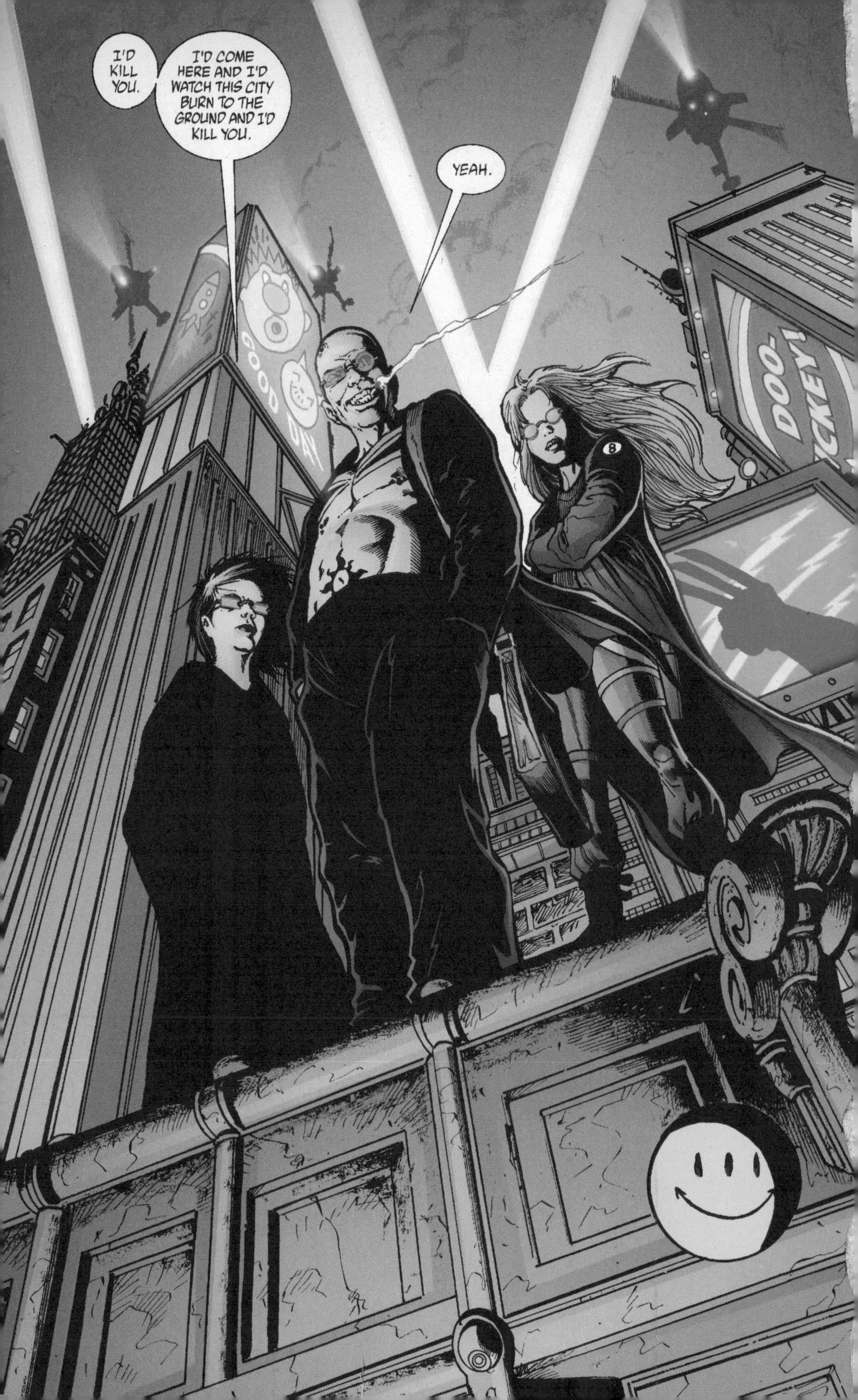
I'D KILL YOU.
I'D COME HERE AND I'D WATCH THIS CITY BURN TO THE GROUND AND I'D KILL YOU.
YEAH.
GOOD DAY
DOO-

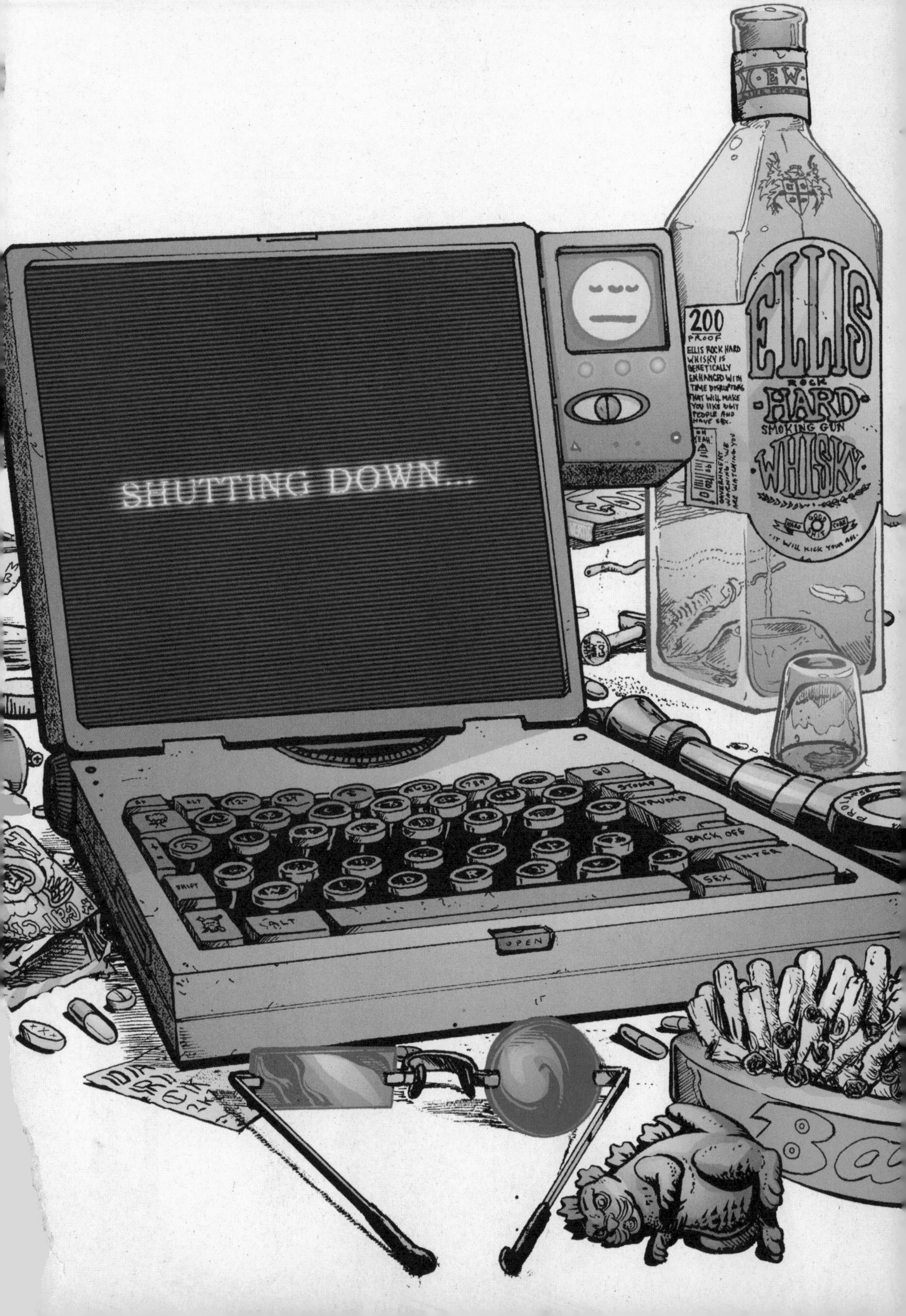
SHUTTING DOWN...
200 PROOF
ELLIS ROCK HARD WHISKY IS GENETICALLY ENHANCED WITH TIME DISRUPTORS THAT WILL MAKE YOU LIKE UGLY PEOPLE AND HAVE SEX.
OH YEAH!
GOVERNMENT WARNING: WE ARE WATCHING YOU
ELLIS
ROCK
HARD
SMOKING GUN
WHISKY
HARD GOOD SHIT CORE
IT WILL KICK YOUR ASS.
GO
STOMP
TRUMP
BACK OFF
ENTER
SEX
SHIFT
ALT
OPEN

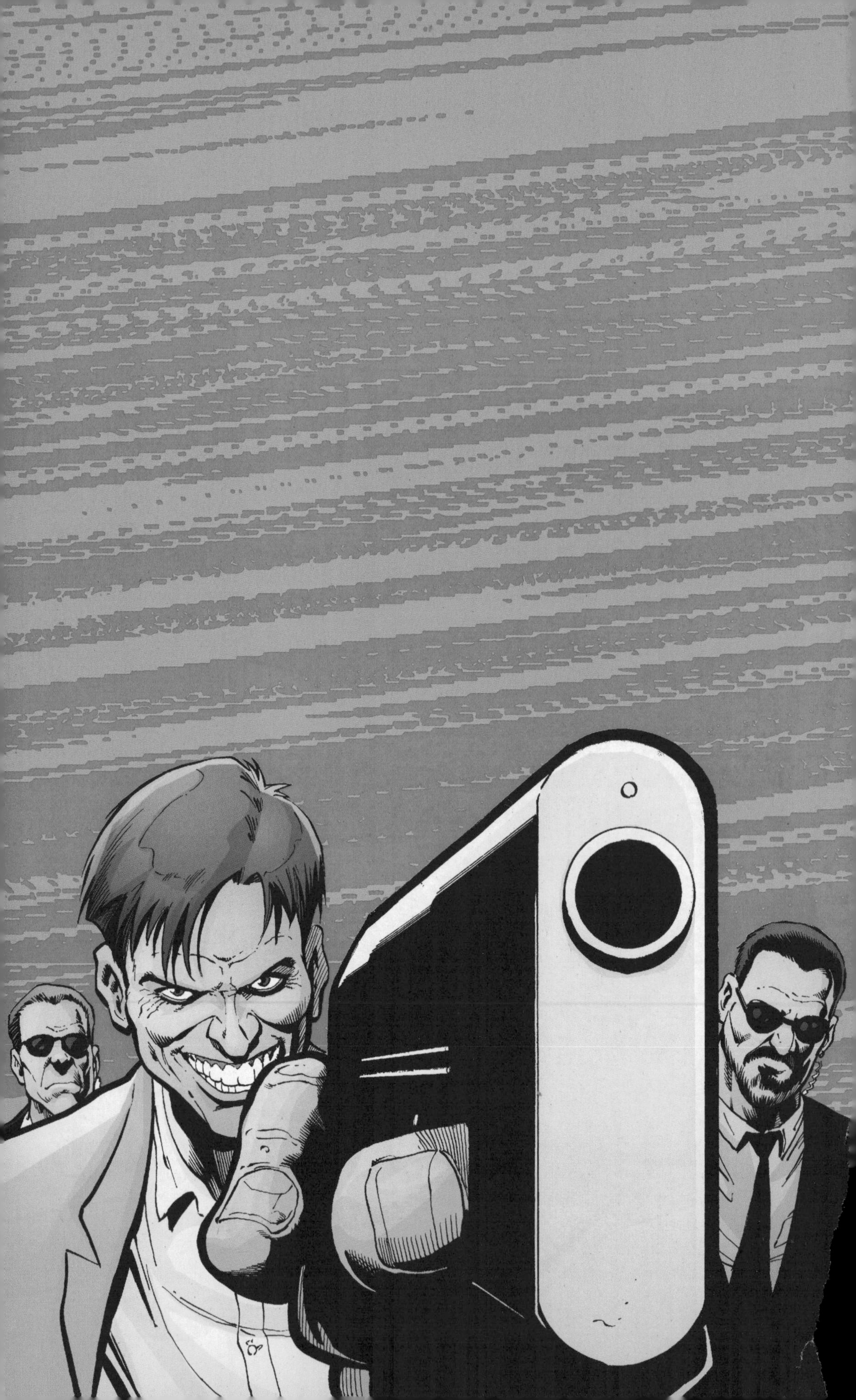

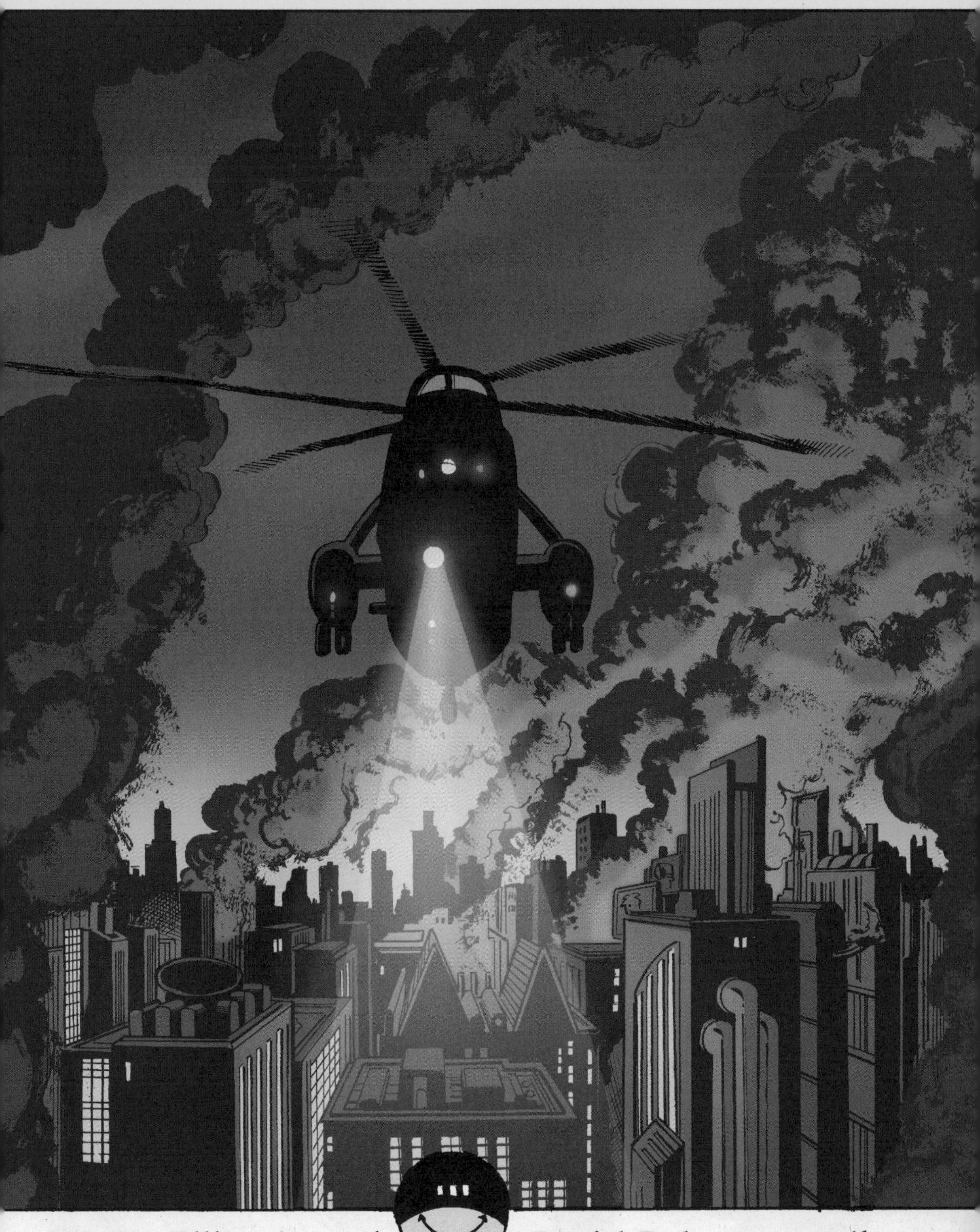

Warren Ellis writes and *Darick Robertson pencils*

The Long Day Closes

***Rodney Ramos**, inker* · ***Nathan Eyring**, color & separations*
***Clem Robins**, letterer* · ***Darick Robertson**, cover* · ***Zachary Rau**, editor*
***Transmetropolitan** created by Warren Ellis and Darick Robertson*

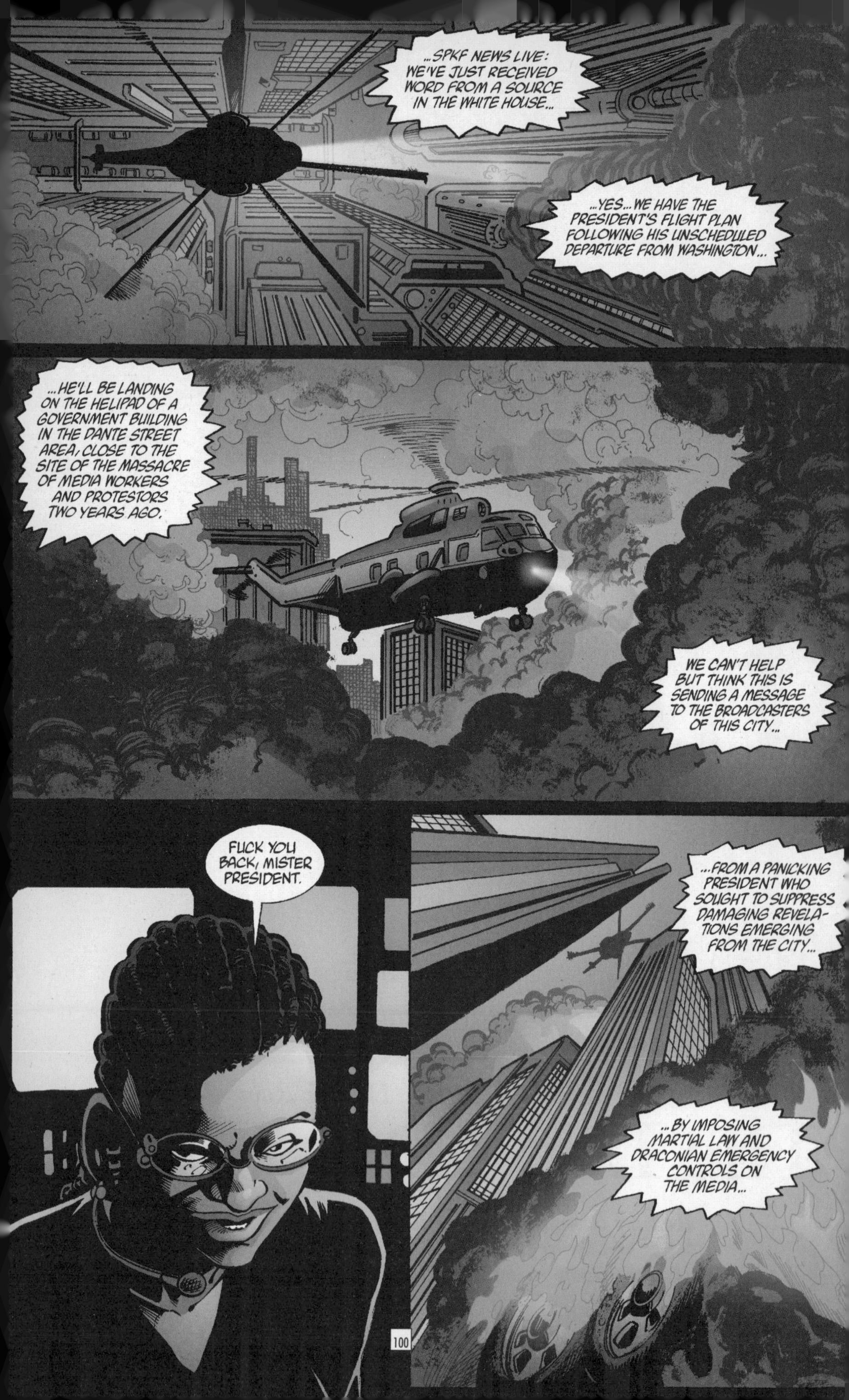

...SPKF NEWS LIVE: WE'VE JUST RECEIVED WORD FROM A SOURCE IN THE WHITE HOUSE...
...YES...WE HAVE THE PRESIDENT'S FLIGHT PLAN FOLLOWING HIS UNSCHEDULED DEPARTURE FROM WASHINGTON...
...HE'LL BE LANDING ON THE HELIPAD OF A GOVERNMENT BUILDING IN THE DANTE STREET AREA, CLOSE TO THE SITE OF THE MASSACRE OF MEDIA WORKERS AND PROTESTORS TWO YEARS AGO.
WE CAN'T HELP BUT THINK THIS IS SENDING A MESSAGE TO THE BROADCASTERS OF THIS CITY...
FUCK YOU BACK, MISTER PRESIDENT.
...FROM A PANICKING PRESIDENT WHO SOUGHT TO SUPPRESS DAMAGING REVELA-TIONS EMERGING FROM THE CITY...
...BY IMPOSING MARTIAL LAW AND DRACONIAN EMERGENCY CONTROLS ON THE MEDIA...

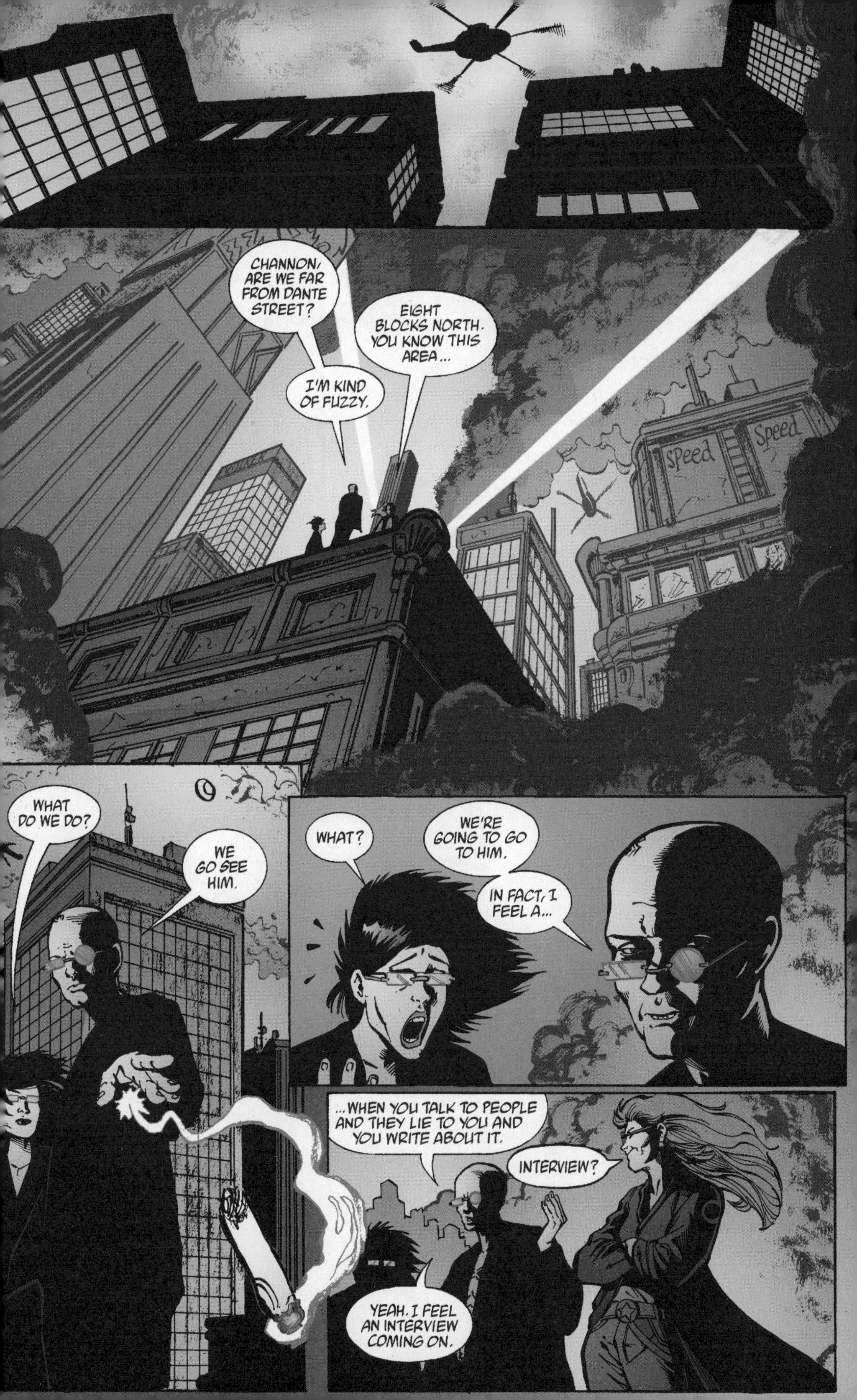
CHANNON, ARE WE FAR FROM DANTE STREET?
EIGHT BLOCKS NORTH. YOU KNOW THIS AREA...
I'M KIND OF FUZZY.
Speed
Speed
WHAT DO WE DO?
WE GO SEE HIM.
WHAT?
WE'RE GOING TO GO TO HIM.
IN FACT, I FEEL A...
...WHEN YOU TALK TO PEOPLE AND THEY LIE TO YOU AND YOU WRITE ABOUT IT.
INTERVIEW?
YEAH. I FEEL AN INTERVIEW COMING ON.

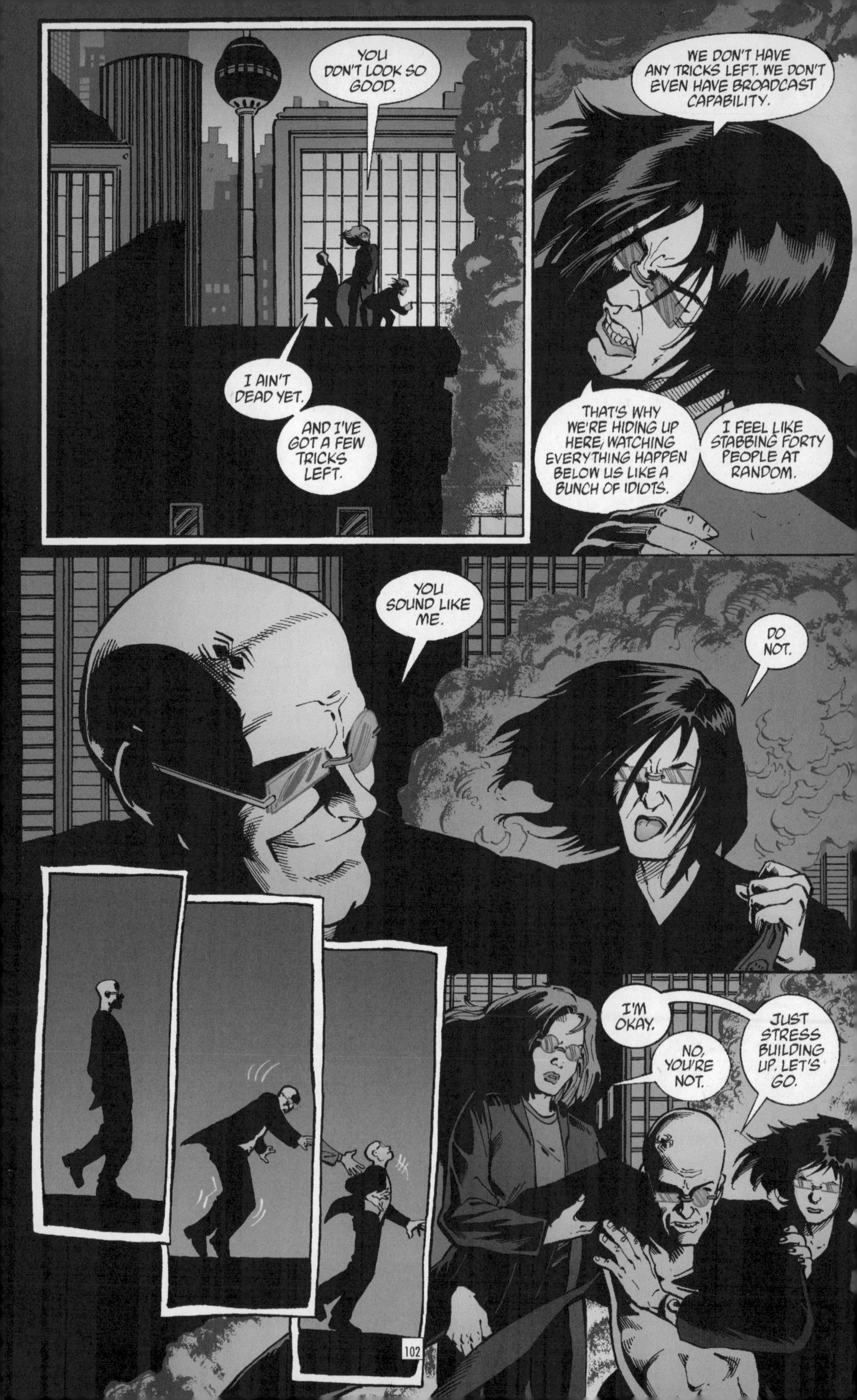
YOU DON'T LOOK SO GOOD.
I AIN'T DEAD YET.
AND I'VE GOT A FEW TRICKS LEFT.
WE DON'T HAVE ANY TRICKS LEFT. WE DON'T EVEN HAVE BROADCAST CAPABILITY.
THAT'S WHY WE'RE HIDING UP HERE, WATCHING EVERYTHING HAPPEN BELOW US LIKE A BUNCH OF IDIOTS.
I FEEL LIKE STABBING FORTY PEOPLE AT RANDOM.
YOU SOUND LIKE ME.
DO NOT.
I'M OKAY.
JUST STRESS BUILDING UP. LET'S GO.
NO, YOU'RE NOT.

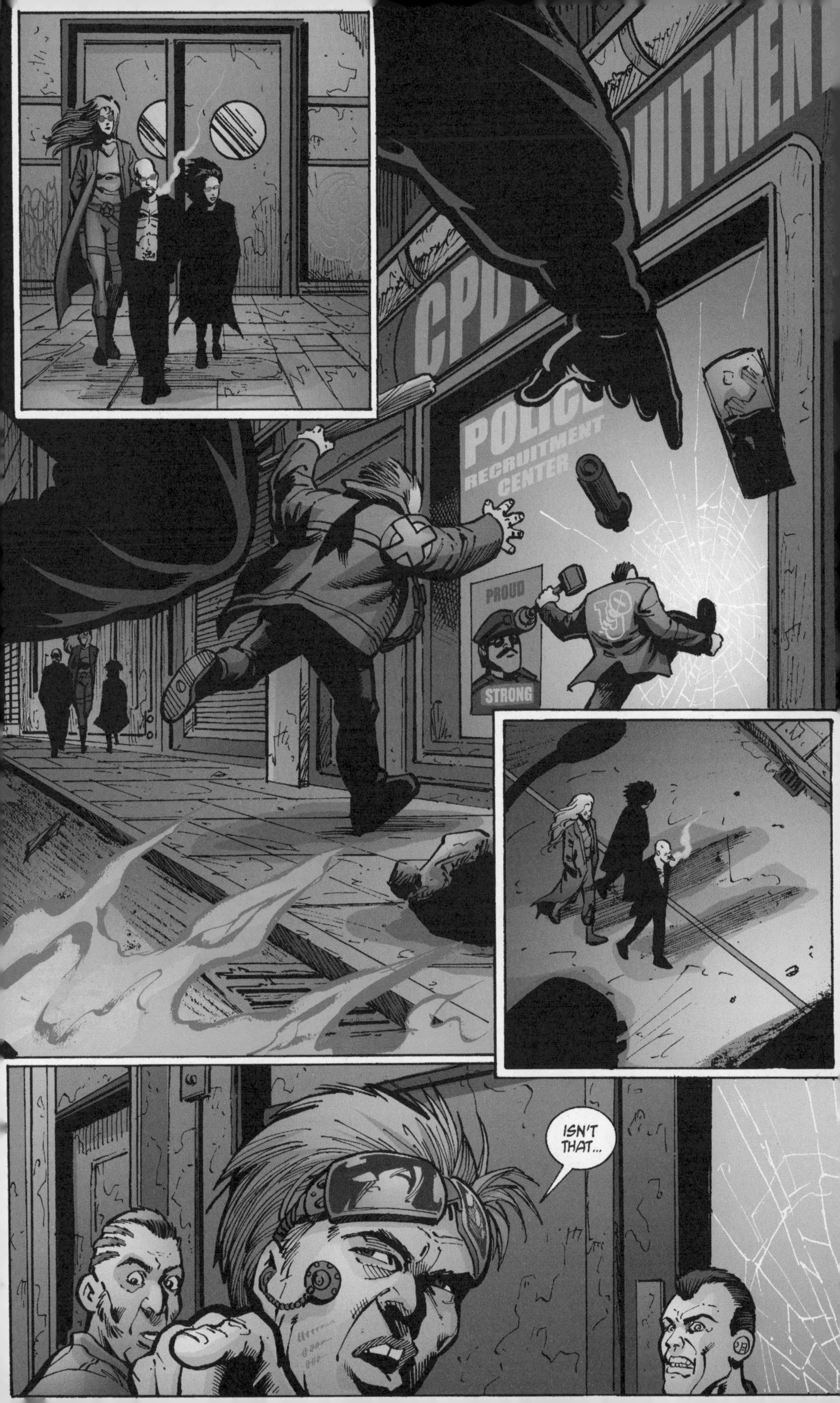

CPD
RUITMENT
POLICE
RECRUITMENT
CENTER
PROUD
STRONG
ISN'T THAT...

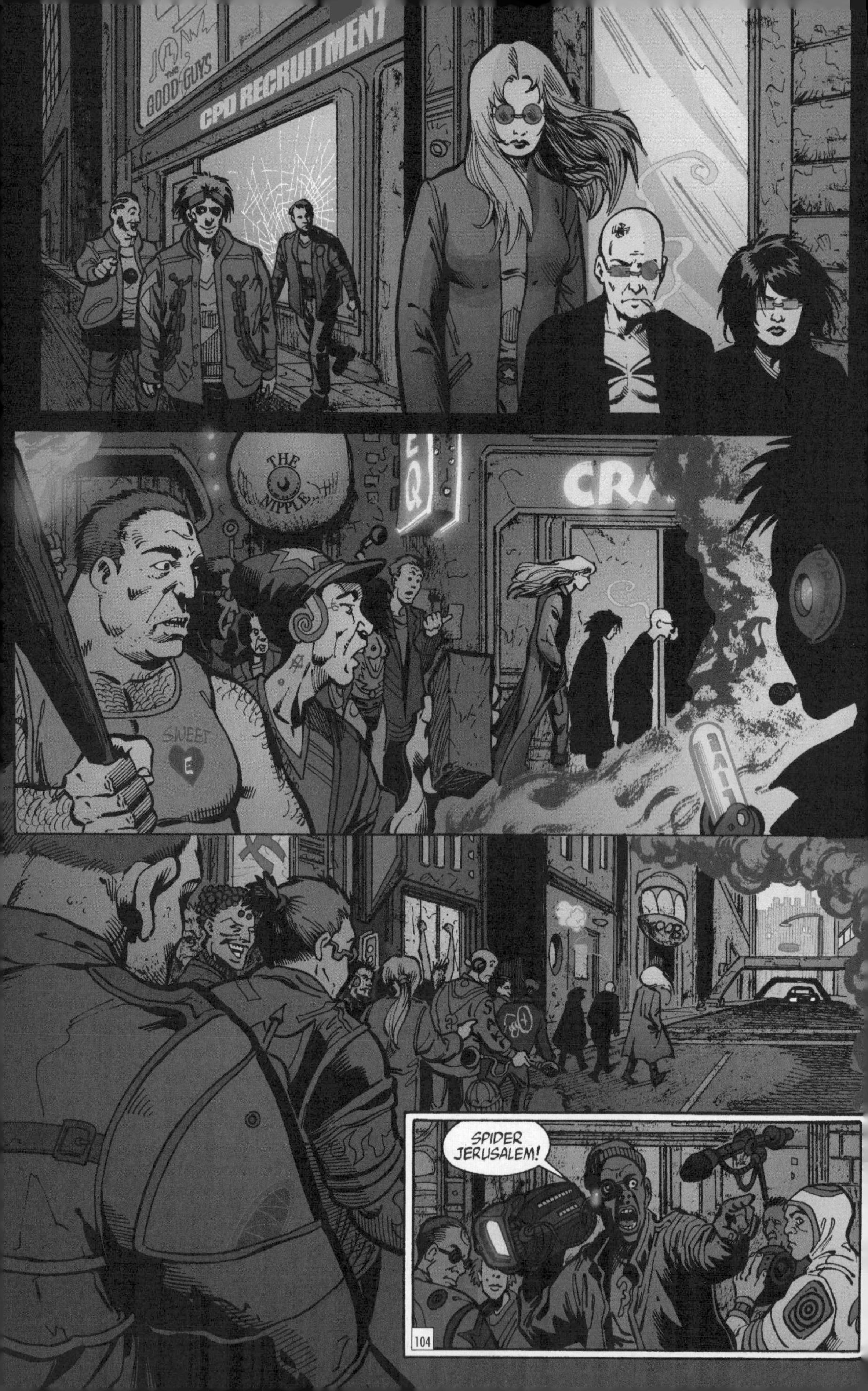

THE GOOD GUYS
CPD RECRUITMENT
THE NIPPLE
SWEET E
SPIDER JERUSALEM!

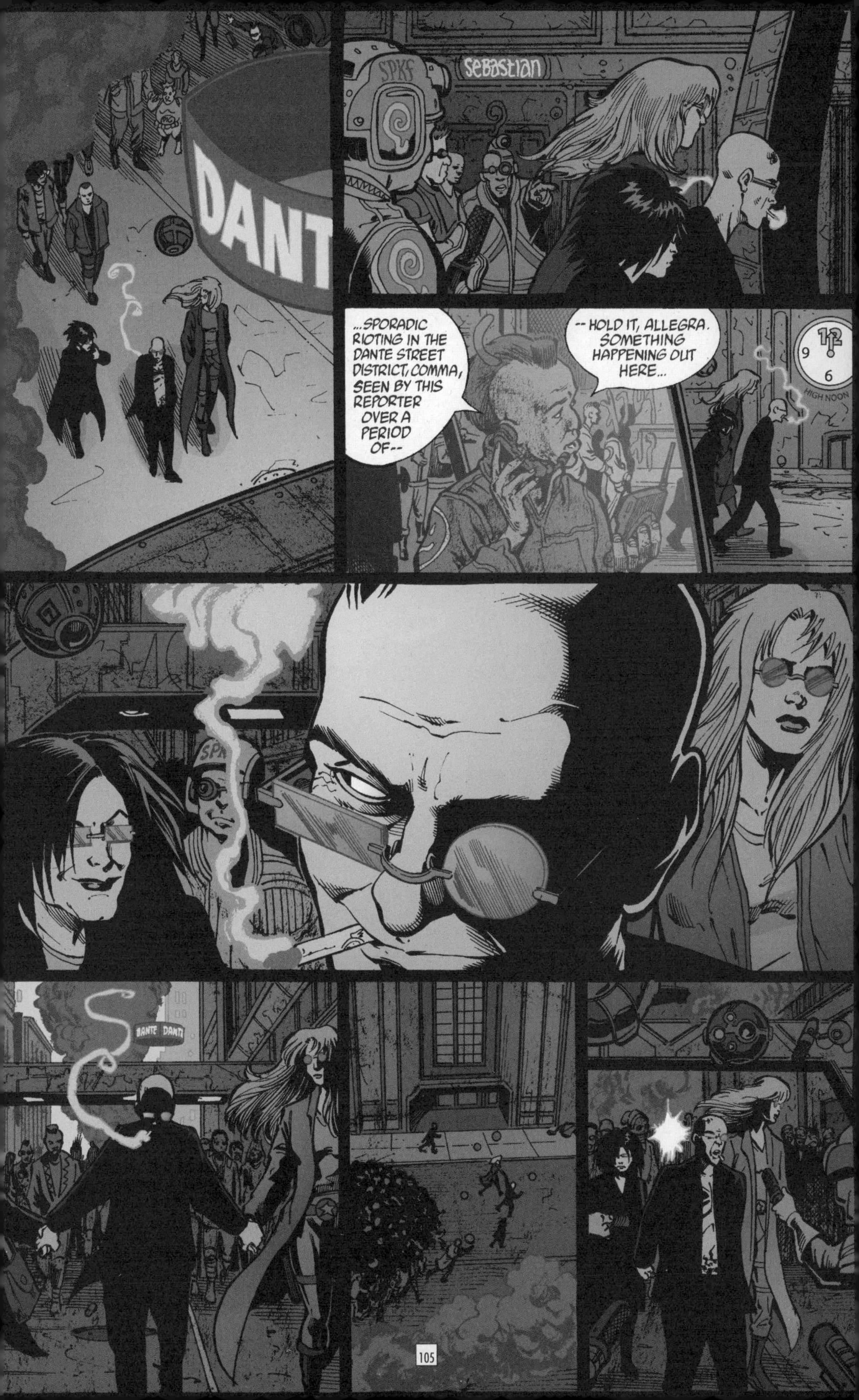
DANT
SEBASTIAN
SPKF
...SPORADIC RIOTING IN THE DANTE STREET DISTRICT, COMMA, SEEN BY THIS REPORTER OVER A PERIOD OF--
-- HOLD IT, ALLEGRA. SOMETHING HAPPENING OUT HERE...
HIGH NOON
DANTE DANTE

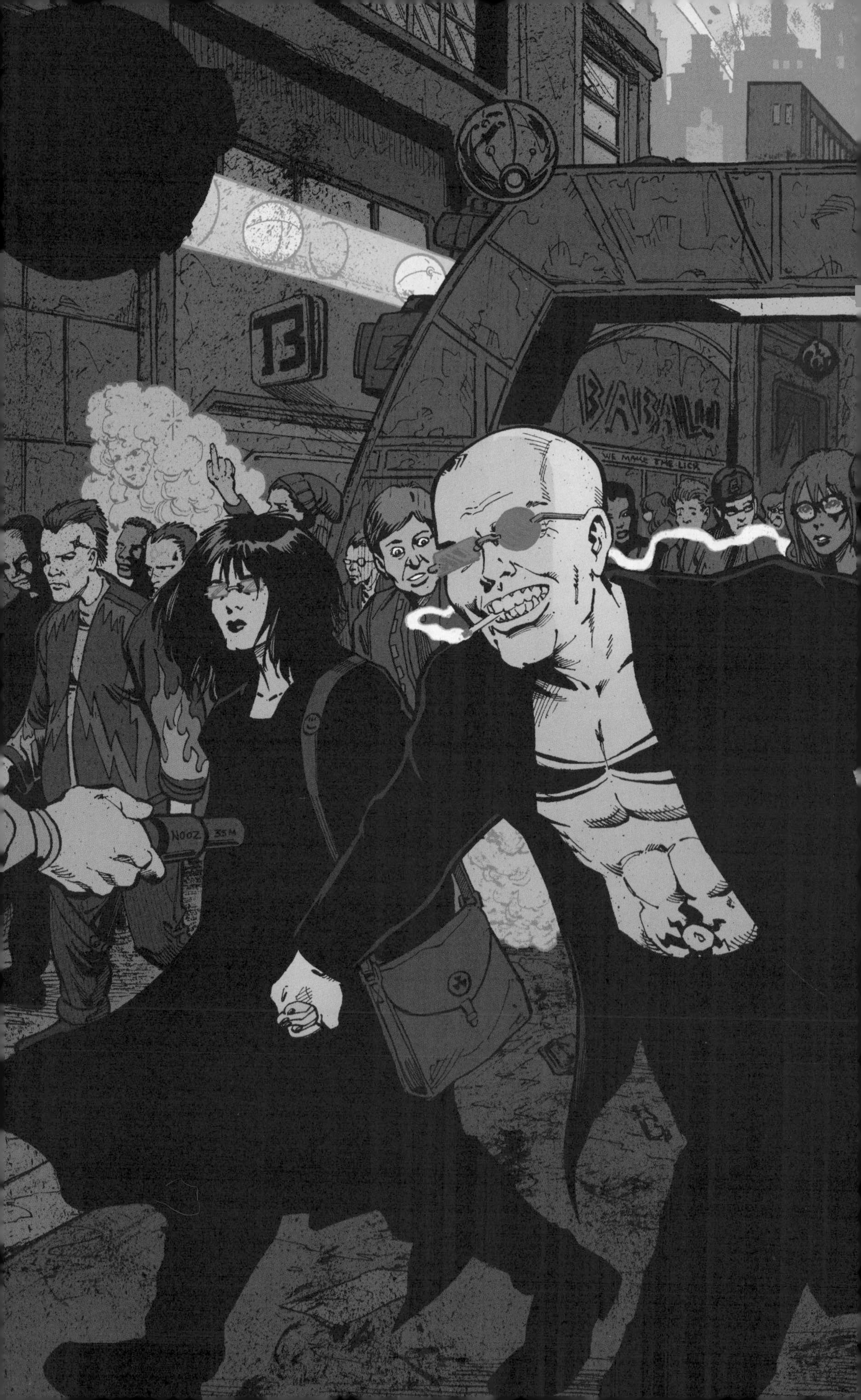
T3
BABALU
WE MAKE THE LICK
NOOZ 35M

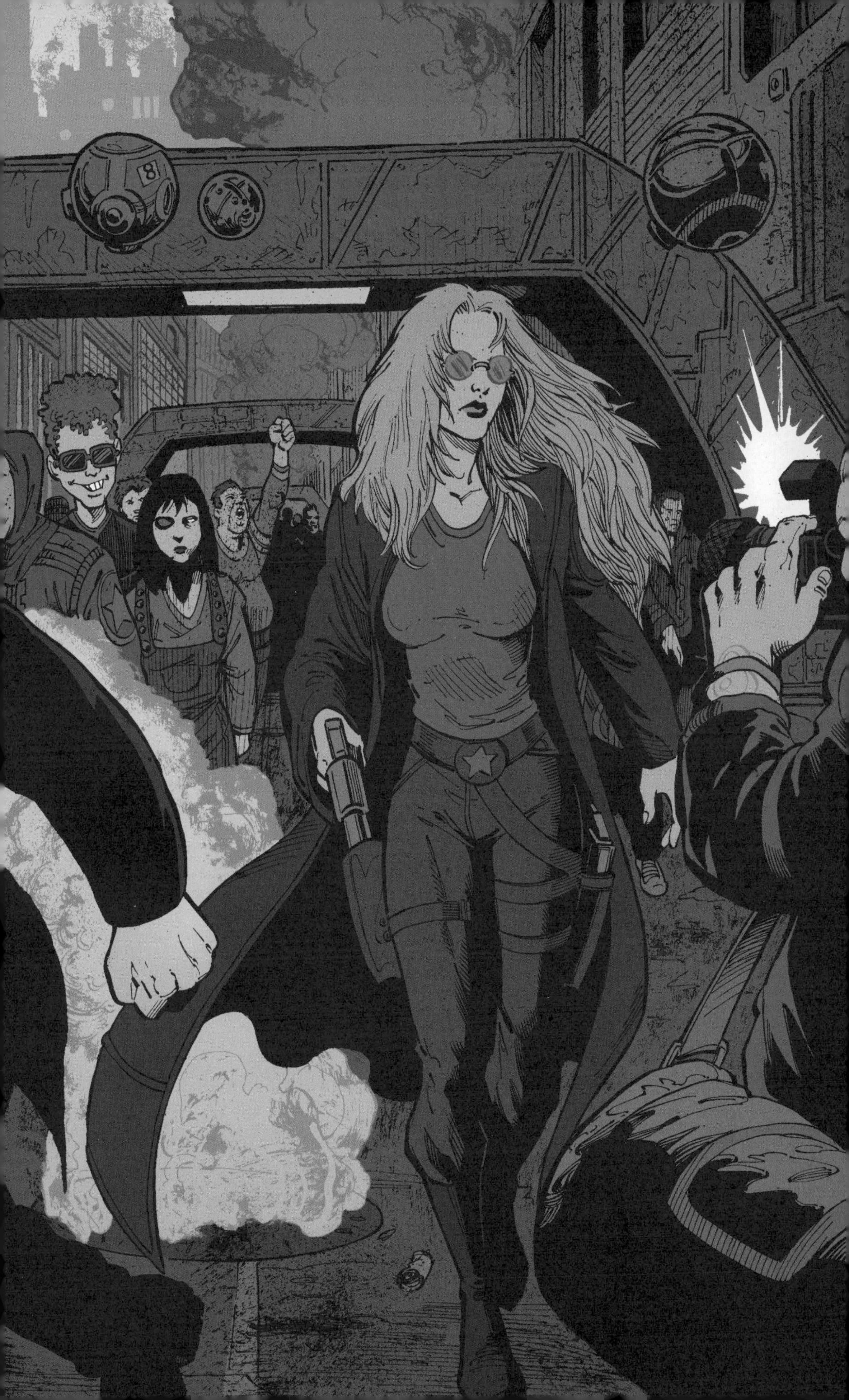
8

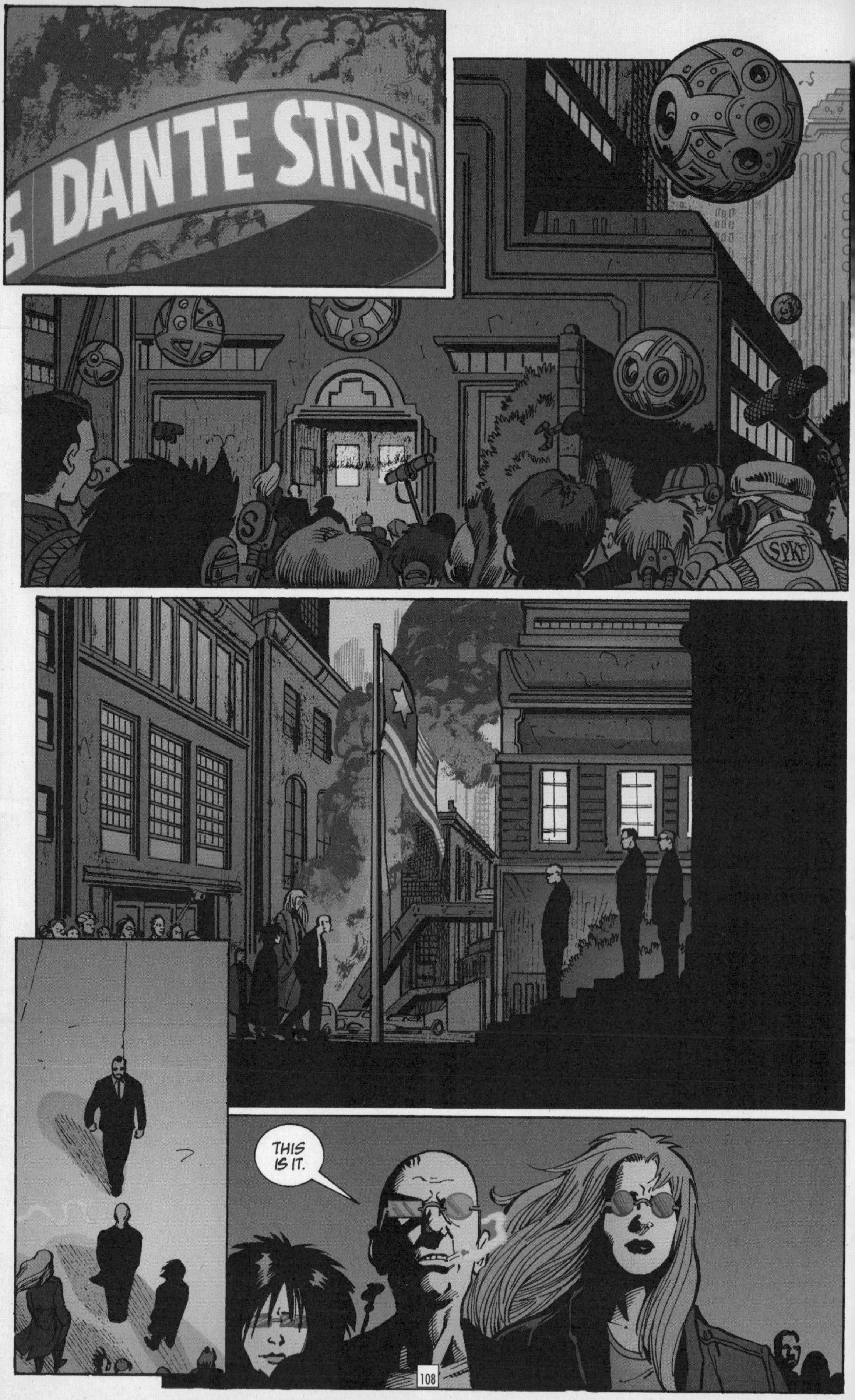

DANTE STREET
SPKF
THIS IS IT.

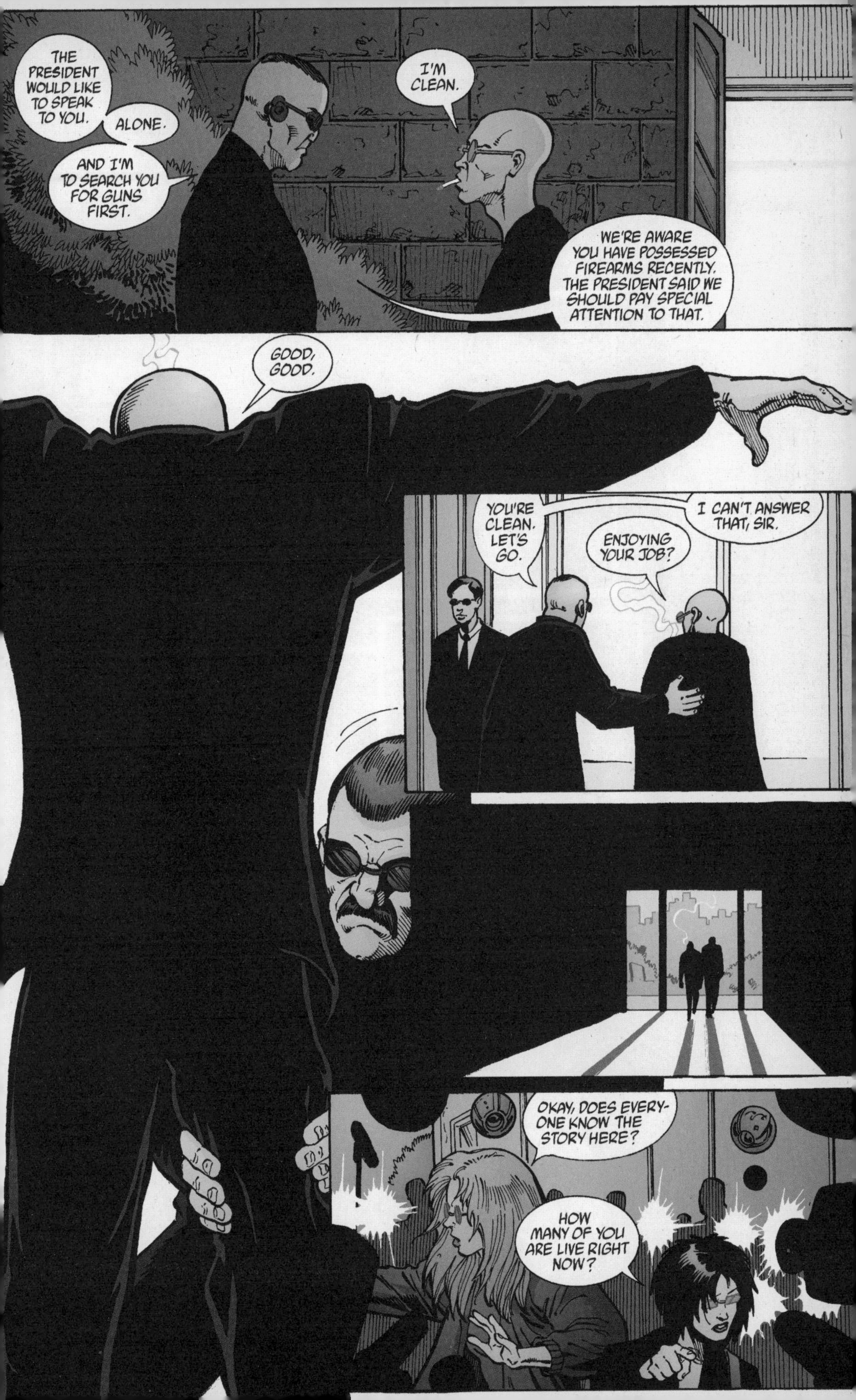
THE PRESIDENT WOULD LIKE TO SPEAK TO YOU.
ALONE.
AND I'M TO SEARCH YOU FOR GUNS FIRST.
I'M CLEAN.
WE'RE AWARE YOU HAVE POSSESSED FIREARMS RECENTLY. THE PRESIDENT SAID WE SHOULD PAY SPECIAL ATTENTION TO THAT.
GOOD, GOOD.
YOU'RE CLEAN. LET'S GO.
ENJOYING YOUR JOB?
I CAN'T ANSWER THAT, SIR.
OKAY, DOES EVERY-ONE KNOW THE STORY HERE?
HOW MANY OF YOU ARE LIVE RIGHT NOW?

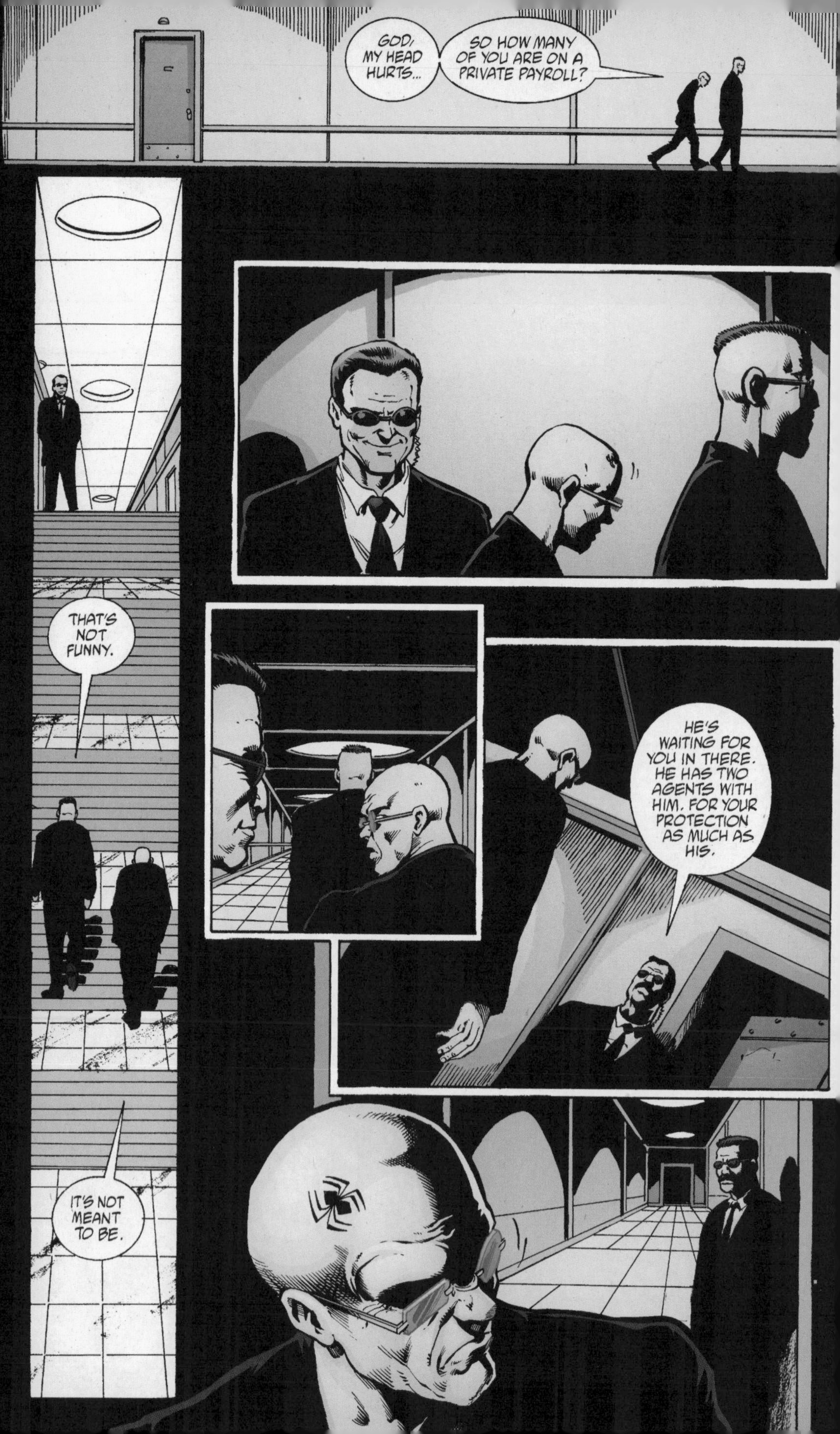
GOD, MY HEAD HURTS...
SO HOW MANY OF YOU ARE ON A PRIVATE PAYROLL?
THAT'S NOT FUNNY.
IT'S NOT MEANT TO BE.
HE'S WAITING FOR YOU IN THERE. HE HAS TWO AGENTS WITH HIM. FOR YOUR PROTECTION AS MUCH AS HIS.

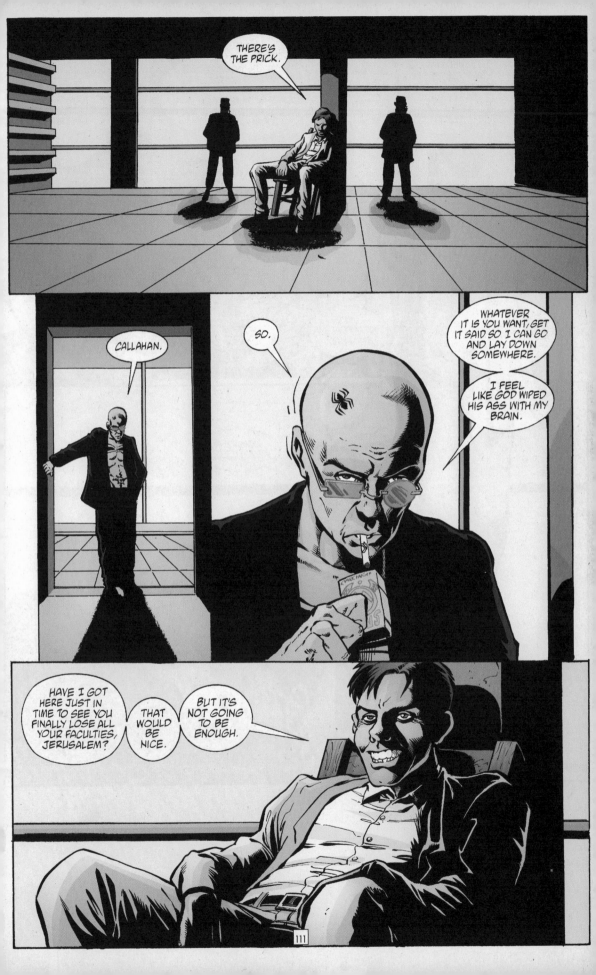

THERE'S THE PRICK.

CALLAHAN.

SO.

WHATEVER IT IS YOU WANT, GET IT SAID SO I CAN GO AND LAY DOWN SOMEWHERE.

I FEEL LIKE GOD WIPED HIS ASS WITH MY BRAIN.

HAVE I GOT HERE JUST IN TIME TO SEE YOU FINALLY LOSE ALL YOUR FACULTIES, JERUSALEM?

THAT WOULD BE NICE.

BUT IT'S NOT GOING TO BE ENOUGH.

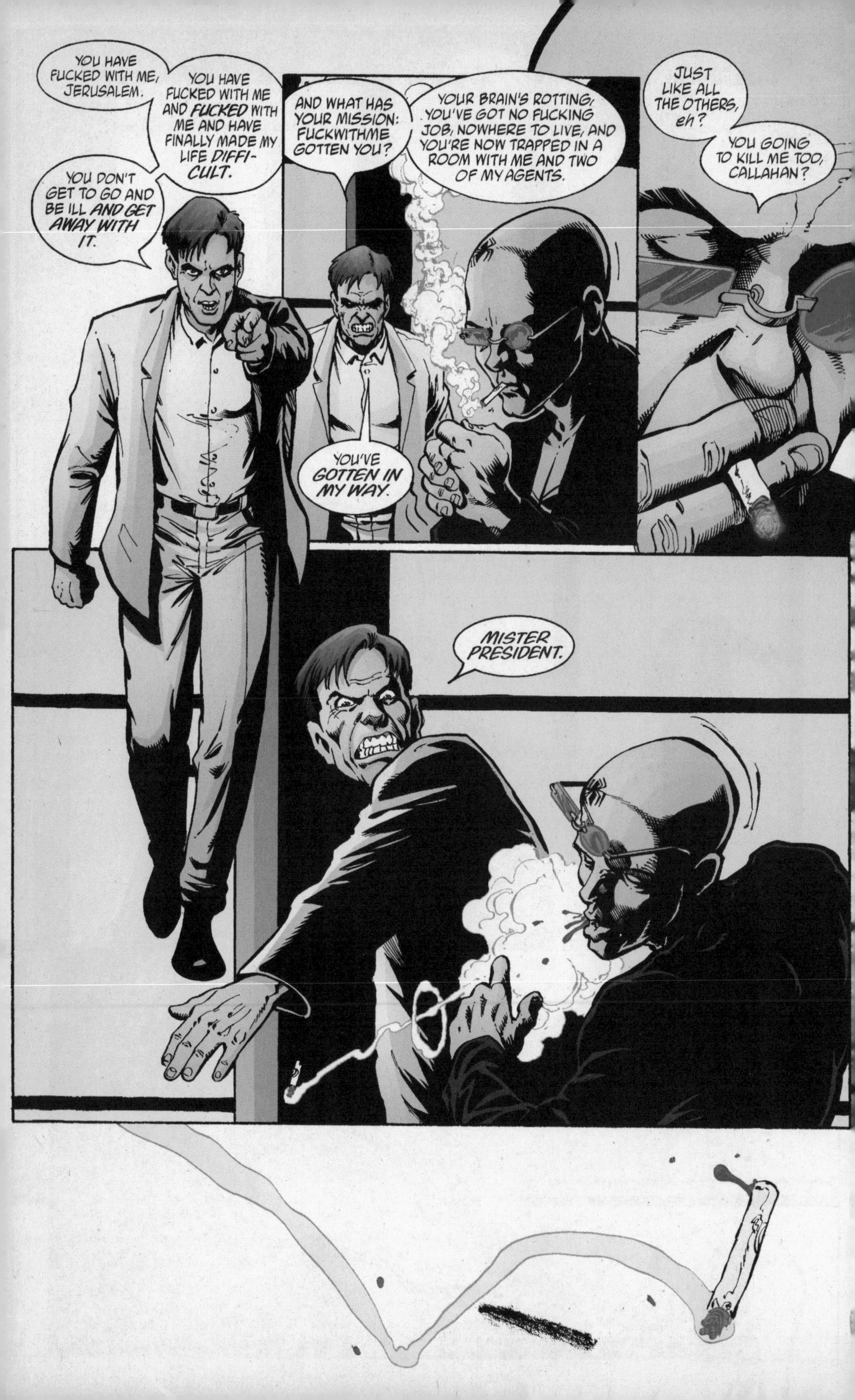

YOU HAVE FUCKED WITH ME, JERUSALEM.
YOU HAVE FUCKED WITH ME AND FUCKED WITH ME AND HAVE FINALLY MADE MY LIFE DIFFICULT.
YOU DON'T GET TO GO AND BE ILL AND GET AWAY WITH IT.
AND WHAT HAS YOUR MISSION: FUCKWITHME GOTTEN YOU?
YOUR BRAIN'S ROTTING, YOU'VE GOT NO FUCKING JOB, NOWHERE TO LIVE, AND YOU'RE NOW TRAPPED IN A ROOM WITH ME AND TWO OF MY AGENTS.
YOU'VE GOTTEN IN MY WAY.
JUST LIKE ALL THE OTHERS, eh?
YOU GOING TO KILL ME TOO, CALLAHAN?
MISTER PRESIDENT.

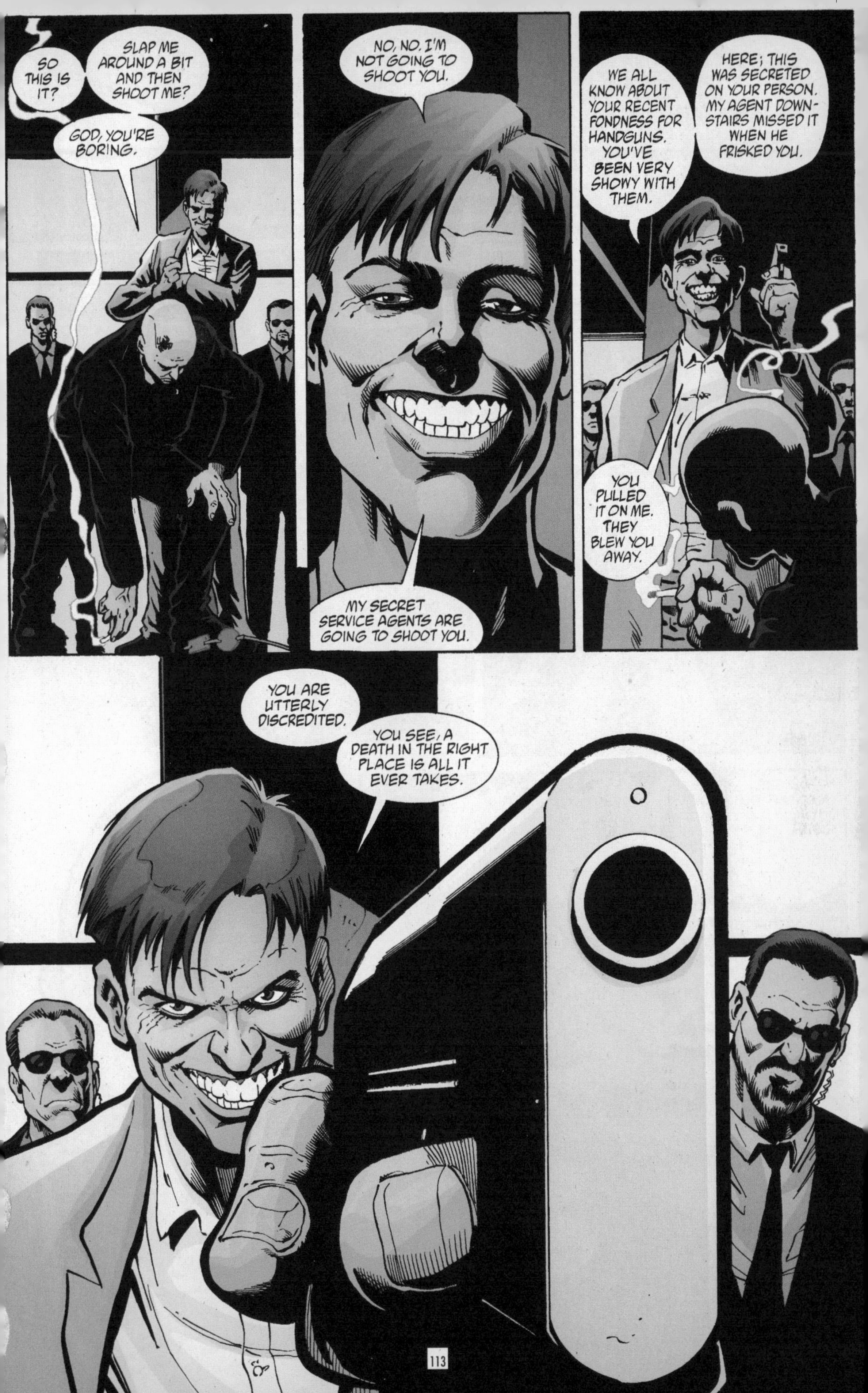

SO THIS IS IT?
SLAP ME AROUND A BIT AND THEN SHOOT ME?
GOD, YOU'RE BORING.
NO, NO. I'M NOT GOING TO SHOOT YOU.
MY SECRET SERVICE AGENTS ARE GOING TO SHOOT YOU.
WE ALL KNOW ABOUT YOUR RECENT FONDNESS FOR HANDGUNS. YOU'VE BEEN VERY SHOWY WITH THEM.
HERE; THIS WAS SECRETED ON YOUR PERSON. MY AGENT DOWN-STAIRS MISSED IT WHEN HE FRISKED YOU.
YOU PULLED IT ON ME. THEY BLEW YOU AWAY.
YOU ARE UTTERLY DISCREDITED.
YOU SEE, A DEATH IN THE RIGHT PLACE IS ALL IT EVER TAKES.

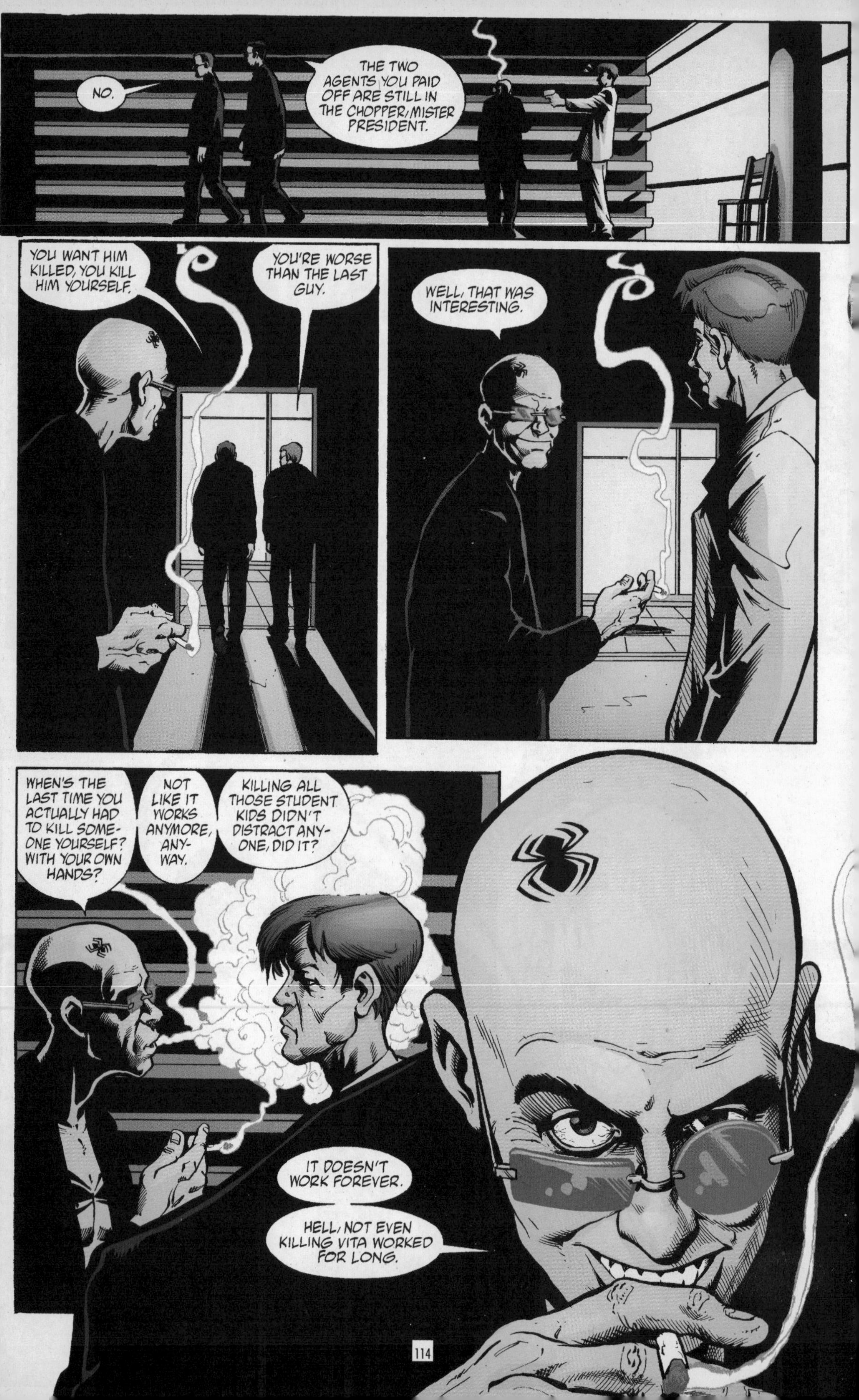
THE TWO AGENTS YOU PAID OFF ARE STILL IN THE CHOPPER, MISTER PRESIDENT.
NO.
YOU WANT HIM KILLED, YOU KILL HIM YOURSELF.
YOU'RE WORSE THAN THE LAST GUY.
WELL, THAT WAS INTERESTING.
WHEN'S THE LAST TIME YOU ACTUALLY HAD TO KILL SOME-ONE YOURSELF? WITH YOUR OWN HANDS?
NOT LIKE IT WORKS ANYMORE, ANY-WAY.
KILLING ALL THOSE STUDENT KIDS DIDN'T DISTRACT ANY-ONE, DID IT?
IT DOESN'T WORK FOREVER.
HELL, NOT EVEN KILLING VITA WORKED FOR LONG.

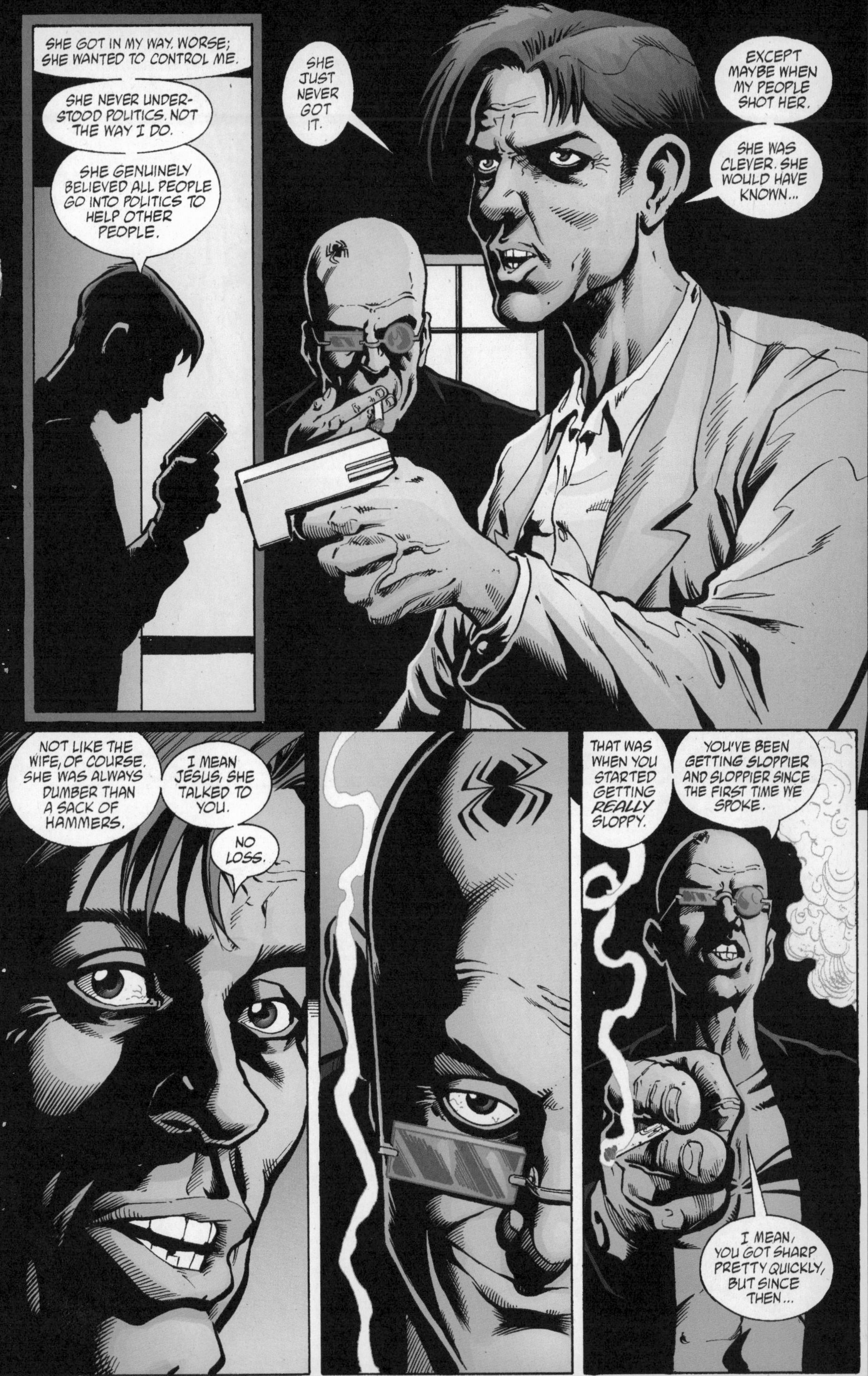
SHE GOT IN MY WAY. WORSE; SHE WANTED TO CONTROL ME.
SHE NEVER UNDERSTOOD POLITICS. NOT THE WAY I DO.
SHE GENUINELY BELIEVED ALL PEOPLE GO INTO POLITICS TO HELP OTHER PEOPLE.
SHE JUST NEVER GOT IT.
EXCEPT MAYBE WHEN MY PEOPLE SHOT HER.
SHE WAS CLEVER. SHE WOULD HAVE KNOWN...
NOT LIKE THE WIFE, OF COURSE. SHE WAS ALWAYS DUMBER THAN A SACK OF HAMMERS.
I MEAN JESUS, SHE TALKED TO YOU.
NO LOSS.
YOU'VE BEEN GETTING SLOPPIER AND SLOPPIER SINCE THE FIRST TIME WE SPOKE.
THAT WAS WHEN YOU STARTED GETTING *REALLY* SLOPPY.
I MEAN, YOU GOT SHARP PRETTY QUICKLY, BUT SINCE THEN...

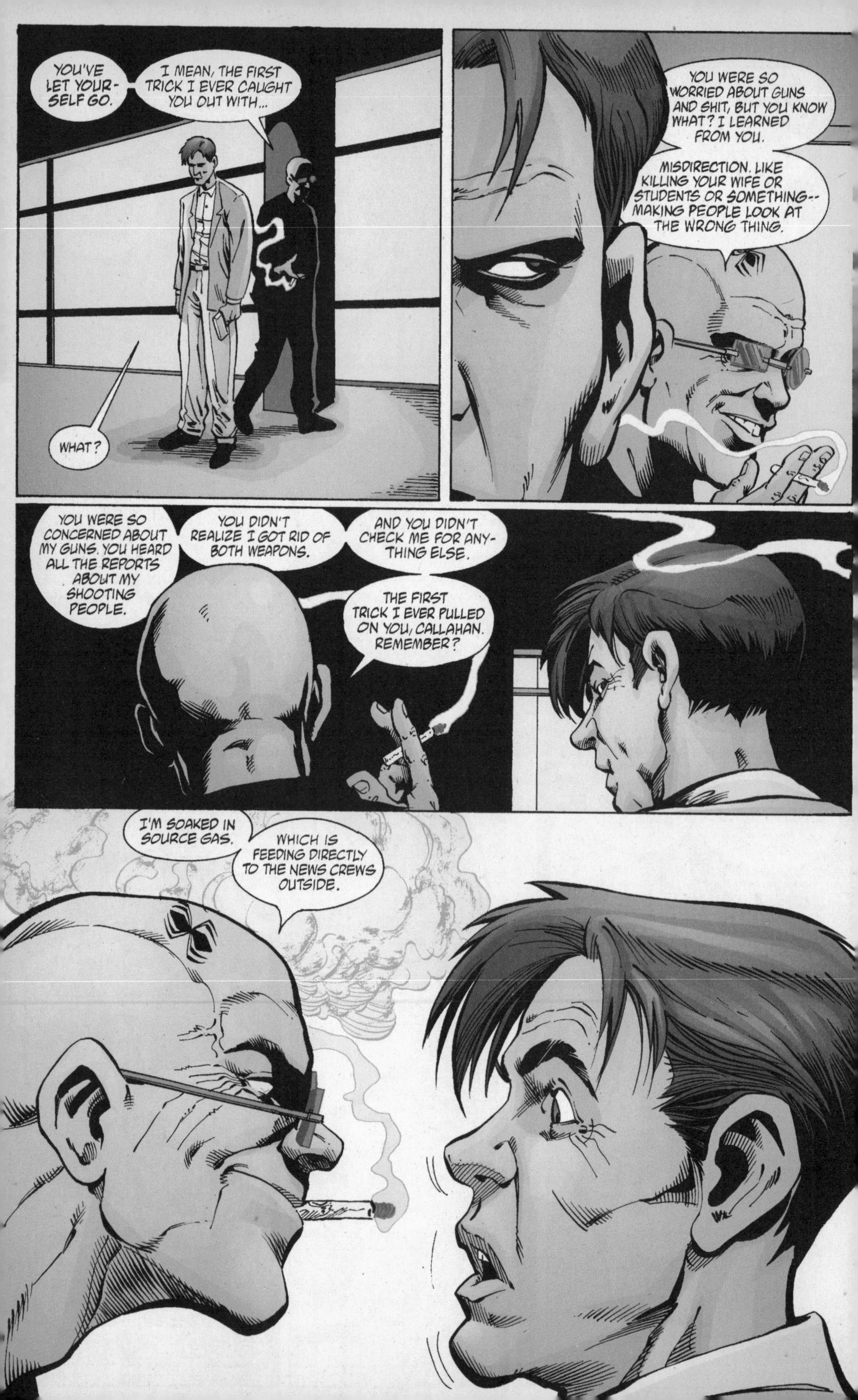

YOU'VE LET YOURSELF GO.
I MEAN, THE FIRST TRICK I EVER CAUGHT YOU OUT WITH...
WHAT?
YOU WERE SO WORRIED ABOUT GUNS AND SHIT, BUT YOU KNOW WHAT? I LEARNED FROM YOU.
MISDIRECTION. LIKE KILLING YOUR WIFE OR STUDENTS OR SOMETHING--MAKING PEOPLE LOOK AT THE WRONG THING.
YOU WERE SO CONCERNED ABOUT MY GUNS. YOU HEARD ALL THE REPORTS ABOUT MY SHOOTING PEOPLE.
YOU DIDN'T REALIZE I GOT RID OF BOTH WEAPONS.
AND YOU DIDN'T CHECK ME FOR ANYTHING ELSE.
THE FIRST TRICK I EVER PULLED ON YOU, CALLAHAN. REMEMBER?
I'M SOAKED IN SOURCE GAS.
WHICH IS FEEDING DIRECTLY TO THE NEWS CREWS OUTSIDE.

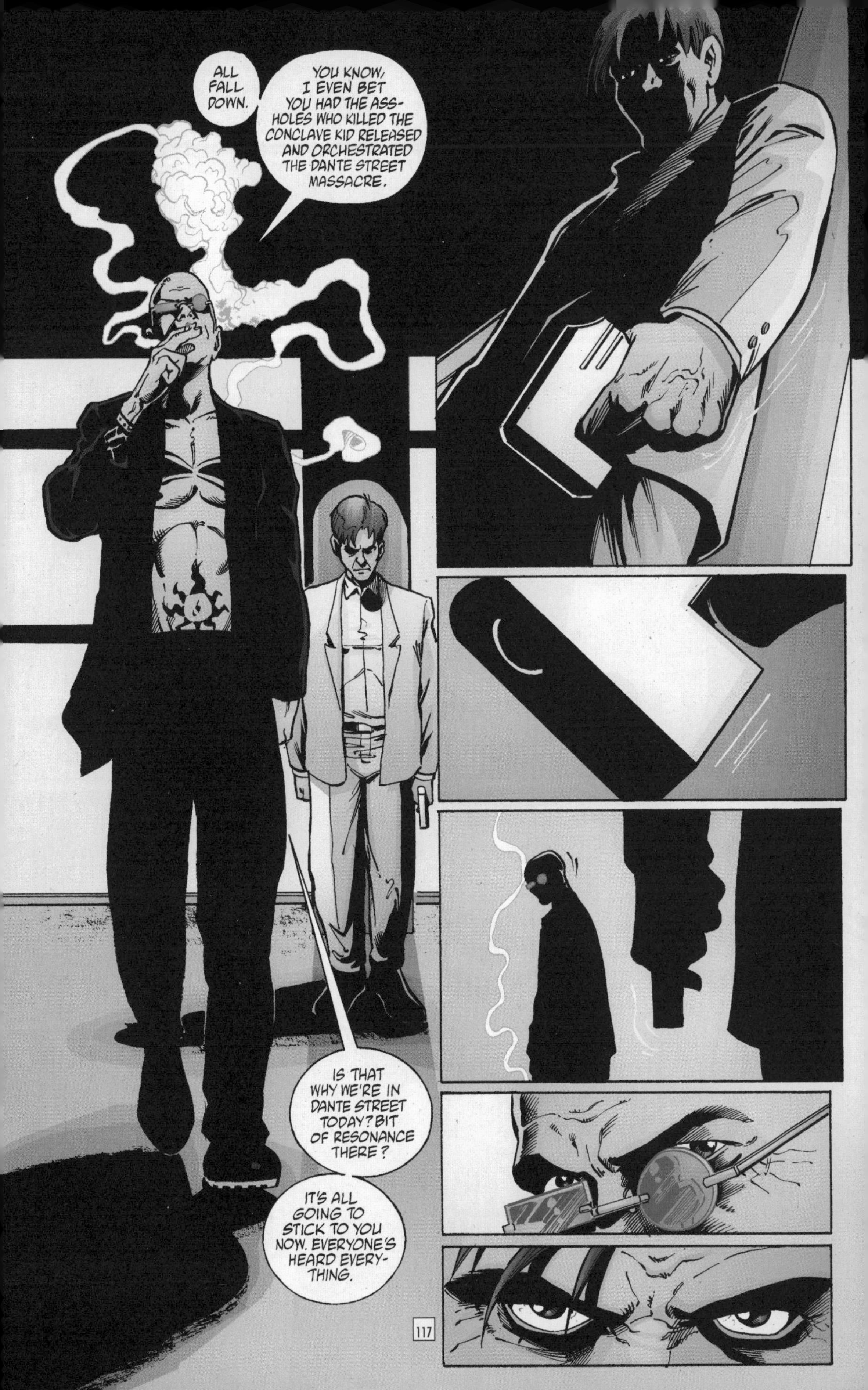
ALL FALL DOWN.
YOU KNOW, I EVEN BET YOU HAD THE ASS-HOLES WHO KILLED THE CONCLAVE KID RELEASED AND ORCHESTRATED THE DANTE STREET MASSACRE.
IS THAT WHY WE'RE IN DANTE STREET TODAY? BIT OF RESONANCE THERE?
IT'S ALL GOING TO STICK TO YOU NOW. EVERYONE'S HEARD EVERY-THING.

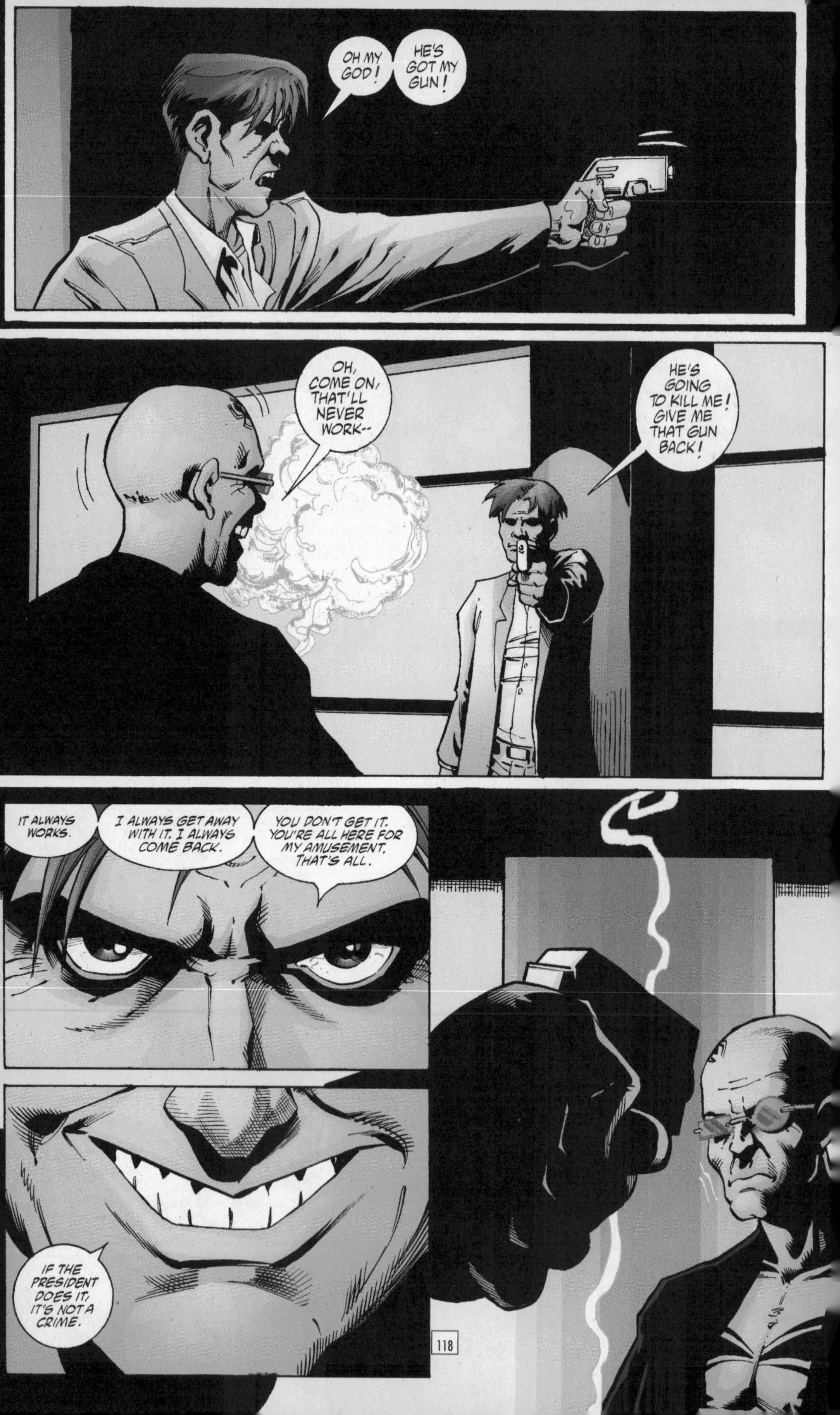
OH MY GOD!
HE'S GOT MY GUN!
OH, COME ON, THAT'LL NEVER WORK--
HE'S GOING TO KILL ME! GIVE ME THAT GUN BACK!
IT ALWAYS WORKS.
I ALWAYS GET AWAY WITH IT. I ALWAYS COME BACK.
YOU DON'T GET IT. YOU'RE ALL HERE FOR MY AMUSEMENT. THAT'S ALL.
IF THE PRESIDENT DOES IT, IT'S NOT A CRIME.

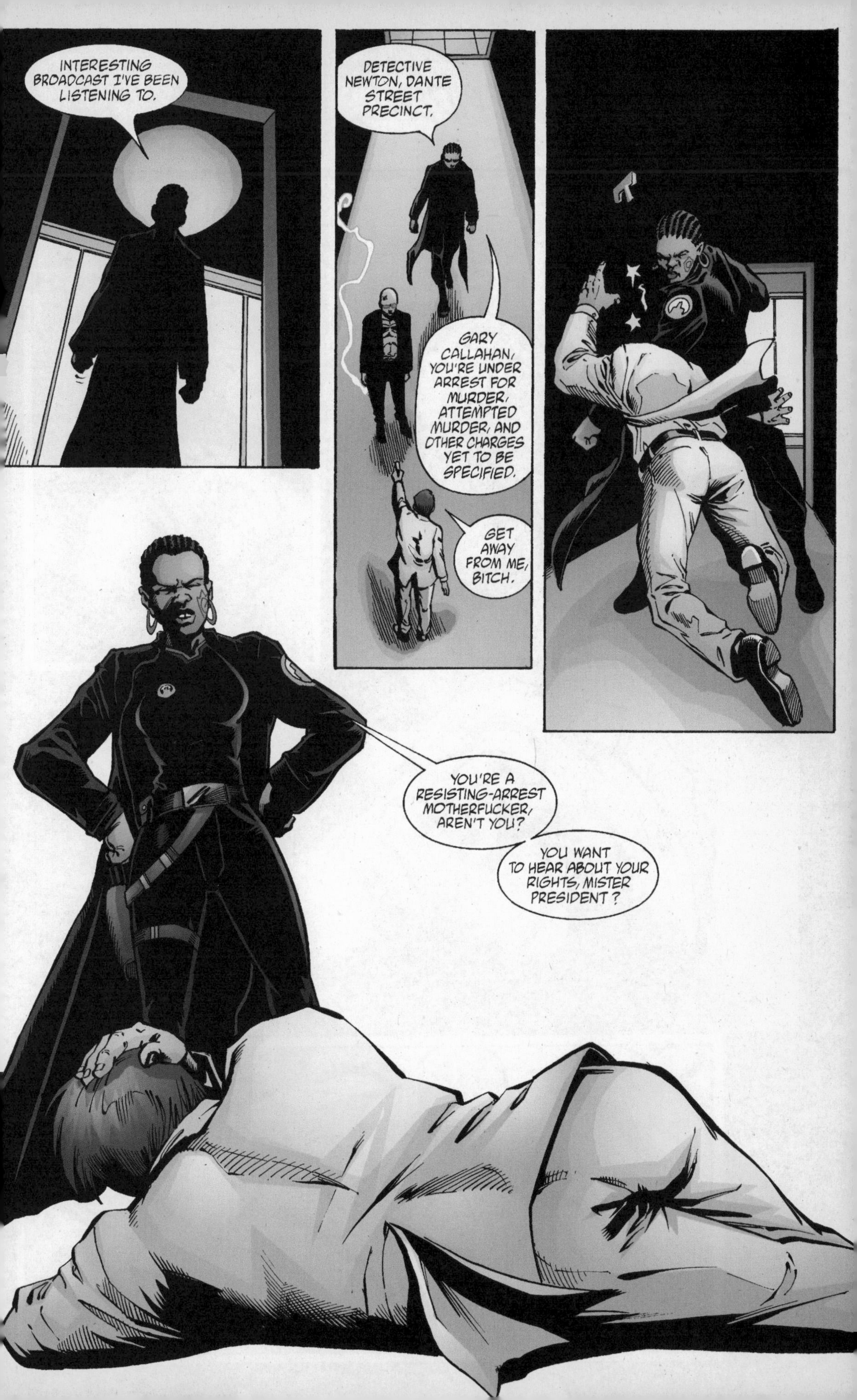
INTERESTING BROADCAST I'VE BEEN LISTENING TO.
DETECTIVE NEWTON, DANTE STREET PRECINCT.
GARY CALLAHAN, YOU'RE UNDER ARREST FOR MURDER, ATTEMPTED MURDER, AND OTHER CHARGES YET TO BE SPECIFIED.
GET AWAY FROM ME, BITCH.
YOU'RE A RESISTING-ARREST MOTHERFUCKER, AREN'T YOU?
YOU WANT TO HEAR ABOUT YOUR RIGHTS, MISTER PRESIDENT?

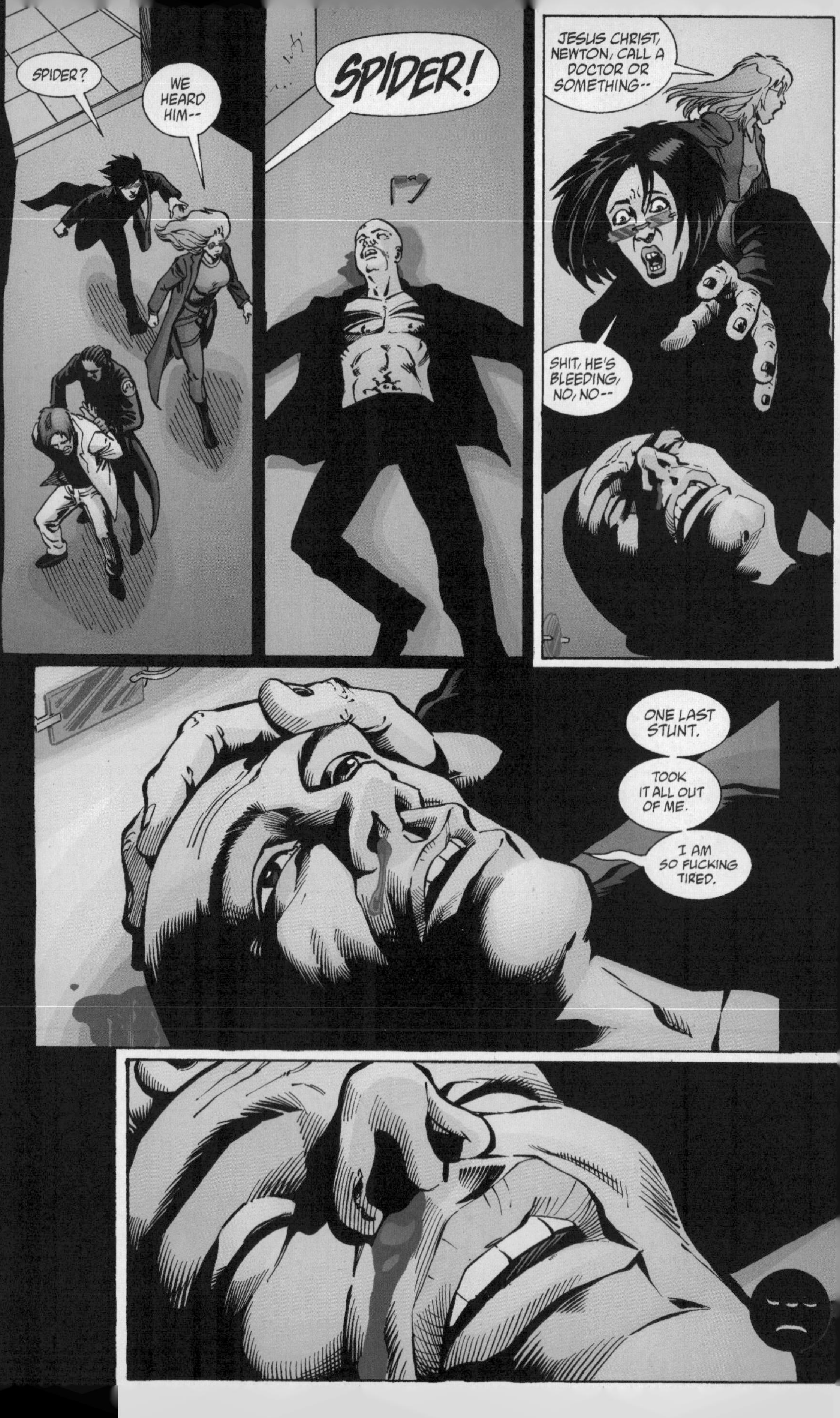
SPIDER?
WE HEARD HIM--
SPIDER!
JESUS CHRIST, NEWTON, CALL A DOCTOR OR SOMETHING--
SHIT, HE'S BLEEDING, NO, NO--
ONE LAST STUNT.
TOOK IT ALL OUT OF ME.
I AM SO FUCKING TIRED.

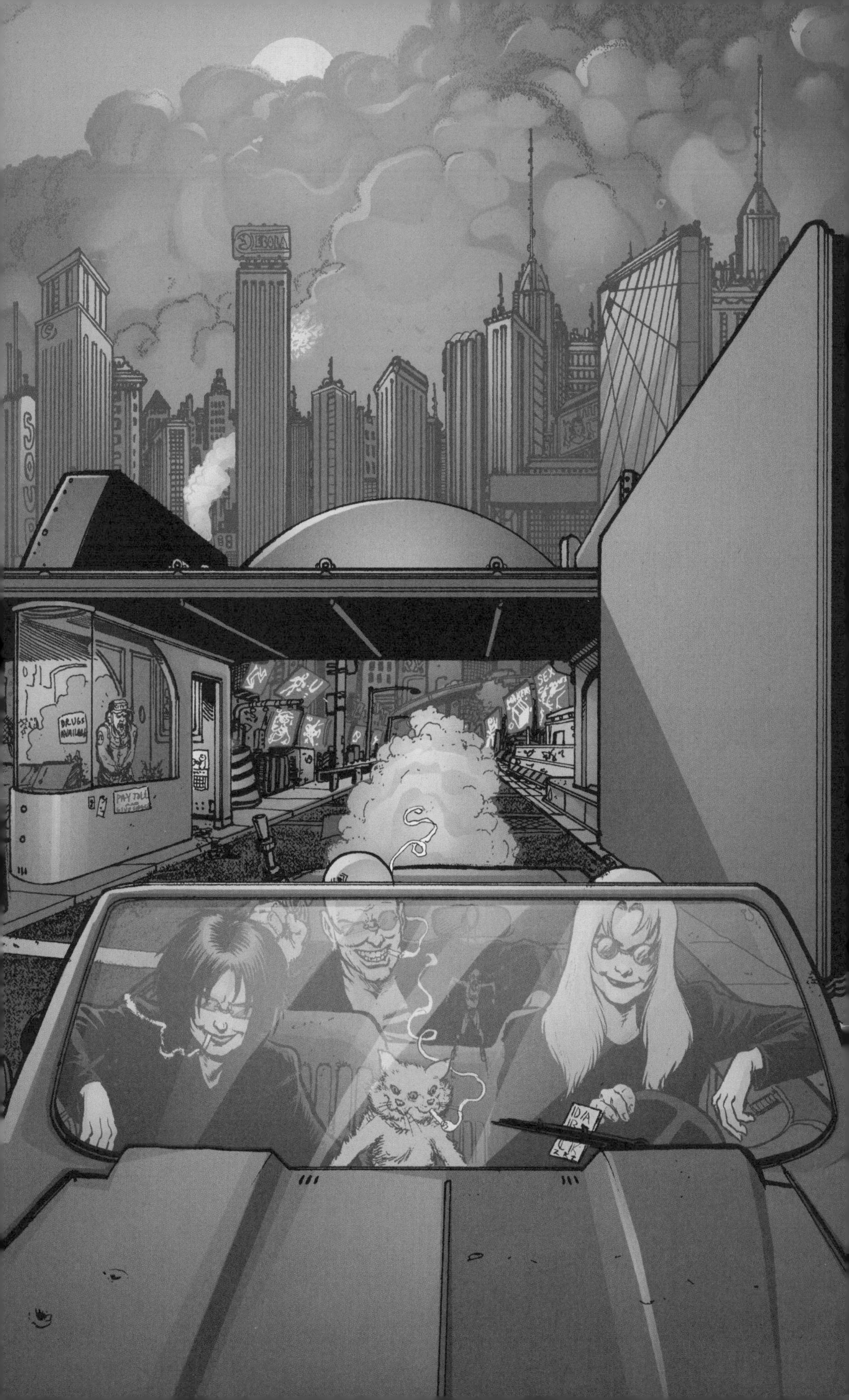
EBOLA
DRUGS AVAILABLE
PAY TOLL
SEX

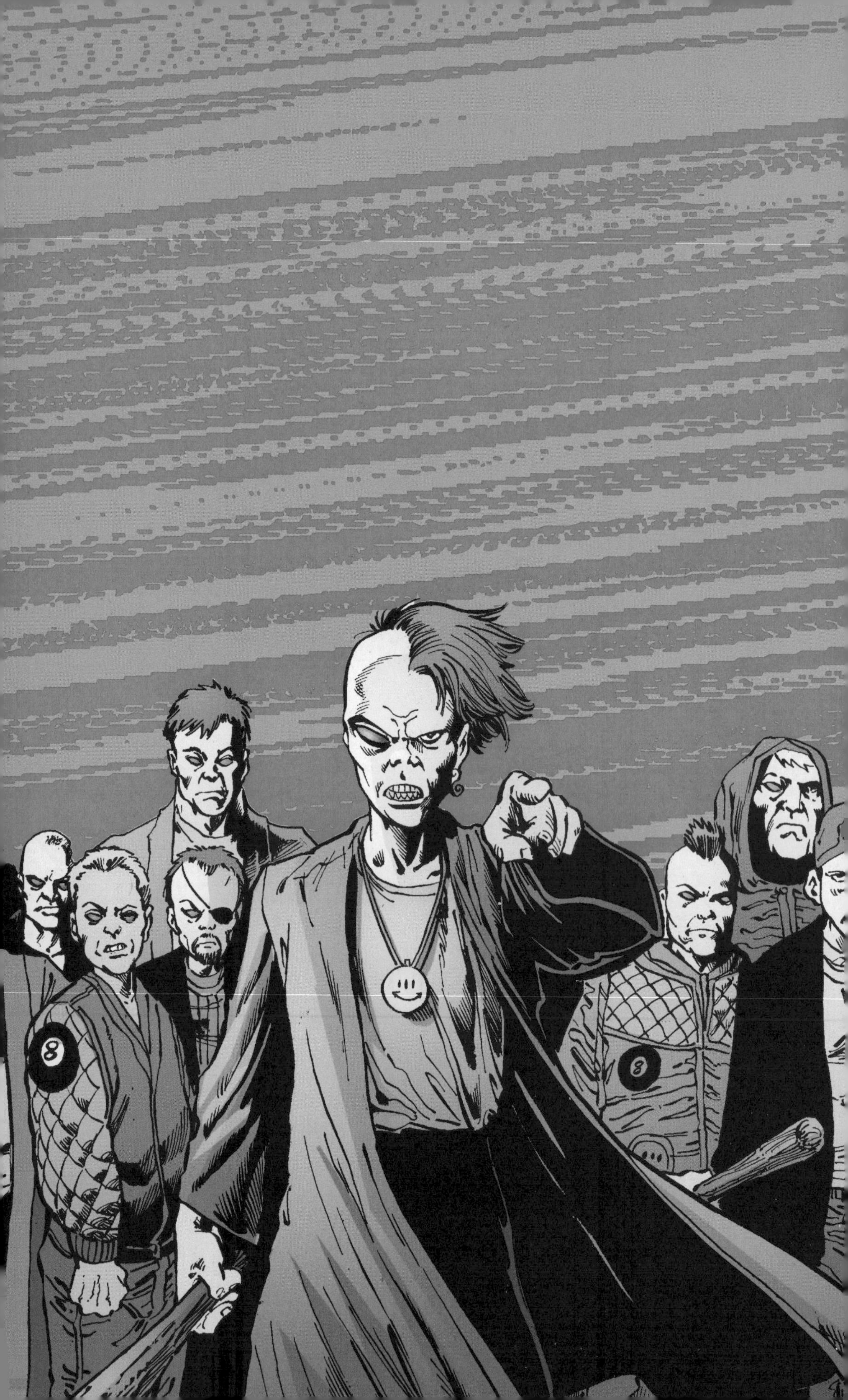

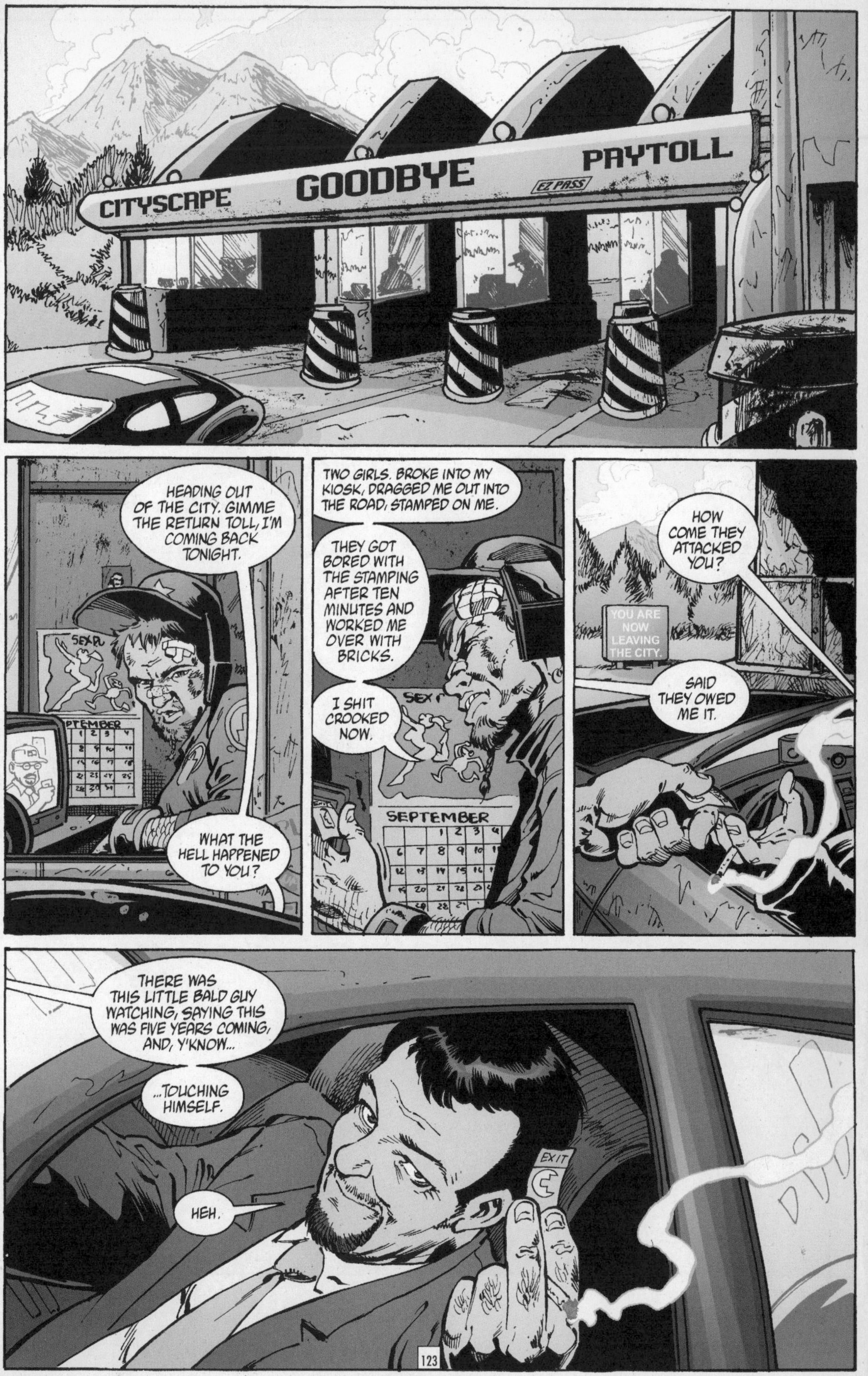
CITYSCAPE
GOODBYE
EZ PASS
PAYTOLL
HEADING OUT OF THE CITY. GIMME THE RETURN TOLL, I'M COMING BACK TONIGHT.
WHAT THE HELL HAPPENED TO YOU?
TWO GIRLS. BROKE INTO MY KIOSK, DRAGGED ME OUT INTO THE ROAD, STAMPED ON ME.
THEY GOT BORED WITH THE STAMPING AFTER TEN MINUTES AND WORKED ME OVER WITH BRICKS.
I SHIT CROOKED NOW.
SEPTEMBER
HOW COME THEY ATTACKED YOU?
YOU ARE NOW LEAVING THE CITY.
SAID THEY OWED ME IT.
THERE WAS THIS LITTLE BALD GUY WATCHING, SAYING THIS WAS FIVE YEARS COMING, AND, Y'KNOW...
...TOUCHING HIMSELF.
HEH.
EXIT

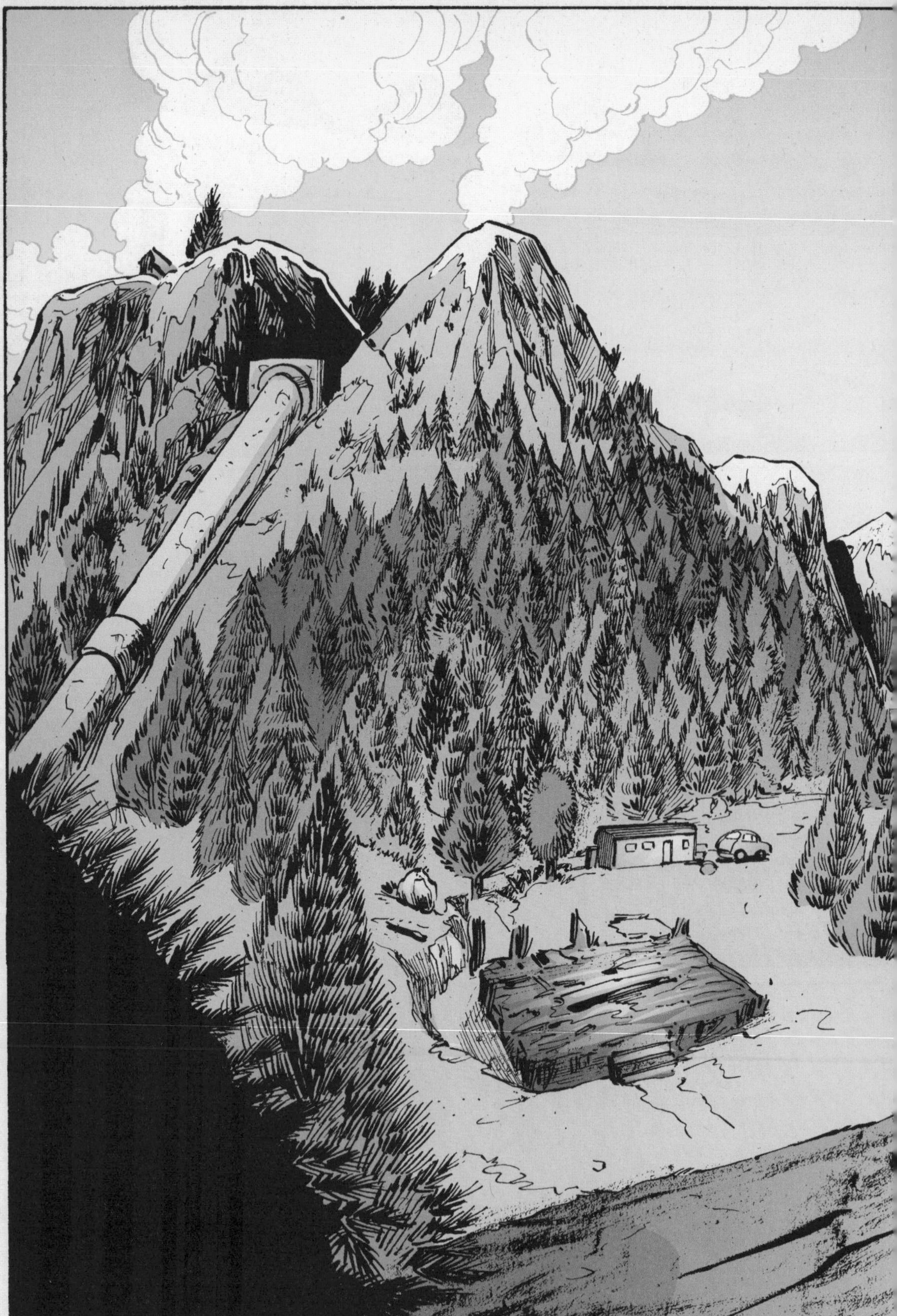

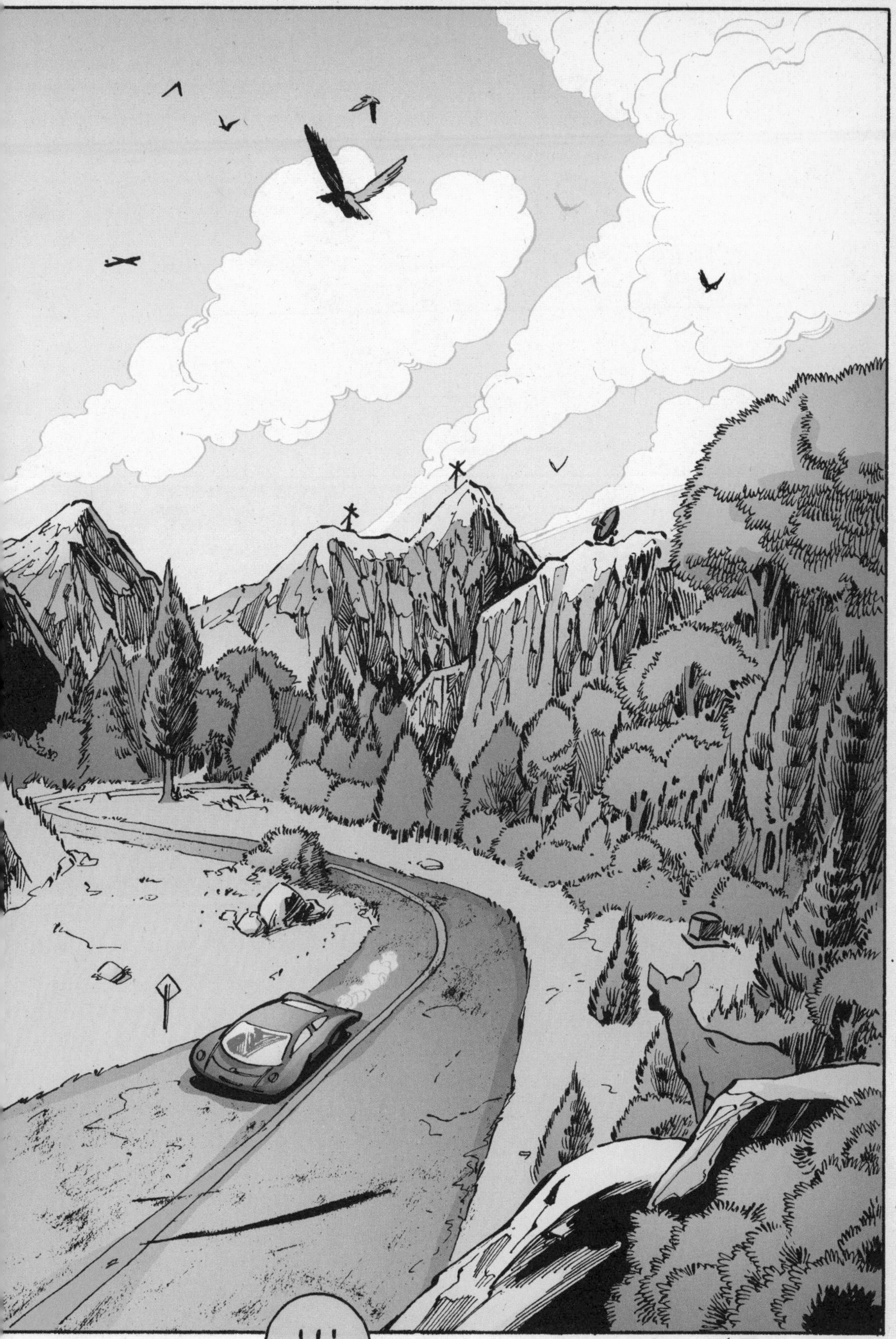

One more time

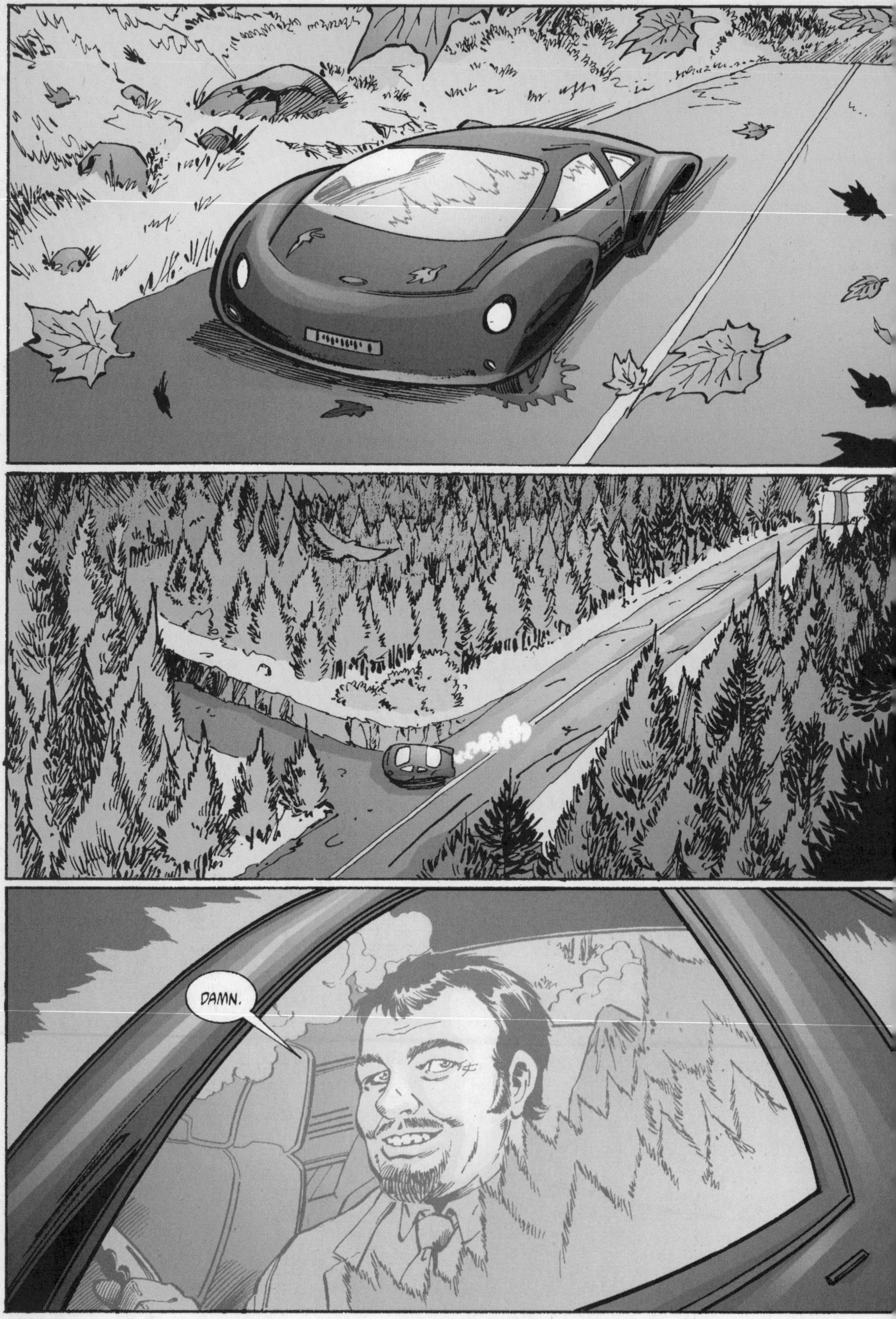
DAMN.

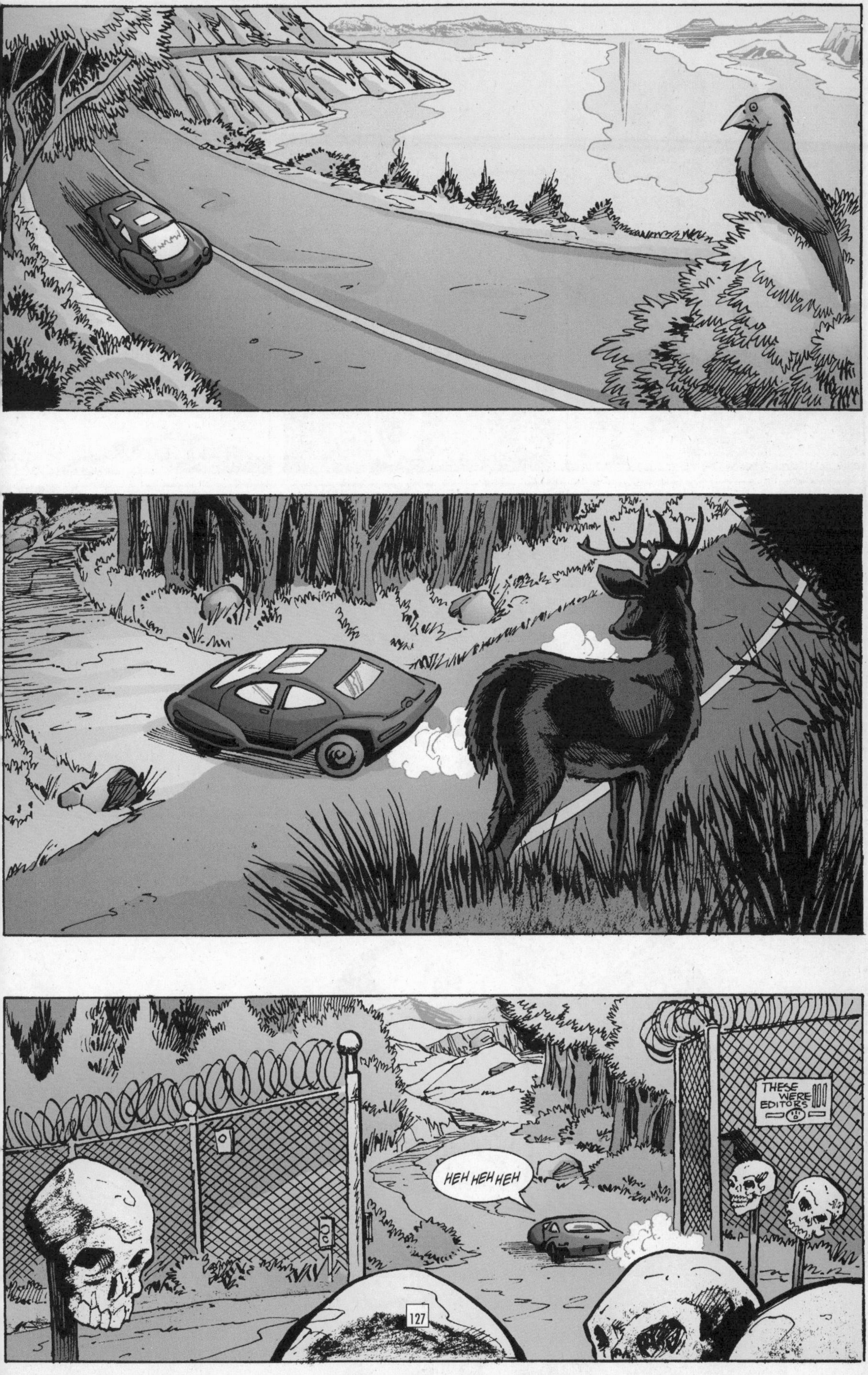
THESE WERE EDITORS
HEH HEH HEH

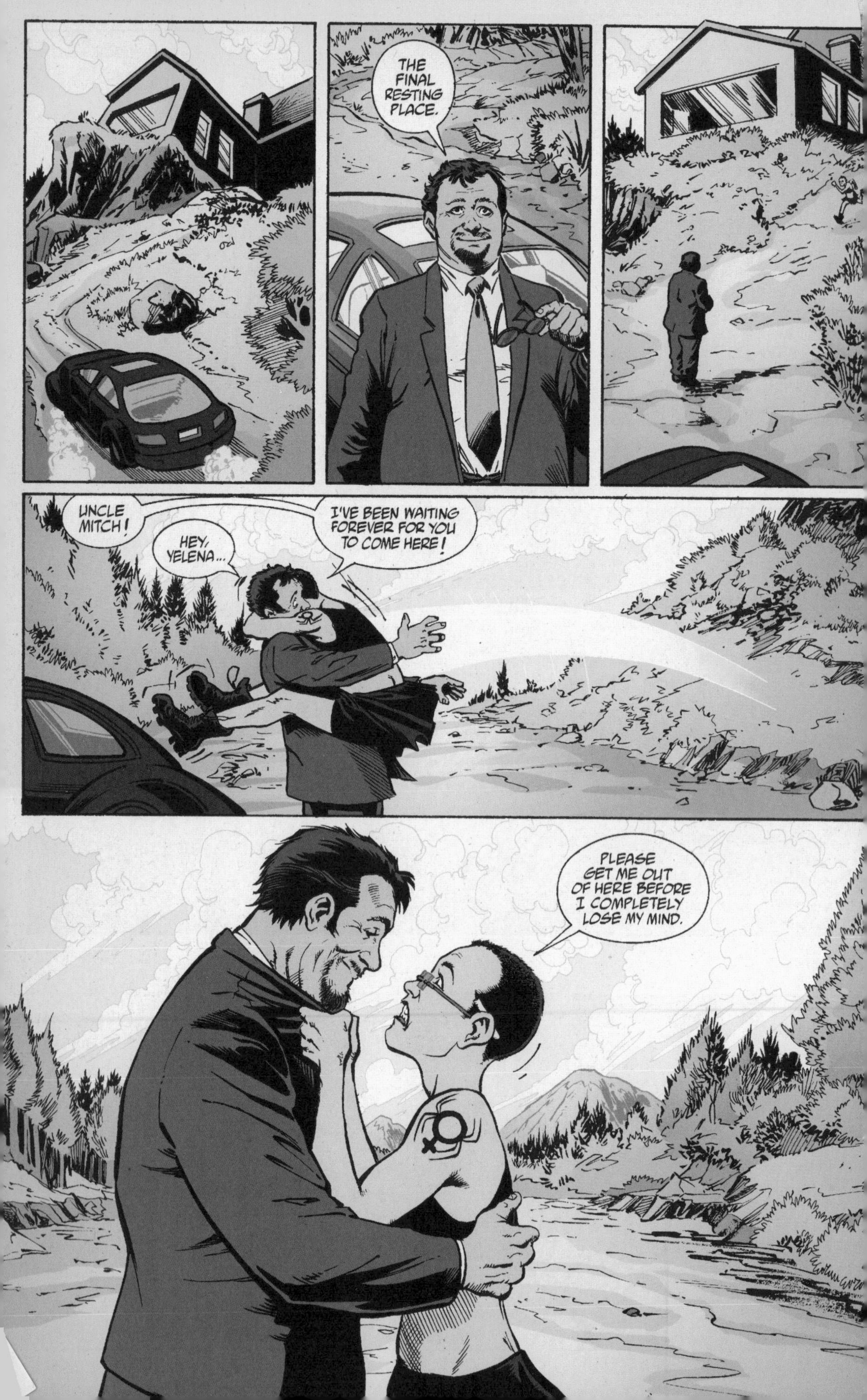
THE FINAL RESTING PLACE.
UNCLE MITCH!
HEY, YELENA...
I'VE BEEN WAITING FOREVER FOR YOU TO COME HERE!
PLEASE GET ME OUT OF HERE BEFORE I COMPLETELY LOSE MY MIND.

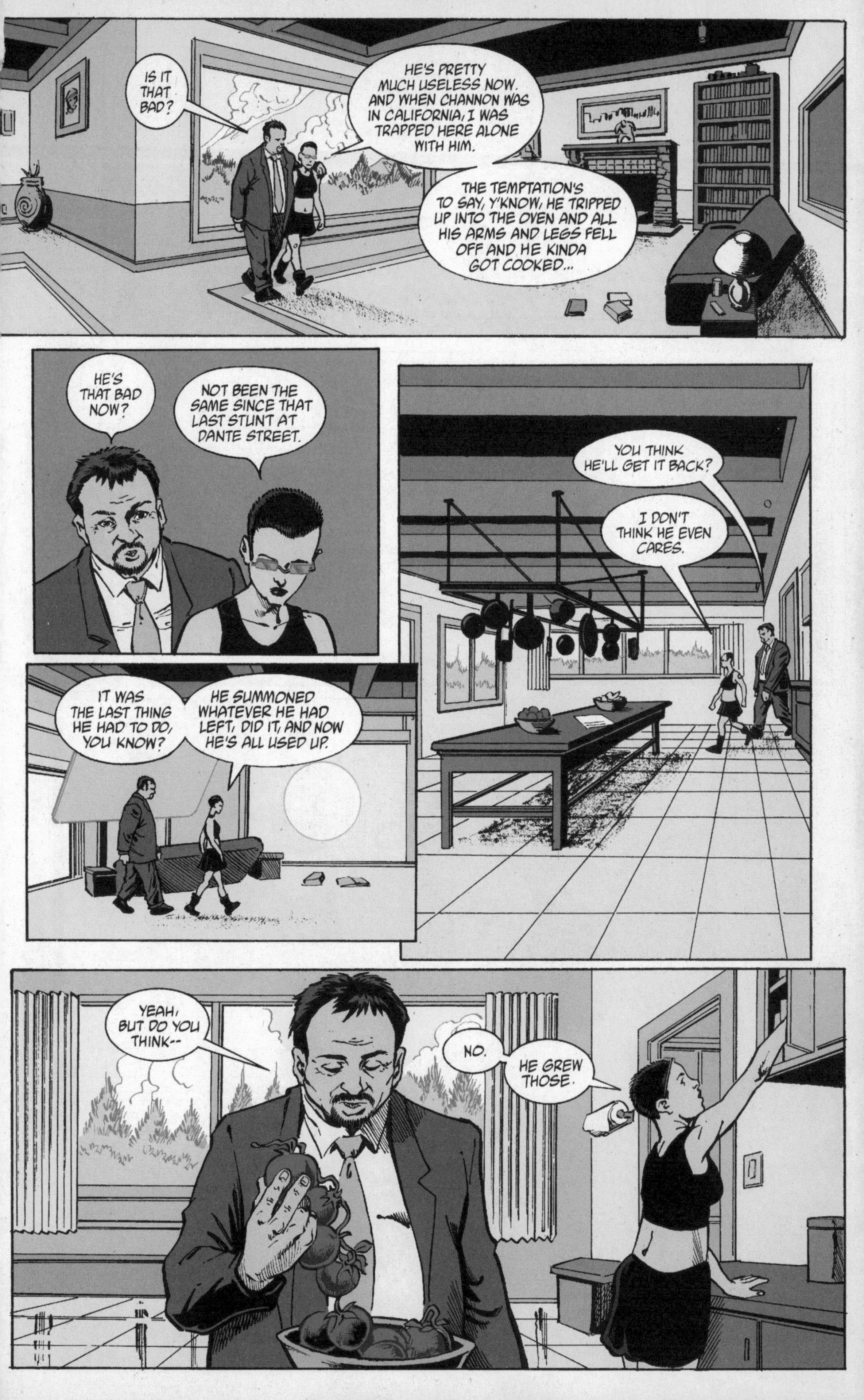
IS IT THAT BAD?
HE'S PRETTY MUCH USELESS NOW. AND WHEN CHANNON WAS IN CALIFORNIA, I WAS TRAPPED HERE ALONE WITH HIM.
THE TEMPTATION'S TO SAY, Y'KNOW, HE TRIPPED UP INTO THE OVEN AND ALL HIS ARMS AND LEGS FELL OFF AND HE KINDA GOT COOKED...
HE'S THAT BAD NOW?
NOT BEEN THE SAME SINCE THAT LAST STUNT AT DANTE STREET.
IT WAS THE LAST THING HE HAD TO DO, YOU KNOW?
HE SUMMONED WHATEVER HE HAD LEFT, DID IT, AND NOW HE'S ALL USED UP.
YOU THINK HE'LL GET IT BACK?
I DON'T THINK HE EVEN CARES.
YEAH, BUT DO YOU THINK--
NO.
HE GREW THOSE.

SHIT!

THEY'RE FINE.

BULL-SHIT.

HE'LL HAVE INFECTED THEM WITH SOME-THING.

LARRY YOUNG OPENS FIRST MOON PUB

ACTUALLY, THEY'RE PRETTY GOOD. HI, MITCH.

HELLO, CHANNON. HOW WAS THE WEST COAST?

WEIRD.

I'M GOING TO FINISH PACKING. CITY AND EIGHT WEEK SPECIAL COLUMN, HERE I COME.

the Wood— STEVE CHUNG SET FREE! MASSIVE GRAFFITI CAMPAIGN SUCEEDS

JUST LEAVE YOUR STUFF BY THE DOOR, I'LL TAKE IT TO THE CAR.

I GET WORRIED ABOUT HIM WHEN I'M NOT AROUND.

I THOUGHT YOU COULDN'T WAIT TO GO.

HE NEEDS ME AROUND.

'KAY, CHANNON, I ALREADY SAID GOODBYE TO HIM. WATCH HIM, ALL RIGHT?

DON'T ASK.

HE JUST DOES, ALL RIGHT?

130

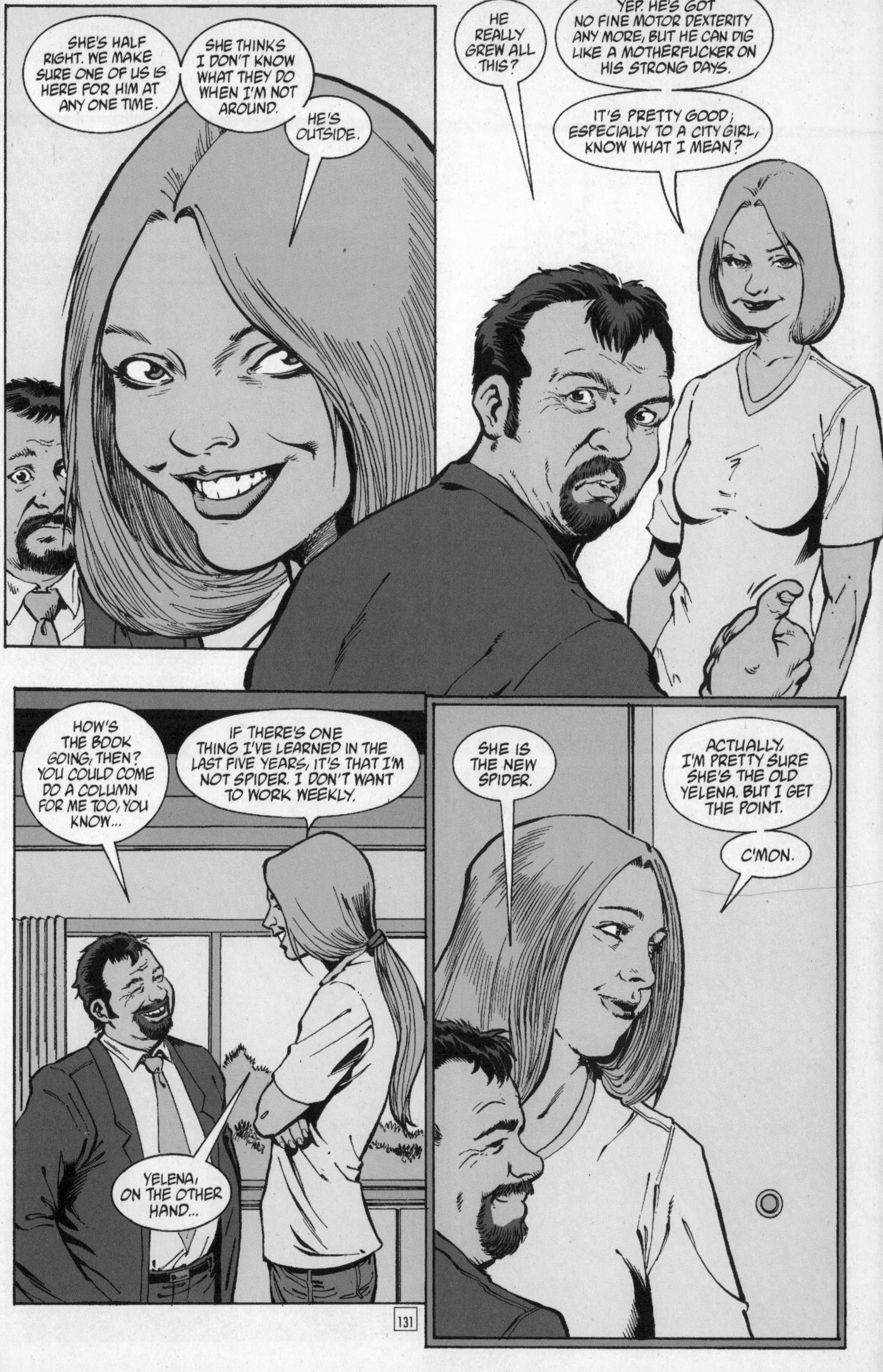
SHE'S HALF RIGHT. WE MAKE SURE ONE OF US IS HERE FOR HIM AT ANY ONE TIME.
SHE THINKS I DON'T KNOW WHAT THEY DO WHEN I'M NOT AROUND.
HE'S OUTSIDE.
HE REALLY GREW ALL THIS?
YEP. HE'S GOT NO FINE MOTOR DEXTERITY ANY MORE, BUT HE CAN DIG LIKE A MOTHERFUCKER ON HIS STRONG DAYS.
IT'S PRETTY GOOD; ESPECIALLY TO A CITY GIRL, KNOW WHAT I MEAN?
HOW'S THE BOOK GOING, THEN? YOU COULD COME DO A COLUMN FOR ME TOO, YOU KNOW...
IF THERE'S ONE THING I'VE LEARNED IN THE LAST FIVE YEARS, IT'S THAT I'M NOT SPIDER. I DON'T WANT TO WORK WEEKLY.
YELENA, ON THE OTHER HAND...
SHE IS THE NEW SPIDER.
ACTUALLY, I'M PRETTY SURE SHE'S THE OLD YELENA. BUT I GET THE POINT.
C'MON.

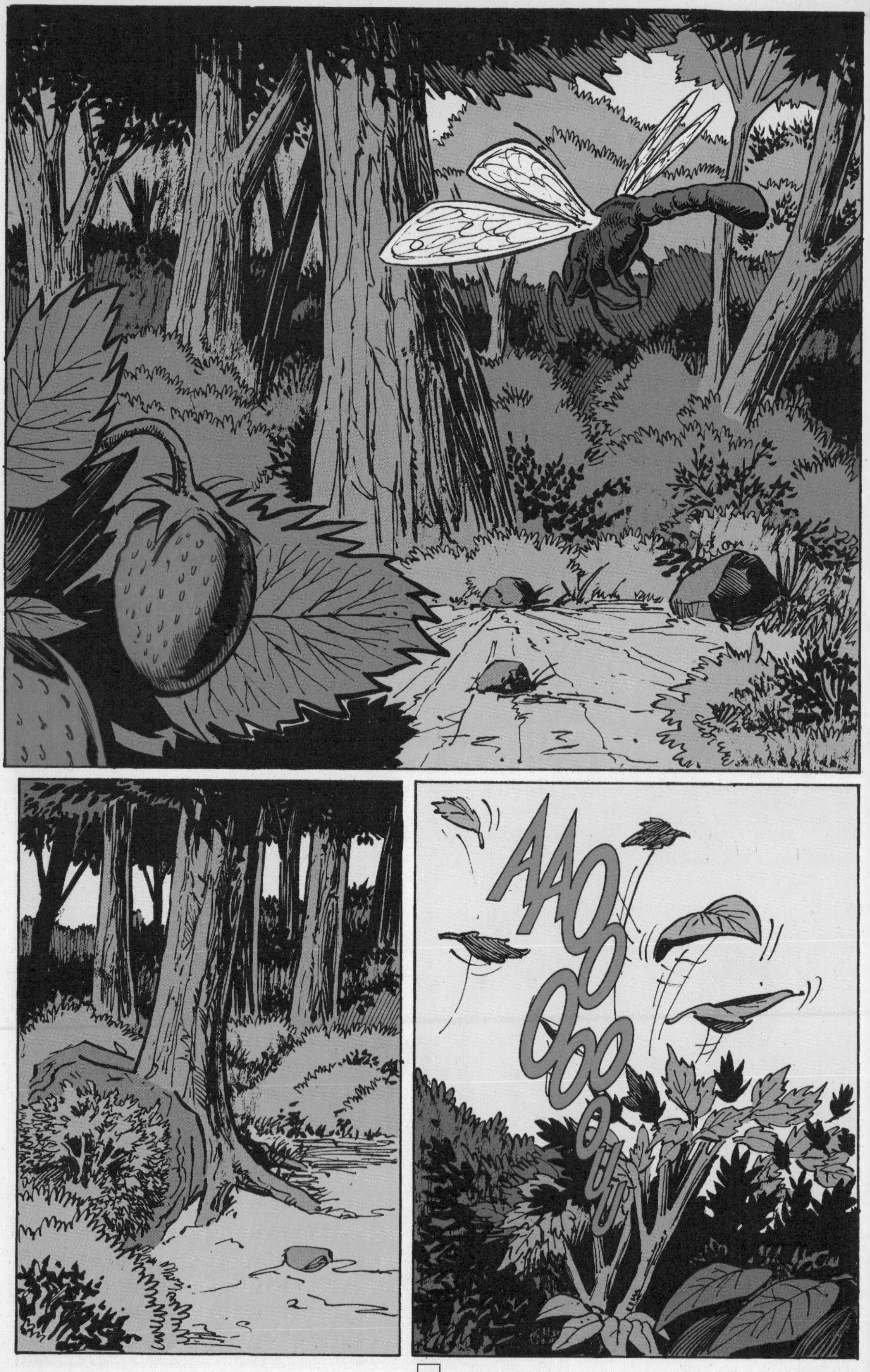
AAOOOOOOUU

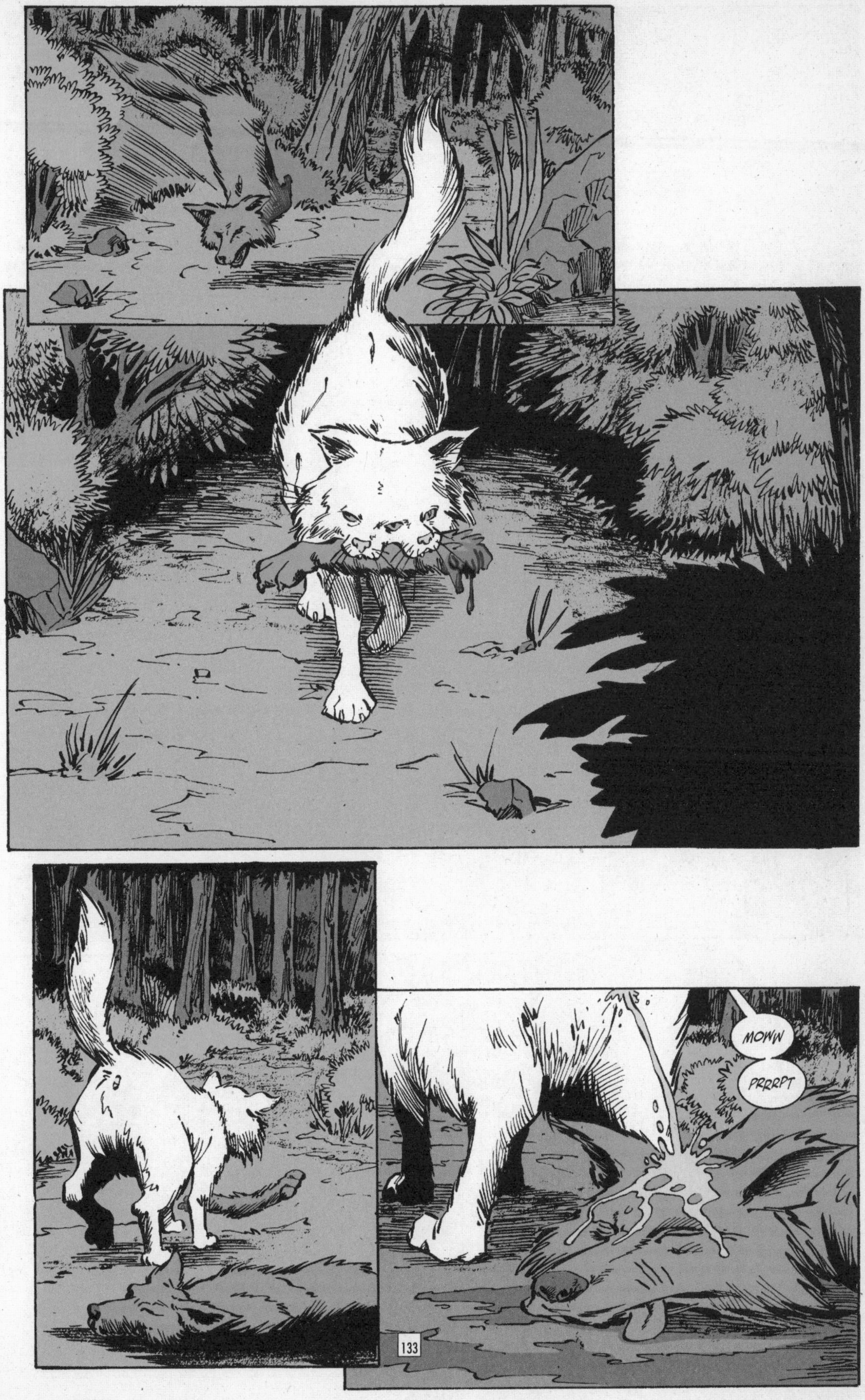
MOWW
PRRRPT

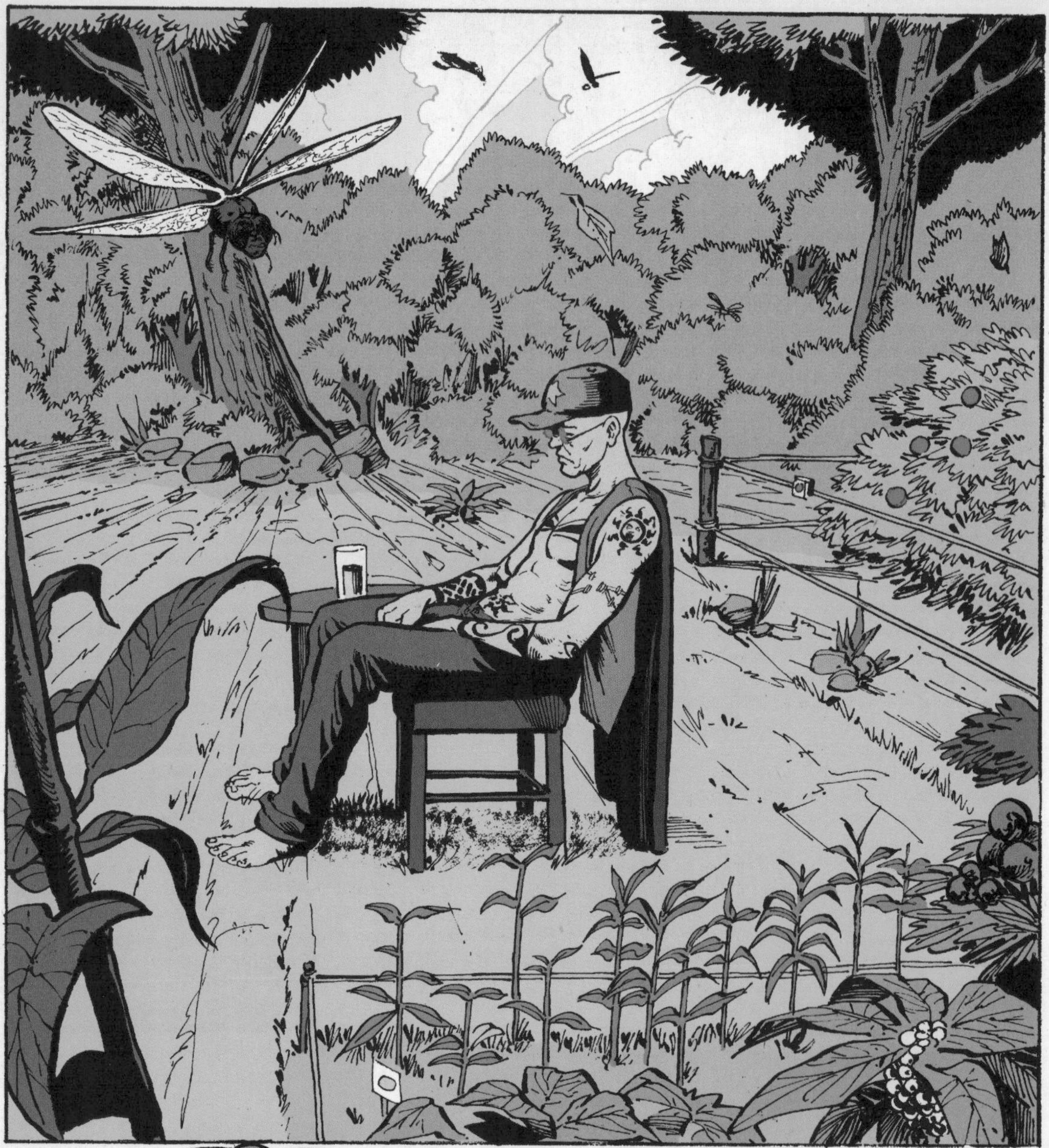

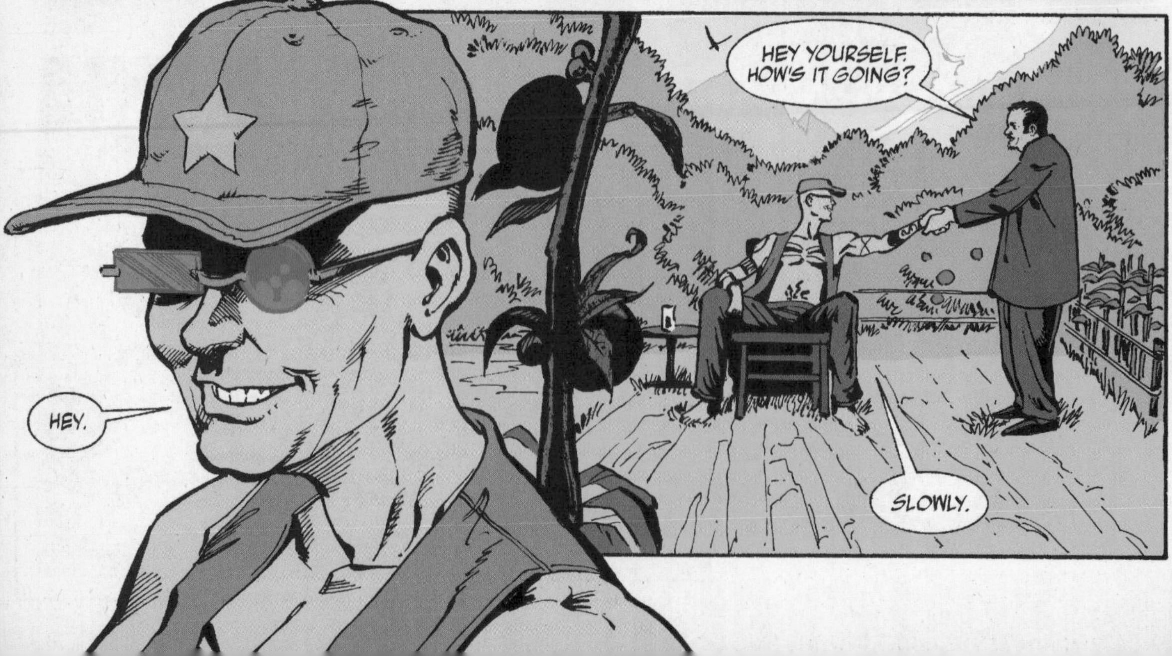
HEY.
HEY YOURSELF. HOW'S IT GOING?
SLOWLY.

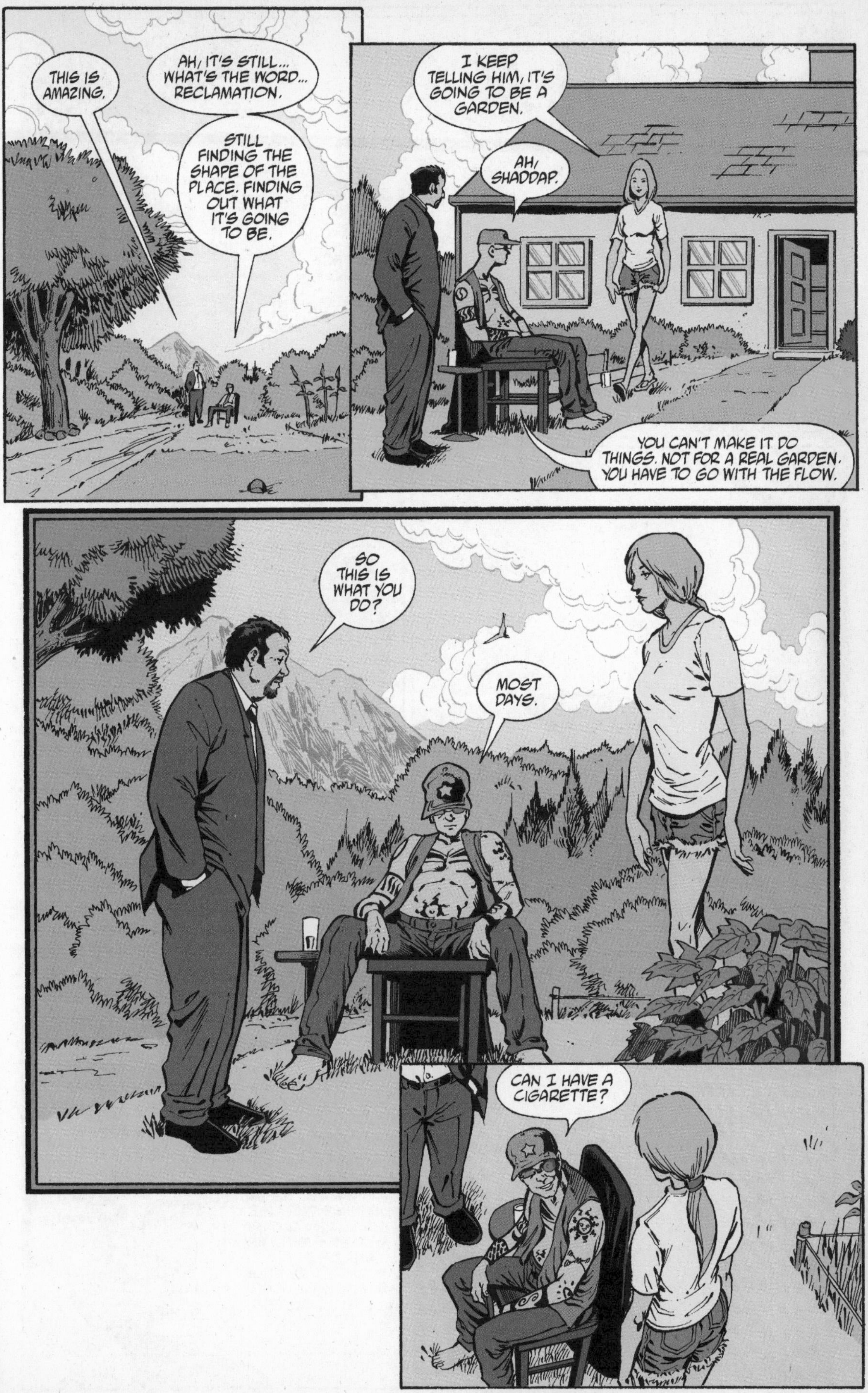
THIS IS AMAZING.
AH, IT'S STILL... WHAT'S THE WORD... RECLAMATION.
STILL FINDING THE SHAPE OF THE PLACE. FINDING OUT WHAT IT'S GOING TO BE.
I KEEP TELLING HIM, IT'S GOING TO BE A GARDEN.
AH, SHADDAP.
YOU CAN'T MAKE IT DO THINGS. NOT FOR A REAL GARDEN. YOU HAVE TO GO WITH THE FLOW.
SO THIS IS WHAT YOU DO?
MOST DAYS.
CAN I HAVE A CIGARETTE?

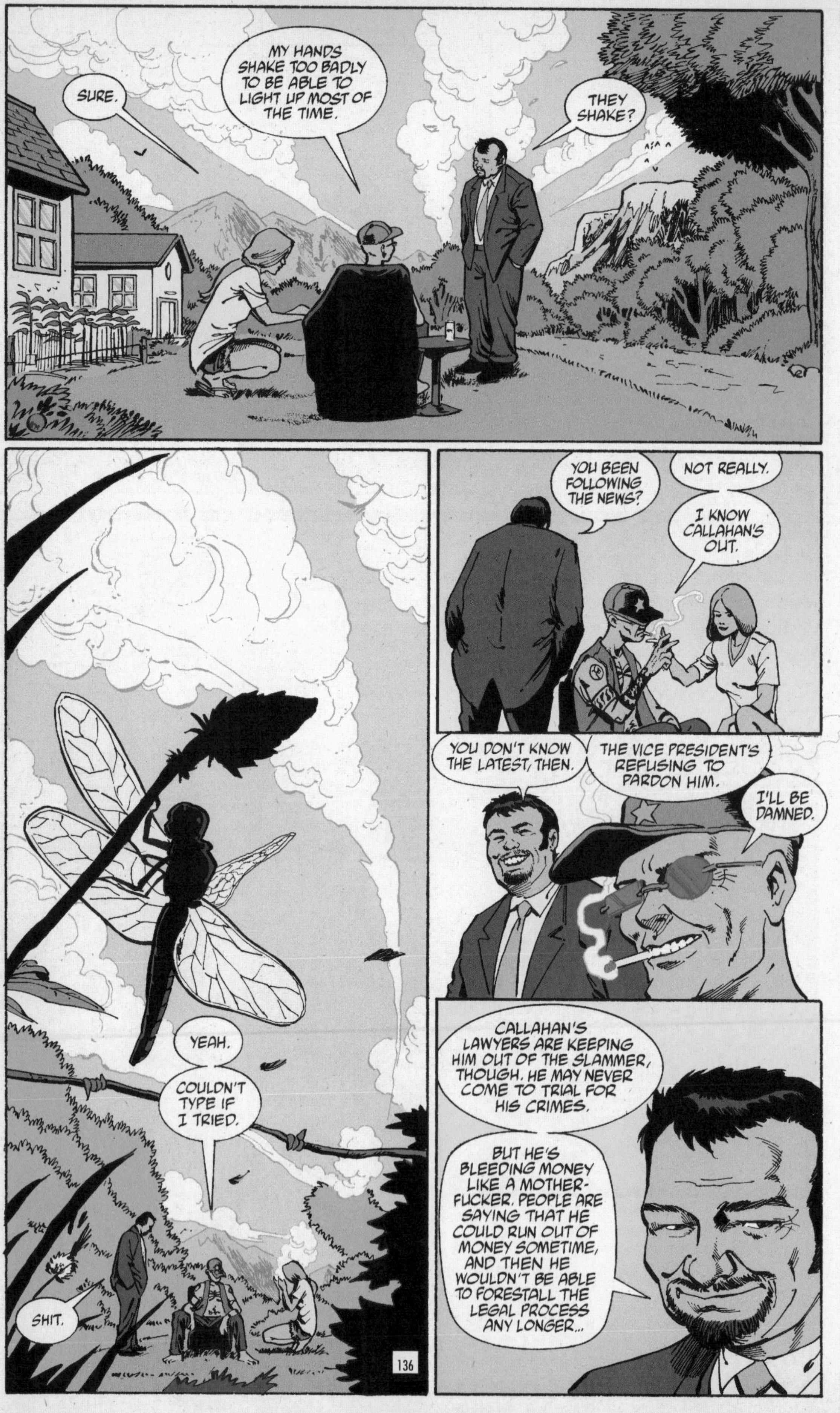
SURE.
MY HANDS SHAKE TOO BADLY TO BE ABLE TO LIGHT UP MOST OF THE TIME.
THEY SHAKE?
YEAH.
COULDN'T TYPE IF I TRIED.
SHIT.
YOU BEEN FOLLOWING THE NEWS?
NOT REALLY.
I KNOW CALLAHAN'S OUT.
YOU DON'T KNOW THE LATEST, THEN.
THE VICE PRESIDENT'S REFUSING TO PARDON HIM.
I'LL BE DAMNED.
CALLAHAN'S LAWYERS ARE KEEPING HIM OUT OF THE SLAMMER, THOUGH. HE MAY NEVER COME TO TRIAL FOR HIS CRIMES.
BUT HE'S BLEEDING MONEY LIKE A MOTHER-FUCKER. PEOPLE ARE SAYING THAT HE COULD RUN OUT OF MONEY SOMETIME, AND THEN HE WOULDN'T BE ABLE TO FORESTALL THE LEGAL PROCESS ANY LONGER...

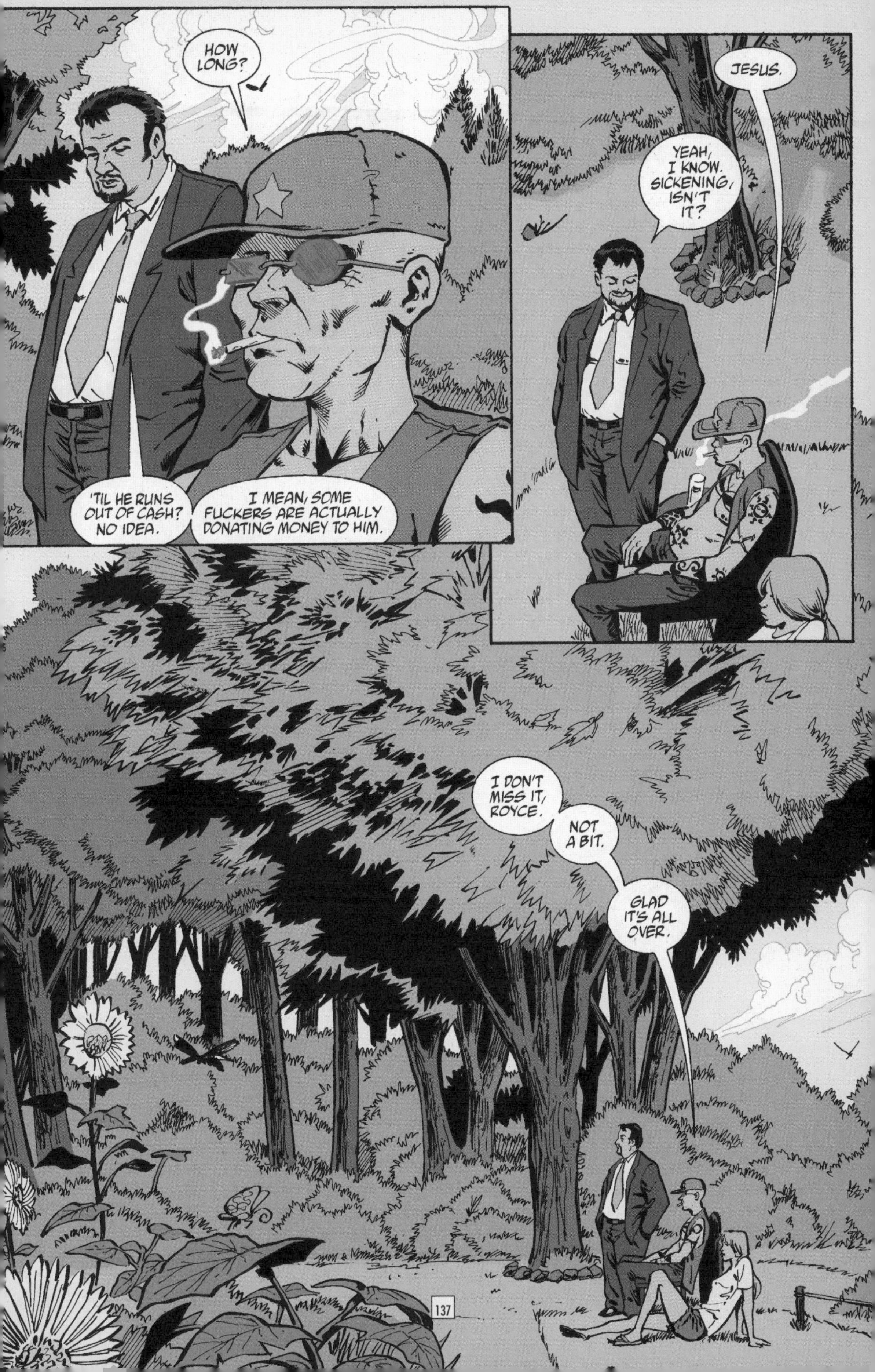
HOW LONG?
'TIL HE RUNS OUT OF CASH? NO IDEA.
I MEAN, SOME FUCKERS ARE ACTUALLY DONATING MONEY TO HIM.
JESUS.
YEAH, I KNOW. SICKENING, ISN'T IT?
I DON'T MISS IT, ROYCE.
NOT A BIT.
GLAD IT'S ALL OVER.

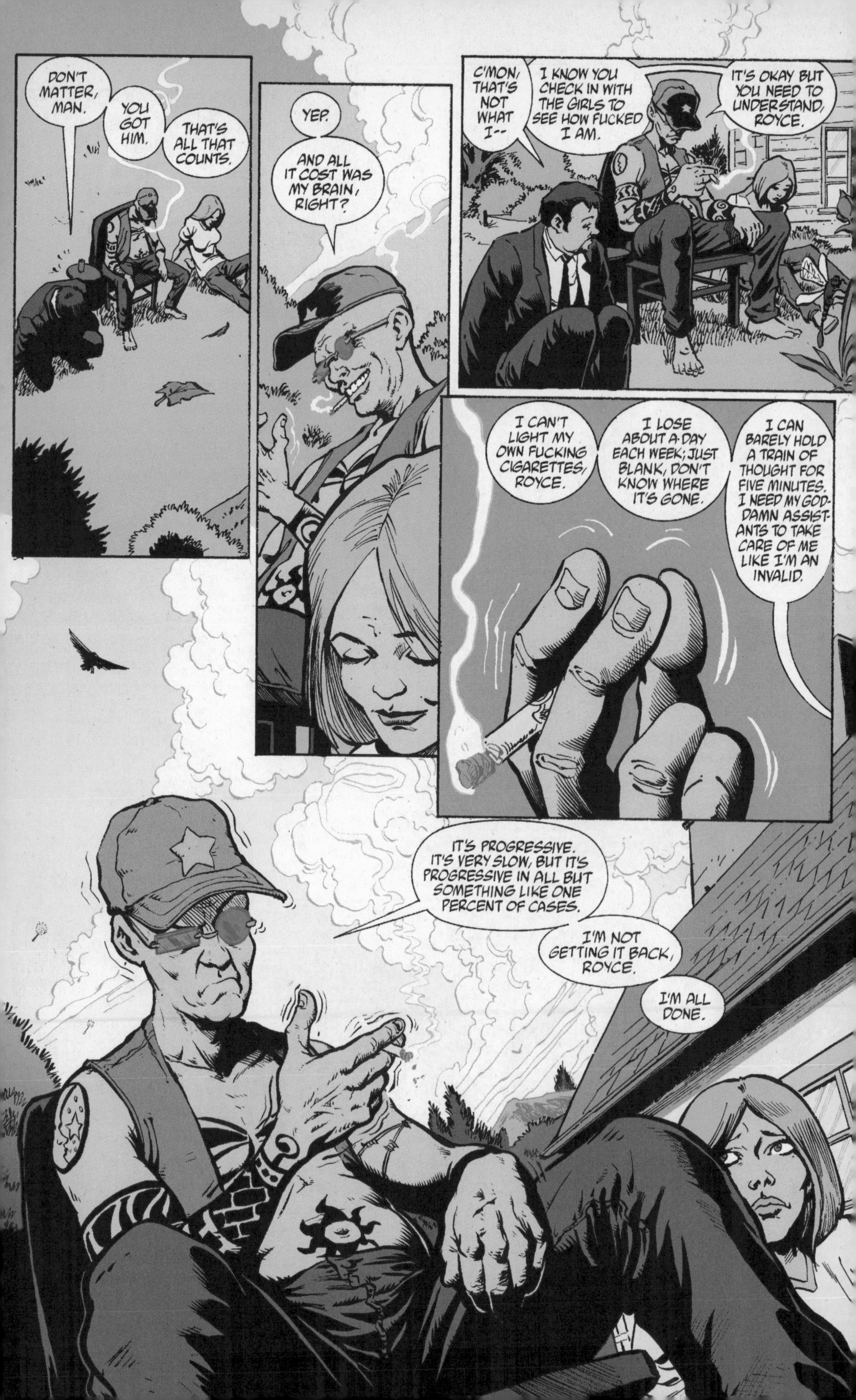
DON'T MATTER, MAN.
YOU GOT HIM.
THAT'S ALL THAT COUNTS.
YEP.
AND ALL IT COST WAS MY BRAIN, RIGHT?
C'MON, THAT'S NOT WHAT I--
I KNOW YOU CHECK IN WITH THE GIRLS TO SEE HOW FUCKED I AM.
IT'S OKAY BUT YOU NEED TO UNDERSTAND, ROYCE.
I CAN'T LIGHT MY OWN FUCKING CIGARETTES, ROYCE.
I LOSE ABOUT A DAY EACH WEEK; JUST BLANK, DON'T KNOW WHERE IT'S GONE.
I CAN BARELY HOLD A TRAIN OF THOUGHT FOR FIVE MINUTES. I NEED MY GOD-DAMN ASSISTANTS TO TAKE CARE OF ME LIKE I'M AN INVALID.
IT'S PROGRESSIVE. IT'S VERY SLOW, BUT IT'S PROGRESSIVE IN ALL BUT SOMETHING LIKE ONE PERCENT OF CASES.
I'M NOT GETTING IT BACK, ROYCE.
I'M ALL DONE.

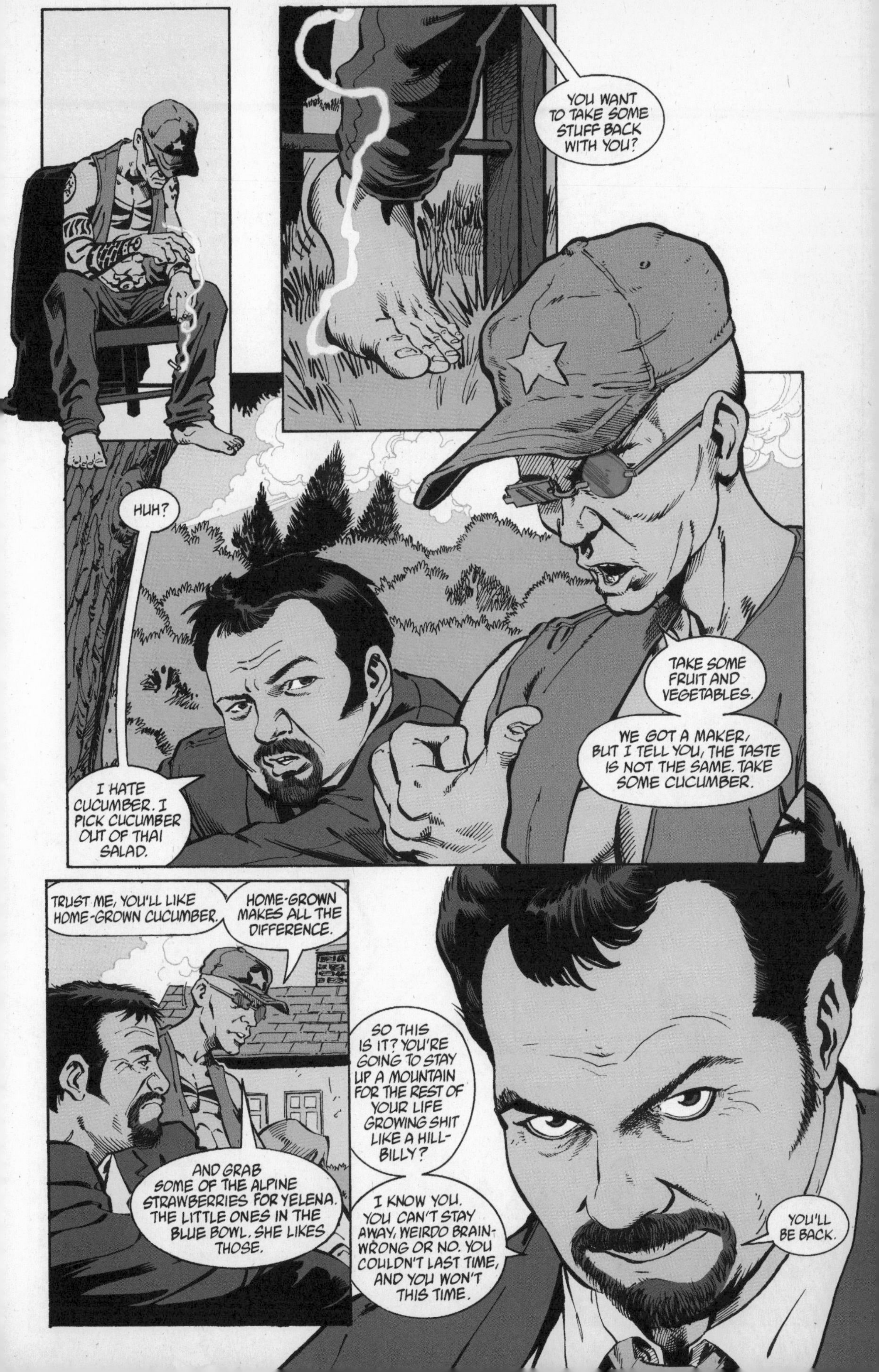
YOU WANT TO TAKE SOME STUFF BACK WITH YOU?
HUH?
TAKE SOME FRUIT AND VEGETABLES.
WE GOT A MAKER, BUT I TELL YOU, THE TASTE IS NOT THE SAME. TAKE SOME CUCUMBER.
I HATE CUCUMBER. I PICK CUCUMBER OUT OF THAI SALAD.
TRUST ME, YOU'LL LIKE HOME-GROWN CUCUMBER.
HOME-GROWN MAKES ALL THE DIFFERENCE.
SO THIS IS IT? YOU'RE GOING TO STAY UP A MOUNTAIN FOR THE REST OF YOUR LIFE GROWING SHIT LIKE A HILL-BILLY?
AND GRAB SOME OF THE ALPINE STRAWBERRIES FOR YELENA. THE LITTLE ONES IN THE BLUE BOWL. SHE LIKES THOSE.
I KNOW YOU. YOU CAN'T STAY AWAY, WEIRDO BRAIN-WRONG OR NO. YOU COULDN'T LAST TIME, AND YOU WON'T THIS TIME.
YOU'LL BE BACK.

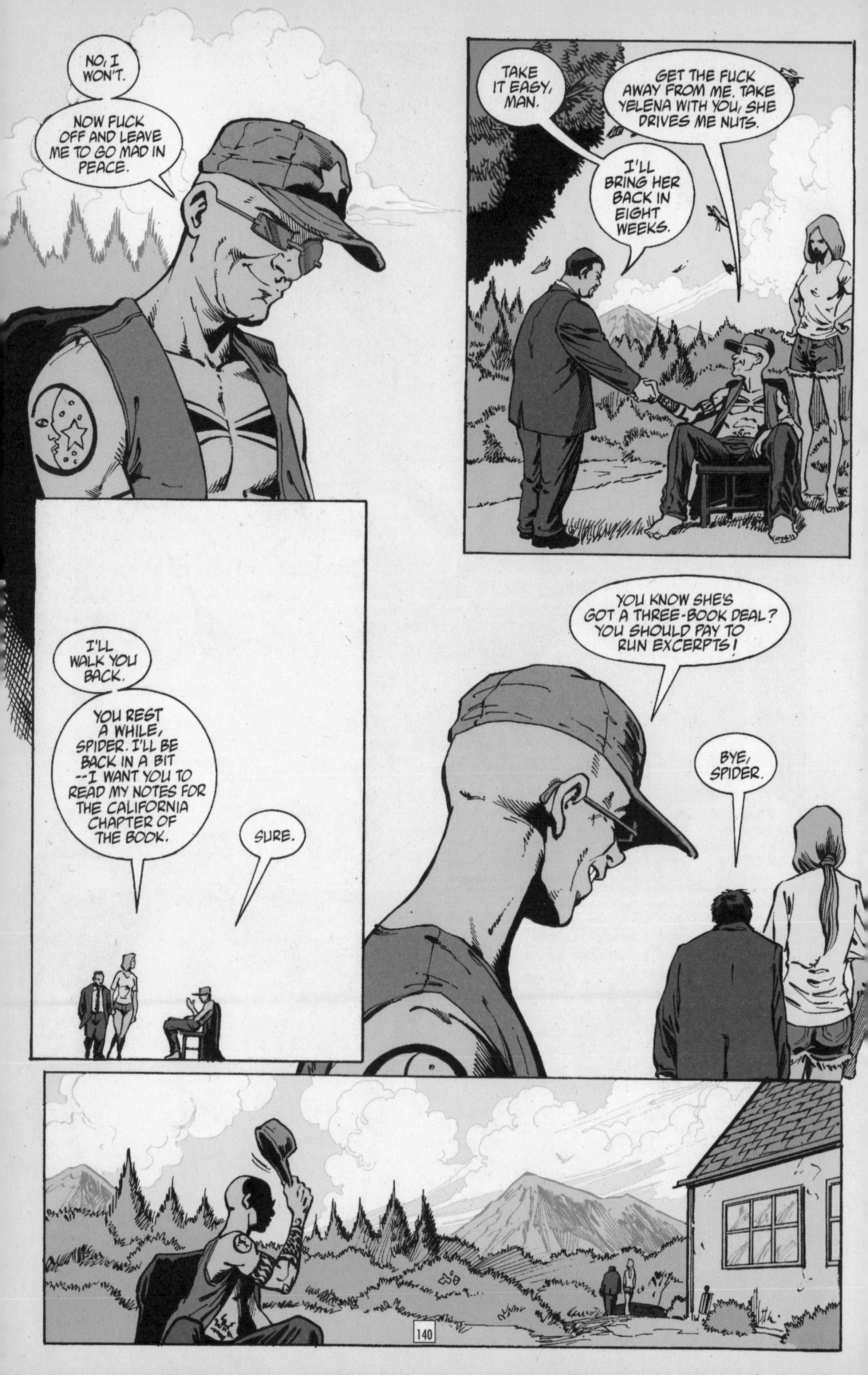
NO, I WON'T.
NOW FUCK OFF AND LEAVE ME TO GO MAD IN PEACE.
TAKE IT EASY, MAN.
GET THE FUCK AWAY FROM ME. TAKE YELENA WITH YOU, SHE DRIVES ME NUTS.
I'LL BRING HER BACK IN EIGHT WEEKS.
I'LL WALK YOU BACK.
YOU REST A WHILE, SPIDER. I'LL BE BACK IN A BIT --I WANT YOU TO READ MY NOTES FOR THE CALIFORNIA CHAPTER OF THE BOOK.
SURE.
YOU KNOW SHE'S GOT A THREE-BOOK DEAL? YOU SHOULD PAY TO RUN EXCERPTS!
BYE, SPIDER.

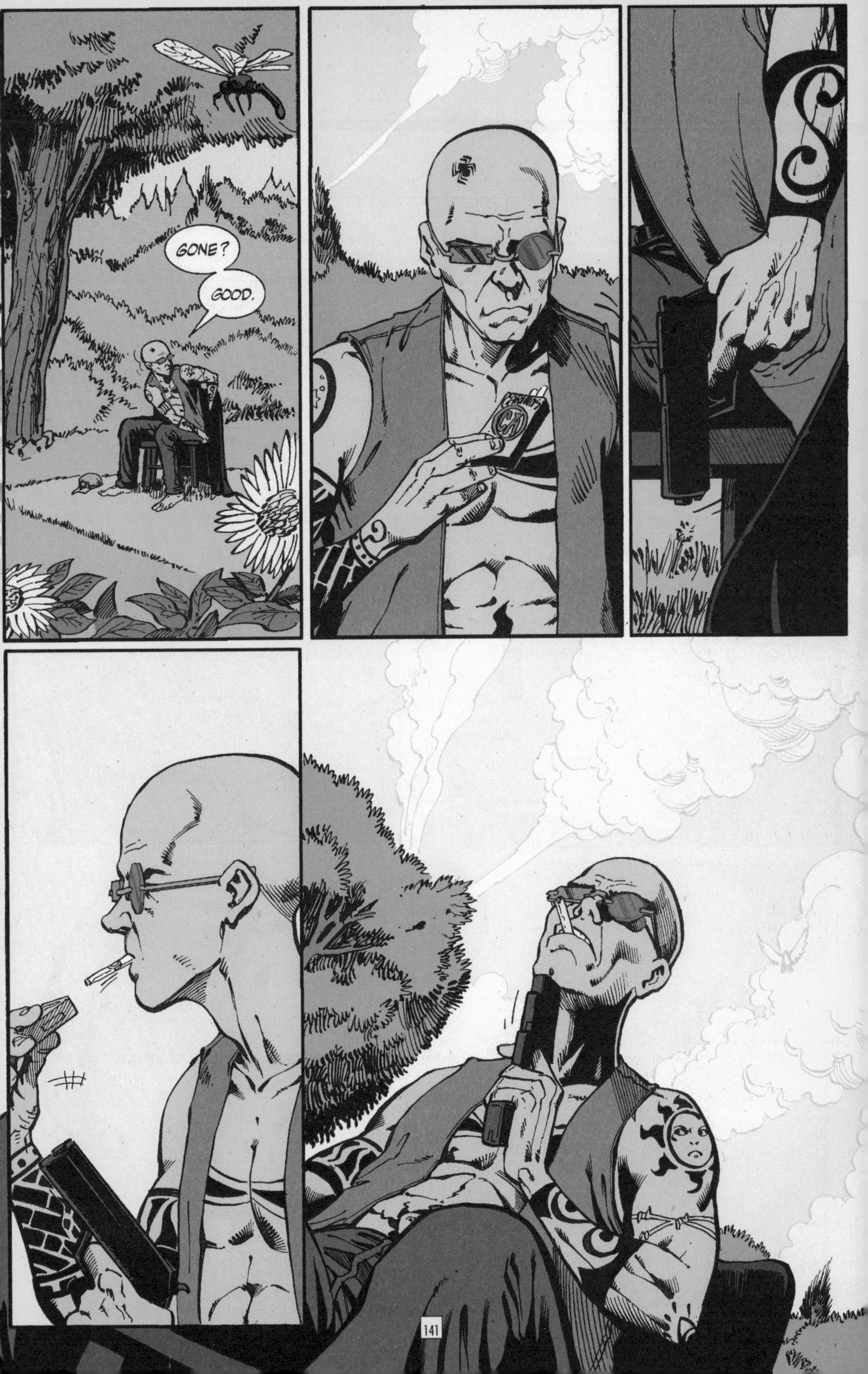
GONE?
GOOD.

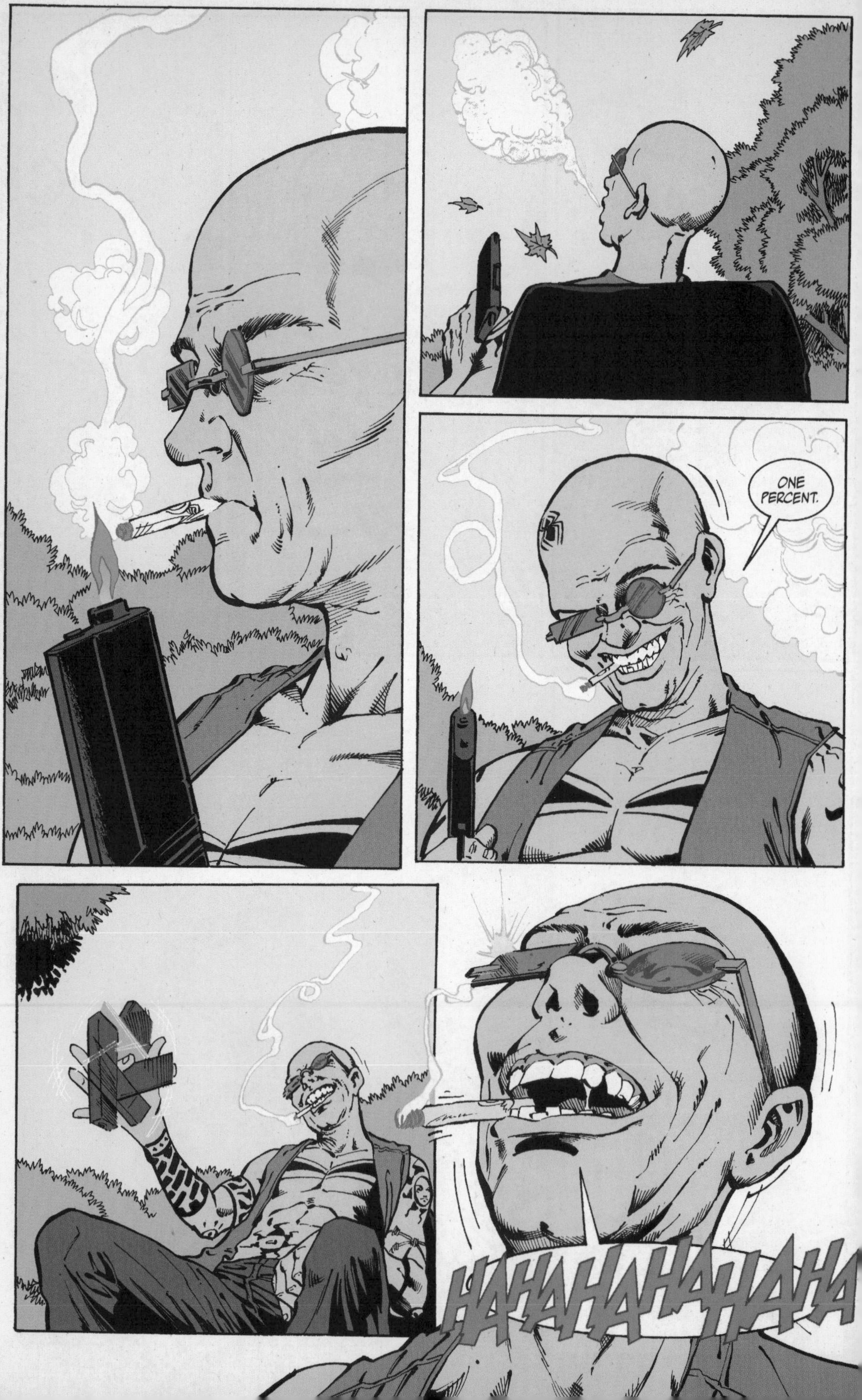
ONE PERCENT.
HAHAHAHAHAHAHA

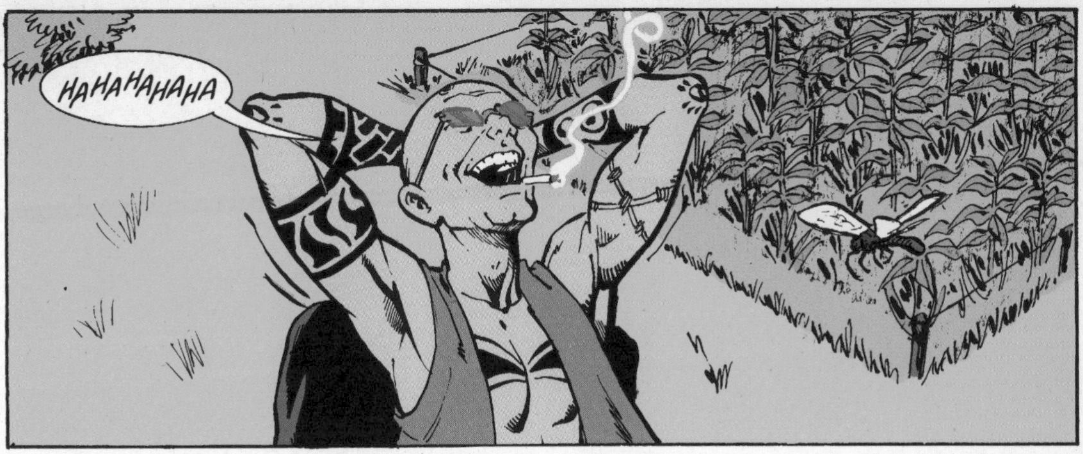
HAHAHAHAHA

EDITED BY **STUART MOORE, CLIFF WU CHIANG, AXEL ALONSO, TONY BEDARD, HEIDI MacDONALD** AND, FINALLY, **ZACHARY RAU**

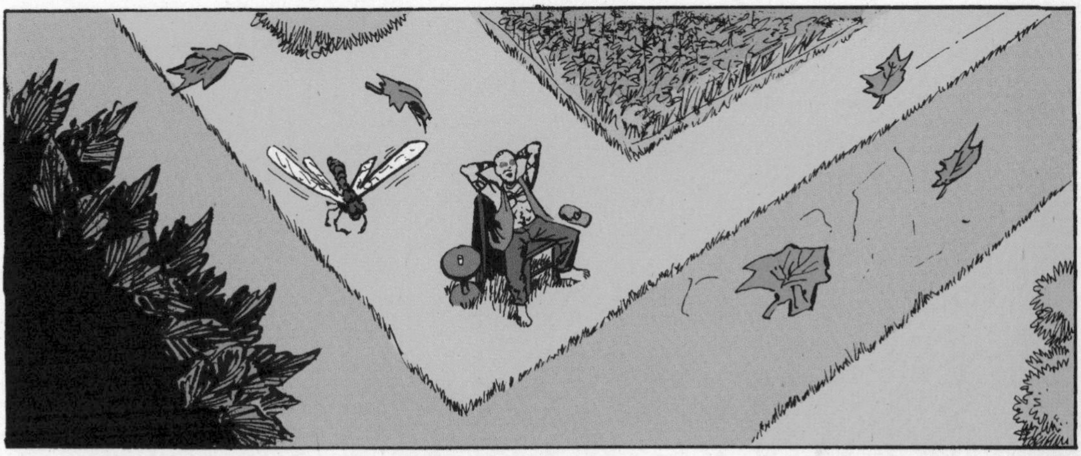

COLORING AND SEPARATIONS BY **NATHAN EYRING**

LETTERING BY **CLEM ROBINS**

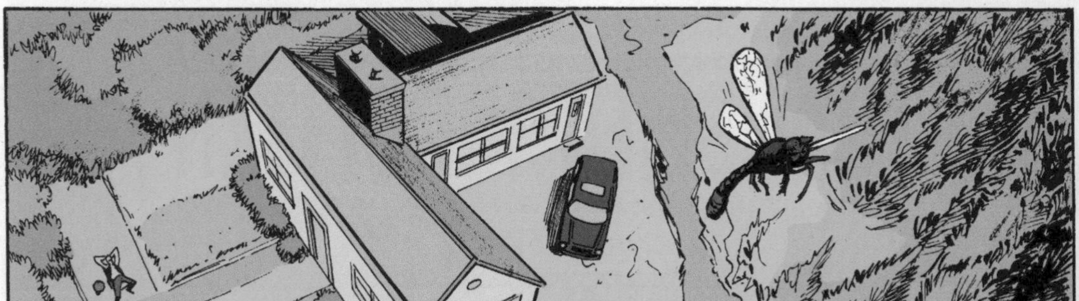

INKING BY **RODNEY RAMOS**

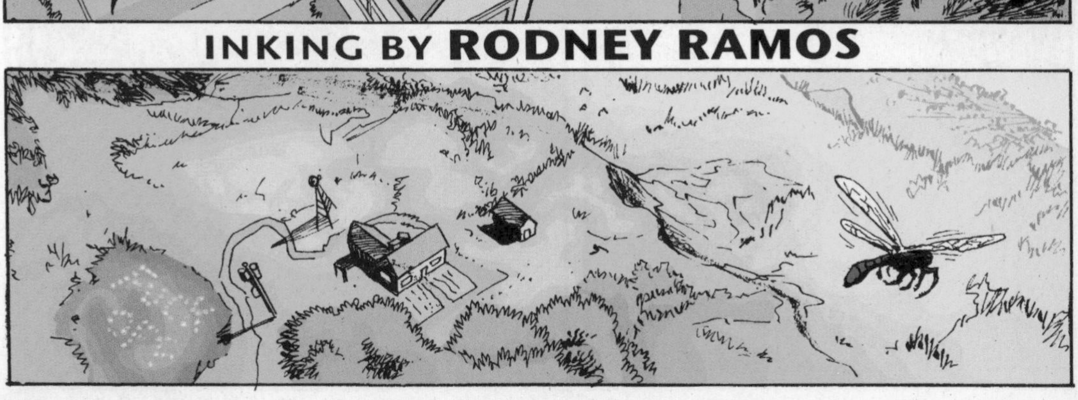

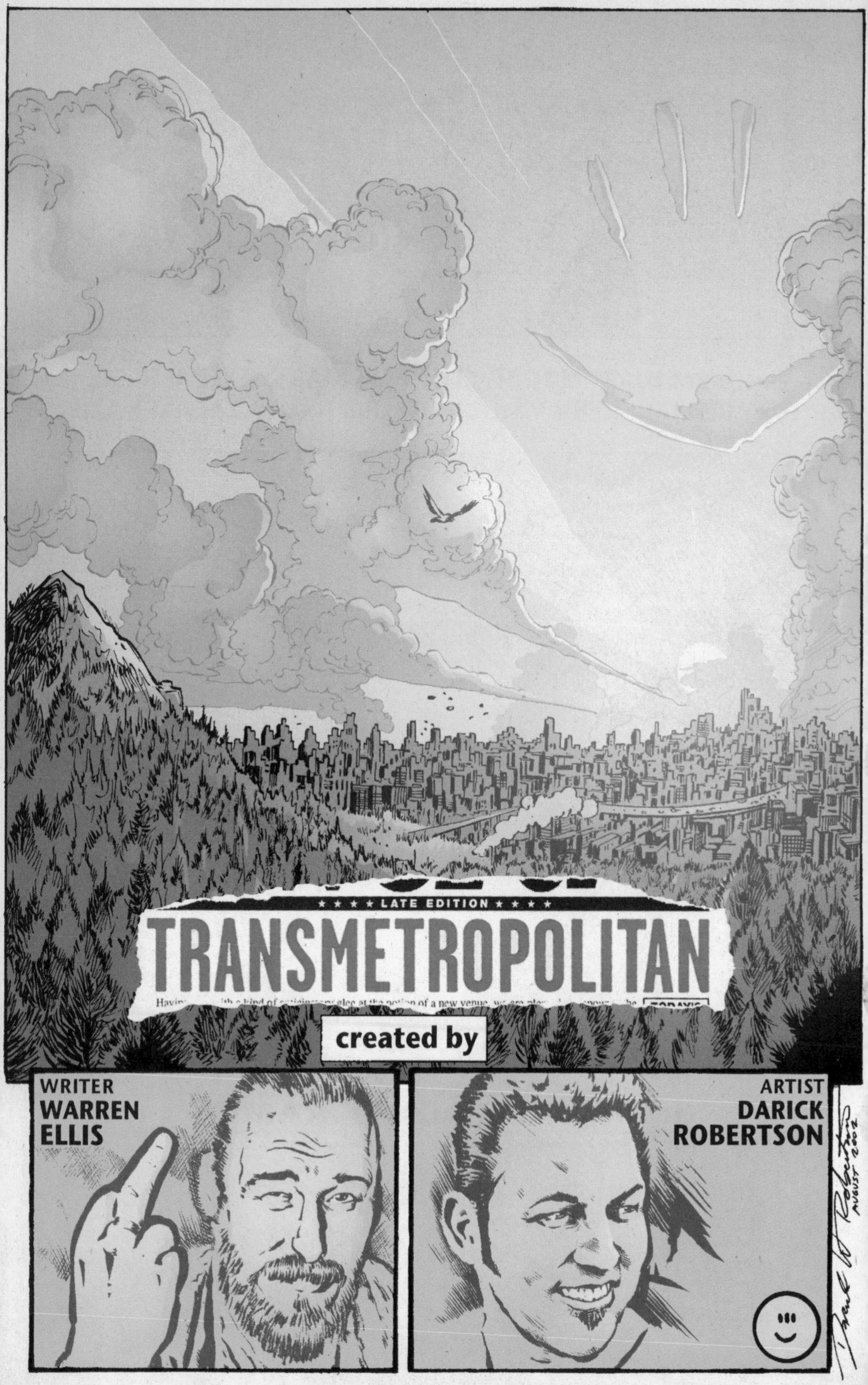
LATE EDITION
TRANSMETROPOLITAN
created by
WRITER
WARREN ELLIS
ARTIST
DARICK ROBERTSON

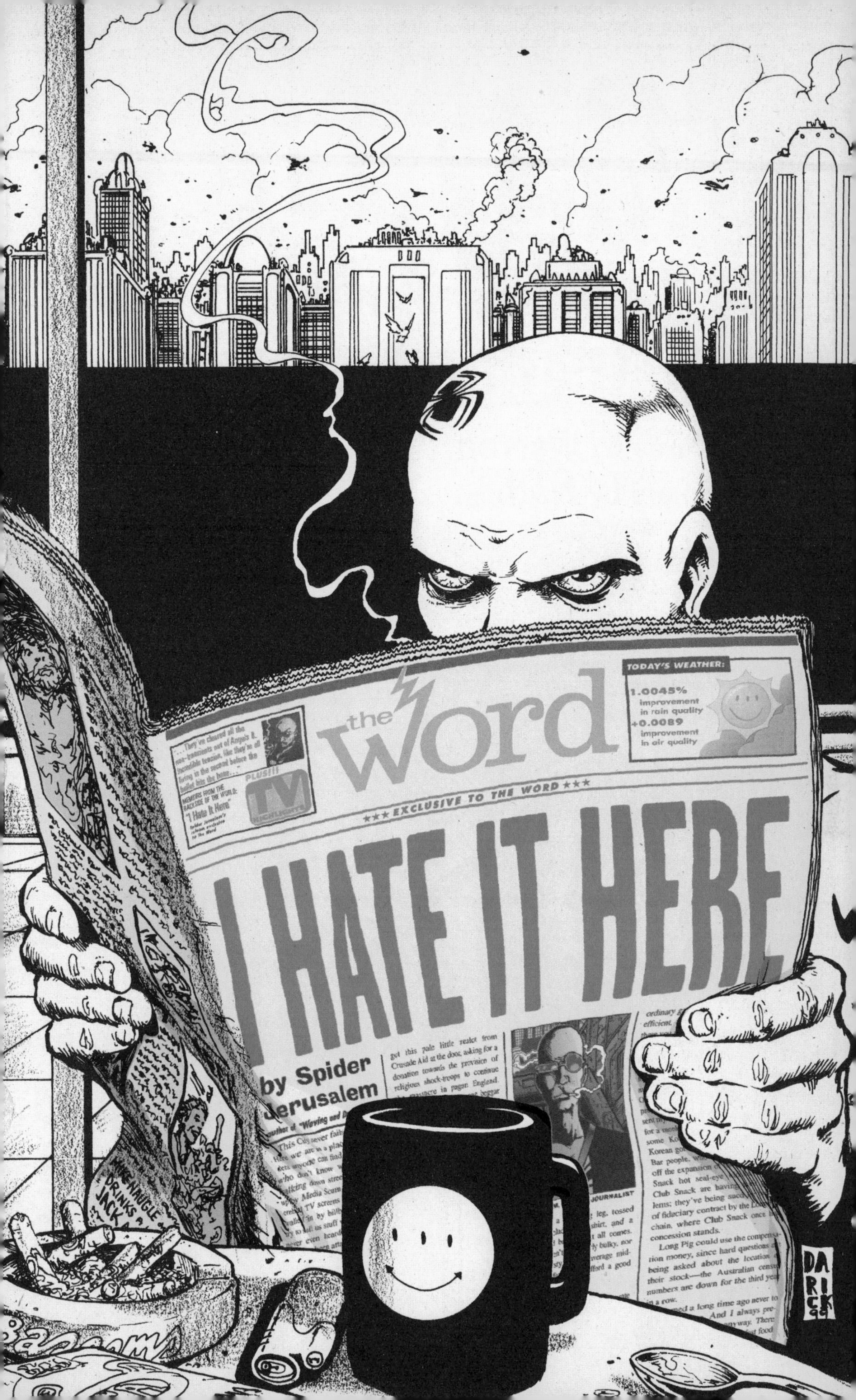

TODAY'S WEATHER:
1.0045% improvement in rain quality
+0.0089 improvement in air quality
the word
PLUS!!!
TV HIGHLIGHTS
★★★ EXCLUSIVE TO THE WORD ★★★
I HATE IT HERE
by Spider Jerusalem
JOURNALIST

TRANS-METRO-POLITAN:

I HATE IT HERE

Words by **Warren_Ellis**
Colors by **Nathan_Eyring**

Art by

INTRODUCTION
by SPIDER JERUSALEM

There's nothing more insulting than having to write the introduction to one of your own books.

I mean, the whole point of these things is that someone else comes in to make nice on you, to hype you up to the audience, to make you sound like you're worth listening to.

But no. Here we are at the hour before the book's shot down the wire to the printer -- and I mean we, I've got two editors, three assistants and a VP Publishing standing behind me as I write this -- and I'm having to write my own fucking introduction to what is essentially an excerpt from two and a half years of unremitting pain and horror.

What? You wanted something cuddly and welcoming? Well, you should have hired someone else to do it then, shouldn't you? I told you to get an actor or a singer or someone else with mental problems. Fuck all of you. Every day since I've been back in this endless shithole has been like being repeatedly hit over the head with a club hammer. Every single day. I wake up in the morning and I can feel my brain swelling, bulging up against the thin parts of my skull. If I look in the mirror really closely, I can see where my skin gets sucked in through the tiny cracks in my skull. One day, big chunks of my head are going to burst off and blood and poison will geyser out of my skull into your faces and you'll all choke on my bile and exploded brain-meat.

Before I am done here, you will all taste my brain-meat.

Get off me, you dogfuckers, I'm on a roll, no, don't take my inhaler away, you bastards

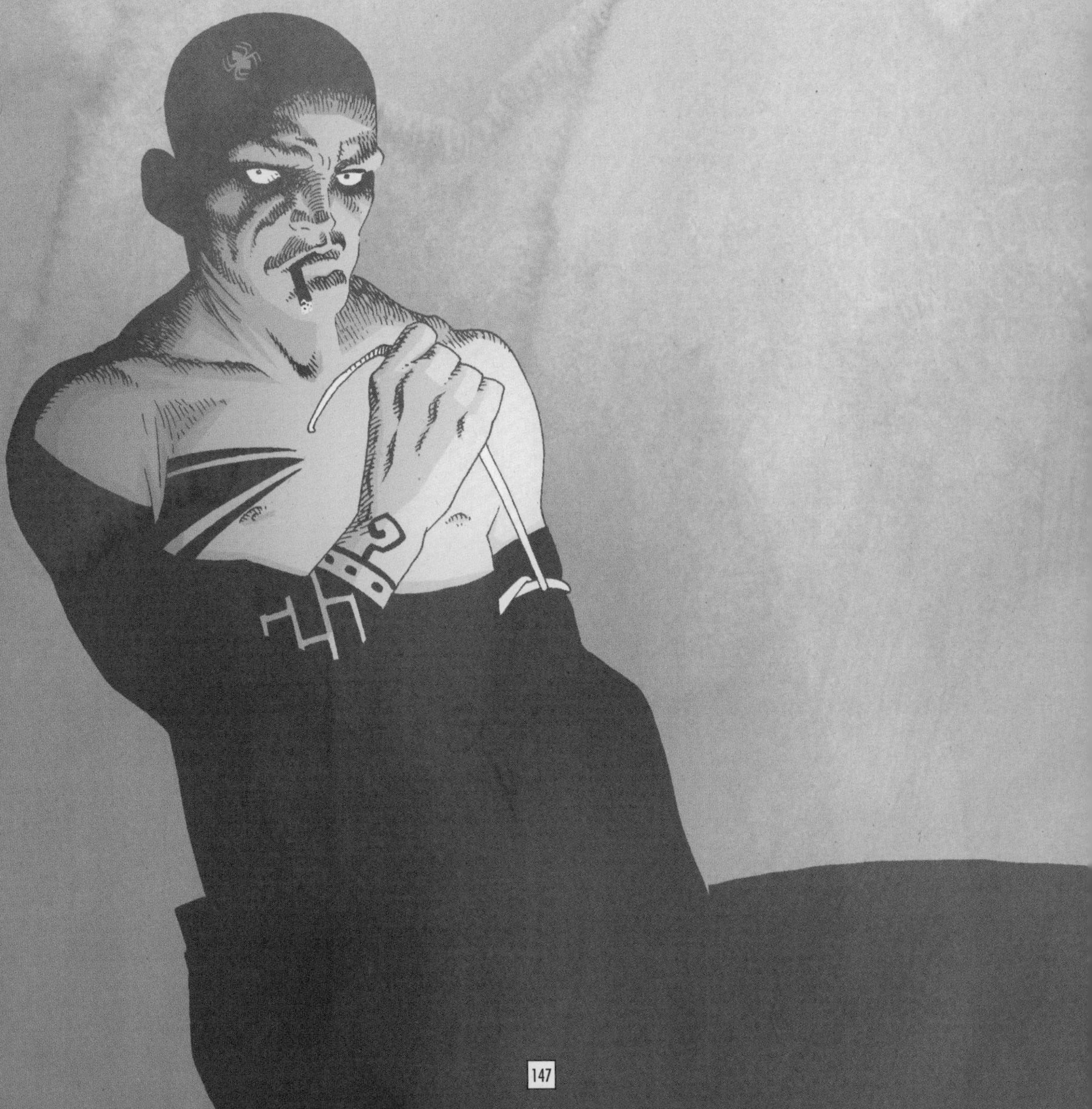

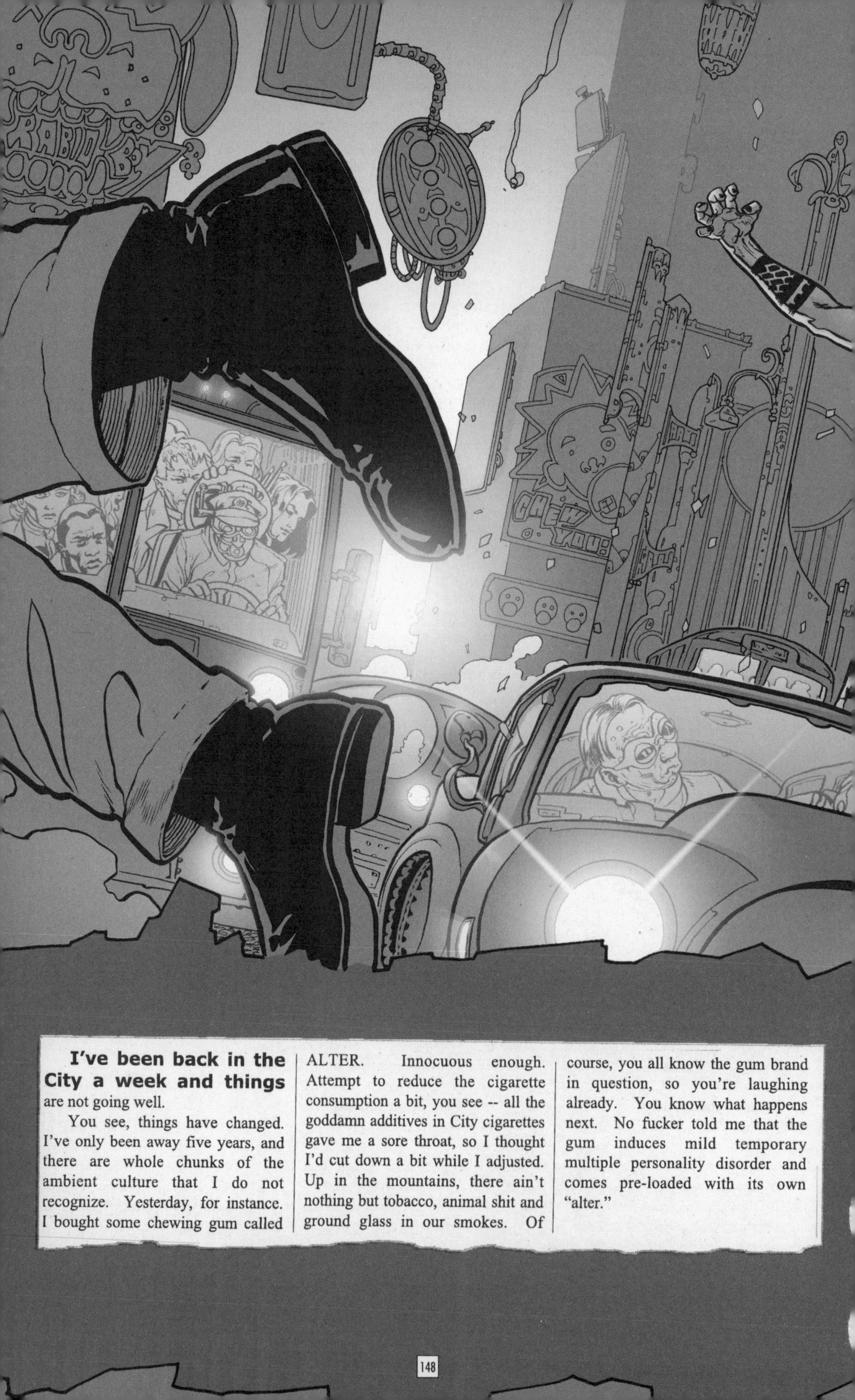
CHEW YOU!

I've been back in the City a week and things are not going well.

You see, things have changed. I've only been away five years, and there are whole chunks of the ambient culture that I do not recognize. Yesterday, for instance. I bought some chewing gum called ALTER. Innocuous enough. Attempt to reduce the cigarette consumption a bit, you see -- all the goddamn additives in City cigarettes gave me a sore throat, so I thought I'd cut down a bit while I adjusted. Up in the mountains, there ain't nothing but tobacco, animal shit and ground glass in our smokes. Of course, you all know the gum brand in question, so you're laughing already. You know what happens next. No fucker told me that the gum induces mild temporary multiple personality disorder and comes pre-loaded with its own "alter."

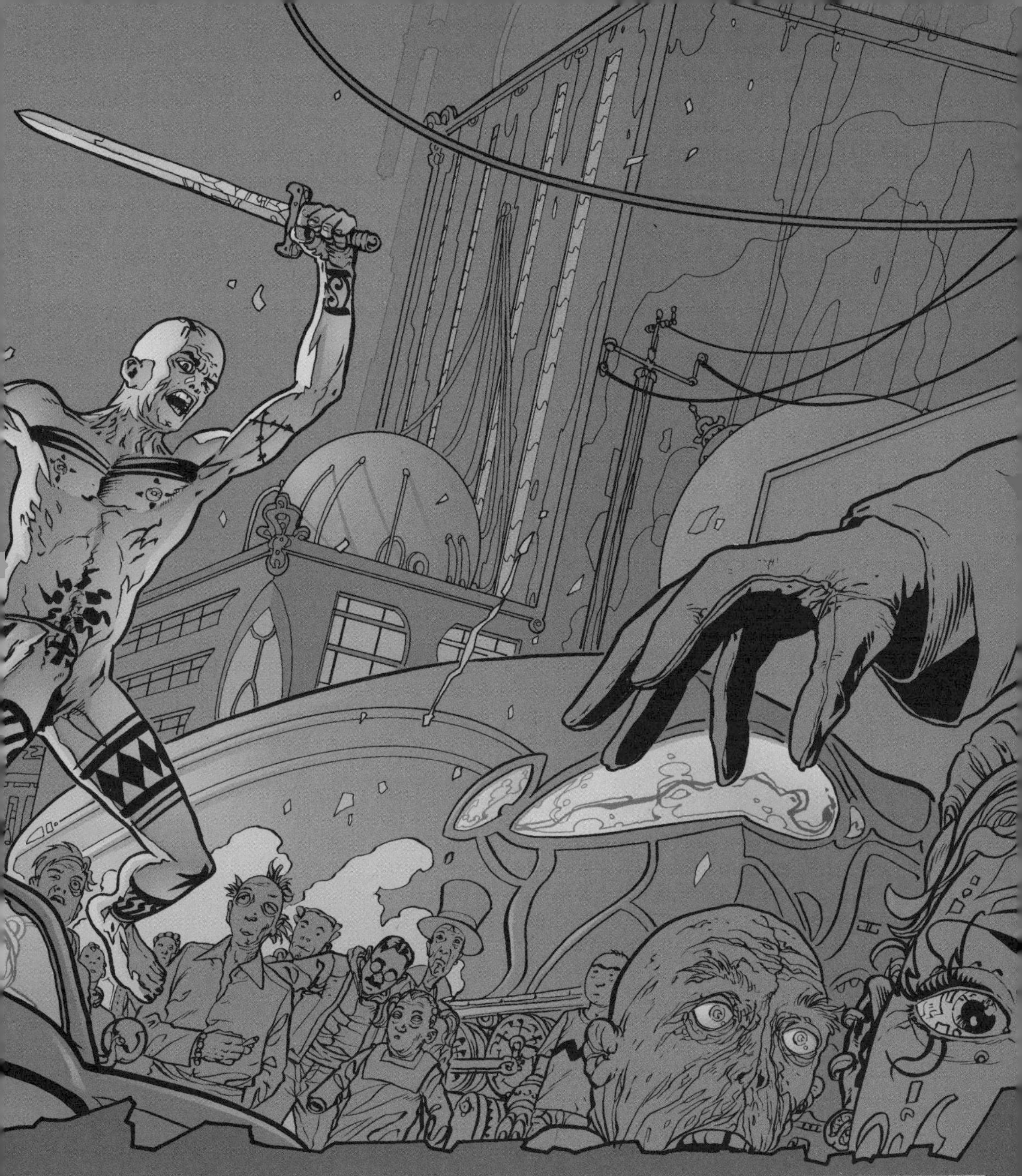

So I spent ninety minutes stark ass naked in the middle of the Print District with my brain trapped in the death-grip of Einarr, syphilis-maddened Norse tribal lawman from the Scando ghetto north of Lugh Bend. No, let's get specific here; I spent ninety minutes naked dispensing ancient wisdom and savage Law up and down the Print District, the alter only wearing off after I brutally beat a deeply unstable ten-year-old boy for pissing in his little sister's pram while mommy was off down the alleyway buying a touch of discreet oral sex from an out-of-work voice-over actor called Giles. These unemployed actors gone bad are the worst. When they're not whoring on streetcorners or trying to look menacing as they loiter around the drama sections of bookstores, they form gangs that relentlessly try to attach themselves to stylish homosexuals and break all the noise laws by bitching about pretty girls and people with talent. The bastards.

My MPD faded away just as I was about to apply my hastily improvised METHOD WHORE brand to Giles' tender bits.

A quick reading of the small print on the gum wrapper crushed into my hand revealed that ingestion of the gum absolved me of responsibility for my actions.

So I branded him and the woman, kicked the kid into passing traffic and had the baby rehomed.

You have no idea how much I hate it here.

I want to travel back time and lop the ddamn heads off all your innocent ommies and daddies.

Come on. Tell me why you serve to live. I mean, I know I've en away, and things have changed, that. But there's absolutely no cuse for the behavior you've all en displaying since I came back.

I am talking specifically about the extensive shrines set up outside my apartment building. I am talking about the two people who attempted to have sex in my shadow to guarantee conception. I am talking about the Conclave who scrabbled through the bag of garbage I couldn't get my Maker to use. I am talking about the people who stole my bathwater and drank it.

This is *America*. I want *money* these things. I mean, I have so especially Holy underpants he shattered and ruined by unus stresses, and I can't let them go t good cause for anything less tha hundred...

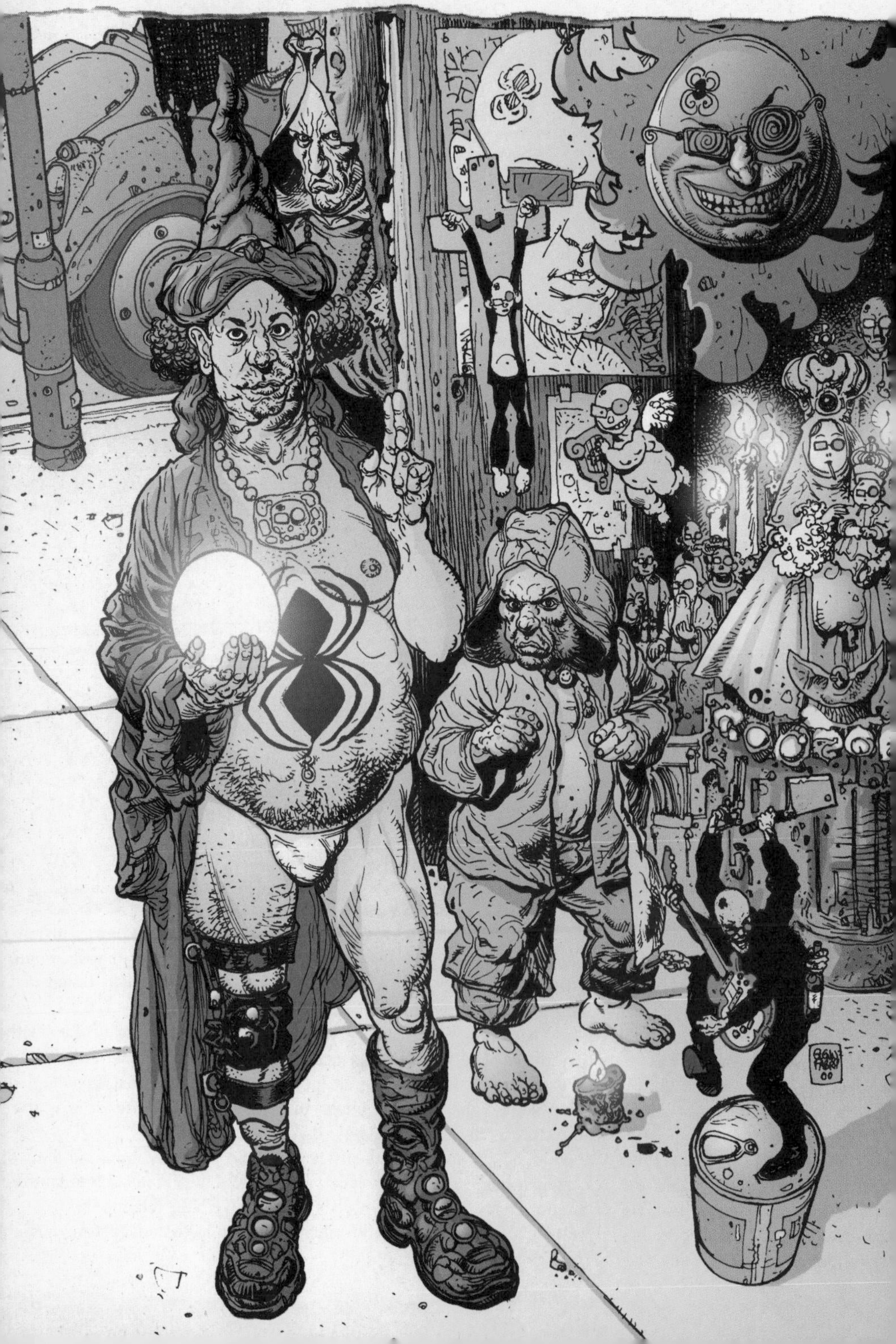

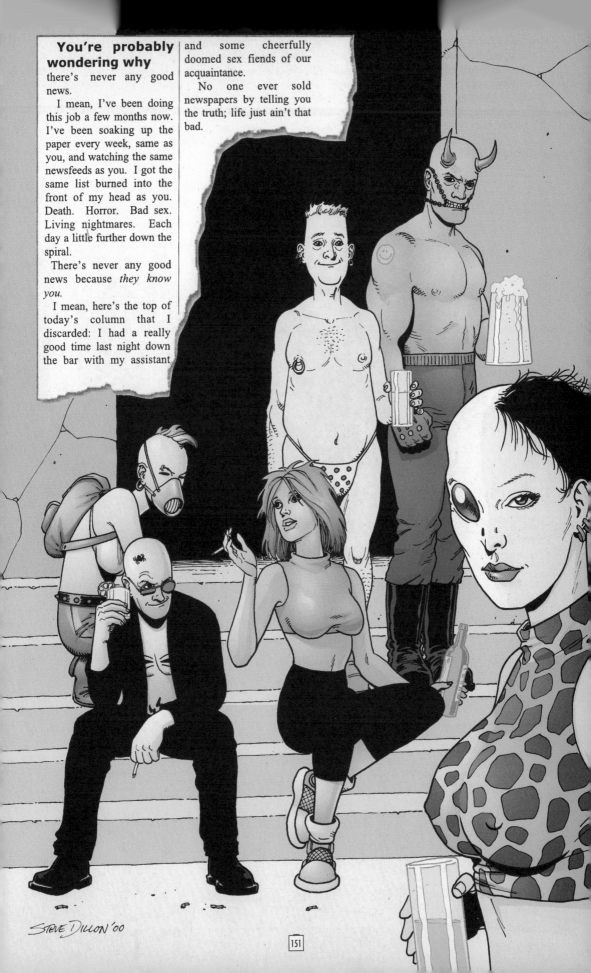

You're probably wondering why there's never any good news.

I mean, I've been doing this job a few months now. I've been soaking up the paper every week, same as you, and watching the same newsfeeds as you. I got the same list burned into the front of my head as you. Death. Horror. Bad sex. Living nightmares. Each day a little further down the spiral.

There's never any good news because *they know you*.

I mean, here's the top of today's column that I discarded: I had a really good time last night down the bar with my assistant and some cheerfully doomed sex fiends of our acquaintance.

No one ever sold newspapers by telling you the truth; life just ain't that bad.

STEVE DILLON '00

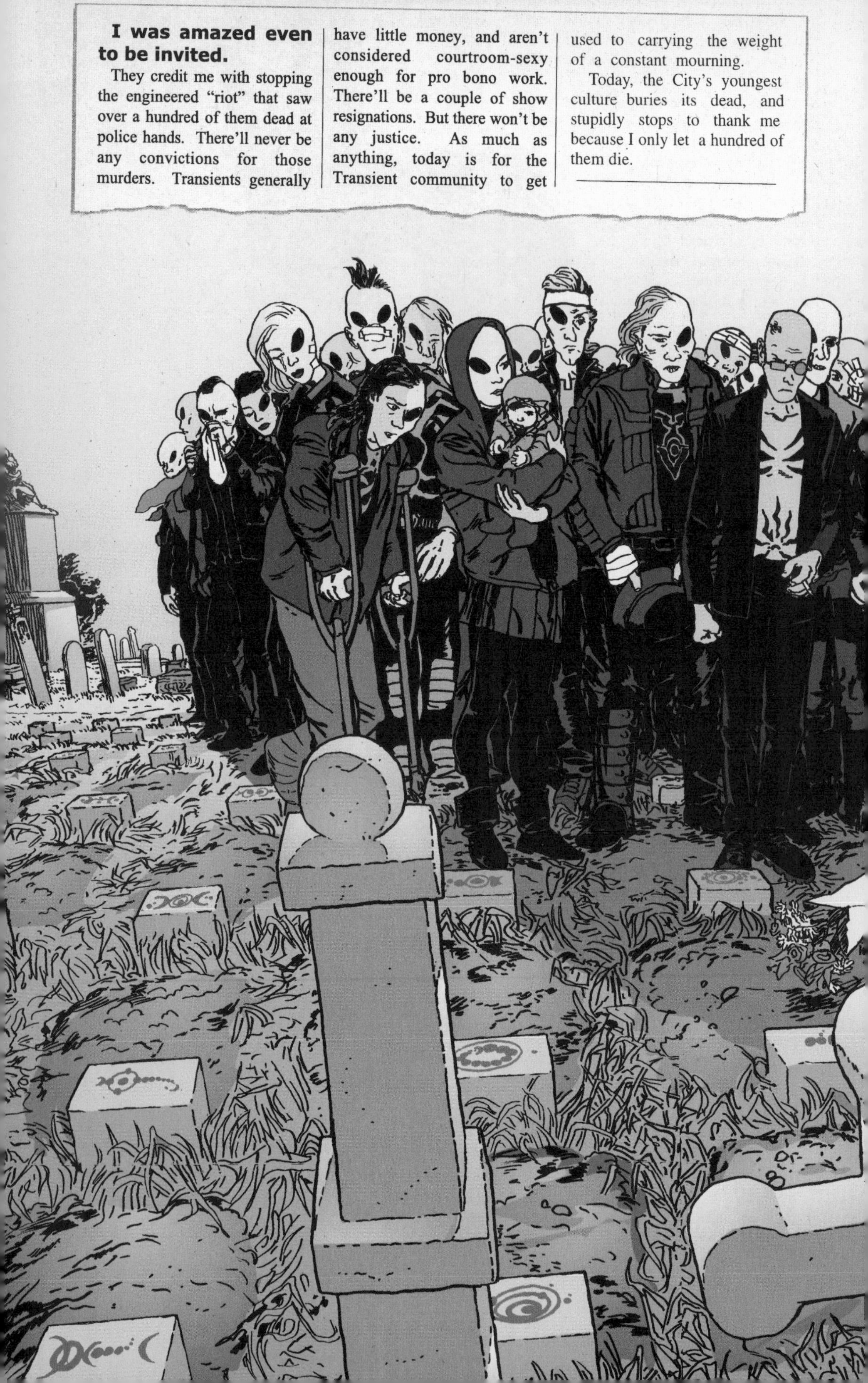
I was amazed even to be invited.
They credit me with stopping the engineered "riot" that saw over a hundred of them dead at police hands. There'll never be any convictions for those murders. Transients generally have little money, and aren't considered courtroom-sexy enough for pro bono work. There'll be a couple of show resignations. But there won't be any justice. As much as anything, today is for the Transient community to get used to carrying the weight of a constant mourning.
Today, the City's youngest culture buries its dead, and stupidly stops to thank me because I only let a hundred of them die.

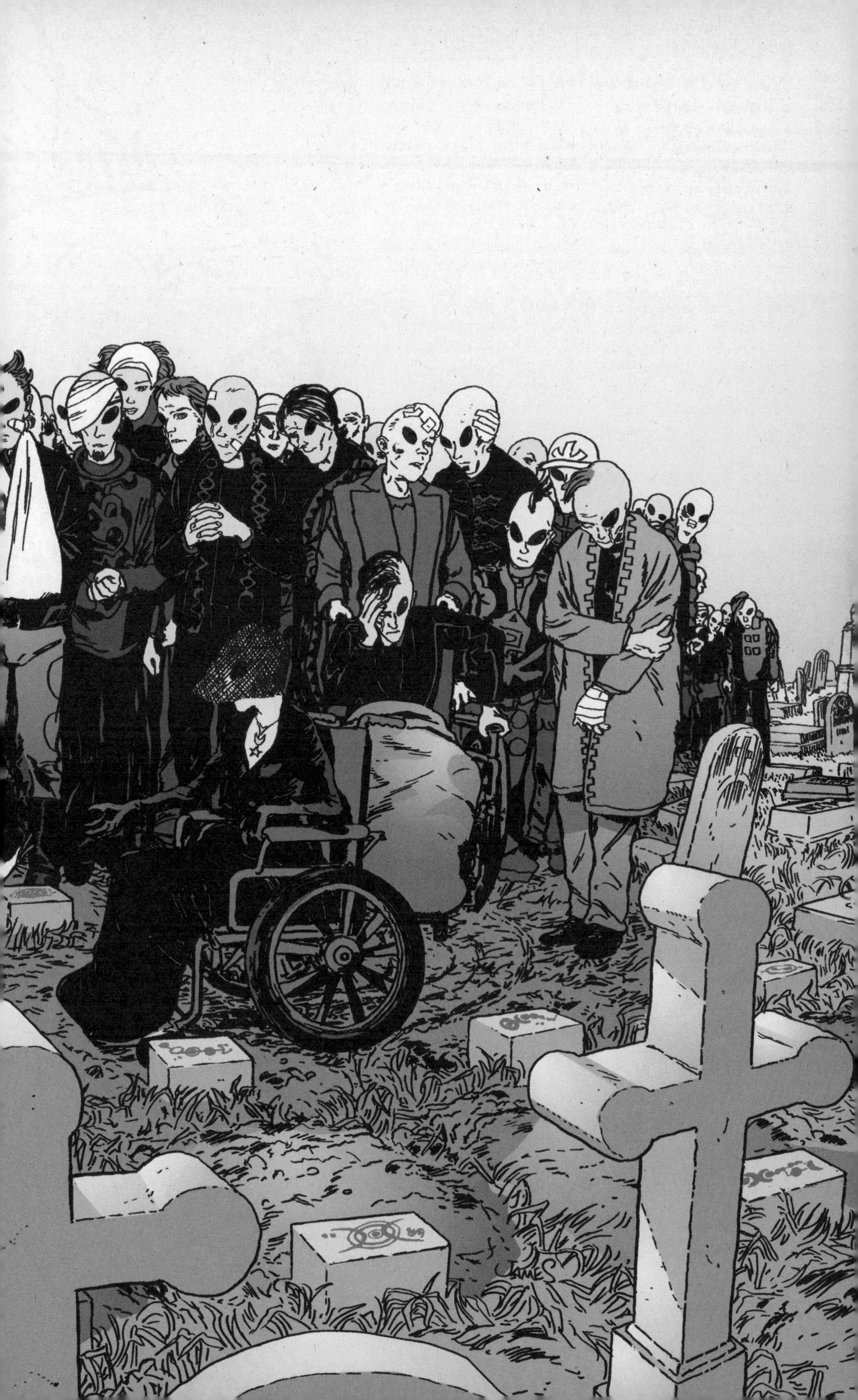
JAMES

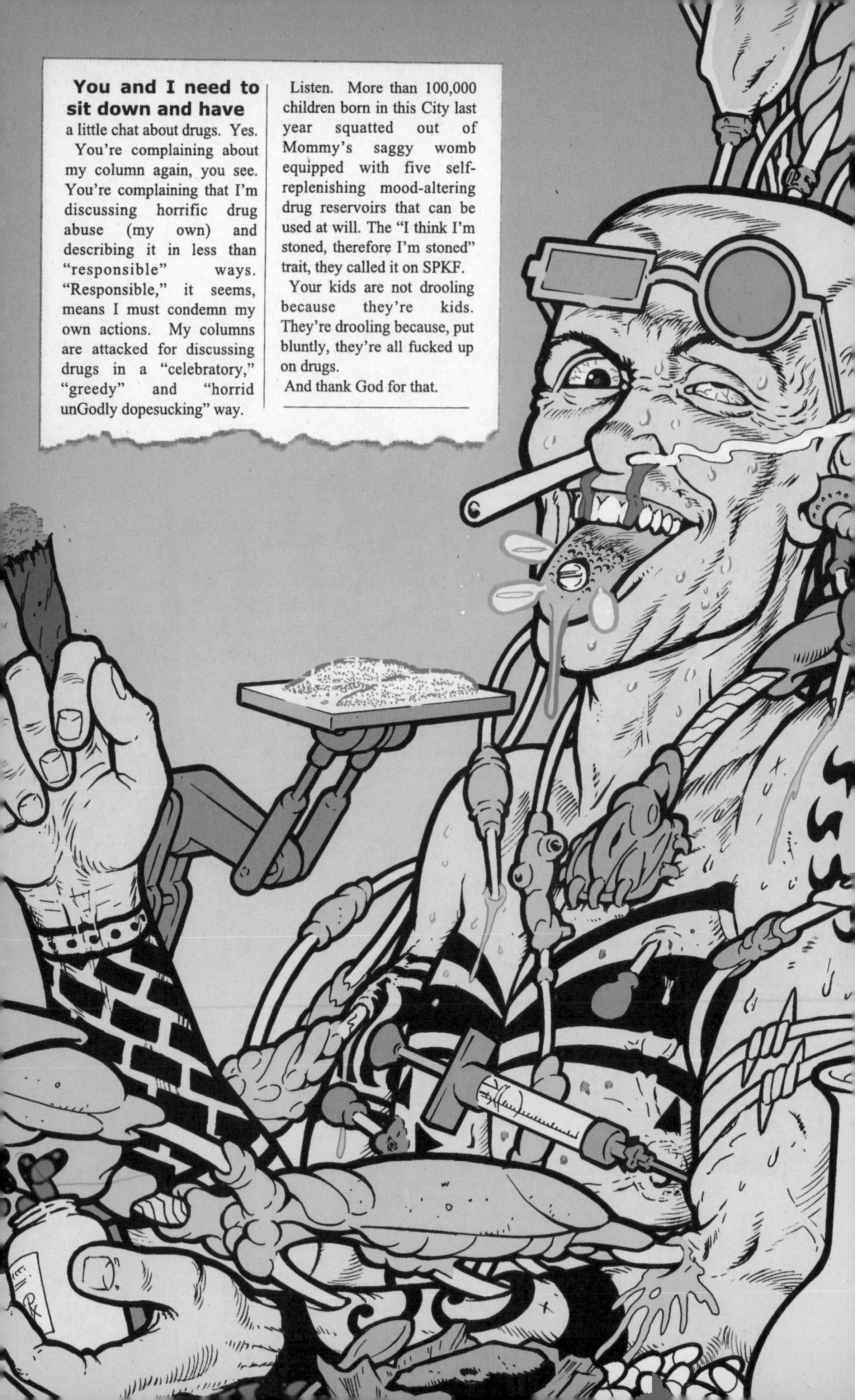
You and I need to sit down and have a little chat about drugs. Yes.
You're complaining about my column again, you see. You're complaining that I'm discussing horrific drug abuse (my own) and describing it in less than "responsible" ways. "Responsible," it seems, means I must condemn my own actions. My columns are attacked for discussing drugs in a "celebratory," "greedy" and "horrid unGodly dopesucking" way.
Listen. More than 100,000 children born in this City last year squatted out of Mommy's saggy womb equipped with five self-replenishing mood-altering drug reservoirs that can be used at will. The "I think I'm stoned, therefore I'm stoned" trait, they called it on SPKF.
Your kids are not drooling because they're kids. They're drooling because, put bluntly, they're all fucked up on drugs.
And thank God for that.

I want to eat a swan. Is that wrong of me?

I can't find anyone who'll sell me a swanburger.

I sent my assistant down to the African for a monkeyburger. I really fancied some Korean dog, but the local Korean got bought out by the Shark Bar people, who are trying to head off the expansion of those tiny Club Snack hot seal-eye kiosks. Mind, Club Snack are having their own problems; they're being sued for breach of fiduciary contract by the Long Pig chain, where Club Snack once had concession stands. Long Pig could use the compensation money, since hard questions are being asked about the location of their stock -- the New Zealand census numbers are down for the third year in a row. I learned a long time ago never to annoy an Incan. And I always preferred caribou eyes, anyway. There used to be loads of Eskimo fastfood stands around here. I wonder what happened to them?

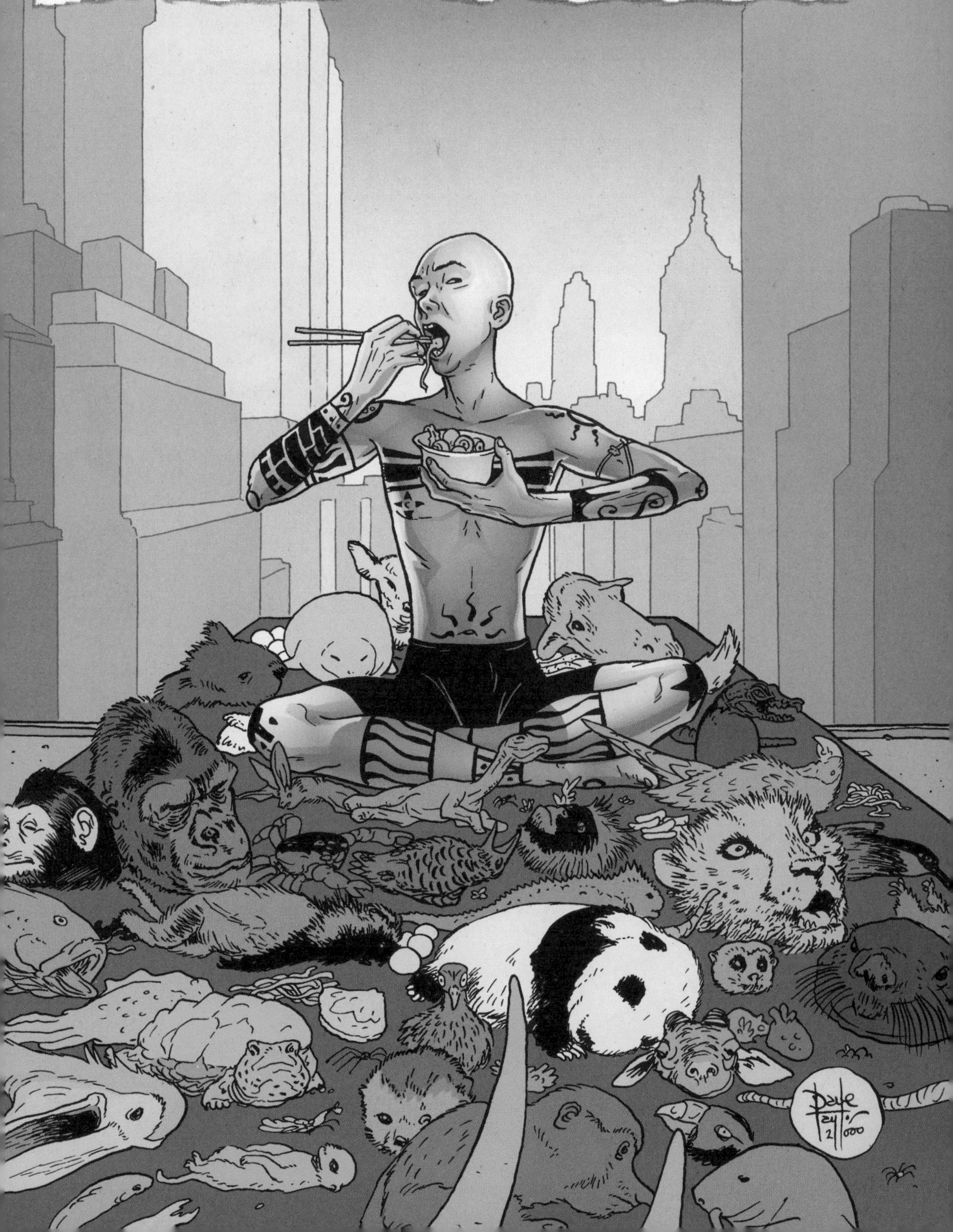

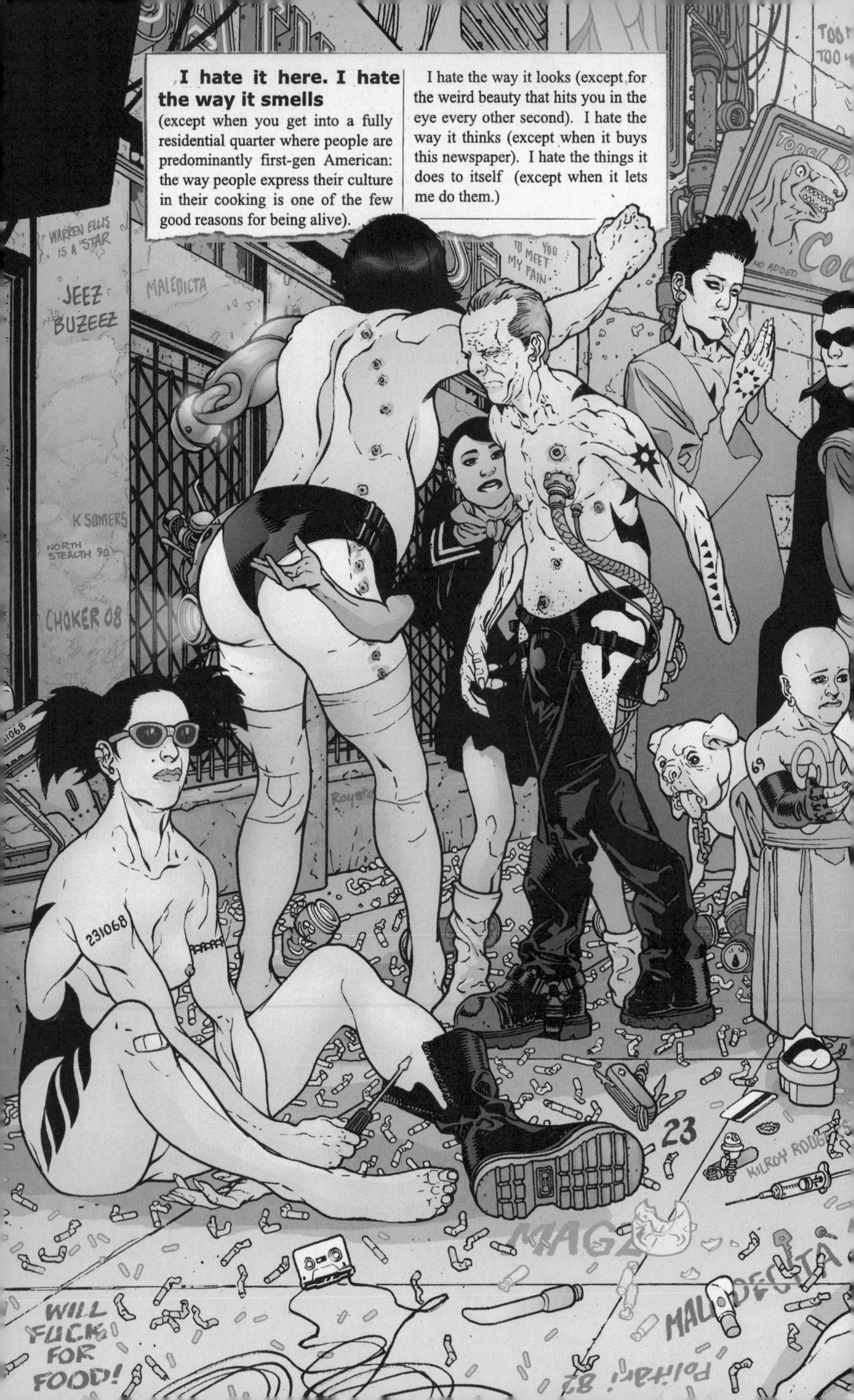
I hate it here. I hate the way it smells
(except when you get into a fully residential quarter where people are predominantly first-gen American: the way people express their culture in their cooking is one of the few good reasons for being alive).
I hate the way it looks (except for the weird beauty that hits you in the eye every other second). I hate the way it thinks (except when it buys this newspaper). I hate the things it does to itself (except when it lets me do them.)
WARREN ELLIS IS A STAR
JEEZ BUZEEZ
MALEDICTA
TO MEET YOU MY PAIN
NO ADDED
K SOMERS
NORTH STEALTH 90
CHOKER 08
231068
69
23
MAGZ
MALEDICTA
WILL FUCK FOR FOOD!

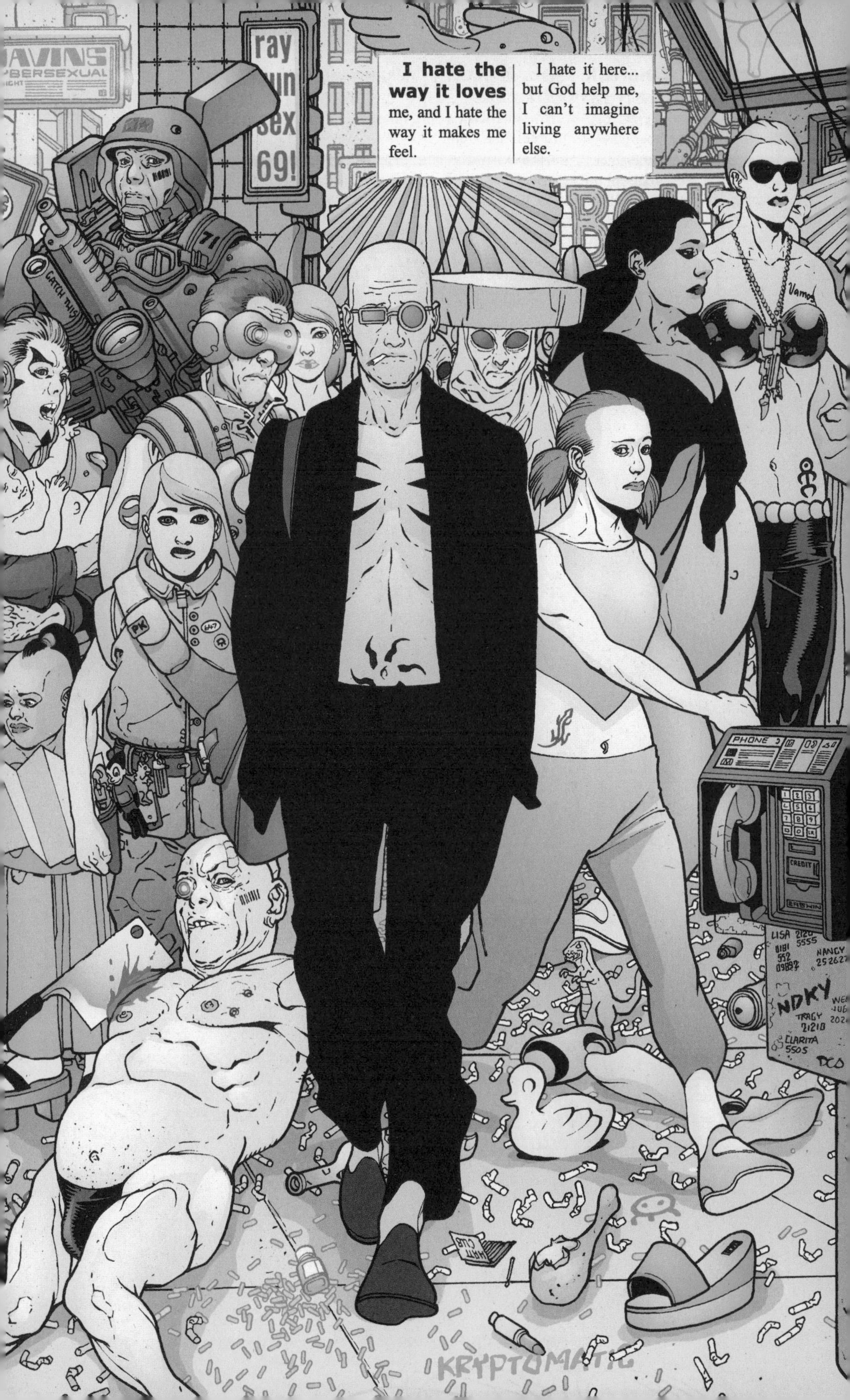
I hate the way it loves me, and I hate the way it makes me feel.
I hate it here... but God help me, I can't imagine living anywhere else.
ray
69!
CATCH THIS
Vamos
PHONE
CREDIT
LISA 2120 5555
NANCY
NDKY
TRACY 21210
CLARITA 5505
KRYPTOMATIC

It was a horrific beating. Biblical ferocity. The vengeful God of the Old Testament flowed in my veins, giving me power, Hate and an erection of uncommon savagery. What else could I do? I was left with no choice.

My journalist's insurance protected me from prosecution. The emergency services unscrewed my victim from the drain I'd attempted to finally dispose of him in. I'm told he'll walk again, with some time and some new legs. And new hips. And new eyes. And an unfried nervous system.

No fucker rewrites *me*.

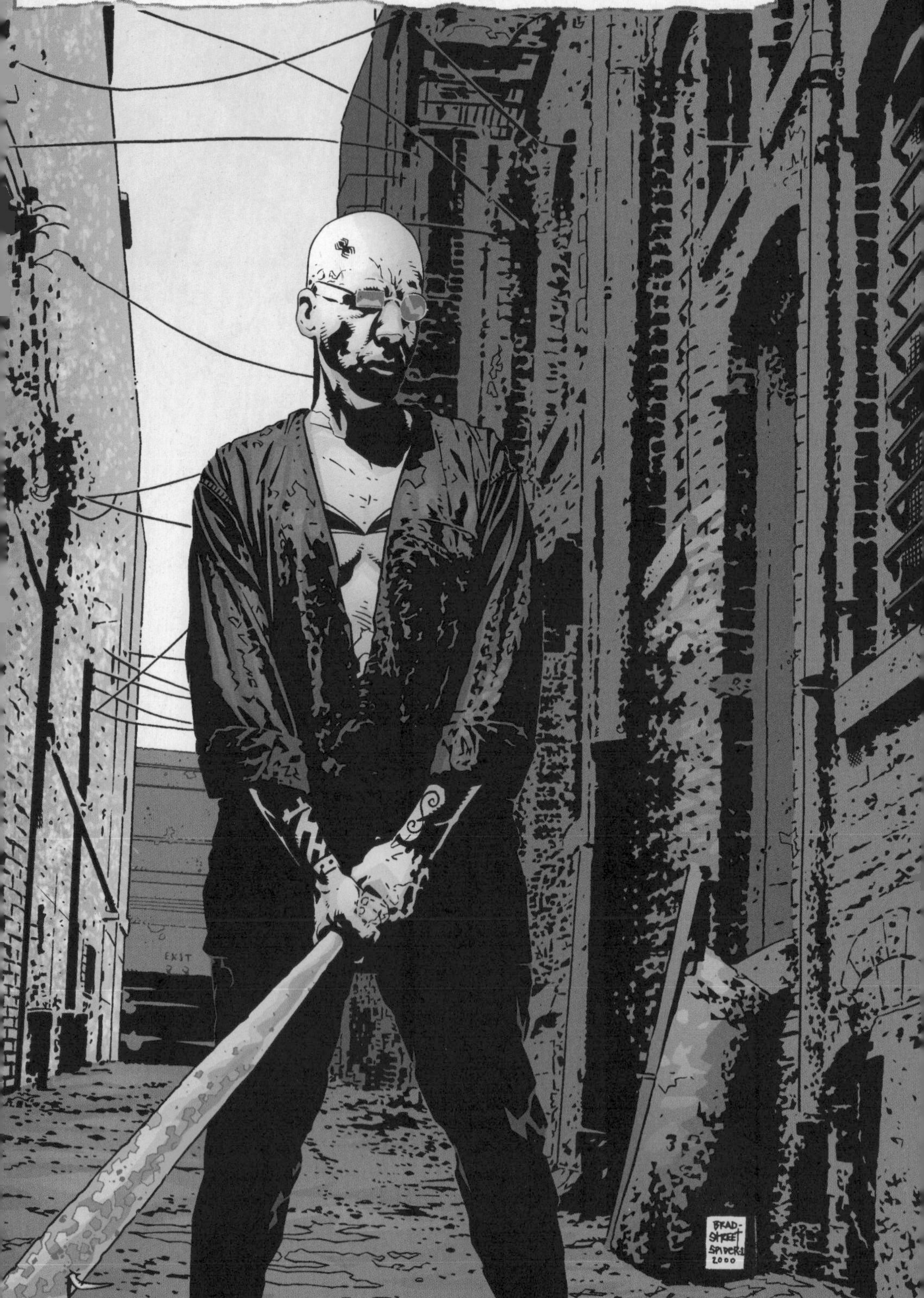

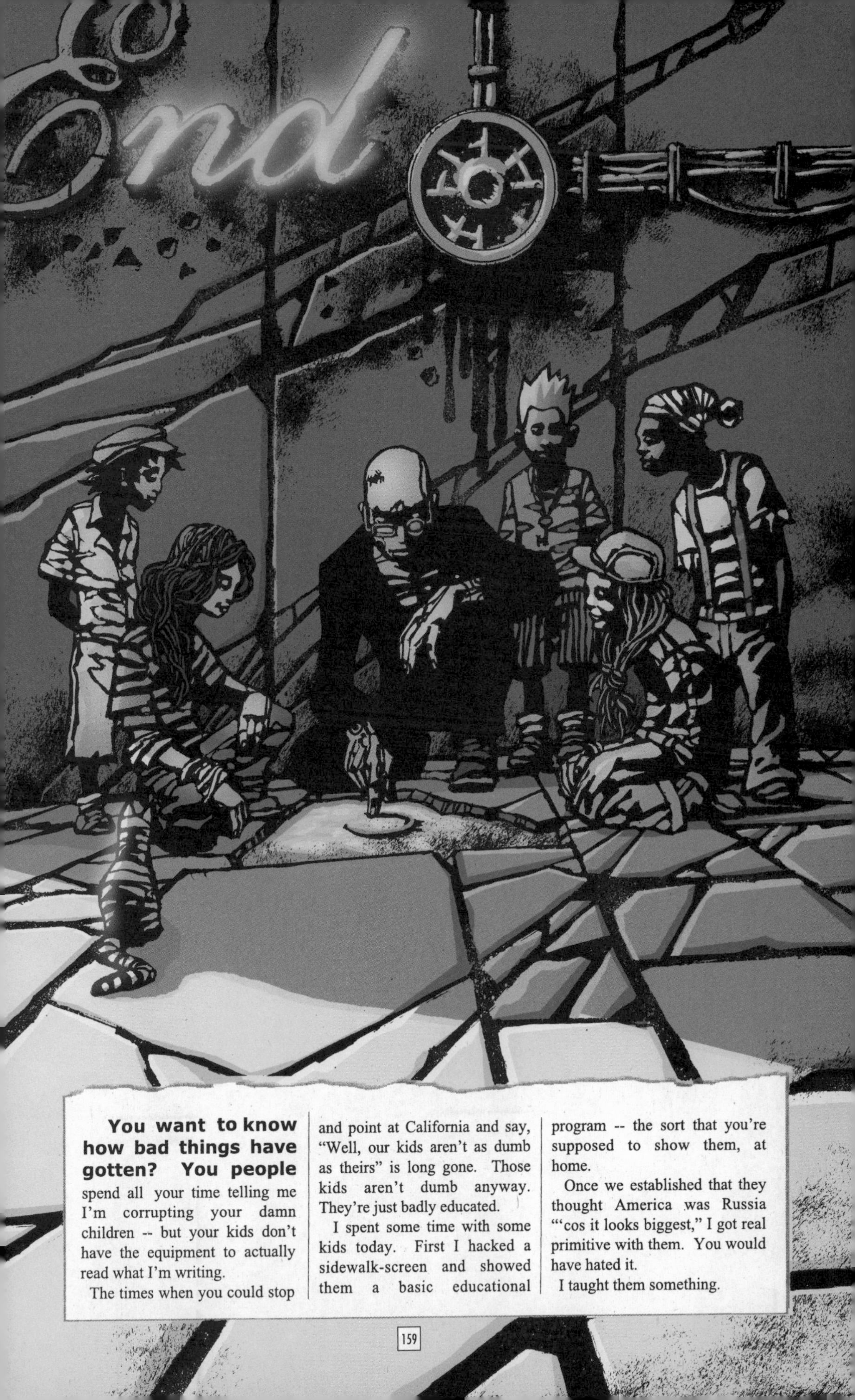
You want to know how bad things have gotten? You people spend all your time telling me I'm corrupting your damn children -- but your kids don't have the equipment to actually read what I'm writing.
The times when you could stop and point at California and say, "Well, our kids aren't as dumb as theirs" is long gone. Those kids aren't dumb anyway. They're just badly educated.
I spent some time with some kids today. First I hacked a sidewalk-screen and showed them a basic educational program -- the sort that you're supposed to show them, at home.
Once we established that they thought America was Russia "'cos it looks biggest," I got real primitive with them. You would have hated it.
I taught them something.

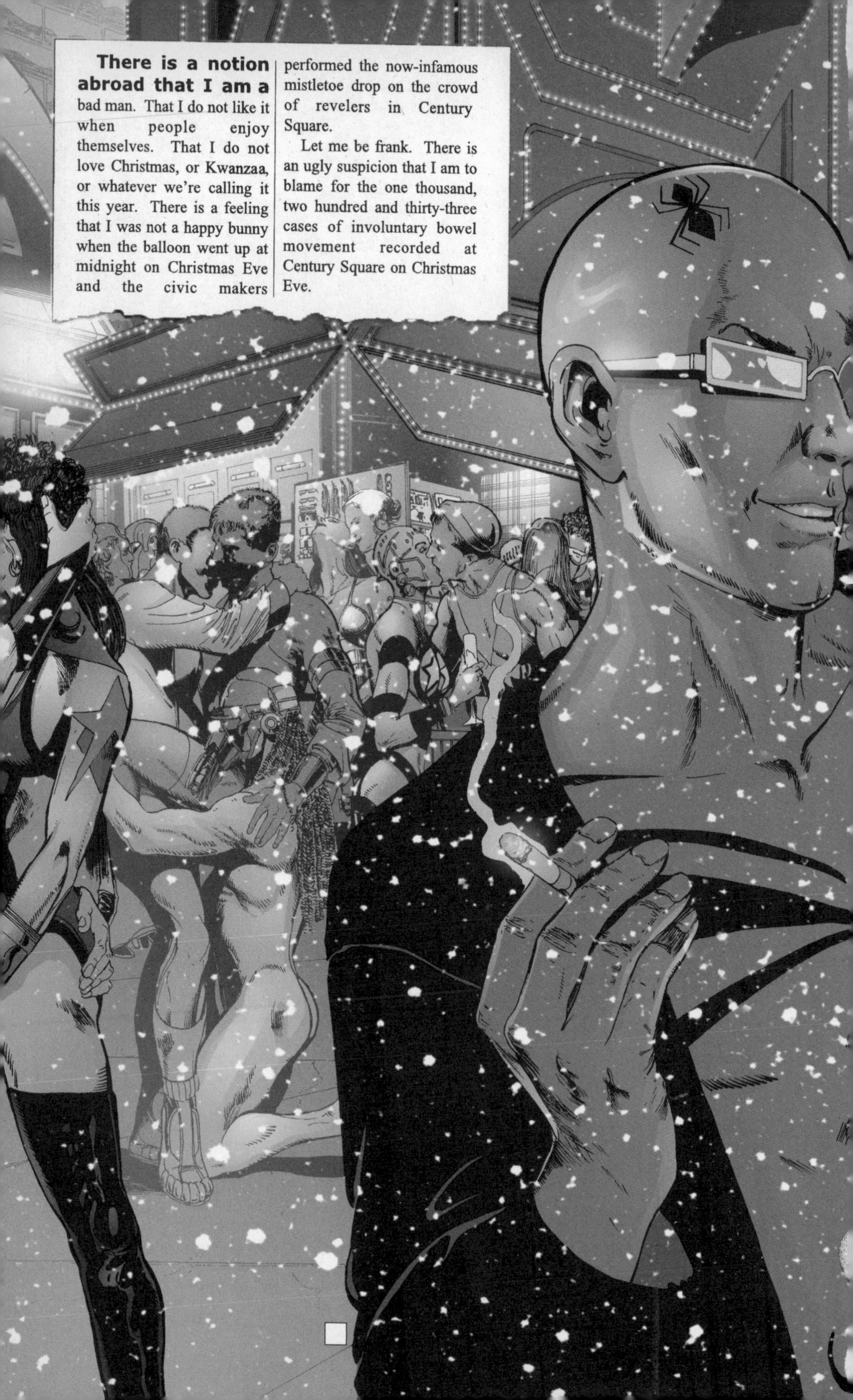

There is a notion abroad that I am a bad man. That I do not like it when people enjoy themselves. That I do not love Christmas, or Kwanzaa, or whatever we're calling it this year. There is a feeling that I was not a happy bunny when the balloon went up at midnight on Christmas Eve and the civic makers performed the now-infamous mistletoe drop on the crowd of revelers in Century Square.
Let me be frank. There is an ugly suspicion that I am to blame for the one thousand, two hundred and thirty-three cases of involuntary bowel movement recorded at Century Square on Christmas Eve.

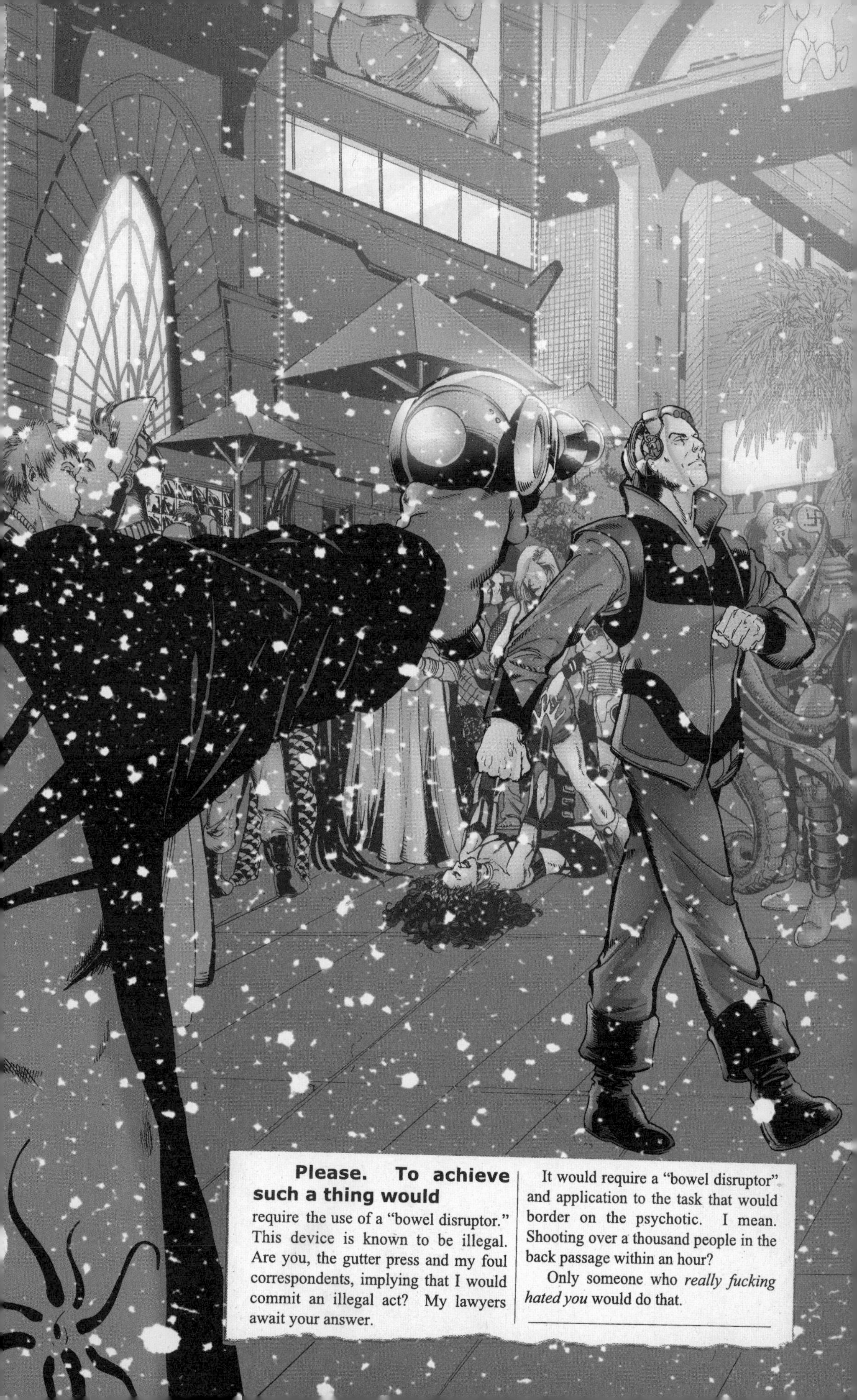

Please. To achieve such a thing would require the use of a "bowel disruptor." This device is known to be illegal. Are you, the gutter press and my foul correspondents, implying that I would commit an illegal act? My lawyers await your answer.

It would require a "bowel disruptor" and application to the task that would border on the psychotic. I mean. Shooting over a thousand people in the back passage within an hour?

Only someone who *really fucking hated you* would do that.

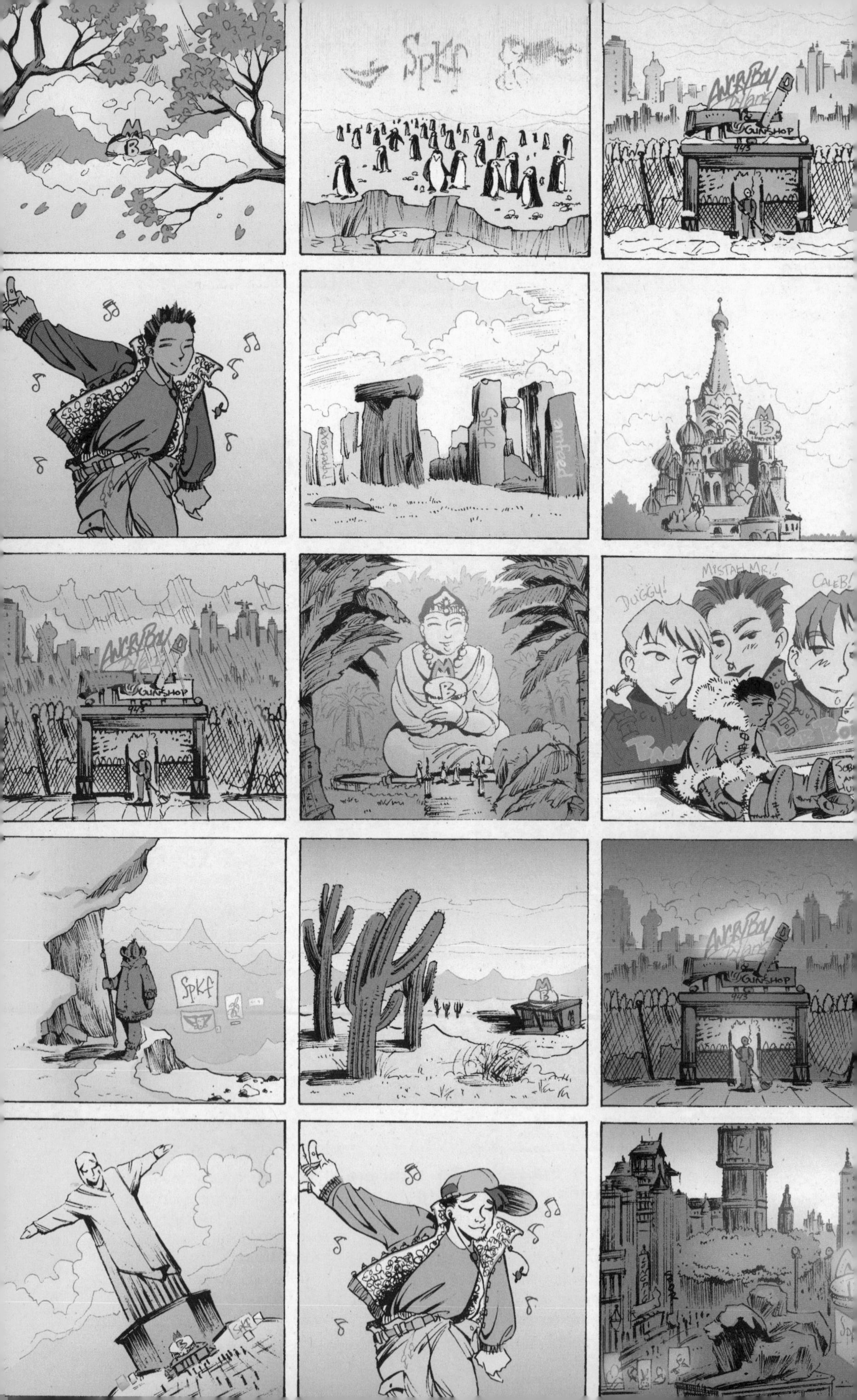
Spkf
AngryBoy
Dylan's
GUNSHOP
443
Puppetseed
Spkf
amfeed
AngryBoy
Dylan's
GUNSHOP
443
DUGGY!
MISTAH MR.!
CALEB!
Spkf
AngryBoy
Dylan's
GUNSHOP
443
Spkf

MISTAH MR.!
CALEB!
BACK
SOBER AND HUNGRY
MISTAH MR.!
CALEB!
BACK
SOBER AND HUNGRY

We live in a monoculture.

What does that mean? Well, go out to your street corner. You'll probably see a Long Pig stand, SPKF on a screen somewhere, an Angry Boy Dylan's Gun Store. You'll go into a record store and see new recordings by the usual suspects, maybe a special Space Culture display rack.

Go out onto a streetcorner in London and you'll see the same thing. Same in Prague. Same in São Paulo. Same in Osaka, and Grozny, and Tehran, and Jo'burg, and Hobart.

That's what a monoculture is. It's everywhere, and it's all the same. And it takes up alien cultures and digests them and shits them out in a homogenous building-block shape that fits seamlessly into the vast blank wall of the monoculture.

This is the future. This is what we built. This is what we wanted. It must have been. Because we all had the fucking *choice*, didn't we? It is only our money that allows commercial culture to flower. If we didn't want to live like this, we could have changed it any time, by *not fucking paying for it.*

So let's celebrate by all going out and buying the same burger.

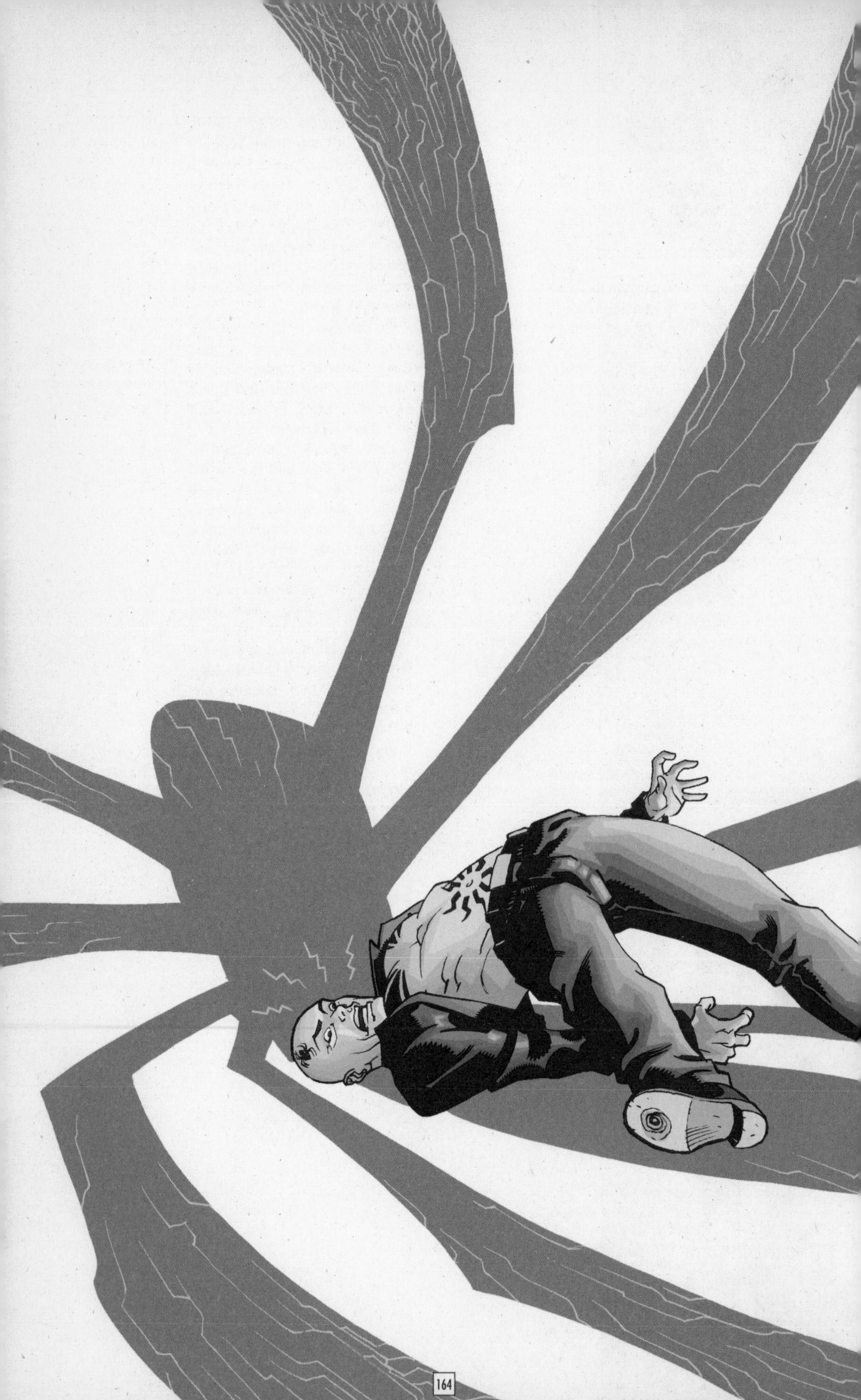

Further to the debate about drug use

(mine and your children's): it's all over. You no longer have anything to worry about.

You know, when I was a kid, we listened to music that made our parents' eyes bleed and took drugs that made us want to dance and fuck and kill things. That is the way things are supposed to be.

It was, therefore, in the spirit of honest investigation that I internalized a heroic dose of Space, the new social drug enjoyed by the young folk of today as part of the youth culture referred to as Supermodernity.

Supermodernity, apparently, is the experience of being between places; that is, not being in a real place at all, but waiting in transit between one place and the other. This is why SM/Space Culture music appears to us to be utterly silent. You have to be on Space -- slowed down, across places, in the zone between ticks of the clock -- to be able to hear it.

This is what they do for fun, apparently: suck up appalling volumes of a drug that traps you in an airport waiting lounge of the mind and doesn't let you go for approximately two hundred years while someone plays an antique handheld electronic keyboard in your ear.

Mr. and Mrs. America, do not be afraid! Your children have finally found a drug that makes it impossible to dance, fuck or kill things. Youth culture has finally sterilized itself. Young America has finally achieved its terminal ambition -- fucking itself before anyone else could.

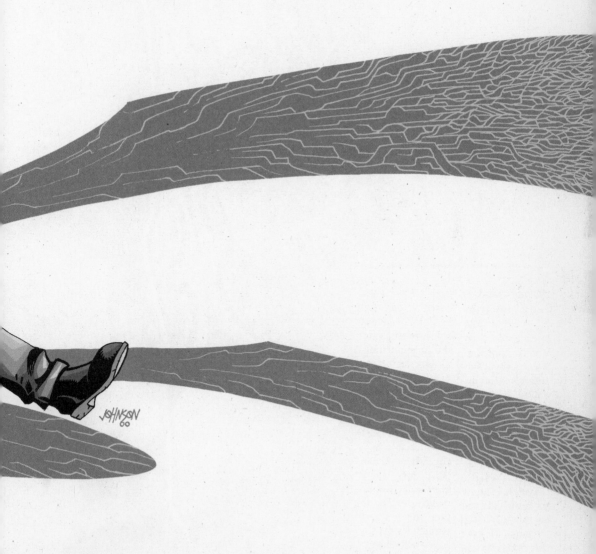

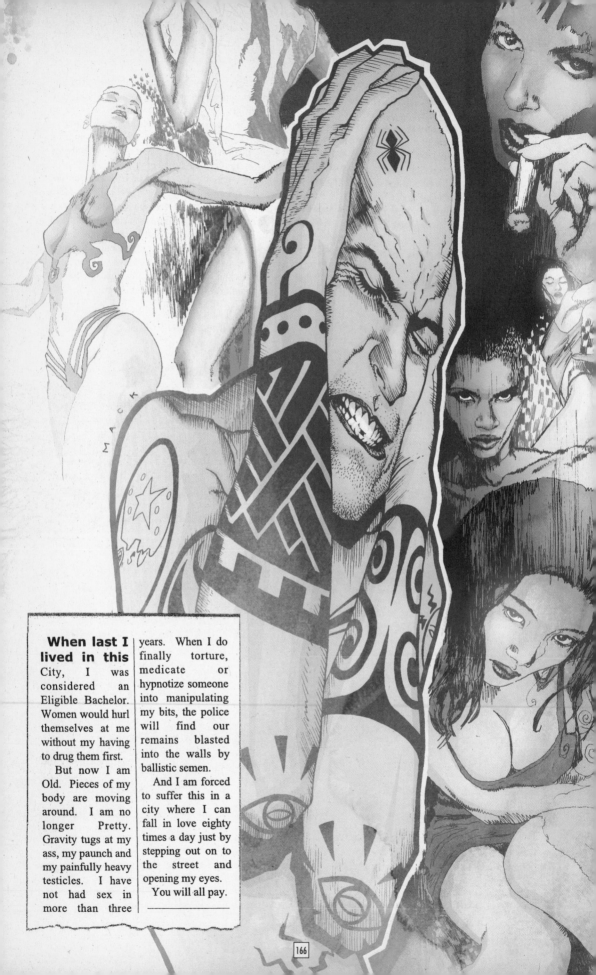

When last I lived in this City, I was considered an Eligible Bachelor. Women would hurl themselves at me without my having to drug them first.

But now I am Old. Pieces of my body are moving around. I am no longer Pretty. Gravity tugs at my ass, my paunch and my painfully heavy testicles. I have not had sex in more than three years. When I do finally torture, medicate or hypnotize someone into manipulating my bits, the police will find our remains blasted into the walls by ballistic semen.

And I am forced to suffer this in a city where I can fall in love eighty times a day just by stepping out on to the street and opening my eyes.

You will all pay.

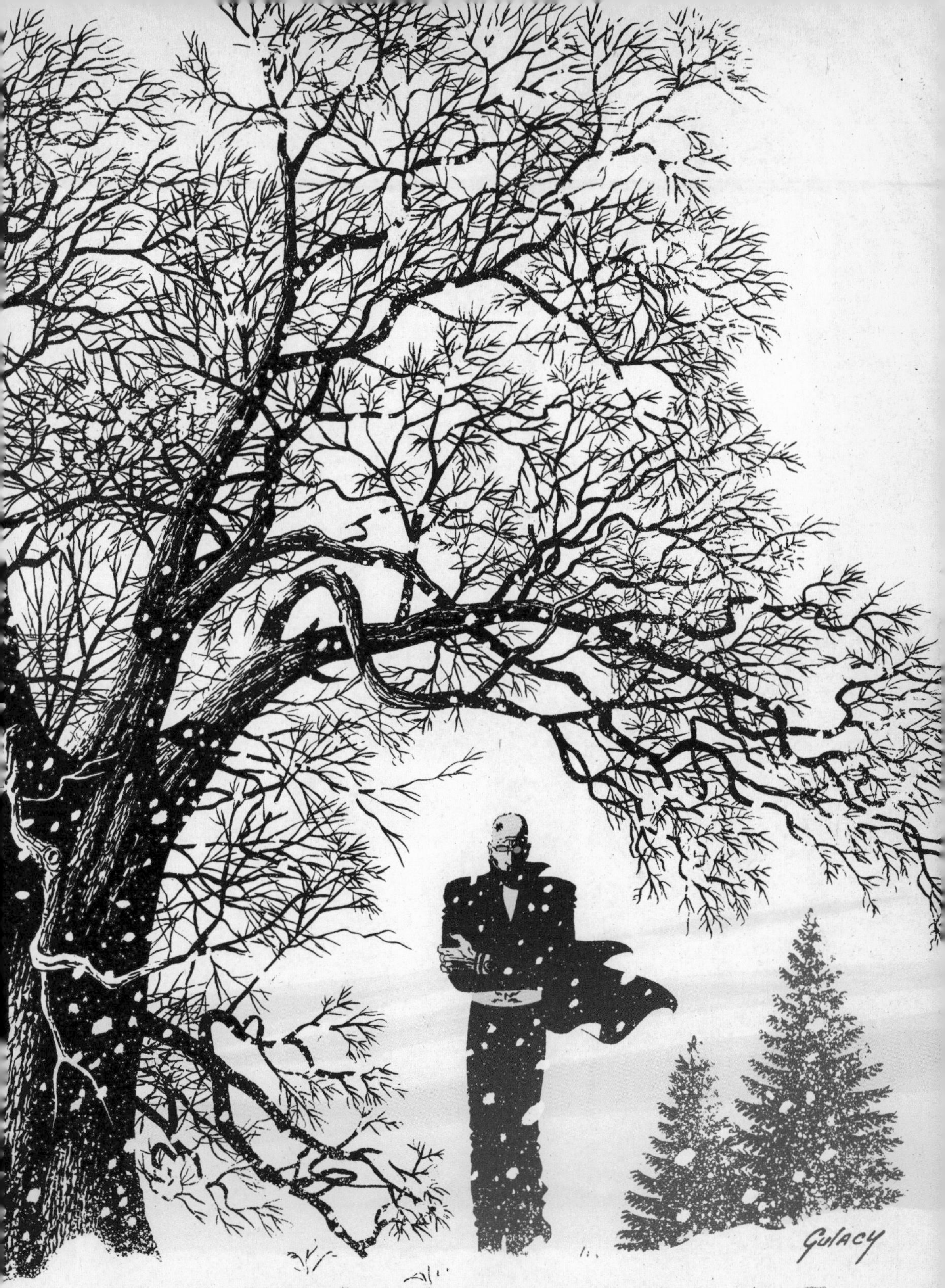
GULACY

I came back down here from a place where the snow would lay for miles, from first fall to thaw, with no mark on it other than the prints of birds, foxes and squirrels.

There's a Reservation under contruction, about ten miles south of Lugh Bend. No people in it yet, but the walls are up, creating the illusion of endless distance, and the environment and weather systems are running. I have friends there, who let me in from time to time.

Sometimes, I can do nothing but stand in constant winter, trying to remember what life is like without all of you.

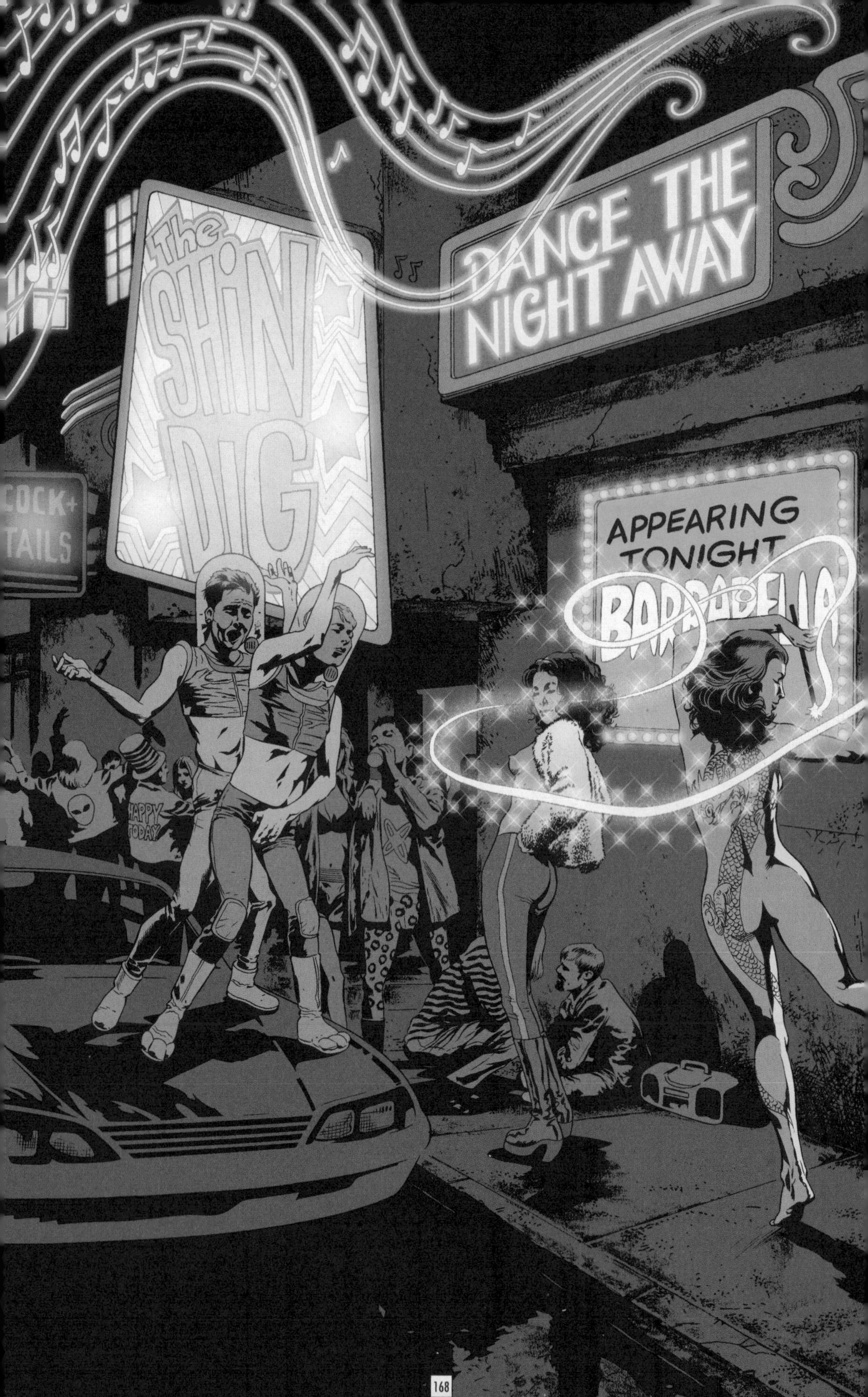

The SHiN DIG
DANCE THE NIGHT AWAY
COCK+ TAILS
APPEARING TONIGHT
HAPPY TODAY

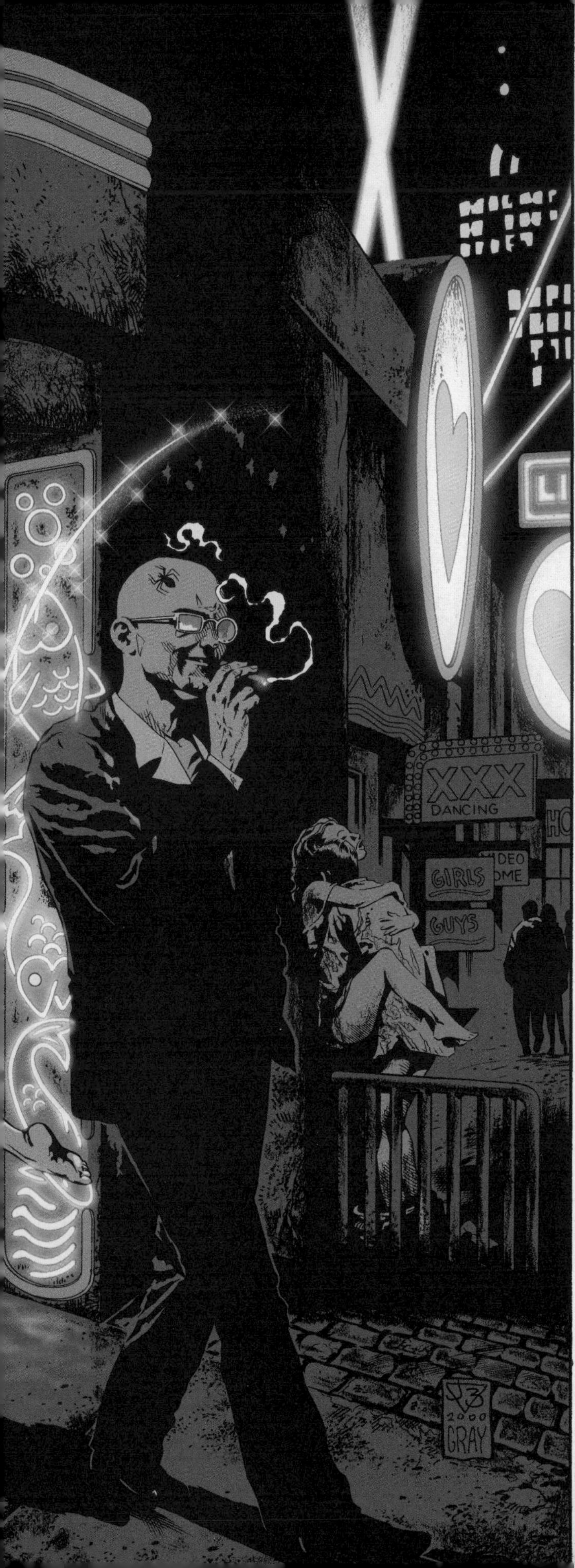
XXX
DANCING
GIRLS
GUYS
2000
GRAY

And then the sun goes down and the night comes up, and I remember why I lived here for so long.

I was born in this City, out on the docks, and as a child I'd see the glow come up in central City as the night fell down on us, and I'd sit there for hours, all happily stained by light pollution, wishing I could be there, dreaming of what I'd do. I built a thousand fantasies of night in the City, sitting there looking at the spotlights and lasers and light-snow and listening to ghost mixes of millions of different musics drifting over...

I had a thousand fantasies of what it was like here. I lived them all out in three months, and spent years coming up with new ones. It's that kind of place. The night brings out those kinds of people.

I hate this place, you know, because I can't let it go. But if you quote me I'll call you a liar.

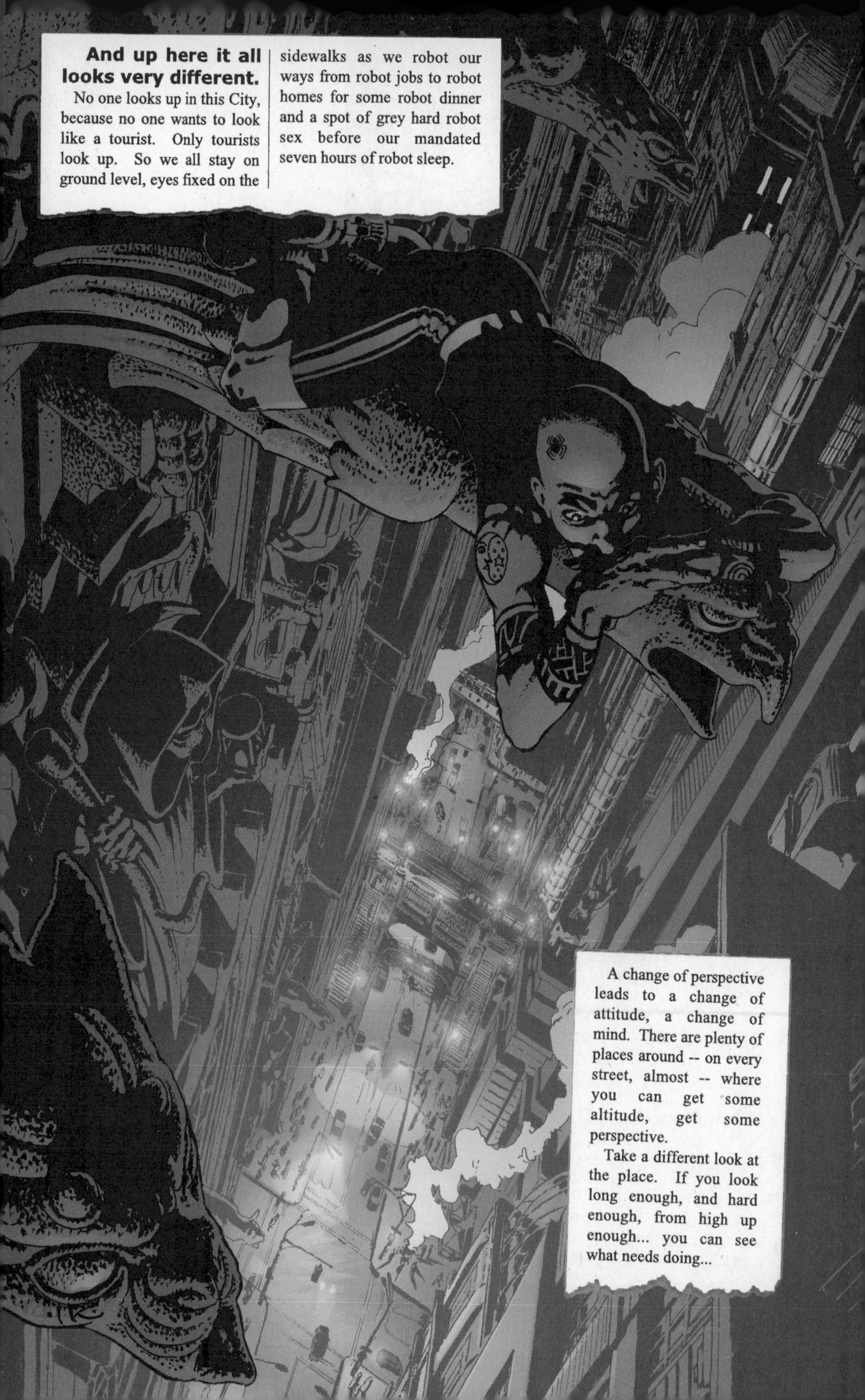
And up here it all looks very different.
No one looks up in this City, because no one wants to look like a tourist. Only tourists look up. So we all stay on ground level, eyes fixed on the sidewalks as we robot our ways from robot jobs to robot homes for some robot dinner and a spot of grey hard robot sex before our mandated seven hours of robot sleep.
A change of perspective leads to a change of attitude, a change of mind. There are plenty of places around -- on every street, almost -- where you can get some altitude, get some perspective.
Take a different look at the place. If you look long enough, and hard enough, from high up enough... you can see what needs doing...

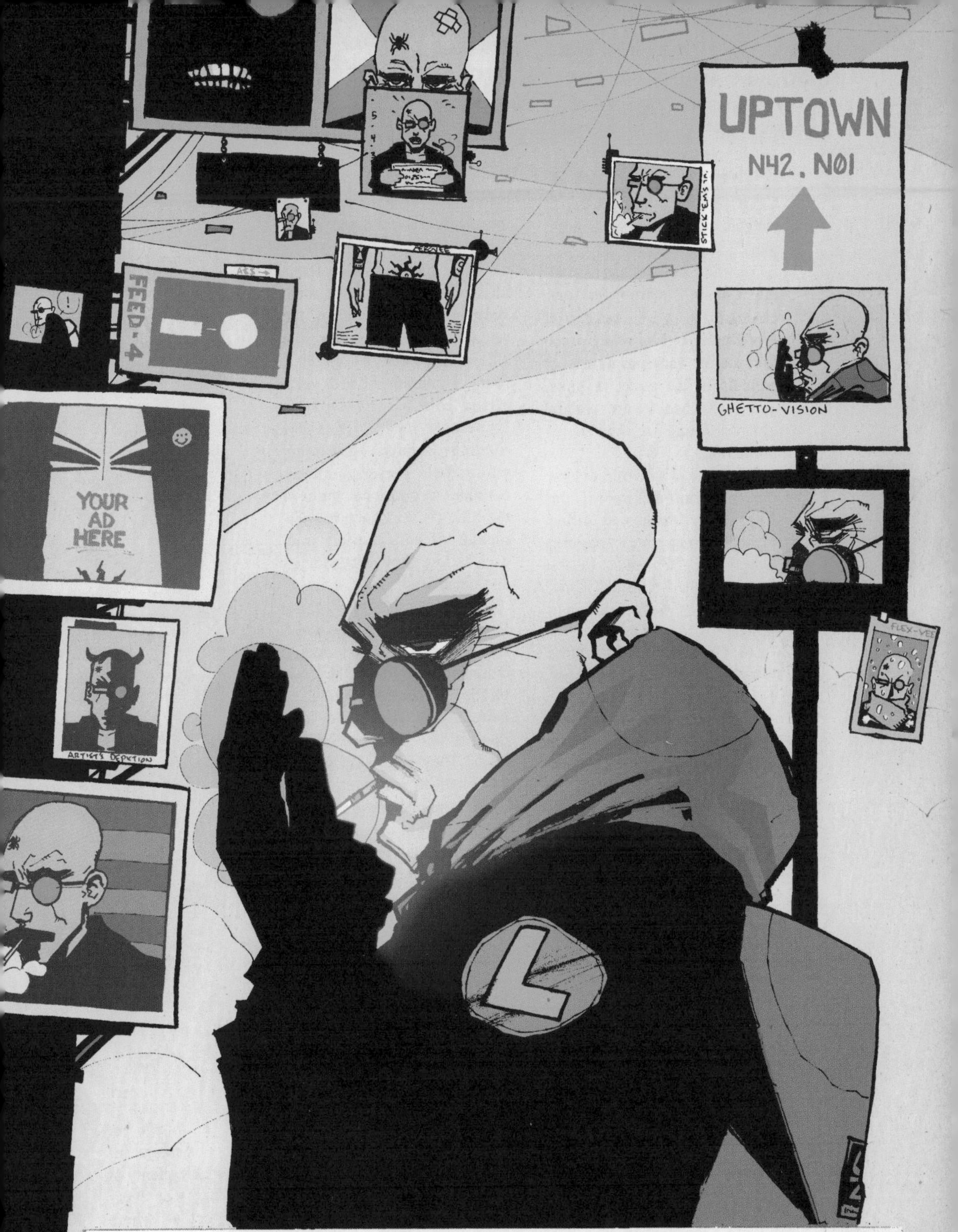
UPTOWN
N42. N01
GHETTO-VISION
FEED-4
YOUR AD HERE
ARTIST'S DEPICTION

I am Famous again.

This development does not please me. But I have found it useful. I have recorded a variety of spots discussing the important things in life. Voting. Truth. Horror. Loss. Being Fucked With Knives.

And now I am being Venerated. I have evidently Energized The Discourse and Made Politics Real Again. Children smile and laugh and rush to me in the street for comfort, singing my name. Old people clasp my hands for luck and to cheat death, and I am Beloved by the whores and the old people, who offer me all they have in return for my countenance, their cheap infected sex and blood products.

I'm back. I have a ragged army hanging on my every word. And I'm pissed off.

The thing about a City is that you can't choose who lives in it with you.

I mean, those of us around the Chase Square area are eminently sensible professionals. Not many of us are caught fucking domestic animals in the street at three a.m., and when we are, we are always found to be using protection.

The same is not true out on the western outskirts of the City, where I happened to find myself during a research trip last week. Oh no. In the district called Gashed Cow, things are very different indeed.

In Gashed Cow, the first thing you notice are the faces. Even in a City like ours, containing the dregs of every gene pool on Earth, you can detect the difference in these people. These are the people of urban myth. The people of the smashed chromosome. The people who play banjos. The people who drank the intellect suppressants in the water supply in preference to the clean water bussed in by the rescue op.

Guys in tan leather flares idly jacking off into the road, keeping a lazy eye on the female newsreader on the sidewalk screen by his left foot. Hundreds of kids with Attention Deficit Hyperactivity Disorder running around screaming while their berserk mothers continue to pump out more of the little fuckers for those few months of soft comfort from each before they start moving and never stop...

I don't want to turn on my fellow human, I really don't. But I saw these people believing everything they saw on the TV. Everything. They believe that The Smiler is a good man. They believe in God. They believe in justice. They believe in *Knight Rider*.

These people are the Enemy. Upgrade your sexual organs today, so that we may leave them behind.

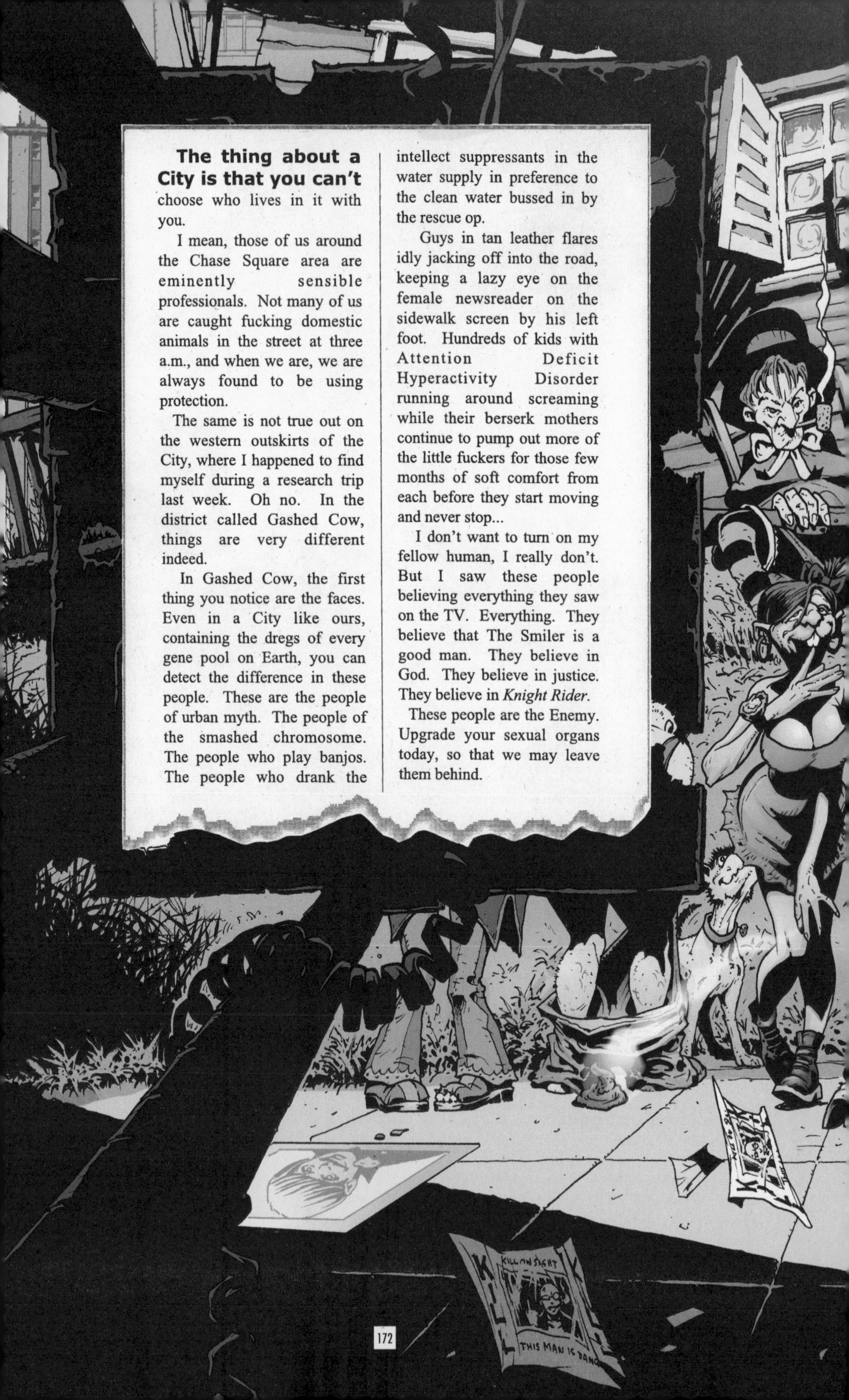
KILL ON SIGHT

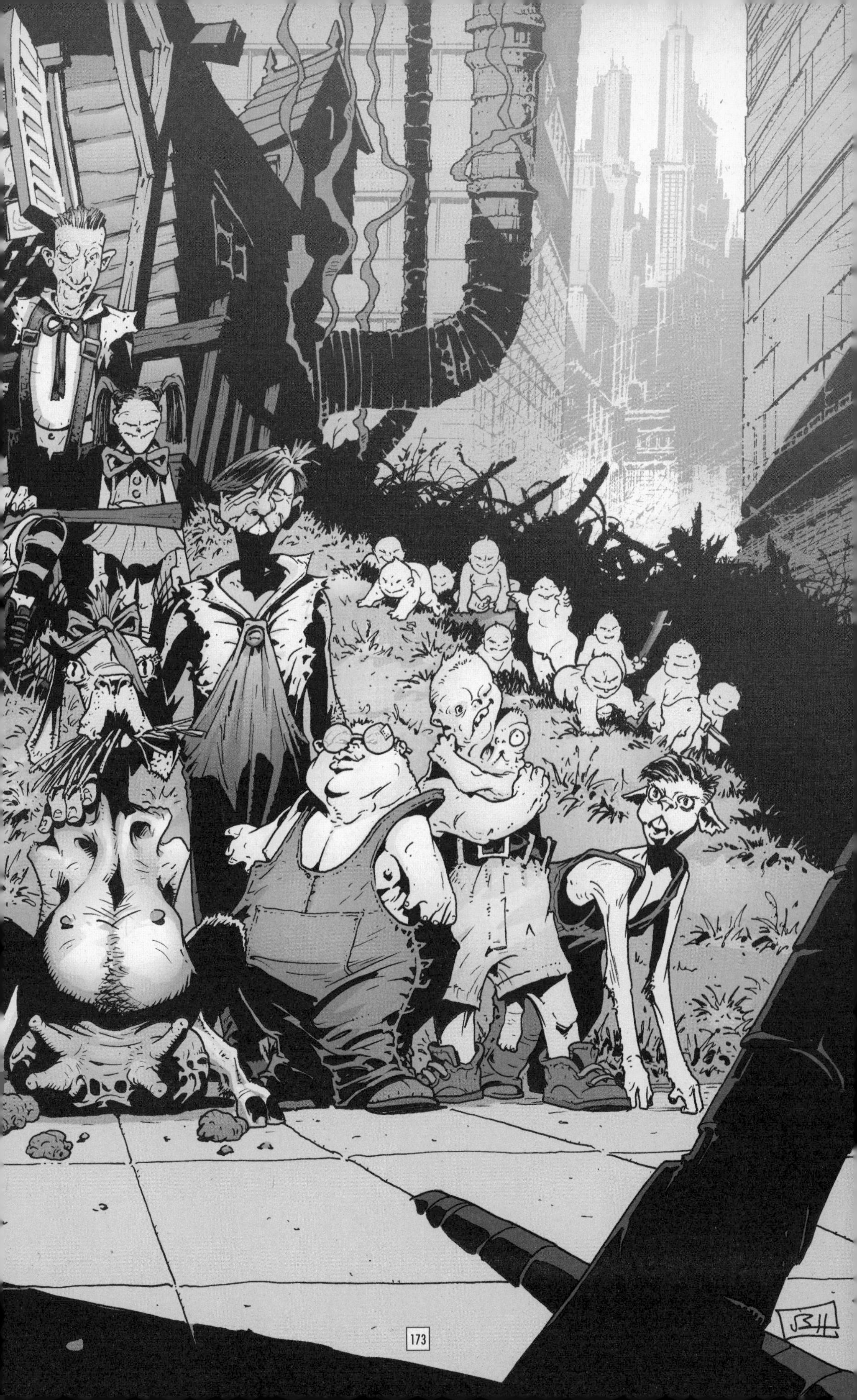

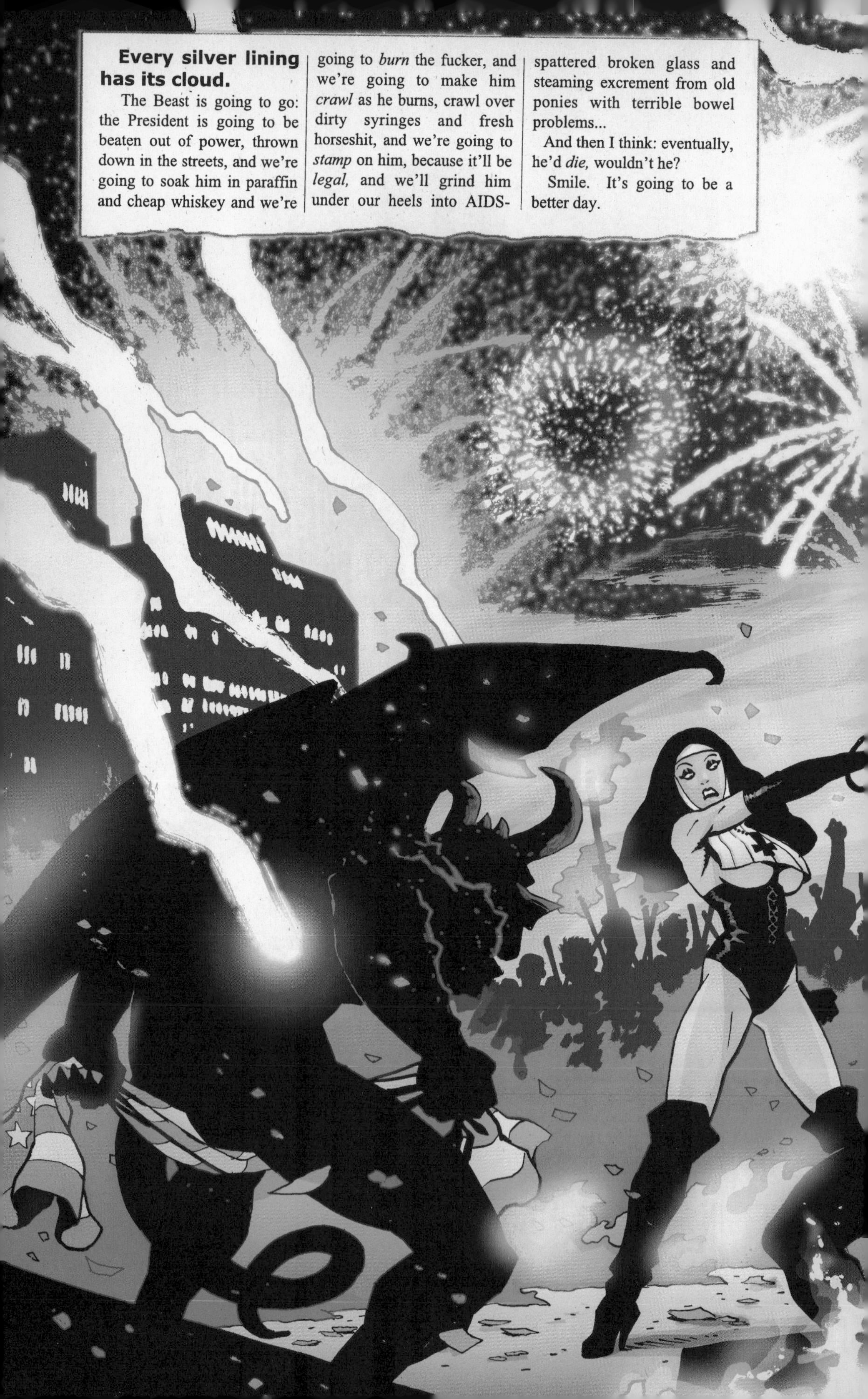
Every silver lining has its cloud.
The Beast is going to go: the President is going to be beaten out of power, thrown down in the streets, and we're going to soak him in paraffin and cheap whiskey and we're going to burn the fucker, and we're going to make him crawl as he burns, crawl over dirty syringes and fresh horseshit, and we're going to stamp on him, because it'll be legal, and we'll grind him under our heels into AIDS-spattered broken glass and steaming excrement from old ponies with terrible bowel problems...
And then I think: eventually, he'd die, wouldn't he?
Smile. It's going to be a better day.

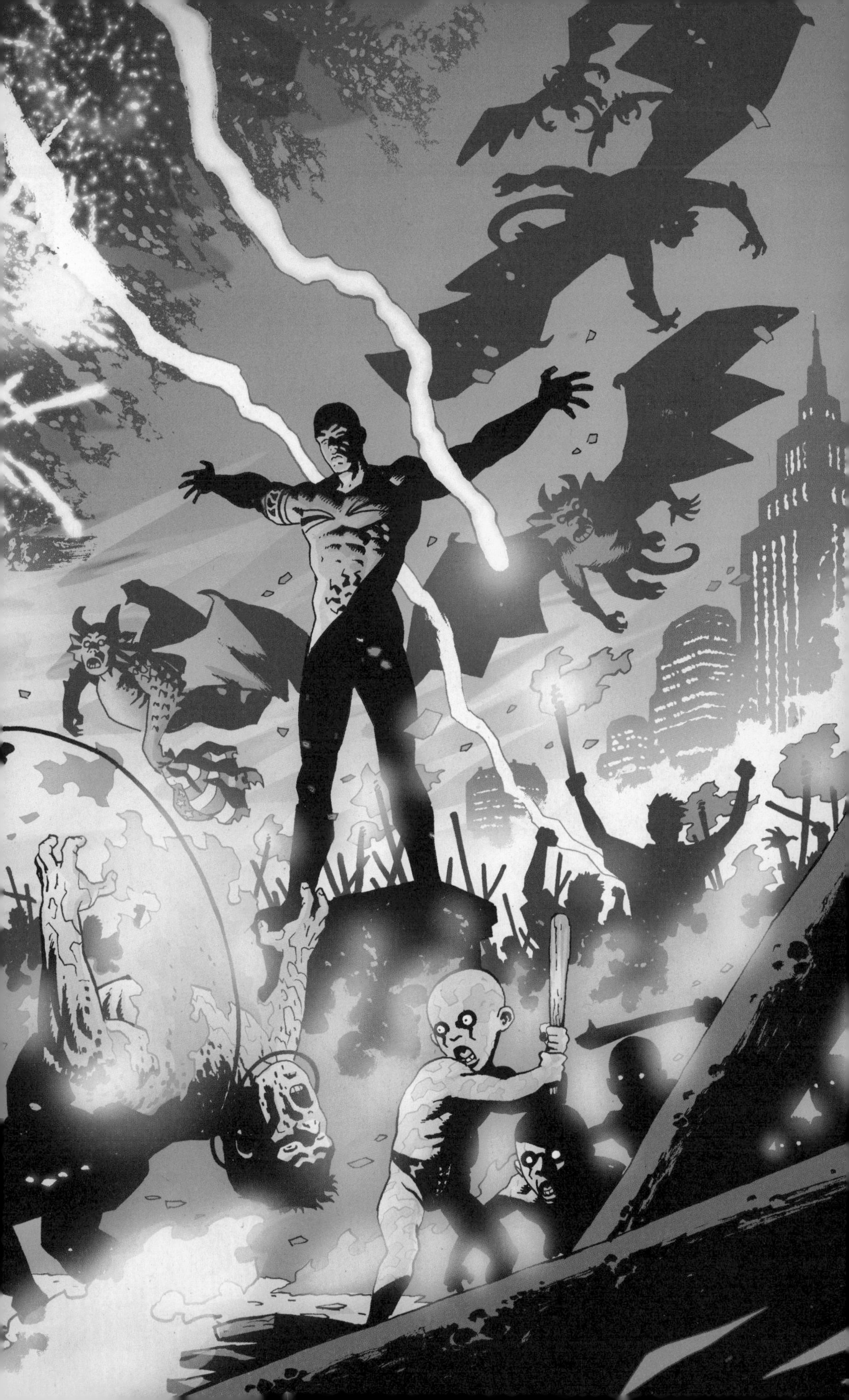

I have developed a new assistant. This is not, as far as she is concerned, a good thing. She hates me immediately. She is intelligent, and comes from a fascinating background. She is fairly quick on the uptake, and will be quicker when the studenty curves on her have been abraded into sharp edges. Frankly, she's far more intelligent than I am and has a genetic inheritance that leaves mine standing in the mire. Actually, now I think about it, my dad used to screw mire.

And she loathes me. No half measures here. She thinks I didn't notice the death trap she set outside my door, or the poison in the coffee.

Her name is Yelena Rossini, and she may well prove to be the best assistant I ever had. I'll tell you how she grows up. If you meet her, tell her none of this. You see, she refuses to read the column...

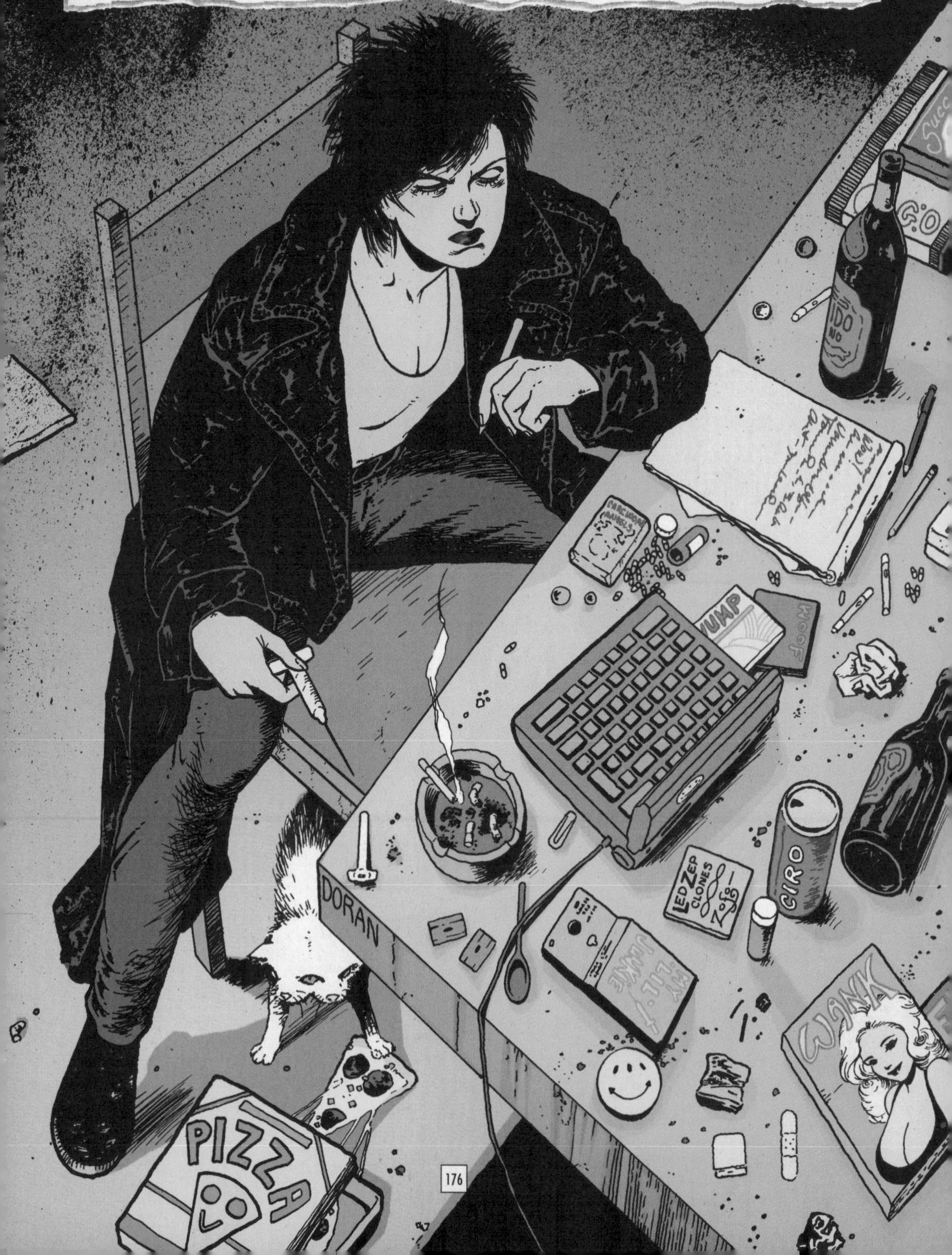

DORAN
CIRO
LED ZEP CLONES
PIZZA
WANK

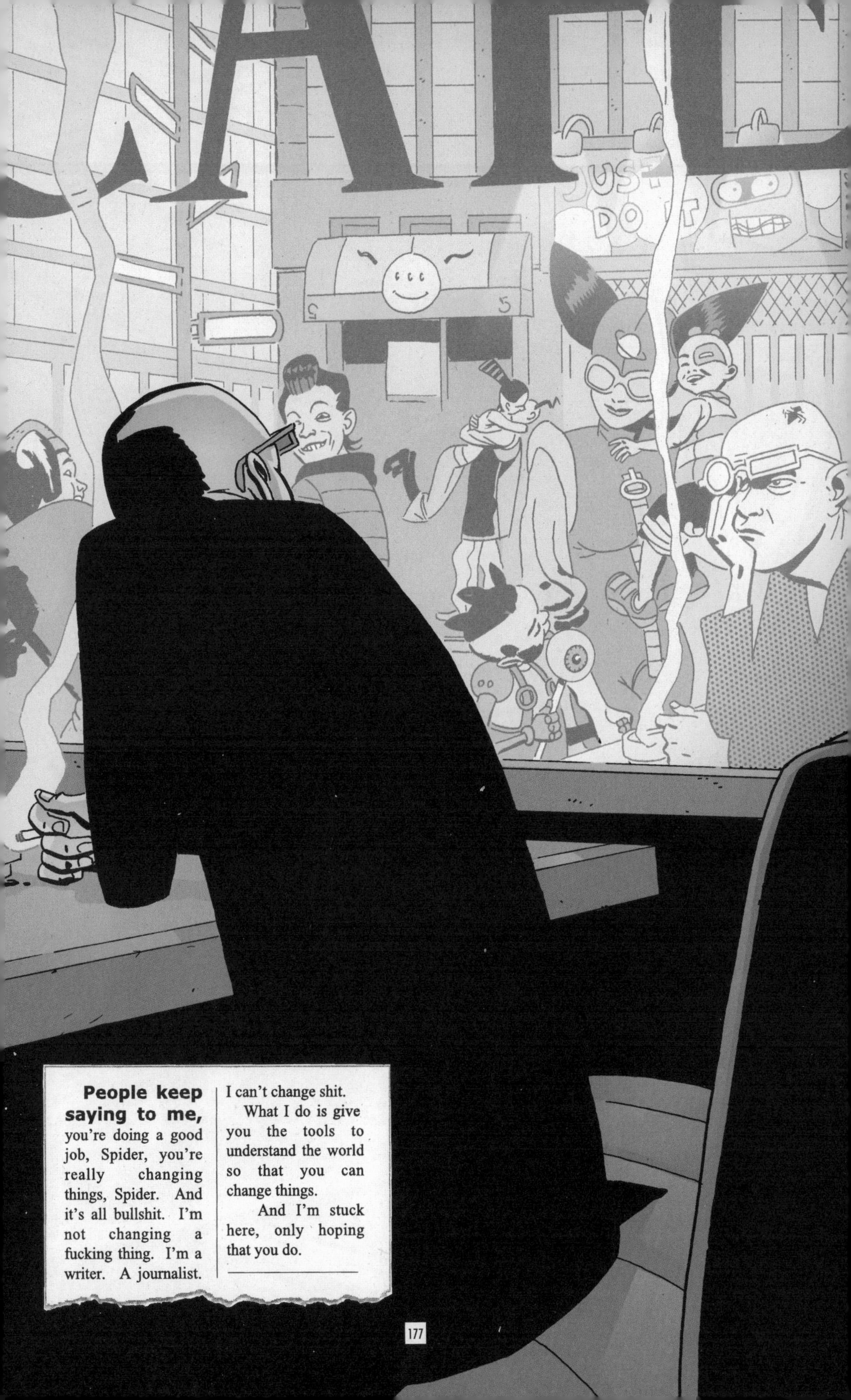
People keep saying to me, you're doing a good job, Spider, you're really changing things, Spider. And it's all bullshit. I'm not changing a fucking thing. I'm a writer. A journalist. I can't change shit.
What I do is give you the tools to understand the world so that you can change things.
And I'm stuck here, only hoping that you do.

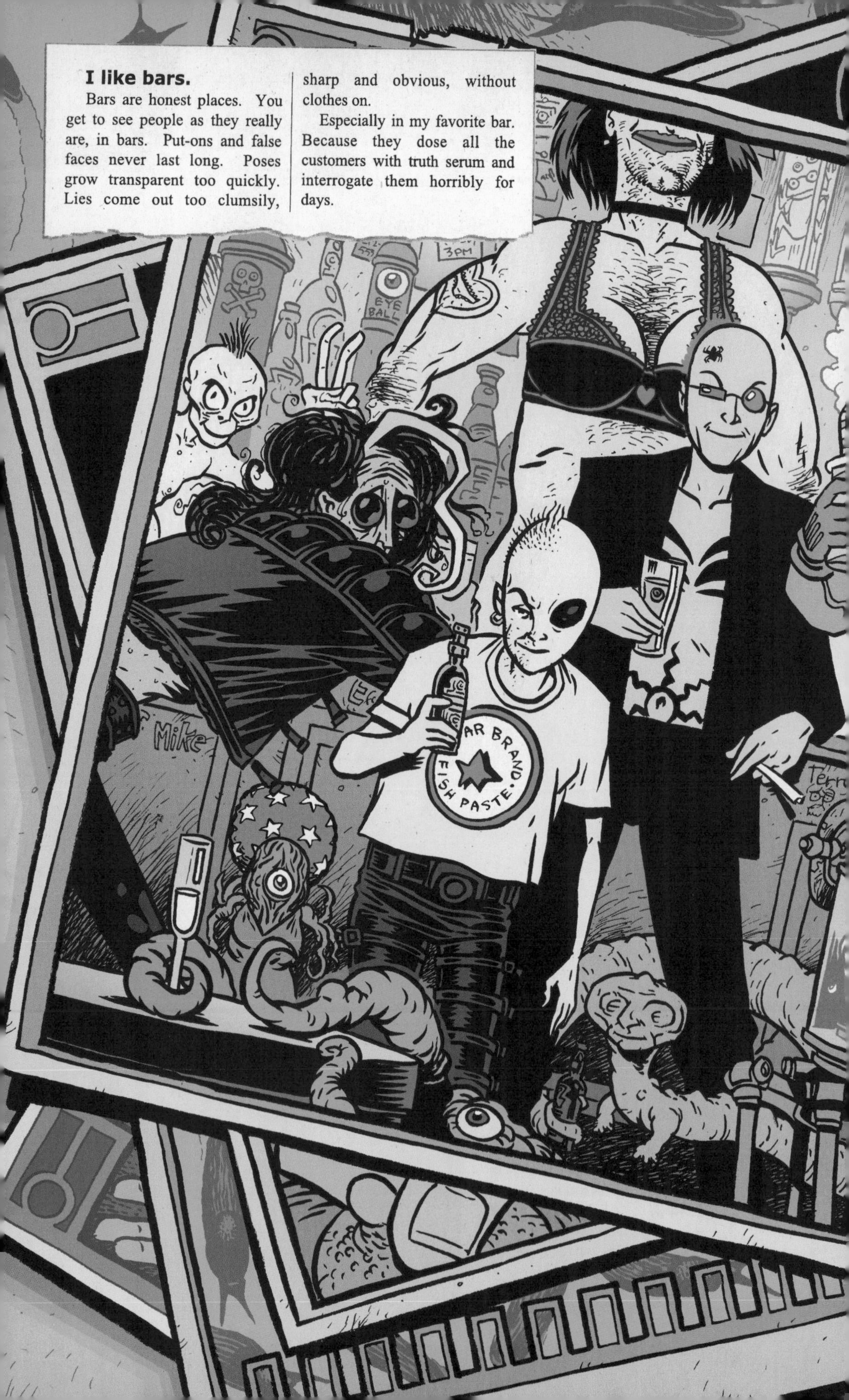
I like bars.
Bars are honest places. You get to see people as they really are, in bars. Put-ons and false faces never last long. Poses grow transparent too quickly. Lies come out too clumsily, sharp and obvious, without clothes on.
Especially in my favorite bar. Because they dose all the customers with truth serum and interrogate them horribly for days.
3PM
EYE BALL
Mike
FISH PASTE.

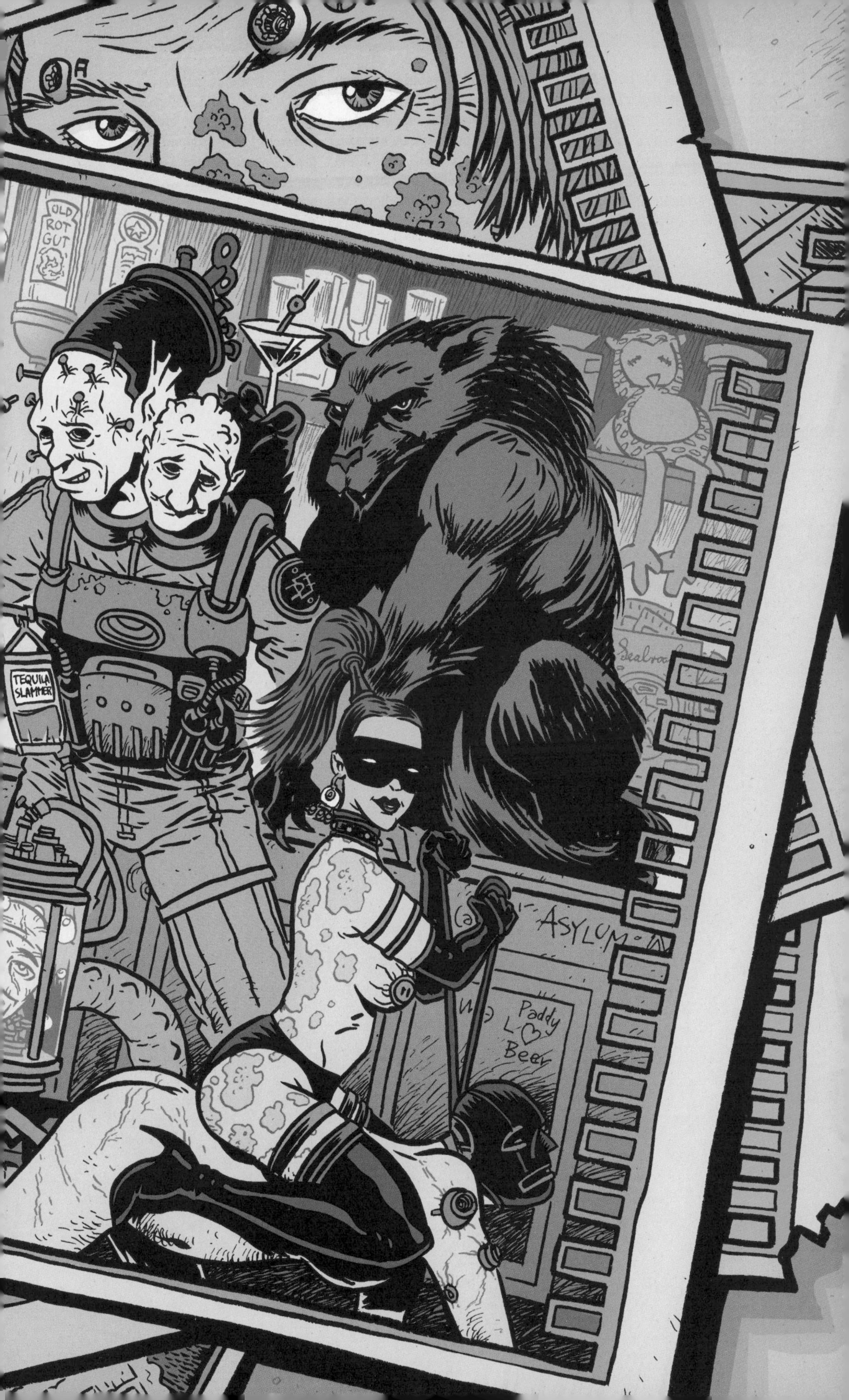
OLD
ROT
GUT
TEQUILA
SLAMMER
ASYLUM
Paddy
L♥
Beer

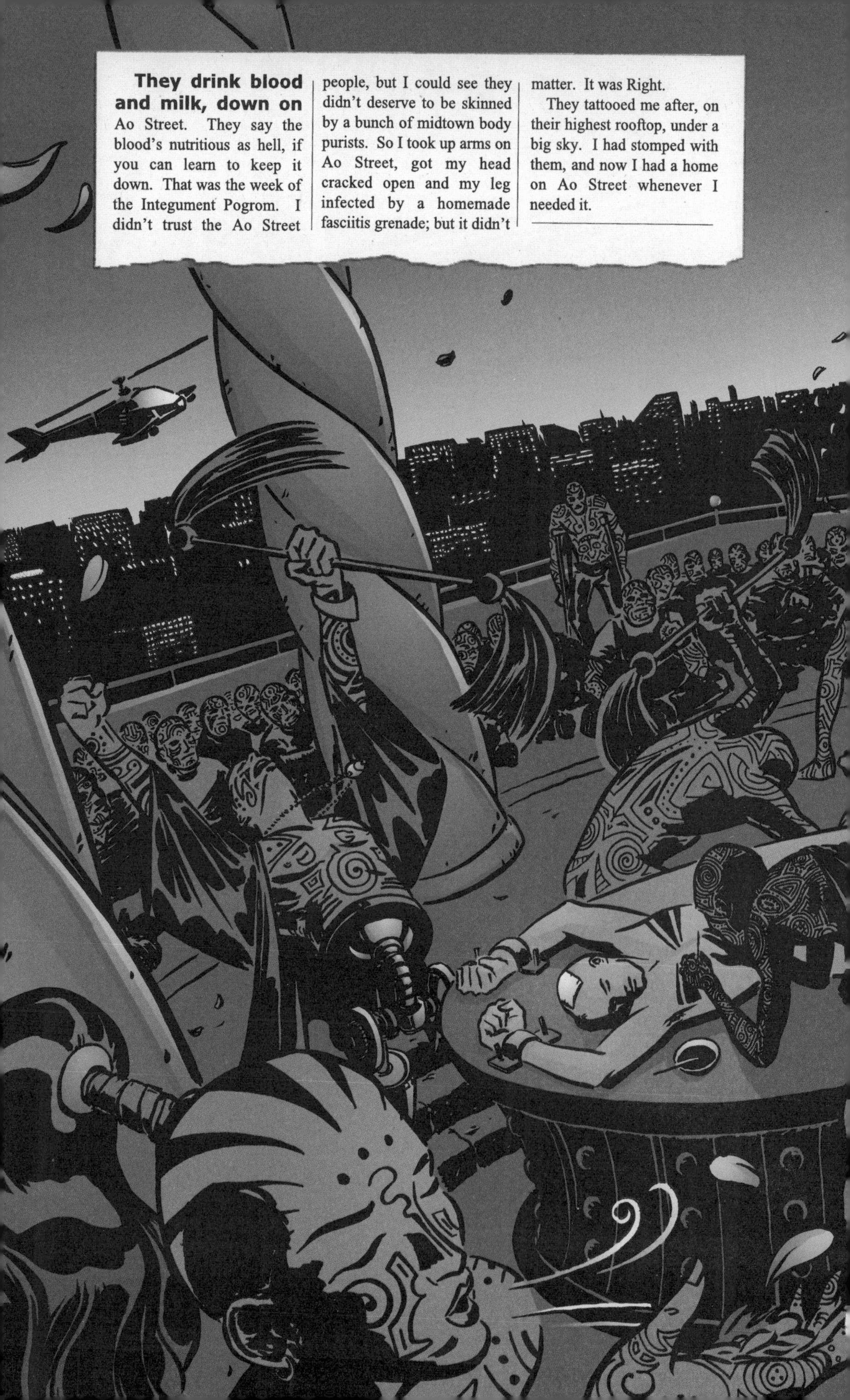
They drink blood and milk, down on Ao Street. They say the blood's nutritious as hell, if you can learn to keep it down. That was the week of the Integument Pogrom. I didn't trust the Ao Street people, but I could see they didn't deserve to be skinned by a bunch of midtown body purists. So I took up arms on Ao Street, got my head cracked open and my leg infected by a homemade fasciitis grenade; but it didn't matter. It was Right.
They tattooed me after, on their highest rooftop, under a big sky. I had stomped with them, and now I had a home on Ao Street whenever I needed it.

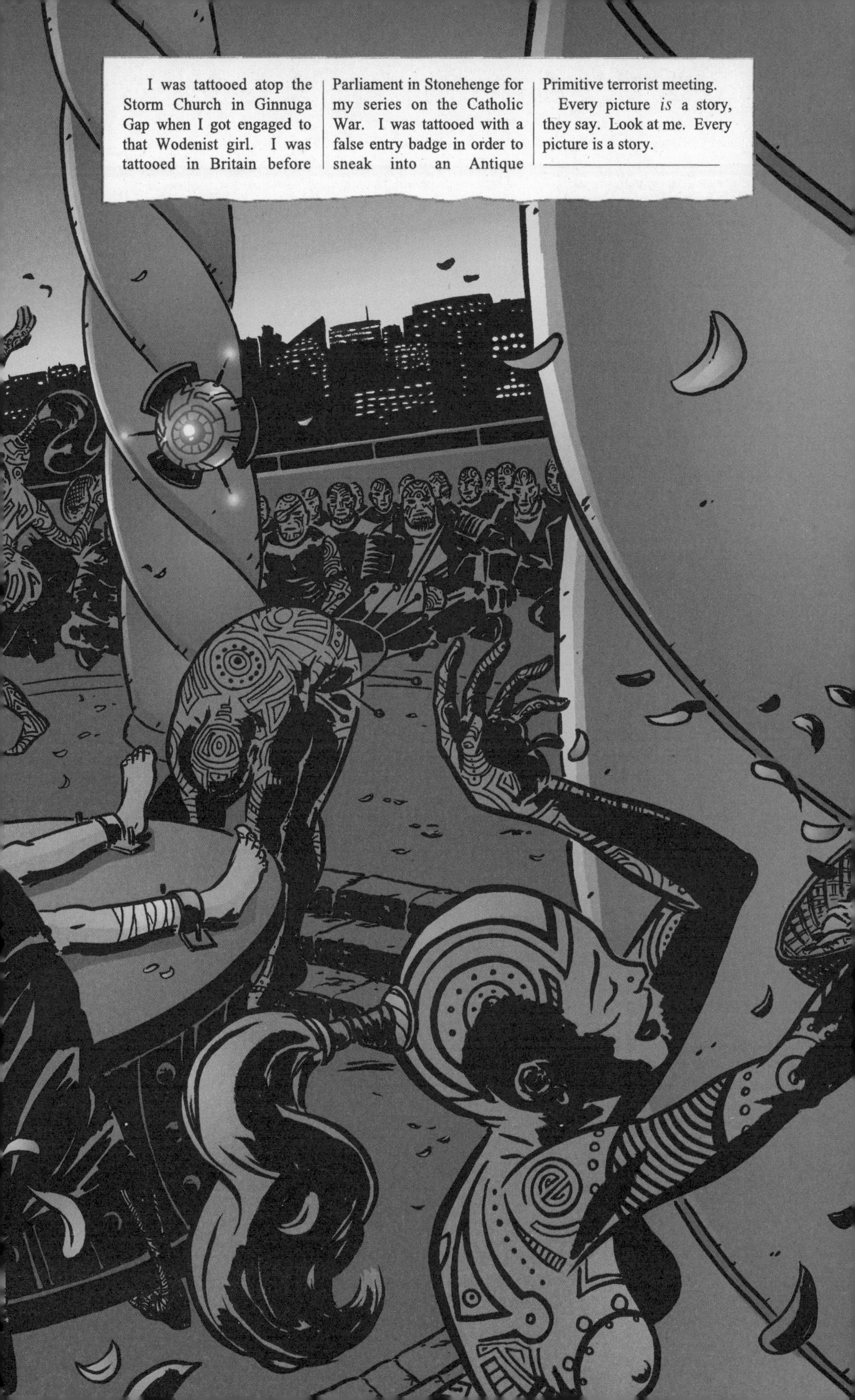
I was tattooed atop the Storm Church in Ginnuga Gap when I got engaged to that Wodenist girl. I was tattooed in Britain before Parliament in Stonehenge for my series on the Catholic War. I was tattooed with a false entry badge in order to sneak into an Antique Primitive terrorist meeting.
Every picture *is* a story, they say. Look at me. Every picture is a story.

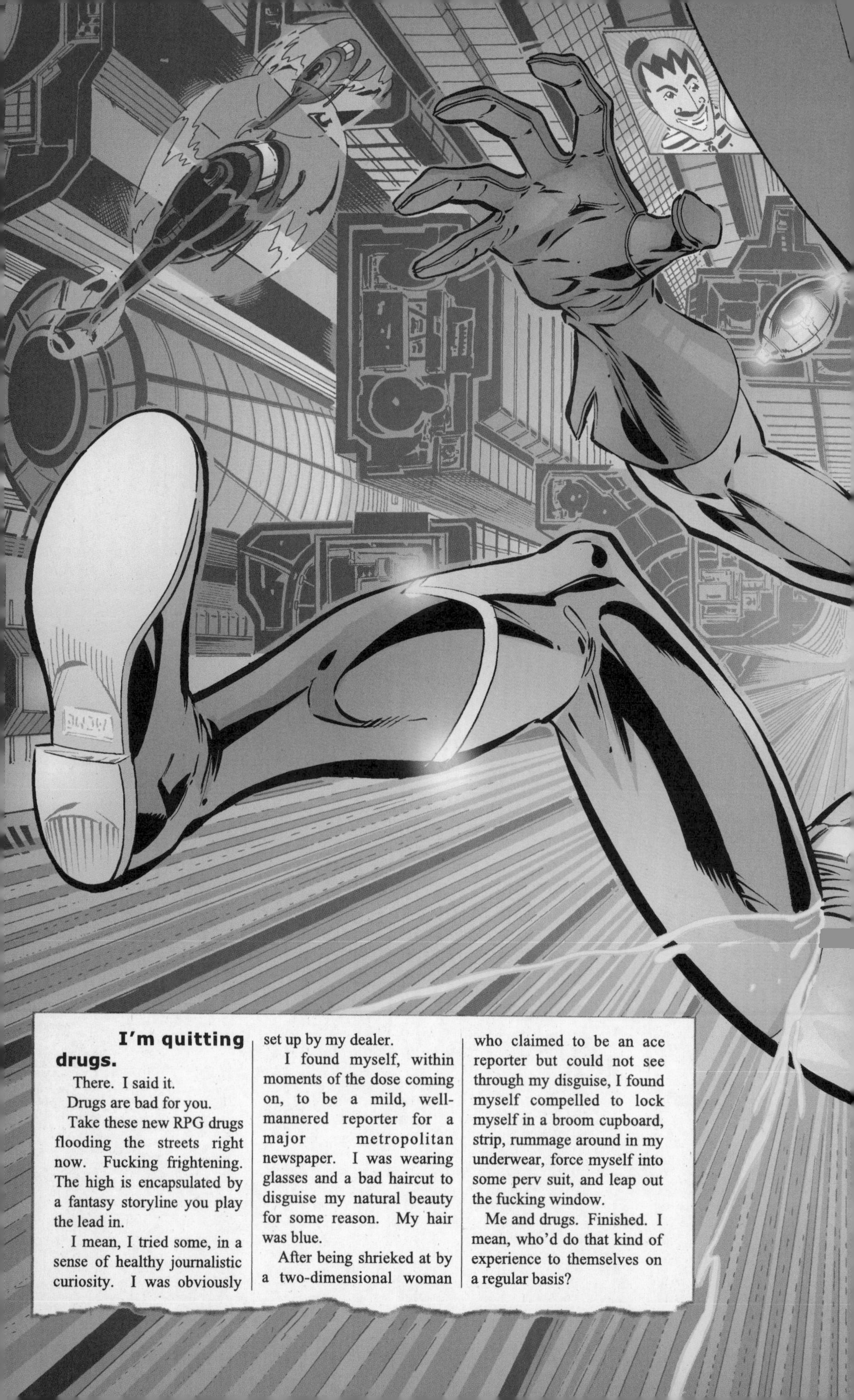

I'm quitting drugs.

There. I said it.

Drugs are bad for you.

Take these new RPG drugs flooding the streets right now. Fucking frightening. The high is encapsulated by a fantasy storyline you play the lead in.

I mean, I tried some, in a sense of healthy journalistic curiosity. I was obviously set up by my dealer.

I found myself, within moments of the dose coming on, to be a mild, well-mannered reporter for a major metropolitan newspaper. I was wearing glasses and a bad haircut to disguise my natural beauty for some reason. My hair was blue.

After being shrieked at by a two-dimensional woman who claimed to be an ace reporter but could not see through my disguise, I found myself compelled to lock myself in a broom cupboard, strip, rummage around in my underwear, force myself into some perv suit, and leap out the fucking window.

Me and drugs. Finished. I mean, who'd do that kind of experience to themselves on a regular basis?

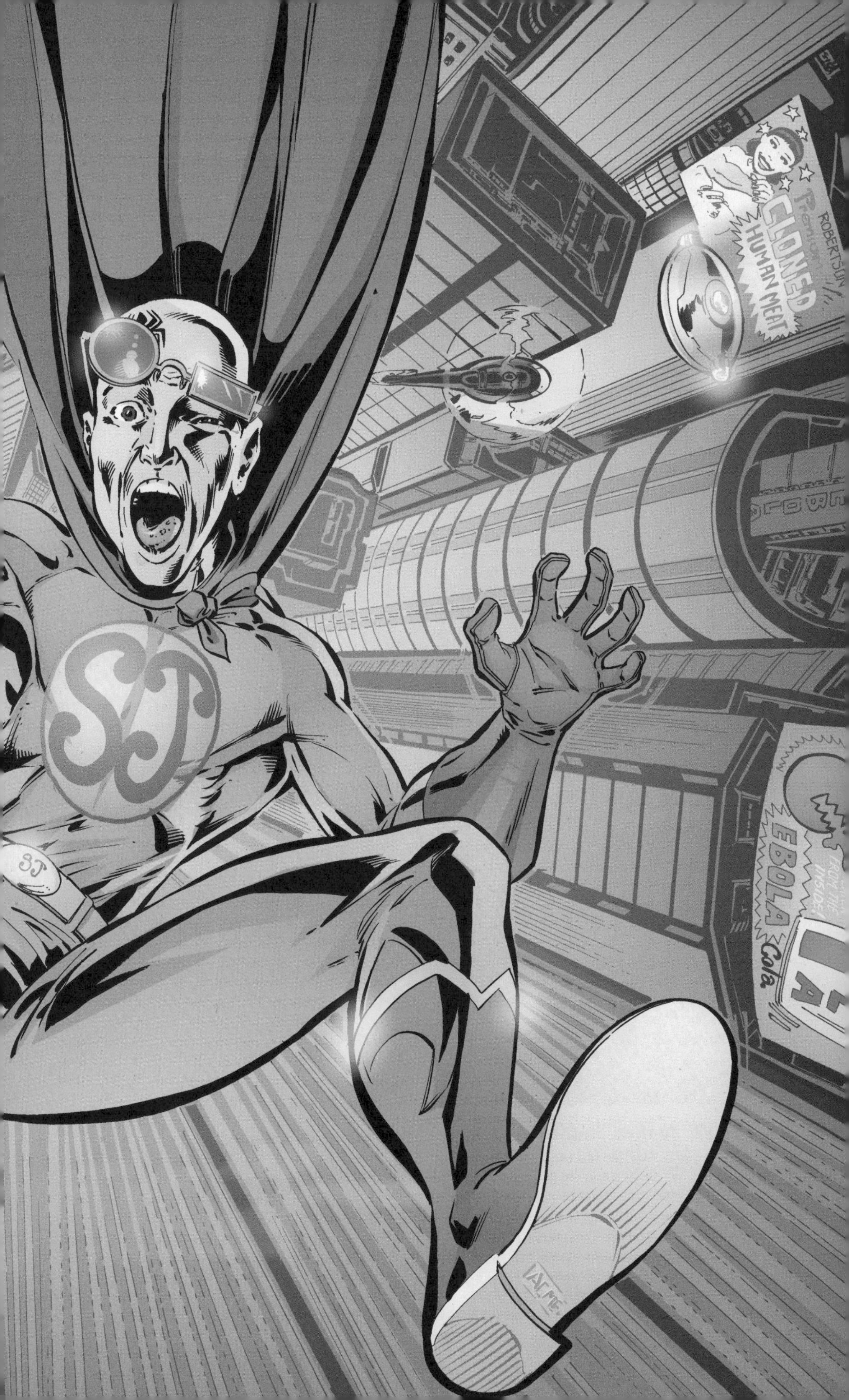
ROBERTSON
Premium
CLONED
HUMAN MEAT
FROM THE INSIDE!
EBOLA
Cola
SJ
ACME

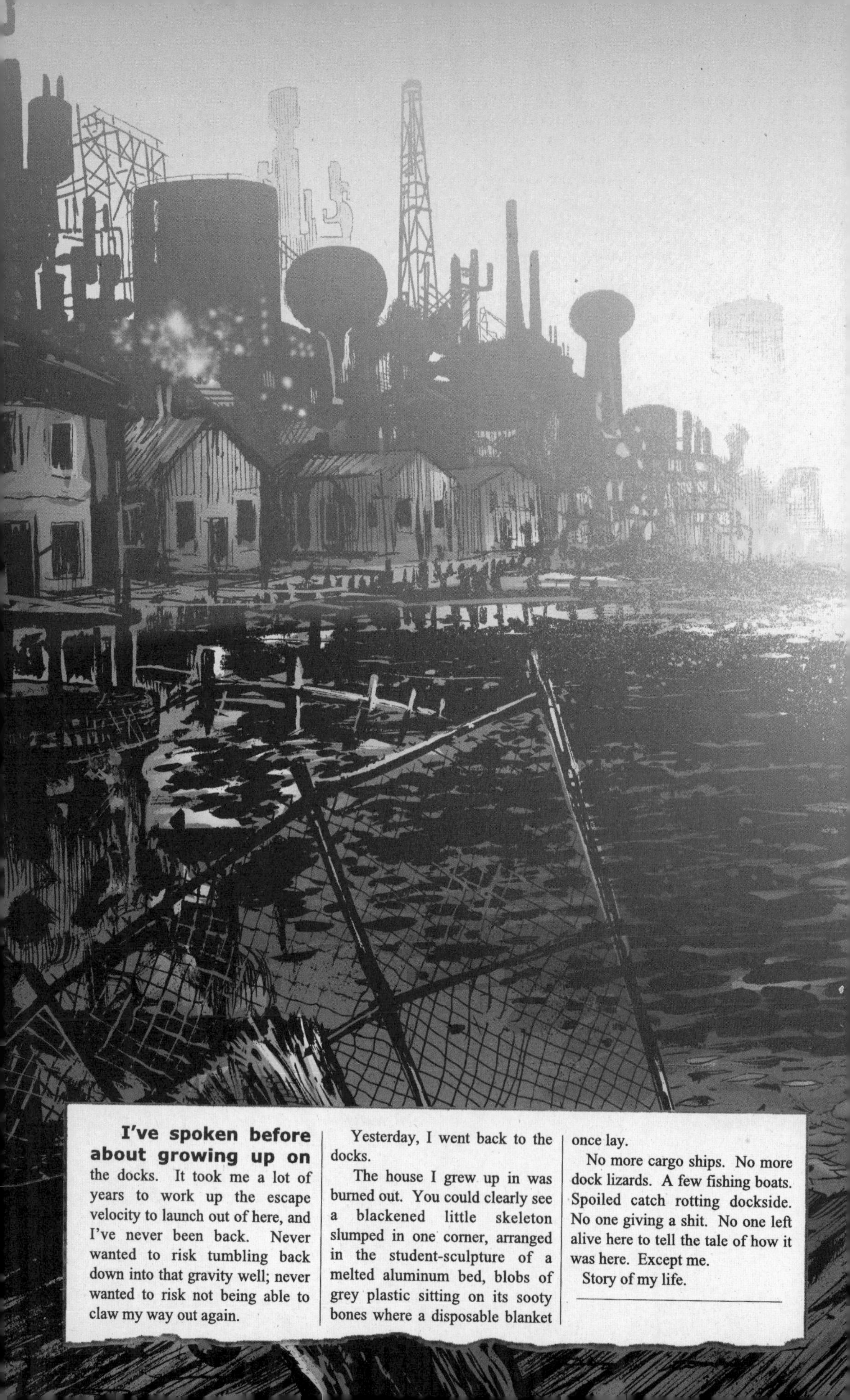

I've spoken before about growing up on the docks. It took me a lot of years to work up the escape velocity to launch out of here, and I've never been back. Never wanted to risk tumbling back down into that gravity well; never wanted to risk not being able to claw my way out again.

Yesterday, I went back to the docks.

The house I grew up in was burned out. You could clearly see a blackened little skeleton slumped in one corner, arranged in the student-sculpture of a melted aluminum bed, blobs of grey plastic sitting on its sooty bones where a disposable blanket once lay.

No more cargo ships. No more dock lizards. A few fishing boats. Spoiled catch rotting dockside. No one giving a shit. No one left alive here to tell the tale of how it was here. Except me.

Story of my life.

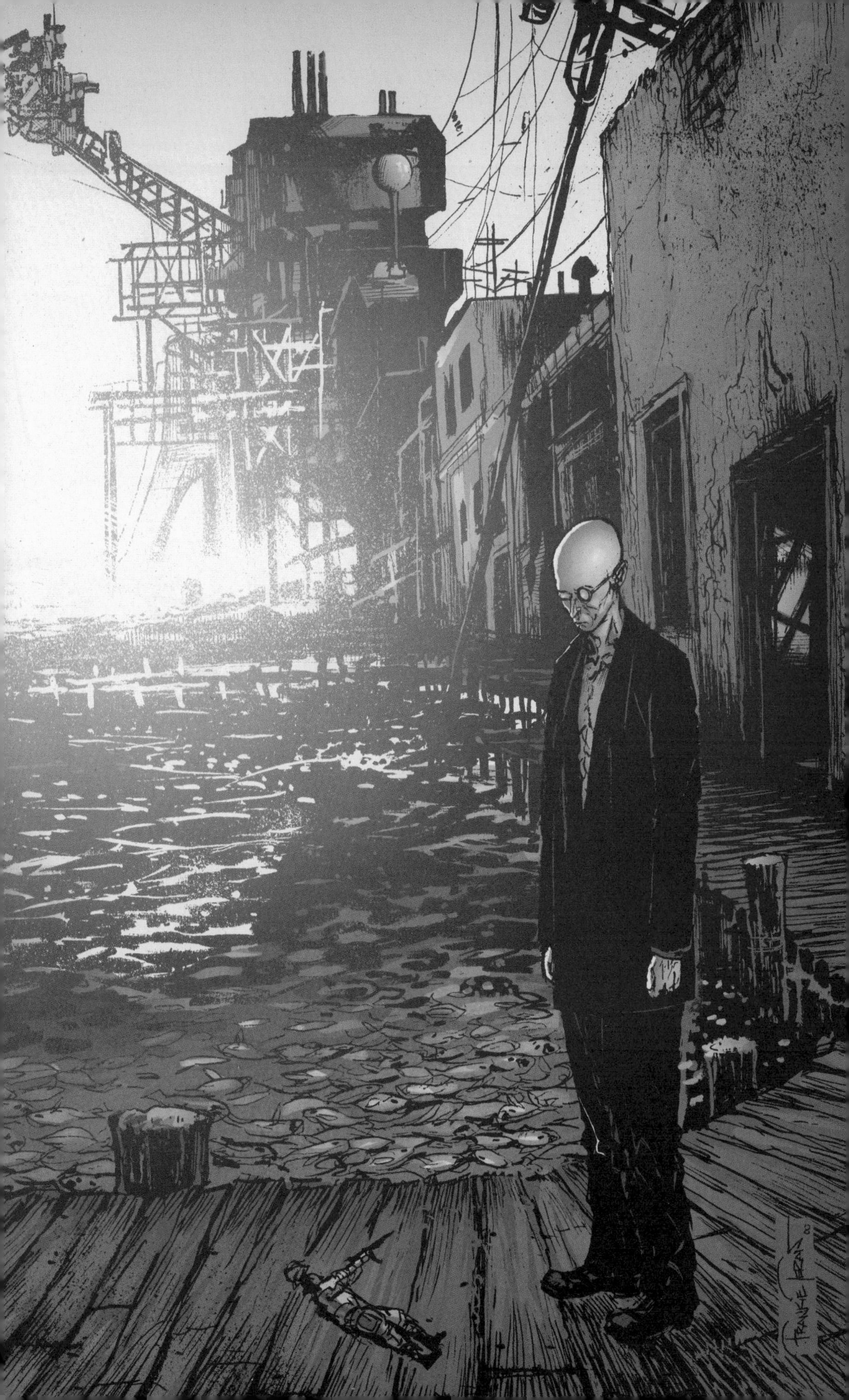

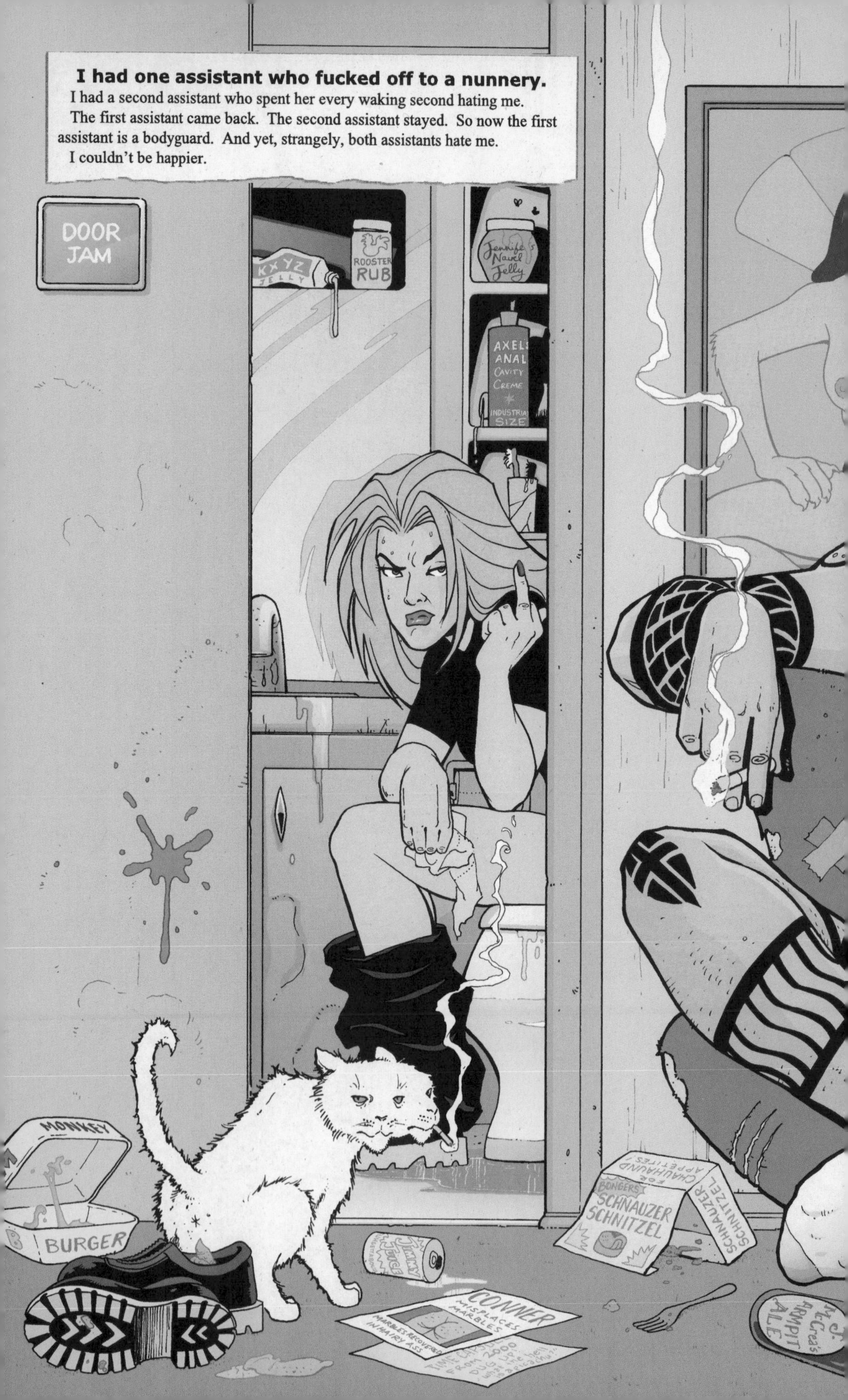
I had one assistant who fucked off to a nunnery.
I had a second assistant who spent her every waking second hating me.
The first assistant came back. The second assistant stayed. So now the first assistant is a bodyguard. And yet, strangely, both assistants hate me.
I couldn't be happier.
DOOR JAM
KXYZ JELLY
ROOSTER RUB
Jennifer's Navel Jelly
AXELS ANAL CAVITY CREME INDUSTRIAL SIZE
MONKEY BURGER
JIMMY JUICE
CONNER MISPLACES MARBLES
MARBLES RECOVERED IN HAIRY ASS
TIME CAPSULE FROM 2000 DUG UP! what the hell is a Pikachu?!
BONGERS SCHNAUZER SCHNITZEL
FOR CHAUHAUND APPETITES!
SCHNAUZER SCHNITZEL
M.J. McCrea's ARMPIT ALE

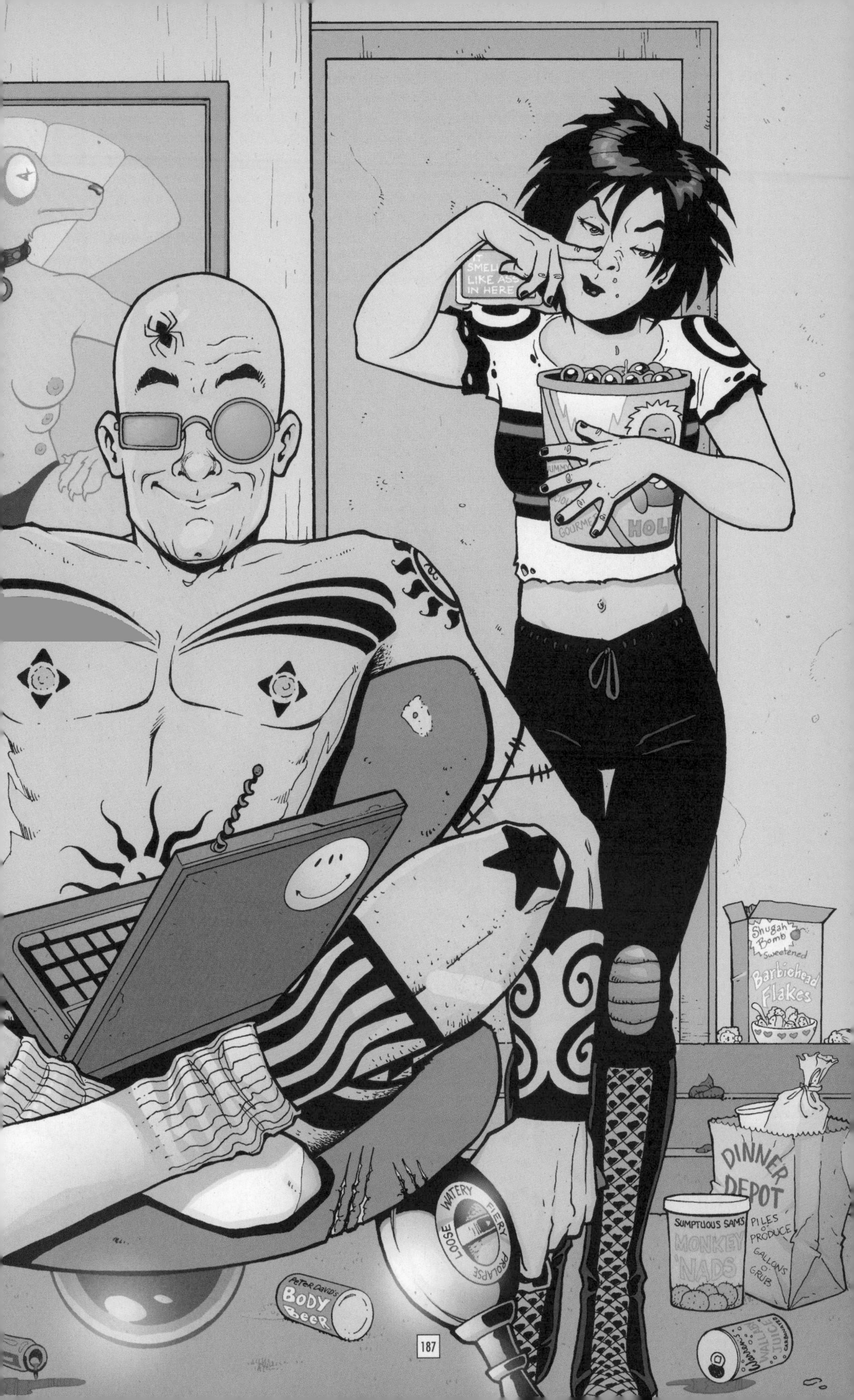
IT SMELL
LIKE ASS
IN HERE
Shugah Bomb
Sweetened
Barbiehead Flakes
DINNER DEPOT
PILES O' PRODUCE
GALLONS O' GRUB
SUMPTUOUS SAM'S
MONKEY 'NADS
LOOSE WATERY FIERY PROLAPSE
PETER DAVID'S
BODY BEER
Warren's
WALLABY JUICE
CARBONATED

I've been on television again. Taping a game show, no less. Now, before you start screaming Sellout and waving your pitchforks and torches in the air, hear me out. It's a game show produced by Pharmatopia. You'll have seen them in the news: the people attempting to bring back the dead by cloning them and reconstructing their electromagnetic auras. Well, they're partway there, and are funding the final big push via this game show. ZOMBIE GLADIATORS. Wherein celebrities engage in arena deathmatches with famous people from the past. So I'm not selling out. I'm helping fund the apotheosis of the human species while beating resurrected power-junkie fame-whores back into the grave.

Don't you wish you were me?

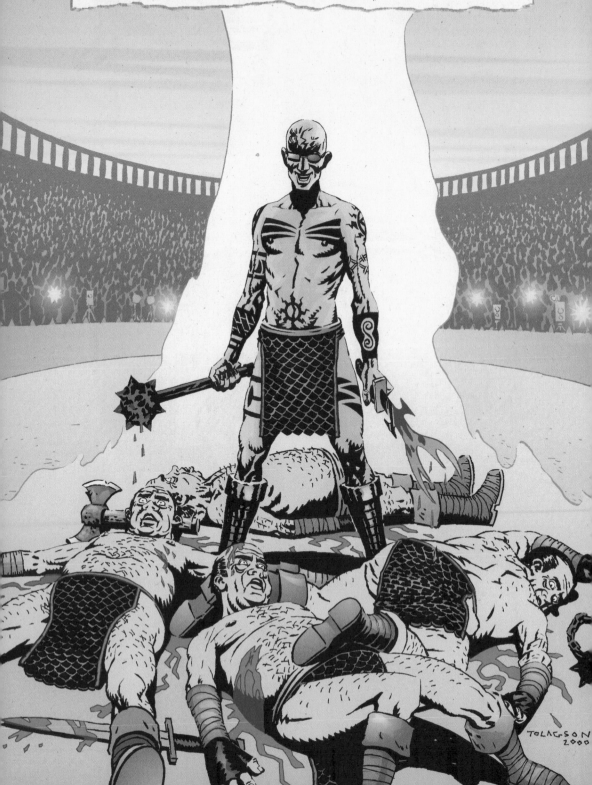

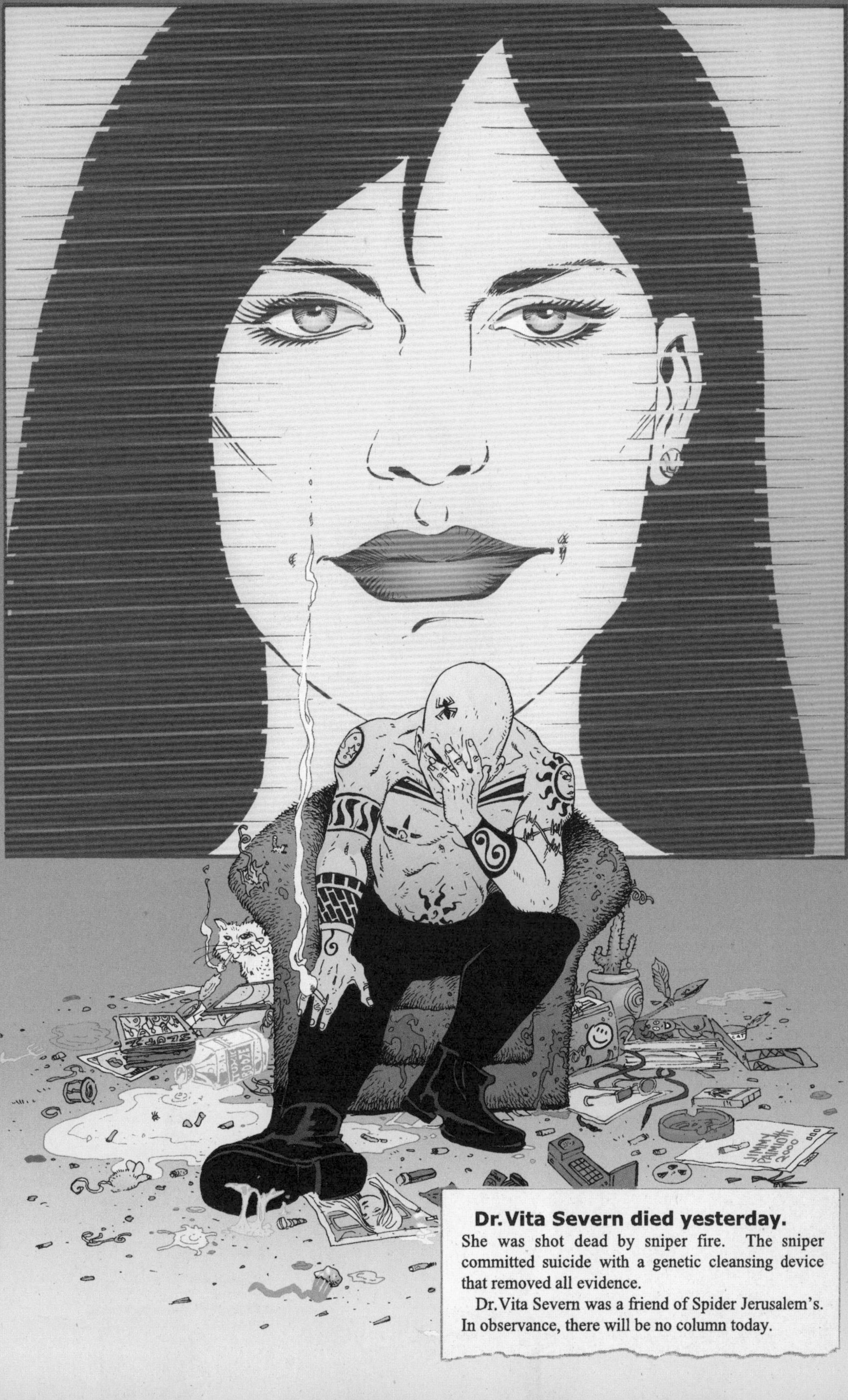

Dr. Vita Severn died yesterday.
She was shot dead by sniper fire. The sniper committed suicide with a genetic cleansing device that removed all evidence.
Dr. Vita Severn was a friend of Spider Jerusalem's. In observance, there will be no column today.

This isn't Spider Jerusalem. I'm Yelena Rossini, and I'm writing Mr. Jerusalem's column in his stead today, at his express invitation. Well. More like an order. He called it a "proclamation," in actual fact. This was during the afternoon he spent dressed as a pharaoh. Some of you may have seen that.

Rather more of you will have seen him two days ago, during what we are calling his "impromptu tour." Which brings me to the subject of this piece. I'd like to clear up a few misconceptions about Mr. Jerusalem's activities during the "tour."

For instance. At no time did Mr. Jerusalem mug anyone. The five elderly citizens who claim that a naked Mr. Jerusalem swooped down from the roof of their hut to lay about them with a large dried bull penis, pausing only to steal their wallets and real teeth before taking flight... well, we've had them checked out. They were all senile, dizzied by an extended session of The Biscuit Game, and confused by ionized swamp-like gas billowing off the nearby Second Canal.

Mr. Jerusalem's admittedly bizarre statements to various feedsite listeners during the two days are not connected to any possible or claimed drug use on his part. He was tired and emotional and suffering unusual brain chemistry due to the trauma of losing his TV remote control.

The bit about his standing on top of the big screen on Century Square and feigning sex with half a Doberman Pinscher is, however, entirely true, and we are in negotiation with the police at this time.

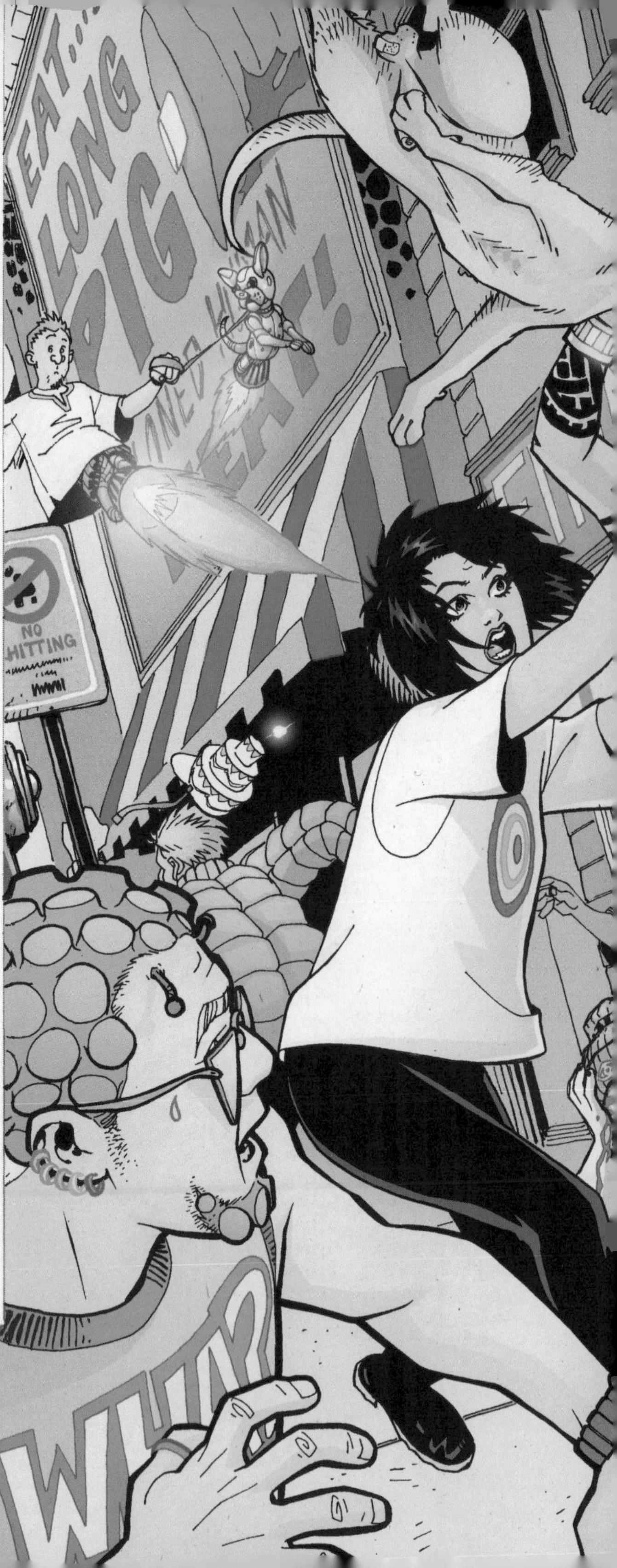
EAT...
LONG
PIG
NO HITTING

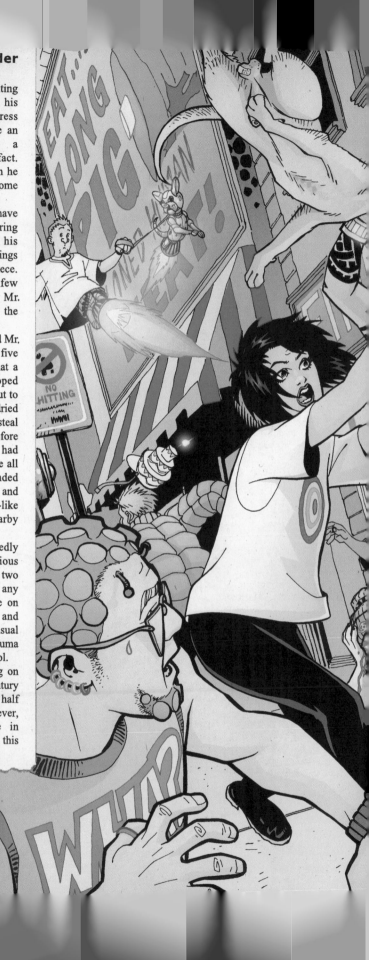

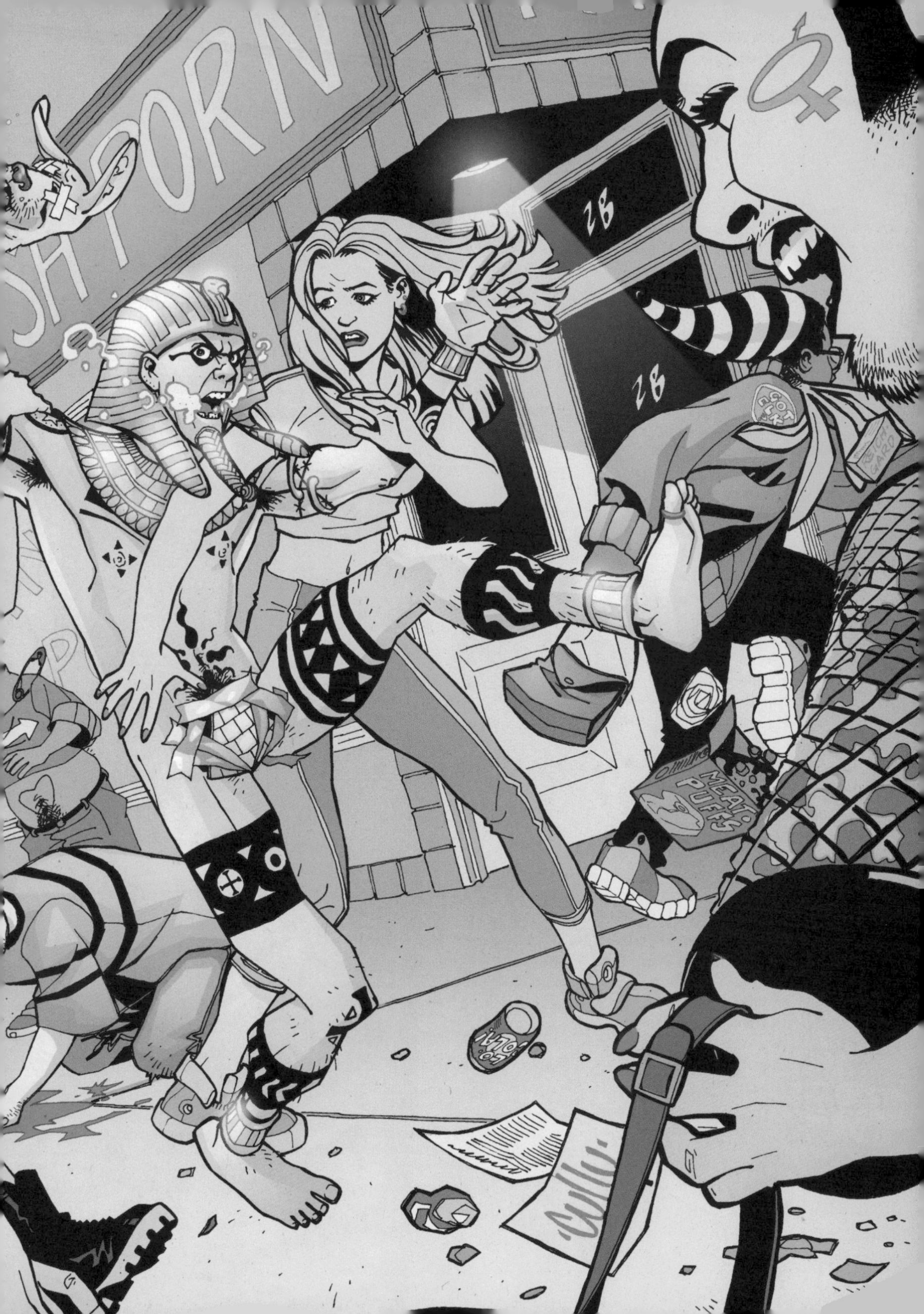
PORN
28
28
MEATY PUFFS

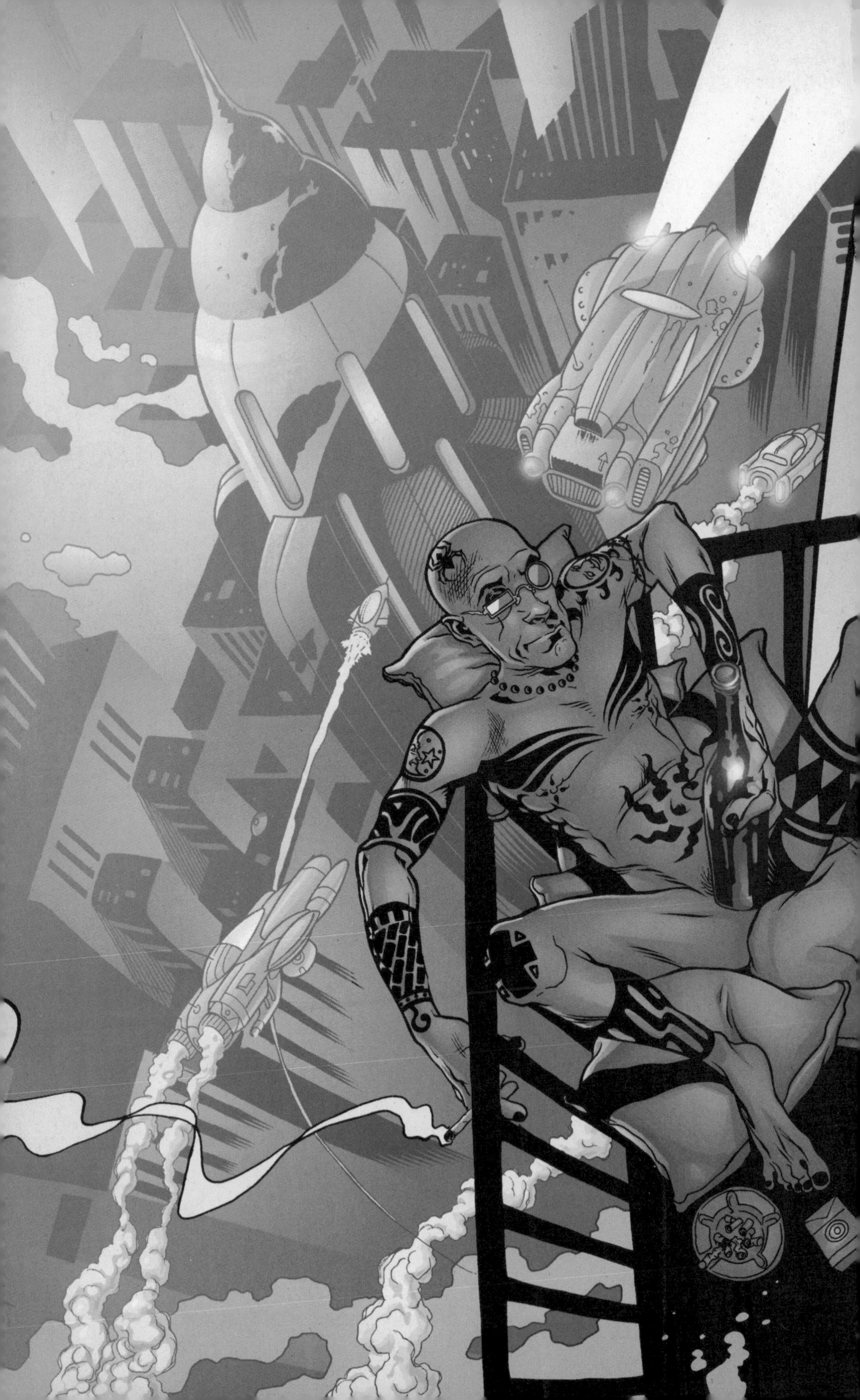

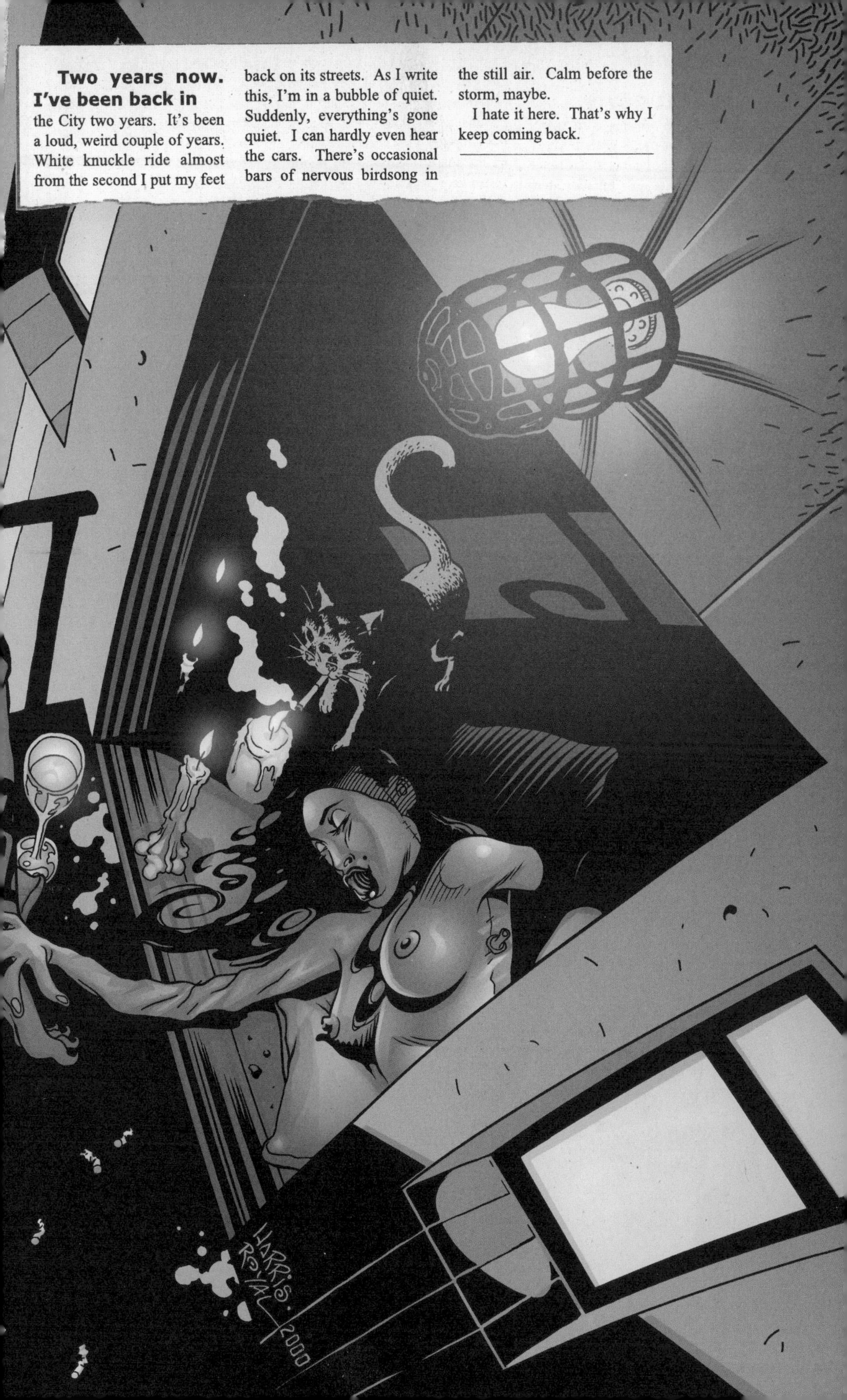
Two years now. I've been back in the City two years. It's been a loud, weird couple of years. White knuckle ride almost from the second I put my feet back on its streets. As I write this, I'm in a bubble of quiet. Suddenly, everything's gone quiet. I can hardly even hear the cars. There's occasional bars of nervous birdsong in the still air. Calm before the storm, maybe.
I hate it here. That's why I keep coming back.
HARRIS. ROYAL 2000

AFTERWORD
by
MITCHELL ROYCE

I have been working with Spider Jerusalem for many years now. It was I who got him into France during the War of Verbals. I was with him in Prague, on The Terrible Night of the Telephone. I kept him alive in St. Lucia when the galloping cockrot threatened to clamber up his spinal column. I got his first column, the column that stopped The Transient Riots, on the major feedsites and public screens. I've known him longer than almost anyone else alive.

And I want you to know that I hate him and I wish he were dead. Now. I mean right fucking now. With harpoons in him. Big fucking harpoons.

Really fucking big ones.

Mitchell Royce
City Editor
The Word

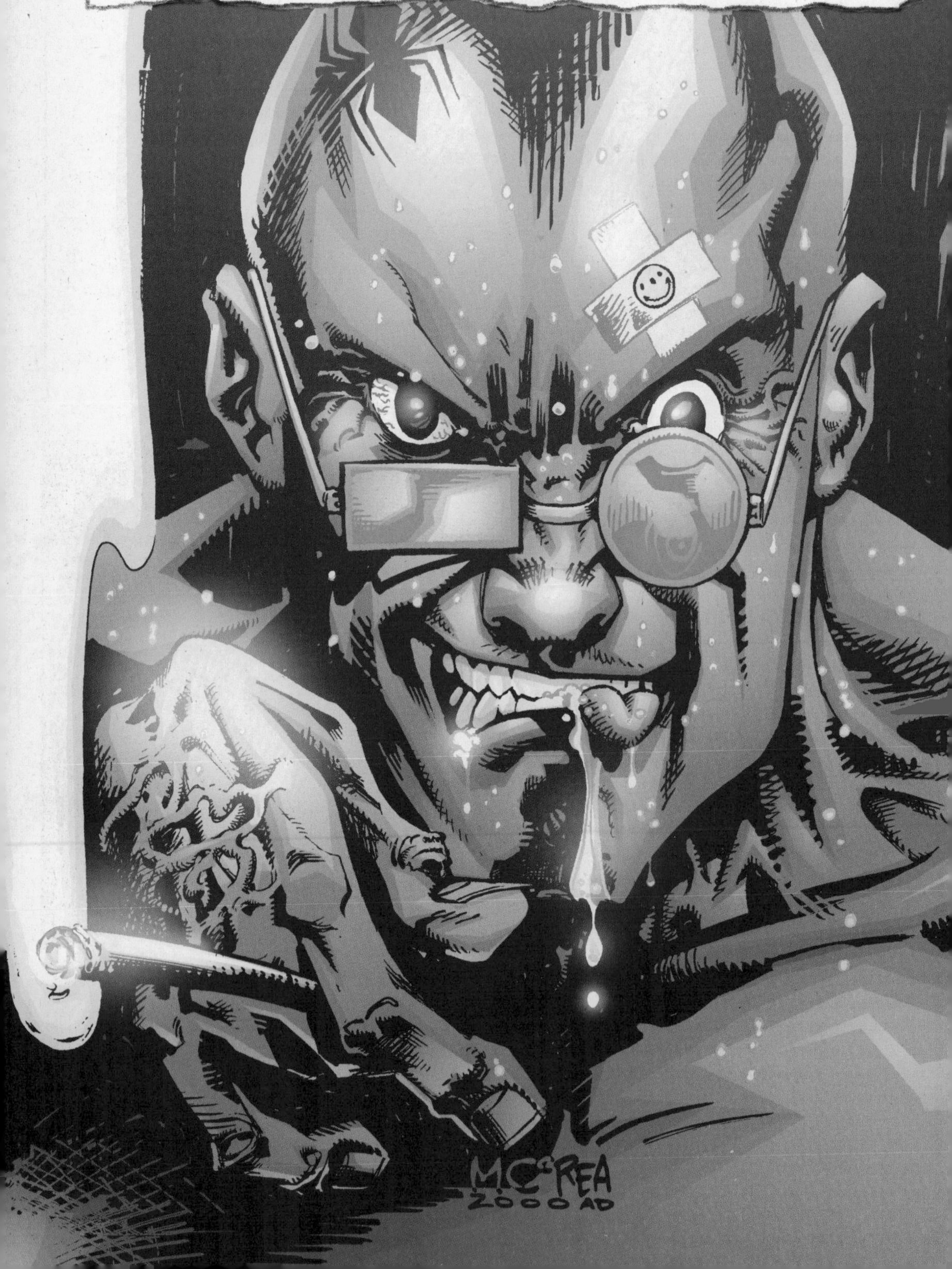
McCREA
2000 AD

Tonight on:

LONELY CITY

"NEXT WEEK'S DRUGS:"

Following the FDA loophole that stops drugs being made illegal until they are actually discovered, our crack team of narcotic-munching investigative reporters tests a spread of fixes invented only hours previous to filming. Includes scenes of FDA troops capturing and taking stomach samples from our staff.

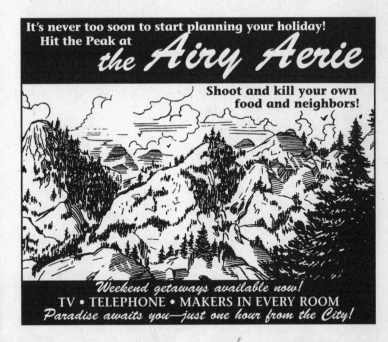

TV HIGHLIGHTS

8:00//78 (comedy)
GOTCHA! Home videos of horrifically bloody and deeply disturbing domestic accidents.

8:30//13.6 (children)
SEX PUPPETS: Delightfully lighthearted educational show. Today, Darleen must decide which Puppet will live and which will die.

9:30//45 (leisure)
SLIDE: Mildly psychoactive visual wave effects combine with Kodo drum patterns and classified subliminal signals to gently chew holes in your frontal lobe.

10:00//1002 (infomercial)
GERIATRICIDE: Killing poverty-stricken old people for fun and profit. This week: arranging a good hard winter to thin the old toads out a bit.

11:00//383 (news)
SPKF: Patching to the Print District offices of the city's prime feedsite for a late-night news and event summary.

11:30//78.4 (music)
LOST: Featuring CFC performing pieces from their new disc, "Dirty Rain." Select interactive subchannel to have holographic simulations of dead, oil-drenched sea gulls tossed at you.

12:00//3 (drama)
CRIMINAL NATION: Adventures of City Police Department detectives. This week — a revived Ernest Hemingway in Sniper Alley! Captain Gacy eats a suspect!

It's never too soon to start planning your holiday!
Hit the Peak at

the Airy Aerie

Shoot and kill your own food and neighbors!

Weekend getaways available now!
TV • TELEPHONE • MAKERS IN EVERY ROOM
Paradise awaits you—just one hour from the City!

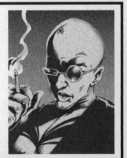

"...They've cleared all the non-transients out of Angels 8. Incredible tension, like they're all living in the second before the bullet hits the bone..."

MEMOIRS FROM THE BACKSIDE OF THE WORLD:
"I Hate It Here" *Spider Jerusalem's column exclusive to The Word : Every month in...*

LATE EDITION
TRANSMETROPOLITAN

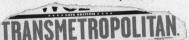

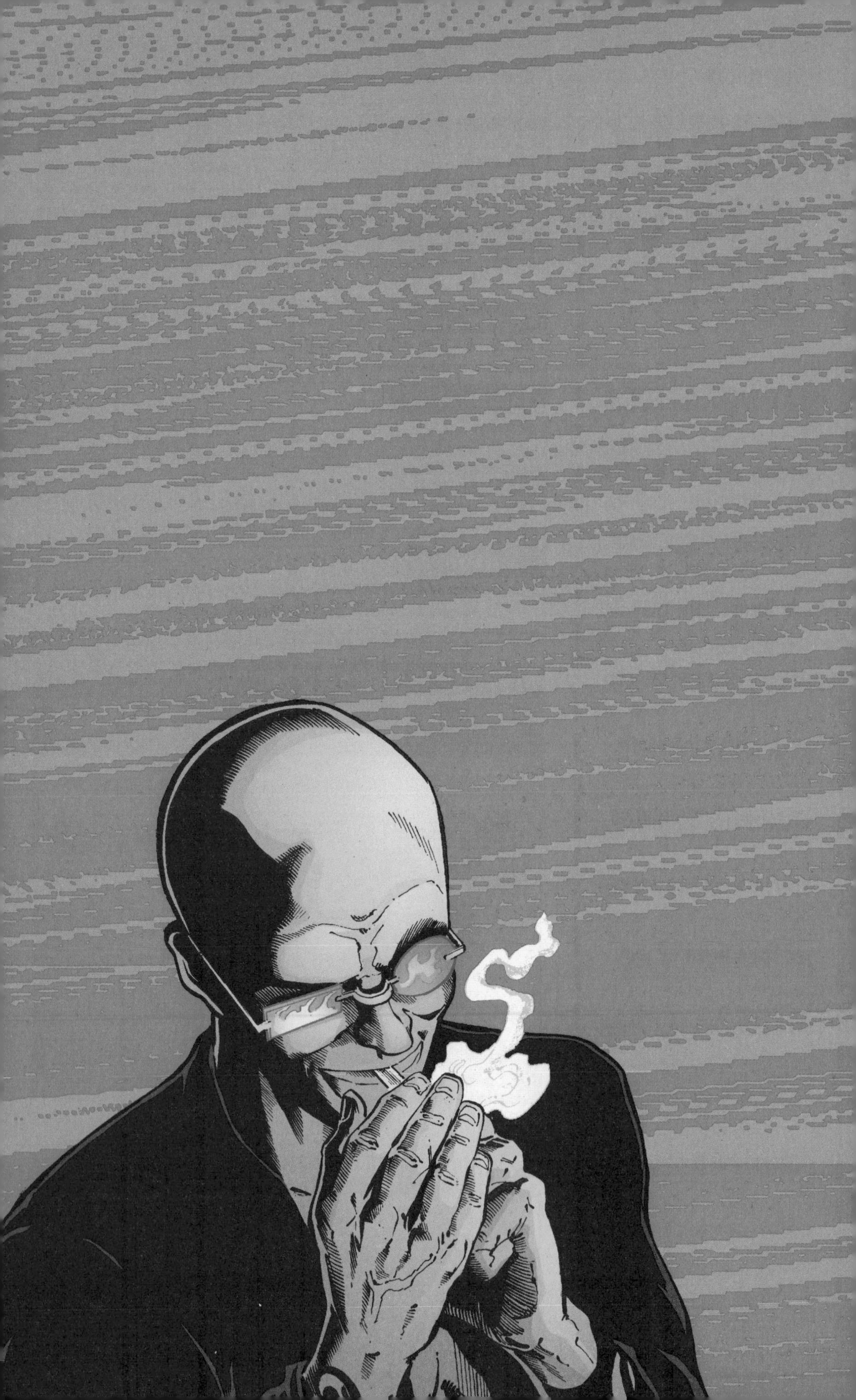

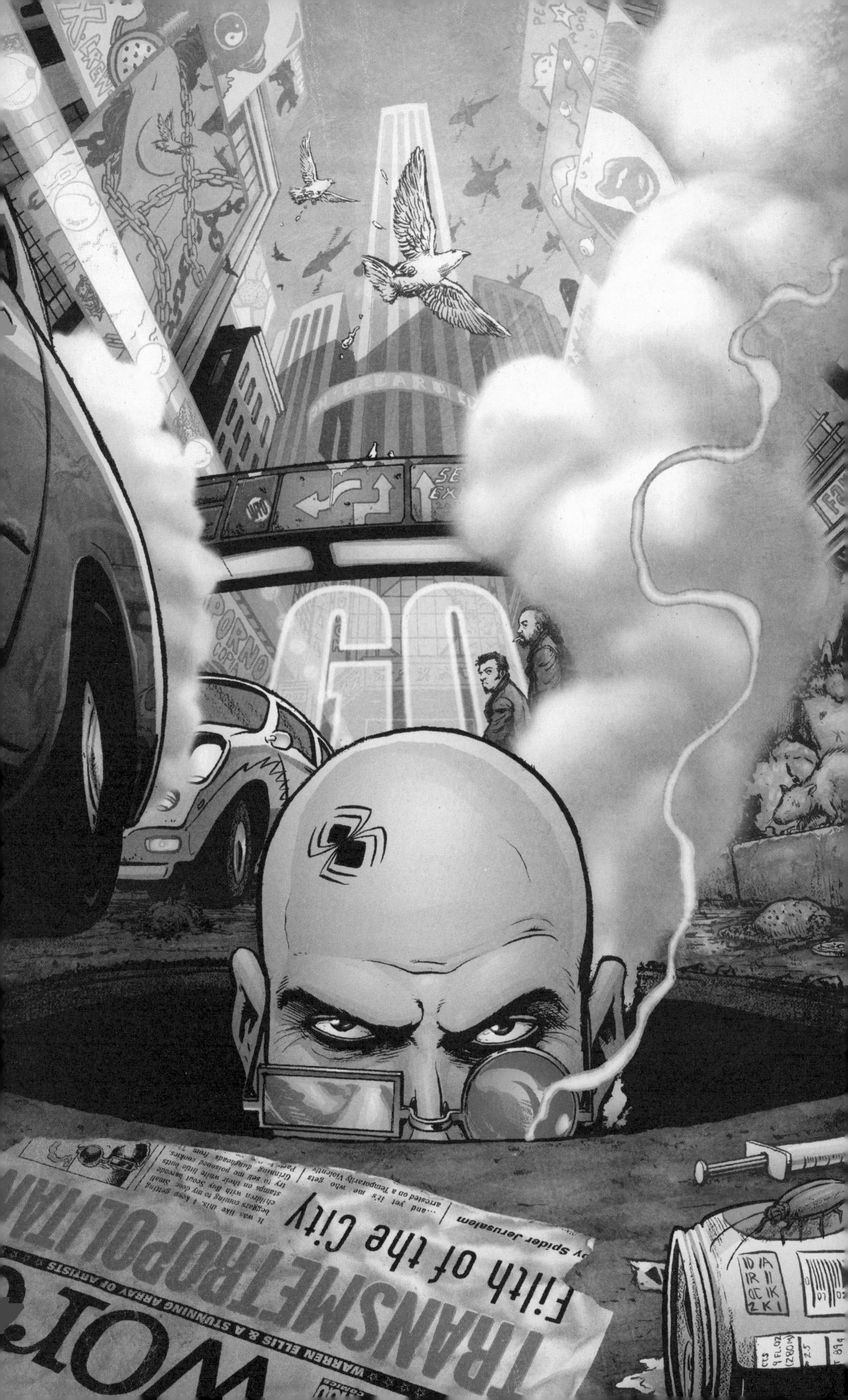

GO
PORNO
COPA
TRANSMETROPOLITAN
WARREN ELLIS & A STUNNING ARRAY OF ARTISTS
Filth of the City
Spider Jerusalem

TRANS-METRO-POLITAN:
FILTH OF THE CITY

Words by Warren_Ellis
Colors by Nathan_Eyring

Art by

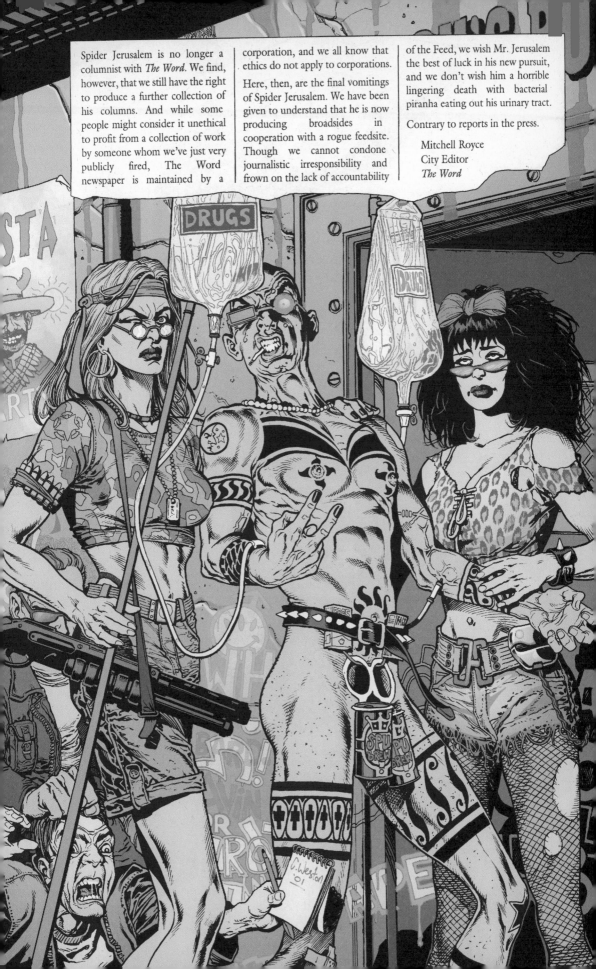

Spider Jerusalem is no longer a columnist with *The Word*. We find, however, that we still have the right to produce a further collection of his columns. And while some people might consider it unethical to profit from a collection of work by someone whom we've just very publicly fired, The Word newspaper is maintained by a corporation, and we all know that ethics do not apply to corporations.

Here, then, are the final vomitings of Spider Jerusalem. We have been given to understand that he is now producing broadsides in cooperation with a rogue feedsite. Though we cannot condone journalistic irresponsibility and frown on the lack of accountability of the Feed, we wish Mr. Jerusalem the best of luck in his new pursuit, and we don't wish him a horrible lingering death with bacterial piranha eating out his urinary tract.

Contrary to reports in the press.

Mitchell Royce
City Editor
The Word

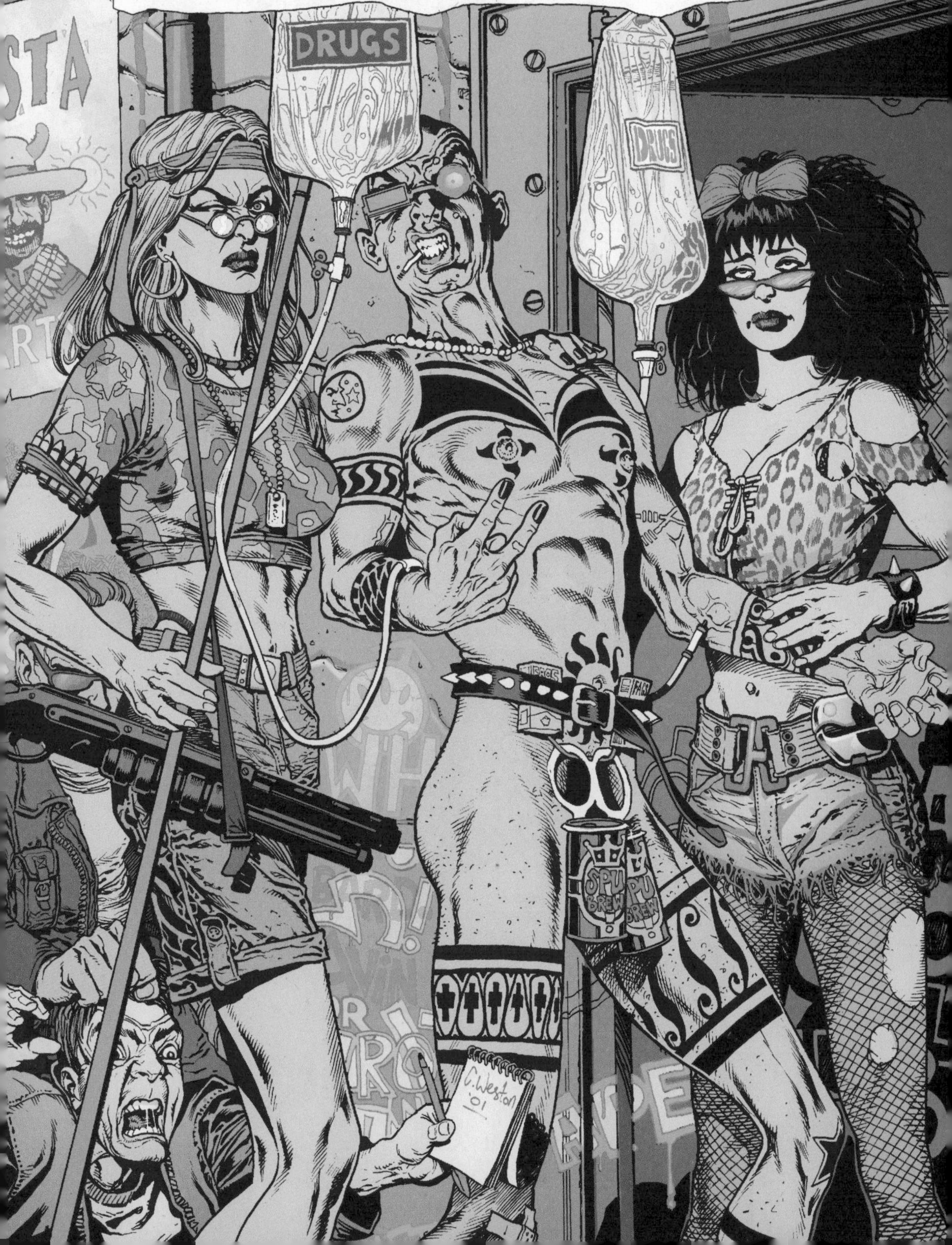
DRUGS
DRUGS
C.Weston '01

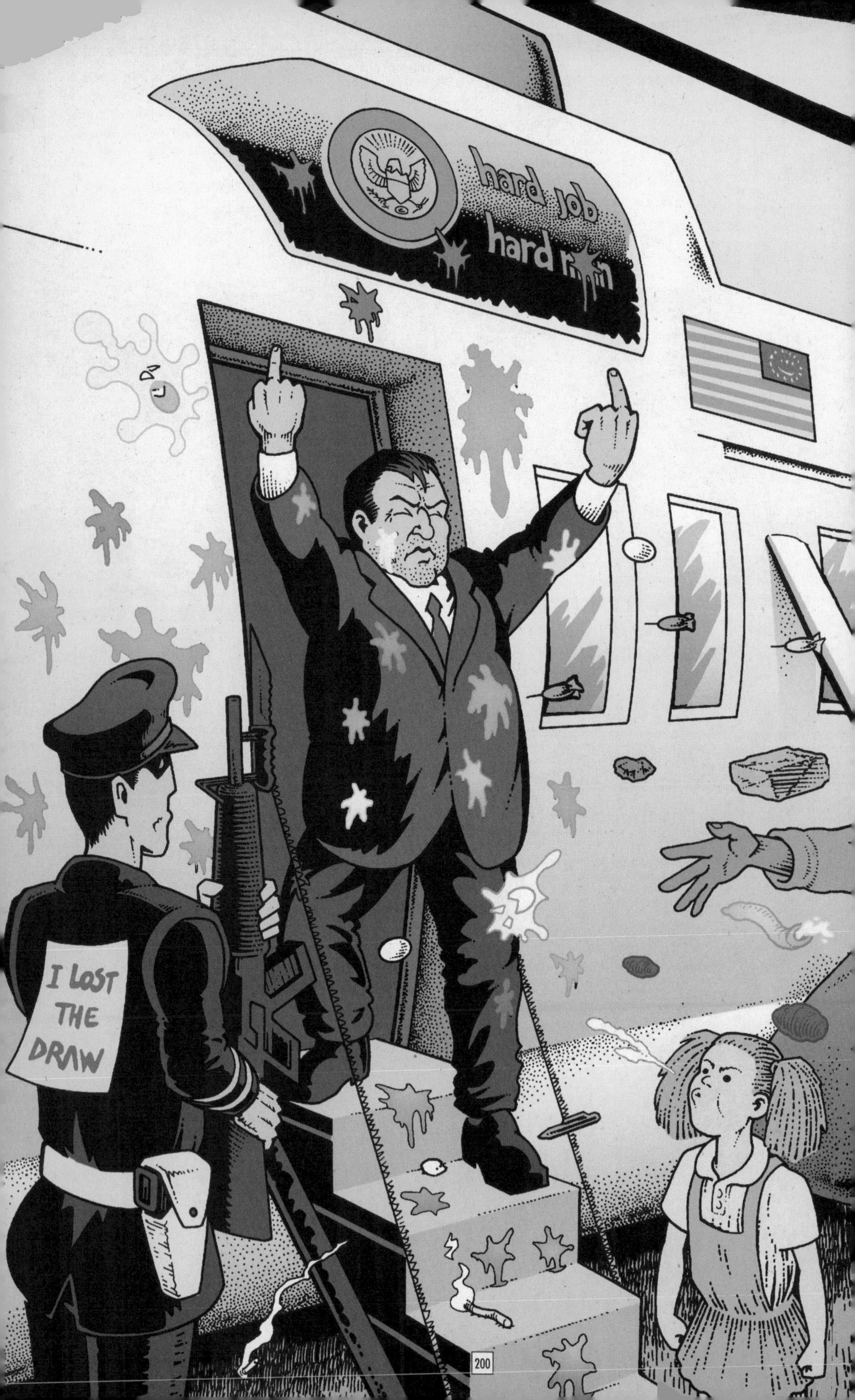
hard job
I LOST THE DRAW

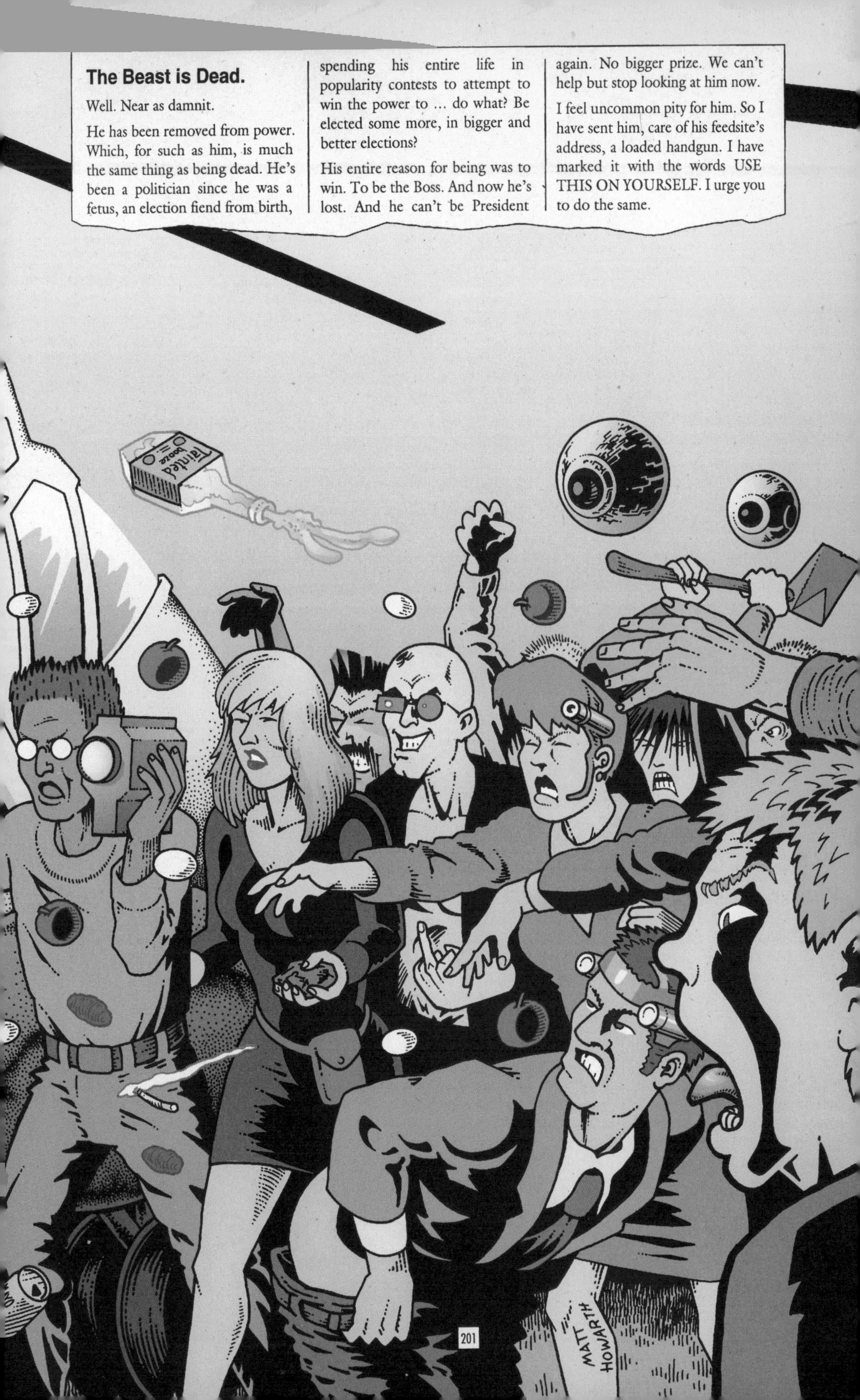
The Beast is Dead.
Well. Near as damnit.
He has been removed from power. Which, for such as him, is much the same thing as being dead. He's been a politician since he was a fetus, an election fiend from birth, spending his entire life in popularity contests to attempt to win the power to ... do what? Be elected some more, in bigger and better elections?
His entire reason for being was to win. To be the Boss. And now he's lost. And he can't be President again. No bigger prize. We can't help but stop looking at him now.
I feel uncommon pity for him. So I have sent him, care of his feedsite's address, a loaded handgun. I have marked it with the words USE THIS ON YOURSELF. I urge you to do the same.
Tainted booze
MATT HOWARTH

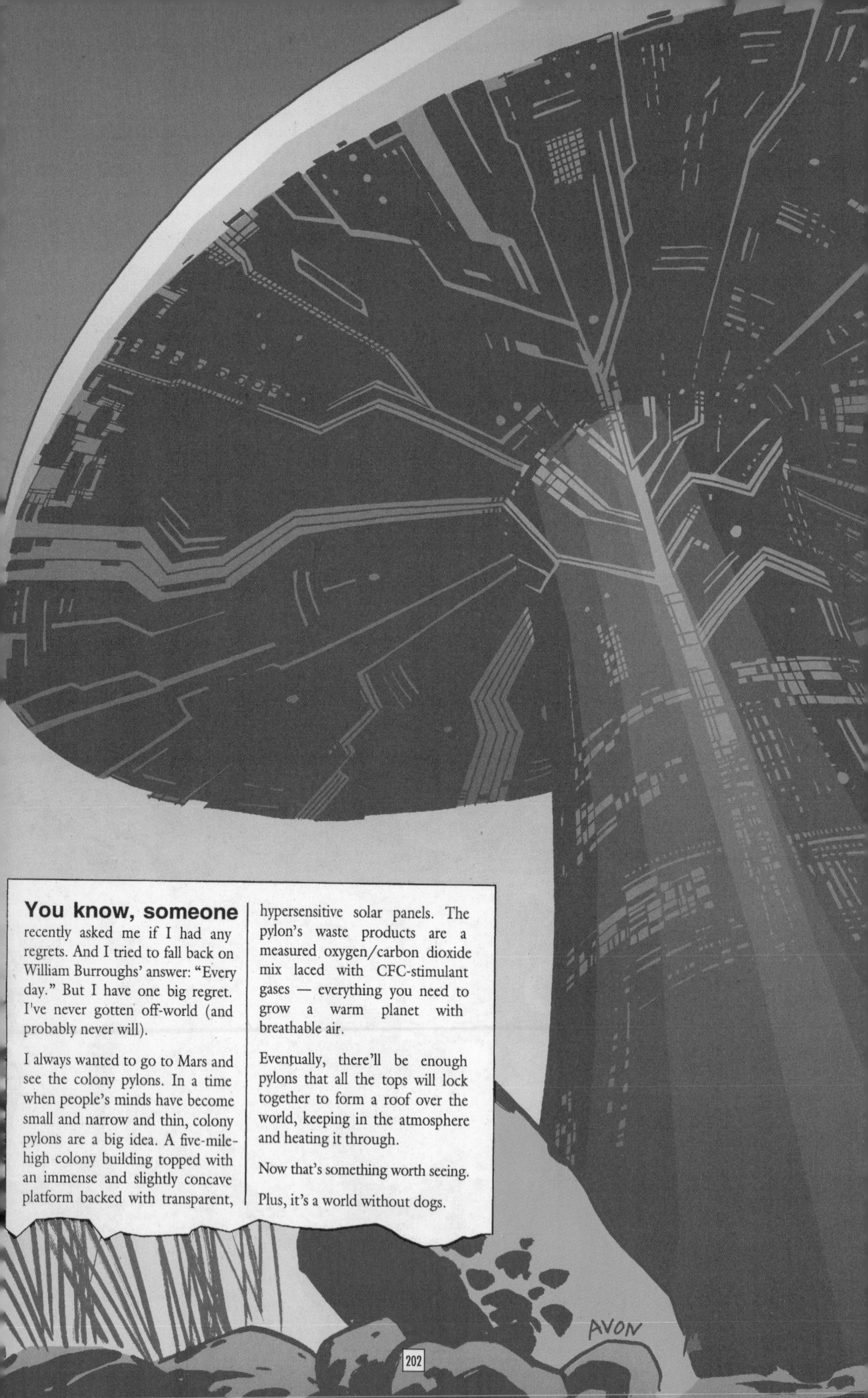
AVON

You know, someone recently asked me if I had any regrets. And I tried to fall back on William Burroughs' answer: "Every day." But I have one big regret. I've never gotten off-world (and probably never will).

I always wanted to go to Mars and see the colony pylons. In a time when people's minds have become small and narrow and thin, colony pylons are a big idea. A five-mile-high colony building topped with an immense and slightly concave platform backed with transparent, hypersensitive solar panels. The pylon's waste products are a measured oxygen/carbon dioxide mix laced with CFC-stimulant gases — everything you need to grow a warm planet with breathable air.

Eventually, there'll be enough pylons that all the tops will lock together to form a roof over the world, keeping in the atmosphere and heating it through.

Now that's something worth seeing.

Plus, it's a world without dogs.

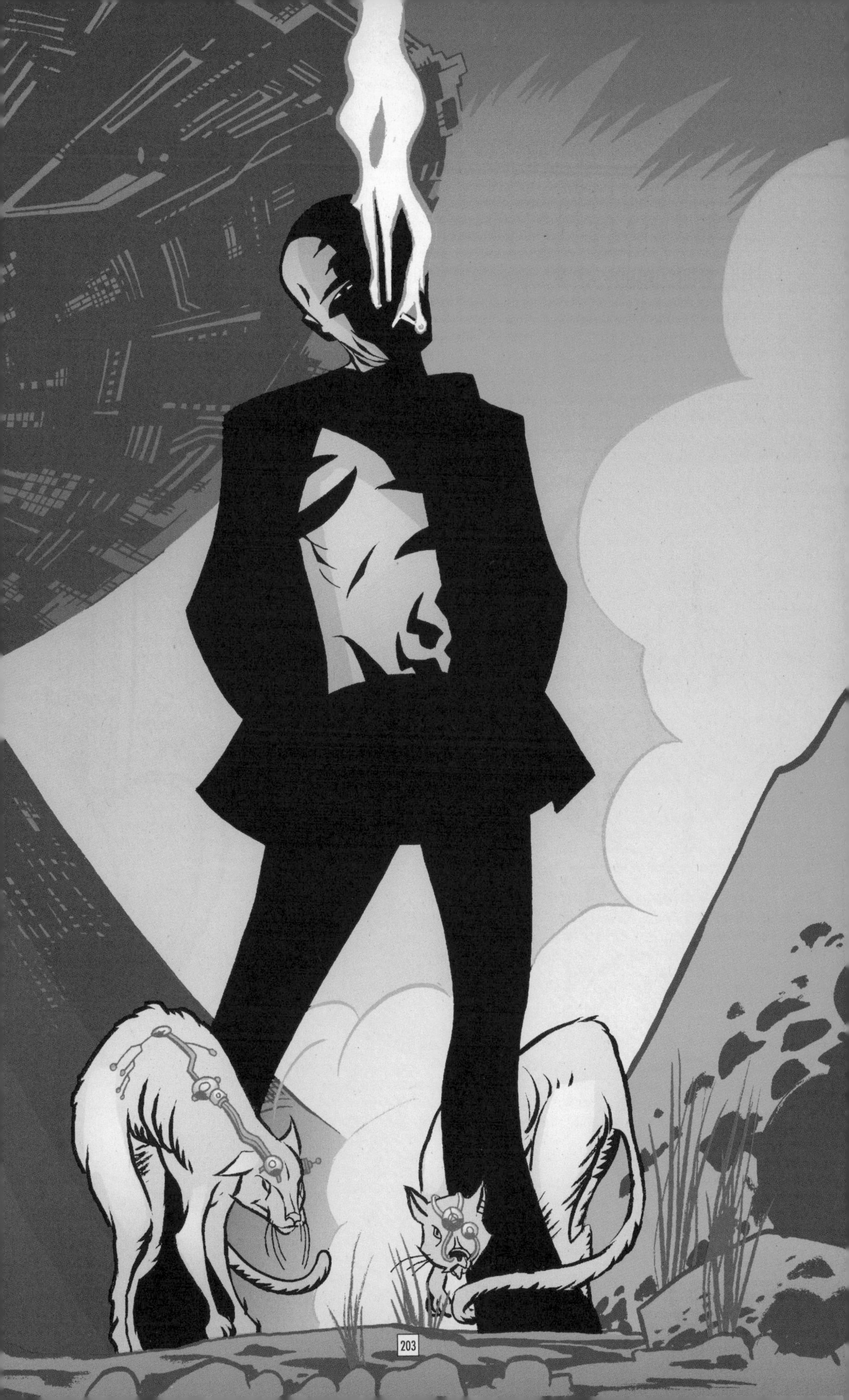

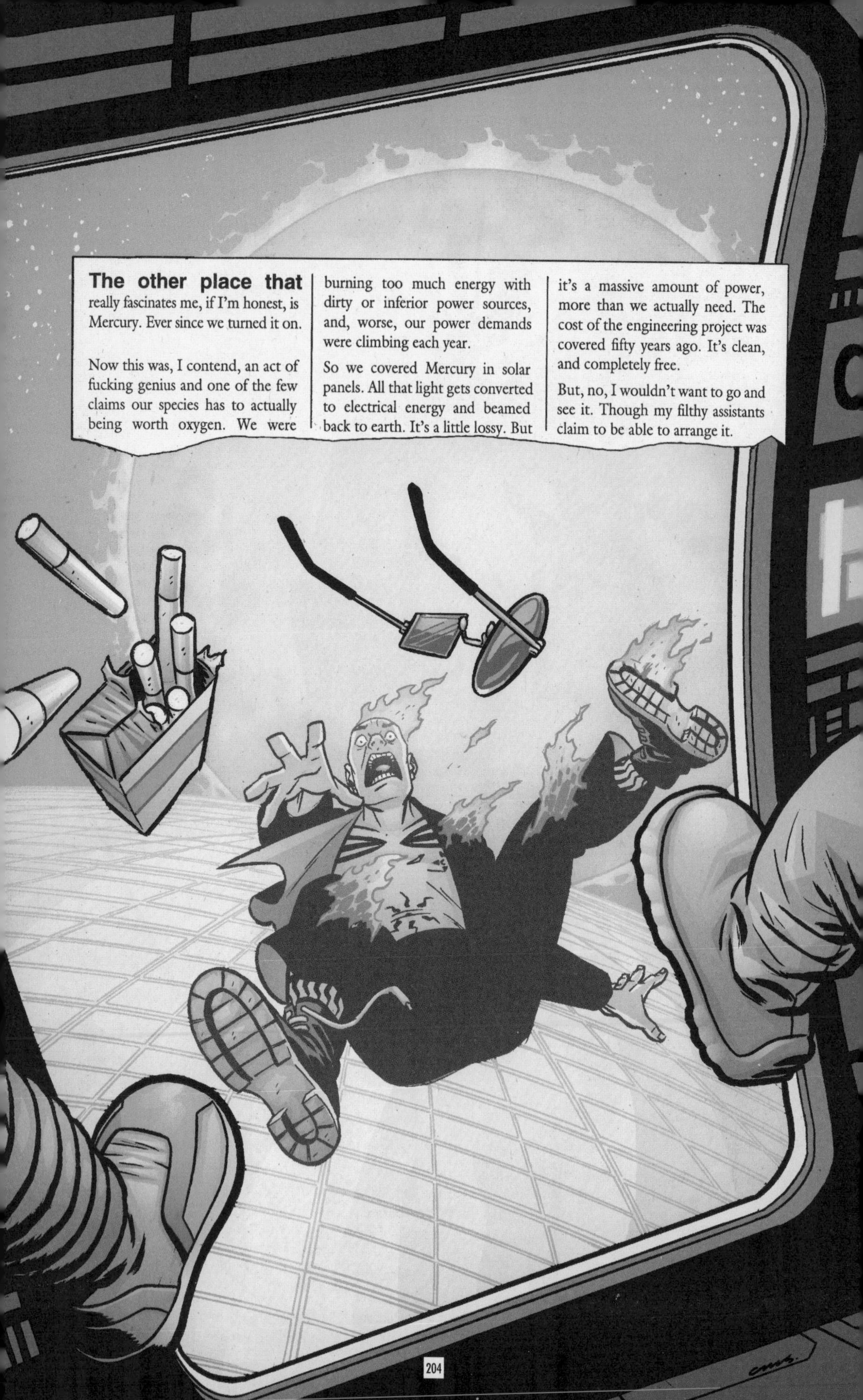
The other place that really fascinates me, if I'm honest, is Mercury. Ever since we turned it on.
Now this was, I contend, an act of fucking genius and one of the few claims our species has to actually being worth oxygen. We were burning too much energy with dirty or inferior power sources, and, worse, our power demands were climbing each year.
So we covered Mercury in solar panels. All that light gets converted to electrical energy and beamed back to earth. It's a little lossy. But it's a massive amount of power, more than we actually need. The cost of the engineering project was covered fifty years ago. It's clean, and completely free.
But, no, I wouldn't want to go and see it. Though my filthy assistants claim to be able to arrange it.

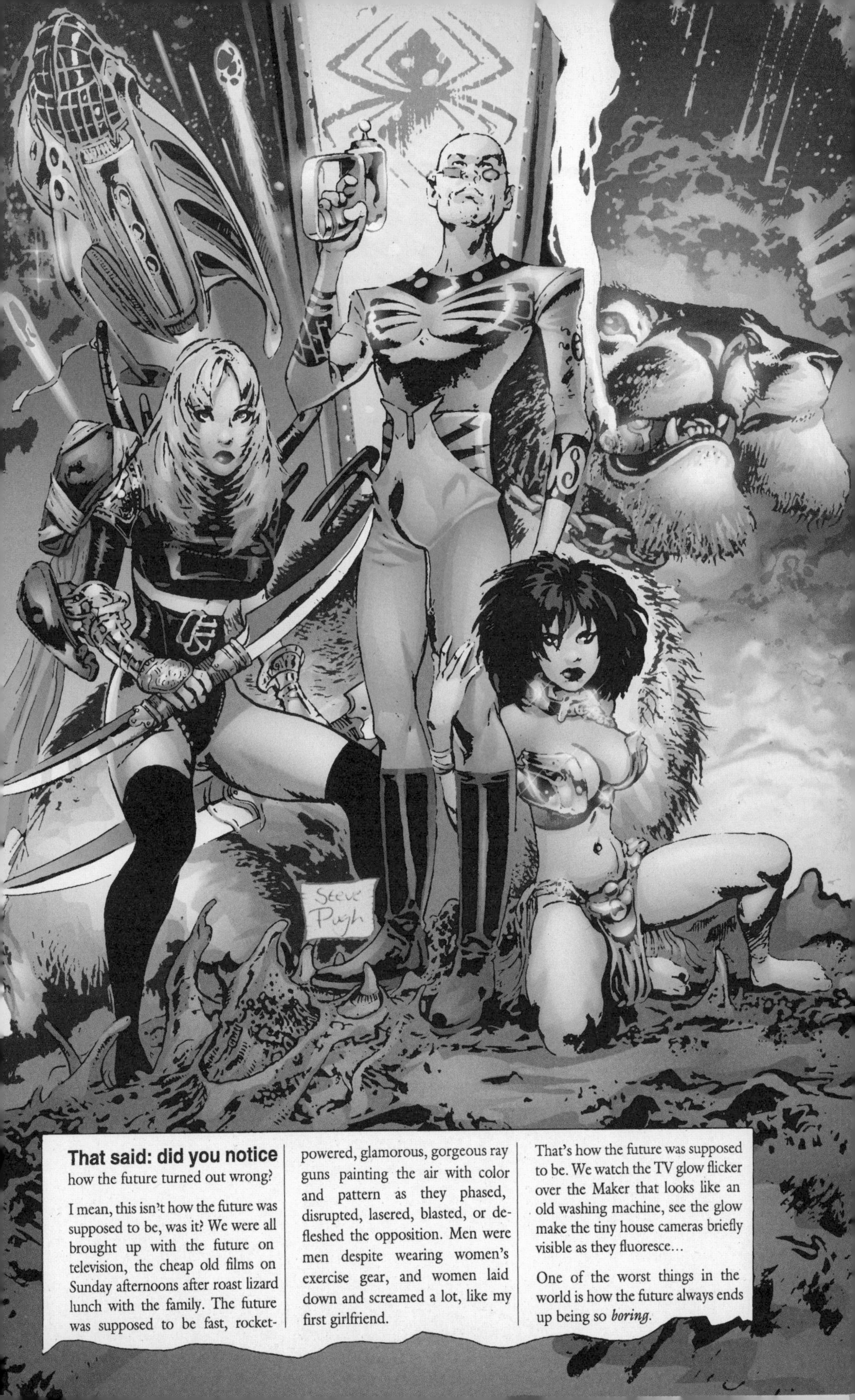
Steve Pugh

That said: did you notice how the future turned out wrong?

I mean, this isn't how the future was supposed to be, was it? We were all brought up with the future on television, the cheap old films on Sunday afternoons after roast lizard lunch with the family. The future was supposed to be fast, rocket-powered, glamorous, gorgeous ray guns painting the air with color and pattern as they phased, disrupted, lasered, blasted, or de-fleshed the opposition. Men were men despite wearing women's exercise gear, and women laid down and screamed a lot, like my first girlfriend.

That's how the future was supposed to be. We watch the TV glow flicker over the Maker that looks like an old washing machine, see the glow make the tiny house cameras briefly visible as they fluoresce…

One of the worst things in the world is how the future always ends up being so *boring*.

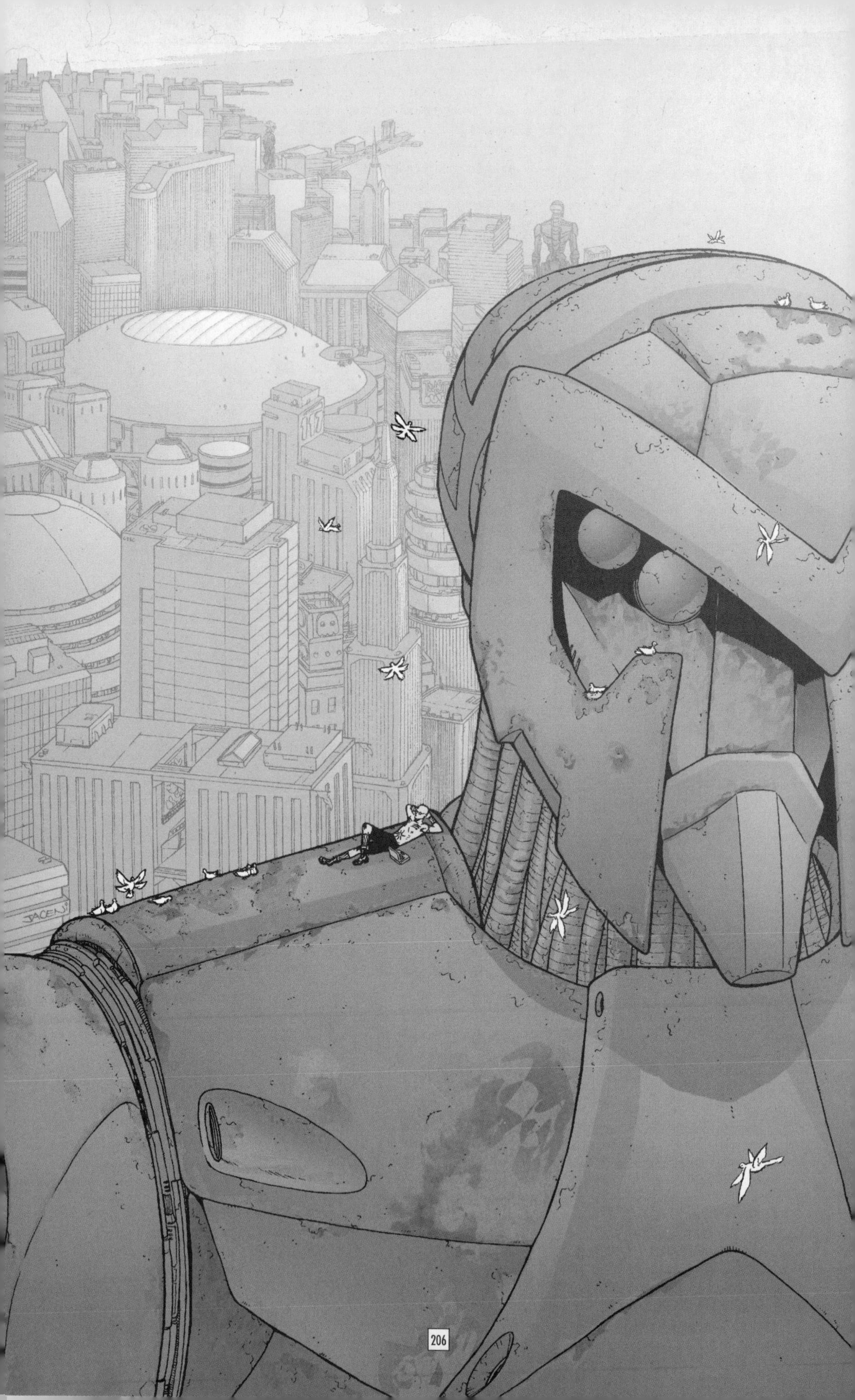

In fact, sometimes we seem to have put the future behind us.

The Gladiator Wall is reckoned to be more than two hundred years old — although, as every schoolkid knows, records aren't to be trusted anymore. Archaeological teams have found crevices in the chest units designed to take human pilots, though no one knows who they were, or even if the things were ever used in anger. They were a defensive measure, back in the days when we still had full-blown wars in America.
Their immense steel penises fell off about thirty years ago, killing over four dozen innocent bystanders caught underneath.

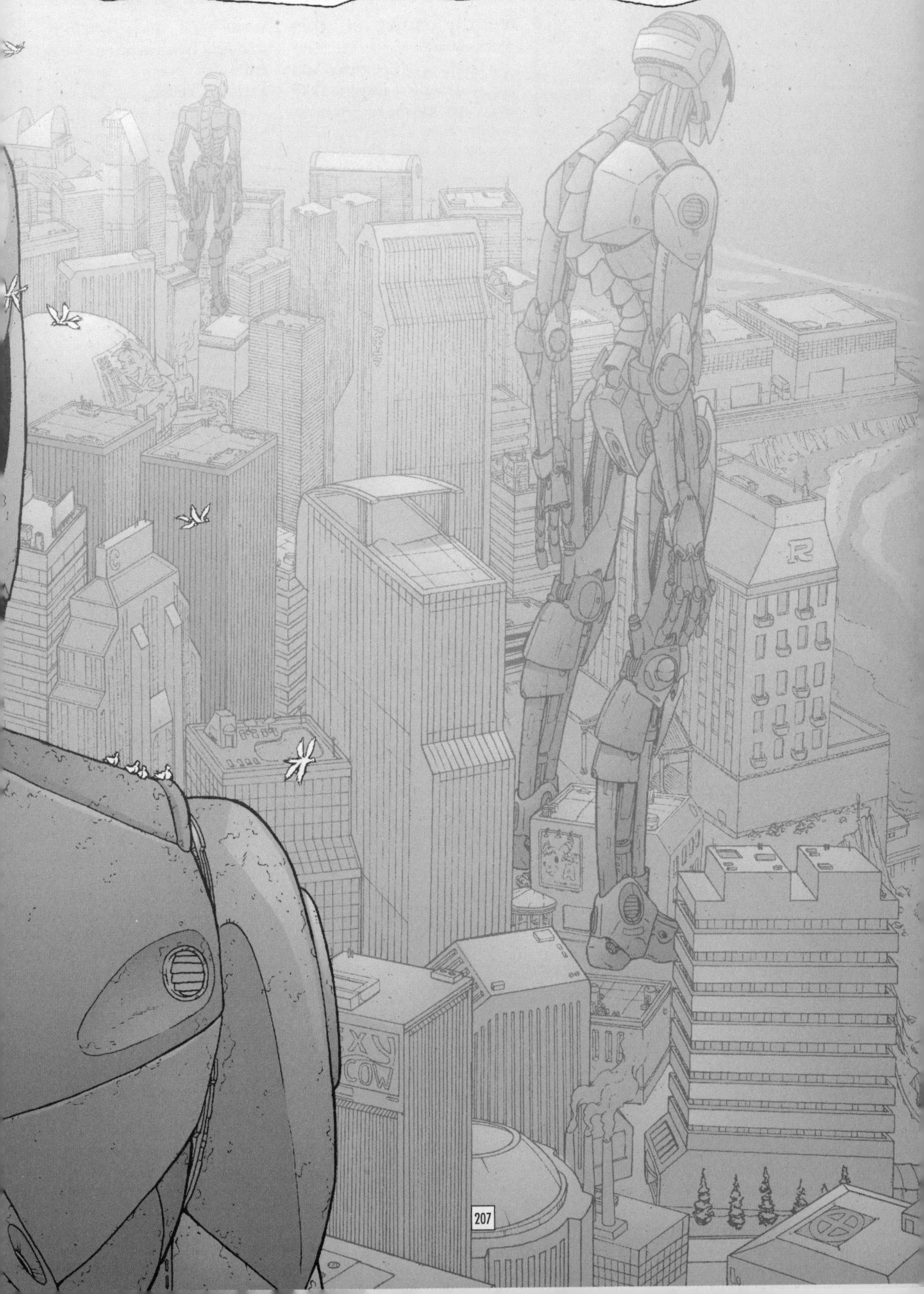

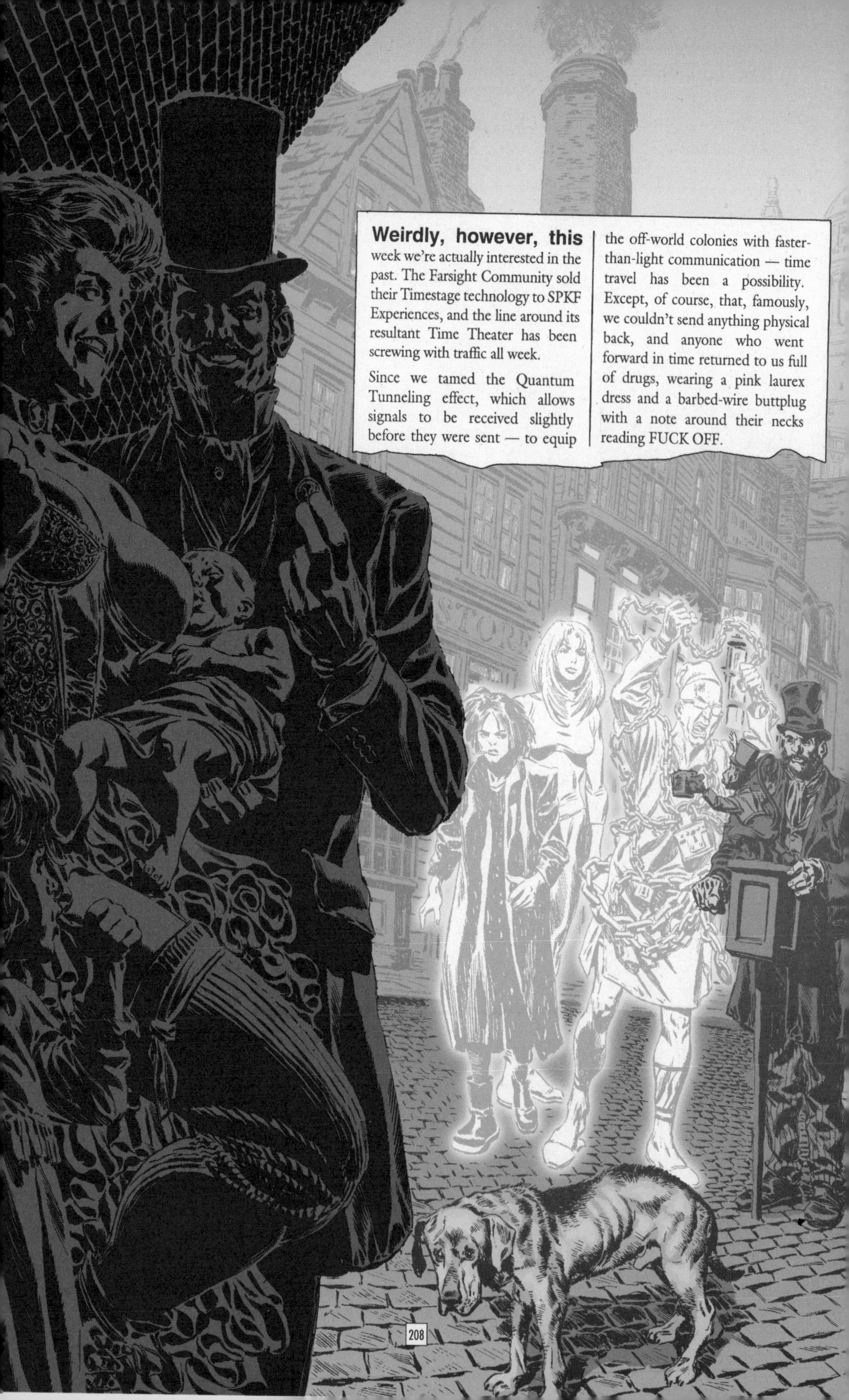

Weirdly, however, this week we're actually interested in the past. The Farsight Community sold their Timestage technology to SPKF Experiences, and the line around its resultant Time Theater has been screwing with traffic all week.

Since we tamed the Quantum Tunneling effect, which allows signals to be received slightly before they were sent — to equip the off-world colonies with faster-than-light communication — time travel has been a possibility. Except, of course, that, famously, we couldn't send anything physical back, and anyone who went forward in time returned to us full of drugs, wearing a pink laurex dress and a barbed-wire buttplug with a note around their necks reading FUCK OFF.

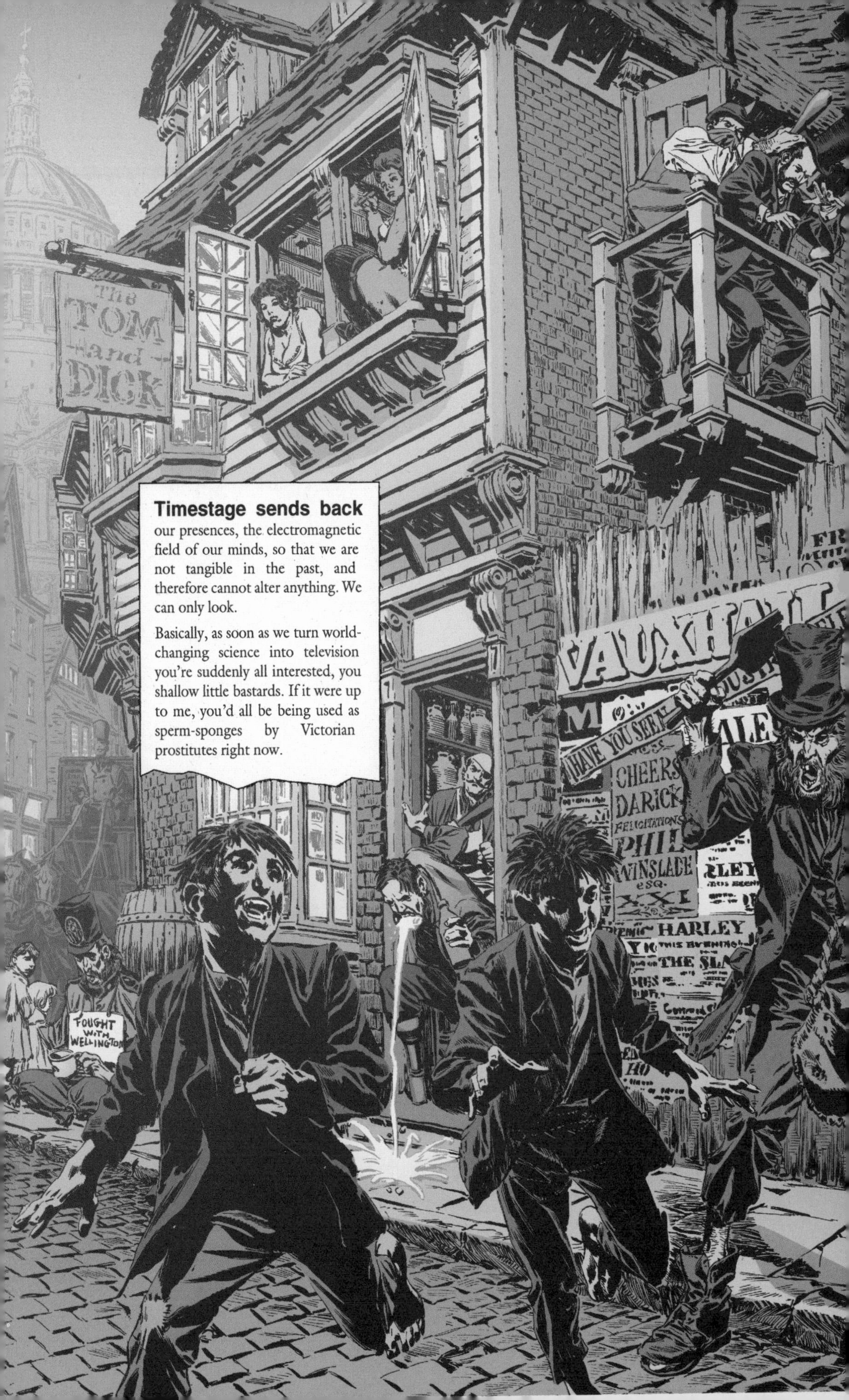
The TOM and DICK
Timestage sends back our presences, the electromagnetic field of our minds, so that we are not tangible in the past, and therefore cannot alter anything. We can only look.
Basically, as soon as we turn world-changing science into television you're suddenly all interested, you shallow little bastards. If it were up to me, you'd all be being used as sperm-sponges by Victorian prostitutes right now.
HAVE YOU SEEN
CHEERS
DARICK
FELICITATIONS
PHIL
WINSLADE ESQ.
HARLEY
FOUGHT WITH WELLINGTON

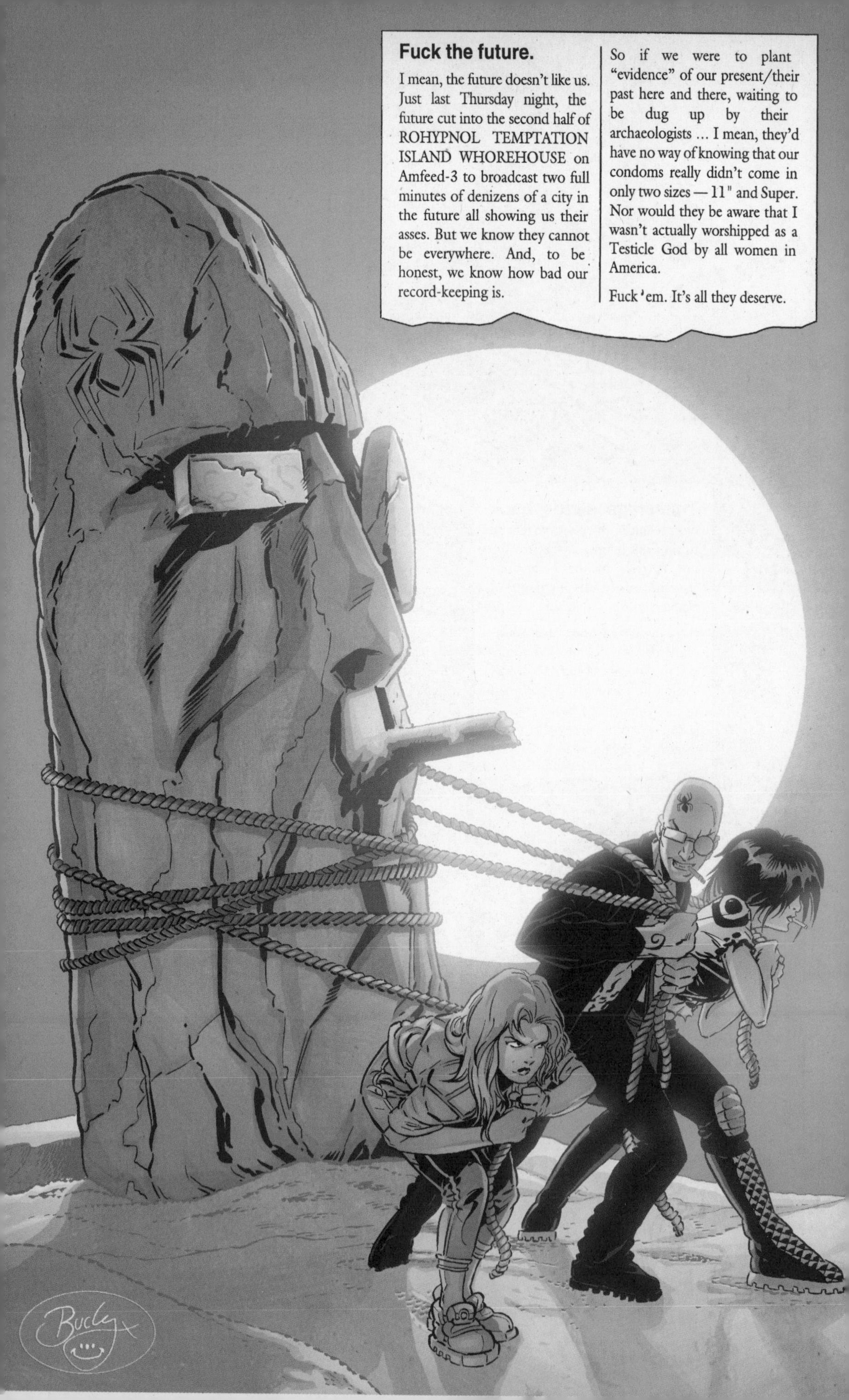
Fuck the future.
I mean, the future doesn't like us. Just last Thursday night, the future cut into the second half of ROHYPNOL TEMPTATION ISLAND WHOREHOUSE on Amfeed-3 to broadcast two full minutes of denizens of a city in the future all showing us their asses. But we know they cannot be everywhere. And, to be honest, we know how bad our record-keeping is.
So if we were to plant "evidence" of our present/their past here and there, waiting to be dug up by their archaeologists ... I mean, they'd have no way of knowing that our condoms really didn't come in only two sizes — 11" and Super. Nor would they be aware that I wasn't actually worshipped as a Testicle God by all women in America.
Fuck 'em. It's all they deserve.

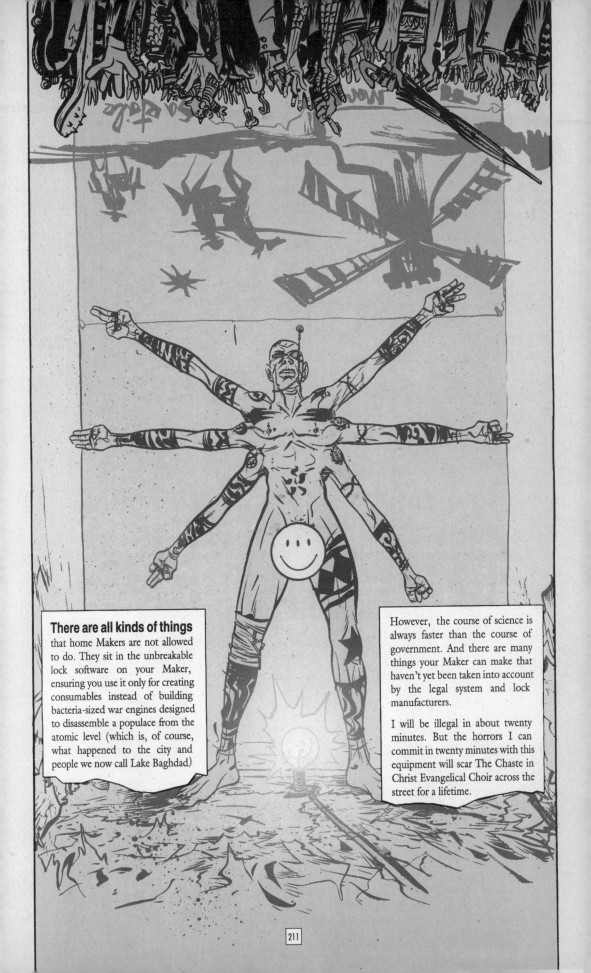

There are all kinds of things that home Makers are not allowed to do. They sit in the unbreakable lock software on your Maker, ensuring you use it only for creating consumables instead of building bacteria-sized war engines designed to disassemble a populace from the atomic level (which is, of course, what happened to the city and people we now call Lake Baghdad)

However, the course of science is always faster than the course of government. And there are many things your Maker can make that haven't yet been taken into account by the legal system and lock manufacturers.

I will be illegal in about twenty minutes. But the horrors I can commit in twenty minutes with this equipment will scar The Chaste in Christ Evangelical Choir across the street for a lifetime.

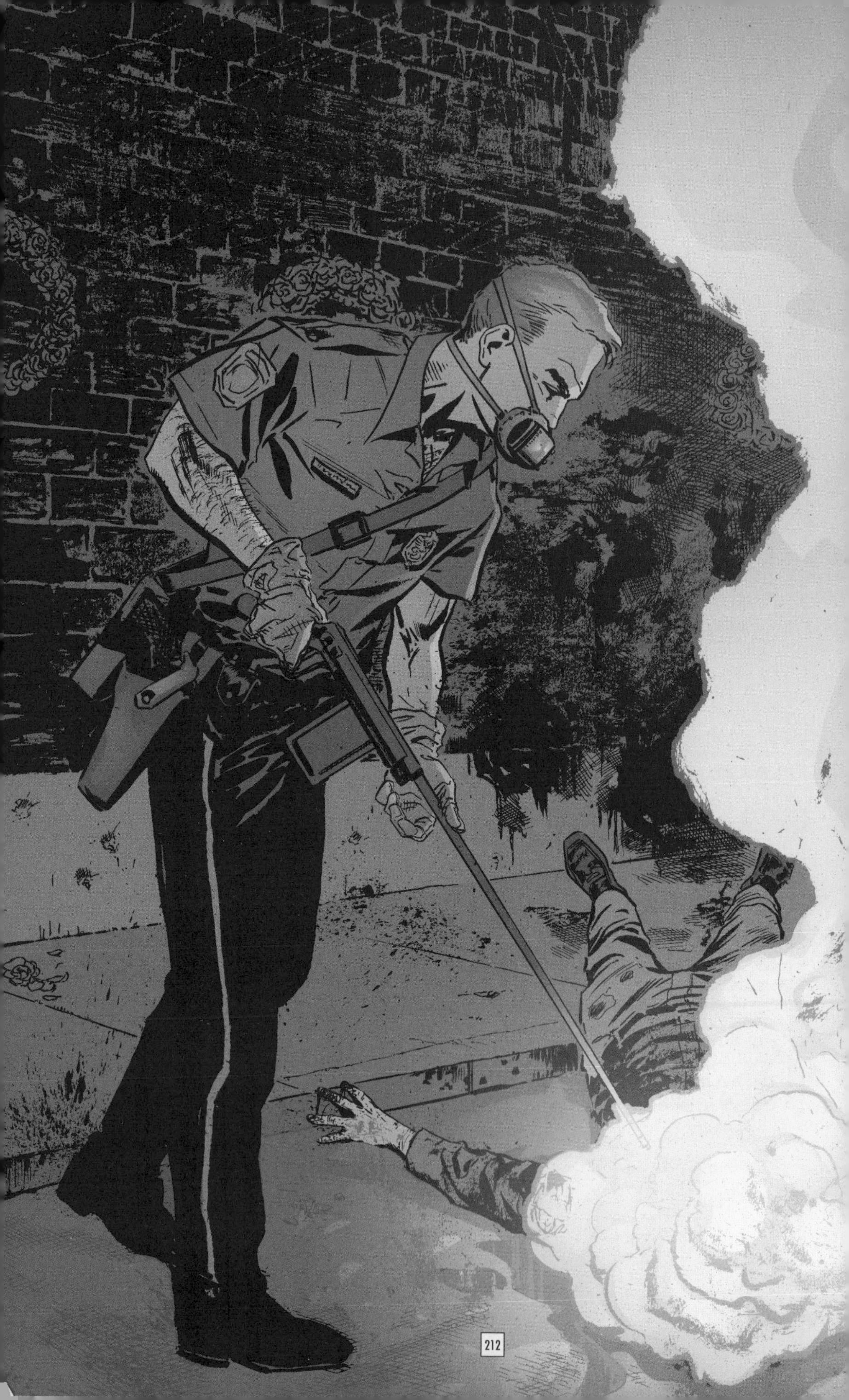

Here lies someone whose name you don't know. He was walking down the street minding his own business when an unmarked car pulled up full of plainclothes cops. There are five witnesses and eight segments of cam footage that show that they did not identify themselves in any way. He put his hand in the back pocket of his jeans, palm facing outwards. Before he could even fully withdraw whatever he was reaching for from his pocket, he was shot dead. In fact, he was shot fifty-two times.

He was reaching for his wallet. He was an American citizen, so he wasn't reaching for a green card or an ID. He was reaching for his wallet because he thought he was being mugged. Accosted by criminals.

Which, in a funny kind of way, he was. Except that they were all cleared of murder by an investigative unit staffed and run by the City Police Department.

It takes six seconds for a CPD standard-issue sidearm to discharge thirteen rounds. Six seconds is a very long time.

Doesn't matter what his name is. There's five like him every week in the City. And you didn't give a shit about them either.

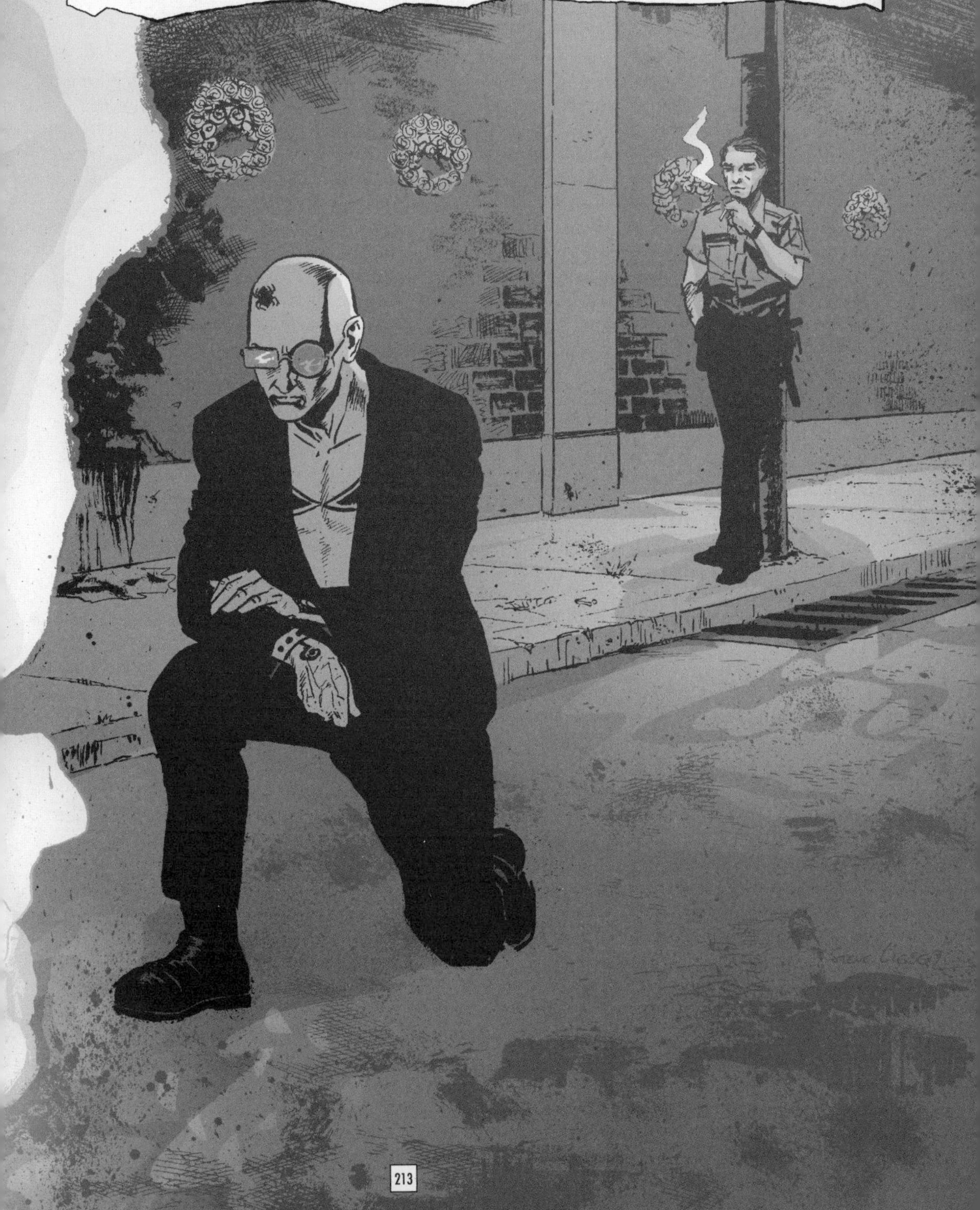

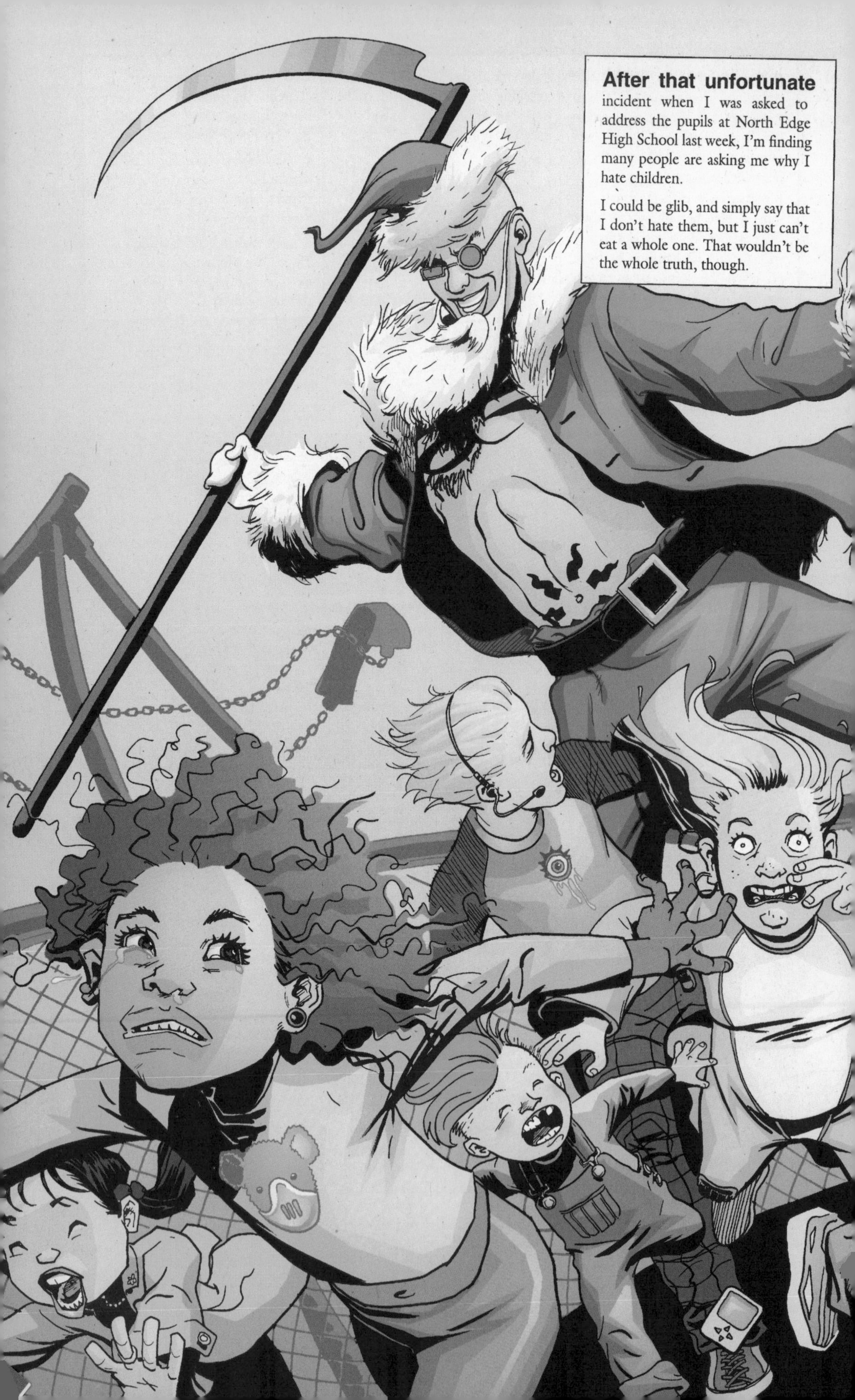
After that unfortunate incident when I was asked to address the pupils at North Edge High School last week, I'm finding many people are asking me why I hate children.
I could be glib, and simply say that I don't hate them, but I just can't eat a whole one. That wouldn't be the whole truth, though.

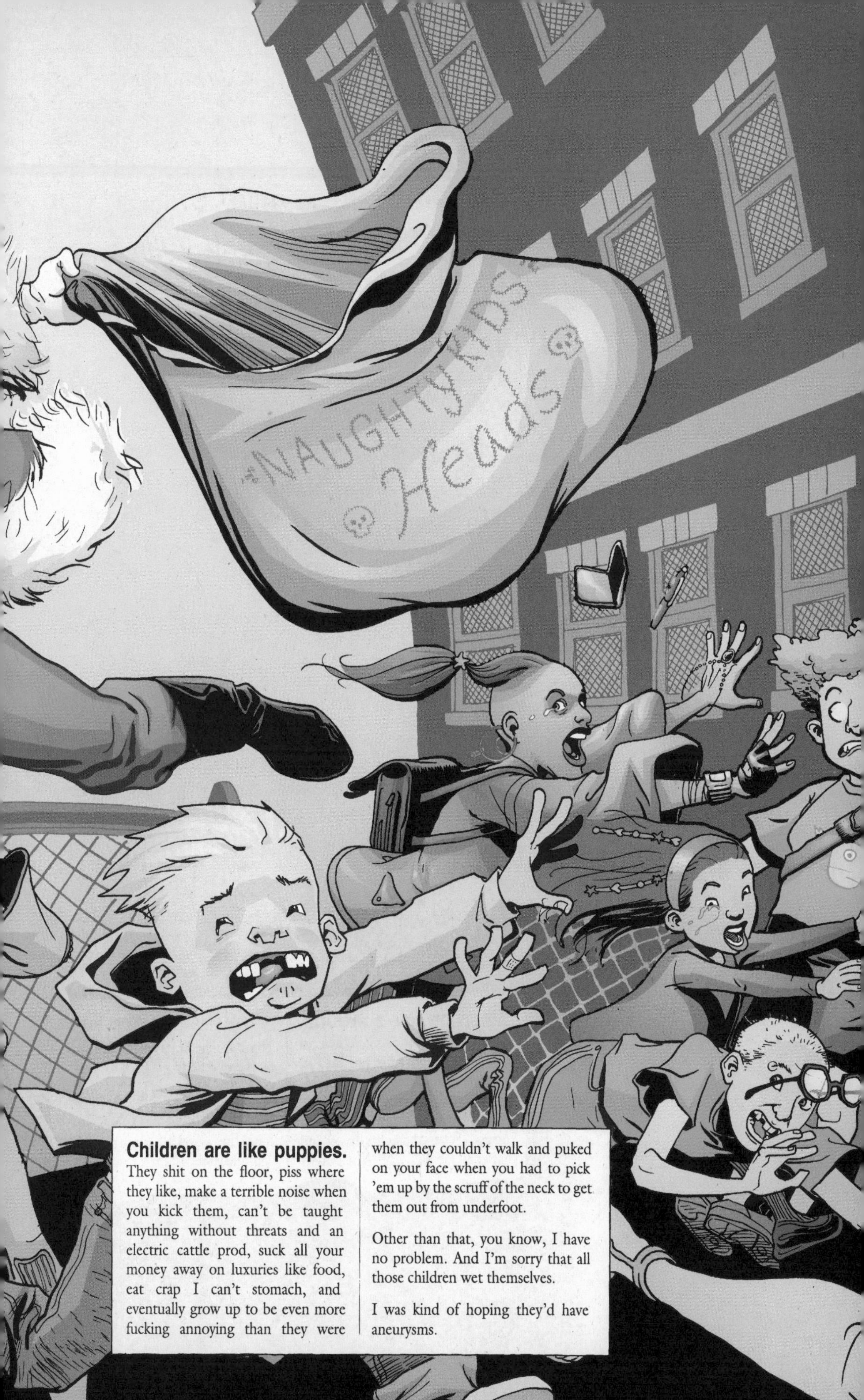
NAUGHTY KIDS'
Heads

Children are like puppies. They shit on the floor, piss where they like, make a terrible noise when you kick them, can't be taught anything without threats and an electric cattle prod, suck all your money away on luxuries like food, eat crap I can't stomach, and eventually grow up to be even more fucking annoying than they were when they couldn't walk and puked on your face when you had to pick 'em up by the scruff of the neck to get them out from underfoot.

Other than that, you know, I have no problem. And I'm sorry that all those children wet themselves.

I was kind of hoping they'd have aneurysms.

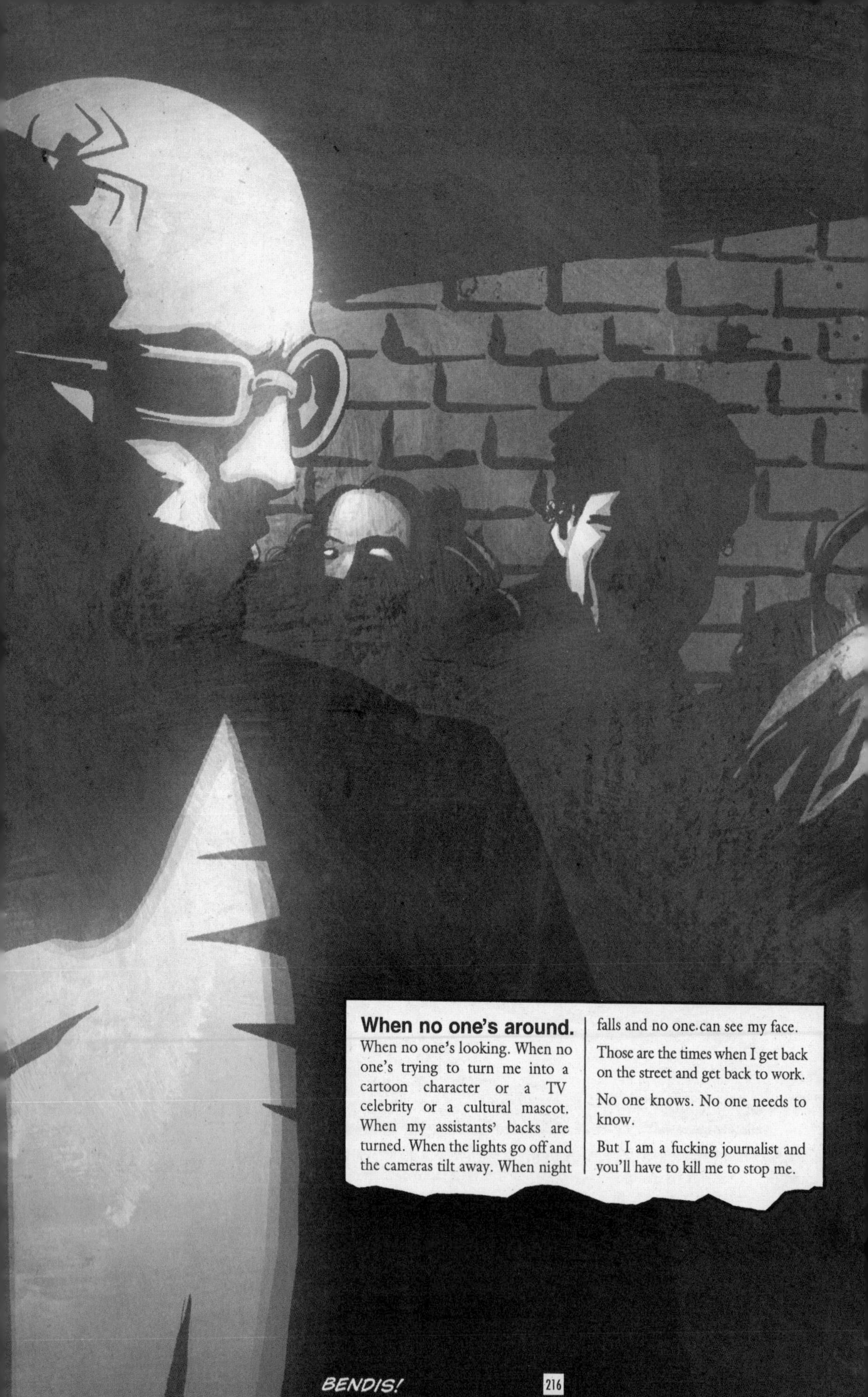
When no one's around.
When no one's looking. When no one's trying to turn me into a cartoon character or a TV celebrity or a cultural mascot. When my assistants' backs are turned. When the lights go off and the cameras tilt away. When night falls and no one can see my face.
Those are the times when I get back on the street and get back to work.
No one knows. No one needs to know.
But I am a fucking journalist and you'll have to kill me to stop me.

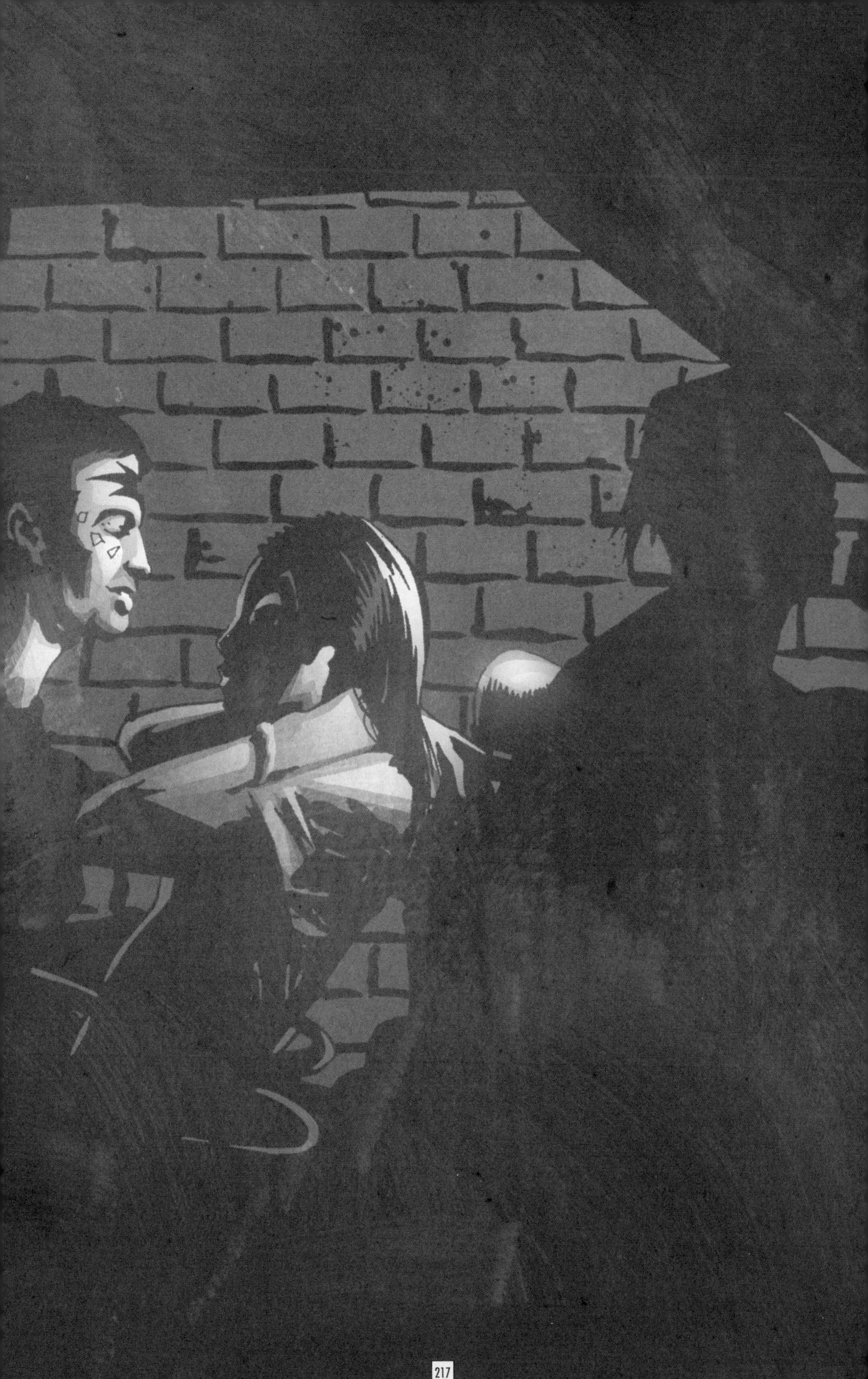

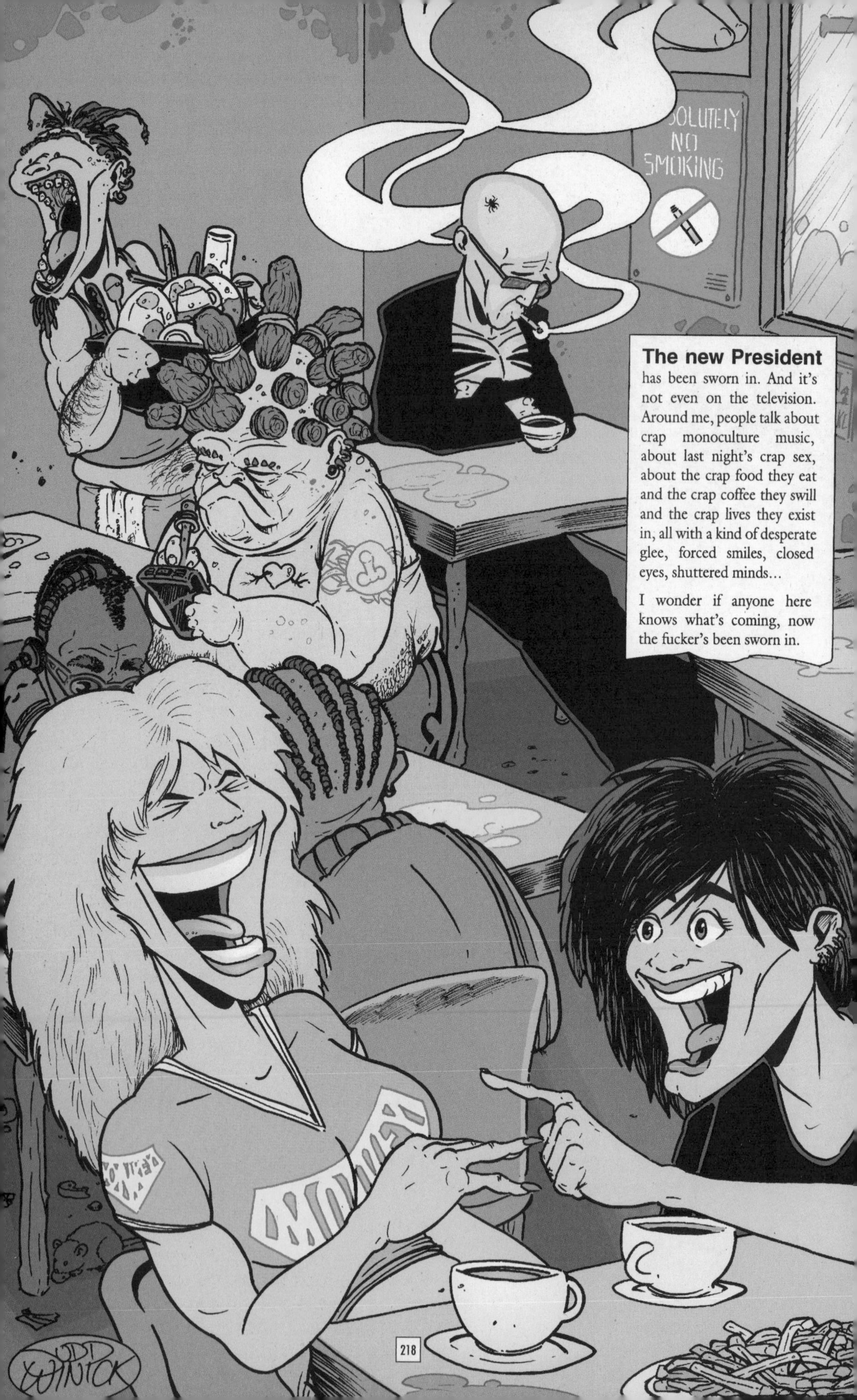
NO SMOKING
The new President has been sworn in. And it's not even on the television. Around me, people talk about crap monoculture music, about last night's crap sex, about the crap food they eat and the crap coffee they swill and the crap lives they exist in, all with a kind of desperate glee, forced smiles, closed eyes, shuttered minds...
I wonder if anyone here knows what's coming, now the fucker's been sworn in.

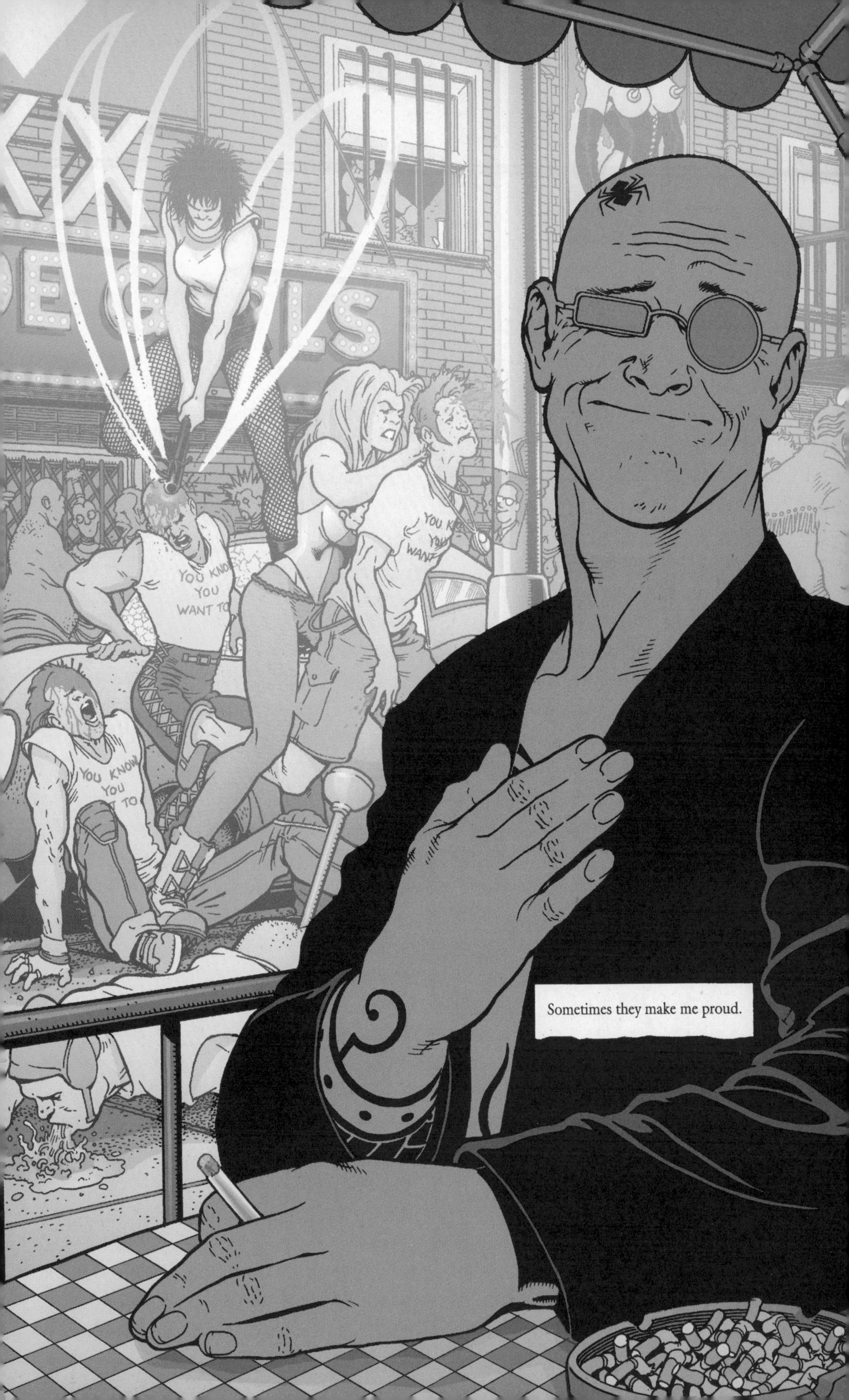
XX
GIRLS
YOU KNOW YOU WANT TO
YOU KNOW YOU WANT TO
Sometimes they make me proud.

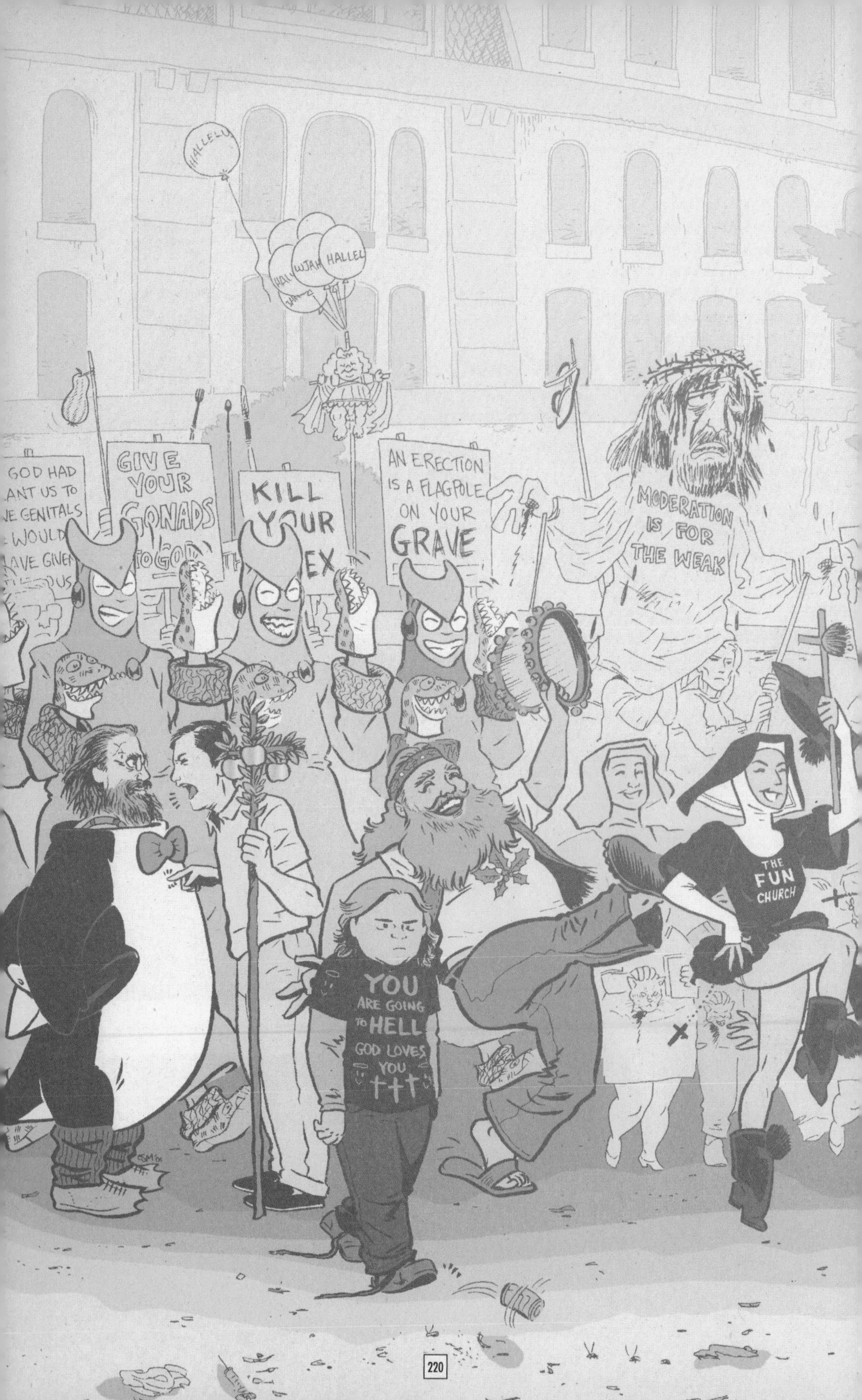

HALLELU
HALLEL
HALLEL
GOD HAD
ANT US TO
E GENITALS
WOULD
AVE GIVEN
GIVE YOUR GONADS TO GOD
KILL YOUR EX
AN ERECTION IS A FLAGPOLE ON YOUR GRAVE
MODERATION IS FOR THE WEAK
THE FUN CHURCH
YOU ARE GOING TO HELL GOD LOVES YOU

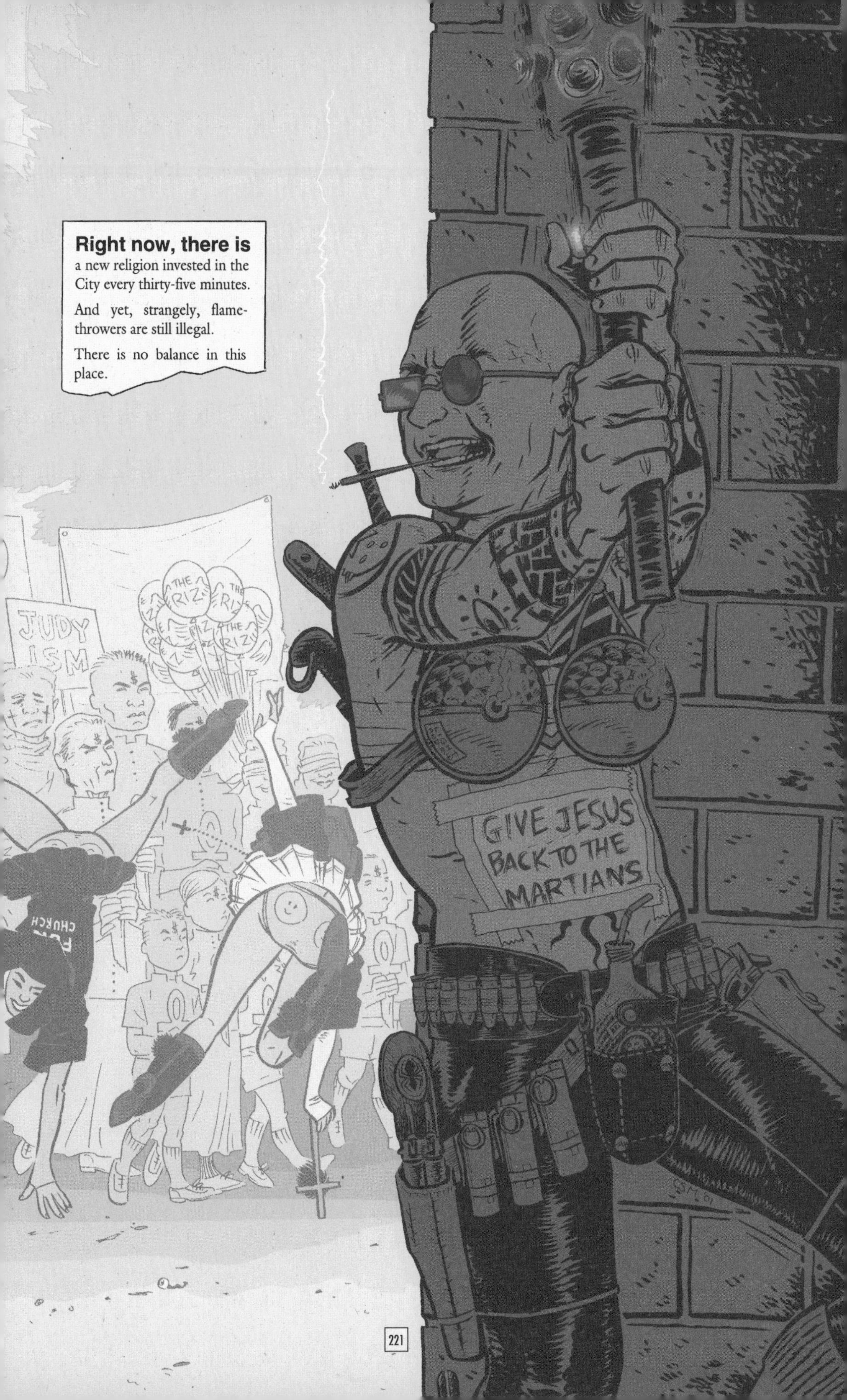
Right now, there is
a new religion invested in the City every thirty-five minutes.
And yet, strangely, flame-throwers are still illegal.
There is no balance in this place.
JUDY ISM
THE RIZ
GIVE JESUS BACK TO THE MARTIANS

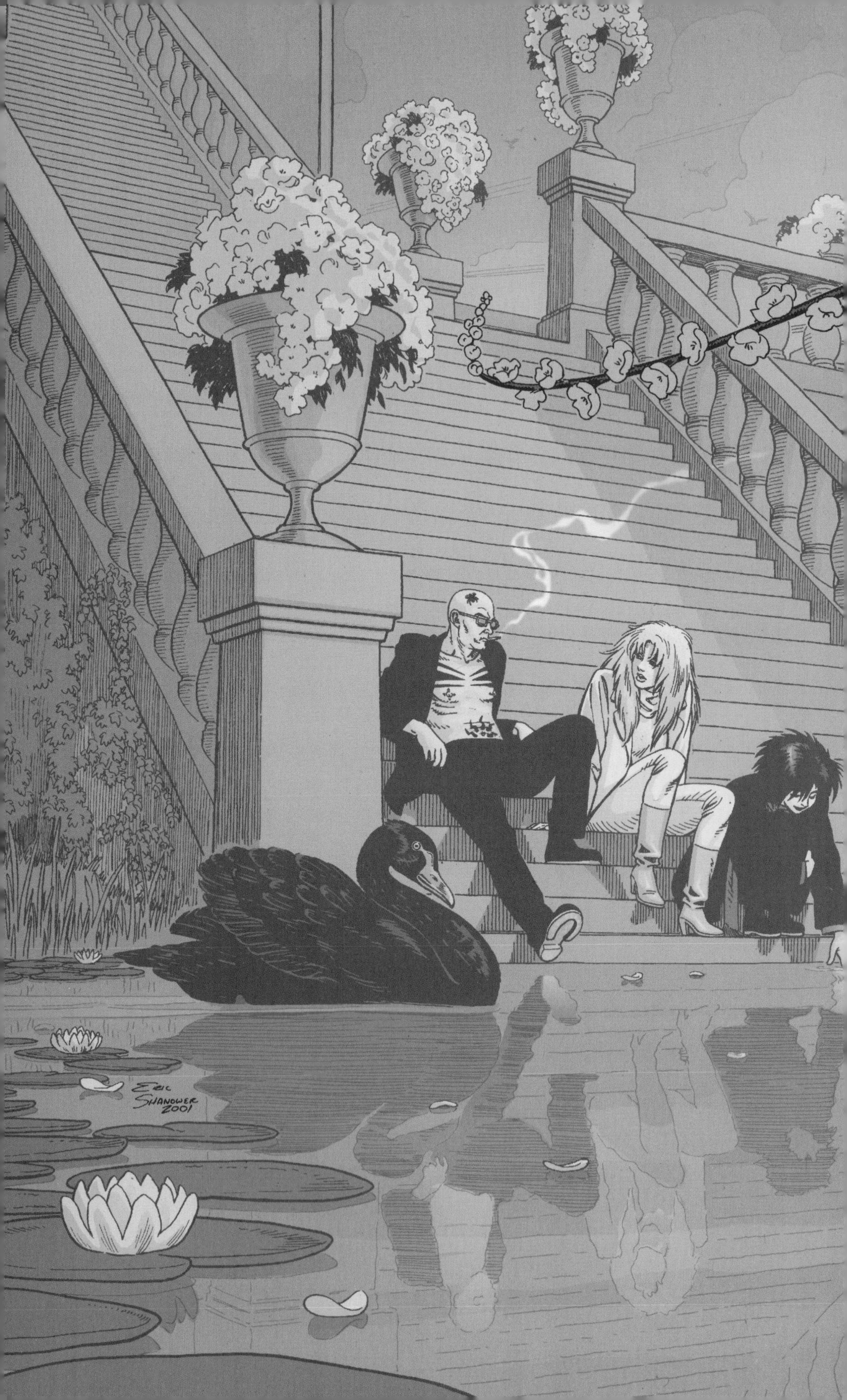
ERIC
SHANOWER
2001

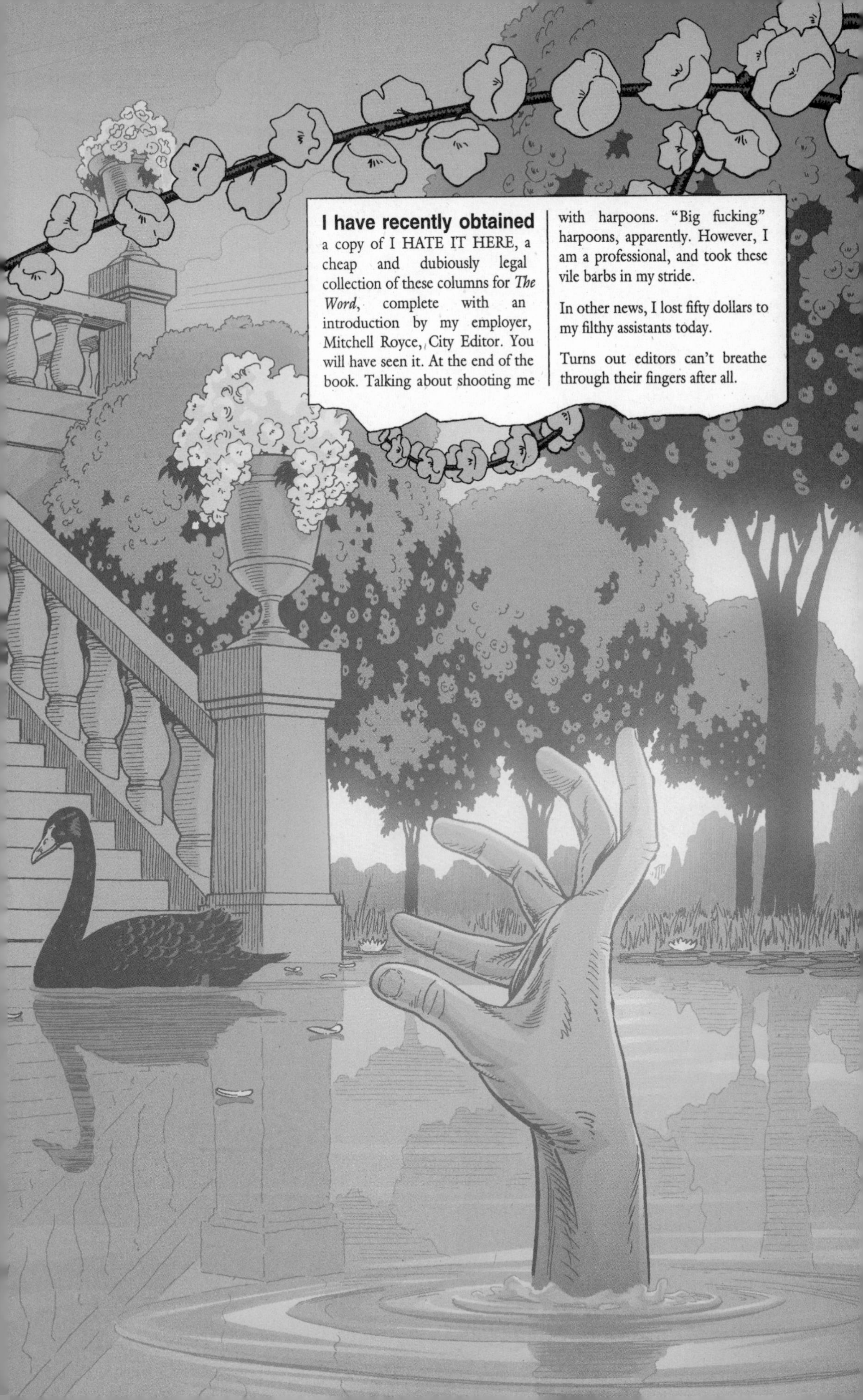
I have recently obtained a copy of I HATE IT HERE, a cheap and dubiously legal collection of these columns for The Word, complete with an introduction by my employer, Mitchell Royce, City Editor. You will have seen it. At the end of the book. Talking about shooting me with harpoons. "Big fucking" harpoons, apparently. However, I am a professional, and took these vile barbs in my stride.
In other news, I lost fifty dollars to my filthy assistants today.
Turns out editors can't breathe through their fingers after all.

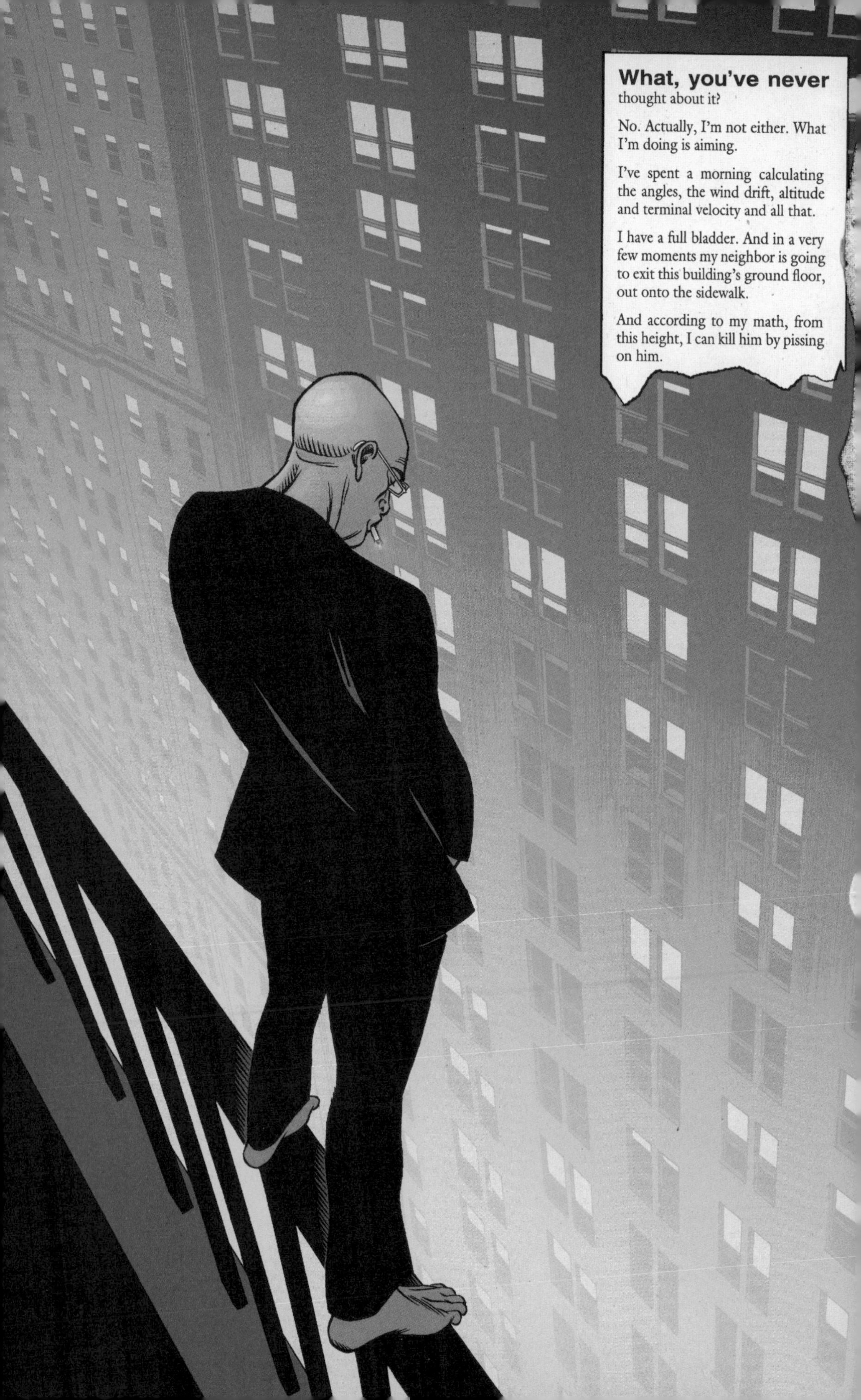
What, you've never thought about it?
No. Actually, I'm not either. What I'm doing is aiming.
I've spent a morning calculating the angles, the wind drift, altitude and terminal velocity and all that.
I have a full bladder. And in a very few moments my neighbor is going to exit this building's ground floor, out onto the sidewalk.
And according to my math, from this height, I can kill him by pissing on him.

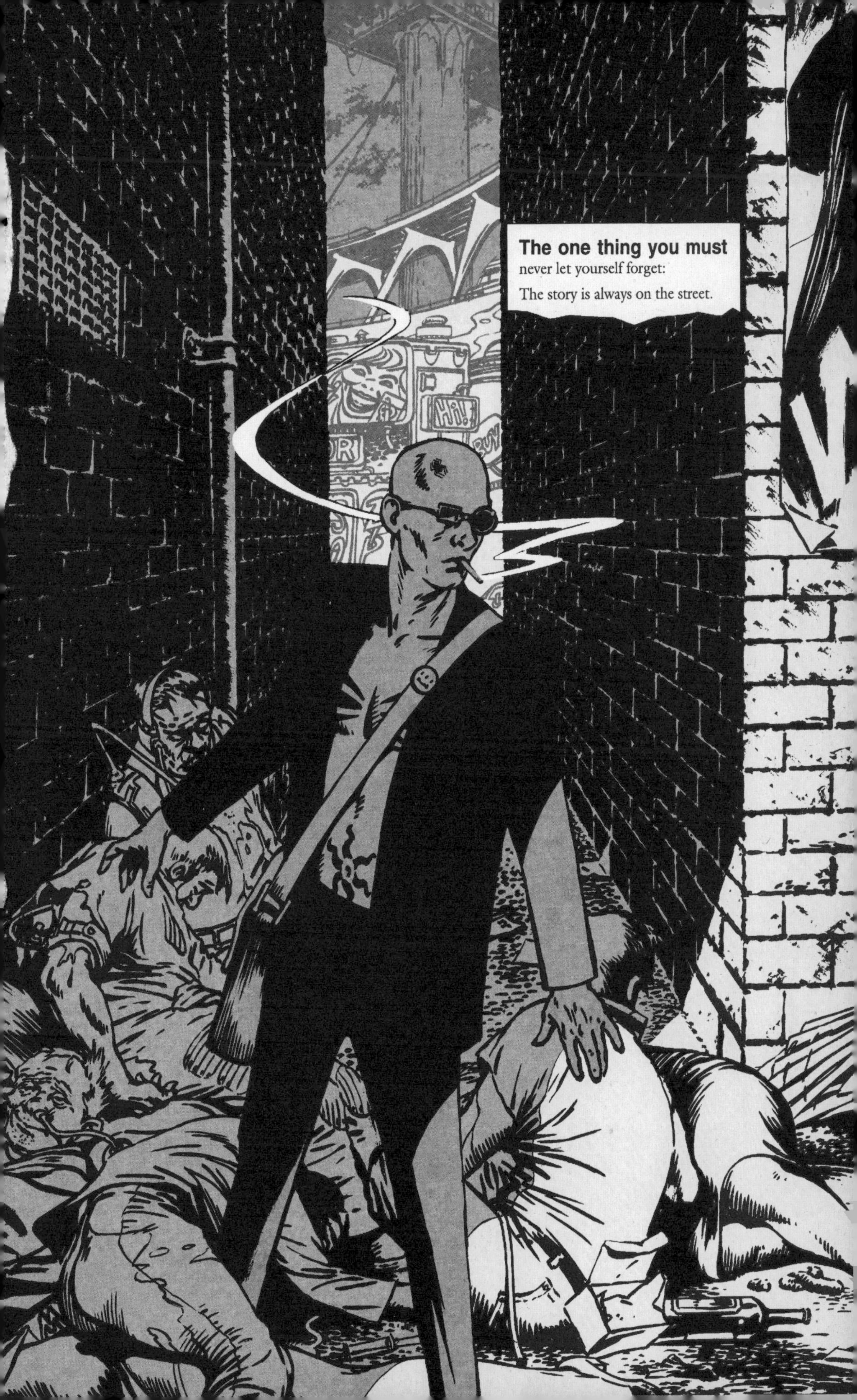
The one thing you must
never let yourself forget:
The story is always on the street.
HI!
BUY

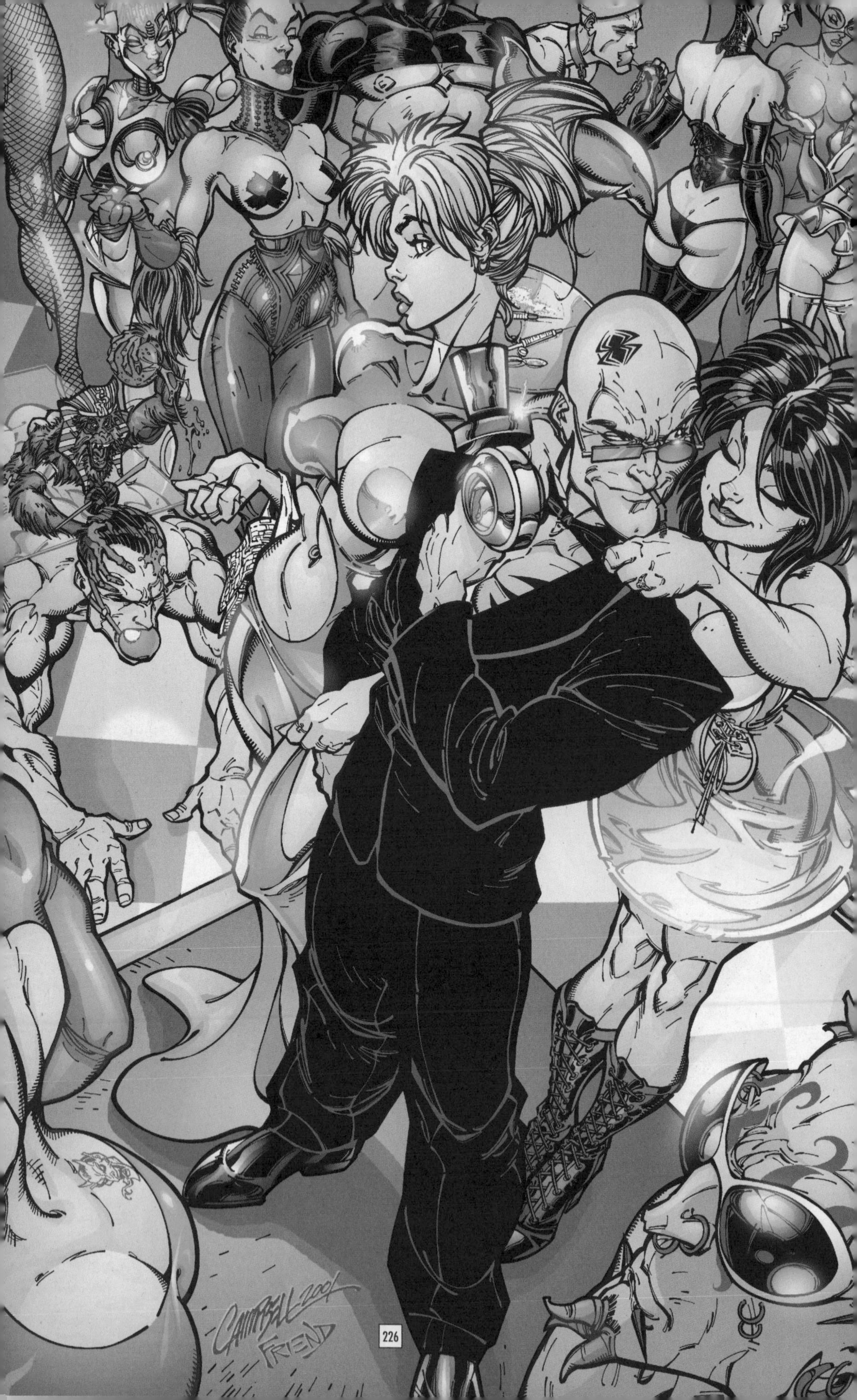
CAMPBELL-2001
FRIEND

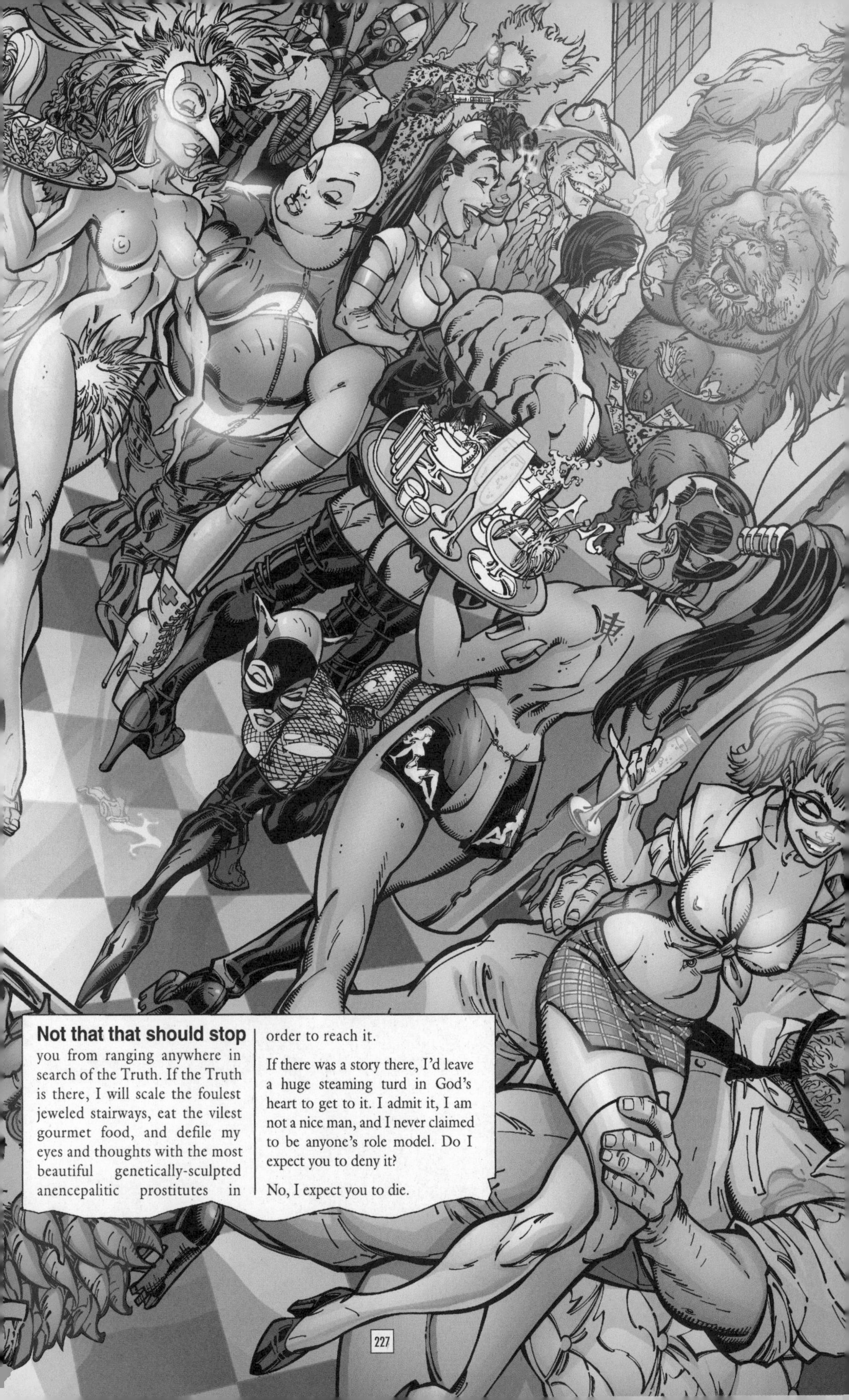
Not that that should stop you from ranging anywhere in search of the Truth. If the Truth is there, I will scale the foulest jeweled stairways, eat the vilest gourmet food, and defile my eyes and thoughts with the most beautiful genetically-sculpted anencepalitic prostitutes in order to reach it.
If there was a story there, I'd leave a huge steaming turd in God's heart to get to it. I admit it, I am not a nice man, and I never claimed to be anyone's role model. Do I expect you to deny it?
No, I expect you to die.

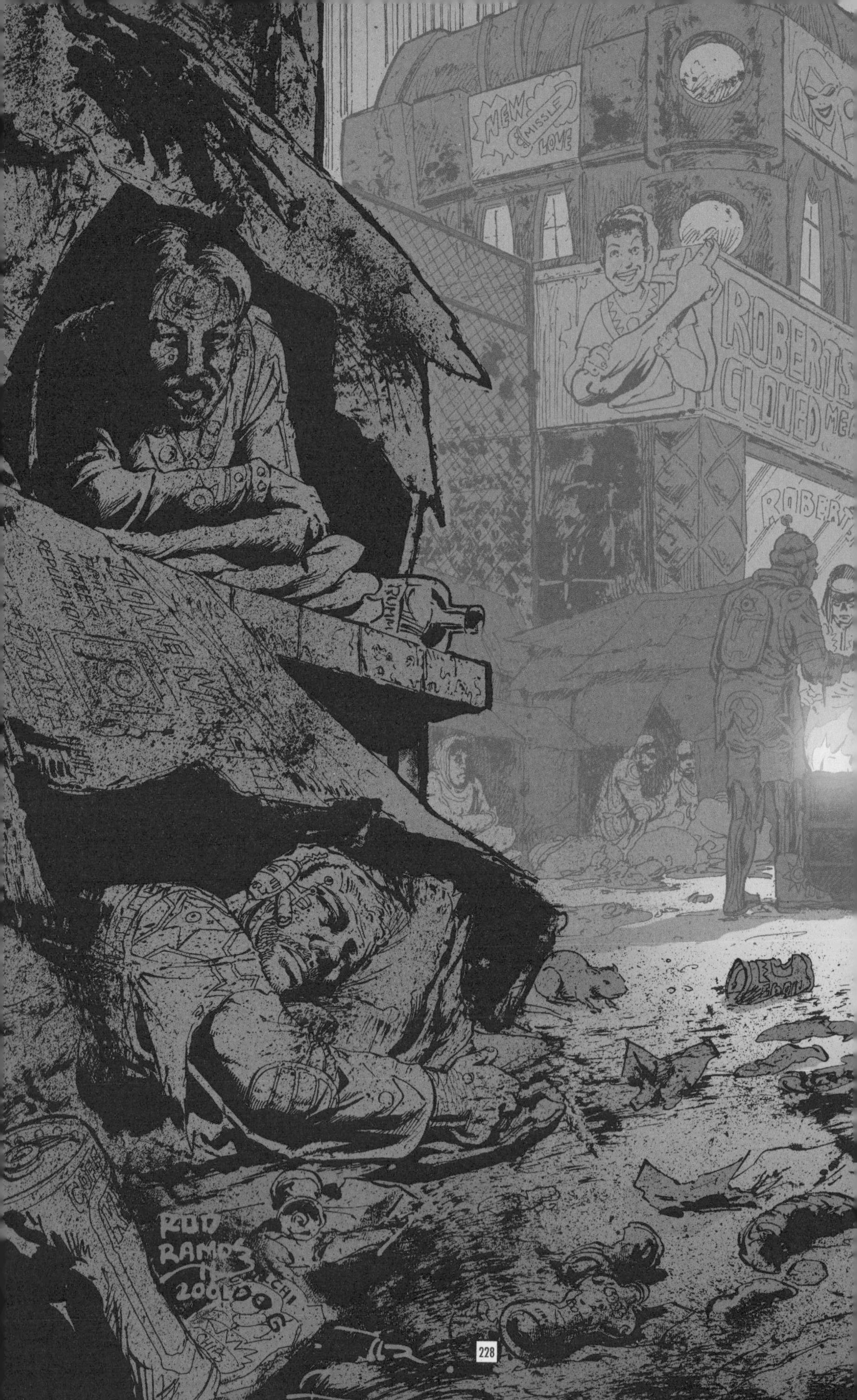
NEW
MISSLE
LOVE
ROBERTS
CLONED MEA
ROBERT
RUM
ROD RAMOS 2001

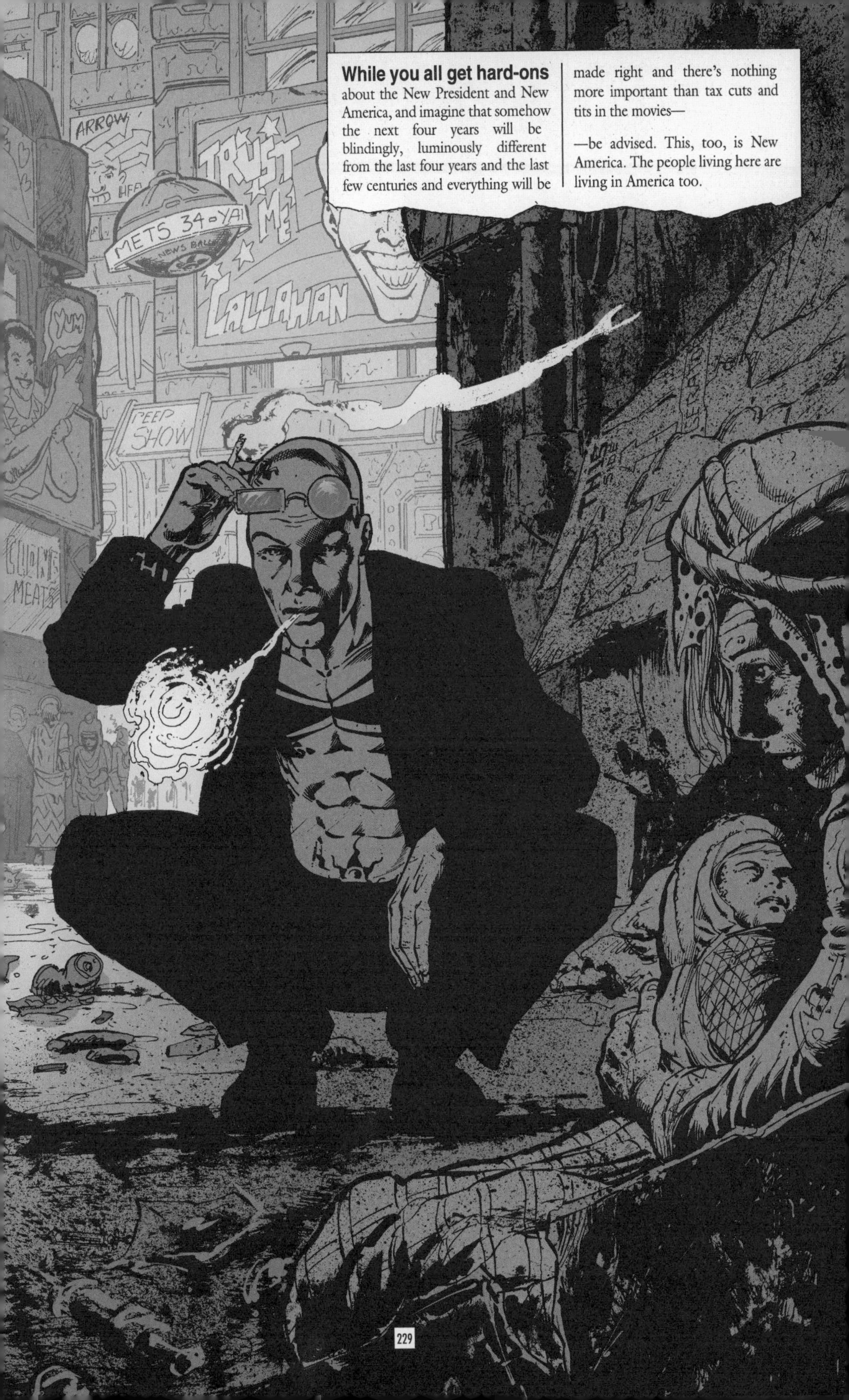
While you all get hard-ons about the New President and New America, and imagine that somehow the next four years will be blindingly, luminously different from the last four years and the last few centuries and everything will be made right and there's nothing more important than tax cuts and tits in the movies—
—be advised. This, too, is New America. The people living here are living in America too.
ARROW
TRUST ME
CALLAHAN
PEEP SHOW
YUM
MEATS

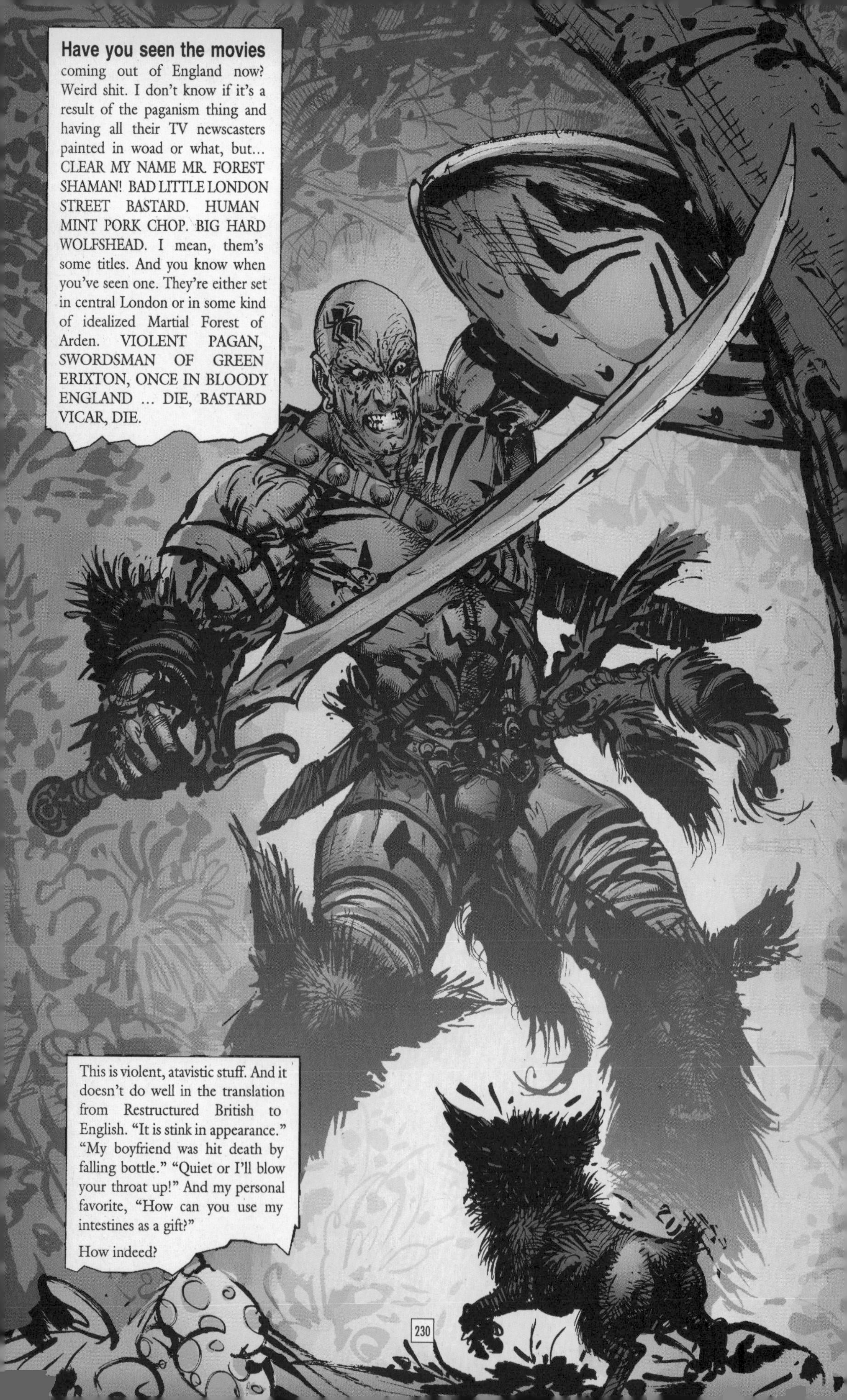
Have you seen the movies coming out of England now? Weird shit. I don't know if it's a result of the paganism thing and having all their TV newscasters painted in woad or what, but... CLEAR MY NAME MR. FOREST SHAMAN! BAD LITTLE LONDON STREET BASTARD. HUMAN MINT PORK CHOP. BIG HARD WOLFSHEAD. I mean, them's some titles. And you know when you've seen one. They're either set in central London or in some kind of idealized Martial Forest of Arden. VIOLENT PAGAN, SWORDSMAN OF GREEN ERIXTON, ONCE IN BLOODY ENGLAND ... DIE, BASTARD VICAR, DIE.
This is violent, atavistic stuff. And it doesn't do well in the translation from Restructured British to English. "It is stink in appearance." "My boyfriend was hit death by falling bottle." "Quiet or I'll blow your throat up!" And my personal favorite, "How can you use my intestines as a gift?"
How indeed?

"Dear Spider, your name sings. Mine sings with it. I've spent entire nites writing them in the blackness with silver bolts of lightning. But the mornings com hard, and I weep in the mirrorr. Lonliness can kill the most nobel intentions. I could have poisoned this letter with combat bacterium and you wouldn't know."

"Dear Spider, I followed you again today and you didnt notice did you? I could have killed you. And I will if I keep seeing you with those slutts. Don't make me kill those slutts too."

"Royce: stop sending me this fan-mail shit. I'll write for the little bastards and I'll do the song and dance to get them to read it. But don't make me look at them."

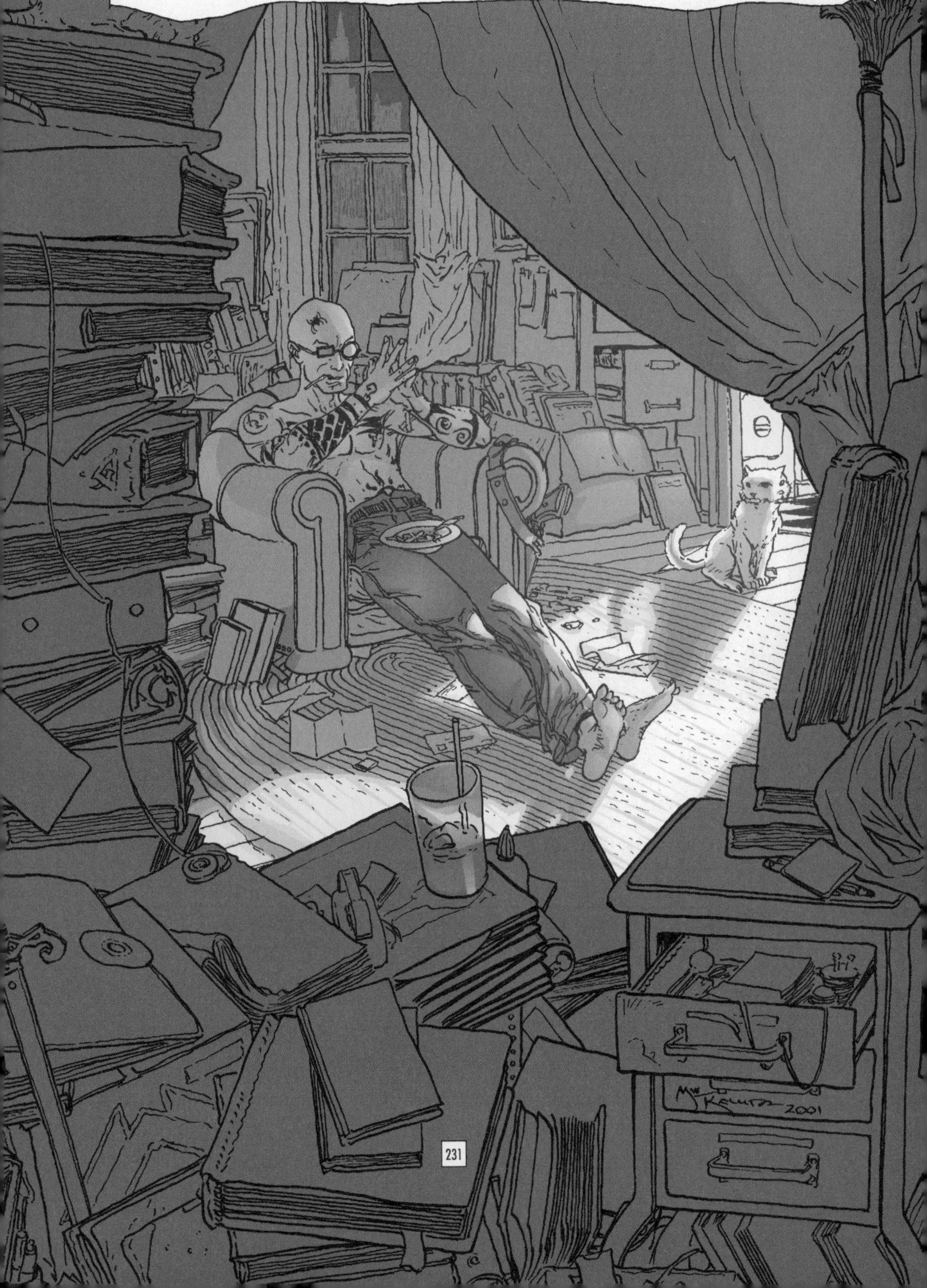

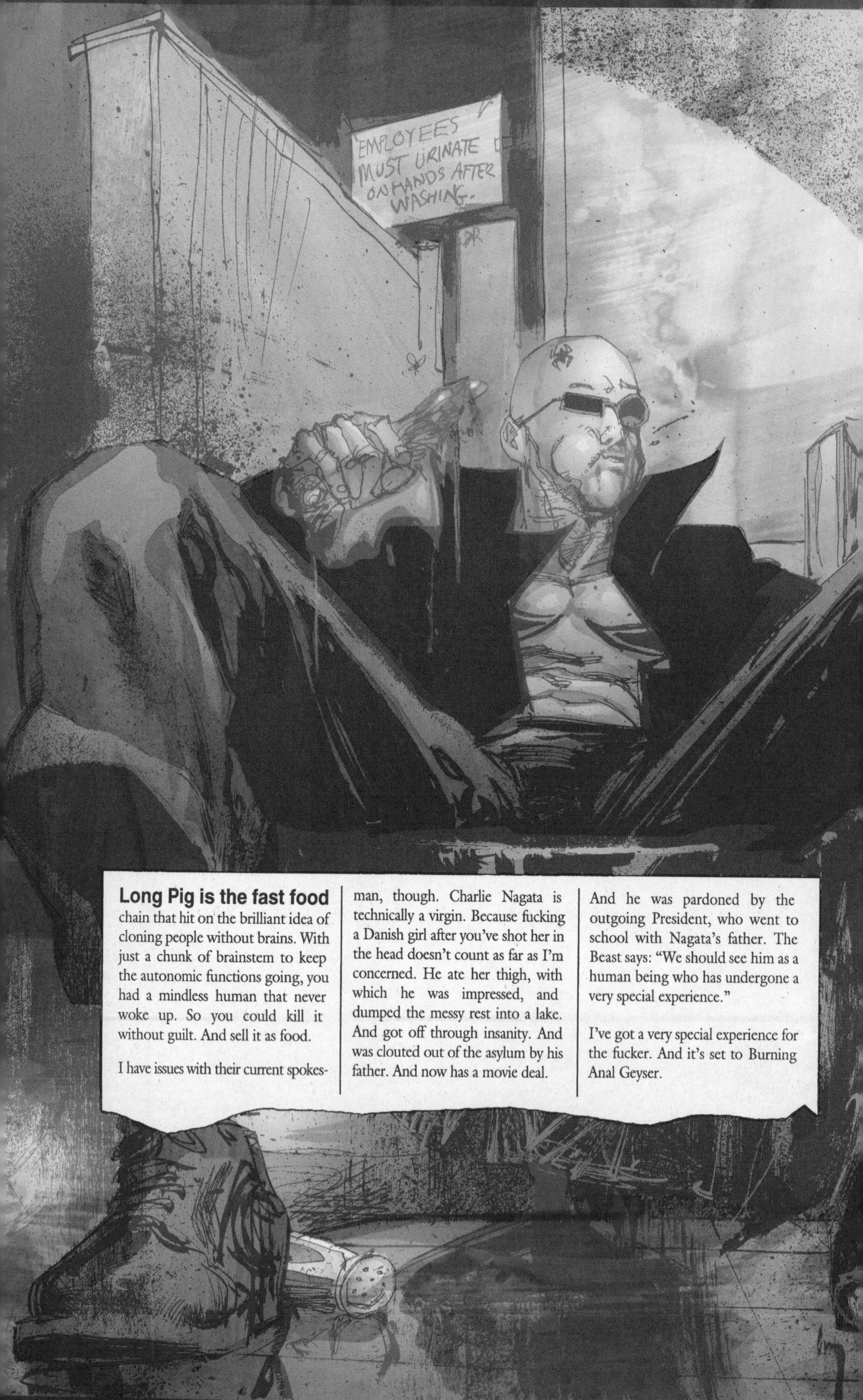
EMPLOYEES MUST URINATE ON HANDS AFTER WASHING.
Long Pig is the fast food chain that hit on the brilliant idea of cloning people without brains. With just a chunk of brainstem to keep the autonomic functions going, you had a mindless human that never woke up. So you could kill it without guilt. And sell it as food.
I have issues with their current spokesman, though. Charlie Nagata is technically a virgin. Because fucking a Danish girl after you've shot her in the head doesn't count as far as I'm concerned. He ate her thigh, with which he was impressed, and dumped the messy rest into a lake. And got off through insanity. And was clouted out of the asylum by his father. And now has a movie deal. And he was pardoned by the outgoing President, who went to school with Nagata's father. The Beast says: "We should see him as a human being who has undergone a very special experience."
I've got a very special experience for the fucker. And it's set to Burning Anal Geyser.

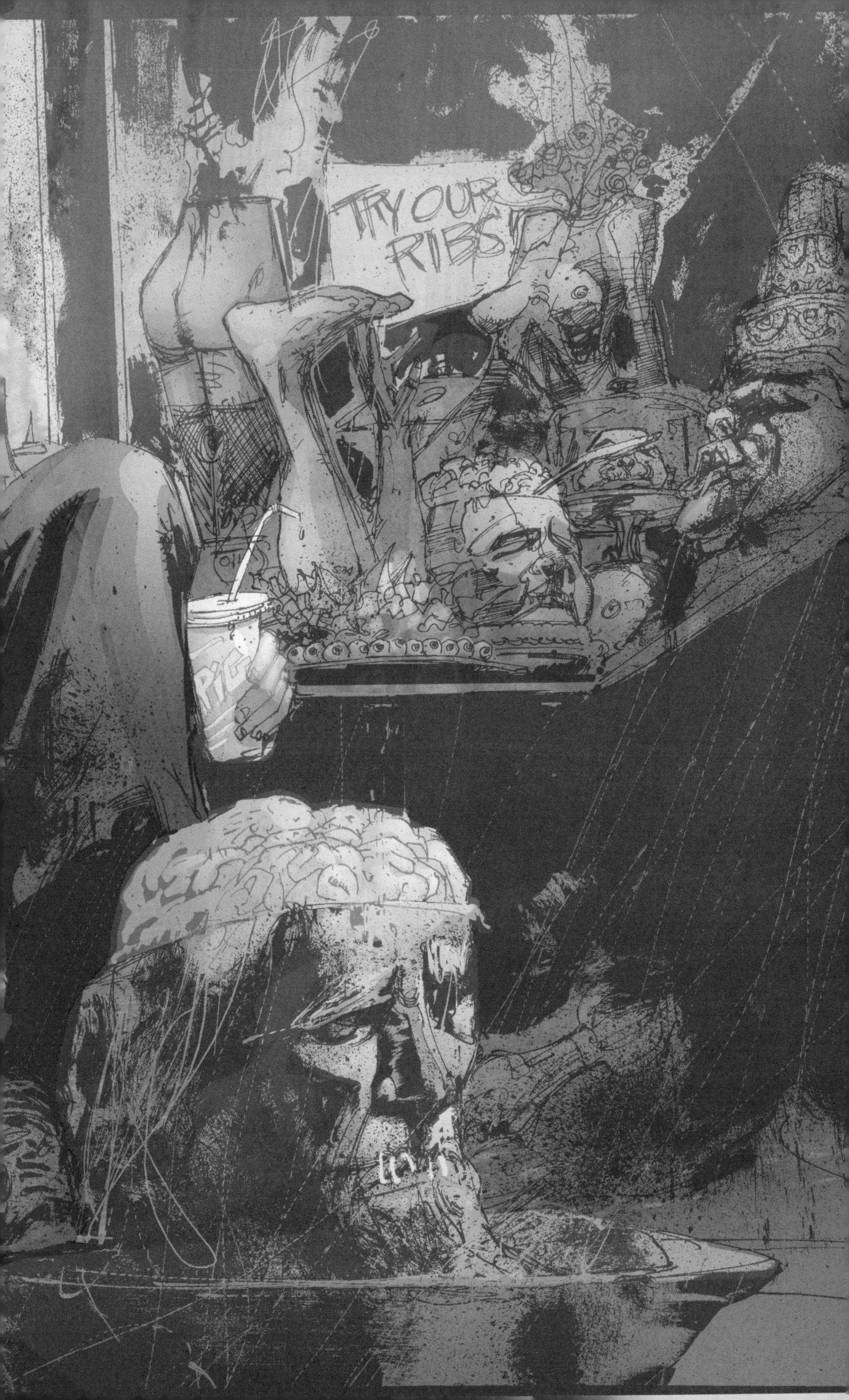
TRY OUR RIBS
PIG

I want you to do some-thing for me tomorrow. I want you to stop. Just stop, and take in the City. Take a breath. Inhale the City's scent. Okay, there s a fair chance that might simply earn you a noseful of dogshit, but give it a try.

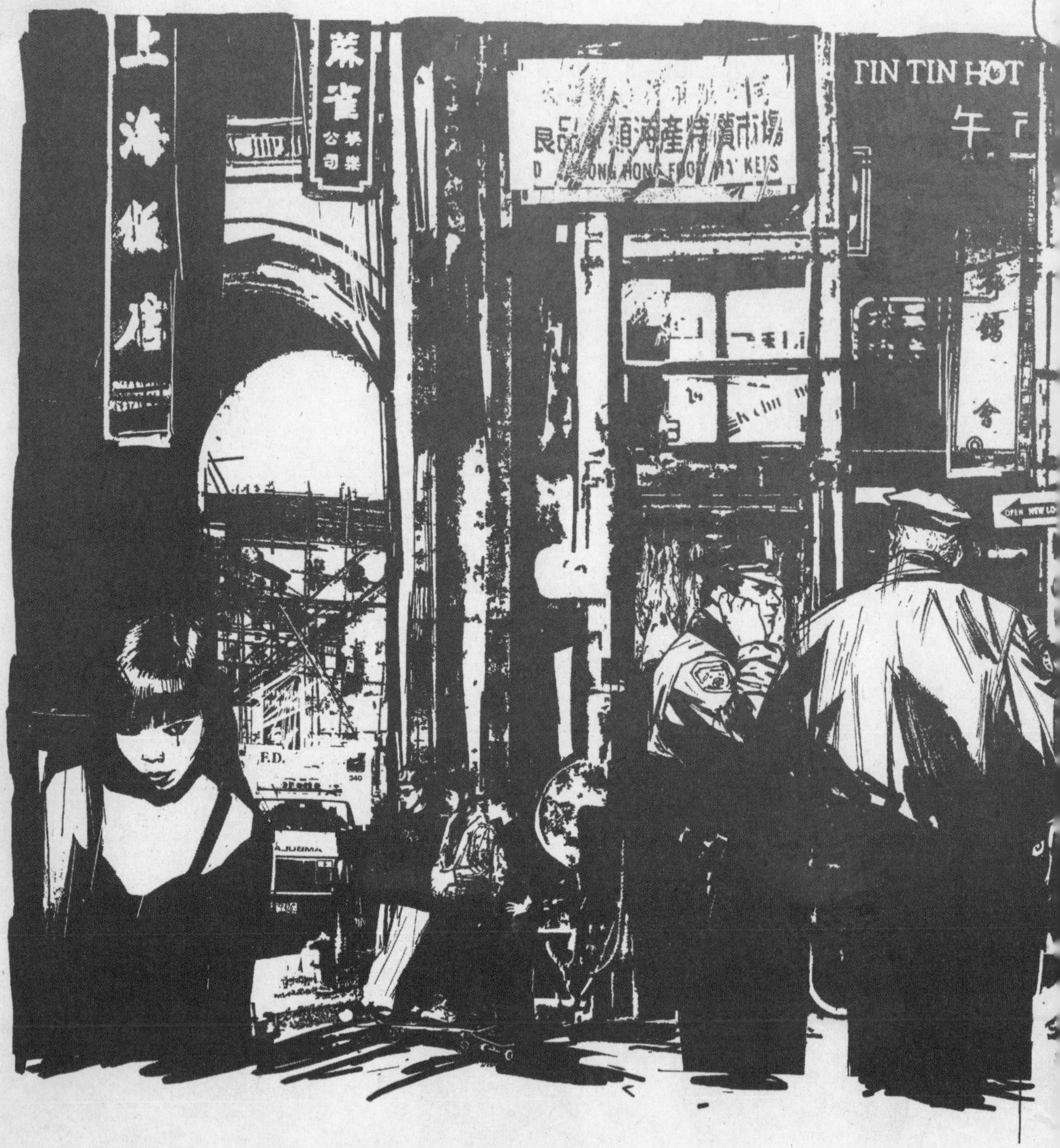
TIN TIN HOT
F.D.

Because it's easy to forget how rich a place this is. How many cultures come here to comprise the place. Take a moment and enjoy it. Because the City will be different tomorrow and that moment will be gone, like a Filthy Assistant's fart in the night...

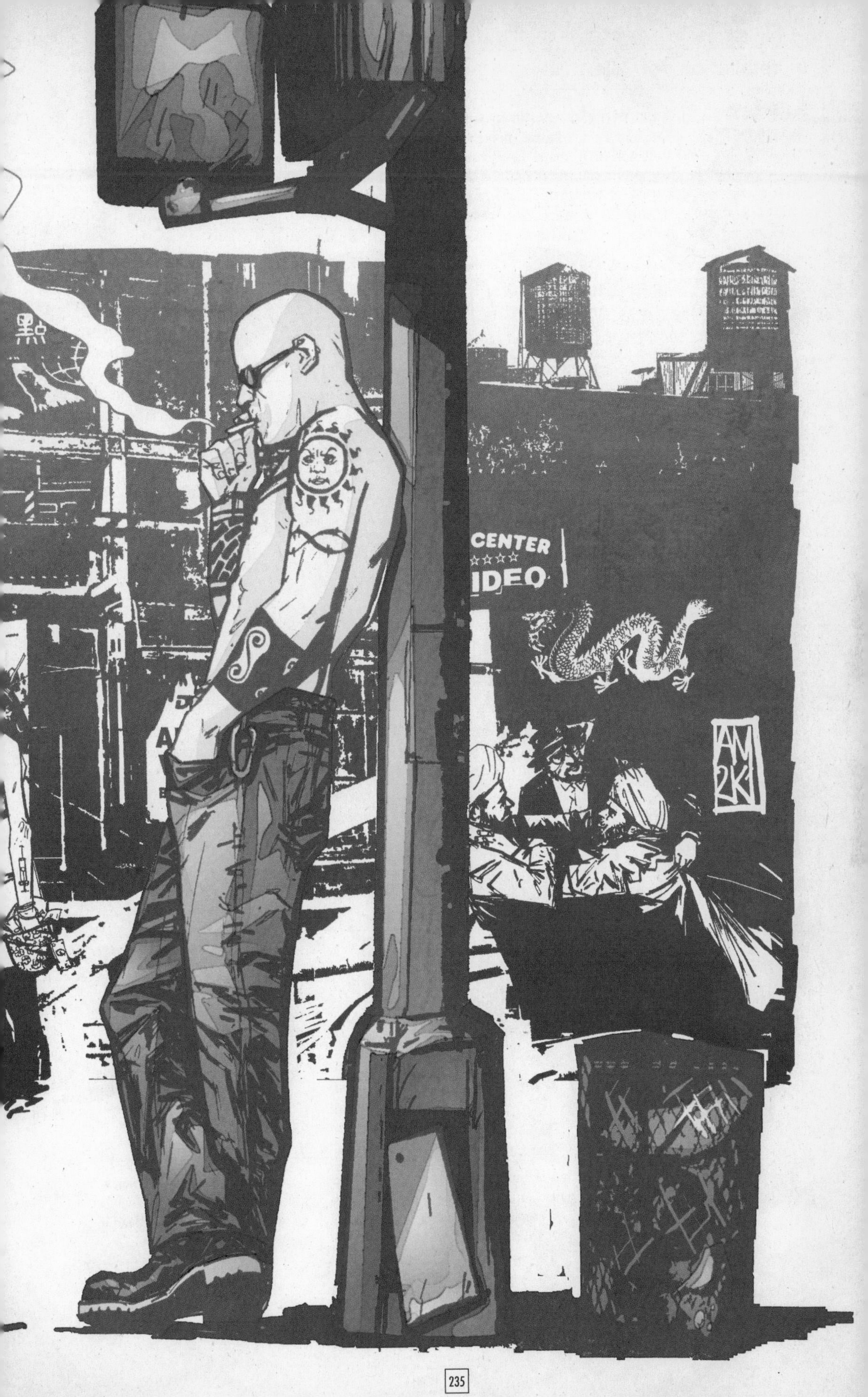
CENTER
IDEO
AM
2K

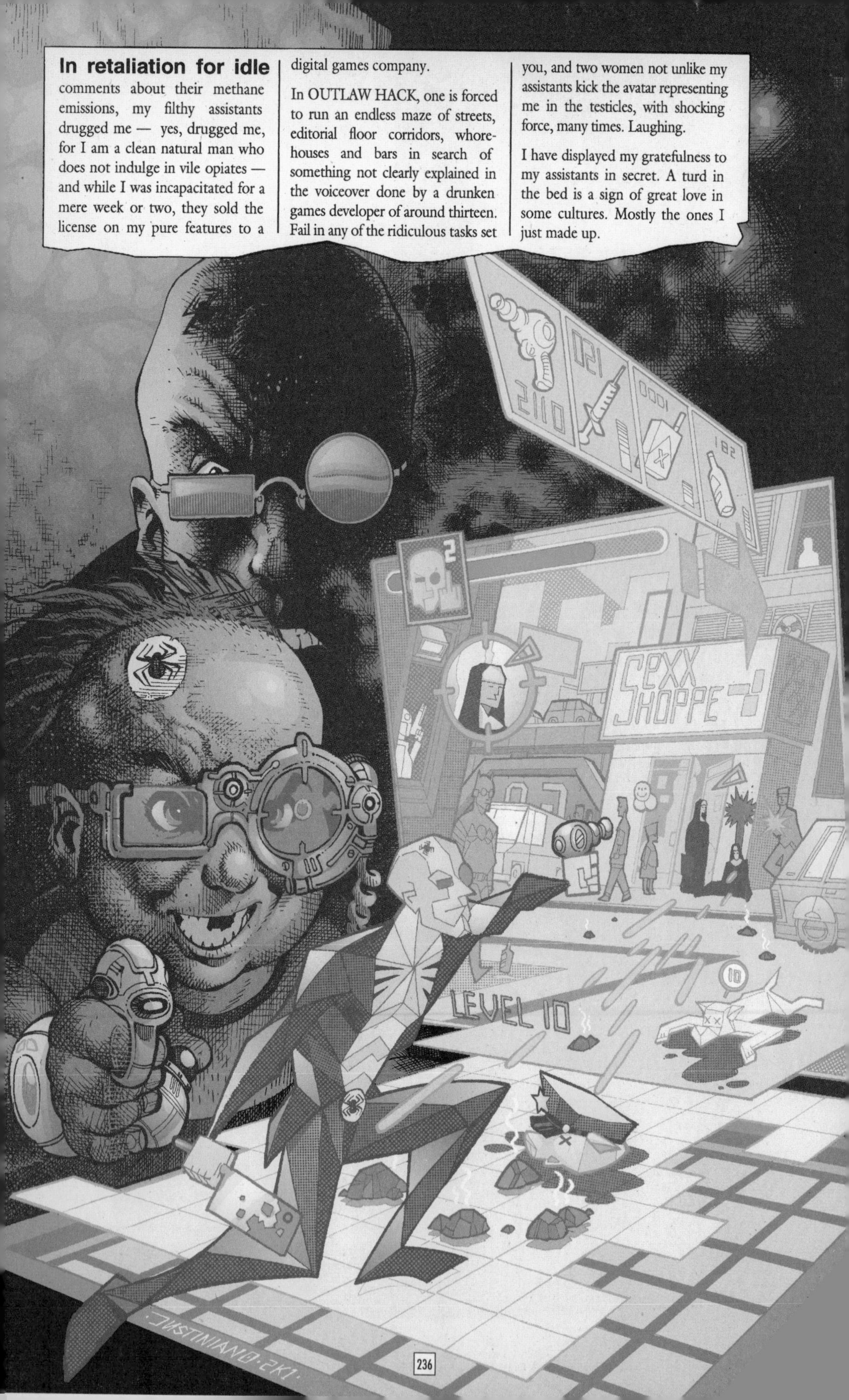
In retaliation for idle comments about their methane emissions, my filthy assistants drugged me — yes, drugged me, for I am a clean natural man who does not indulge in vile opiates — and while I was incapacitated for a mere week or two, they sold the license on my pure features to a digital games company.
In OUTLAW HACK, one is forced to run an endless maze of streets, editorial floor corridors, whorehouses and bars in search of something not clearly explained in the voiceover done by a drunken games developer of around thirteen. Fail in any of the ridiculous tasks set you, and two women not unlike my assistants kick the avatar representing me in the testicles, with shocking force, many times. Laughing.
I have displayed my gratefulness to my assistants in secret. A turd in the bed is a sign of great love in some cultures. Mostly the ones I just made up.
SEXX SHOPPE
LEVEL 10
JUSTINIANO·2K1

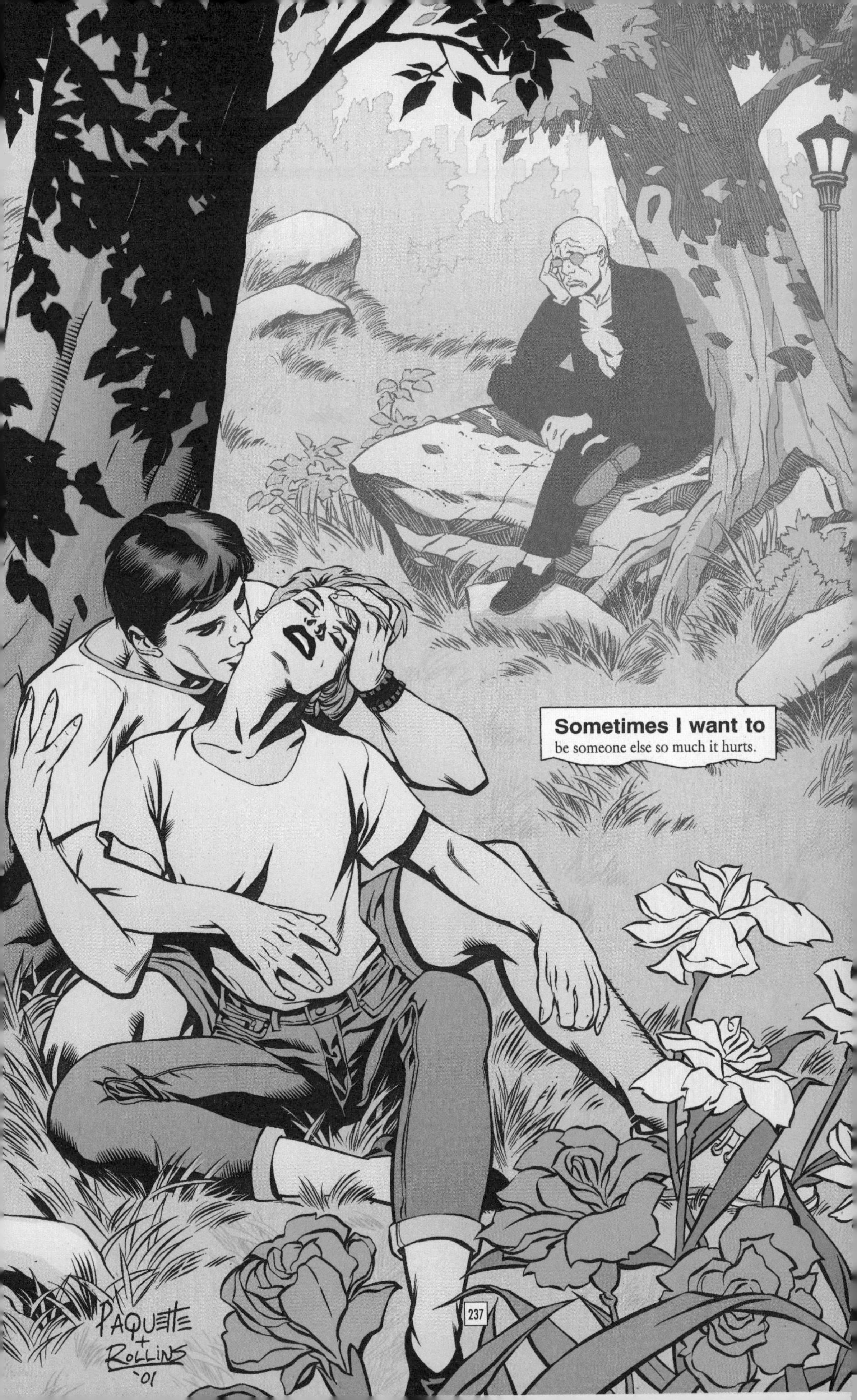
Sometimes I want to
be someone else so much it hurts.
PAQUETTE + ROLLINS '01

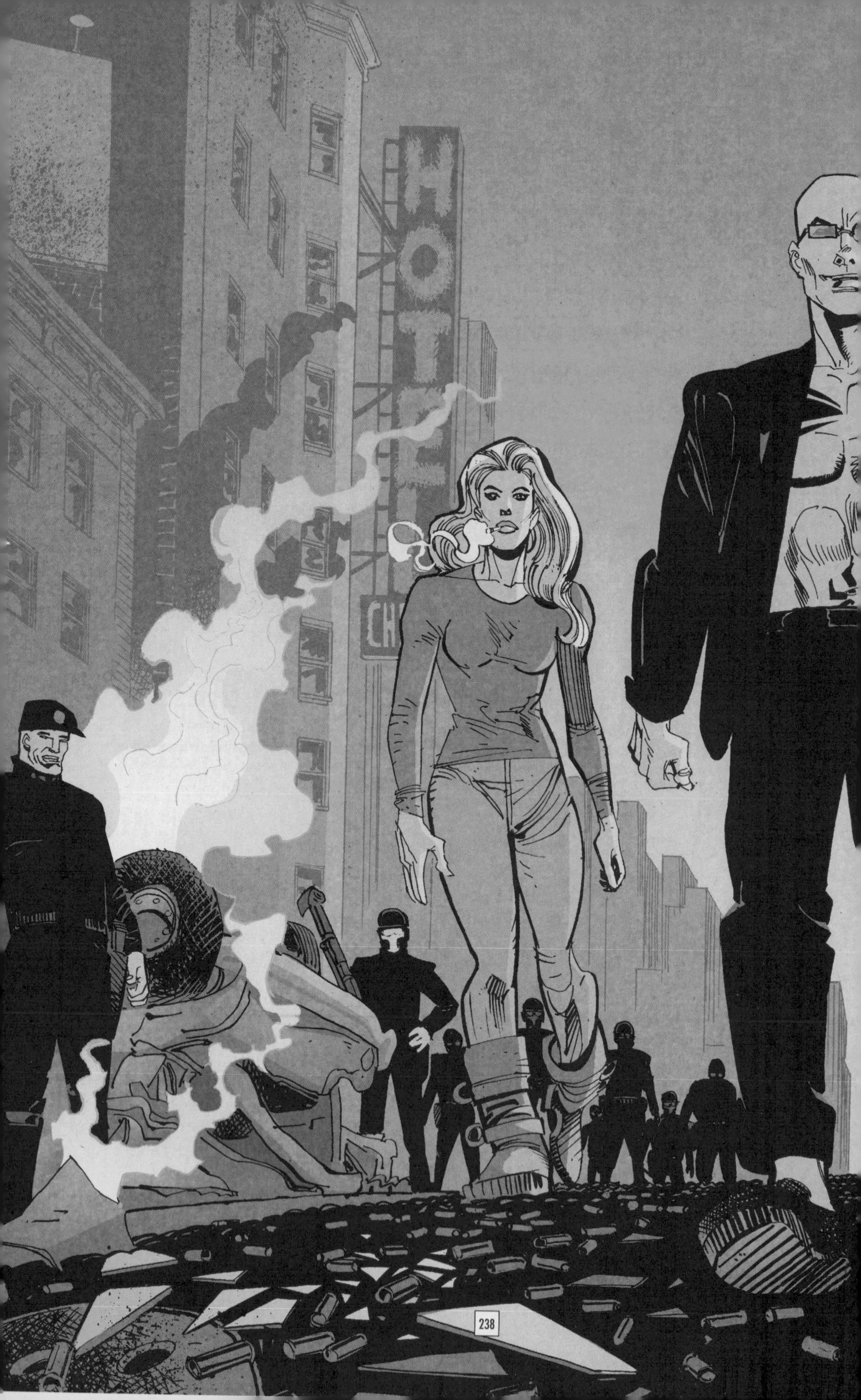

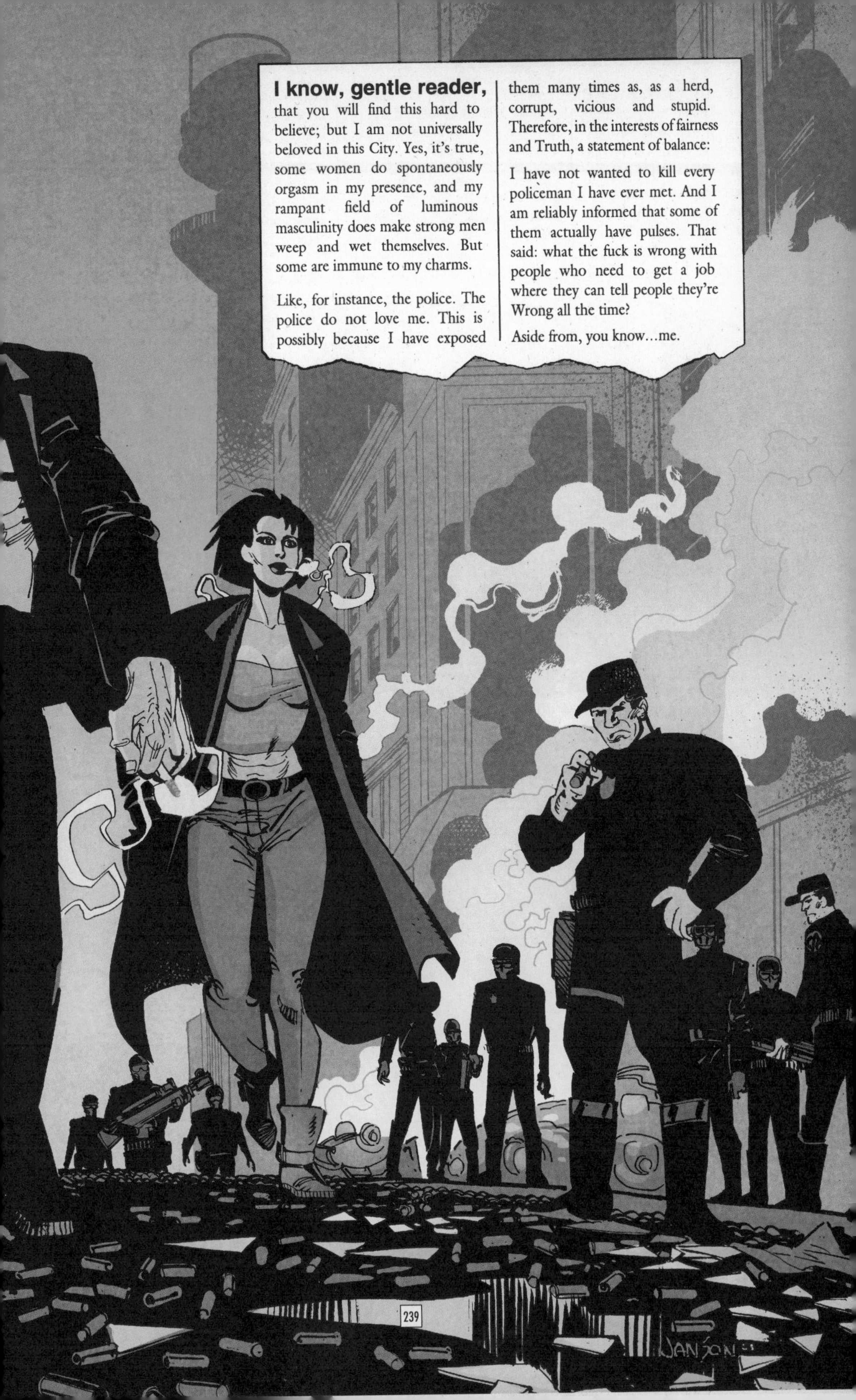
I know, gentle reader, that you will find this hard to believe; but I am not universally beloved in this City. Yes, it's true, some women do spontaneously orgasm in my presence, and my rampant field of luminous masculinity does make strong men weep and wet themselves. But some are immune to my charms.
Like, for instance, the police. The police do not love me. This is possibly because I have exposed them many times as, as a herd, corrupt, vicious and stupid. Therefore, in the interests of fairness and Truth, a statement of balance:
I have not wanted to kill every policeman I have ever met. And I am reliably informed that some of them actually have pulses. That said: what the fuck is wrong with people who need to get a job where they can tell people they're Wrong all the time?
Aside from, you know…me.
JANSON

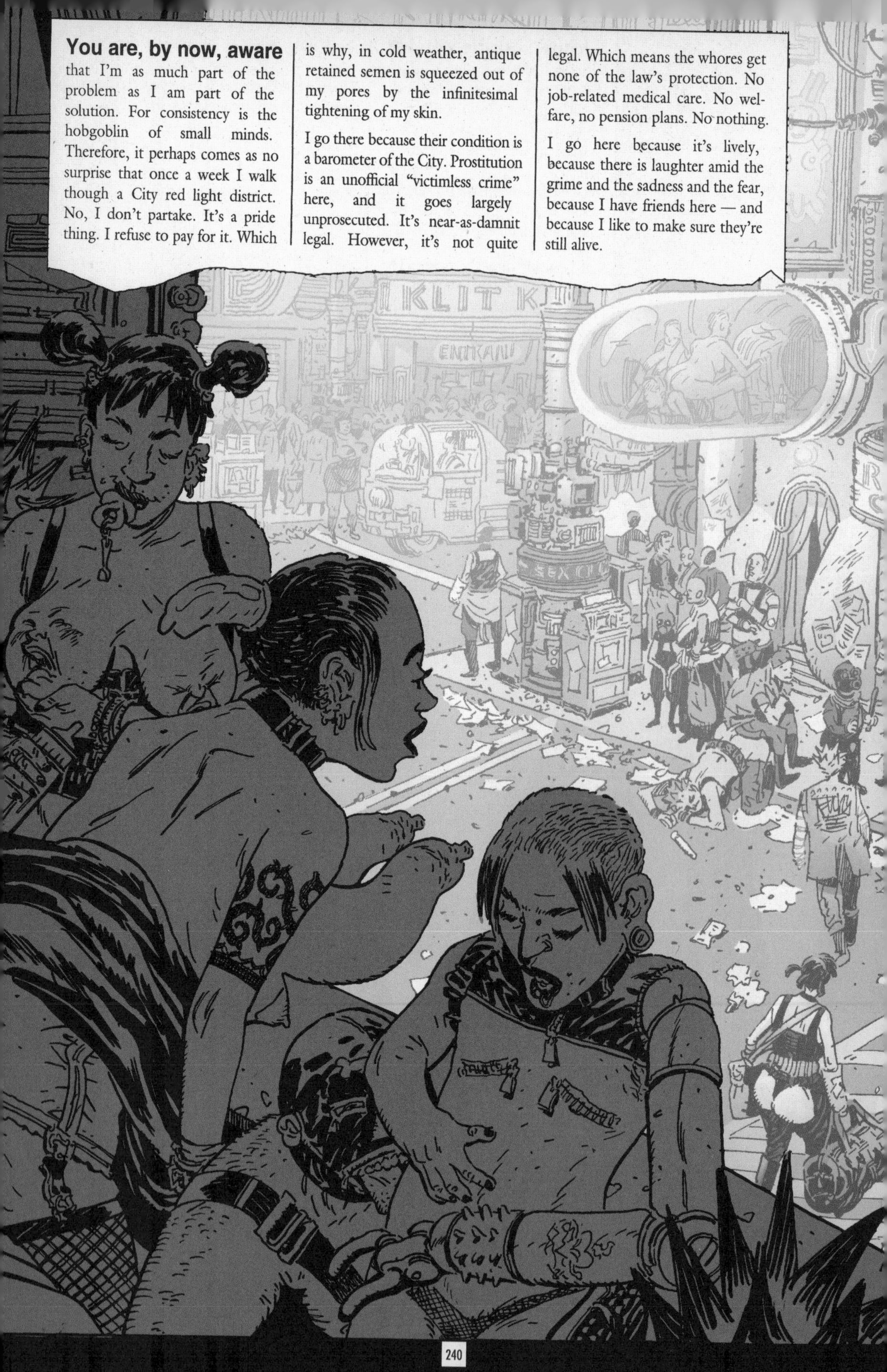
You are, by now, aware that I'm as much part of the problem as I am part of the solution. For consistency is the hobgoblin of small minds. Therefore, it perhaps comes as no surprise that once a week I walk though a City red light district. No, I don't partake. It's a pride thing. I refuse to pay for it. Which is why, in cold weather, antique retained semen is squeezed out of my pores by the infinitesimal tightening of my skin.
I go there because their condition is a barometer of the City. Prostitution is an unofficial "victimless crime" here, and it goes largely unprosecuted. It's near-as-damnit legal. However, it's not quite legal. Which means the whores get none of the law's protection. No job-related medical care. No welfare, no pension plans. No nothing.
I go here because it's lively, because there is laughter amid the grime and the sadness and the fear, because I have friends here — and because I like to make sure they're still alive.
KLIT K

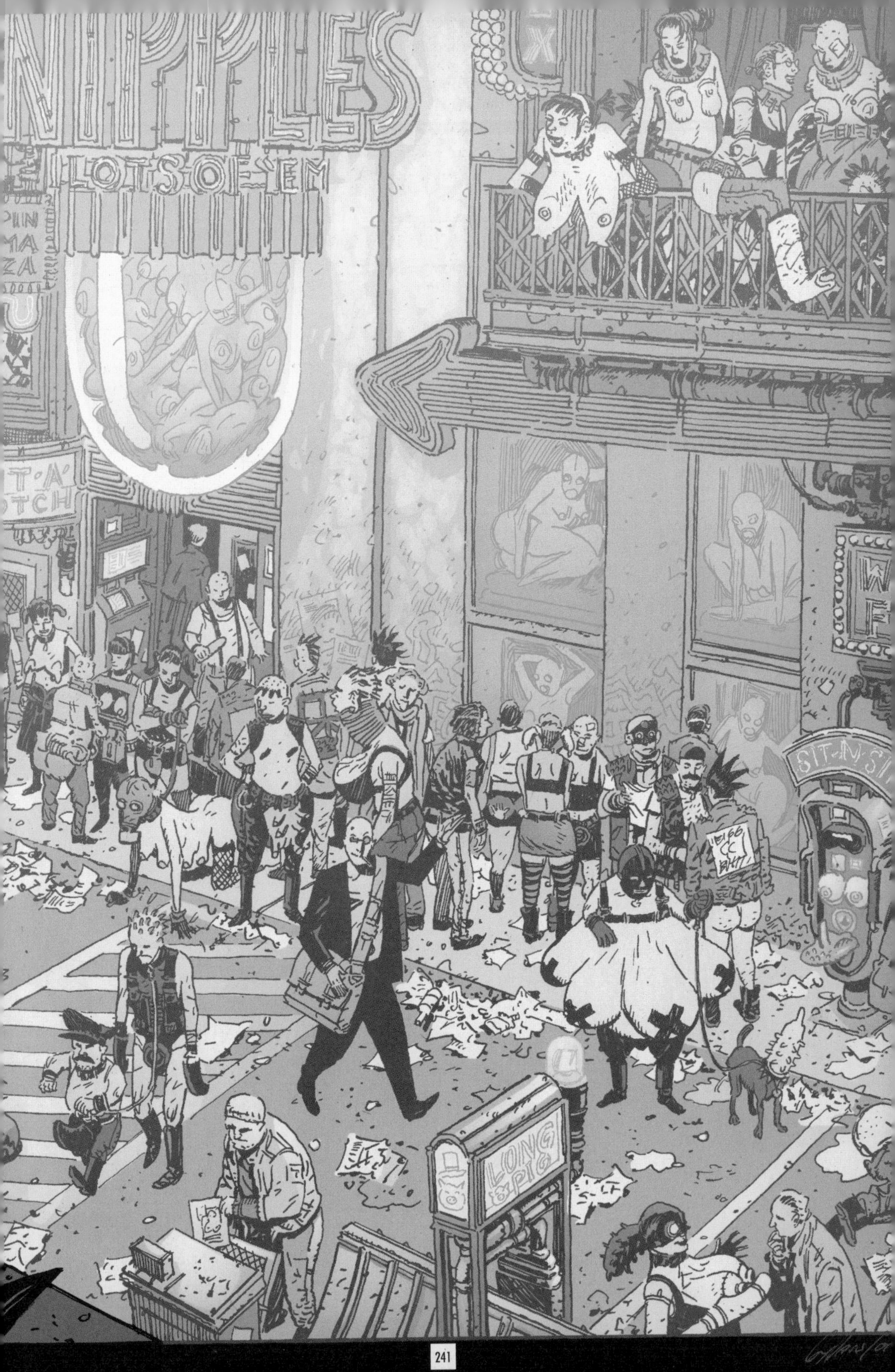
NIPPLES
LOTS OF 'EM
LONG PIG

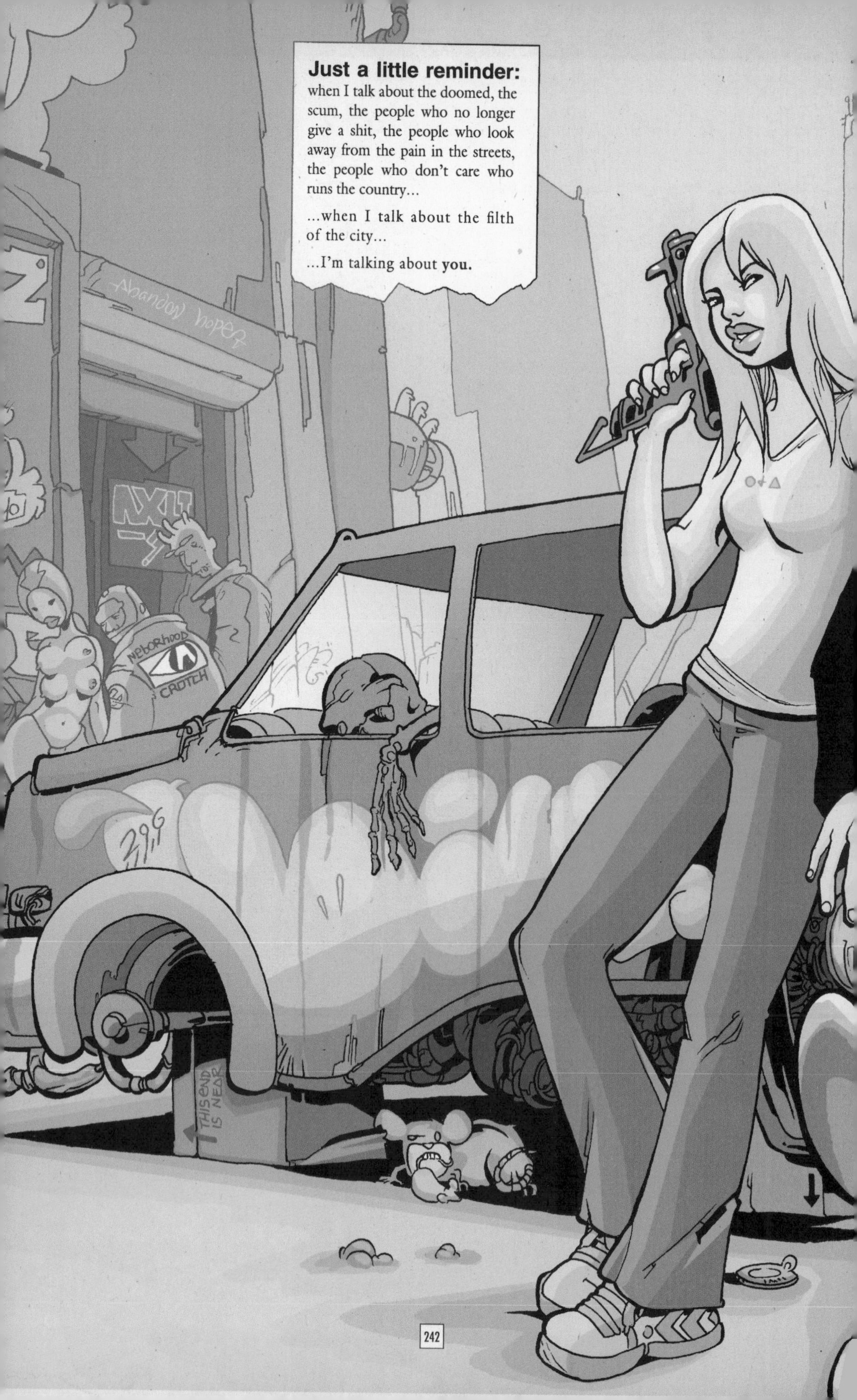
Just a little reminder:
when I talk about the doomed, the scum, the people who no longer give a shit, the people who look away from the pain in the streets, the people who don't care who runs the country...
...when I talk about the filth of the city...
...I'm talking about **you.**
NEBORHOOD CROTCH
THIS END IS NEAR

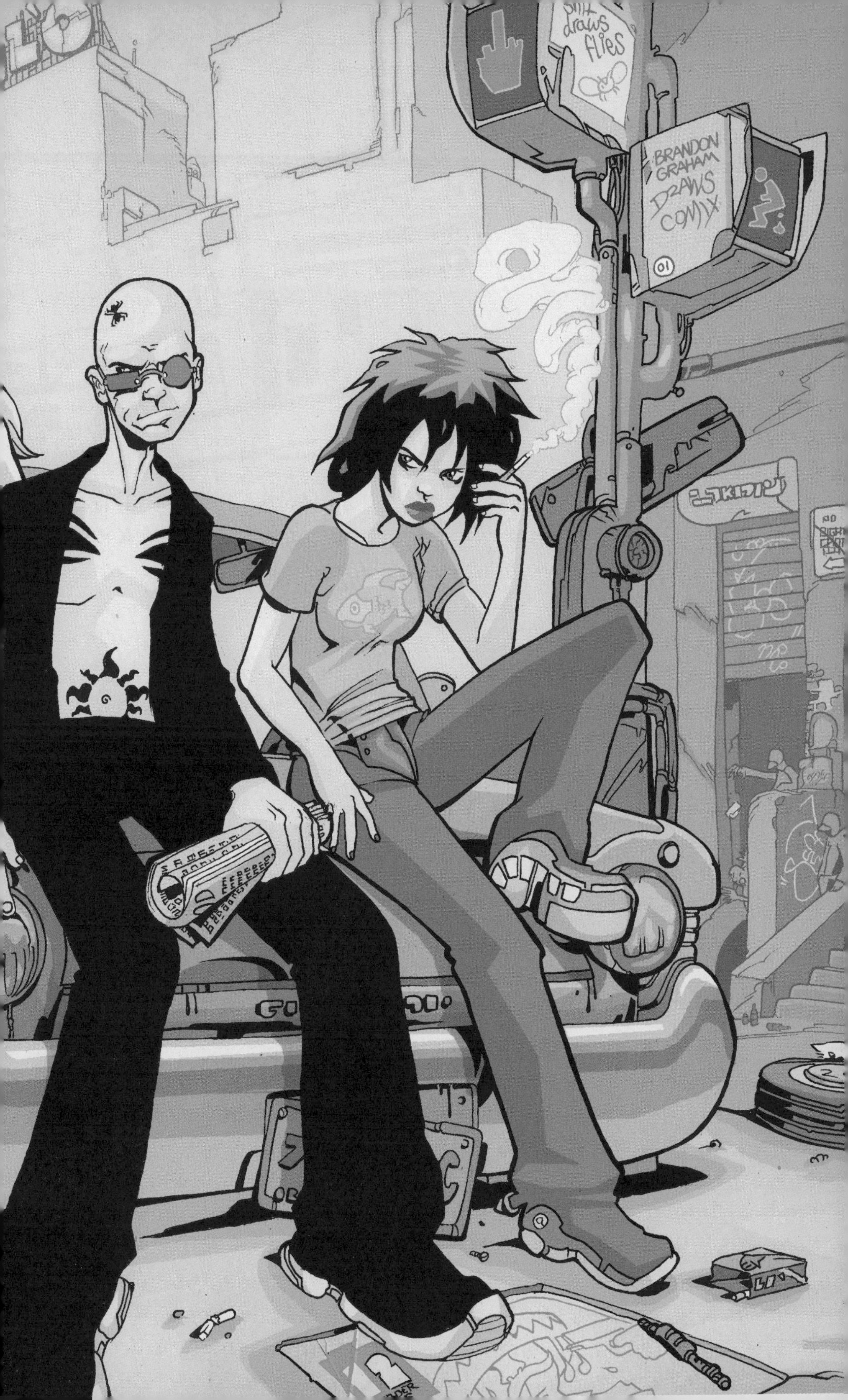
draws flies
BRANDON GRAHAM DRAWS COMIX
01

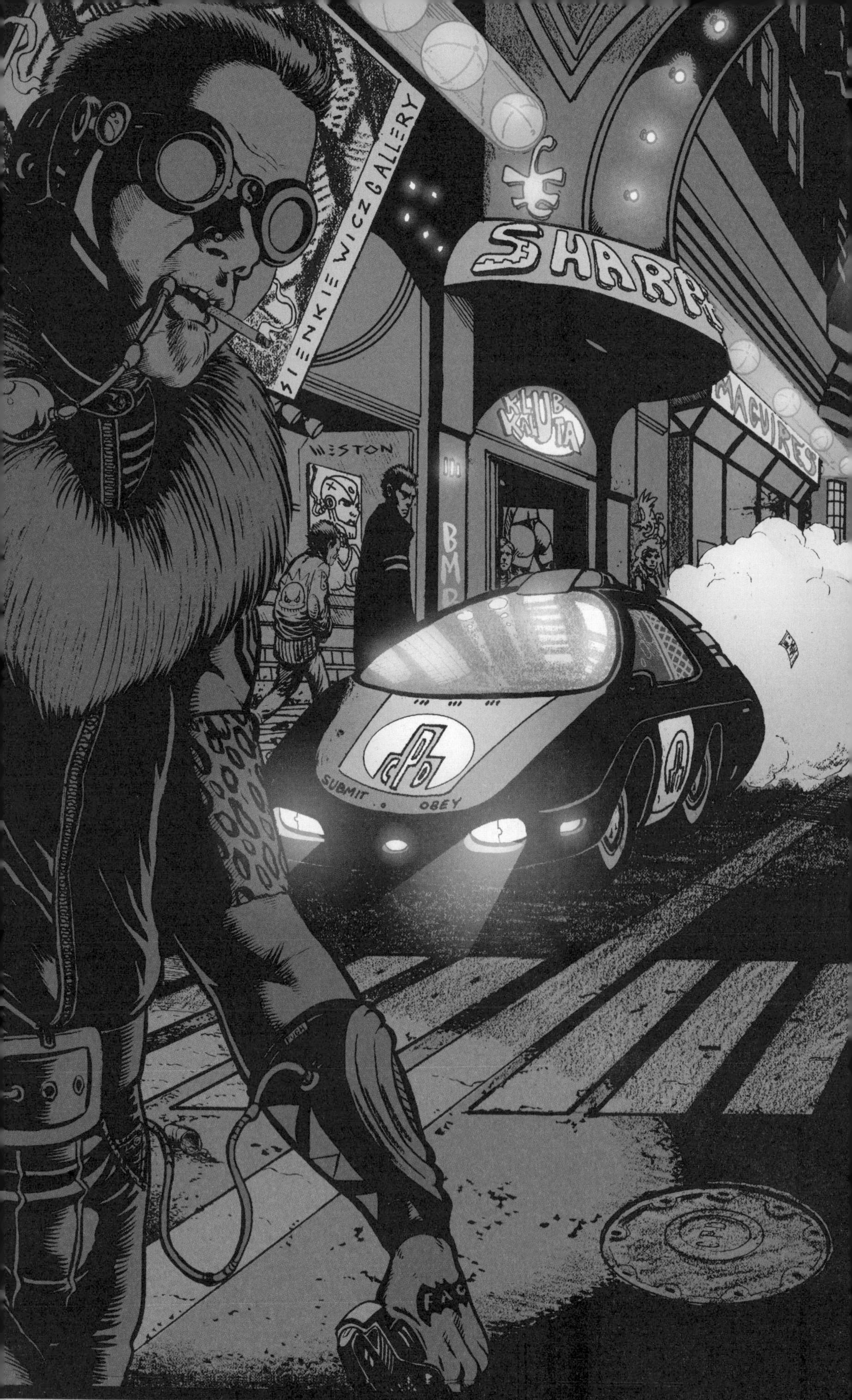
SIENKIEWICZ GALLERY
SHARP
KLUB KALUTA
MAGUIRES
WESTON
SUBMIT
OBEY

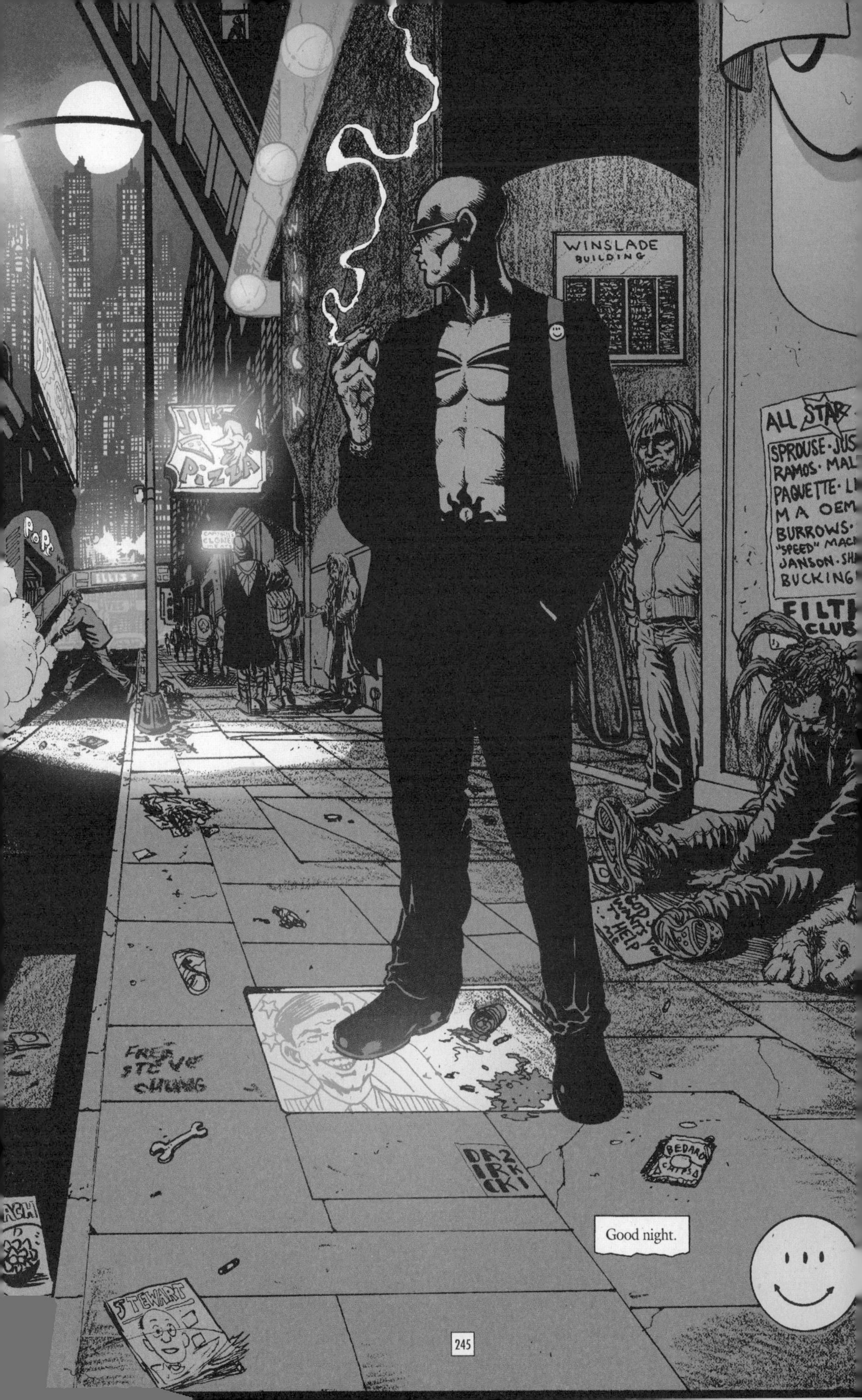
WINSLADE
BUILDING
PIZZA
ALL STAR
SPROUSE · JUS
RAMOS · MAL
PAQUETTE · LI
BURROWS ·
JANSON · SHA
BUCKING
CLUB
FREE
STEVE
CHUNG
STEWART
Good night.

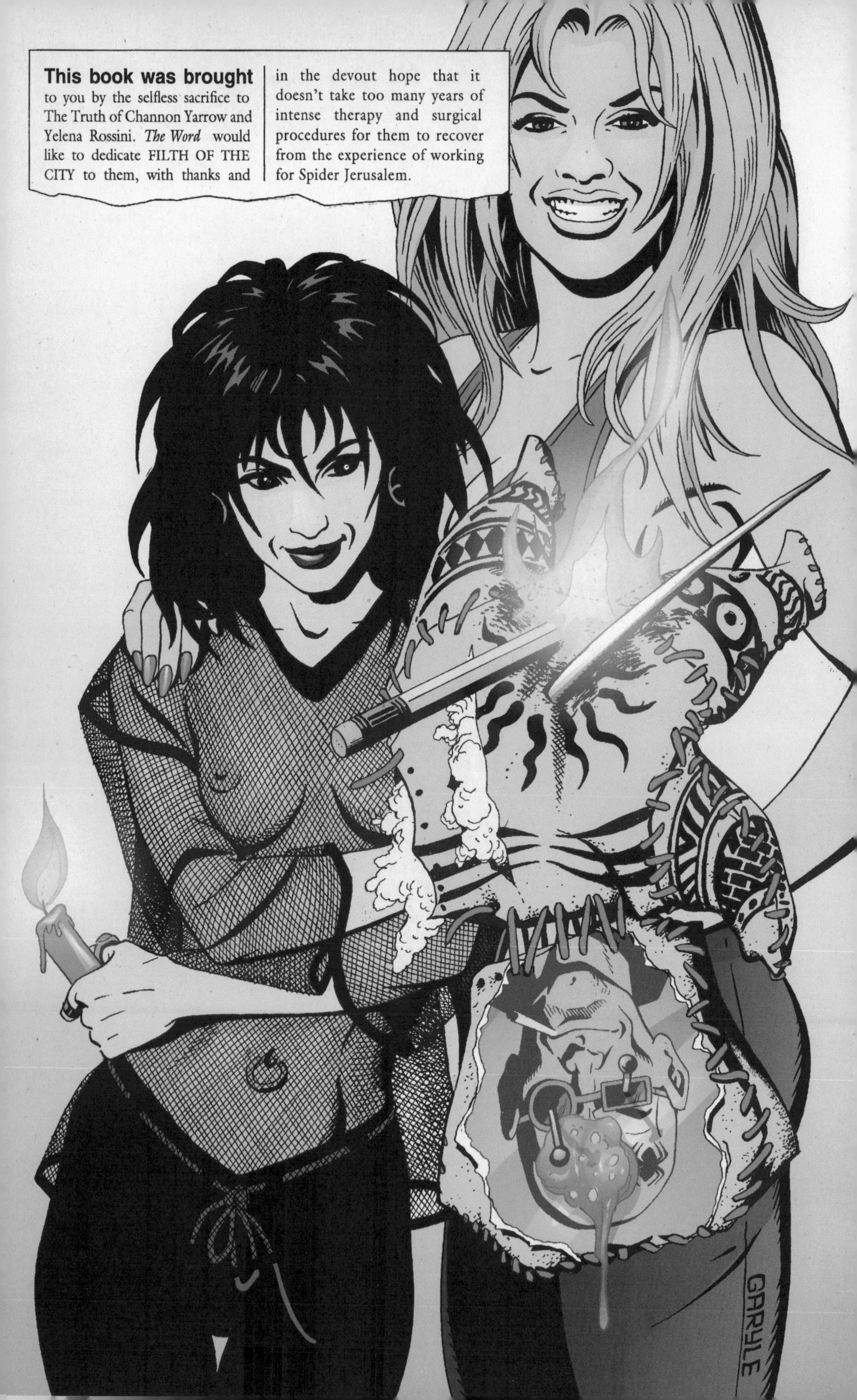
This book was brought to you by the selfless sacrifice to The Truth of Channon Yarrow and Yelena Rossini. *The Word* would like to dedicate FILTH OF THE CITY to them, with thanks and in the devout hope that it doesn't take too many years of intense therapy and surgical procedures for them to recover from the experience of working for Spider Jerusalem.

LOOK BACK IN ANGER

The following pages showcase cover art created by Darick Robertson for the original trade paperback editions of TRANSMETROPOLITAN, which were released between 1998 and 2004. They include the covers from Volumes 2-10 (the first edition of Volume 1 used art from an interior story page as its cover image).

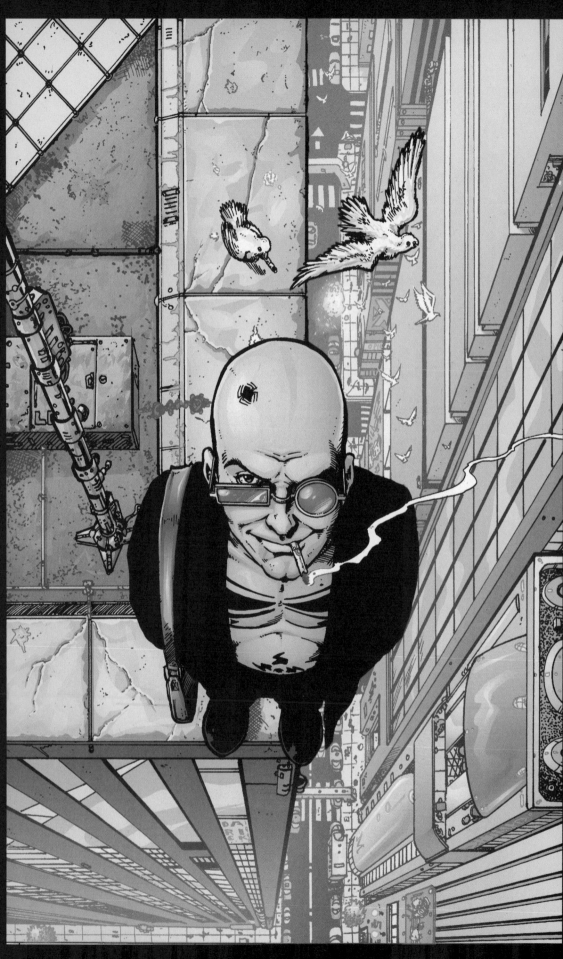

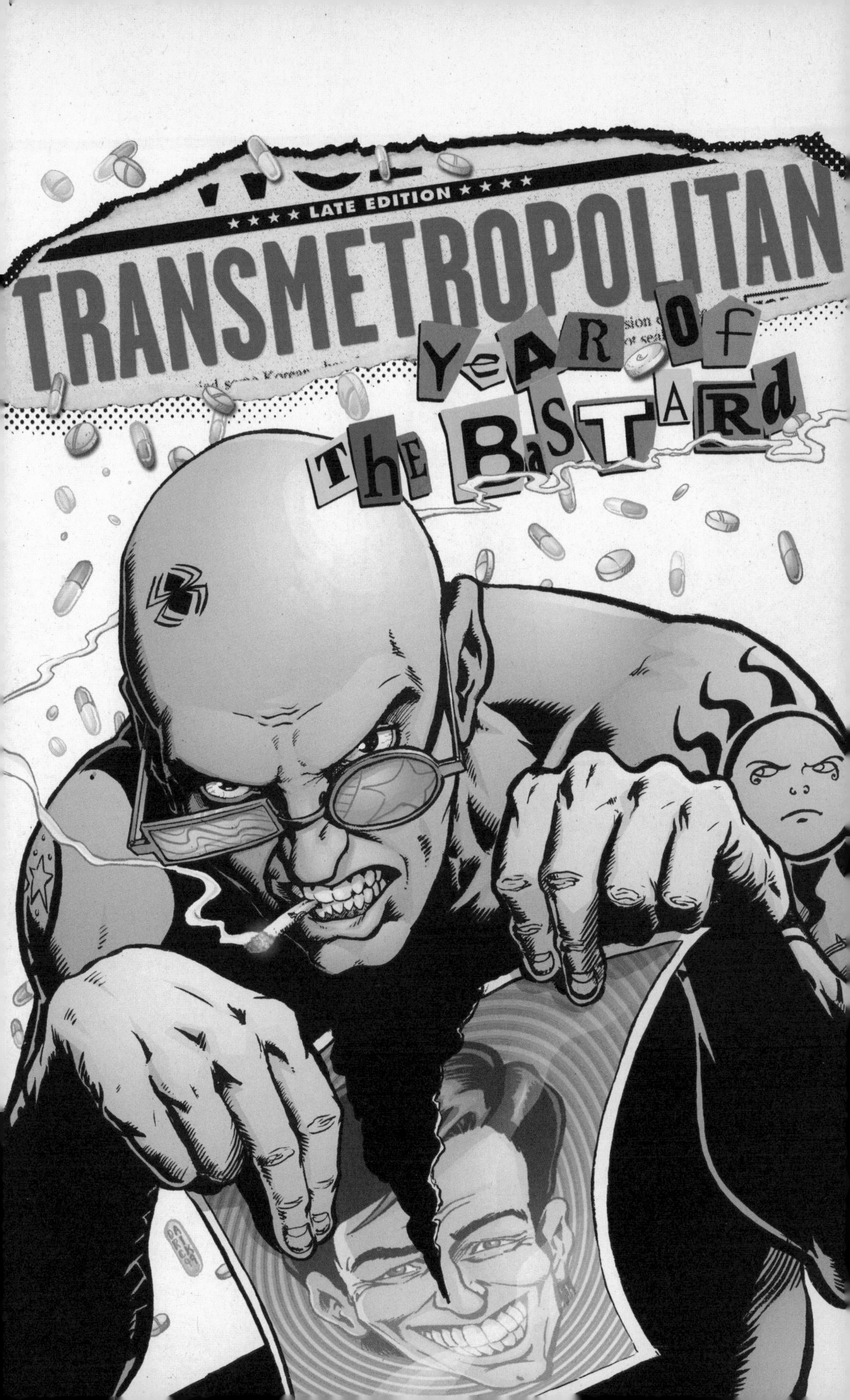
LATE EDITION
TRANSMETROPOLITAN
YEAR OF THE BASTARD

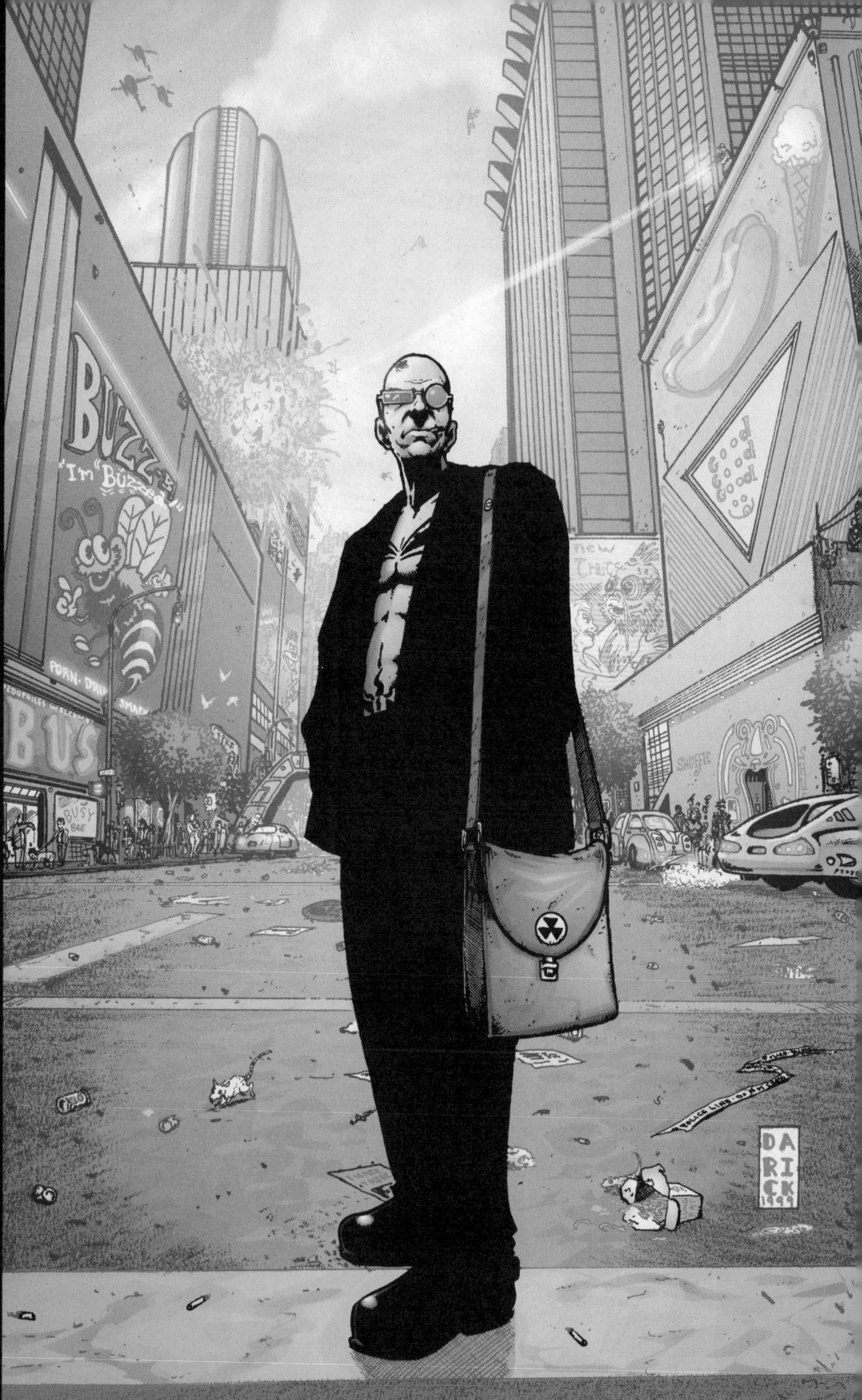
BUZZ
"I'm" Buzzed
BUSY BEE
Good Good Good
SHUFFLE
DARICK 1999

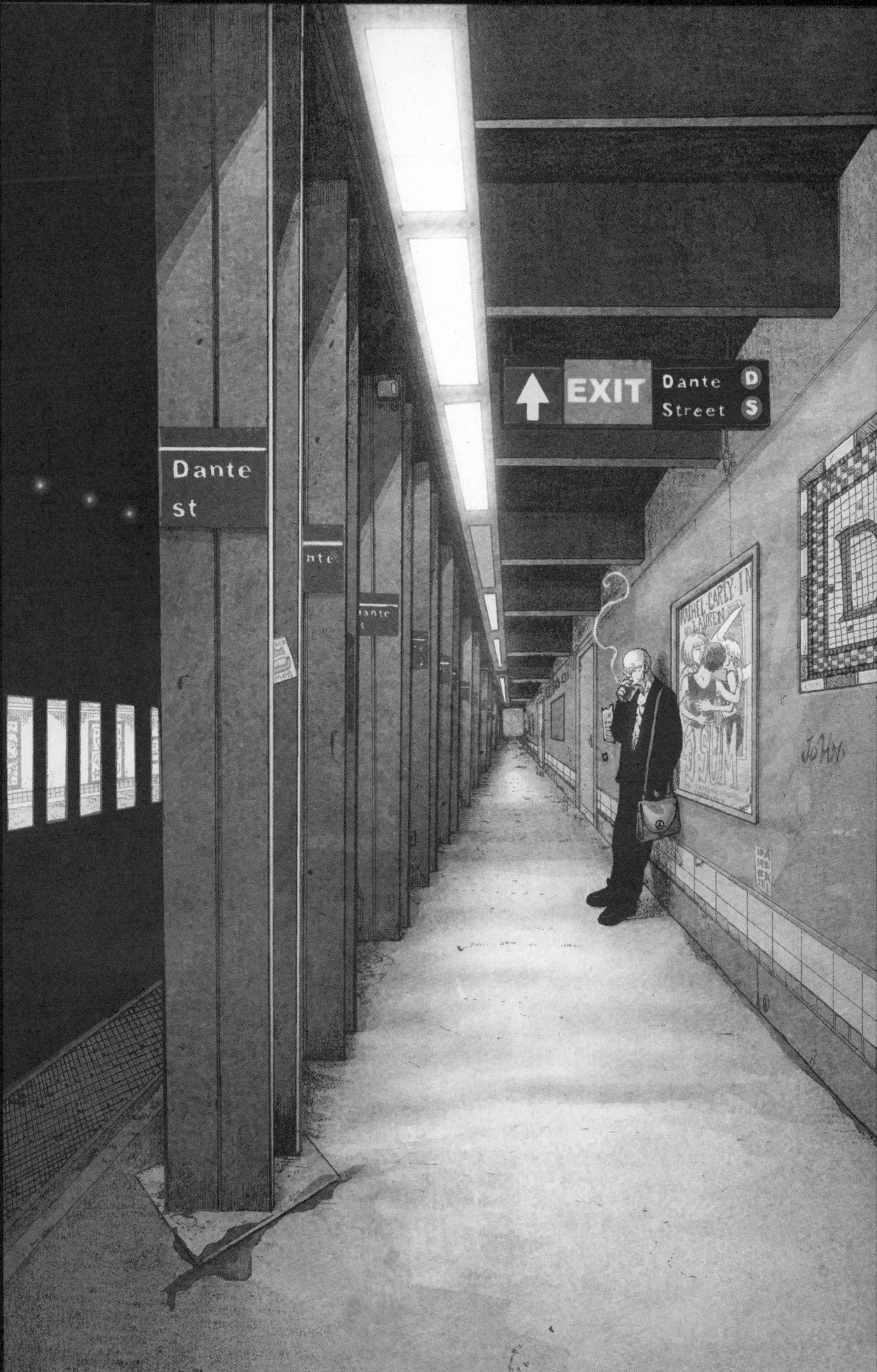
Dante
st
EXIT
Dante
Street
D
S

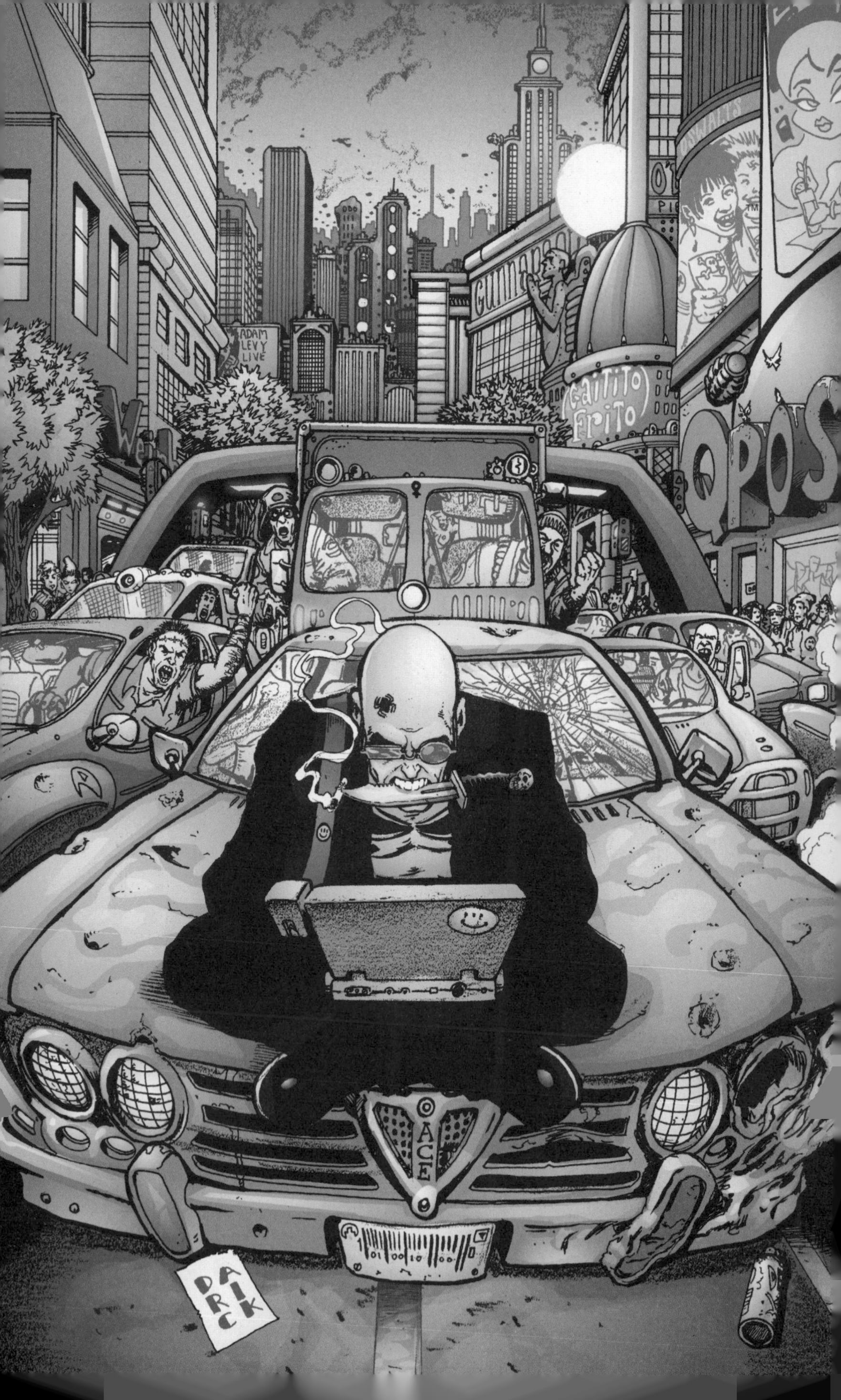
ADAM
LEVY
LIVE
QPOS
ACE

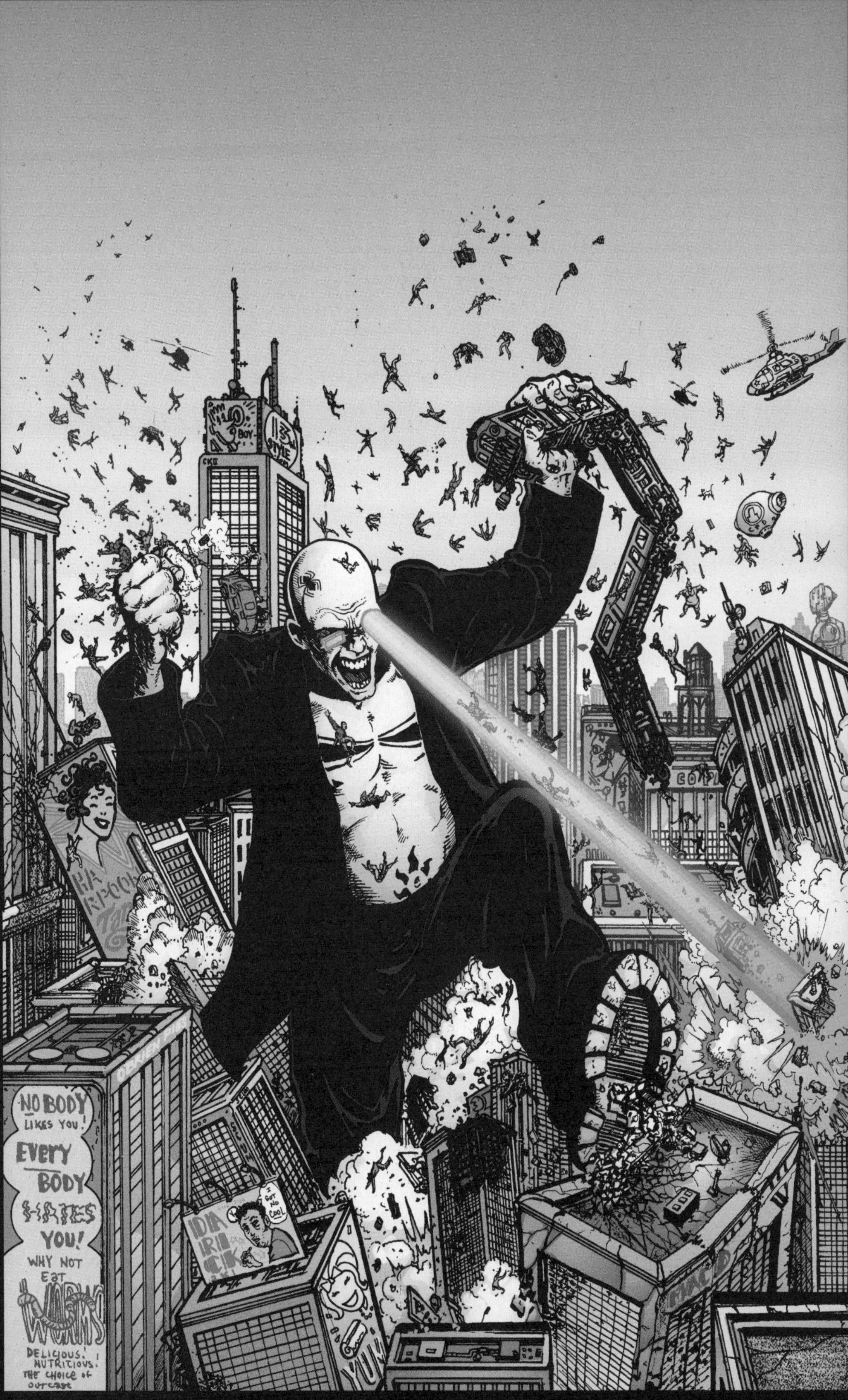
NO BODY
LIKES YOU!
EVERY
BODY
HATES
YOU!
WHY NOT
EAT
WORMS
DELICIOUS!
NUTRITIOUS!
THE CHOICE OF
OUTCASTS
I GOT NO COOL
13 STYLE

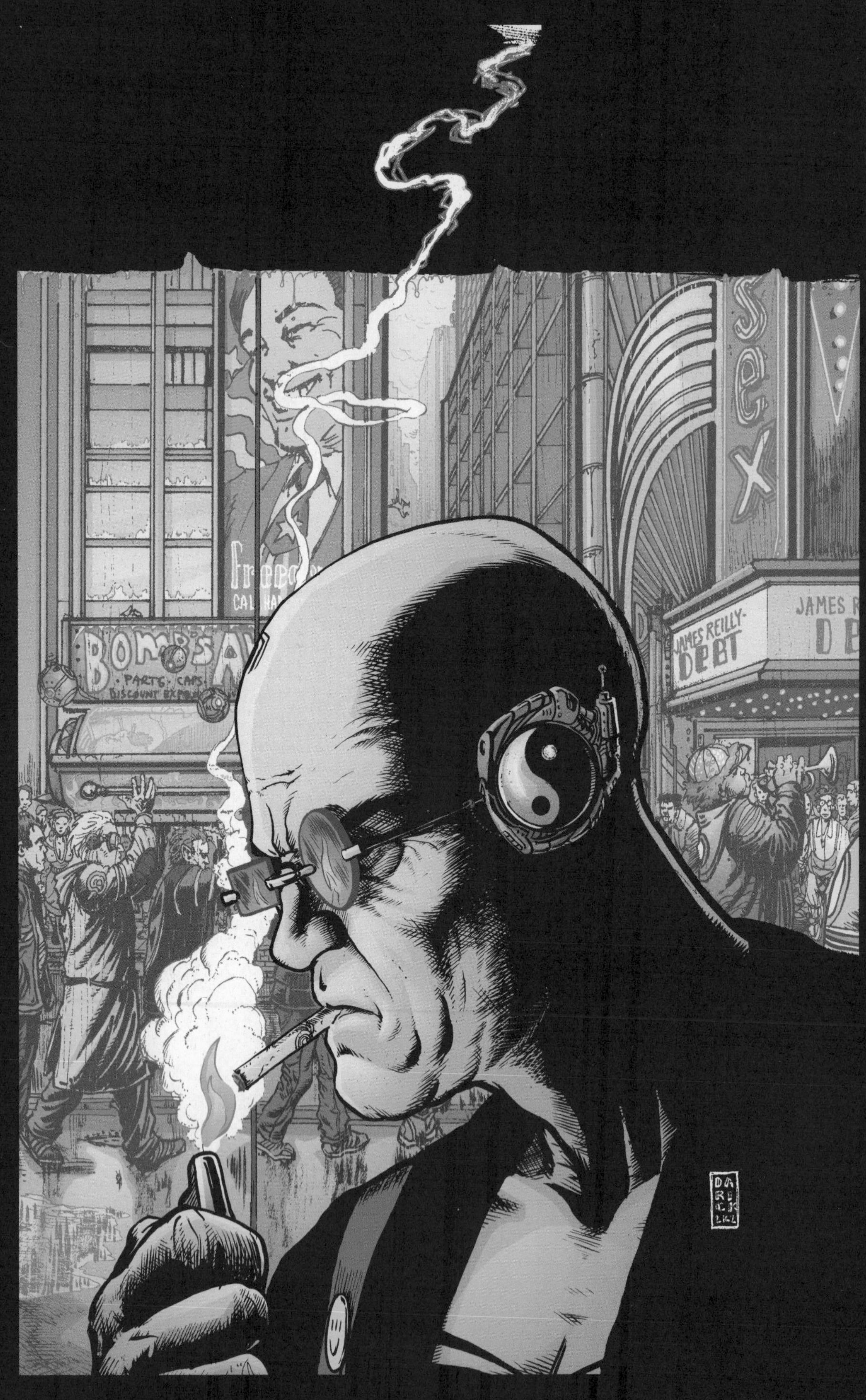
sex
JAMES REILLY-
DEBT
PARTS. CAPS.

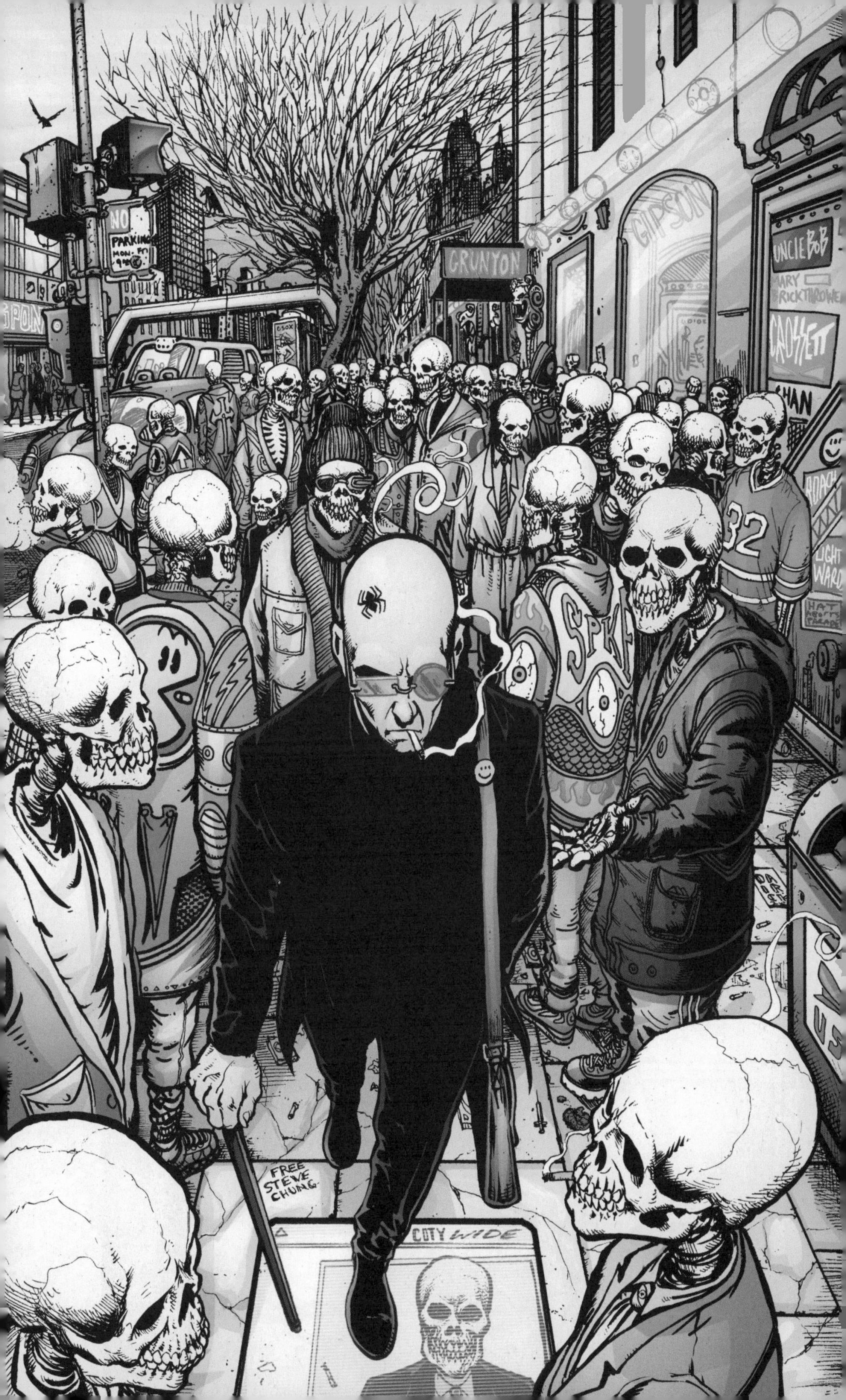
NO
PARKING
GRUNYON
GIPSUN
UNCLE BOB
CROSSETT
CHAN
32
LIGHT WARD
FREE STEVE CHUNG
CITY WIDE

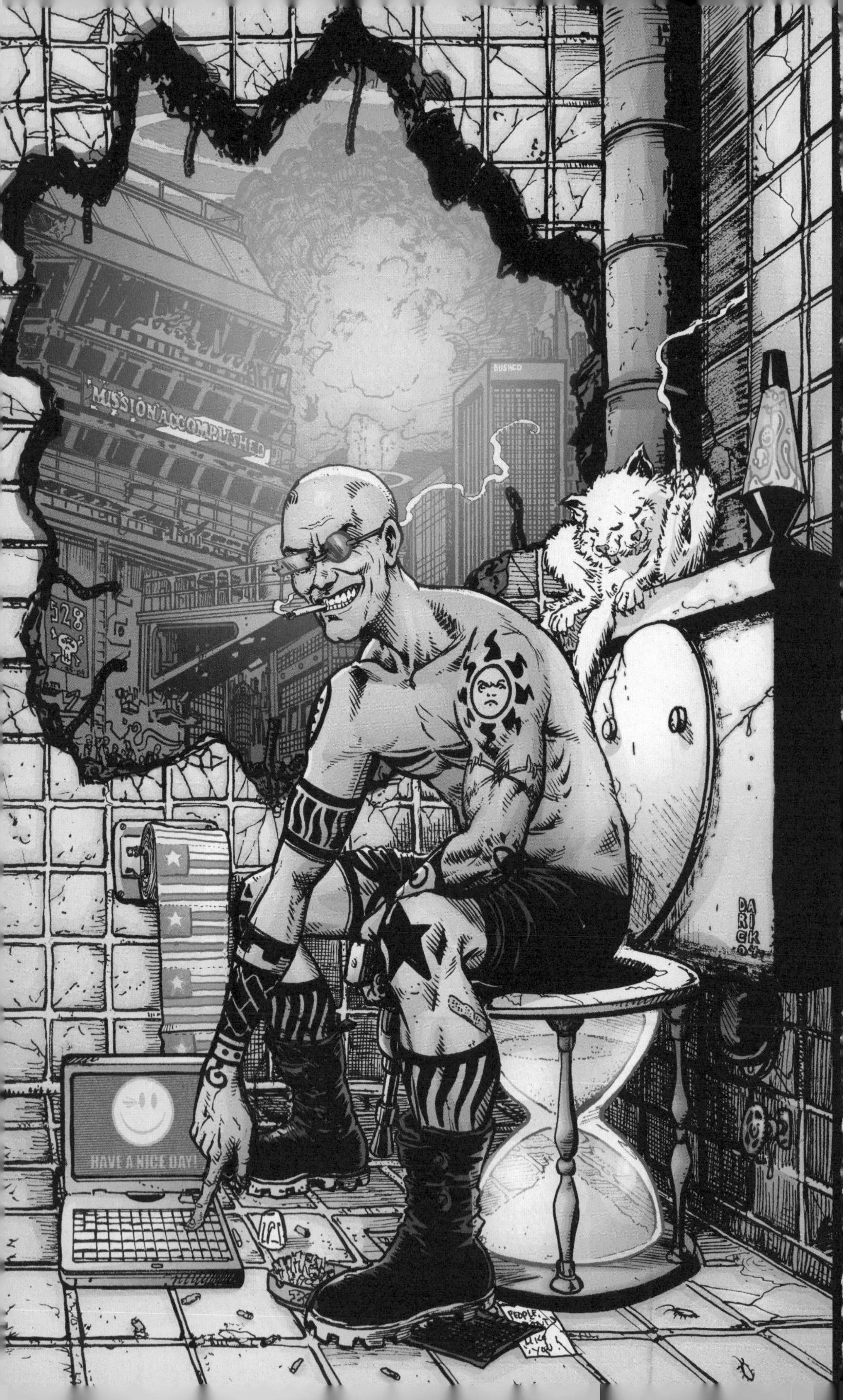
MISSION ACCOMPLISHED
BUSHCO
528
HAVE A NICE DAY!
DARICK 04